*"Why do the nations rage,
So furiously together?"*

Psalm 2, as adapted by
George Frideric Handel, *Messiah*

*"All the seas, in every quarter,
are as brothers to one another.
Why, then, do the winds and waves of strife
rage so turbulently throughout the world?"*

Emperor Meiji of Japan

*"Do you know why this century has seen such terrible events happen?
The Turks killing two million Armenians, the Holocaust, Hitler killing
most of the Jews of Europe, Stalin killing fifteen million Ukrainians,
nuclear destruction unleashed, the final war apparently inevitable? It
is because God agreed to let the Great Prince Satan have his way with
men for a hundred years — this one hundred years, the twentieth century. And he has. How did he do it? No great evil scenes, no demons —
he's too smart for that. All he had to do was leave us alone. We did it."*

Walker Percy,
The Thanatos Syndrome

D1556085

THE WORLD IN THE TWENTIETH CENTURY

VOLUME 1

The Rage of Nations

Edward R. Kantowicz

WILLIAM B. EERDMANS PUBLISHING COMPANY
GRAND RAPIDS, MICHIGAN / CAMBRIDGE, U.K.

Printed in the United States of America

04 03 02 01 00 99   7 6 5 4 3 2 1

Library of Congress Cataloging-in-Publication Data

Kantowicz, Edward R.
The rage of nations: the world in the twentieth century / Edward R. Kantowicz.
p.   cm.
Includes bibliographical references and index.
ISBN 0-8028-4455-3 (paper: alk. paper)
1. History, Modern — 20th century.   I. Title
D421.K325   1999
320.5′09041 — dc21   98-35887
                                      CIP

Maps are based on originals provided by
Mountain High Maps®
Copyright © 1993 Digital Wisdom, Inc.

For Jane, Chris, and Greg

Contents

Maps   xi

Acknowledgments   xiii

Introduction   xv

PART ONE
EUROPE AND THE WORLD IN 1900

1. Europeans under Siege   3
   The Boer War; The Boxer Rebellion

2. The Terrible "Isms"   13
   Imperialism, Nationalism, Socialism, Anarchism

3. East and West, North and South   28
   Colonialism in India and Africa; The Fifth Ism, Ethnocentrism

4. East Asian Responses to Europe   45
   Decline of the Manchus in China; Meiji Restoration in Japan

5. War and Revolution: The Preview   61

   Russo-Japanese War; Russian Revolution of 1905

PART TWO
THE FIRST WORLD CATASTROPHE

6. A Murder in Bosnia   81

   Austro-Hungarian Empire; Sarajevo

7. The Fatal Alliances   100

   Causes of World War I

8. The War of Exhaustion   118

   World War I

9. Peace and Consequences   138

   *Results of World War I; Paris Peace Conference;
   Pacifism and War Resistance*

PART THREE
REVOLUTIONS ON THE RIM OF WAR

10. Revolutions in Red, White, and Black   159

    *Russian Revolutions of 1917; the Counterrevolution and Civil
    War; the Makhno Anarchist Movement in the Ukraine*

11. Gray Wolf on the Prowl   176

    *The Young Turks; Kemal Ataturk; the Turkish Revolution;
    The Armenian Genocide*

12. A Tangle of Promises   196

    The Arab Revolt; Zionism

13. The Beginning of the End   216

    Irish Nationalism; The Easter Rising; Irish Independence

14. Revolutions, Constitutions, and Institutions   234

    The Mexican Revolution

PART FOUR

EUROPEAN CIVILIZATION JUMPS THE TRACKS

15. The Intoxicated Engineers   255

    The Great Crash and Depression; John Maynard Keynes;
    Franklin Delano Roosevelt

16. Italy's "New Deal"   272

    Benito Mussolini and the Rise of Italian Fascism

17. A Delayed-Action Fuse   291

    Adolf Hitler and the Rise of German Nazism

18. Socialism in One Country   309

    Joseph Stalin and the Consolidation of Russian Communism

19. The Spanish Tragedy   326

    The Spanish Civil War

PART FIVE

THE SECOND WORLD CATASTROPHE

20. Incidents and Accidents in East Asia   347

    Chinese Nationalism and the Sino-Japanese War of 1937

21. The Onset of Hitler's War   365

    The Origins of World War II in Europe

22. The Coming of the Greater East Asia War   384

    The Origins of World War II in the Pacific

23. Coalition Warfare, Unconditional Surrender   403

    World War II in Europe and the Pacific

24. The War of Extermination   422

    War Crimes; The Holocaust; Strategic Bombing of Cities;
    The Atom Bomb

25. The Search for Alternatives   440

    The Plot to Kill Hitler; The Pacifist Alternative;
    The United Nations

Afterword — Volume 1   457

Suggestions for Further Reading   458

Index   497

Maps

1. Southern Africa c. 1900   4

2. China c. 1900   9

3. World Empires c. 1900   14

4. Africa c. 1914   35

5. China c. 1900   46

6. Japan c. 1900   56

7. East Asia at the Time of the Russo-Japanese War   62

8. Austria-Hungary c. 1900   89

9. The Triple Alliance and the Triple Entente   108

10. Front Lines on the Western Front at the end of 1914   120

11. The Gallipoli Peninsula   129

12. New States of Eastern Europe, 1920   154

13. The Ottoman Empire at the Time of Its Greatest Extent c. 1700   177

14. Historic Armenia   185

15. The Sykes-Picot Agreement, 1916   206

16. Palestine at the Time of the Balfour Declaration   210

17. The Historic Four Provinces of Ireland   218

18. Mexico in the Twentieth Century 237

19. Italy after World War I 273

20. Germany c. 1920 292

21. The Division of Spain in July 1936 335

22. The Japanese Empire after the Manchurian Incident, 1931 356

23. The Chinese Communists' Long March, 1934-35 360

24. Changes in Europe, 1935-39 370

25. Japan's Greater East Asia Co-Prosperity Sphere 387

26. The Greatest Extent of Hitler's Conquests 409

Acknowledgments

Kathleen Alaimo, history professor and chair of the department of history and political science at Saint Xavier University, Chicago, Illinois, took a great deal of time out of her busy schedule to read the entire manuscript of this book. I can't thank her enough for her insightful comments and suggestions. Her husband, Dominic Pacyga, a historian from Columbia College Chicago, pointed me toward the Walker Percy quote on the frontispiece of the book. Several of my former colleagues at Carleton University, Ottawa, Canada, read chapters of this book — Fred Goodwin, Ray Jones, and Carter Elwood. I also want to thank several other former colleagues at Carleton who have not seen a word of this book but helped me devise and teach a course on the World in the Twentieth Century, giving me many ideas and suggestions which I later followed up on my own — Peter Fitzgerald, Blair Neatby, and Nicoll Cooper. Peter d'A. Jones, from the University of Illinois at Chicago, Janet Nolan from Loyola University, Chicago, and Ellen Skerret, an independent scholar, also read individual chapters.

Chapter three, which explores the fifth "ism," ethnocentrism, and tries to lay out a roadmap for world history, had more readers than any other chapter of the book. Jim Sack and Mel Holli, from the University of Illinois at Chicago, originally suggested that I needed such a chapter. Michael Fuller and Leo Lefebure, from St. Mary of the Lake Seminary, and Anne Serafin, from Newton North High School, Massachusetts, gave me many frank suggestions for improving it. One of the unexpected joys of working on a project such as this was the assistance I received from people that I have never even met. Ned Rossiter, Gail Marcus, and Lenny Markowitz all offered comments on chapter three after it reached them through an unusual grapevine. Thanks to them all.

Two institutions of higher education helped immensely in making this work possible. The University of Chicago, where I received my Ph.D. in history, granted me alumni privileges for the use of their world-class Regenstein Library, where I did nearly all the research for the book. St. Mary of the Lake Seminary in Mundelein, Illinois, the graduate school of theology for the Catholic Archdiocese of Chicago, granted me the Chester and Margaret Paluch Chair for 1995-96, enabling me to refine many of my ideas about the twentieth century with intelligent and like-minded students.

Three artists have greatly enhanced the appearance of this book: David Zylstra, who conceived and drew the cover illustration; Tracey Gebbia, who summarized a great deal of information in the numerous maps; and Greg Kantowicz, who unleashed his imagination on the twentieth century to produce the illustrations at the beginning of each section.

Finally, the dedication indicates my deep gratitude to my family, who lived through a significant portion of this century with me and put up with my obsession with this book.

INTRODUCTION

The World in the Twentieth Century

The twentieth century has been the most explosive and destructive in human history. The first half of the century was marked by two world wars, the Holocaust and other acts of genocide, plus a host of violent revolutions. The second half, though a bit less bloody, also saw its share of wars and atrocities. As we enter the twenty-first century, it is vital that we understand what went wrong in the preceding hundred years.

Four terrible "isms" — anarchism, socialism, imperialism, and nationalism — drove the events of the twentieth century. Anarchists seemed most threatening at the turn of the century, for they had launched a wave of assassinations that struck down kings and empresses, presidents and prime ministers. Anarchism has persisted as an undercurrent of protest against organized bigness, but it has registered relatively little impact on the shape of the century as a whole. For much of the past hundred years, the interplay between socialism and imperialism dominated events in many areas of the world, with socialism seemingly rising and imperialism waning. The Russian Bolshevik Revolution of 1917 and the Chinese Communist Revolution of 1946-49 brought more than a billion people under the sway of dictatorships inspired by Marxist socialism. Socialism and imperialism, however, both collapsed toward the end of the century, while nationalism remains as the most powerful "ism," a worldwide force for good and evil.

Yet the most explosive ideological forces of the century were the hybrids of nationalism and socialism. Mussolini, Hitler, and Stalin all created unstable amalgams of these two "isms," with more in common than is often recognized. There is no satisfactory generic term to describe this phenomenon. The obvious compound phrase, National Socialism, is forever compromised by its association with Hitler. A less controversial terminology was contributed by the Indonesian independence leader Sukarno, who coined the phrase "socio-nationalism" to describe one of the principles of his revolution. Until a better term can be devised, therefore, I use the made-up word "socio-nationalism," or simply "nationalism plus socialism." In combination, these two "isms" ignited the bonfires of atrocity that scarred the first fifty years of this century, and more positively, they also sparked the independence struggles of Asia and Africa during the second half of the century.

Along with this combination of "isms," a new social class also played a major role throughout the century, the "intellectual proletariat." The spread of literacy and higher education has often produced a group of overeducated but underemployed men and women in many different countries. Filled with rising but frustrated expectations, the intellectual proletariat has been the most dangerous social class in the world of the twentieth century. Hitler and Mussolini both belonged to this class and drew much of their support from it, as did the leaders of the Third World who rebelled against European imperialism.

Underlying the history of the past century has been a fifth "ism," more terrible than all the rest because it remained largely unrecognized. This was ethnocentrism, the belief that one's own culture and society is superior to all others. In recent years scholars have focused a powerful spotlight on ethnocentrism and have tried to replace it with a more relativistic approach which considers all cultures and societies of the world equally good and refuses to make value judgments. This causes as many problems as it solves, however, for some societies have been more successful than others, by a variety of criteria. An important intellectual task, therefore, remains: the construction of a road map, navigating between a bigoted ethnocentrism on the one hand and a value-free cultural relativism on the other.

As a new century opens, humanity must find a way to avoid the atrocities that marked the past hundred years. While I do not believe that history has all the answers or that historians can predict the future based on what happened in the past, I do agree with historian J. H. Jackson that "the object of historical study is to enable one to understand what is happening now." A hundred years ago, a group of American historians, including Charles Beard and James Harvey Robinson, began writing what they called the "New History." Their oft-stated goal was "to help people understand the morning newspaper." Their new history long ago became old, but their aim remains valid. In today's world, perhaps we should rephrase it "to help people understand the nightly news."

I have written this book in that spirit, as a primer, a *TV Guide for the newscast*, enabling citizens of the world to make sense of what is happening now by learning what happened in the recent past. When I was a university teacher I often shocked my students by telling them that I rarely watched the evening news on television. "How can you stay informed?" they asked. "You tell me what the headlines are," I shot back. "I'll tell you what they mean." That is the power of history.

Though citizens of the world need to know the facts about the twentieth century — the who, what, when, where, and why — it is even more vital that they ask the next question, so what? Why should anyone care about these events? What is the context that makes them meaningful? What connections do they have with everyday life? How do they challenge or confirm our deepest values? I have attempted, therefore, in these two volumes to highlight the peak events, key personalities, and driving "isms" of the twentieth century; and I have further attempted to provide context, connections, and values so a reader can understand the meaning of events.

I should briefly mention how I derived my own point of view and what my own values are. As a grandson of immigrants and an immigrant myself, I have always been acutely aware of how important national culture is in forming personal identity and of how much damage can be done to individuals by insensitivity to their culture. Anyone who has lived in more than one country is in some sense a "marginal" man or woman, never completely accepted wherever he or she goes. Such marginality can lead either to madness or creativity. In my case, I think, it has simply made me curious.

I was also raised and educated with Catholic Christian values and a deep revulsion against warfare, based on Christian teachings about war and peace. In the pages that follow, I often express shock and dismay at the atrocities of the twentieth century. I have approached the events of this century from a point of view that is moral and ethical, but, I sincerely hope, not moralistic. I explore alternatives to violence in the spirit of a quest, not as a dogmatist dictating answers.

In the final analysis I believe that the best hope for overcoming the violent excesses of nationalism lies with one further "ism," federalism. States must become simultaneously smaller and larger. As empires and artificially contrived countries fragment into smaller units based on ethnic nationalism, this tendency should not be resisted. Small-scale communities are the most natural objects of human reverence, and there is no point in trying to suppress them. One of the most humiliating events of recent American diplomacy was President George Bush's so-called "Chicken Kiev" speech, when on August 1, 1991, he addressed the Ukrainian parliament and urged the legislators not to secede from the Soviet Union. Less than six months later, not only Ukraine but fourteen other republics had fragmented the former Soviet colossus into its constituent parts.

Yet such small and mid-sized national communities must and can be brought into larger regional federations or economic common markets. The coming century certainly possesses the transportation and communications technology to make such federations possible. The slow creation of a European Union out of the wreckage of two world wars marks a first step in the forging of these new political unities. Africa, the Americas, the Pacific Rim of Asia, and the former Soviet republics are prime candidates for further integration.

Something similar has already happened in the realm of computer technology. In economically prosperous countries today, millions of individuals possess more computing power on their own desks than governments used to command just a few decades ago. Yet, these personal computers are often linked together with those of co-workers in Local Area Networks (LANs) and also with the World Wide Web of information on the Internet. So in technological terms, computer users have been "flying apart, yet coming together." This phrase has furnished the title for my second volume, and it can provide a model for the political future of world society, a system of dual loyalties that may temper the excesses of nationalism.

The French journalist, Jean Jacques Servan-Schreiber, once commented that he embraced two patriotic loyalties, Alsace (his local province, or *pays*) and the world. (I would say Chicago and the world.) The intermediate loyalty to nation-states, such as France or the United States, has proven tremendously powerful for mobilizing the economic and military energies of large groups of people. Such mobilization, however, is highly dangerous, as the history of the twentieth century amply illustrates. A federalist strategy that recognizes the power of national feeling but tries to break it down into smaller bits, while rearranging those pieces into larger, more useful, and more peaceful wholes, holds out hope for the twenty-first century. The past hundred years have been marked by a ferocious rage of nations, but as we approach the coming century the world seems to be flying apart, yet coming together.

PART ONE

EUROPE AND THE WORLD IN 1900

"The world may politically, as well as geographically, be divided into four parts [Asia, Africa, Europe, and America], each having a distinct set of interests. Unhappily for the other three, Europe . . . has in different degrees extended her dominion over them all." One of the founding fathers of the United States, Alexander Hamilton, wrote these lines in 1789, but his lament rang even truer a hundred years later. Though the Americas had established their political independence, the United States remained an overseas offshoot of European culture and the Latin American republics were controlled by European capital. Furthermore, Europe carved Africa into colonies in the late nineteenth century and reduced most of Asia to a state of dependence. As the nineteenth century turned into the twentieth, the North Atlantic states of Western Europe and the United States dominated the world. Europe and North America formed the "center" of the world economy with the other countries ranged around them on the "periphery."

CHAPTER ONE

Europeans under Siege

In the first year of the new century,[1] Europeans were fighting for their lives in two far-flung outposts on the "periphery." At the southern tip of Africa, English settlers, with their worldwide empire approaching its zenith, found themselves besieged in three dusty provincial cities of the South African *veldt*. On the other side of the world, not only the English, but all the foreign consular staff and their families, Americans, Germans, French, and Japanese, were walled up in Peking's embassy compound by enraged Chinese militants. The *Times* of London was surely correct when it editorialized "that this century, like the last, is likely to witness momentous changes in the relative importance of the nations of the world."

In South Africa, the revolt against the English came not from native black Africans but from another "white tribe," the Boers. Descended from Dutch adventurers who had settled at the Cape of Good Hope in the seventeenth century, the Boers were rugged backcountry farmers and herders. The word *Boer* meant farmer or peasant. The tough Dutch farmers wore this label, originally intended as an insult, proudly. The Boers had killed off, pushed aside, or enslaved the origi-

---

1. There was a sharp public debate over the date when the new century really began, January 1, 1900, or January 1, 1901. Technically, the year 1900 was the one-hundredth year of the old century and the new one only began with the year 1901. This is the usage adopted by the *Times* of London, by the *New York Times*, and by "official" keepers of the calendar. Yet on January 1, 1900, the *Times* of London printed a letter from a correspondent who argued on practical grounds that as "a matter of nomenclature and usage" the new century began that day. I agree. In popular parlance, 1900 was, and is, viewed as the first year of the century, just as 1920 was the first year of the decade of the twenties, and so forth. I shall use this more popular terminology throughout the book, dating the "turn of the century" to 1900.

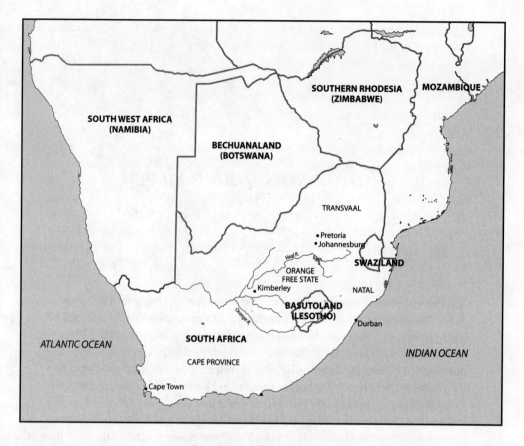

Southern Africa c. 1900

nal black inhabitants of the Cape, the Khoi and the San, whom they called Hottentots or Bushmen; and they fought endless wars against the more powerful Bantu-speaking tribes they encountered in the interior. The English navy seized the Cape for strategic reasons during the Napoleonic Wars and acquired legal control of the Cape Colony at the Congress of Vienna in 1815. Yet the Boer farmers stayed, for they no longer considered themselves Dutch but Afrikaners, that is, white Africans.

When the English became too meddlesome and abolished slavery at the Cape in 1834, the Boers packed their families into wagons, and like American pioneers at the same time, they embarked on the Great Trek of 1836-38, eastward along the coast to Natal. Though the Trekkers decisively defeated the Zulus at the Battle of Blood River on December 16, 1838, the English would not leave them alone, annexing Natal in 1843. So the Boers packed up again, heading deep into the interior, beyond the Orange and Vaal Rivers and the Drakensberg Mountains. South African historian Leo Marquard has written: "The Trek created a gulf between Britain and the Afrikaners that has not yet been bridged. . . . Even now the Afrikaner cannot quite shake off the illusion that he is being followed."

Indeed, the English followed once again when diamonds were found at Kimberley in 1867 and gold was discovered on the Witwatersrand River in 1886. So many Outlanders, as the Boers termed the English, came flocking into the republics of the Transvaal and the Orange Free State that they threatened to overwhelm the Boers' agricultural way of life. By 1897, Johannesburg, the major city in the gold fields, counted 120,000 Outlanders to only 30,000 Boers. During the 1890s, a British robber baron and adventurer, Cecil Rhodes, built a railroad north from the Cape and established new English colonies that nearly encircled the Boers. Rhodes manipulated public opinion back home, decrying the lack of political rights suffered by the Outlanders within the Boer republics, to create a pretext for war and annexation. The war finally began in October 1899, when the Boers launched a preemptive strike against the English. Like the Americans in 1776, they fired "a shot heard 'round the world," hoping to convince the English to stop following them.

The Boer commandos, like the earlier American revolutionaries, were volunteers, mounted frontiersmen accustomed to hard riding and straight shooting. Their spirited resistance to English rule attracted adventurers from around the world (much as the Spanish Civil War would later in the twentieth century), including a corps of 500 fiery Irishmen eager to settle scores with their hereditary enemy. Initially outnumbering the regular British soldiers, whose reinforcements would have to come by ship from India or from England, the Boers rode toward Durban, a port in Natal, which would give their landlocked republics an opening to the outside world. Other detachments drove westward to Kimberley and Mafeking, key points on Cecil Rhodes's railway.

After initial Boer victories in Natal, over 13,000 British soldiers took refuge in the city of Ladysmith, on the road to Durban. Rather than bypass them and leave such a large force in their rear, the Boer generals besieged the city, capturing the surrounding hilltops and raining artillery fire downward. Meanwhile, in Kimberley, Cecil Rhodes himself rallied the civilian population, and the British showed more foresight than in Ladysmith, establishing a defense perimeter on the heaps of debris from the diamond mines that surrounded the city. The Boers began an extended siege of Kimberley on November 7, 1899; and they also invested Mafeking, farther north "on the borders of nowhere." There a young English colonel, Robert Stephenson Smyth Baden-Powell, who in later life would organize the Boy Scouts, took command of the defense.

"A siege is a war in microcosm, expressed in heightened, theatrical form," historian Thomas Pakenham has aptly written. "Boredom, discomfort, anxiety, funk, bravery, hope, humiliation — above all, discomfort and boredom." Typhoid fever ravaged the garrison at Ladysmith. More than 10,000 of the 13,000 soldiers holding the town spent some time in field hospital during the siege, and 551 died. Food ran short in all three besieged cities, with the death rate from starvation highest among women and children, and among the African population, who were deliberately put on short rations. At Mafeking, Baden-Powell executed Africans caught stealing food, flogged others almost daily, then finally cut off African rations entirely, driving them out of town to run the gauntlet of Boer soldiers. By saving food for the white officers and townspeople, this ingenious Boy Scout leader held out for 271 days until Mafeking was finally relieved.

By the turn of the year, and the new century, the British Cabinet realized they had a real war on their hands, so in January 1900 they sent out their two most famous generals, Field Marshal Lord Roberts, who had spent forty-one years solidifying English rule in India, and Major General Lord Kitchener, the conqueror of Egypt and the Sudan. With reinforcements constantly debarking at the Cape, Roberts and Kitchener encircled one Boer army and forced its surrender, then lifted the sieges of the three embattled cities. In March 1900 the British captured Bloemfontein, capital of the Orange Free State; then on June 5 the Boers surrendered the Transvaal capital, Pretoria, without a fight.

From that point on, the outcome of the war no longer remained in doubt. The Boers could not win against the larger British forces, but they could harass them, make them miserable, and humiliate them. For the first, but by no means the last time in this warlike century, small bands of highly motivated men, supported by the heroic sacrifices of women and children, mounted effective guerrilla raids against technologically superior armies.

The war dragged on for two more bloody years. Frustrated by an enemy who did not play by the rules, the British threw the rulebook out the window. They organized guerrilla bands of their own, such as the Bushveldt Carbineers, who took no prisoners and retaliated savagely after each Boer raid. Roberts and Kitchener authorized the burning of 30,000 farms and about twenty villages to punish collaborators with the enemy.

After Roberts returned to England at the end of 1900, Kitchener established what he called "camps of refuge," where wives and children of Boer commandos were interned so that they could no longer support the guerrilla fighters. Opponents of the war in England borrowed a term from the Spanish repression in Cuba during the previous decade, dubbing Kitchener's prison compounds "concentration camps." A crusading Englishwoman, Emily Hobhouse, toured the camps in the early months of 1901 and revealed that disease and poor sanitation were decimating the lives of internees. The British government dismissed Hobhouse's revelations but was forced to send an official commission to South Africa, led by the feminist Millicent Fawcett, to investigate further. The Fawcett Commission confirmed Emily Hobhouse's worst reports and concluded that most of the sickness and death in the camps was preventable if elementary rules of hygiene were observed. Civilian authorities finally took control from the military and cleaned up the camps, but in the meantime 26,000 prisoners, 20,000 of them under age sixteen, died.

Besides establishing the first concentration camps of the new century, General Kitchener also strung 3,700 miles of barbed wire around strategic railways and "pacified" districts. Foraying out from these bastions, British soldiers treated the *veldt* as a "free-fire zone" and reported a monthly body count of killed, wounded, or captured guerrillas. Kitchener termed this tally the "bag," as if he were engaged in a fox hunt.

In Bruce Beresford's 1979 film *Breaker Morant,* the title character, an officer in the infamous Bushveldt Carbineers, enlightens a comrade on the realities of warfare in South Africa: "It's a new war for a new century. I suppose this is the first time the enemy hasn't been in uniform. They're farmers, they're people from small towns, and they shoot at us from houses and from paddocks. Some of them are women, and some of them are children. . . . The tragedy of war is that these horrors are committed by normal men in abnormal situations."

It would be hard to imagine a more abnormal, or ironic, situation than the Anglo-Boer War of 1899-1902. A white African tribe fought for freedom and national independence against European conquerors, while denying the more numerous black African tribes any rights of their own. The savage struggle between whites and the brutal oppression of blacks foreshadowed many of the horrors of the twentieth century.

The British won the war, but the Hobhouse and Fawcett revelations had given them a guilty conscience, so they soon relinquished effective control back to the Boers. When a Liberal government came to power in London in 1905, it repudiated the warlike policies of its Conservative predecessors and apologetically

7

granted self-government to the Transvaal and the Orange River Colony (as the Orange Free State had been renamed). Led by one of their most skillful generals, Louis Botha, the Boers united their two colonies with Natal and the Cape in the Union of South Africa, proclaimed on May 30, 1910. Boer and Briton conspired together to build a prosperous, democratic state that segregated the black African majority, while exploiting its labor on their farms and in the mines and factories. Thus the twentieth century began with one white tribe in Africa under siege by another, but ultimately united against the black Africans.

Halfway around the world in East Asia, Europeans were beleaguered by inhabitants of the world's largest and oldest civilization. The Chinese Empire remained technically independent, under the aloof rule of a Manchu Ch'ing (Qing)[2] ruler and a corps of scholar-gentry in the Forbidden City of Peking (Beijing). Yet in the mid-nineteenth century the British had fought two wars against the Chinese, winning the right to trade with the empire, and they had come to dominate large sectors of the country. Other European powers, as well as Japan and the United States, followed the British lead, extracting trade concessions from the Chinese and carving out spheres of influence in various port cities and their surrounding hinterlands.

The Chinese had fitfully imitated the foreign invaders, importing European weapons and adopting some features of European education; but it was a halfhearted effort at best. The Dowager Empress (or Queen Mother) Ts'u-hsi (Cixi) staged a palace coup in 1898, imprisoning the young reforming emperor Kuang-hsu (Guangxu) on an island within the Forbidden City and terminating all attempts to imitate European practices.

At the turn of the century the greatest empires of the world, China and Great Britain, both had female monarchs. Yet Ts'u-hsi actually ruled her realm, whereas Queen Victoria of England, though she gave her name to an age, was a constitutional monarch without political power. A curious paradox marked twentieth-century politics. More strong female leaders have ruled over Asian countries, despite their traditions of patriarchy, than in the more "feminist" nations of Europe or America. The dowager empress of China is the first example, but later in the century Indira Gandhi in India, Benazir Bhutto in Pakistan, and

---

2. In the late 1970s the Chinese government introduced the *pinyin* system of transliterating their language into English, and many Western scholars have adopted it. I have chosen to retain the older system for two reasons. First, the older form of city names, such as Peking and Canton, and personal names, such as Chiang Kai-shek and Mao Tse-Tung, are more familiar to most readers and were used in the majority of historical works I consulted. Second, while advocates of the new system contend that their spellings are closer to the actual sound of the words in Chinese, the widespread use of the letters Q and X in the *pinyin* system makes English pronunciation difficult. The new form of spelling is included in parentheses the first time a Chinese name appears.

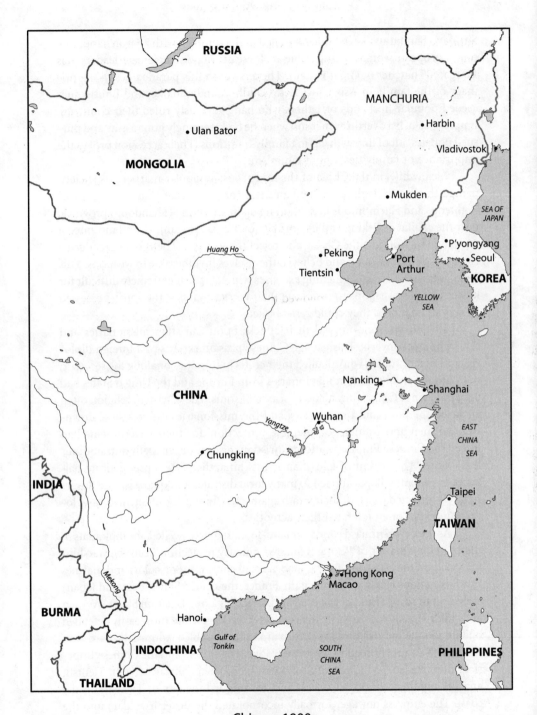

China c. 1900

Sirimavo Bandaranaike in Sri Lanka ruled their countries with an iron hand. The only European woman comparable to these strong Asian female leaders was Margaret Thatcher of Great Britain. The answer to this paradox lies in the primacy of the family in Asian societies. Gandhi, Bandaranaike, and Bhutto succeeded popular husbands or fathers who had previously ruled their countries. Empress Ts'u-hsi overthrew her son when he had seemingly gone astray and pursued policies out of line with Ch'ing family traditions. Their accession proves the importance of family ties, not of feminism.

Meanwhile, in the China of the mid-1890s, a popular martial arts society, named the Boxers United in Righteousness (often translated as the Society of Righteous and Harmonious Fists), sprang up in Shantung (Shandong) province, near the capital of Peking and its port city of Tientsin (Tianjin), and mounted a campaign to "support the Ch'ing and reject the foreign." The Boxers practiced a ritual of spirit possession and believed themselves invulnerable to weapons. This belief was based on strengthening exercises which made it extremely difficult for knives or other weapons to penetrate their tensed muscles; the spirit-possessed Boxers also believed they could resist bullets.

The Boxers concentrated their attacks upon Christian missionaries and their Chinese converts. The average Chinese peasant rarely saw a foreign diplomat, soldier, or trader, who all plied their crafts in the cities or along the seacoast; but Catholic and Protestant missionaries from Europe and the United States had penetrated into China's heartland in search of souls. The Christian religion often attracted the poor and the outcasts, and the missionaries offered these downtrodden men and women considerable protection, for their governments had forced the Chinese Empire to afford Christians a separate, virtually autonomous legal status. The advent of Christianity in China, therefore, upset delicate balances in peasant villages and led to many local disputes and quarrels. The Boxers naturally directed much of their wrath against the foreign "soul catchers," and local authorities often tolerated their activities.

As the new century dawned and anti-foreign frenzy swelled, the diplomats in the Legation Quarter of Peking requested military protection from the warships stationed off the coast. On June 1, 1900, a small contingent of sailors and marines from six nations (Russia, Great Britain, France, the United States, Italy, and Japan) arrived in the capital and began erecting barricades along Legation Street. Women and children withdrew to the British embassy, the largest and most easily defended building in the quarter, and the British ambassador cabled Admiral Edward Seymour with an urgent request for more troops. The Boxers and the Chinese Imperial troops stalled Seymour's force of nearly 2,000 men halfway between Tientsin and Peking, then cut off his retreat and surrounded the city of Tientsin on the coast. The empress dowager formally incorporated the Boxer irregulars into the Imperial Army and declared all-out war to drive the foreigners into the sea.

Sailors and marines from the ships in the harbor forced their way into Tientsin on June 24, and a detachment relieved Admiral Seymour's force, which had lost more than 10 percent of its men while fighting its way back to the coast. More foreign troops poured into China, particularly from nearby Japan and Russia, and in mid-July they cleared the Chinese forces from Tientsin, burning and looting much of the city. The Chinese viceroy, disgraced by defeat, committed suicide along with his entire family.

Since communications had been cut between Peking and the coast, the foreign soldiers assumed that the diplomats and their families in the capital had all been killed. In fact, about 1,000 foreigners and 3,000 Chinese Christians had come under siege in the Legation Quarter on June 20, 1900, but they had brought in enough provisions to hold out for several months, including 150 racing ponies that they slaughtered and ate. They piled sandbags around the British embassy and shored up the barricades to keep the Chinese artillery and rifle fire as far away as possible. The empress brought in a strongly anti-foreign general from the south to direct the siege of the legations, and she ordered the execution of five advisers who counseled making peace with the foreigners. Nevertheless, several local commanders may have dragged their feet and prevented an all-out assault on the compound.

After a month of siege, the diplomats smuggled out a message, and on August 4 a strong relief column of nearly 20,000 soldiers set out for Peking. The Japanese provided nearly half the troops, while the Russians, British, French, and Americans contributed the rest. With the Japanese in the van, the invaders drove the Chinese back relentlessly, reaching the walls of Peking by August 13. On a reconnoitering mission, Russian troops discovered an unguarded gate and, disregarding orders, rushed in to find the besieged diplomats, their families, and the Chinese Christians unharmed.

The dowager empress and the captive emperor fled to a mountain stronghold in western China on August 15 as the foreign troops seized and looted the city. A year later, the Chinese signed a humiliating treaty, pledging to execute, imprison, or exile about 100 of the Boxer ringleaders, and then pay an indemnity to the various foreign states equivalent to 67 million British pounds sterling. This sizeable sum (equivalent to about 300 million dollars) ate up nearly all the revenue gathered by Chinese customs receipts for a number of years, further retarding China's ability to compete economically with Europe.

The Boxer Rebellion provides a classic example of what anthropologist Anthony F. C. Wallace has labeled a "revitalization movement." Often in the last several centuries, when a militarily stronger people came into contact with a weaker group, the subject people underwent a sort of religious revival. New leaders arose preaching a gospel of anti-foreignism and claiming that if their followers abandoned all foreign customs and returned to the traditions of their ancestors, they

11

would be invincible — even foreign bullets would not harm them. Perhaps the most famous example of such a revitalization movement was the Ghost Dance religion among the Sioux tribe in the western United States. The Ghost Dancers gained numerous adherents in 1889-90 until their gathering at Wounded Knee Creek in South Dakota led nervous American troops to open fire on December 29, 1890, killing several hundred, including women and children.

Though the Boxers were routed and China's exploitation continued, the siege of the legations provided a powerful foretaste of the forthcoming century, when the dominance of Europe and the United States over Asia and Africa would come under attack and finally crumble. Like the complicated war in South Africa at the same time, the Boxer Rebellion prophesied a century of rage among nations.

CHAPTER TWO

The Terrible "Isms"

The twentieth century pulsed and throbbed with boundless energy. Artists and philosophers loosed the energy of willpower and imagination against all received wisdom, while scientists probed the life force of living beings and unlocked the energy of atoms. Inventors built flying machines and cast waves of sound and light through the air. Electricity turned night into day. Yet the most powerful energies unleashed in this century were the terrible "isms," great ideas that inspired Europeans to dream of better worlds, to conquer ancient civilizations they found overseas, and to kill each other with ferocity and abandon.

Four "isms," four clusters of ideas — imperialism, nationalism, socialism, and anarchism — haunted Europe and the world in 1900. The French Revolution of 1789, that mother of modern ideologies, spawned all four, and throughout the nineteenth century they grew in intensity. All but anarchism would persist as major forces throughout the twentieth century.

A map of the world in 1900 reveals that Western Europe and the Americas looked much the same then as they do today. However, four giant empires (the German, the Habsburg, the Russian, and the Ottoman Turk) dominated Eastern Europe; and the various Western European countries had carved the continents of Asia and Africa into colonies, protectorates, and spheres of influence.

The name for this phenomenon is imperialism, which international historian Akira Iriye has defined simply as "the dominance of one group of people over another by force." A specific form of this impulse to dominate marked the nineteenth and twentieth centuries. Economically advanced European states spread their influence around the world, penetrating less technically complex and less prosperous countries in Asia, Africa, and the Americas. Europe became the metropolitan center of a world economy, with the other continents as the pe-

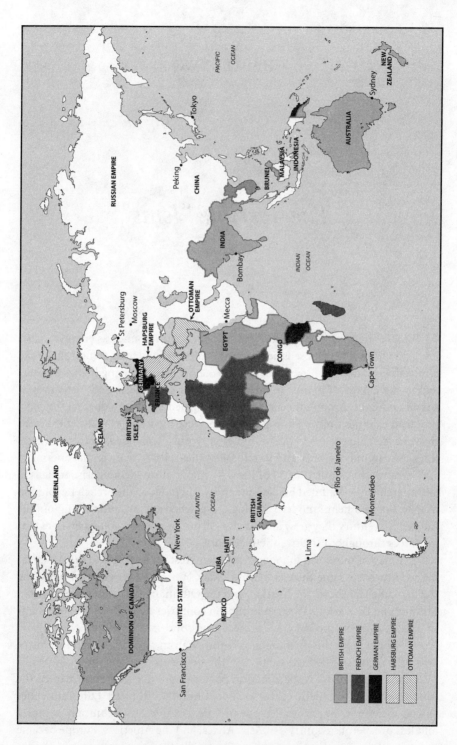

World Empires c. 1900

RUSSIAN EMPIRE

PACIFIC OCEAN

NEW ZEALAND

Sydney

AUSTRALIA

Tokyo

Peking

CHINA

BRUNEI

MALAYSIA

INDONESIA

INDIA

Bombay

INDIAN OCEAN

St Petersburg

Moscow

OTTOMAN EMPIRE

Mecca

HAPSBURG EMPIRE

GERMANY

FRANCE

EGYPT

CONGO

Cape Town

BRITISH ISLES

ICELAND

GREENLAND

ATLANTIC OCEAN

BRITISH GUIANA

Rio de Janeiro

Montevideo

New York

CUBA

HAITI

Lima

DOMINION OF CANADA

UNITED STATES

MEXICO

San Francisco

BRITISH EMPIRE
FRENCH EMPIRE
GERMAN EMPIRE
HABSBURG EMPIRE
OTTOMAN EMPIRE

riphery. Imperialism, then, can also be defined as the "growth of metropolitan control."

At first the stronger nations, particularly Great Britain, exercised their influence indirectly, through trade and missionary activities, finding willing collaborators among the elite of the non-European states. This "informal imperialism" of free trade and Christian evangelization profoundly disrupted the economies, governing mechanisms, and patterns of thought in the hinterlands of the periphery, giving rise to revolts against the Europeans and their collaborators. For example, the Boxers in China attacked European missionaries and Christian converts, not because the Chinese hated other religions, but because the missionaries had disturbed age-old patterns of status, power, and justice in the villages. Missionaries converted the outcasts of Chinese society and brought them under the legal protection of the European powers. They intervened frequently in lawsuits against Christian villagers, short-circuiting the processes of Chinese law. To the Boxers, Christianity seemed a mechanism for protecting bandits and exalting pariahs, upsetting the norms of settled society.

Such local crises frequently moved Europeans toward the next step in modern imperialism: formal colonial rule over faraway territories they could no longer dominate indirectly. No master plan drove this final stage of imperialism. Rather, the actions of ambitious Europeans out on the periphery and the inevitable reactions and revolts against them built up the colonial empires piecemeal. In sum, as historian Wolfgang J. Mommsen has said, "imperialism was primarily the consequence of the overflowing energy of European societies in the economic, military and political fields."

The results of this excess energy are striking. In the last three decades of the nineteenth century, the European powers gobbled up one-fifth of the land area and one-tenth of the people on earth. In 1878 Europeans had penetrated only a few coastal areas of Africa, but by 1912 they had grabbed the entire continent except for Ethiopia and Liberia. France and England captured the lion's share of Africa, with laggard Germany just beginning to stake its claims. Even the king of tiny, neutral Belgium, Leopold II, kept the Congo basin in the center of the continent as a gigantic rubber plantation, worked by forced African labor. The land mass of Asia was not so neatly parceled out. Continent-sized countries such as India and China, with ancient, complex civilizations of their own, retained some autonomy or independence, but Europeans influenced and ultimately controlled them.

The economy of Western Europe powered this final burst of imperialism in the late nineteenth century. The industrial revolution created giant industries with giant needs, so European industrialists were constantly seeking new markets for their burgeoning supply of manufactured goods. English textile manufacturers dreamed of putting a cotton shirt on the backs of 400 million Chinese. Industrialists also required huge quantities of raw materials to feed their machines. European mills processed cotton from Egypt, copper from Australia, tin from Bolivia, nickel from Canada, and rubber from Malaya. So in the late nineteenth century, Europeans roamed the world searching for raw materials and new markets. Bigness was the hallmark of imperialism — giant empires based on giant economic enterprises.

The Russian Bolshevik leader, V. I. Lenin, reflected on this scramble for colonies in his 1916 book *Imperialism: The Highest Stage of Capitalism*. In Lenin's view, economic laws inevitably push capitalist states into colonial expansion, which leads to rivalries between the imperialist powers and eventually to the collapse of the whole system. Imperial rivalries did increase international tension throughout the twentieth century; but it is worth stressing, in the words of historian Laurence Lafore, that "the flurry of overseas expansion and its accompanying tensions never led to war between European Powers."

Nevertheless, the imperial outreach of Europe devastated many countries and peoples that it touched. Pierre Savorgnan de Brazza, who explored the Congo basin for France in the 1880s, returned twenty-five years later to investigate abuses by colonial administrators and discovered that much of "his" colony had become a wilderness, depopulated by predatory trade wars and slave-hunting expeditions. In 1904 the cattle-herding Herero of German South West Africa, driven to desperation by disease and forced labor, revolted against their colonial masters. General Lothar von Trotha, sent out by Kaiser Wilhelm II, drove the rebels and their families into a waterless waste of desert then issued a formal "extermination order," authorizing wholesale slaughter of all Hereros who did not surrender. Though the kaiser tardily countermanded the order, the military in Africa carried out this first genocide of the twentieth century. Out of 80,000 Hereros, about 60,000 died of thirst, starvation, or German bullets. Perhaps 9,000 survived the desert and escaped to a neighboring British colony; 15,000 surrendered, but more than half of them died in prison camps.

Though greed was the strongest force behind these imperialist outrages, other motives besides economics impelled Europeans outward. Missionaries and colonial administrators believed they were doing the "backward peoples" of the world a favor by spreading Christianity and European culture to them. The English poet of empire, Rudyard Kipling, christened this impulse "The White Man's Burden," to uplift and civilize the savages.

Imperialism was also a status symbol for nations. Even if colonies did not pay well (and many of them did not), every economically advanced country desired them as proof that it was an important nation. So, at the turn of the century, upstart nations such as Germany, the United States, and Japan jumped into the race for overseas colonies out of a desire for national prestige. This leads us to the second great "ism," nationalism.

16

Though Lenin called imperialism the highest stage of capitalism, it might better be labeled the highest stage of nationalism. National pride pushed countries toward a colonialist version of conspicuous consumption, collecting conquests and colonies like so many jewels in a crown. As historian Carlton Hayes remarked:

> Flags of European imperial powers were seemingly hoisted by an explorer or ship captain as a national competitive sport with about the same indifference to any practical consideration as characterized the later planting of American and other flags on cakes of ice around the North or South Pole.

When the English boasted that the sun never set on their empire, they were expressing national pride more than economic greed.

National sentiment is a sense of cohesion, a "we-feeling" among a relatively large group of people. Ordinarily, we assume that this "we-feeling" is based on a common racial origin, a common language, and a common religion. So, for example, we assume that Swedes have blond hair and blue eyes, speak a common language, and belong to the Lutheran church; Italians have dark hair and swarthy complexions, speak their own language, and are all Catholics. Yet, in reality, national cohesion is rarely this tidy. Germany, for instance, is divided into many religious groups, Catholics, Lutherans, Calvinists, and Jews; and Switzerland embraces the speakers of four official languages, German, French, Italian, and Romansch. Other European nationalities, such as the French, which look so homogeneous from a distance, are amalgamations of several different peoples, including Normans, Bretons, and Provencals. They are not biologically or racially "pure," like thoroughbred horses or genetically engineered plants. And what are we to make of countries such as Canada and the United States, composed of many different immigrating peoples with no common origin at all? What holds these countries together and makes them nations?

Ultimately, national consciousness is based on cultural identity more than racial inheritance. It is primarily emotional. The nineteenth-century French philosopher Ernst Renan provided the single most penetrating analysis of national sentiment, which can be paraphrased as "a feeling that we have done great things together in the past, are continuing to do great things together in the present, and shall do great things together in the future." This feeling need not be based on a common biological origin or a common religion, but it must be firmly grounded on striking common experiences: wars, revolutions, conquests — great deeds that make people swell with pride.

The emotion of nationalism requires heroes, myths, and great events (either real or imaginary) linking people to something bigger than themselves. Unfortunately, historic enemies (either real or imaginary) are also required to define the national identity. A small band of similar people isolated on a desert island would feel no national consciousness, for they would have no one with whom to compare themselves. They would simply call themselves "the people," as small tribes in isolated regions of the world still do. It is only when different groups bump against one another that they develop national consciousness.

Words can seriously mislead us, for an unconscious form of imperialism surrounds much discourse about nationalism. Europeans in this century generally call an ethnic group in Africa that does not possess a nation-state of its own a *tribe*. Yet they would designate a group of similar size in Europe, which happens to form the majority of a country's population, a *nation*. Both ethnic groups (the Greek root, *ethnos*, means people) are basically the same — collections of people united by a sense of common origin.

Nearly all people in every time and place feel ethnic or tribal consciousness, but nationalism as a full-blown ideology requires a high degree of self-consciousness. Mass education played a major role in directing popular patriotism away from local clans, villages, cities, or provinces and toward the nation as a whole. Carlton Hayes, one of this century's foremost students of nationalism, concludes:

> Patriotism, therefore, while instinctive in its origin and root, is much more naturally and readily associated with a small community in a restricted area than with a large nationality in a broad expanse of territory. Only through an intensive and extensive educational process will a local group of people become thoroughly aware of their entire nationality and supremely loyal to it.

Nationalism also has a political aspect that is lacking in more instinctive, less self-conscious forms of human identity. As soon as national consciousness has emerged and been disseminated through mass education, the people of a nation, if they are not politically independent, begin agitating for a state, a country, a *nation-state* of their own. Mature nationalism, therefore, links a sense of identity with the notion of power. Political power as a nation-state confers status, prestige, and dignity on a self-conscious group of people.

We take nationalism for granted today and often forget that it is a comparatively recent historical phenomenon, beginning to develop only about five hundred years ago and not reaching full flower until the last two hundred years. Throughout all of human history, people have given their primary loyalty to small groups and localities: the family, the clan, the neighborhood, or the region. Hayes labels these small-scale patriotisms "feline" loyalties to familiar places and "canine" loyalties to familiar persons. When people did feel a need to be part of something larger, they usually looked to religion or to multinational empires. In past centuries, Europeans considered themselves part of Christendom or the Islamic world, subjects of the Habsburg or the Ottoman Empires, not citizens of France, Italy, or Turkey. Nationalism developed out of the breakdown of Christian unity at the time of the Protestant Reformation. Later, as religious fervor declined and society became more secular, nationalism replaced religion as a unifying force. Nationalism is a substitute religion, an emotional force that unites people who do not even know each other.

The French Revolution made nationalism the most powerful force in Europe. The French overthrew their king and their church in 1789, then under the Emperor Napoleon their armies marched through Europe. These stunning events provided the "great deeds" needed for a full-blown French nationalism and persuaded other European people to emulate the French. Nationalism was seen as a liberating force. Ironically, rebellions against Napoleon and the French by the conquered peoples of Europe fueled their own national consciousness. Throughout the nineteenth century, whenever Europeans felt oppressed by kings or priests, they would appeal for a revolution of national liberation. Nationalism seemed to go hand-in-hand with political liberalism. A similar process of nation-state formation was well developed in North and South America and had also begun in a few regions of Africa and Asia, but national self-consciousness reached its fullest development worldwide as a reaction to European imperialism.

Yet nationalism could be a conservative or oppressive force as well, as rulers shamelessly exploited the emotion for militarist or imperialist goals. Unfortunately, too, once an oppressed nation gained its independence, it often oppressed other nationalities in turn. So, for example, the largest subject nationality in the Austrian Empire, the Hungarians, finally forced the Habsburgs to grant Hungary self-government and autonomy in 1867. The Habsburg Empire became a dual monarchy, a double state called Austria-Hungary. But the Hungarians were no sooner free than they began ruthlessly oppressing and trying to assimilate the Slovaks, Rumanians, and other minorities within their borders. Nationalism, then, can be a powerful force for either liberation or oppression.

By 1900 in Europe, the impulse of nationalism had narrowed to a more rigid form, emphasizing a supposed racial homogeneity of the nation over cultural identity. Europeans equated national consciousness with race and power. They identified themselves as members of a biologically distinct English "race" or French "race," and they assumed that only "races" who controlled their own nation-states were worthy of respect. The "tribes" of Africa, therefore, or the subject nationalities of Eastern Europe were decidedly second-class citizens in a world of racially conceived nation-states.

At the turn of the century, nation-states were considered the highest form of society in Europe; yet the continent fell far short of this ideal. Four multinational empires still dominated Eastern Europe, and even in Western Europe many anomalies and exceptions could be discovered. Nearly every European state encompassed one or more "Irelands" or "Alsaces," in the striking terminology fashioned by historian Laurence Lafore.

Ireland did not exist as a political entity in 1900; it formed part of the United Kingdom. Yet the Irish, though they had largely lost their language, still felt like a separate people. They practiced a militant form of Catholicism and cherished their own history of heroes, saints, and martyrs, while hating their ancient enemy, the Protestant English, who had been meddling in Irish affairs for more than seven hundred years. The Irish clearly enjoyed a national consciousness, and they wanted their own nation-state. An "Ireland" in the generic sense, therefore, was a subject nation within another people's nation-state. As such it posed a constant threat to the state's political stability. Every country in Europe embraced one or more "Irelands" in this sense.

Nearly every state in Europe also contained an "Alsace." Alsace was a province along the Rhine River that had frequently changed hands between the French king and the German emperor during the Middle Ages. Peasants and even knights cared little who their overlord was, so long as he protected religion and public order. However, in the age of nationalism, a lost province was not a pawn in a game but a part of a body, living flesh severed from the nation. After Alsace was seized by Germany in the Franco-Prussian War of 1870, the French lusted for *revanche*, revenge against Germany, and the recovery of the lost province. "Alsace," then, in the generic sense, referred to a part of a nation forcibly separated from its nation-state.

Europe, then, was a continent of imperfect nation-states in 1900, filled with "Irelands" and "Alsaces" and loaded with nationalist dynamite. Europe had also extended its imperialist sway over the rest of the world, stimulating nationalist movements of resistance and liberation in Africa and Asia. Imperialism and nationalism, therefore, kept the world of 1900 in a constant state of tension.

Yet they were not the only disruptive forces at work. The progress of industry and commerce, which had transformed much of Europe and North America, gave birth to "the social question," and this in turn spawned two more "isms," socialism and anarchism.

The social question dealt with the gap between rich and poor in industrial society. As the wealth of nations increased and capitalists grew prosperous, peasants were forced off their land to become wage laborers in factories, working twelve to fifteen hours a day, seven days a week at pitifully low wages. Men, women, and children all toiled to keep the industrial wheels turning. The harshness of social conditions for workers led many to despair. A young Parisian who lost his job tried to take his life by jumping into the Seine. When bystanders pulled him out alive, he kept crawling back in.

20

Others conquered their despair by dreaming new visions of a better society; the two most prevalent visions were socialism and anarchism. These two "isms" shared much in common. Both, like nationalism, were inspired by the example of the French Revolution. Though the revolution of 1789 had been neither socialistic nor anarchistic in its goals, it was indisputably a successful revolution. Therefore it inspired nineteenth-century radicals to believe that revolution was possible and that the next time it would be a social revolution.

Anarchism and socialism both indicted the industrial-capitalist system as hopelessly corrupt and worked to destroy it. Both "isms" envisioned the abolition of private property and the establishment of a system of collective ownership of the world's goods. Both ideologies held out the classless society as the ultimate goal, but they disagreed sharply over the means for reaching this goal. They also differed in the temperament and personality of their leaders.

The great founder and theorist of socialism, of course, was Karl Marx. Born in the German Rhineland to a Jewish family that had converted to Christianity, Marx studied philosophy at several German universities, became a committed socialist in Paris during the 1840s, then spent the rest of his life after 1849 in England. Before going to England he had already met his indispensable collaborator, Friedrich Engels, who often ghostwrote Marx's articles in English. Though Karl Marx enjoyed a loving relationship with his own father, his wife, and his father-in-law, Engels became his only close friend outside the family circle. A warm, light-hearted man in love with life, Engels perfectly complemented the cold, morose Marx, who cared only for ideas. Engels, who had lived among the industrial workers of Manchester, portrayed in vivid, concrete detail the problems of the English working class, which Marx had only grasped through statistics he had gleaned at the British Museum.

In 1848 Marx and Engels authored a short but influential pamphlet titled *The Communist Manifesto,* which contained the famous rallying cry: "Workers of the world unite, you have nothing to lose but your chains." Then in 1867 Marx produced his philosophic masterpiece, the massive volume called *Capital.* In the meantime, he helped found and eventually dominated the International Working Men's Association, the First International, a federation of socialist workers' organizations dedicated to the overthrow of capitalism.

Marx spun out a thoroughly materialistic philosophy of history. There is no God, and all human events are determined by economic motives. His philosophy, furthermore, was evolutionary: human society progresses through various stages of economic development. The present stage of capitalism, which Engels so vividly sketched out for him in England, had succeeded feudalism; and it in turn would inevitably give way to socialism, the collective ownership of property. Engels summed up Marx's philosophy most cogently in the eulogy he delivered at his friend's funeral in Highgate Cemetery:

21

As Darwin discovered the law of evolution in organic matters, so Marx discovered the law of evolution in human history — the single fact, previously hidden in ideological growths, that human beings must first of all eat, drink, shelter and clothe themselves before they can turn their attention to politics, science, art and religion; that therefore the production of the immediate means of life and consequently the given stage of economic development of a people or of a period forms the basis on which the State institutions . . . have developed.

Marx claimed to have discovered the exact process by which the inevitable triumph of socialism would take place. Capitalism, by its very nature, must result in increasing poverty for the masses. Capitalists, no matter how well intentioned, can only pay their workers a bare subsistence wage because of the iron laws of economics. Therefore, as poverty and exploitation increase, the working class will become more class conscious. The task of the socialist revolutionary is to organize the working class to overthrow its oppressors, seize the means of production, and socialize the production and consumption of goods. The increasing poverty of the working class and the inevitable collapse of capitalism were the two key ideas of Marxist socialism.

Anarchism, on the other hand, was less well worked out intellectually than socialism. The two key anarchist thinkers of the nineteenth century, Pierre-Joseph Proudhon and Michael Bakunin, had none of Marx's systematic, penetrating rationalism. Temperamentally, they were more emotional. Still, the basic ideas of anarchism are reasonably clear.

Anarchists shared the socialists' contempt for private property. One of Proudhon's first pamphlets, published in 1840, contained the most famous revolutionary slogan of the nineteenth century: "What is property? Property is theft." Anarchists, however, also believed in the immediate abolition of government. The social question was not purely economic, as it was for Marx. In *The General Idea of the Revolution in the Nineteenth Century,* Proudhon raged at the very idea of government:

To be governed is to be at every operation, at every transaction, noted, registered, enrolled, taxed, stamped, measured, numbered, assessed, licensed, authorized, admonished, forbidden, reformed, corrected, punished. It is, under pretext of public utility, and in the name of the general interest, to be placed under contribution, trained, ransomed, exploited, monopolized, extorted, squeezed, mystified, robbed; then, at the slightest resistance, the first word of complaint, to be repressed, fined, despised, harassed, tracked, abused, clubbed, disarmed, choked, imprisoned, judged, condemned, shot, deported, sacrificed, sold, betrayed; and to crown all, mocked, ridiculed, outraged, dishonored.

In essence, anarchism was a philosophy of pure liberty — no king, no church, no state, no landlord. Freed from oppressive institutions, individuals would prove more productive than formerly, and they would join together voluntarily in mutual associations for the sharing of the earth's goods.

Socialism and anarchism differed in important respects. Marxist socialism was highly organized, centralized, dogmatic, and authoritarian; whereas anarchism was, by definition, opposed to coercion, organization, and centralism. Socialists advocated political action by the workers to take over the state. The largest socialist party in Europe, the German Social Democratic Party, polled a million and a half votes and earned thirty-five seats in the Reichstag as early as 1890. The anarchists, on the other hand, opposed political action and wanted to destroy the state. Both aimed at the classless society as the ultimate goal, but they differed sharply over the transition from the existing order to the classless society. During the transition, socialists would forge a powerful, centralized state under control of the working class party (the dictatorship of the proletariat), whereas anarchists insisted on the destruction of the state at the earliest possible moment without any transitional dictatorship. Anarchist theory tried to match the means (voluntary mass action) to the end (the classless society).

These important philosophic and organizational differences reflected the different backgrounds of the leaders. Though Marx suffered much hardship and family tragedy during his years of exile in London, his roots were in the educated professional class, and his wife was the daughter of a wealthy nobleman. His wife's inheritance finally solved his personal financial problems. Proudhon, on the other hand, the son of a provincial laborer, was often close to starvation throughout his life. His personal boast about his origins and aspirations hit the mark:

> Born and bred in the bosom of the working class, belonging to it still in my heart and affections and above all in common suffering aspirations, my greatest joy [is] . . . to be enabled henceforth to work without cease, through science and philosophy, with all the energy of my will and all the powers of my spirit, for the betterment, moral and intellectual, of those whom I delight to call my brothers and my companions.

Proudhon sensed the differences between himself and Marx after meeting him for the first time in Paris in 1844. Shortly thereafter, he wrote to Marx: "Let us by all means collaborate in trying to discover the laws of society . . . but for God's sake, after we have demolished all the dogmatisms *a priori*, let us not of all things attempt in our turn to instill another kind of dogma into the people." Bakunin, too, found Marx insufferable. Shortly before his own death, Bakunin recalled: "Marx called me a sentimental idealist, and he was right. I called him morose, vain, and treacherous; and I too was right." The dictatorial dogmatism of the triumphant Communists in Soviet Russia flowed not only from Marxist theory but also from Marx's own vindictive, intolerant personality.

In historical perspective, socialism is far and away the more important of these two ideologies. Marxists led the most important revolutions of the twentieth century, the Russian Revolution of 1917 and the Maoist Revolution in China after World War II, and for much of this century they ruled over half the world. Despite the collapse of the Soviet empire in 1989, socialism is still a potent force in many parts of the globe today. Not so anarchism. Anarchism no longer exists as a conscious movement or philosophy, and only for two brief moments in the twentieth century did anarchists ever succeed in putting their ideas into practice — in parts of Ukraine just after the Russian Revolution in 1918-19, and in Barcelona and surrounding areas during the Spanish Civil War in 1936-37. In short, anarchism failed.

And yet it did not seem this way in 1900. In some ways, socialism seemed to be a spent force at the turn of the century, whereas anarchism caused nightmares for the bourgeoisie. By 1900, Marx's predictions seemed clearly wrong. The working class was not getting progressively poorer; rather, their standard of living was rising. Slow, piecemeal reform had made modest gains through trade union activity and democratic politics, so that the capitalist system seemed far from collapse. When a leading German Socialist, Edward Bernstein, asked his colleagues to face these facts squarely, he was condemned as a revisionist (the socialist term for heretic) at his party's congress in 1899. Though the socialist parties of Western Europe were large and growing, many believed they were paper tigers, too closely enmeshed in the existing political order to overthrow it. The situation of the socialists in Eastern Europe seemed far more dire. The Social Democratic Workers Party of Russia had just been founded at a congress of nine delegates who represented practically nobody but themselves. This party — which eventually started the revolution of 1917 — was, at the turn of the century, a tiny Marxist minority of an already minuscule left wing in tsarist Russia. No one — capitalist or socialist alike — took it seriously.

If you asked most Europeans at the turn of the century which of the "isms" most concerned them, they would probably have responded anarchism. To put the matter bluntly, Europeans were preoccupied with anarchism because anarchist guns and bombs were going off all over Europe and the Americas.

In the twenty years before 1914, anarchists assassinated six heads of state or government — a president of France, a president of the United States, two prime ministers of Spain, the empress of Austria, and the king of Italy. Anarchists also attacked other class enemies and agents of the state. On December 9, 1893, a young man named August Vaillant hurled a homemade bomb filled with nails from the gallery of the French Chamber of Deputies. Amazingly, no one was killed, but a number of deputies were wounded by the flying metal fragments.

Most chilling were the seemingly random anarchist attacks on innocent by-standers. On November 8, 1893, opening night at the Lyceo, the elegant opera house of Barcelona, two men tossed bombs from the balcony, one of which ex-ploded, killing twenty-two spectators and maiming fifty more. The following year, a French anarchist, Emile Henry, detonated a bomb in the Cafe Terminus at a busy Paris train station, killing one and wounding twenty. The terrorists, how-ever, did not consider their violence to be random. At his trial, when Henry was asked why he killed innocent bystanders, he replied with cool logic: "There are no innocent bourgeois." Similarly, another anarchist, Leon-Jules Leauthier, argued: "I shall not strike an innocent man if I strike the first bourgeois to come along."

So at the turn of the century, and ever after, the word "anarchism" called up visions of terror, violence, and chaos. The typical anarchist, immortalized in thousands of political cartoons, was a madman with a bushy mustache and a smoking bomb. This stereotypical anarchist really existed, for anarchism enjoyed its greatest appeal among desperate men, women, and nations. Proudhon, unlike Marx, defined the working class very broadly to include the unemployed, drifters, and down-and-outers as well as the factory workers. Anarchism waxed strongest in Spain, Italy, and Russia, countries on the less advanced fringes of Europe where the state and the upper classes were most oppressive. It appealed to those who had nothing to lose.

Yet the individual terrorists formed a tiny minority in the anarchist move-ment. There were many kinds of anarchists, and the movement functioned at many different levels. This would have been news to the average European, but most anarchists were moral men and women — indeed, they were *moralists,* who agonized over questions of right and wrong. In particular, they asked whether it was permissible to use immoral means to bring about a just end. In this they dif-fered from Karl Marx, who despised moralizing and believed that all human ac-tions were determined by economic laws. Lenin, too, was thoroughly amoral. He titled his most famous published work simply and pragmatically, *What Is to Be Done?* Anarchists, however, also worried about *how* it, the revolution, was to be done.

Obviously, the individual terrorists gave one answer to the question of means and ends. Yet even their case is not so simple. Emile Henry, who declared that there were no innocent bourgeois, did not believe he was using immoral means toward revolution. With the logic of the fanatic, he foreshadowed a terri-ble commonplace of this rage-filled century, demonization of the class enemy or the national enemy. Most anarchists, from Proudhon onward, delivered another answer: it was not permissible to use immoral means to achieve a moral end. In particular, they feared the use of authoritarian organizations to hasten the revo-lution. Centralized revolutionary parties were governments by another name, and all governments trampled on fundamental rights. The anarchists saw more clearly than most that a dictatorship of the proletariat is still a dictatorship. They would have appreciated the last line of the 1960s rock anthem, "Won't Be Fooled Again": "Say hello to the new boss, the same as the old boss."

The terrorist stereotype of anarchism is unfortunate; yet the bomb-throwing image does illustrate the basic dilemma that faced all anarchists: How were they to make a revolution without the disciplined, centralized workers' party which they found anathema? Anarchists relied primarily on agitation and propaganda. They believed that revolution would spring spontaneously from the working class. Only two things were required to cause this spontaneous combustion: constant propaganda to educate the workers and some sort of spark to set off the masses.

Different anarchists viewed the propaganda problem in differing ways. Intellectuals rested content with propaganda in words, hoping that the spark would come automatically in a strike, a bread riot, or a police atrocity. Some desperate individuals went further and determined to provide the spark themselves; these were the assassins and bomb-throwers. They called their acts of terrorism "propaganda by the deed." Neither form of propaganda, by word or deed, worked. The masses did not rise up. Indeed, the terror campaign proved counterproductive, for it increased government repression.

After the turn of the century, some anarchists compromised a bit and began to organize. They organized trade unions, or *syndicats* in French, and thus were called anarcho-syndicalists. Anarchist unions did not agitate for bread-and-butter gains, they still rejected politics, and they still advocated revolution. Their distinctive technique, which they added to the anarchist's arsenal of weapons, was the general strike. Rather than words or individual terrorism, the general strike would spark off the revolution.

So anarchism was a great kaleidoscope of personalities, ideas, and techniques, not a tightly organized movement. It included psychopathic killers and saintly dreamers. Yet at all levels, anarchism failed. So why bother discussing it?

First of all, anarchism, though largely forgotten today, loomed large at the turn of the century. Anarchists helped raise people's consciousness of the social question, and their very extremism may have inadvertently assisted more moderate socialists and liberal democrats. Also, their individual acts of terror provided the model for the spark that set off the First World War and for other terrorist outrages later in the century. Propaganda by the deed has been a basic fact of life in the twentieth century.

Furthermore, there is always value in studying losers because the loser reveals, as in a mirror, major features of the winners. If we understand why a person, an idea, or a movement failed, we will learn a great deal about the society surrounding it. So it is with anarchism. The anarchists believed in individual liberty and resisted government or organized bigness of any kind. Yet the twentieth century has been preeminently the century of organized bigness — big government, big corporations, big unions, big armies, vast bureaucracies of all kinds. So the failure of anarchism shines a spotlight on the central tendency of the twentieth century — the trend toward centralized giantism.

One of the most popular historians of the century, Barbara Tuchman, summed up the matter very well: "Anarchism was the last cry of the individual man, the last movement among the masses on behalf of individual liberty, the last hope of living unregulated, the last fist shaken against the encroaching State, before the State, the party, the union, the organization closed in."

Four "isms" stalked the world in 1900. Anarchism was the most sensational and seemingly the most threatening at the time, but it soon faded. Imperialism and socialism, and the reactions against them, dominated much of the twentieth century. Yet, nationalism, the "ism" often taken for granted, proved the most basic and persistent. After the colonial empires had fallen and the Berlin Wall crumbled, revealing the wreckage of imperialism and socialism, nationalism still raged in human hearts and shaped the end of the century as it had the beginning.

In the human orchestra of the twentieth century, anarchists crashed the cymbals and banged the drums, but their raucous noise clanged only intermittently. The sounds of imperialists and socialists swelled impressively, like two massed groups of strings and brasses, in chorus after chorus. Yet when their last crescendo faded, the steady beat of nationalism continued throbbing, like a *basso continuo* throughout the century.

CHAPTER THREE

East and West, North and South

When Europeans looked out at the rest of the world in the early twentieth century, they judged other peoples by European nationalist standards and thus found them inferior. They calculated the degrees of supposed inferiority on a scale calibrated by race and power. The closer that peoples of Asia, Africa, and the Americas approximated the European racial type and the militarily or industrially powerful nation-state, the more favorably they were viewed. Might plus white made right.

In North America, where the native Amerindian population had been killed or pushed aside, most citizens of Canada and the United States were transplanted Europeans, and thus formed a part of "Western civilization."[1] The countries of South America were also independent nation-states, largely ruled by creole descendants of European settlers, but these countries retained large numbers of Amerindian and mixed-race inhabitants and thus were considered "backward" by Europeans and North Americans.

The vast populations of Asia and Africa, however, seemed truly benighted

---

1. The terms "West" and "East" are, of course, Eurocentric. China and Japan were the Far East, as viewed from Europe; Persia and the eastern shore of the Mediterranean were the Middle East; and Turkey and the Balkans formed the Near East. "Western civilization" traces its roots to the religious cultures of Judaism and Christianity and the civic cultures of Greece and Rome and is often contrasted with "Oriental civilizations" such as the Islamic states of the Arabs and Turks or the Hindu and Buddhist cultures of Asia. Since these terms are loaded with connotations of "Western" superiority and are, furthermore, not geographically very useful (Asia, after all, is west of the United States, not east), I will try to avoid them throughout this book. I will employ, wherever possible, simple geographical terms, such as "East Asia" rather than "the Far East."

by European standards. Africa had long been known as the Dark Continent, not only for the color of its inhabitants' skin but also for their non-Christian religious practices and unfamiliar physical environment. Europeans knew more, or thought they knew more, about Asian societies such as China and India, but they considered their inhabitants backward and childlike, suitable for colonization and improvement by European conquerors. They were able to harbor such illusions because of the vast preponderance of power and physical force enjoyed by European nation-states. In India, for example, the British numbered only 156,500 — including soldiers and civilians, men and women — in 1921, but they ruled over 305.7 million Indians. Despite lingering fears and doubts, the British could always console themselves with a little bit of rhyme:

> Whatever happens, we have got
> The Maxim gun, which they have not.

It is important to recall that Europe was not always stronger than the rest of the world. For more than a thousand years after the fall of the Roman Empire in the fifth century, Christian Europe was weaker than the Chinese and other Asian empires and was constantly threatened with invasion by its Islamic neighbors. Arabs conquered nearly all of Spain in the eighth century, built a brilliant civilization there, and were not finally expelled until the year that Christopher Columbus set sail on the Atlantic. Nomadic warriors from the steppes of Asia periodically overran Eastern Europe, and the Islamic Turks ruled most of the Balkans and the Hungarian plain well into modern times. As late as 1683 the Turks were still threatening to capture Vienna.

Europeans set sail on their epic voyages of discovery in the fifteenth and sixteenth centuries, not from a position of overwhelming strength, but in compensation for their weakness. Traders such as Marco Polo had made contact with China during the Middle Ages, when the Mongol Khan enforced peace and order along the land routes, and Europe had developed an appetite for the silk and spices that could be obtained only in Asia. Yet as the Mongol Empire weakened and the Turks blocked the caravan routes between Europe and East Asia, this contact was interrupted. The European kingdoms facing the Atlantic Ocean — Portugal first, then Spain, England, and France — developed new types of sailing ships in an attempt to outflank the power of Islam. Portuguese navigators inched down the west coast of Africa and finally rounded the Cape of Good Hope at the continent's southern tip in 1488, reaching Asia ten years later. The Spanish took a chance on Columbus's westward voyage in 1492. The "Admiral of the Ocean Sea" was grossly in error about the size of the earth. When he "discovered" the Americas, he thought he had reached Asia. The European age of discovery was born in weakness and ignorance.

The swift and relatively easy conquest of the Americas by Spain and the other European nations owed less to overwhelming firepower or technological superiority than to disease. Isolated from the linked continents of Asia, Africa, and Europe, where human beings first evolved, the inhabitants of North and South America lacked natural immunity to many Old World diseases, such as smallpox. Not a policy of conscious genocide, as is often alleged, but the ruthless, unseen workings of tiny microbes devastated Amerindian populations after the first contact with Europeans. The population of North America around 1600, when the English first began colonization, has been estimated at about one million. The number of original inhabitants, however, had already crashed from an estimated total of 10 to 12 million at the time of Columbus — a 90 percent reduction due to disease before most Amerindians had even seen a white settler. The English thought they were colonizing virgin land, but as historian Francis Jennings has pointed out, "the American land was more like a widow than a virgin. Europeans did not find a wilderness here; rather, however involuntarily, they made one."

In the sixteenth century, firearms gave Europeans relatively little advantage in battle. Muskets and pistols made a loud noise and fired a single shot, very inaccurately. The native populations of the Americas soon got over their shock at the noise and realized that well-aimed arrows and spears could be just as lethal as European shot. What did give Europeans a battle advantage was their greater mobility, through the use of horses on land and sailing ships on the sea. Horses were not native to North America, and the canoes of the Amerindians, though well suited to riding the surf of coastal waters, could not transport large numbers of warriors great distances. Europeans could therefore deploy and concentrate their troops against the disease-weakened Amerindians in battle.

In Asia and Africa, Europeans did not enjoy the same advantages. Asians and Africans already employed horses in temperate plains environments; and in less hospitable climates, such as deserts and jungles, they made use of camels or elephants. Europeans, therefore, enjoyed no greater mobility in land warfare. Disease, which had unwittingly smoothed the European path in the Americas, worked against them in tropical Africa and India, where intense heat and unfamiliar diseases devastated them. The only advantage Europeans could rely on was greater mobility by sea. Not surprisingly, therefore, European trade and settlement in Africa and Asia were initially limited to islands and seacoasts.

In their first seagoing forays outside their own continent, Europeans were not infected by the virus of racism as strongly as they would be in later centuries. Impelled by a love for God, gold, and glory (not necessarily in that order), the conquerors and settlers in Asia, Africa, and the Americas certainly found the natives' customs strange, exotic, even disgusting. Yet they were repulsed more by the pagan religion of the peoples they encountered than by the color of their skin.

30

Over the centuries of intercontinental contact, however, a more biological, seemingly scientific judgment of dark-skinned peoples developed. The mainstay of commerce between Europeans and Africans was the slave trade. Economic need in the newly conquered territories of North and South America gave rise to the transatlantic practice of African slavery. Conquering Europeans had no intention of performing the backbreaking labor required on sugar, rice, indigo, or cotton plantations in the Americas, yet their imported diseases had so decimated the native population as to create an acute labor shortage. Therefore, European traders bought Africans captured in battle from their fellow Africans on the west coast of the continent, transporting them in filth and squalor to the Americas. From the 1500s to the 1800s more than 12 million African slaves were landed in the Western Hemisphere; millions more died en route.

The only Africans that most Europeans encountered were slaves or slave-traders. This did not create a positive impression of the black race. Gradually, the Europeans began to consider Africans as a slave race and blackness as a mark of slavery. In the mid-nineteenth century, this growing feeling received inadvertent scientific support from the publication of Charles Darwin's *On the Origin of Species,* which accustomed educated Europeans to think in racial terms. Darwin theorized that animal species evolve through a process of random mutations preserved by the survival of the fittest. Less rigorous scientists applied these insights to human communities and concluded that the dominant nations of Europe must therefore be the fittest in both a biological and a moral sense. Africans and Asians, reduced to servitude or colonization, must be "beaten men from beaten breeds." Racism, therefore, was more the consequence than the cause of African slavery.

The bonded labor of millions of Africans not only cultivated racism among Europeans; it also increased their power. Plantation agriculture swelled the profits of Europeans and Americans, enabling them to reinvest in trade and industry. By the nineteenth century, when slavery and the slave trade were abolished in most parts of the world, Europeans and Americans no longer needed slave labor, since they had undergone an industrial and agricultural revolution, greatly increasing their productivity and their power. As the age of imperialism reached its apex in the late nineteenth and early twentieth century, white men and women believed they were destined to rule the world.

Imperialism, the dominance of one people over another, had always gone hand in hand with another phenomenon, colonialism, a psychological state, an emotional feeling that this dominance was just and permanent. Racism greatly enhanced the European feeling of superiority over conquered peoples, and the greater military and technological power of the Europeans caused many Asians and Africans to reciprocate with feelings of inferiority. Octave Mannoni, the French author of a pioneering book on the psychology of colonization, has argued:

31

A *colonial situation* is created, so to speak, the very instant a white man, even if he is alone, appears in the midst of a tribe, even if it is independent, so long as he is thought to be rich or powerful or even merely immune to the local forces of magic, and so long as he derives from his position, even though only in his most secret self, a feeling of his own superiority.

The colonialist interplay of race and power can be traced in the history of British rule in India. The British East India Company began trading along the coasts of the Asian subcontinent around 1700; but far from enjoying any natural superiority, the English had to compete with Portuguese, French, and Dutch traders from Europe as well as local Arab and Indian merchants. British traders were restricted to "factories," that is, fortified trading posts along the coast. Historian Michael Edwardes has characterized the existence of the early British factories as "a generally boring life in an alcoholic haze of varying opacity."

Since about 1500, the Muslim Mogul emperor had ruled the subcontinent from Delhi, the capital of Hindustan, but the local village life of Indians was not affected greatly by either Moguls or Europeans. The British traders gradually fitted themselves into the economic life of the Mogul Empire as middlemen, particularly in the three major cities of Calcutta, Bombay, and Madras. As they made more contacts outside the coastal factories, they exhibited little interest in Indian culture but also very little racial prejudice. Since there were few white women in Asia, Englishmen married Indian women, or else kept them as concubines, producing mixed-race Eurasians who, in an early form of affirmative action, were given preference for employment by the British East India Company. The company did not try to disrupt local Indian customs, since that would be bad for business, and they discouraged Christian missionaries from entering India and rocking their profitable boat.

Toward the middle of the eighteenth century, however, the English muscled aside the other European contenders for India's trade and began to exercise political power, particularly in the province of Bengal surrounding Calcutta. During the next century, following their victory over the Nawab of Bengal in 1757, the British gradually extended their *raj* (rule) over most of the subcontinent. They conquered various Indian states in battle, then recruited the losers into their own army in order to lessen the sting of defeat and cement the loyalty of the defeated. The Mogul emperor and many other princes, whose domains covered a full third of the subcontinent, remained on their thrones. The British paid the *rajahs* (rulers) and *maharajahs* (high rulers) exaggerated respect to earn their loyalty, but they stationed a British resident at their courts to guide their policies. Either directly or indirectly, therefore, Great Britain became the paramount power in India by the mid-nineteenth century.

The British conquered India with relatively few troops. The only obvious power advantage they enjoyed was control of the sea and the ability to reinforce their armies at key points when necessary. The main reason they succeeded was the divided Indian resistance. As the Mogul Empire waned in strength, ambitious princes jockeyed for position and spent more time fighting each other than the European invaders. The British, therefore, divided and conquered the subcontinent, employing minority ethnic or religious groups, such as the Gurkhas of Nepal and the Sikhs of the Punjab, as shock troops.

British soldiers did not have better weapons or more skillful leaders than their Indian opponents, but they did possess a stronger esprit de corps, growing out of their sense of nationalism. Most Indians believed that emperors and kings would come and go, and that this did not matter greatly so long as village customs were respected. They fought, therefore, without great commitment to a cause. The British soldiers came largely from the riff-raff of their nation, but they possessed strong national pride. In time of battle or siege, they stuck together, closed ranks, and fought for queen and country, both of which they believed in with a nearly religious fervor. Many historical accounts of colonial battles give the impression that Asians or Africans were crazed religious fanatics who would charge the Europeans irrationally. The reverse was closer to the truth. European soldiers did not charge willy-nilly; they were better disciplined than that. Yet they did fight with a national pride and solidarity bordering on the fanatical. As historian V. G. Kiernan has pointed out: "Britain's conquest of India was one of the most abnormal, unnatural events in history; only individuals somewhat unbalanced, as well as full of energy and drive, could have accomplished it."

With power came a change in attitude. White women and Christian missionaries appeared in India, both disapproving of the free-and-easy life of the early English traders. Though interracial sexual unions continued, the Eurasian offspring were now frowned upon and limited to low-level jobs grudgingly bestowed by their "betters." The British began to withdraw themselves into a closed, privileged caste, waited on by numerous poorly paid Indian servants, whom they despised but depended on for all the amenities of daily life. An Englishwoman would not so much as pick up a dropped handkerchief, but would call for her servant to fetch it. Racial solidarity completely overwhelmed any sexual equality between white women and their female servants.

In 1857, this unreal Victorian society was rocked by the Sepoy Mutiny. British troops had long been outnumbered at least two to one by native Indian soldiers, or sepoys, who nursed many grievances against their officers. Some complaints were common to any army — poor pay, harsh discipline, unease at being posted far from home — but the more important grievances were produced by the clash of cultures. Indian soldiers feared that the British would force them to convert to Christianity or at least to suffer ritual pollution from policies offensive to Hindu or Muslim morality.

33

A classic case of cultural blindness sparked the mutiny. In 1857 the British army replaced its ancient muskets with new breech-loading Enfield rifles. In order to load these weapons, the soldiers greased the cartridges with animal fat, then bit off the ends before inserting them into the rifle. If the grease came from pigs it offended Muslims, if from cows it polluted Hindus. When eighty-five sepoys stationed at Meerut, forty miles northeast of Delhi, refused to load the new rifles, they were arrested and scheduled for execution. On May 10, 1857, the Meerut garrison revolted, freed the prisoners, and slaughtered the few resident English soldiers and their families. They then marched on Delhi and vowed their loyalty to the eighty-two-year-old Mogul emperor, Bahadur Shah, who seemed more startled than the British. Full-scale revolt spread across the plain of the Ganges River in northern India, but by the spring of 1858 reinforcements from Europe marched upcountry from Calcutta and ended the mutiny in a bloodbath of reprisals and lynchings.

The British deposed the last Mogul emperor in 1858 and dissolved the British East India Company, transforming India into a directly ruled Crown colony. Two decades later, in 1876, Queen Victoria formally assumed the title empress of India. More importantly, the army increased the ratio of British to Indian soldiers (though the latter still outnumbered the former) and strictly reserved control over artillery and ammunition to British troops. British civilians closed ranks against the Indians even more strongly, denying them upper-level posts in the government administration. In 1909 only sixty Indians served in the Indian Civil Service, which numbered about 1,200 officers in all. When a Liberal viceroy tried to pass a law permitting Indian judges to adjudicate cases involving Europeans, he faced a storm of controversy back home and was forced to back down. An English newspaper published the telling query: "Would you like to live in a country where at any moment your wife would be liable to be sentenced on a false charge, the magistrate being a copper-coloured Pagan?" The British had erected and defended a barricade of imperial power and racial separation against both the masses and the educated elite of India.

Europeans did not conquer Africa until long after they had mastered the Indian subcontinent, but when they finally invaded Africa in the late nineteenth century they applied racist power even more nakedly. Direct contact between Africans and Europeans had first been limited to factories and forts along the coast of West Africa where the slave trade was transacted. No single African emperor claimed to rule all of the continent, as the Moguls did in India, but powerful kingly states such as Ghana, Mali, and Songhai blocked any European attempts to conquer inland in West Africa. Yet over the centuries slave trading weakened and divided the various African states, and the profits of worldwide trade and slave-grown produce vastly strengthened Europe. Historian Basil Davidson has summed up the power equation between Europe and Africa: "The gap in effec-

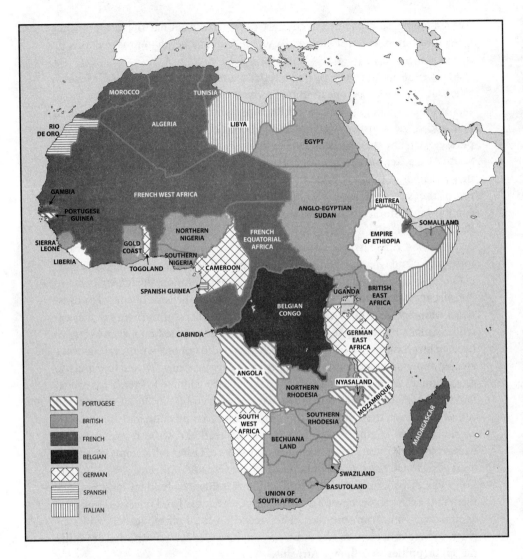

Africa c. 1914

tive technological capacity and military power had been narrow in the Middle Ages, and barely existent earlier. Now [in the nineteenth century] it was an abyss."

The European states conquered Africa after 1880, not so much for its own sake, but because of European imperial rivalries. Each expanding empire feared that another would grab a strategically important territory if they did not take it first, and so there ensued what has always been called the "scramble for Africa," a phrase coined by the English Lord Derby in 1884. Only in a few regions, such as South Africa, Kenya, and Algeria, did sizeable numbers of European colonists settle permanently, pushing aside the natives as in the Americas. Throughout the rest of the continent, a handful of soldiers and administrators ruled the newly conquered colonies, relying heavily on native troops and indigenous rulers as the British did in India.

In West Africa, where European contact with Africans had the longest history, France and Great Britain started building their colonies from slightly different premises. Fired with the idealism of their great revolution, the French believed that all people possessed a natural human equality, and they exhibited far less overt racial prejudice than the British. In their earliest African colony of Senegal, they extended French citizenship to all male inhabitants and pursued a policy of assimilation to French culture. (Natural equality, however, did not mean political rights for women, either in France or in French Africa.) Senegalese males elected a deputy to the National Assembly in Paris and sent some of their children to France for education. When the French extended their West African empire in the late nineteenth century, however, they retreated from this policy of assimilation and granted citizenship only to a hand-picked few who could read and write French and had worked for many years in the colonial civil service. Other inhabitants of French West Africa were ruled as subjects, decidedly second-class citizens.

The British, on the other hand, perhaps influenced by their long involvement in the slave trade, never held Africans in high regard and rejected a policy of assimilation right from the start. They relied on local village leaders and clan chiefs to keep order among the populace, but provided few educational or political opportunities to ordinary Africans.

Despite their different theoretical starting points, French and English policy in the West African colonies converged in the economic sphere. Both imperial nations wished to rule their African colonies as cheaply as possible and extract whatever raw materials and agricultural products they could through the use of native labor. The British stated their contempt for the Africans more openly than the French, avowing that the typical African likes "to do nothing for six days in the week and to rest on the seventh." Both the British and the French, however, shared this stereotype of the "lazy African" and thus imposed compulsory labor to carry out public works and cultivate plantations.

36

Europeans prided themselves on the abolition of slavery and the slave trade, but at the same time they refined new methods for extracting labor from Africans. Sometimes they presented quotas to village leaders and demanded that they provide able-bodied men to work for a period of time constructing roads or railways. More indirectly, they impelled African farmers to serve European economic interests by imposing a head tax or land tax on each inhabitant. In order to earn money to pay this tax, the African farmer had to grow cash crops for the market, rather than food for the family, or else seek work on large plantations or in the cities. If an African male attempted to evade the payment of the tax, he would be arrested and forced to work as a prison laborer. In all these ways, therefore, Europeans impressed their African subjects, whom they held in contempt, to work for them.

In summary, then, Europeans at the beginning of the twentieth century perceived three kinds of countries outside their own continent: settler societies, such as Canada, the United States, Australia, and South Africa, where white Europeans had replaced the native inhabitants; mixed-race societies, comprising most of Central and South America; and subject societies, such as India and West Africa, where a tiny cadre of white Europeans ruled over the presumably inferior and backward masses of natives.

At the root of colonial relations between the rulers and the ruled, in all three kinds of societies, lies another "ism," perhaps more fundamental and universal than the European "isms" considered in the previous chapter. Not just Europeans, not just colonial rulers, but most human beings, when confronted by a culture different from their own, recoil in shock and indignation, proclaiming it strange, alien, and inferior. This self-centered feeling of superiority is called ethnocentrism.

An early contact between the British and the Chinese can illustrate the mutual nature of ethnocentrism. In 1793 Lord George Macartney, an Irishman who previously served as British governor in the Caribbean and in India, arrived in Peking, the imperial capital of China. The British government had instructed him to expand trade relations with China and to establish a permanent exchange of ambassadors. Macartney sailed into Chinese waters in a squadron of five ships, including a sixty-four-gun man-of-war, with a retinue of seven hundred soldiers, sailors, diplomats, and merchants. Yet only one Englishman, the twelve-year-old page, Thomas Staunton, bothered to learn Chinese on the nine-month sea voyage.

The British brought with them a cornucopia of new, technically advanced products. Their prize exhibits were astronomical instruments and fine Wedgewood porcelain, which they believed would interest the Chinese, who had long ago invented the clock and perfected the making of fine porcelain, called "china" by all the world. Alain Peyrefitte, who has written a richly detailed account of Macartney's mission, described the full array of goods as "a preview of the British pavilion at an international exhibition." Yet the Emperor Ch'ien Lung (Qianlong), in the fifty-eighth year of his reign, considered them merely the usual tribute offered by barbarians and hardly glanced at them. His written reply to King George III, which he began composing before he even received Macartney, stated: "The Celestial Empire, ruling all within the four seas, simply concentrates on carrying out the affairs of government properly, and does not value rare and precious things. . . . Nor do we have the slightest need of your country's manufactures." The emperor firmly and none too politely refused all the British requests.

Macartney, for his part, lauded his own king as "the sovereign of the seas" and "the most powerful monarch of the globe," and insulted the Chinese by refusing to perform the ritual kowtow to their emperor. Peyrefitte vividly describes the scene when the party met the emperor face to face at his summer residence north of the Great Wall:

> It was still dark in Manchuria at four in the morning on September 14, 1793. In the capital encampment in Jehol, where the Imperial Court was spending the summer, paper lanterns lit the emperor's tent, to which only four members of the large British mission were to be granted entry: Lord Macartney; his deputy, Sir George Staunton; his interpreter, Father Li, a Tartar priest and a graduate of a Naples seminary; and the twelve-year-old page, Thomas Staunton. . . . At seven o'clock they were brought before the emperor. All those present — court attendants, Tartar princes, envoys from vassal nations — performed the kowtow: three genuflections, each accompanied by three acts of prostration, the forehead touching the ground nine times in all. Except for the English, who merely went down on one knee: Lord Macartney insisted on shunning a ritual he considered humiliating for his country.

Steeped in ethnocentrism, the British and the Chinese talked past each other. If Ch'ien Lung thought Macartney a barbarian, the British lord surely considered the Chinese a backward people.

Who was right? Was the Chinese civilization superior? Or was European culture more advanced? What about Great Britain versus Mogul India, or the Africans and Europeans who met on the coast of West Africa to deal in slaves? Who was advanced and who was backward? Should we even ask these questions, or must we retreat into a fashionable cultural relativism, asserting that each culture was correct for its own people and we have no right to judge either one superior? It would be pleasant if we could dodge the issue in this fashion. A student of mine once wrote on an examination paper: "In comparing two cultures and their histories the goal should be to learn from the similarities and the differences. It

38

should not be a question of which one is better." In theory, I agree with him; yet, consciously or unconsciously, we all make judgments about different cultures, for ethnocentrism is deeply imbedded in human responses to the Other. It is best to bring these feelings to light and make our judgments explicit. A road map is necessary to navigate through the minefield of cross-cultural contacts, in order to avoid the two extremes of ethnocentrism and complete cultural relativism. A fairly objective starting point can be found in the different physical environments of various societies. Obviously, a temperate climate, fertile soil, and abundant natural resources provide more possibilities for a high standard of living and a highly developed material culture than a desert waste or tropical jungle. Inhabitants of North America, for instance, possess environmental advantages over those living in sub-Saharan Africa. This is not due to any innate superiority of Americans over Africans but is a free gift from God or Mother Nature. A glance at the globe reveals that most of the temperate land regions of the earth stretch across the Northern Hemisphere in Europe, Asia, and North America. There is less land mass south of the equator, and much of it lies in more difficult tropical climates. So the sharp contrast between societies, which Europeans long characterized as a cultural conflict between "East" and "West," is more often viewed today as an economic distinction between "North" and "South."

Yet, this geographical or environmental approach does not go very far in explaining differences between societies. Physical environment sets limits to human endeavor but does not determine the results. The southern tip of Africa, for example, with a relatively temperate climate and abundant agricultural and mineral resources, has been settled by four different groups of humans — Khoi-San hunter-gatherers, Bantu-speaking pastoralists and agriculturalists, Boer farmers, and English industrialists — and each made something different out of the same environment. In the words of African historian Walter Rodney: "This capacity for dealing with the environment is dependent on the extent to which they [different groups of humans] understand the laws of nature (science), on the extent to which they put that understanding into practice by devising tools (technology), and on the manner in which work is organized."

A functional approach offers some hope of comparing objectively the different ways in which societies apply science and technology to their material environment. Without making moral judgments, we can assess whether a particular culture performs some specific function better than another culture. For example, traditional Chinese medicine, including acupuncture, herbal remedies, meditation, and exercise, has attracted much favorable attention in recent years because of its holistic approach to healing. Chinese medicine treats the whole person, both mind and body, and it has shown some astonishing results in stress reduction, alleviation of pain, and the retardation of aging. However, traditional Chinese doctors never developed much skill at surgery, since Confucian teaching frowned on voluntary cutting of the body. As a result, when Chinese soldiers were mangled by modern weapons in a war against Japan in 1894-95, they relied on European missionary doctors to patch up the seriously wounded. European surgery proved superior for some purposes, but Chinese medicine has shown itself better for others.

West African agriculture provides another example. Africans had adopted iron tools and implements during the first millennium A.D., but when Europeans first encountered African agricultural societies around 1500 they discovered that the natives used iron hoes to cultivate the soil, not horse-drawn plows as in Europe. Naturally, the ethnocentric Europeans judged the African farmers backward. Yet West Africans had learned from long experience that their native soil was relatively thin and could not endure extensive and repeated plowing. So they rotated their planting and worked the earth with hoes, rather than digging deeper with plows. When Europeans later introduced their own methods, they quickly exhausted the soil. The African hoe proved superior to the European plow for the function of growing food crops in the particular environment of West Africa. This example thus combines our first two criteria for assessing different cultures, the nature of the environment and the function being performed.

Another approach to cultural differences will make judgments according to the individual society's own standards. Sometimes a society declines and becomes inferior, even by its own standards. Returning to China's confrontation with Europe as an example, we can state that Chinese rulers valued order and stability above all; their primary duties were to keep the peace and feed the populace. By those standards, the nineteenth century marked a period of decline as China was plagued by numerous rebellions and widespread famines. Europeans, on the other hand, experienced an increase in military power and economic wealth, standards by which they judged themselves in that same century. Therefore, historical realism, not ethnocentrism, prompts us to conclude that China was declining and Europe ascending in the nineteenth century.

In sum, then, geographical or environmental factors, a functional approach, and an assessment using each society's own standards can inject some objectivity into cultural comparisons. These approaches, however, work best when comparing the material and economic development of different societies. Even the strongest cultural relativist will probably admit that industrial society provides more wealth and a higher standard of living than a hunter-gatherer society. Yet is an industrial worker happier, more moral, or more spiritually exalted than a hunter-gatherer? European and American farmers have tamed whole continents to produce food and extract minerals, but earlier settlers who hunted game or herded flocks may have lived in closer harmony with their natural environment and enjoyed greater spiritual satisfactions. It is much harder to reach objective judgments in the realm of human values.

Every human society possesses deeply felt beliefs dealing with the relationship of the individual to the group; the proper balance between liberty and order; the nature of truth, beauty, justice, and virtue; and the ultimate source of existence. The content of these beliefs, however, and the customs and practices based upon them, vary sharply from one society to another. The relationship of the individual to the group provides an outstanding example of this "values gap." By the time they began to contact the inhabitants of other continents, Europeans had exalted the individual over the group. Mariners sailed out into the unknown seeking personal glory; entrepreneurs bought and sold slaves and plantations to amass personal wealth; Christians confronted their God and worked out their eternal salvation doing individual deeds of charity and avoiding personal sins. The European quest for God, gold, and glory was a highly individualistic one.

In Africa and Asia, and indeed in many parts of Europe as well, the individual's life was embedded in a rich network of family, kin, and caste associations. India provides the most extreme example of a highly developed caste society. The Hindu scriptures defined four classic caste divisions: Priests (Brahmins), Warriors (Kshatriyas), Traders (Vaishyas), and Cultivators (Shudras). Yet between the Brahmins on the top and the Shudras on the bottom, everyday village society embraced about a dozen more specific castes, based primarily on the traditional occupation of a given family. Those whose ancestors had performed "unclean" trades such as the removal of human or animal waste existed outside the caste system altogether, as Untouchables.

Europeans often attacked this caste system as unjust and degrading to the individual, but the Indian sense of justice was built upon it. Christian missionaries made their initial converts among those of the lowest caste (we saw a similar phenomenon among the Chinese in Chapter 1), but this simply stigmatized their religion among most Indians. Europeans, with their individualist ethics, offended the Indian (and Chinese and African) sense of just relations between the individual and the group.

It is possible to apply the functional approach to this particular values gap. Individualism, in the guise of entrepreneurial capitalism, has served well to amass wealth, but it has often destabilized the peace of societies. Rigid family or caste regulations, on the other hand, usually make for more stable societies, but at a lower standard of material wealth. Still, this functional approach falls short in assessing different value systems. There will always be a wide range of beliefs and behaviors which will cause conflict and misunderstanding between cultures.

Three final examples — from China, India, and Africa — will illustrate the depth of the values gap. Because of a male sexual fetish for small feet, Chinese parents tightly bound their daughters' feet during their growing years, permanently deforming them. This practice of foot-binding often produced grown women who could only hobble painfully about the house as they pursued their

41

domestic duties. It was finally abandoned when the Communists applied great pressure after their revolution in the mid-twentieth century. In India, the upper castes observed the practice of *suttee,* the suicide of a widow on her husband's funeral pyre. Such self-immolation symbolized the sanctity of the marriage bond and ensured that an economically useless, non-productive member of society, the widow, would not become a burden to her extended family. The British tried to stamp out suttee as early as 1829, but, like foot-binding in China, it persisted well into the twentieth century. Hindu fundamentalists have recently attempted to revive it. The third example, female circumcision or female genital mutilation, still remains common in more than twenty African states, as well as some regions of the Arabian peninsula and South Asia. Before a girl reaches the age of puberty, her parents "circumcise" her genital organs. Sometimes this means little more than cutting a fold of skin from the clitoris, a procedure somewhat similar to the circumcision of the male penis. More commonly, however, the parent or another relative cuts off the entire clitoris then sews up the vagina to preserve the young girl's virginity before marriage.

These three time-honored practices of Asian and African societies have long disgusted Christian Europeans, and female circumcision remains under strong attack from Europeans and Americans, who find it not just demeaning, but painful and damaging to women's health, as Chinese foot-binding was. Asians and Africans, in turn, often consider European and American customs immoral and radical. In the nineteenth century, the Chinese condemned the public relations between European men and women, openly holding hands and kissing in public, as barbarous and animalistic. East African parents resist attacks on female circumcision, believing that an uncircumcised girl will become wild and immoral like American girls. Similarly, Indians frequently condemn European feminism for disrupting family solidarity and the proper order of society.

For all our attempts to remain scholarly and objective, there is little a historical observer of different cultures can do when the values gap yawns widely except agree to disagree. Nothing is gained by pretending to a cultural relativism that the observer does not truly believe in. Those Europeans and Americans who most strongly proclaim the equality, or even the superiority, of African to European culture would probably be the first to condemn female circumcision. We all judge such matters by our own moral or ideological standards. The best we can do when confronted by such cultural conflicts is to state clearly our own values and then attempt to start a dialogue with those who disagree.

My own values are based on Christian training and belief, yet I do not believe that the members of all other religions are destined for eternal damnation. Pope John Paul II, in his best-selling book *Crossing the Threshold of Hope*, wrote: "From the beginning, Christian Revelation has viewed the spiritual history of man as including, in some way, all religions, thereby demonstrating *the unity of humankind with regard to the eternal and ultimate destiny of man.*" In line with this point of view, I reject any attempt to impose Christianity, or other values, by force or coercion. The recently published *Catechism of the Catholic Church* states that "the missionary task implies a *respectful dialogue* with those who do not yet accept the Gospel." This phrase, "respectful dialogue," describes the task of world history.

Such a dialogue can be assisted by a number of international statements of human rights and human values that have received at least nominal approval by nations and religious bodies. As early as 1948, the General Assembly of the United Nations adopted a "Universal Declaration of Human Rights," which begins with the statement that "all human beings are born free and equal in dignity and rights." The declaration includes thirty articles in all, many of them startlingly specific. Articles 3 through 6, for example, state: "Everyone has the right to life, liberty and security of person; No one shall be held in slavery or servitude . . . ; No one shall be subjected to torture or to cruel, inhuman or degrading treatment or punishment; Everyone has the right to recognition everywhere as a person before the law." These rights have been widely ignored in the half century since the UN declaration was adopted, but the very fact that every nation of the world has recognized them, at least on paper, gives them a presumption of universality that was previously absent in political, ethical, or religious statements.

More recently, the Parliament of the World's Religions met in Chicago at the end of summer in 1993 and adopted a "Declaration Toward a Global Ethic." The Roman Catholic archbishop of Chicago agreed with representatives of Protestant, Jewish, Muslim, and even "neo-pagan" religious groups on a statement of principles that they all shared. These religious leaders declared forcefully that "every human being must be treated humanely" and agreed upon the "Golden Rule" that is common to nearly all religions: "What you wish done to yourself, do to others!" These basic principles are very general, of course, and members of the various religious bodies would interpret them in highly diverse ways. Yet the very fact that religious leaders can meet and discuss such matters holds out promise of a wider understanding between cultures.

Finally, while engaging in dialogue between cultures, we should recognize that change is inevitable when two societies with different values come into contact. A principle of modern physics, the so-called Heisenberg or uncertainty principle, can be applied metaphorically to the contact of human cultures. It is axiomatic in particle physics that one cannot observe a subatomic particle without changing its position. The energy contained in any instrument of observation, such as an electron microscope, will inevitably alter the position of the observed particle.

Something like this happens when two societies meet. Vasco da Gama and Christopher Columbus initiated a process of change in the societies they encountered. Africa, Asia, and the Americas were not unchanging, eternal societies in any case, but contact with another culture was bound to "change their positions" in a sort of cultural Heisenberg principle — that is, to disrupt established customs and accelerate change.

In the historical contacts between East and West, North and South, such accelerated change actually led to much conflict and violence. The study of world history, employing the techniques of respectful dialogue, may help to make such an outcome less likely in the future. In this book, I will try to understand different twentieth-century societies within the context of their physical environment and to assess their strengths and weaknesses according to functional criteria and their own cultural standards. Yet when a values gap appears, I will try to define it clearly and then engage the reader in a dialogue, based on my own deepest values, but respecting the values of others.

CHAPTER FOUR

East Asian Responses to Europe

The twentieth-century dialogue between "Eastern" and "Western" cultures can begin with the response of China and Japan to European domination. Both countries had a long history of political independence and economic development, but by the nineteenth century each felt threatened by European penetration of East Asia. The two countries responded quite differently to the political and economic challenge of Europe.

The Chinese did not think of themselves as one nation among many, but as the civilized center of the whole universe. The very name of China literally means "middle country" or "middle kingdom": the very center of everything under heaven. The Chinese considered themselves the only civilized people; all others were mere barbarians. Their emperor, the Son of Heaven, was a universal ruler, presiding over the whole human family. Barbarians could only stare in amazement at the greatness of China and offer tribute to her emperor. The Italian Jesuit, Matteo Ricci, who spent several decades at the court of the Chinese emperor in the sixteenth century, noted this Chinese self-absorption:

> To them the heavens are round but the earth is flat and square, and they firmly believe that their empire is right in the middle of it. They do not like the idea of our geographies pushing their China into one corner of the Orient.

Throughout most of her long history, China was not isolated from foreign, outside influences; she was merely unaffected by them. The Chinese absorbed barbarians. During the three hundred years of the Ch'ing (Qing) dynasty (1644-1912), the country was ruled by an alien race, the Manchus. Though the Manchus kept themselves rigidly apart from the native Chinese, they swiftly assimilated

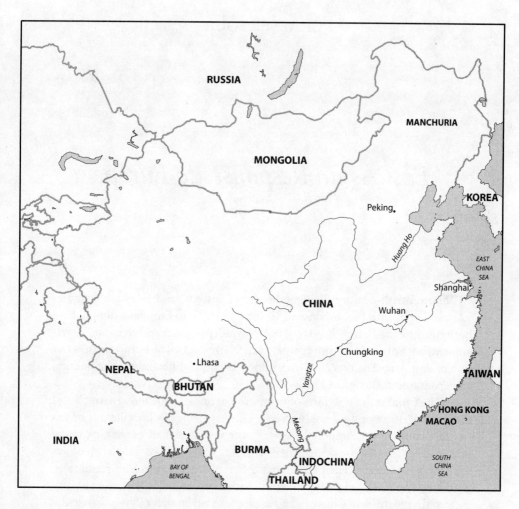

China c. 1900

their culture and ruled by traditional Chinese bureaucratic methods. It is difficult to say who was the conqueror and who the conquered.

Imperial China, therefore, was not a nation-state in a world of competing nation-states. It was a multinational, continent-sized country, stretching from the latitude of Canada in the north to that of Cuba in the south, encompassing many different climates and peoples. As John King Fairbank, the preeminent American historian of China, has pointed out, "Early travelers compared China with Europe in the variety of its languages and the size of its different provinces." Like Europe in the Middle Ages, China possessed a cultural unity and a universal self-consciousness. To medieval Christians, Europe was the world and all other peoples were infidels; so, too, the Chinese considered themselves the only civilized people and all others barbarians.

The Manchus had also conquered Mongolia and Tibet, spreading China's boundaries far into Central Asia. A number of surrounding kingdoms, such as Nepal, Burma, Vietnam, and Korea, paid tribute to the Chinese emperor. Yet by the nineteenth century, when the European powers thrust their tentacles into Asia, China had ceased to be expansionist and was threatened by barbarian invasions on its borders and peasant rebellions in the interior. Under the later Manchu or Ch'ing rulers, China lapsed into a self-centered passivity alien to the dynamism of European imperialist powers.

The Chinese guided their lives by an "ism" of their own, Confucianism. Confucius himself lived from 551 to 479 B.C. at a time of moral and political disorder in China. Not a religious leader or a messiah, Confucius was primarily a political and moral philosopher who taught a conservative code of conduct for rulers and ruled alike. Though he enjoyed relatively little success in his own lifetime, his disciples collected and codified his writings; and by the time of the Han dynasty, two centuries before Christ, Confucian ethics had become the guiding principles of Chinese society. Interpreted and reinterpreted numerous times over the centuries and eventually hardened into a rigid orthodoxy, Confucius's thoughts still provided norms of conduct for the Chinese at the time when Europeans first arrived in Asia.

Hierarchy ruled the Confucian cosmos, and the patriarchal family furnished a model for all of society. The family, not the individual, was the primary social unit, and filial obedience to the father was the prime virtue. Confucian philosophers emphasized three bonds that held China together: the bond of loyalty between subject and ruler, the bond of obedience between sons and their fathers, and the duty of chastity and obedience that wives owed their husbands. Confucian ethics prescribed a conservative, hierarchical code of virtue, obedience, and harmony.

This harmony was disrupted by the English shortly after the unsuccessful trade mission of Lord George Macartney. Chinese tea and silks were in great demand in Europe, but there was no European product that the Chinese desired in sufficient quantity to make for a profitable two-way trade. Opium produced in British India filled the trading vacuum. Indian opium was traded in Canton (Guangzhou), the one port where the Chinese allowed outsiders to trade, for Chinese tea, which was then shipped to Europe.

Opium poppies were grown locally in China, but British traders gave the consumption of the drug a powerful push. Historians Jonathan Spence and John King Fairbank have estimated that by 1900 forty million Chinese smoked opium, and perhaps fifteen million of these were addicts. "This meant that for every Chinese converted to Christianity there were some 15 addicted to opium." The widespread addiction was a sign of China's decline, by its own standards. As poverty and disorder increased in the late Ch'ing dynasty, many Chinese searched for escape and release by smoking opium. John King Fairbank has concluded provocatively that "the Chinese demand grew up in situations of demoralization not unlike the American inner cities of today." Though opium is not as powerful or addictive as present-day heroin or crack, it did destroy the health of many individuals and wreck the unity of numerous families. Opium smoking was not a quaint, traditional Chinese custom that Europeans simply misunderstood. The Chinese themselves viewed it as a curse.

When the Chinese tried to ban the opium trade in 1839, Britain responded by going to war. With only a few thousand soldiers and a handful of heavily armed gunboats, the English routed the disorganized imperial forces and struck the first of many unequal treaties. The Treaty of Nanking (Nanjing) in 1842 handed over Hong Kong to the British, opened five new treaty ports to foreign trade, and granted the right of "extraterritoriality" to foreigners in the treaty ports. This latter right meant that foreigners could not be tried in Chinese courts but would remain under the jurisdiction of their own consulates. The Americans and the French swiftly claimed the same rights as the British. The British and the French finally fought another war with China, from 1856 to 1860, to enforce their new treaty privileges, occupying and sacking the capital city of Peking itself in 1860. The Chinese Maritime Customs were placed under the direction of a foreigner, the Englishman Sir Robert Hart, as inspector general.

Stunned by these events, the Manchu rulers of China asked themselves what had gone wrong. "Why are they small and yet strong?" a Chinese scholar named Feng Kuei-fen (Feng Guifen) mused in 1860. "Why are we large and yet weak?" The question remains a puzzle. The ancient Chinese Empire of the Han dynasty was an exact contemporary of the Roman Empire, only larger. A thousand years later, when Marco Polo and other European travelers visited the Great Khan in Peking, they were astounded by the wealth and power of the Chinese Empire. When Prince Henry the Navigator of Portugal first sent his sailing vessels down the west coast of Africa looking for a path to Asia, a Chinese admiral named Cheng Ho (Zheng He) took a grand fleet all around the Indian Ocean. As is well known, China invented many important implements of human civilization, such as gunpowder, paper, and the compass. So why did China decline relative to Europe? Using a functional approach, why was China inferior in wealth, power, and technology by the nineteenth century? In short, why did China not modernize at the same rate as Europe?

The answer lies deep within the cultures of the two contending parties. China was inward-looking and self-satisfied, whereas modern Europe looked outward with a restless thirst for novelty. Even when China was clearly superior in wealth and power, during the Middle Ages, the seeds of the European advantage can be detected. European Christians considered Jerusalem the center of the universe, and so they ventured out to conquer the Holy Land. China, on the other hand, deemed itself the center of the universe, its own Jerusalem, and thus felt no compulsion to crusade outward.

The grand voyages of Cheng Ho illustrate how strongly inward-looking China was. The admiral took his navy on seven expeditions from 1405 to 1433, and more than twenty countries paid tribute to the Chinese. But as Daniel Boorstin has pointed out in his epic tale *The Discoverers:*

> Cheng Ho's navy came from another world. The purpose of his vast, costly, and far-ranging expeditions was not to collect treasure or trade or convert or conquer or gather scientific information. . . . The voyages became an institution in themselves, designed to display the splendor and power of the new Ming dynasty.

The Chinese neither sought nor gained any material advantage from these fifteenth-century voyages. Indeed, rather than trading with or looting the tributary states, Cheng Ho showered gifts upon them, showing his emperor's magnificence and generosity. The admiral accepted mainly curiosities in return, such as a giraffe from east Africa by way of the kingdom of Bengal in India. He could never admit that China wanted or needed anything from other countries. The Ming emperor finally took this logic to its final conclusion and ended the voyages in 1433, thereafter forbidding the Chinese to leave the country on trading expeditions. While never completely isolated or closed off from the world, China remained inward-looking until the British crashed into their country in the nineteenth century. Ironically, China's very superiority in earlier centuries may have led to its decline, as it remained self-satisfied and saw no need to change.

Chinese culture was also collective rather than individualist, prizing the collective strength of the family more than the individual's quest for wealth or prestige. The Chinese sought to live in harmony with nature rather than to dominate it. Many observers have noticed the different relation between human beings and nature in Chinese and European art. The individual stands at the center of European paintings, with nature as either a neutral background or an enemy. In China, however, landscape art developed very early, emphasizing the grandeur and the harmony of nature, with human beings as tiny appendages barely visible in the scene. Europeans try to dominate, to conquer nature. In the Confucian universe, a human tries to fit into nature, to conquer himself or herself.

Collective and inward-looking, Chinese culture was, in the final analysis, profoundly conservative. The Chinese did not believe in progress, but in an endless round of historical cycles. Both rulers and peasants valued order and stability above all other virtues. When the Manchus conquered the country, they reinforced this conservativism. As outsiders, they felt insecure on the imperial throne and thus exaggerated the tendency to perform every official act exactly as it had always been performed. They tried to earn legitimacy by changing nothing. Alain Peyrefitte, who chronicled the visit of Lord George Macartney to the Ch'ing court, labeled China "the immobile empire."

Jerome Ch'en, a European-trained Chinese scholar, has cleverly noted the difference between British and Chinese forms of conservatism: "the British preserved the old bottle while changing the wine; the Chinese changed the bottle while preserving the old wine." England retained its monarchy and aristocracy and has remained a class-conscious society up to the present, but in the process the English whittled away the duties and functions of the monarch and nobles and profoundly transformed the sources of wealth in their economy. While still appearing stuffy and aristocratic, they became the most dynamic country on earth — the same ancient bottle but with a totally new wine in it. The Chinese, however, when finally shocked into action after the so-called Opium Wars of the mid-nineteenth century, tried to adopt a few of the most important European innovations without changing anything fundamental — a new bottle but the same old wine.

After the Opium Wars, the Ch'ing dynasty attempted to renew itself and save China from foreign dominance. In the so-called Ch'ing Restoration, the vigorous Dowager Empress Ts'u-hsi (Cixi) took control of the government and instructed her officials to discover the secrets of the Europeans. In 1867 Chinese scholars at the Ch'ing court conducted a lively written debate over whether they should introduce courses in astronomy and mathematics. They finally compromised, by introducing the modern courses but at the same time reaffirming the primacy of traditional Confucian scholarship.

Out of this debate came a formula that set the terms for the "self-strengthening" movement that was to follow — Chinese learning as the essence, with European learning only for application. The Ch'ing dynasty attempted to preserve the stem or root *(t'i)* of Chinese culture and graft onto it the branch *(yung)* of European technology. Following the *t'i/yung* formula over the next thirty years or so, the Chinese adopted European weapons and military techniques, as well as modern means of manufacture and transportation. They built factories, railways, and telegraph lines, mainly with foreign capital. At the same time, however, they believed they were changing nothing essential, and the government never made a wholehearted commitment to adopt the totality of European culture. John King Fairbank has summed up the weakness of the self-strengthening movement admirably:

> This movement . . . was posited on the attractive though misleading doctrine of "Chinese learning as the fundamental structure, Western learning for practical use." . . . In retrospect we can see that gunboats and steel mills bring their own philosophy with them. But the generation of 1860-1900 clung to the shibboleth that China could leap halfway into modern times, like leaping halfway across a river in flood.

The bankruptcy of this policy became evident in the last decade of the nineteenth century. Japan, which, as we will see in a moment, pursued a much more vigorous modernization policy than China, invaded Korea, which technically still owed allegiance to the Chinese Empire. When the Chinese tried to counter this move, the imperial troops were slaughtered and fell back in disarray. The Chinese governor Li Hung-chang (Li Hongzhang) capitulated and signed the humiliating Treaty of Shimonoseki on April 17, 1895, ceding control of Formosa to the Japanese and granting them a monetary indemnity of 30 million British pounds sterling (roughly 150 million dollars). The treaty also recognized the predominant interest of the Japanese in Korea and ceded them a portion of South Manchuria.

At this point the European powers smelled blood and moved in. First of all, Russia, Germany, and France, in what became known as the Triple Intervention, pressured Japan to give up its gains in Manchuria. Then these three, along with the British, carved spheres of influence out of the weakened Chinese Empire. Within each of these spheres one of the European powers claimed a monopoly on trade and new railway investments. Many observers at the turn of the century believed that the powers would eventually partition China and that it would disappear from the political map the way Poland did a century before. This did not happen, partly due to rivalries between the imperialists, and partly because the Chinese fought back, blindly in the Boxer Rebellion, then more effectively with governmental reforms and revolutionary activities.

Historian Michael Gasster has concluded: "Around 1900 China paused at a fork in the road. Looking over its shoulder along the path of traditionalism, the government could see forty years of defeat." Mary Clabaugh Wright adds: "Rarely in history has a single year marked as dramatic a watershed as did 1900 in China.

The weakness laid bare by the Allied pillage of Peking in the wake of the Boxer Rebellion finally forced on China a polar choice: national extinction or wholesale transformation."

Belatedly, the imperial government accelerated the rate of modernization after 1900, beginning first with the army, which successfully beat off challenges by the British and the Russians on the far borders with Tibet, Burma, and Mongolia. An imperial edict of 1906 launched an aggressive program to eradicate the opium poppy. This campaign, which Mary Wright calls "the most vigorous effort in world history to stamp out an established social evil," converted to food crops 80 percent of the land where poppies had grown. The government also installed a modern system of education, intensified the pace of railroad building, and promised a European-style constitution and representative assemblies. This final decision, to study and emulate other governments, symbolized a profound change of mind by the Chinese, for no aspect of their culture had been more highly prized than the Confucian style of government.

These changes came too late for the Manchu Ch'ing dynasty. Chinese students sent to study in Japan, Europe, and the United States grew increasingly dissatisfied with China's weakness, and in 1905 a group of students meeting in Japan formed the Revolutionary League, with Sun Yat-sen (Sun Yatsen)[1] at its head.

Sun Yat-sen, born in 1866 in Kwangtung (Guangdong) province, studied at European schools in Hawaii and Hong Kong and became a medical doctor. After the first of his abortive anti-Manchu uprisings in 1895, he spent years in exile raising money among the overseas Chinese in America and Southeast Asia. Mostly he relied on small donations from laundrymen or shopkeepers, but he kept hoping for a large loan from foreign bankers for his "capital-intensive" revolutionary activities. During an English sojourn in 1896-97, he was kidnapped and imprisoned at the Chinese legation in London until outraged English public opinion sprung him loose. Amid the hubbub, he spent fifty-nine days studying in the British Museum; but unlike Karl Marx he did not emerge from the museum with

---

1. Both Chinese and Japanese names customarily are written with the family name first, then the given name. Thus Sun was the family name of Sun Yat-sen, just as Chiang was the family name of Chiang Kai-shek. Sun actually had several given names. He was originally called Sun Wen by his parents, but he adopted Yat-sen upon his Christian baptism in 1884. While hiding in Japan during the last years of the nineteenth century, he assumed the pseudonym Chung-shan, "Central Mountain," and it was as Sun Chung-shan that he became best known in China.

Europeans and Americans have long misunderstood the order of these names. When Sun Yat-sen made contact with the Second International in Europe, the socialists called him "Comrade Sen." Later, an American diplomat reportedly embarrassed himself and his country by debarking from an airplane, shaking the hand of the Nationalist Chinese leader, and saying briskly: "Glad to meet you, Mr. Kai-shek."

a coherent, hard-edged ideology. Instead, he espoused a grab bag of modern philosophies he called the Three Principles of the People — nationalism, democracy, and "people's livelihood" (an uncertain amalgam of socialism and reformed capitalism).

Among all the "isms" the Chinese revolutionaries encountered in their overseas studies, only nationalism and imperialism made much impression. Nationalism inflamed the radical students to inveigh against imperialism and to call for the overthrow of the foreign Manchu dynasty. Boycotts against European goods advanced the first aim, and symbolic acts such as cutting off the queue or pigtail (the traditional sign of loyalty to the Manchus) showed their dedication to the second.

The Ch'ing dynasty had come to the end of the line. The dowager empress died in 1908, just a day after the emperor she had dominated. The new emperor, Pu-Yi (Puyi), was merely a boy, and his regent lacked vigor or courage. In 1911 a protest broke out against a foreign loan to pay for railway building. Sun Yat-sen had instigated ten unsuccessful revolutions between 1895 and 1911. Now a nearly spontaneous outburst succeeded, while Sun was in the United States on yet another fund-raising expedition. He read about the 1911 revolution in an American newspaper.

The Chinese revolutionaries forced the Manchus to abdicate in February 1912, and a prestigious general, Yuan Shi-kai (Yuan Shikai), was named president after a short-lived provisional presidency by Sun Yat-sen (who had arrived back in China in December 1911). The general, however, short-circuited the revolution, established a dictatorship, then died in 1916. For the next decade, China fragmented into a collection of feuding provinces ruled by warlords.

Looking back on the century and a quarter following Lord George Macartney's mission to Peking in 1793, we can conclude that China did not modernize swiftly enough because the Ch'ing rulers and the Chinese scholar-gentry that served them did not really want to. Some historians believe that the final efforts of the last Manchus after 1900 might have succeeded in the long run, but there proved to be no long run. The revolutionaries refused to wait any longer; yet their own efforts, driven by raw nationalism, were equally confused and ineffective. China entered the twentieth century as the "sick man of Asia."

China's island neighbors in the Pacific, the Japanese, conducted a much swifter and more thorough forced march to modernization. By 1900 Japan had bested the Chinese in the Sino-Japanese War and had taken a leading role in the punitive expedition during the Boxer Rebellion. The smaller country had also begun to extricate itself from unequal treaties with European powers, eliminating the Europeans' right of extraterritoriality. The Chinese took notice, and after 1900 they patterned their modernization efforts on the Japanese success story.

China's imitation of Japan marked a profound change in the order of the universe, for Japan's culture and society were derived from Chinese civilization. In ancient times, the Japanese adopted from China their written language, most of their literary forms, their concepts of kingship, family, and social structure, and many tenets of Confucianism. The island kingdom had narrowly escaped total dominance by China in 1281 when an invasion from the mainland was stymied by a typhoon, called the *kamikaze* or "divine wind."

Japan's swift transformation looked even more remarkable because the country had isolated itself from all outside influences for so long. After numerous contacts with European explorers and missionaries in the sixteenth century, the Japanese government sealed off the country in the 1630s. In Japan the emperor reigned as a remote figurehead, and the *shogun,* or military commander, generally exercised the effective power. In 1603 a vigorous warlord, Ieyasu, seized the shogunate and declared it hereditary in his family, the Tokugawa. Then he set out to end the civil wars between *daimyo,* or lords of different provinces, with their numerous *samurai* retainers. The presence of foreign traders and missionaries had exacerbated the civil wars in Japan, as the factions enlisted one or another of the foreign powers in their cause.

In 1636 the shogun forbade the Japanese to travel overseas and closed off the ports to foreign trade, allowing just one tiny window to remain open, an island in Nagasaki harbor where only the Dutch were allowed to trade. The Tokugawa *bakufu,* or tent government as it was called in recollection of its military origins, brought more than two centuries of peace to the island kingdom. The shogun not only prevented foreign influences; he also kept close watch over the feudal lords of the kingdom by requiring them to spend six months of each year in the capital of Edo (present-day Tokyo), leaving family members behind as hostages for the other six months. Meanwhile, the emperor remained the source of legitimate authority, but in fact the shogun kept him on a small pension, a virtual prisoner in his palace at Kyoto.

The Tokugawa shoguns succeeded in isolating their country because it lay at the other end of the world from Europe. Russia was still digesting the vast land mass of Siberia, the British were busy penetrating the two most populous countries in the world, India and China, and the French and the Dutch had colonies and interests elsewhere. Germany and the United States were not yet major players on the world scene. But by the middle of the nineteenth century this began to change. Russia was moving southward from its base in Siberia, and the British, having finally hammered open the China trade in the Opium Wars, were spreading their commercial interests even farther. Too many ships were sailing by the Japanese islands for contact not to increase.

Interestingly, it was the young nation of the United States, which had just begun to receive its first English colonists when the Tokugawa closed off Japan, that finally pried the island kingdom open again. Commodore Matthew C. Perry anchored his two steamships and two sailing vessels off the port of Uraga on July 8, 1853, and delivered a virtual ultimatum to the Japanese. American textbooks have often portrayed Perry's voyage as a classic case of Yankee luck and pluck, as if the commodore had just been out sailing with the boys and then blundered into the most important event of the century in East Asia. Actually the American government, which had recently acquired California and Oregon, thus becoming a Pacific power, had carefully planned the expedition, announcing it to the world beforehand so that Perry, who was reluctant to take the assignment, would not back down or compromise.

Perry demanded the proper treatment of shipwrecked sailors, the opening of ports of refuge for provisioning and refueling, and the opening of trade. He threatened the Japanese officials that if these "very reasonable and pacific overtures" were not accepted, he would return the following spring with a larger force. As the Japanese stalled, Perry withdrew to Okinawa for the winter, then returned as promised in February 1854 with eight ships. On March 31 the Japanese reluctantly signed the Treaty of Kanagawa by which they opened two cities as ports of refuge, promised to treat castaway sailors humanely, and authorized an exchange of diplomatic representatives and the opening of trade negotiations in the near future.

We should not exaggerate the American role in the opening of Japan. British and Russian admirals visited the country shortly after Perry and obtained identical terms from the Japanese. The prior American arrival was largely accidental. If the United States had not opened Japan, someone else would have. The Americans pressed their advantage, however, and sent a canny Yankee businessman, Townsend Harris, as the first American consul to Japan. Harris cajoled the Japanese to strike a commercial treaty and pledge that trade would be free of government intervention, that more ports would be opened to outsiders, and that the foreign traders would enjoy the right of extraterritoriality. News that British and French naval squadrons were approaching convinced the Japanese to sign the Treaty of Shimoda on July 29, 1858.

More gunboats proved necessary to confirm the opening of Japan. In August 1864 a combined flotilla of seventeen ships (nine British, three French, four Dutch, and one American) bombarded the forts on the Shimonoseki Straits, and as a result the Japanese opened even more ports to the foreigners. The emperor, who had been reluctant to legitimize the change in policy up until then, finally signed the various treaties with the European and American powers on November 22, 1865. This marked the formal and official end of Japan's isolation policy.

The Tokugawa shogunate suffered a fatal loss of face by opening the country to foreigners. A movement sprang up to restore the emperor to formal authority, while overthrowing the shogun and expelling the foreigners. In any case, some kind of change was inevitable since Japan was bursting with energy and

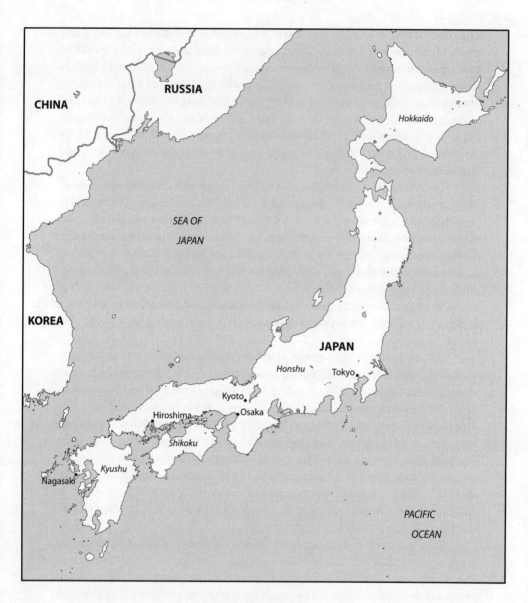

Japan c. 1900

could not be kept much longer in the seventeenth-century straitjacket of the shoguns. Merchants and rural landowners had grown rich over the centuries but did not enjoy comparable status or power in the feudal kingdom. Low-ranking samurai could not exercise their military skills during the long Tokugawa peace, and they grew bored and increasingly impoverished as petty bureaucrats serving the shogun. Finally, the rich provinces of Satsuma, Chosu, Tosa, and Hizen at the southwestern end of the island chain desired a greater role in governing the country. All these forces came together in the movement to topple the shogun and restore the emperor.

The last shogun, Yoshinobu, resigned on November 9, 1867, and in January 1868 troops from Satsuma marched into Edo in the name of the emperor. Some of the shogun's followers tried to mount a last stand in loyal provinces; but Yoshinobu, as a final Tokugawa contribution to the peace of Japan, declined to engage in civil war. The emperor, who took the name Meiji (enlightened peace), assumed formal authority and moved his headquarters to Edo, which was renamed Tokyo (eastern capital).

The Meiji Restoration had been fueled in part by anti-foreign sentiments, but the lords and warriors who overthrew the shogun were realistic men. The bombardment at Shimonoseki had opened their eyes to the military power of Europe, and they concluded that it would be suicidal to resist. The Meiji leaders, therefore, launched a thoroughgoing program of modernization to make Japan "a rich country with a strong army." The Japanese used the term *ishin* (renovation) for the restoration of the emperor, but it is better understood as the Meiji Revolution. The emperor, in the charter oath he swore on April 6, 1868, promised to unite the country and consult widely with the lords of all provinces; but more importantly the emperor also pledged that "knowledge will be sought for all over the world and thereby the foundations of the imperial rule shall be strengthened." This took place just one year after the astronomy-mathematics debate at the Ch'ing court in Peking, which resulted in the equivocal, halfway policies of self-strengthening in China. Meiji Japan, by contrast, embarked on a steadfast, thoroughgoing campaign to borrow the best from all over the world and thus renew the country.

The emperor himself, just a boy of fifteen at the time of the restoration, exercised little more effective power than he had under the shogun's thumb, but Japan was fortunate to have him as an alternate source of authority. When the Ch'ing dynasty went into decline in China, it still hung on to power indefinitely for lack of an alternative. But in Japan, when the shogun lost face, the emperor and his followers were ready to take command. The actual leaders of Meiji Japan were a new elite from the four provinces that had led the revolt. They filled the lower ranks of government according to ability, not inherited rank or status, drawing heavily on the rising merchant class and the lower samurai whose ambitions had been frustrated under the Tokugawa. They formed a coherent ruling class, an oligarchy acting with a sense of urgency, for they believed, quite rightly, that the country was in danger of foreign dominance and only a revitalized economy and a strong military could save them. As W. G. Beasley, the English historian of the Meiji Restoration, has stated: "The Meiji leaders were from the start engaged in building a new Japan, not merely a new regime."

The first decisive step was the abolition of the feudal domains in 1870. The lords could no longer exercise local governmental jurisdiction and were required to disband their private armies. A few years later, the samurai were forbidden to wear their swords in public, and the central government bought out the remaining privileges of lords and samurai with government bonds. The former feudal warriors now became directly dependent for their economic survival on the success of the central government. All of this did not go unchallenged. The warrior class particularly resented the cancellation of a proposed invasion of Korea. The samurai therefore revolted in Satsuma province in 1877, but the new conscript army with modern weapons defeated them easily. For a generation thereafter, the central government pursued a consistent policy of reform at home and peace abroad. Though the rebellions ceased, numerous government officials were assassinated over the next few decades.

In the 1870s and 1880s, the government built railroads, adopted the Gregorian calendar, and inaugurated universal military service. They divided up the old provincial domains into centrally governed prefectures and instituted a stiff land tax to pay for reform. Local assemblies at the town, village, and prefectural level were established, and in 1881 the government promised to convene a national assembly within the next decade. Finally, in 1889 the emperor proclaimed a constitution, and the following year the first elections for the Diet, or parliament, were held.

Ito Hirobumi from Choshu province fashioned the new Japanese constitution more on the German model than on the English, French, or American. The ruling cabinet was responsible to the emperor, as in the kaiser's Germany, not to the parliament. The elected representatives were envisioned as outlets for popular dissatisfaction rather than as policymakers. Yamagata Aritomo from Satsuma, the outstanding military leader among the Meiji oligarchs, also imitated the Germans in the building of the army, including, for example, a general staff responsible directly to the emperor, not the government. However, the Japanese also followed other examples. The British Royal Navy tutored Japanese sailors and took pride in the rapid development of Japanese sea power. The Japanese also looked closely at American business and manufacturing methods and British and French models in law, banking, and education.

Less than forty years after the Meiji Restoration, Japan succeeded where China had failed. It had taken giant steps toward becoming a "rich country with a strong army." The unification and renewal of the country led to a powerful surge of nationalism among the Japanese people, who felt ready and willing to confront the imperialist powers on their own terms. As W. G. Beasley concludes:

> China, after all, also adopted something of the West's military methods in the nineteenth century and learned to use the telegraph and railways, but the Chinese did not thereby achieve a revolution in their way of life. That the Japanese did so was due in large measure to the readiness of their leaders to reform radically and fundamentally in every field. For this they had to be imaginative as well as ruthless.

The Japanese leaders felt free to imitate other nations because they harbored no illusions that their small country on the rim of the world was the center of the universe. From ancient times they had always emulated a more vigorous civilization, usually China; and now that other, stronger countries had intruded into East Asia it seemed imperative to imitate them. Furthermore, as we have already seen, Japan possessed a credible source of authority, the emperor, and a cohesive, new ruling class ready to take over after the fall of the old regime. The Meiji generation followed a consistent policy and never looked back. Leaders such as Ito and Yamagata alternated the prime ministership and other key government offices, and even in their old age they still dominated policymaking as *genro*, or elder statesmen.

Yet the Meiji Revolution was not all centrally planned from the top down. The Japanese people responded willingly to the proddings of the leadership class and readily adopted new ways of thinking and earning a living. As historian Cyril E. Black has pointed out, the Japanese were "able to achieve high levels of conformity with relatively low levels of coercion." Japan seemed remarkably ready for modernization, for despite its isolation the economy of the Tokugawa period had not been stagnant. Indeed, the three large cities of Edo, Osaka, and Kyoto contained about 1.8 million people, and the countryside produced a sizeable agricultural surplus to feed these city dwellers. The male populace was about 40 percent literate, and almost 25 percent were engaged in occupations other than agriculture.

The frustrated merchants, of course, were poised to leap forward; but the samurai, too, seemed prepared for new opportunities. The samurai had lost most of their military functions in Tokugawa Japan and had become mostly administrators. Their *bushido* code of behavior transformed the warrior's field virtues of austerity and endurance into economic virtues of diligence and frugality. The result was a mental outlook remarkably similar to the Protestant work ethic of Europe. A code prescribing maximum effort and minimum consumption admirably suited the Japanese for economic growth.

59

Once Japan had set its new course, the people became fiercely nationalistic. Edwin O. Reischauer, a former American ambassador to Japan and a lifelong student of that country, argues cogently: "Indeed, Japan constitutes what may be the world's most perfect nation-state: a clear-cut geographic unit containing almost all of the people of a distinctive culture and language and virtually no one else." Unlike the European nation-states, Japan was not troubled by Alsaces and Irelands. Yet the insults and incursions of the imperialist powers rubbed nationalistic emotions raw. In particular, the Triple Intervention of Russia, Germany, and France, which deprived Japan of some of the spoils from its victory over China, rankled deeply.

The pamphleteer Thomas Paine wrote at the time of the American Revolution that it was absurd for an island (Great Britain) to rule over a continent (America). Similarly, we might find it remarkable that a small island kingdom (Japan) became a powerful nation-state in the late nineteenth century while the continent-empire of China lagged behind. Yet the very smallness of Japan (and Great Britain, too) gave it an advantage. Cyril Black has concluded:

> Japan began with great advantages of scale. . . . Developments at the central port cities were quickly felt in even remote parts of the country. Its population was concentrated along a coastal strip in such a way as to maximize advantages from development of modern transportation.

The population of Japan was also relatively small and stable, about 31 million, having increased hardly at all since the seventeenth century, whereas China's huge populace quadrupled within that time period to about 400 million, putting enormous pressure on its government and economy.

In short, it is easier to turn a torpedo boat than an aircraft carrier. Shaped like a torpedo aimed at the continent of Asia, Japan greeted the twentieth century with confidence, but also with lingering grievances and unsatisfied ambitions.

CHAPTER FIVE

War and Revolution: The Preview

Japan's rapid rise in East Asia ignited the first war of the twentieth century and unexpectedly provided a preview of the century's greatest revolution.

Among their many borrowings from the European powers, the Japanese had absorbed the prevailing imperialist fever. After a generation of reform at home and peace abroad, Japan was now looking to expand its influence onto the mainland of Asia, but its imperialist outreach ran headlong into the Russian Empire. The interests of the two countries met and clashed in Manchuria and Korea, thus leading to war.

Russia had become an Asian power centuries before as the tsar's empire spilled over from Europe across the top of Asia to the Pacific. At one time it even included part of North America, for Russians had claimed Alaska before finally selling it to the United States in 1867. In the late nineteenth century, Russia intensified its interest in Asia as a rich storehouse of minerals and an outlet for surplus population. The tsar's government began building the Trans-Siberian Railway, Asia's first transcontinental, in 1891. The railway's main line took it on a roundabout route north of Manchuria's Amur River to the port of Vladivostok on the Pacific. The Russians realized, however, that the acquisition of a warm-water port in Manchuria or Korea and the construction of a straight-line shortcut for the railway through Manchuria would gain an advantage in the great power rivalries of East Asia.

The Japanese, for their part, had long harbored interests in Korea, which lay about a hundred miles across the Straits of Tsushima from Japan's home islands. Indeed, Japan had invaded Korea in the sixteenth century but had withdrawn when the Tokugawa initiated their isolationist policy. Now, as an emerging great power, the Japanese viewed events in Korea the way Great Britain looked at oc-

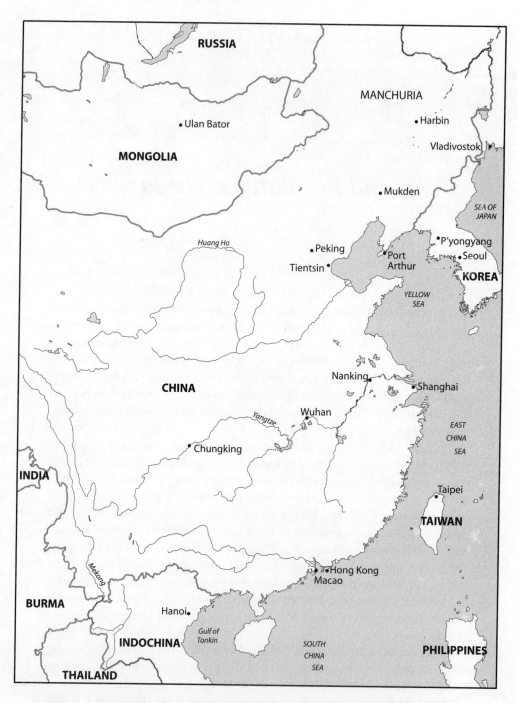

East Asia at the Time of the Russo-Japanese War

currences in Flanders and Holland. Just as England could never permit a hostile power to entrench itself across the English Channel, so too the Japanese declared that Korea affected Japan's vital interests.

The Koreans had been just as reclusive as the Tokugawa Japanese; indeed, nineteenth-century European travelers dubbed Korea the Hermit Kingdom. But in the 1870s the Japanese employed Commodore Perry's tactics of gunboat diplomacy, forcing a trade treaty on the Koreans and narrowly avoiding a full-scale invasion of the kingdom. In fairness to the Japanese, we should note that something more than predatory greed motivated their interventions. They feared that Korean reclusiveness would hamper their own efforts to catch up with the modern economies of Europe and America. Diplomatic historian Richard Storry has summed up this point well: "In the Japanese view Korean (and Chinese) conservatism amounted to a betrayal of the one cause, that of reform and modernisation, that held any future for Japanese, Korean, and Chinese alike in face of the presence and pressure of the Western powers." For the first time, the Japanese began to view themselves as leaders of Asia in competition with Europe and America.

The events that prompted the first Japanese intervention on the mainland illustrate this point. In May 1894 the Tonghak rebellion swept through southern Korea, the portion closest to Japan. The rebels were anti-Western conservatives, somewhat akin to the Chinese Boxers, who aimed to restore *tonghak,* or Eastern learning, and expel all foreign influences. The Korean king requested aid from China, which was still nominally his overlord, and when the Chinese sent troops the Japanese followed suit, according to a previous treaty with China. After crushing the Tonghaks, however, the Japanese pressed the Korean monarch for internal reforms and drove the Chinese out of Korea. The results of this Sino-Japanese war, as we have already seen, were devastating for the Chinese, who relinquished all rights in Korea, ceded Formosa to Japan, and paid a stiff monetary indemnity. The Japanese also seized the fortified harbor of Port Arthur (Lushun), at the tip of the Liaotung (Liaodong) Peninsula in South Manchuria.

Russia, Germany, and France, who were all fishing in East Asian waters, stepped in immediately and forced a Japanese withdrawal from Port Arthur and the Liaotung Peninsula. Germany's Kaiser Wilhelm added a touch of bizarre and insulting humor to this highhanded intervention by drawing a cartoon of a bloodthirsty Japanese samurai, which he entitled the "Yellow Peril," and sending it off to his "Cousin Nicky," Tsar Nicholas II, for his amusement. The Russians added injury to insult in 1898 by leasing Port Arthur and the nearby port of Dairen (Dalian) from the Chinese as their own sphere of influence. Obviously, neither Germany nor Russia took the Japanese seriously. Richard Storry has concluded that "no understanding of twentieth-century Japanese nationalism is possible without some comprehension of the bitterness and sense of humiliation that swept the country in the wake of the Triple Intervention."

Later events leading to the Second World War have imprinted on the minds of Americans an indelible image of crazed Japanese militarists implacably leading their nation to conquest, war, and ultimate ruin. So it is worth emphasizing that, at this early stage in Japan's expansion onto the mainland of Asia, the Japanese government showed itself more cautious than Japanese public opinion. The People's League had been founded in Japan in 1900 to pressure the government for more aggressive actions in Korea. By 1903 it had renamed itself the Anti-Russia Comrades' Society. The most recent historian of the Russo-Japanese War, J. N. Westwood, has pointed out that the Japanese education system produced literate citizens who were trained not to ask too many awkward questions, so they were ripe for nationalist propaganda. Westwood concluded: "On the Japanese side, therefore, the Russo-Japanese War would belong to a category hardly recognised by modern historians, that of the people's imperialist war."

Furthermore, in the events of the next few years, which finally led to the Russo-Japanese War, Russia acted far more aggressively than Japan did. Following the kaiser's lead, the Russians treated the Japanese with contempt. Russian soldiers quarreled with their Japanese counterparts in the Allied expedition during the Boxer Rebellion, and the Russian press caricatured the "Japs" as stunted dwarfs. Nicholas II had visited Japan in 1891, while still crown prince, and had narrowly survived an assassination attempt by a saber-wielding Japanese patriot. Ever after he carried a scar on his forehead and a chip on his shoulder against the people he referred to, in private, as "yellow monkeys."

After the Triple Intervention, the Russian seizure of Port Arthur, and the carving of China into spheres of influence by the European powers, Japan moved to protect itself by striking a treaty with the English. England was still the leading power in the world at the turn of the century, but its difficulties with the Boers of South Africa had sobered it. The strategic dangers of the new century appeared formidable enough that the English decided to abandon the lone wolf role they had played during most of Queen Victoria's glorious reign. They had already reached informal understandings with the United States that virtually ceded supremacy in the Western Hemisphere to the Americans. Now they decided that an alliance with the rising power of Japan would be the best way to protect their interests in China.

The Anglo-Japanese Alliance, signed in London on January 30, 1902, recognized Japan's preponderant interests in Korea and Britain's extensive rights and privileges throughout China. Article 3 prescribed that if either country went to war to protect its interests in East Asia, the other would remain neutral, unless a third party joined the fray, in which case the alliance partner would join in. W. G. Beasley astutely sums up the significance of the Anglo-Japanese Alliance:

> The agreement, despite the care taken in its wording, meant something different to each of the parties to it. From the British viewpoint it was to be a warning

to Russia, but not a provocation, as the public announcement of its contents took pains to show. To Japan it was a triumph, this not merely because it gave her an alliance on a footing of equality with the greatest of the powers, but also because it enabled her to treat with Russia on more even terms. There could be no repetition of the Triple Intervention, it was clear.... In this sense, Japanese extremists saw the alliance as an invitation to aggression.

Nevertheless, the Japanese government continued to act cautiously. In August 1903 they opened negotiations with the Russians, offering a Manchuria-Korea deal. If the Russians would recognize Japan's "preponderating interests" in Korea, the Japanese in turn would respect Russia's "special interests" in Manchuria. The Russians, however, stalled and showed no great desire to strike a bargain with Japan.

The Japanese broke off negotiations with Russia on February 4, 1904; then on the night of February 8, without first issuing a declaration of war, they launched a sneak attack on the Russian fleet at Port Arthur, Manchuria. Around midnight, ten Japanese destroyers fired their torpedoes at the heavy ships of the Russian fleet, which were anchored outside the harbor since they could enter the narrow channel only at high tide. Three torpedoes found their marks, crippling two battleships and a heavy cruiser. Meanwhile, the Japanese landed troops at Chemulpo (later named Inchon), the port for the Korean capital of Seoul, and secured a protectorate over that kingdom.

The surprise attack on Port Arthur seems so similar to the "day of infamy" thirty-seven years later when the Japanese bombed Pearl Harbor that we have to make an effort to understand it in the context of its times. In 1904, public opinion in the English-speaking capitals applauded the Japanese for their daring strategy and judged that the Russians deserved a comeuppance for their unwillingness to bargain in good faith.

Furthermore, unlike Pearl Harbor, the lightning strike in 1904 did not destroy the Russian fleet. The Japanese repeated their torpedo attacks and launched artillery barrages, but the powerful Russian shore batteries kept the Japanese ships too far away to strike a decisive blow. Three separate attempts to bottle up the Russians by scuttling ships in the harbor channel failed. The Japanese therefore committed a sizeable number of ground troops to finish off Port Arthur and drive all Russian troops from Manchuria. They eventually succeeded in the first goal, but not in the second.

On May 25 Japanese troops cut across the Liaotung Peninsula, blocking land access to Port Arthur. While keeping a Russian garrison bottled up in the port, three Japanese armies then fought northward along the Russian-built South Manchuria railway toward Mukden (Shenyang), the ancient mud-walled capital of the Manchus. Their ultimate goal was the city of Harbin (Haerhpin), where they could cut the Chinese Eastern Railway, the four-hundred-mile shortcut on the Trans-Siberian rail route to Vladivostok. Japan's three armies converged near the city of Liaoyang in August, and Field Marshal Oyama Iwao arrived to take command of the combined forces. From August 26 to September 3, Oyama commanded 115,000 infantry, 4,000 cavalry, and 470 artillery pieces against General A. N. Kuropatkin's 135,000 infantry, 12,000 cavalry, and 599 guns in the twentieth century's first great battle. The Russians eventually retreated, in good order, toward Mukden, after inflicting more than 20,000 casualties on the Japanese.

At Liaoyang, and elsewhere in the Manchurian campaign, Marshal Oyama tried to outflank the Russians as the German army had encircled the French in the Franco-Prussian War of 1871; but General Kuropatkin's strategic retreats kept him one step ahead of the advancing Japanese. Kuropatkin was a cautious, bureaucratic general. In the Russian army system it was always safer for the officer's career ambitions to remain on the defense and then retreat rather than to attack. Though this strategy, retreating before the enemy to stretch out his lines of communication while building up one's own forces, had helped the Russians outlast Napoleon and would later have the same happy result against Hitler's panzers during the Second World War, it proved overly conservative in 1904. The Japanese were numerically inferior to the Russians, with scanty reserves and little hope of reinforcement. They also made enough tactical mistakes to open the way for successful counterattacks. Yet the Russians rarely took advantage of this. The repeated retreats from strongly held positions sapped the morale of the Russian soldiers and may have turned the balance against them.

After the retreat from Liaoyang, both sides dug in before Mukden, and the twentieth century witnessed its first extended siege of trench warfare. The advent of the smokeless, magazine-loading, long-distance rifle had revolutionized infantry warfare, as both sides in the Boer War had discovered. The Boers were the first to realize that concealing and protecting their soldiers in trenches and arming them with the new rifles gave defenders a decisive advantage over attacking troops. As Thomas Pakenham, the historian of the Boer War, points out: "This was the new rule of war — dig your own trench now, or they'll dig you a grave later." Yet the war in South Africa changed so rapidly from a conflict of set-piece battles to guerrilla warfare that too few military men learned its lessons. Now the Japanese and the Russians discovered for themselves the bitter truth — dig or be damned.

Meanwhile, on August 10 the Russian fleet came out of Port Arthur, fleeing to its home port of Vladivostok. In the ensuing Battle of the Yellow Sea, Togo Heihachiro, the English-trained admiral commanding the Japanese navy, drove the Russian battleships back into the anchorage of Port Arthur and chased the cruisers and destroyers until they took refuge in neutral ports. The Japanese fleet did not sink a single ship, but they neutralized Russian naval power in East Asia.

By the autumn of 1904, the war of movement had ended, and the land troops settled down to a fierce siege at Port Arthur and a bloody stalemate before Mukden. On December 5, the Japanese captured a hill overlooking Port Arthur, then hauled eleven-inch howitzers up to the heights. These gigantic guns, transferred from the coastal defenses of the Japanese home islands, fired five-hundred-pound shells into the harbor, systematically sinking every ship of the Russian fleet.

With the destruction of the Russian ships, the Japanese had accomplished their first strategic goal. They could, then, have transferred most of the 100,000 soldiers investing the port to reinforce Marshal Oyama at Mukden. Port Arthur, however, held great symbolic significance as the naval base stolen from Japan by the Russians at the time of the Triple Intervention. General Nogi therefore continued to press the siege of Port Arthur, burrowing trenches closer and closer to the port and eventually losing about 60,000 men, almost the equivalent of a full army. Finally, on January 2, 1905, General A. M. Stoessel surrendered Port Arthur. Stoessel was later court-martialed and found guilty of premature surrender; but clearly the garrison of 30,000 starving Russians, more than half of them sick or wounded and many suffering from scurvy, could not have held out much longer.

In February 1905 the Japanese at Mukden pressed forward in the largest battle ever waged up to that time. Over 400,000 Japanese troops faced 350,000 Russians over a front that stretched for more than ninety miles. In the early days of the war, the Japanese had followed the Prussian doctrine of massed frontal infantry assault, but by the time of Mukden they had grown more cautious, with the infantry advancing slowly at night and digging in for cover during the daytime. Nevertheless, heavy fighting raged all along the line as the battle dragged on for almost three weeks, with each side trying to outflank the other. The general slaughter resulted in more than 100,000 dead and injured. On March 9 the Russians began a retreat northward toward Harbin, defeated but not shattered.

Russia still had one last hope. The tsar ordered his Baltic Sea fleet, including four brand-new battleships, to weigh anchor in St. Petersburg and sail halfway around the world to reinforce the beleaguered forces in East Asia. This heroic effort seemed doomed from the start. Since international law prevented neutral nations from assisting belligerents, the Russians had to bring coal and supply ships with them, thus slowing their progress. When the Russian fleet left the Baltic in October 1904, the sailors were so jittery that they fired at English fishing boats on the Dogger Bank, fearing they might be Japanese torpedo boats. This caused an international incident and nearly persuaded the English to join the war (Great Britain was not obliged to do so by the terms of the Anglo-Japanese Alliance, since no third party had yet supported Russia). The largest Russian ships rounded the Cape of Good Hope at the tip of Africa and rendezvoused in Madagascar with the smaller ships that had taken the Suez Canal route. At this point

(January 1905) the Russian government received news of Port Arthur's fall and reconsidered whether it should risk another sea battle; so the fleet holed up in Madagascar for two months, with the sailors losing their fighting edge day by day. Finally, the tsar ordered the fleet to sail on.

Having come around the world in eight months, the Russians met the Japanese on May 27, 1905, in the Straits of Tsushima. Admiral Togo's navy destroyed the Russian fleet in a single afternoon, sinking about half of its fifty ships and either capturing or chasing the rest into neutral ports. In one battle, Japan had erased Russia from the ranks of the world's sea powers. The English, who had trained the Japanese navy, took great pride in the victory of Tsushima, as Richard Storry notes:

> The completeness of the Japanese victory off Tsushima in the centenary year of Trafalgar filled British hearts with victorious pride. Togo's battleships came from British yards. Togo himself had been a cadet on *HMS Worcester;* and his captains had either received their training in England or from instructors in Japan steeped in the doctrines of the Royal Navy.

The two island empires, one in the East and one in the West, rejoiced together in their naval supremacy. Admiral Togo was lionized as the "Nelson of the East."

Though the Japanese won stunning victories on land and sea, they suffered heavy casualties in the land battles and used up most of their reserves. Russia, on the other hand, could pour in endless numbers of troops, given enough time. The final link on the Trans-Siberian Railway was completed in September 1904, and by the end of the war sixteen troop trains daily were rolling into Manchuria. Most important, Japan was broke. It was still a small, developing country, and it had used up most of its resources and financial credit in the fighting. Since an exhausted victor faced a vanquished foe, a negotiated peace seemed the logical result.

The Japanese government, which had known all along that its only hope lay in a swift victory, had prudently laid plans for peace even while the fighting raged. Baron Kaneko Kentaro, a Harvard classmate of Theodore Roosevelt, arrived in Washington in March 1904 and conducted private talks with the president throughout the war. When the Japanese wired an official request for mediation after the Battle of Tsushima, the president responded swiftly and invited representatives of the warring parties to meet with him at Portsmouth, New Hampshire, in August.

Teddy Roosevelt's role as a peacemaker seems surprising and incongruous at first sight, given his usual warlike bluster and his reputation as the Rough Rider hero of San Juan Hill. Indeed, he assumed the role almost by default. Britain's alliance with Japan and France's alliance with Russia disqualified them as neutral mediators, and Germany's Kaiser Wilhelm appeared even more unsuitable temperamentally than Roosevelt. Actually, the American president, despite his cow-boy image and some superficial resemblance to the kaiser, practiced the arts of diplomacy in a sophisticated manner. He sought a greater role for the United States in world affairs, of course, but he also worked toward a balance of power in areas where the U.S. could not predominate, such as East Asia. He hoped to end the war before a total Japanese victory and thus preserve some kind of balance in Manchuria that would permit other countries, like the United States, to continue trading there.

Russia and Japan signed the Treaty of Portsmouth on September 5, 1905. The Russians ceded the southern half of Sakhalin Island, which the Japanese had seized near the end of the war, and handed over their leasehold rights in Port Ar-thur and the Liaotung Peninsula to Japan. The Russians also withdrew their troops from the rest of South Manchuria and recognized the Japanese protector-ate over Korea, but they adamantly refused to pay any monetary indemnity.

Considering the scope of the Japanese victory, the spoils they earned in the treaty seemed relatively modest. The Japanese government knew how physically and financially exhausted its army was; but the Japanese populace, who had al-ways been more imperialist than the ruling class and had been prevented by cen-sorship from gauging the actual course of the war, did not know this. The people of Tokyo therefore rioted in Hibiya Park when the terms of the Treaty of Portsmouth were published.

Yet despite the disappointment of the mobs in Hibiya, the Russo-Japanese war marked an epochal change in world affairs. For the first time, an Asian coun-try had bested a European power in a major war. Colonized peoples were inspired by the first defeat of the white race in Asia. The Chinese revolutionary leader, Sun Yat-sen, was passing through the Suez Canal shortly after the Japanese naval vic-tory at Tsushima. Arab laborers at the canal, taking him for a Japanese, hailed him as a liberator. Europeans, on the other hand, noted with dismay the arrival of a new power in the world. Naturally enough, the shock waves from the Japanese victory struck most immediately in the country Japan defeated.

Russia was the last absolute monarchy in Europe. The Fundamental Laws of 1832 stated: "The Emperor of all the Russias is a sovereign with autocratic and unlimited powers. To obey the commands not merely from fear but according to the dictates of one's conscience is ordained by God himself." Though Peter the Great borrowed administrative methods and industrial techniques from Western Europe in the early eighteenth century, Russia's modernization had proceeded in fits and starts. Generally speaking, when the country felt threatened militarily the Russian government accelerated the growth of its economy, but when the foreign challenges subsided economic progress also halted. In the mid-nineteenth centu-ry, Russia was still considered hopelessly backward by the citizens of Western Eu-rope, and it was in fact not much more advanced economically than the isolated

Japanese. Cyril Black's comparative study of Russia and Japan estimated that in 1870 both countries had a per capita gross national product only about one-quarter to one-third that of Great Britain.

Russia initiated policies to catch up with the rest of Europe about the same time Japan did. The Russian defeat in the Crimean War (1853-1856) exposed the meagerness of the country's productivity and the weakness of its transportation system. In a series of "Great Reforms" the tsar emancipated the serfs (1861-64), revamped the military and the legal system, and accelerated the development of railways and heavy industry. Manufacturing output grew almost 7 percent a year from 1885 to 1900.

Nevertheless, the country's economic growth remained sluggish and was hindered by the lack of freedom and mobility in the political system. Though the peasants had been emancipated, they were burdened with heavy redemption payments — in effect, paying for their own freedom. The government also saddled the peasantry with heavy taxes. Most eked out only the most meager living from the soil. About 80 percent of the Russian populace remained untouched by the government's modernization policies, and those who were affected were scarcely better off. By 1910 more than half the industrial workers labored in factories that employed more than five hundred people. As Cyril Black concludes: "They were poorly paid, terribly overcrowded, had little education; they were a destitute and exploited labor force."

Tsar Nicholas II, who succeeded to the throne in 1894, presented a truly dangerous combination of traits: he was a weak man with absolute power. Though something of a playboy as a youth, he became deeply religious when he assumed the throne and married the puritanical Alix of Hesse-Darmstadt, a German Protestant who converted to Russian Orthodoxy and became Empress Alexandra. Nicholas was sincerely devoted to his wife, four daughters, and only son, the hemophiliac Tsarevich Alexei. He paid scant attention to the details of government but devoted himself to the duty of passing on all his autocratic powers intact to his heir. According to French historian Marc Ferro:

> Nicholas had been brought up in the English way: sport, modern languages, sport, deportment, *savoir-faire*, sport, dancing, horseriding. A well-made body, a head with not too much in it. . . . Above all, he was always at the receiving end of events, never their initiator. History never stopped hustling him. He believed that he had a duty to oppose change.

In 1903 the tsar dismissed his most capable official, Finance Minister Count Sergei Witte. A former railway administrator, Witte had risen to the top of the transport ministry and then served as the closest approximation to a prime minister that the Russian monarchy allowed. Witte was the prime mover in the building of the Trans-Siberian Railway and in the push for industrialization. After his removal, Russia remained what it had always been, an inefficient dictatorship. The rector of Moscow University astutely commented that "the government is believed neither when it threatens nor when it promises."

As the disasters of the war in Asia reverberated halfway around the world, they sparked a series of events usually called the Revolution of 1905. Adam Ulam, historian of the Russian revolutionaries, sums up the mood in Russia that year:

> The striving for political freedom had become universal. Russian autocracy was felt not only to be an anachronism and a national shame as in the previous generation, but the source of all evils beginning with her backwardness and ending with her defeat at the hands of a petty Asiatic state.

Yet it was a strange revolution, and ultimately an unsuccessful one. Ironically, it began with a peaceful protest, led by an Orthodox priest in the pay of the tsar.

Father Georgi Gapon headed a group of labor unions that were secretly sponsored by the police to co-opt labor organizers and defuse unrest. Yet sometime in the course of his double life, Father Gapon started thinking more like a labor leader than a police informer. Furthermore, he discovered depths of leadership ability neither he nor anyone else had previously suspected. So in January 1905, shortly after the fall of Port Arthur, Father Gapon marched to the tsar's Winter Palace in St. Petersburg at the head of a crowd numbering between 50,000 and 100,000. The working people of the capital carried a petition that addressed the tsar most reverentially, blaming the ills of the country on his bureaucratic ministers. The petition affirmed: "Popular representation is essential; it is essential that the people help themselves and govern themselves. . . . This is our principal request, upon which everything else depends." The document also requested normal civil liberties, such as freedom of speech and assembly, and many economic measures, including the eight-hour day and a raise in wages. Finally, the petitioners begged for "termination of the war in accordance with the will of the people."

The tsar refused to meet with the protesters or entertain their petition. Indeed, he was not even in town but was residing at Tsarkoe Selo, his fairy-tale country estate fifteen miles south of the capital. The mounted police in St. Petersburg charged the crowd, firing live ammunition and killing several hundred people. This event of January 9/22, 1905,[1] ever after known as Bloody Sunday, sparked

---

1. Russia still followed the Julian calendar, which at that time was thirteen days behind the Gregorian calendar followed in most of the rest of the world. Bloody Sunday, therefore, occurred on January 22, 1905, according to the Gregorian calendar. In the text, I have given both Old Style and New Style dates, separated by a slash.

a year-long string of strikes, riots, mutinies, and peasant revolts throughout Russia. Father Gapon fled the country, but he returned several times and was eventually murdered by the revolutionaries in 1906.

In June 1905 the sailors of the battleship *Potemkin,* bottled up in the Black Sea and unable to join the war in the Pacific, staged a mutiny that was later made famous by the Sergei Eisenstein silent film. The sailors cruised about for eleven days, setting off bloody riots in the port of Odessa and briefly shelling that city. When other ships failed to join the mutineers and their food and fuel ran low, they sought asylum in the Rumanian port of Constanza. The Rumanians let the sailors stay but returned the battleship to Russia. The tsar's government, fearing more mutinies, granted the sailors of the Black Sea fleet extended shore leave and deactivated the ships temporarily. The revolution disabled the one remnant of Russia's sea power left intact by the Japanese.

Strikes in the cities remained largely spontaneous and unplanned throughout 1905, and the workers made no clear-cut distinction between economic demands and political protests. Indeed, since collective action against employers remained illegal in tsarist Russia, any strike was, by definition, an act of political protest. Workers in Ivanovo-Voznesensk, a textile mill city in central Russia often dubbed the "Russian Manchester," formed an assembly or strike committee in May 1905, which is usually considered the prototype of a workers' soviet, although it did not use that name. A larger and more important workers' council, the Soviet of Workers' Deputies, came into being in St. Petersburg, and about forty other cities also formed workers' soviets (the word *soviet* means council). When a number of stoppages on the railways developed spontaneously into a general strike in October, the St. Petersburg Soviet became the headquarters for the strike and took on quasi-governmental powers. The organizing vigor of the workers surprised the socialist parties of Russia almost as much as it did the tsar. Only one prominent Marxist socialist, Leon Trotsky, played a major role in the activities of the St. Petersburg Soviet. Lenin did not arrive in Russia until after the October general strike.

In desperation the tsar turned again to Count Witte, who had already served in August as peace plenipotentiary at Portsmouth, New Hampshire. Though Nicholas still despised the man, he took his advice and issued the October Manifesto, which granted civil liberties to the populace and promised to convoke a legislative assembly, the State Duma. He then named Witte chairman of the Council of Ministers, in effect the prime minister.

The populace took these concessions as a sign of weakness in the government and for a time general lawlessness prevailed in Russia. Workers continued to strike and riot spontaneously, peasants seized their landlords' estates, military companies mutinied. In retaliation, pro-tsarist gangs, called the Black Hundreds, attacked workers, and religious fanatics mounted bloody pogroms against the

Jews. The workers in Moscow attempted an armed uprising to topple the government in December, but the tsar's troops, liberally firing their artillery into the working-class neighborhoods, quelled it.

Count Witte then decided on a course of thoroughgoing repression. Even the tsar seemed surprised, commenting in a letter to his mother: "As for Witte, since the happenings in Moscow he has radically changed his views; now he wants to hang and shoot everybody." The most effective instruments of repression were the punitive expeditions, highly organized attacks by small, specially selected bands of soldiers, who took no prisoners and ruthlessly shot, flogged, or beat anyone suspected of opposing the government or causing disorder. These brutal expeditions, though limited in scope, intimidated the populace. Two or three months into 1906, the revolution ended and the soviets became only a memory.

The tsar proclaimed a new Fundamental Law for the State, which merely changed the word "unlimited" autocratic power to "supreme" autocratic power. Still, the convocation of an assembly afforded the regime's opponents a platform. After the first elections in April 1906, the Duma fought constantly with the government until the latter dissolved it three months later. The second Duma, elected in 1907, proved even worse from the tsar's point of view and was also dismissed after only a few months. Finally, in June 1907 the government changed the election laws, greatly restricting the franchise; this finally produced a tame and cooperative body of legislators. Russia remained an autocracy, yet the Revolution of 1905 had snapped the mystic bond between tsar and people.

Both the Russo-Japanese War and its strange and unexpected revolutionary sequel foreshadowed numerous events of the coming century. Most obviously, these events were a dress rehearsal for World War I and the Russian Revolution of 1917.

The conflict in Asia was the first large-scale war between major powers since the Franco-Prussian War of 1870-71, and it was the first war ever fought with completely modern weapons. Artillery and machine guns raked the battlefield, cutting down the ranks of charging infantrymen. Field telephones and railways aided the commanders in coordinating troop movements. Cavalry, even the vaunted Russian Cossacks, proved of little use in this new-style warfare, and only one traditional lance charge was mounted in the course of the war.

Journalists and military attachés from all over the world descended on the front in Manchuria to observe, take notes, and report on the strategy and tactics of the combatants. They learned some important lessons. The battle of Tsushima, for example, which destroyed almost the entire Russian fleet in a single day, made such an impression on European naval officers that they grew extremely cautious about risking full fleet battles. Consequently, the German and English fleets spent most of the First World War in port, and naval battles played little role in that war.

Other valuable lessons could have been learned but were not. Field artillery and machine guns had transformed the nature of land warfare. The enormous casualties the Japanese suffered while assaulting the Russian trenches should have made clear how great an advantage the defense enjoyed at this stage in the development of modern warfare. The carnage in Manchuria signaled that a lightning victory on land had become nearly impossible and a long, bloody war of attrition, over a wide front, was the most likely outcome. Nevertheless, the powers in World War I struggled for decisive land victories with the thoroughly predictable result of wholesale slaughter in the trenches.

Jumping further ahead in this century, many observers point out that the Japanese sneak attack on Port Arthur prefigured their strategy at Pearl Harbor in 1941. Therefore, Americans should have learned the lessons of history and been on the alert at Pearl. This argument is accurate enough as far as it goes; however, the Japanese also failed to learn from their own experience. For all its shock value, the undeclared attack on Port Arthur did not destroy the Russian fleet. Only a year-long siege by land troops succeeded in that. Yet the Pearl Harbor raid in 1941 was a pure hit-and-run attack. The Japanese did not follow up their lightning strike, which badly damaged the American fleet but did not totally destroy it, with troop landings in Hawaii. So ultimately they failed to eliminate American power in the Pacific.

Diplomatically, as well as militarily, the war of 1904-5 contained a warning that was not heeded. The Russo-Japanese War could easily have turned into a world war since so many powers had interests in East Asia. The only reason it did not is that the other powers worked very hard to keep it limited. The Anglo-Japanese Alliance of 1902 required England to stay neutral if Japan went to war so long as no other country entered the fray. France had earlier struck a similar defensive alliance with Russia. All the European powers respected these treaties, and eventually the Americans stepped in and brokered a peace. Yet, if the powers ever became entangled in alliances that called for automatic military support of their allies, general war would be much more likely. This is what happened in the decade after the Russo-Japanese War.

The Revolution of 1905 also whispered prophecies of the future. Nearly the same circumstances that set off revolt in 1905 recurred in 1917: defeat in war, massive disaffection of the intellectuals, peasant unrest, and workers marching in the streets. In the latter year as in the former, the initial risings were spontaneous and unplanned; but by 1917, a few revolutionary leaders had learned the lessons of 1905. Orthodox Marxists did not expect the revolution to occur in backward Russia, but in one of the more advanced capitalist states. Lenin, however, almost alone among the European socialists, read the events of 1905 correctly and determined not to be caught by surprise the next time. As a result, he and his small band of Bolsheviks seized the moment in October 1917 and made the most of it.

The events of 1904-5, therefore, contain many hints and warnings of the greater events from 1914 to 1918. They also illustrate three major trends of the twentieth century: the revolt against European imperialism, the emergence of the United States as a world power, and the globalization of war and politics.

The Russo-Japanese War marked the first time that an Asian, non-white nation defeated a European power. As Japan pressed its advantages in Asia over the following decades, the prestige of the colonial powers slowly crumbled. The arrogant militarism of the Japanese in World War II eventually fostered a deep hatred against Japan in Southeast Asia, but the immediate result was different. The opening months of World War II showed in an even more startling manner than the Russo-Japanese War the hollowness of European imperialism. Richard Storry sums up the impact:

> Apologists for imperialism always claimed, when under fire from critics of the system, that in the final analysis its ethical justification was the ordered peace and security it provided for the native inhabitants of the colonies and protec-torates. Thus failure to repulse an enemy invasion destroyed the *raison d'etre* of colonial governments. . . . It was doubly so when colonial rulers were over-thrown, not by their own kind, but by invaders racially akin to the ruled.

Japan's victory in 1905, and its greater string of victories in 1941, prompted the re-volt of "the Third World" against Europe.

The events of 1905 also marked the emergence of the United States on the world stage. For the first one hundred years of its independent existence, the United States had confined most of its political and military activities to the Western Hemisphere. Though the word "isolationism" has often been used by historians to describe American policy, the United States was never so thor-oughly isolationist as Japan and Korea were. Indeed, Americans believed their own revolution held a universal message of political freedom for the world, and they arrogantly hoped they could reform the world by example. In addition, American merchant ships roamed the world in search of trading opportunities. In both the commercial and ideological realms, therefore, the early United States was universalist, not isolationist. However, the American government, pragmatically following the counsel of George Washington's Great Rule of Con-duct, confined their military activities to the Western Hemisphere and stayed out of European alliances and conflicts. American foreign policy in the nine-teenth century, therefore, can be summed up in three principles: reform the world by example, trade with everyone, but steer clear of entangling alliances and observe a strict "spheres of interest" policy. Viewed in this light, Commo-dore Perry's expedition to Japan was quite unusual, and it was strictly limited in its aims and methods. Americans wanted to open up Japan for trade, but they remained content to let England and the other European powers perform most of the gunboat diplomacy.

Around 1900, however, the U.S. government initiated military and diplomatic interventions outside its traditional sphere of interest in North and South America. The war with Spain in 1898 yielded the first American colonies outside the continent of North America — most surprisingly, the Philippine Islands, which gave the United States an interest in Asian affairs. Theodore Roosevelt, who engineered the seizure of the Philippines while assistant secretary of the navy, harbored grandiose visions of his country's role in the world. As president, Roosevelt readily grasped the opportunity to intervene in the Russo-Japanese War, thus marking a milestone in American world involvement. The U.S. government never would have offered to mediate the Franco-Prussian War of 1870, for example, and if they had, no one would have taken them seriously. Yet by 1905 American mediation proved both necessary and successful. The U.S. president earned the Nobel Peace Prize for midwifing the Treaty of Portsmouth.

Finally, the Russo-Japanese War illustrates the globalization of politics in the twentieth century. For the first time, European, American, and Asian interests and policies interacted in the same theater. When conflict broke out, the whole world was watching. Cable dispatches from the Manchurian front were printed in the world's newspapers the following day. Ever since, there has been no such thing as a local war. The global age had begun.

The events of 1904-5 also show clearly how the four "isms" galloped across this new global stage. Nationalism and imperialism, of course, played front and center. National pride and racism caused the Russians to take the Japanese lightly and ignore their attempts to negotiate and head off the coming war. The Japanese, for their part, exhibited a rising national feeling and were eager to prove themselves in the game of imperialism and the test of battle. National pride, far more than mere economic interests, pushed the two countries to imperial outreach and war. In the Russian Empire, suppressed nationalities stimulated and intensified the revolutionary agitation against the tsar. Some of the fiercest fighting of the 1905 revolution occurred in conquered Poland, the Baltic provinces, and the region of the Caucasus.

Socialism and anarchism stalked the scene more furtively, but burst forth in Russia in 1905. The Japanese were well aware of European left-wing movements. Indeed, they employed a network of intelligence agents who secretly encouraged and subsidized socialists and anarchists in the Russian Empire as a means of weakening the enemy. Ironically, though, it was one of the Russians' own agents, not the Japanese, who sparked the revolution. This first Russian Revolution owed little to Marxist ideology or socialist organizing; in fact, it unfolded largely along the lines the anarchists had sketched out. It was a spontaneous rising of the unorganized masses, prepared by constant agitation and propaganda then set off by the horrors of Bloody Sunday. The workers' soviets, informal, voluntary bodies of working-class delegates, sound far closer in spirit to the anarchist ideal than the socialist. The very bewilderment and surprise of most Russian socialists when faced with the revolt highlights the anarchic nature of that rising.

So we end this prologue to the twentieth century as we began it, with four "isms" stalking Europe and the world, and with a foretaste of modern warfare and social revolution. The first years of the twentieth century forecast a uniquely ferocious rage of nations.

PART TWO

THE FIRST WORLD CATASTROPHE

Europe had enjoyed a long peace since the Congress of Vienna settled the Napoleonic Wars in 1815. The nations that defeated Napoleon's France — England, Russia, Prussia, and Austria — fashioned the Concert of Europe, an informal consortium of great powers that attempted to preserve both internal order and a balance of power internationally. The system worked. Though countries forged temporary alliances and wars occasionally broke out, the great powers always gathered in congress after each war to settle the outstanding issues and prevent further fighting. The Concert of Europe did not effect perfect justice between nations. It was more interested in preserving stability than doing the right thing, and thus it often sacrificed the interests of smaller nations to the general peace of Europe. Yet it prevented any general war from breaking out for almost a century.

Toward the end of the nineteenth century, however, the concert of great powers broke down into two competing, rival alliances. The rise of a strong, united Germany in the center of Europe caused the other powers to fear it and to look for permanent partners for protection. Alliances are like weapons. Though statesmen disavow any hostile intent, eventually they will use the implements of war they have forged. Europe's long peace eventually turned out to be simply a long fuse.

CHAPTER SIX

A Murder in Bosnia

Imperialism collided with nationalism in 1914, striking a spark that ignited the First World War. This bonfire of the "isms," however, was not kindled in China, India, or Africa, but in Europe's own "third world," the Balkan Peninsula. Austria-Hungary, the weakest of the five great European powers and the only one without an overseas empire, grabbed its sole colony, Bosnia-Hercegovina, in 1878. Chancellor Bismarck of Germany warned that "some damn fool incident in the Balkans" might set off a general war. He was right. On June 28, 1914, Gavrilo Princip, a Serbian nationalist, murdered Archduke Franz Ferdinand of Austria in the Bosnian capital of Sarajevo. A month later, the European powers fell upon each other in a war that stretched around the world.

The twin provinces of Bosnia-Hercegovina,[1] which have troubled Europe and the world both at the beginning and now also at the end of the twentieth century, sit astride rugged mountains in the west-central sector of the Balkan Peninsula. A Bosnian folk tale relates that God, at the time of the creation, carried two sacks, one full of earth and the other full of stones. While passing over the Balkans

---

1. Since Bosnia, which takes its name from the Bosna River, and Hercegovina, which means "the duchy" in Serbo-Croatian, have been politically and administratively joined since 1878, I shall refer to them collectively as Bosnia for the sake of convenience. Bosnia is the northerly of the two territories, with its capital at Sarajevo, and Hercegovina lies immediately southwest, with its capital at Mostar. The boundaries of the united provinces are well defined on three sides: the Drina River separates them from Serbia in the east, and the Sava River from Croatia in the north; and the Dinaric Alps lie between them and the Dalmatian coast of the Adriatic Sea on the west. At one point, a narrow finger of Hercegovina cuts Dalmatia in two and touches the sea. The southern boundary with Montenegro is not well defined geographically.

the second sack burst and the stones tumbled out, creating Bosnia. Though the rocky soil of the province makes for poor farmland, it is rich in minerals, heavily forested, and wildly beautiful. The English novelist Rebecca West, who traveled through the Balkans in the 1930s and fell in love with both countryside and people, emphasized the stunning variety of Bosnia's mountains: "These heights and valleys run neither north nor south nor west nor east, but in all ways for a mile at a time. . . . Because of the intricate contours of its hills it is for ever presenting a new picture, and the mind runs away from life to its setting." The terrain resembles Switzerland, but its history has been far less peaceful.

The Slavic people who inhabit Bosnia were part of the medieval kingdom of Croatia until it was conquered by Hungary in 1102. Thereafter, the Bosnians withdrew into the mountains, anchoring their own kingdom on the natural fortress of Jajce, which sits upon an egg-shaped hill (*Jajce* means "little egg," or in some translations, "testicle"). In their isolation, Bosnians developed a distinctive style of Christianity which used the vernacular language, forbade landholding by the church, and blurred the boundaries between bishops, priests, and laypeople. They called themselves "true Christians," but they were also nicknamed Bogomils, which roughly translates as "God be merciful."

It is not clear whether the Bogomil brand of Christianity was heretical or schismatic in the technical, theological sense. A clearly heretical group of Bogomils existed in Bulgaria. These sectarians were dualist in theology, intellectual descendants of the ancient Manicheans who held that there are two first principles in the universe: a good spirit who created heaven and the human soul, and an evil spirit who created earth and the human body. Since most of what historians know about the Bosnian Bogomils comes from papal condemnations issued in Rome, we cannot be certain that they too held these same dualist beliefs. A modern-day Croatian priest, Ivo Sivric, argues forcefully that the Bosnians were not heretics, but "primitive Christians," living a life modeled after the early church. Franciscan friars who settled in Bosnia reinforced the New Testament simplicity of the native Christians. Thereafter, the Bosnians of the Middle Ages wanted nothing so much as to be left alone.

They never got their wish. Pope Honorius III preached a crusade against Bosnia in 1237, and the Hungarians took it upon themselves to invade the province in the name of the pope. Both the Orthodox emperor of Constantinople and the Orthodox prince of Serbia burned Bogomils at the stake when they discovered them in their domains. Then the Ottoman Turks, having conquered Constantinople and brought the Eastern Orthodox Empire to an end, swept westward through the Balkans, conquering Bosnia in 1463 and Hercegovina in 1482.

After the Turkish conquest, many Bosnians converted to Islam. Since the Bogomils had been persecuted by both Roman Catholic and Orthodox Christians, they saw submission to Islam as the least of three evils. Their primitive

Christianity had built few strong institutions that might have held out against the Ottoman state. As historian John V. A. Fine Jr. has argued, "*Acceptance* is a better word than *conversion* to describe what occurred in Bosnia. Probably few Bosnians in accepting Islam underwent any deep changes in patterns of thought or way of life." Furthermore, since only Muslims could hold land in the Ottoman Empire, conversion allowed the Bosnian nobles to keep possession of their estates and the peasants to become freeholders. Whatever the motivations of these Islamic converts, their descendants remain Muslims to this day, and Bosnia is, perhaps, the only country in the world with snow-covered mosques.

Bosnia remained on the front lines between competing empires. The long, irregular, boomerang-shaped boundary between Croatia and Bosnia marks the furthest advance of the Turkish armies into the Balkan Peninsula. The Habsburg emperors, who ruled Austria and Hungary from the late Middle Ages, transformed much of Croatia into a military frontier, with Croatians and refugee Serbs providing shock troops to guard against Muslim invasion and help suppress internal uprisings. The Croatian Frontiersmen became the "Cossacks of the Habsburgs." On the other side of the line, the Turks seized young male Bosnians, transported them to Constantinople for their upbringing, and trained them as Janissaries, that is, their own elite army corps. Slavs from the Bosnian mountains, therefore, fought each other as the vanguards of their respective conquerors.

As the Turkish empire disintegrated in the nineteenth century, the Christian Bosnian peasants chafed under the feudal dues owed their Muslim landlords and the heavy taxes due to the state. This dual burden ordinarily took at least 44 percent of the serf's produce. Then in 1875 the Turkish sultan increased the taxes by 25 percent and the peasants finally revolted. The Austrians, however, marched their own troops into Bosnia and Hercegovina in 1878; and the Treaty of Berlin, which regulated the aftermath of these events, granted them the right to occupy and administer the two provinces under nominal Turkish suzerainty. The Bosnians had merely exchanged one set of masters for another. Finally, in 1908 Austria-Hungary made it official by formally annexing Bosnia-Hercegovina.

The population of Bosnia in 1910 stood at just under 2 million, including 825,000 Eastern Orthodox Serbs (43 percent), 612,000 Muslims (33 percent), and 442,000 Roman Catholic Croatians (24 percent). The Croatians had long enjoyed a symbiotic relationship with the Austrian Empire, and many of them remained loyal to the House of Habsburg. In the German phrase of the time, they were *kaisertreu,* the emperor's people. Some of the Slavic Muslims also gave firm allegiance to Austria, though most were probably indifferent. The Serbian plurality in Bosnia, however, was disaffected from Austria, and with good reason. Just across the Drina River, their fellow Serbs had succeeded in throwing off Turkish rule and carving out an independent kingdom. The Serbs of Bosnia wished to unite with their compatriots and form a Greater Serbia.

Serbia, like Bosnia, had been an independent kingdom until conquered by the Turks in the fourteenth and fifteenth centuries. The decisive battle took place in the Kosovo Plain on the feast of St. Vitus, June 28, 1389. The forces of the Sultan Murad I captured the Serbian Prince Lazar, but another Serbian nobleman, Miloš Obilić, crept into the Turkish camp and assassinated the sultan. In retaliation, the Turks beheaded Prince Lazar. The Battle of Kosovo became the central legend of the Serbian people, later spiced with a tale of treason by the Serb Vuk Branković which made the defeat easier to understand and accept.

The Kosovo legend illustrates very clearly the definition of nationalism as "a feeling we have done great things together in the past." Even a defeat in battle could provide the great deeds as historical memories became richer and more complexly layered through the centuries. The Serbian Orthodox revered both Prince Lazar and Miloš Obilić as saints; and the cult of Miloš, the noble warrior who committed tyrannicide, eventually inspired the Serbs to revolt against Turkish rule. Serbian historian Dimitrije Djordjević has analyzed the Kosovo legend: "We do not know how deep the historical heritage rested in peasant memory. But we know that the epic popular poetry expressed the deeds of heroes, the strength of the Orthodox faith, and the martyrdom of a conquered nation." Though the main body of Serbian population migrated into the Morava valley in the central Balkans and Muslim Albanians gradually replaced them on the Kosovo Plain, Kosovo remained sacred ground, a Mecca or Jerusalem, for the Serbs.

In 1804 Karadjordje (Black George) Petrović mounted a revolt against the Turks, calling on his followers "to throw off, in the name of God, the yoke which the Serbs carry from Kosovo to this day." Though the Turks regained control in 1813, a second revolt in 1815 led by Prince Miloš Obrenović proved successful, and Serbia gained autonomy under an increasingly nominal Turkish suzerainty. To curry favor with the Turkish overlords, Prince Miloš murdered his rival, Karadjordje, and sent his stuffed head to the sultan. An oligarchy of nobles held the real authority in this turbulent country during the first half of the nineteenth century, forcing Prince Miloš to flee the country in 1838, and naming Alexander Karadjordjević (the murdered Karadjordje's son) as prince. Alexander lost a power struggle with the oligarchy in 1858 and was replaced by Michael Obrenović, who was, in turn, assassinated in 1868 and succeeded by his second cousin Milan, who kept the Obrenović dynasty in power.

Serbia joined the war against the Turks that the Bosnian revolt of 1875 ignited. The Russians, acting like big brothers to all Slavs, marched their armies down the Balkan Peninsula and nearly swept the Turks out of Europe. Serbian soldiers even managed to reach Kosovo in January 1878. However, the great powers who gathered at the Congress of Berlin to sort out the wreckage left by this war forced Serbia to withdraw from Kosovo and the Russians to disgorge some of their gains as well. The Congress of Berlin granted Serbia international recognition of its full independence from Turkey, but the Serbs gained little else. Despite the Pan-Slavist propaganda, Russia abandoned its tiny Slavic ally at the great power congress and conceded that Serbia lay within Austria-Hungary's sphere of influence.

For the rest of the century, therefore, Serbia functioned as a virtual satellite of the Austro-Hungarian Empire. A trade treaty in 1881 locked Serbia into the Austrian economy, which accounted for over 80 percent of the small kingdom's foreign trade. The Serbs traded agricultural produce, mainly pigs and plums, in return for manufactured goods. Also in 1881, Prince Milan Obrenović signed a secret convention with Austria-Hungary that nearly yielded Serbia's status as an independent nation. The Serbian prince pledged himself to remain neutral if Austria-Hungary should go to war and not to conclude any treaty or military alliance with another country without consulting the Austrians first. He also promised not to tolerate any political or military agitation against Austria either in Serbia itself or in Bosnia. In return, Austria promised to recognize Milan as king, rather than merely a prince, if he should choose to assume that title. Accordingly, Milan Obrenović proclaimed Serbia a kingdom in 1882; but he soon grew weary of ruling over the people he called "my damn subjects," and in 1889 he abdicated so that he could live in Paris with his mistress. His son Alexander Obrenović, a boy of thirteen, assumed the throne under the guidance of a three-man regency.

The waning days of the Obrenović dynasty played out like a bad comic opera. Finding nothing but ennui in exile, Milan Obrenović returned to Belgrade in 1891. The government of Serbia, which had wrested a constitution from the monarchy and was trying to transform the country into a parliamentary democracy, paid off Milan's debts and convinced him to leave again; but he did not stay away long. For the rest of the decade he engaged in a tug-of-war with his estranged wife, Natalia, for the dominant influence over their son, King Alexander. Serbian historian Michael Petrovich, author of a sober two volumes on modern Serbia, has stated in frank disbelief, "It is astonishing how much of the political energy of Serbia was spent in the quarrel between King Milan and Queen Natalia."

The old king (actually he was only thirty-eight) engineered a military coup in 1893 that allowed his son to assume his majority status two years early, at age sixteen, and for Milan to exercise decisive influence. The young king grew tired of his father's bullying and went to visit his mother in exile at Biarritz in 1895. There he fell hopelessly in love with Natalia's lady-in-waiting, Draga Masin, with ultimately fatal consequences. King Alexander convinced his mother to return to Belgrade and his father to depart, but this lasted only until 1897 when father returned and mother left for good. Alexander tried to strike out on his own and exercise personal authority over the kingdom, but he was finally dragged down by his love for Draga Masin, whom he married in 1900.

Draga was a thirty-four-year-old widow, twelve years older than Alexander.

Her father had ended his life in an insane asylum and her mother was an alcoholic. Draga had apparently supported herself in the early days of widowhood by discreet liaisons with wealthy gentlemen. She had never borne children to her first husband and was believed to be barren. For all these reasons, she made an appalling choice for the wife of a king. Alexander did not care. He loved Draga passionately and tried to develop a cult of personality around her (something like Eva Peron later in Argentina), naming schools, streets, and edifices after her. Immediately after her marriage, Draga declared that she was pregnant, but this proved to be a false alarm. Rumors spread that she planned to pass off one of her sister's children as her own, or if that ploy failed, Alexander might declare one of Draga's brothers heir-apparent.

A group of junior officers in the Serbian military decided that Draga and Alexander were bringing shame upon the country and had to be eliminated. Colonel Dragutin Dimitrijević, nicknamed Apis, the busy bee, for his incessant activity, was the ringleader of the conspiracy that eventually encompassed over a hundred individuals, including some civilians. On the night of June 10-11, 1903, the conspirators stormed into the royal palace in Belgrade and invaded the king and queen's bedroom about 2:00 A.M., only to find it empty. After frantic searching throughout the palace, at 3:50 A.M. they found the fugitives cowering in a hidden closet. The soldiers emptied their rifles into the unfortunate couple, then hacked their bodies with sabers and threw them over the balcony into the courtyard. Rebecca West has commented, melodramatically: "When Alexander and Draga fell from that balcony the whole of the modern world fell with them. It took some time to reach the ground and break its neck, but its fall started then." Indeed these horrendous murders marked a watershed in Serbia's history and in the destiny of Europe and the world, for they initiated a series of events that ultimately culminated in war.

On June 15 the parliament invited Peter Karadjordjević, the sixty-year-old pretender from Serbia's other royal family, to become monarch. He accepted immediately, arriving in Belgrade to assume the throne on June 25, 1903. The new king, a well-read man of liberal inclinations who had spent most of his life in Western Europe, was more of a Serbian nationalist than any of the recent Obrenovićes had been. Through the years of its decline, the Obrenović dynasty had remained committed to close relations with Austria. When the old king, Milan, died in 1901, shortly after his son's ill-fated marriage, he was buried, according to his written request, at a Serbian monastery in Austria. Petrovich, the Serbian historian, coldly concludes that "Milan's funeral was less that of a Serbian king than of a vassal of the Habsburgs." King Peter Karadjordjević, on the other hand, felt a special affection for the Russian tsar as leader of the Slavs and an inspiration for Orthodox Christians. Therefore, he sought to escape the Austrian dominance and reorient Serbia's foreign relations towards Russia.

This melodramatic series of events in Serbia followed a pattern that was very common during the centuries when Europe dominated the world. Europeans usually ruled their colonial possessions and dependencies through willing collaborators among the elites of the subject countries, such as the Obrenovićes in Serbia. Such collaboration, however, often stimulated a rival elite family or faction, such as the Karadjordjevićes, to cultivate nationalist sentiments and lead resistance to the imperialist powers. Thus the counterpoint between the Karadjordjevićes and Obrenovićes was not uniquely Serbian; it happened in Africa and Asia as well as in the Balkans. It reflected the struggle between imperialism and nationalism.

Under the Karadjordjević dynasty, the Serbian intelligentsia and middle class burned with a nationalist fervor for liberation from Austrian influence. Serbian nationalists cherished two ultimate goals: the incorporation of all Serbs into a Greater Serbia and the unification of all South Slav peoples (Serbs, Croats, Slovenes, and maybe even the Bulgarians) into a Yugoslav (South Slav) federation. The second goal seemed little more than a dream in the first years of the twentieth century, and it could possibly conflict with the first. Therefore, practical politicians in Belgrade, especially Nikola Pašić who headed most of the governments under the Karadjordjević monarchy, pursued the ideal of a Greater Serbia. The military also supported this goal; indeed, the conspirators of 1903 justified their regicide on nationalist grounds, charging that King Alexander had neglected the "Serbian cause." From the Greater Serbia point of view, Kosovo remained the holy grail, though few of its inhabitants were Serbs, and Bosnia was an "Alsace," that is, a severed branch from the Serbian tree. The Serbs also wanted to annex Macedonia, which was still ruled by the Turks, and whose people were not yet recognized as a separate nationality.

These Greater Serbian stirrings thoroughly alarmed the Austrian government. In order to pressure its former client state, Austria suspended negotiations on a new trade treaty at the end of 1905 and closed its borders to Serbian produce. A tariff war between the two states, more picturesquely described as the Pig War, subsequently raged for five years, from 1905 to 1911. The Austrians also proposed to build a railroad from Bosnia through the Sanjak of Novipazar, a narrow strip of Turkish territory separating Serbia from the independent principality of Montenegro. This railroad, which was never built, would have virtually encircled the landlocked kingdom of Serbia and cut it off from access to the sea. Finally, in 1908 Austria annexed Bosnia-Hercegovina outright, though it simultaneously renounced any rights in the Sanjak of Novipazar and declined to pursue its railroad scheme. The Serbian public was outraged and called for a war of liberation in Bosnia, but the Russians made it clear they still desired peace with Austria and would not support Serbia. The Serbian goverment, therefore, backed down and signed a humiliating capitulation, pledging once again not to stir up nationalist agitation in Bosnia.

Denial of the Austrian market hurt many Serbs, especially the pig farmers who could not export their pork across the border, but it also occasioned a frantic and long-overdue search for new trading partners and new communication links with other countries. The Pig War also stimulated home-grown industries and attracted foreign investment. Austria's economic warfare backfired, strengthening Serbia rather than crippling it; and its highhanded annexation of Bosnia gave Serbs a burning, uncompromisable grievance.

In the wake of the Bosnian annexation crisis, a Serbian patriotic organization named *Narodna Odbrana* (National Defense) sprang into being. Though this secret society originally aimed at overthrowing Austrian rule in Bosnia, the Belgrade government reined it in and limited it to cultural activities. The National Defense, however, did retain a network of sympathizers, virtually an underground railroad for spies, across the Drina in Bosnia. Then in 1911, a group of army officers, including Colonel Dimitrijević-Apis and other regicides, formed a secret society named *Urjedinjenje ili smrt* (Unity or Death). Its enemies, however, called it the Black Hand, after the Italian mafia, and it was generally known by this name.

Many members of the Black Hand held high positions in the Serbian government, and they agitated continually for the liberation of Bosnia. Before their plans could come to fruition, however, the continuing disintegration of the Turkish Empire provided a more tempting target for Greater Serbian ambitions. In 1912, the small Slavic states of Serbia, Montenegro, and Bulgaria formed a Balkan League with Greece, and the four states attacked Turkey, driving the Ottoman forces all the way to the gates of Constantinople. The Balkan allies soon fell to quarreling over the spoils of war, and in 1913 Bulgaria attacked Serbia with disastrous consequences as all Bulgaria's former allies, as well as the Turks and the Romanians, piled on against it. Serbia came out of the Balkan Wars of 1912-13 with major territorial gains in Kosovo and Macedonia. For the first time in over five hundred years no Serbs were living under Turkish rule. The defeat at Kosovo in 1389 had finally been avenged.

Serbian nationalists, however, deemed their job only half-done. After the Balkan Wars, the population of Serbia swelled to about 4.4 million, but another 2.5 million Serbs remained outside the kingdom, mainly in Bosnia and in other provinces of the Austro-Hungarian Empire. Belgrade was swarming with demobilized soldiers and with Bosnians of peasant origin who came to study in the Serbian capital. Colonel Dimitrijevic and other advocates of a Greater Serbia cultivated these two discontented groups, fed them nationalist propaganda, trained them in the use of firearms, then smuggled them across the Austrian border. Inspired by their Serbian patrons, the Bosnian students organized revolutionary secret societies, collectively known as *Mlada Bosna* (Young Bosnia). Having finally expelled the Turks from Europe, these young nationalists now took deadly aim at the remaining imperial occupier, Austria-Hungary's Habsburg dynasty.

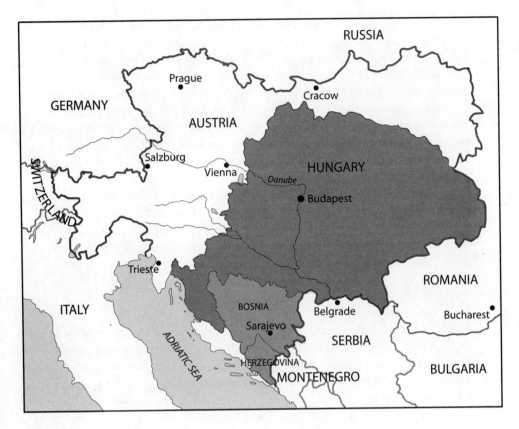

Austria-Hungary c. 1900

Austria-Hungary, as its double name implies, was not an ordinary European nation-state. Rather, it was a multinational empire composed of formerly independent kingdoms and principalities which the German-speaking Habsburg family had accumulated over the centuries by war, by treaty, or by felicitous dynastic marriages. In 1867 an *Ausgleich,* or compromise, with the largest non-German nationality, the Magyars, split the realm into two self-governing parts, Austria and Hungary. Each half of the Dual Monarchy, as it was called, had its own prime minister and parliament and enjoyed total autonomy. They shared, however, a single monarch, the Habsburg Franz Joseph, who was known as emperor of Austria and king of Hungary. The emperor/king commanded a common army and navy for the Dual Monarchy as well as a foreign ministry and a finance ministry. There was no prime minister at the federal level. Each country elected a delegation to debate and approve common imperial policies, but the two delegations did not meet together and did not form a truly common parliament. A customs union linked the economies of Austria and Hungary, but the terms of this economic partnership were negotiable every ten years. The Dual Monarchy, therefore, had to reinvent itself every decade.

Two-headedness marked only the beginning of Austria-Hungary's complexity. Besides Germans and Hungarians, the empire also embraced nine other major nationalities. A 1910 census in the Austrian lands counted a total population of 28 million. Thirty-five percent of these were Germans, concentrated mainly in the Austrian heartland around Vienna; 23 percent were Czechs, in Bohemia and Moravia; 18 percent Poles in Galicia; 13 percent Ruthenians (or Ukrainians), beyond the Carpathian Mountains towards Russia; 4 percent Slovenes, just south of Austria proper; and 3 percent Italians, in the high Alpine passes near the town of Trent. Hungarians formed a bare majority of the 22 million people in their half of the empire, with very large minorities of Slovaks, Romanians, Croatians, and Serbs. Croatia enjoyed a certain amount of autonomy in the Hungarian kingdom, and the Polish landowners of Galicia remained satisfied with their local political power. Slovenes had never enjoyed a homeland of their own and possessed relatively little national consciousness. However, the Czechs, Slovaks, Italians, Romanians, and Serbs felt alienated from the rulers of Austria-Hungary. The Czech lands formed an "Ireland" within Austria, and Slovakia was Hungary's "Ireland." The neighboring kingdoms of Italy, Romania, and Serbia viewed their compatriots within the Dual Monarchy as "Alsaces," waiting for liberation.

Much has been written about Austria-Hungary's anomalous status as a multinational, two-headed empire in a Europe of nation-states. Many observers at the beginning of the twentieth century viewed the Dual Monarchy as a hopelessly anachronistic dinosaur, lumbering inevitably toward extinction. Others called it the "dungeon of nations." English Liberals, such as Henry Wickham Steed, the foreign editor of the *Times,* and the historian Robert Seton-Watson, championed the subject nationalities of the Balkans and railed against their jailers, the Habsburgs of Austria-Hungary.

Other points of view, however, prevailed in the capitals of Central Europe. In a much-quoted phrase, the Czech leader Frantisek Palacky once remarked, "Truly, if the Austrian empire had not existed for ages, it would be necessary, in the interest of Europe, in the interest of mankind itself, to create it with all speed." The Habsburg empire served as a buffer between more powerful states such as Germany and Russia. Indeed, it is important to recall the context of Palacky's famous quote. He was writing in the revolutionary year of 1848, at a time when Germans and Czechs in central Europe were contemplating a much enlarged, Greater Germany at the expense of Austria. Palacky declined to sit as a delegate at the German National Assembly in Frankfurt and penned his classic response by way of explanation. He was worried that Russia would swiftly expand into Eastern Europe and the Balkans if the Habsburg Monarchy disintegrated. "Austria divided into a number of republics and miniature republics. What a welcome basis for a Russian universal monarchy!" Palacky concluded.

Chancellor Otto von Bismarck of Germany, whose armies defeated the Habsburgs in 1866, held the power to partition or destroy the Austrian monarchy. Yet he too believed it worth preserving. The alternative would be revolutionary chaos, as each of the subject nationalities tried to carve out as much living space as possible. Conservatives like Bismarck viewed Austria as a welcome buffer against the nationalist passions of the Balkan nations. Even the English Liberal, Seton-Watson, before he became disillusioned with Austria argued that "the Habsburg monarchy is the pivot of the balance of power, and its disappearance would be a European calamity. . . ."

For a variety of reasons, therefore, if Austria-Hungary did not exist in the nineteenth century, it would have been invented. Indeed, its disappearance after World War I has proven how important the Habsburg monarchy really was. Certainly Palacky's prophecy that, in the absence of Austria, Russia would dominate Eastern Europe proved true for much of this century. A rage of nationalities has also erupted periodically, as Bismarck feared.

Historian Joachim Remak has ably summed up the case in favor of Austria-Hungary in a pathbreaking 1969 article, "The Healthy Invalid: How Doomed the Habsburg Empire?" Remak believes that the Dual Monarchy's gradual, historical accretion of territories was not so haphazard and random as it might seem. Though the empire was not ethnically homogeneous, its expansion could be viewed as a "gradual spreading of roots." Furthermore, a customs union of 50 million people living in the basin of a great river, the Danube, made good economic sense. The Habsburg dynasty was revered by many of these 50 million. Franz Joseph's incredibly long reign, beginning in 1848 and ending only with his death in 1916 at age eighty-six, proved important in cementing the loyalty of his subjects. As Sigmund Freud, a citizen of Habsburg Vienna, would be the first to point out, sons revolt against their fathers; but Franz Joseph ruled as an imperial grandfather.

Furthermore, a large dose of tolerance and broadmindedness leavened the Viennese temperament. It is vital to remember that Franz Joseph was no Hitler and the Austrian Germans were not Prussians. Nineteenth-century politicians described Habsburg rule as "absolutism mitigated by sloppiness." In a probably apocryphal tale, a Viennese diplomat once reported the empire's military situation as "desperate but not serious." Austrians were not noted for their efficiency.

A passage describing a Viennese mansion, written by the novelist Robert Musil, may serve as a metaphor for Franz Joseph's Austria-Hungary:

> Its original structure was seventeenth-century, the garden and the upper storey had an eighteenth-century look, and the facade had been restored and somewhat spoilt in the nineteenth century, so that the whole thing had a faintly bizarre character, like that of a superimposed photograph. But the general effect was such that people invariably stopped and said: "Oh look."

The book from which this passage is taken provides a perfect example of Habsburg Austria's ramshackle elegance. Musil's multivolume novel, *The Man without Qualities,* chronicles the life of Vienna in the last years before World War I, with a relentless completeness akin to James Joyce's *Ulysses.* Published in stages between 1930 and 1945, it became a cult favorite among historians of Central Europe during the second half of the century. Yet alert readers will note that virtually all quotations from Musil's work (including the passage I quoted above) come from the first few pages of the book. Quite possibly no one has ever finished it, including Musil himself, who left only fragments of a third volume when he died in 1942. The writing is not difficult — indeed it has a lucid brilliance so typical of Habsburg Vienna — but nothing much happens. Intelligent but anguished people stand around striking poses and displaying exquisite sensibilities. This epitomizes Habsburg Vienna.

Though it is easy to criticize or satirize the Dual Monarchy, historian Remak concludes: "It was, when all was said and done, a rather good empire over which Franz Joseph presided. It was . . . a tolerant, open society, without forcible Germanization or blind centralism." Even the English historian A. J. P. Taylor, who generally harbored little love for the Habsburg monarchy, conceded: "The Austrian citizen after 1867 had more civic security than the German and was in the hands of more honest and more capable officials than in France or Italy. . . ."

I would go one step further and argue that the Habsburg empire provides a possible model for the contemporary restructuring of Europe. Not the Habsburg empire as it actually existed in 1910, but an ideally reformed empire as envisioned by European federalists. In the early years of this century, a Romanian intellectual, Dr. Aurel Popovici, wrote a book called *Die Vereinigten Staaten von Grossosterreich* (The United States of Greater Austria) that proposed the abolition of the Dual Monarchy and its replacement by a thoroughly federal system of fifteen or sixteen regional governments, based on national autonomy. Robert Seton-Watson toyed with this federalist idea as well. While visiting the coast of Dalmatia in 1910, he expressed a wish that Dalmatia might enjoy the same fate as his native Scotland, peaceful coexistence in a United Kingdom, without loss of national feeling and identity.

An empire, kingdom, or commonwealth that would draw many peoples together in an economic and political union, while still conceding them regional autonomy and cultural self-determination, has much to recommend it. This is what the Eurocrats who shaped the European Common Market have been aiming at in the latter half of the century. The alternatives — trying to draw individual countries' borders so precisely that they coincide perfectly with nationality or else trying to destroy the national consciousness of minorities — have proven impossible and disastrous throughout the twentieth century. The lost example of Austria-Hungary deserves a second look.

However appealing a multinational common market might be in theory, the actual Dual Monarchy of Austria-Hungary failed to satisfy its subjects in the early twentieth century for two reasons. First, the Hungarian half of the empire proved far less tolerant and broadminded than the Austrian half. Budapest was not Vienna. Indeed, the Hungarian capital bisected by the Danube River was a virtual boomtown in 1900, the fastest growing city in Europe. Journalists routinely commented on the "American tempo" of its life, and one of its working-class neighborhoods was nicknamed *Csikago* (Chicago) due to its flimsy and rapid construction. The Hungarian nobility, gentry, and intelligentsia were prosperous, proudly nationalistic, and overconfident as the century began. They pursued a policy of forced Magyarization on their Slovak and Romanian minorities and resisted all appeals for universal manhood suffrage or increased democracy. Any attempt to undo the *Ausgleich* and decentralize the empire into a federal system would have foundered on the rock of Hungarian opposition. Indeed, they were more likely to secede, taking their suppressed minorities with them, than to agree to federalism, just as the American South attempted secession in order to preserve slavery.

The Dual Monarchy's only colony, Bosnia, provided the second stumbling block to a solution of the nationalities question. Not even the most pro-Austrian apologist could describe the empire's grab of Bosnia in 1878 as "a gradual spreading of roots." The populace of that province, having thrown out the Turks, resisted fiercely when the Habsburg armies rolled in. It eventually took a full summer and fall of campaigning by an army of 250,000 men to make good the occupation of Bosnia.

Adding one more anomaly to the Habsburg monarchy, Bosnia belonged to neither Austria nor Hungary. It was the sole colony "occupied and administered" by the common imperial authorities. The colonial bureaucracy in the province, which reported to the common finance minister, grew swiftly from the 180 government agents employed by the Turks to a total of 9,500 Habsburg functionaries by 1908. It took so much political effort to win taxing and spending approval from both Austrians and Hungarians that the Dual Monarchy did not even try in the case of Bosnia. The emperor decreed instead that the costs of governing the new province must be met from taxes within Bosnia itself. The slender resources of this agrarian province therefore limited Austrian attempts to modernize it. So even the usual justification for imperialism, the "White Man's Burden" of technological and economic development in the colonies, fell flat in this case.

Benjamin von Kallay, a member of the Hungarian gentry, ruled Bosnia as a virtual proconsul or dictator during his long tenure as common finance minister from 1882 to 1903. Kallay hoped to win the loyalty of the people by hastening the material progress of the province, and he declared a thoroughly patriotic goal for his governance: "As long as I shall remain the head of the administration of these lands I will always strive to increase in the Bosnians the feeling that they belong to a great and powerful nation." A master of propaganda, Kallay gave his superiors in Vienna and Budapest as little information as possible but ensured that he received good press throughout Europe.

Nevertheless, the economic development of Bosnia under Kallay's administration proved very modest, largely due to the meager resources available in the province itself. The Austrians built military fortifications and a few railways and constructed a lavish health spa and race course at the town of Ilidze near Sarajevo. Rebecca West found that the humiliation of this imperial tourist establishment still rankled more than sixty years later, when an aged gardener shouted at her: "Yes, yes, and they had our men and women brought in to dance the *kolo* to them, we were for them the natives, the savages, and we had to dance for them as if we were bears at a fair." Peter Sugar, the economic historian who has studied Kallay's administration most thoroughly, concluded: "Austria-Hungary planned to conquer its own subjects through economic progress, for which these people themselves had to pay."

The Austrian colonial authorities followed the tried and true imperialist strategy of divide and conquer, playing the Christian and Muslim populations in Bosnia against each other. Finding Muslims in control of most of the agricultural land, the Habsburgs confirmed the title of these landlords and resisted agrarian reforms that would have subdivided estates and granted land to the Serbian Orthodox serfs. Ironically, the Austrians, who had justified their occupation in part on religious grounds as Christian protectors against the Turks, consciously favored their Muslim subjects, who appeared conservative and loyal, over the Orthodox Christians, who harbored Greater Serbian aspirations.

The occupation and later annexation of Bosnia constituted a colossal blunder by Austria-Hungary. The border between Bosnia and Croatia had served for centuries as an international boundary, a great divide between empires. Breaching that border projected the Dual Monarchy farther south into the Balkans than was safe and brought it into conflict not only with the new, small Balkan states but also with their Pan-Slavic protector, Russia. When the heir apparent to the throne, Archduke Franz Ferdinand, visited Bosnia to observe military maneuvers in the early summer of 1914, he paid the ultimate price for the Habsburg's misguided colonial venture.

The archduke's itinerary for his 1914 trip included a ceremonial visit to Sarajevo on June 28, the feast of St. Vitus and the Serbian national holiday commemorating the battle of Kosovo. This was an appallingly naive and inflammatory choice of dates, for the Young Bosnians were nurtured on the Serbian tradition of tyrannicide, harking back to Kosovo. In 1910 a youth from Hercegovina named Bogdan Zerajić fired five shots at the Austrian governor in Sarajevo but failed to even nick him. He then shot himself with the sixth bullet. A revolutionary pamphleteer, Gaćinović, transformed Zerajić into a hero for Young Bosnia. Now four years later, two trios of assassins awaited the archduke.

Franz Ferdinand von Osterreich-Este was Emperor Franz Joseph's nephew, who had come into the line of succession after the emperor's only son, Crown Prince Rudolf, killed himself at his hunting lodge of Mayerling in 1889. Franz Ferdinand's own father died of typhoid on a pilgrimage to the Holy Land in 1896, but his official designation as heir apparent was delayed a few years by a battle with tuberculosis. Then the archduke fell in love with a lady-in-waiting at court, Sophie Chotek, an impoverished member of a Czech noble family. In an eerie parallel to the star-crossed Serbian lovers, Alexander Obrenović and Draga Masin, Franz Ferdinand overcame the emperor's opposition and married his beloved Sophie in 1900, but only after disavowing any claim to the throne by her or their children (a morganatic marriage).

His long illness and the unpleasantness surrounding his marriage left the archduke a stubborn, bitter man, who got carried away with whatever he was doing. He turned the usual aristocratic fondness for hunting into a love of slaughter for its own sake. By 1910 he had personally killed 5,000 stags; often he would bag 2,000 pheasants in a single hunt. He took his antique collecting hobby to similar extremes, acquiring, for example, over 3,000 representations of St. George and the Dragon.

After 1900 the archduke became increasingly involved in the military affairs of the empire, and he took a special interest in strengthening the navy. He struck up a personal friendship with Kaiser Wilhelm II of Germany, who shared his love for military might and display, and championed the appointment of General Franz Conrad von Hötzendorf as Austrian Chief of Staff. Conrad advocated an aggressive policy, even a preventive war, in the Balkans.

Nevertheless, some liberals within the empire deluded themselves that Franz Ferdinand might solve the nationalities question when he assumed the throne. He had flirted with the idea of trialism early in the twentieth century, that is, autonomy for the South Slavs (Croatians and Serbians), which would transform the empire into a Triple Monarchy. He may also have carried his speculation along these lines one step further and explored the idea of a thoroughgoing federalism. Yet no one knew for sure what policies the archduke was ruminating by 1914, and his rigid authoritarian personality would not seem well suited to assuaging the subject nationalities. One thing was known for sure about Franz Ferdinand: he hated the Magyars. The Englishman Seton-Watson once heard him remark, "it was an act of very bad taste of those gentlemen [the Hungarians] ever to come to Europe at all." Few within the empire loved the archduke, and many had good reasons to wish him dead.

The Young Bosnian assassins, however, were prompted by an extremely simple motive, the desire to kill a tyrant. Vladimir Dedijer, who has written the most exhaustive account of the murder in Bosnia, calls the archduke's assassins "primitive rebels." This phrase is not intended in a derogatory sense but simply implies that the Young Bosnians were innocent of ideology. Though they resemble the anarchists in their ascetic dedication and their practice of "propaganda by the deed," a combination of personal problems and simple nationalism provided their motive force. They should be understood primarily as troubled individuals growing up in an oppressed colonial society. Gavrilo Princip had dropped out of school in 1912 and tried to join the Serbian army during the Balkan Wars, but he was rejected as too small and frail. Obviously suffering from a "Napoleon complex," Princip "carried to extremes a tendency to feel the sufferings of people around him as though they were his own." His comrade, Nedjelko Cabrinovic, had suffered under a tyrannical, patriarchal peasant father, and Dedijer suggests that "his revolt against his father became identified with his revolt against society."

Princip, Čabrinović, and a third Young Bosnian, Trifko Grabez, obtained hand grenades, revolvers, and poison capsules from the Black Hand in Belgrade. It is unlikely that Colonel Dimitrijević and his aide, Major Voja Tankosić, took these would-be assassins too seriously, for they were all still teenagers, they were frail and consumptive, and only Princip showed much aptitude for his shooting lessons. Nonetheless, the Black Hand's officers wished to stir the pot in Bosnia, and even an unsuccessful attempt on the heir apparent's life might provoke Austrian repression and thus radicalize the Serbs of Bosnia. Black Hand customs agents and border guards, therefore, smuggled the three back to Sarajevo, the

Bosnian capital, in early June 1914; there they waited for the Austrian archduke's visit.

The Serbian government did not initiate or approve the assassination plot. King Peter Karadjordjević and Crown Prince Alexander naturally feared the influence of the Black Hand. Colonel Dimitrijević and his cohorts had killed a Serbian king before and might do so again. Prime Minister Nikola Pašić was engaged in a tug-of-war with the military, trying to establish civilian authority over them in the territories newly conquered in the Balkan Wars. Furthermore, those wars had exhausted the country's resources, so the Serbian government did not wish to provoke Austria at this time. Pašić's own spies informed him that assassins had passed into Bosnia; the Serbian government made some discreet attempts to warn the Austrians, but their warnings were not understood or taken seriously.

In Sarajevo, Gavrilo Princip stayed with his best friend, Danilo Ilić, a leader in Young Bosnia who recruited three more assassins as a backup team. Vaso Čubrilović and Cvijetko Popović were Sarajevo high school students, and the final recruit, Muhamed Mehmedbasić, gave the group a touch of ethnic balance, for he was a Bosnian Muslim. Perhaps Ilić felt that an all-Serbian plot would implicate Belgrade too directly.

Franz Ferdinand and his wife, Sophie, journeyed to Bosnia by separate routes, arriving at the Austrian spa of Ilidze on June 25. For the next two days, the Archduke inspected troop maneuvers in the mountains while Sophie paid goodwill visits to churches and orphanages. The couple actually made an unscheduled shopping trip to Sarajevo on the evening of June 25. Gavrilo Princip caught a good look at his quarry but decided to wait and carry out the plan during the official visit to the city on June 28.

St. Vitus Day, Sunday June 28, 1914, dawned sunny and hot after several days of unusually cool and rainy weather. The archduke and his wife attended Mass in a room of the Hotel Bosnia in Ilidze, then took a special train to Sarajevo at about ten o'clock in the morning. A motorcade of six open cars drove along the Appel Quay, an Austrian-built boulevard flanking the Miljacka River, to a reception at the city hall. Security precautions were light and seemingly casual. Four years previously, when the Emperor Franz Joseph visited Sarajevo, troops had lined both sides of the street; but no military detachment entered the city this day. Franz Ferdinand objected to heavy security and did not want soldiers between him and the people.

Danilo Ilić had positioned his six assassins along the Appel Quay. The first three froze and did nothing as the motorcade passed by; but at 10:10 A.M., Nedjelko Čabrinović, who the Black Hand officers had believed to be the least reliable, pulled a hand grenade from beneath his coat, knocked its firing pin off on a metal lamppost, and lobbed it at the archduke's open car. The bomb bounced off the folded rooftop and exploded in the street, wounding two soldiers in the car behind as well as several bystanders. Čabrinović jumped the embankment into the river and swallowed his cyanide capsule, but neither the fall nor the poison killed him, and he was swiftly arrested.

The two remaining assassins, Princip and Grabez, heard the bomb blast but were uncertain what had happened and failed to act as the archduke's car sped by. Arriving at the ugly pseudo-Moorish city hall, Franz Ferdinand burst out to the lord mayor: "I come to Sarajevo on a friendly visit and someone throws a bomb at me. This is outrageous." He quickly regained his composure, however, and the reception continued as planned. The governor and the police chief convinced the archduke to alter the rest of his route, driving swiftly along the broad Appel Quay rather than turning into narrow Franz Joseph Street in the heart of town, but they neglected to inform the chauffeur of the change. So Franz Ferdinand's car slowed and started to turn off the Quay, in front of Schiller's store where Gavrilo Princip was standing.

Princip stared directly at Franz Ferdinand, raised his pistol and took aim. A policeman saw him and made a grab for the pistol, but a bystander kicked the policeman, throwing him off balance. Princip fired two shots at point-blank range, hitting the archduke in the neck and his wife Sophie in the groin. The car sped off to the governor's residence across the river where both imperial visitors died of internal bleeding. The crowd nearly lynched Princip before he was rescued and arrested by the police.

The lax security and the incredible mix-up by the archduke's driver have led to many conspiracy theories about the assassination. It is not impossible that Austrian or Hungarian authorities connived with the Black Hand to eliminate Franz Ferdinand. He had certainly made enough enemies. Yet no evidence has ever turned up to support such speculation. Vladimir Dedijer's conclusion still seems the best: "This narrative of the Sarajevo assassination shows that it was one of the most amateurish regicides of modern times. . . . The success of the conspiracy was mainly due to sheer luck."

The next day a mob of Croats and Muslims rampaged through Sarajevo attacking Serbs and destroying Serbian-owned shops. One man was killed and fifty injured in the rioting. Meanwhile, the police and troops arrested thousands of Serbs for questioning about the assassination. Princip and Čabrinović both concocted plausible stories to protect their co-conspirators and hide their ties to Belgrade, but when Danilo Ilić was picked up in the police sweep he panicked and named names. The police found Čubrilović and Popović, but Mehmedbasić escaped across the border to the tiny kingdom of Montenegro. Many others were arrested as accomplices, most of whom had innocently assisted Princip, Čabrinović, and Grabez on their journey from Serbia and knew nothing of the plot.

Princip impressed his judges and jailers with his calm demeanor and steely determination. When asked at his trial whether he felt any remorse, he replied: "I

am not a criminal, for I have removed an evildoer. I meant to do a good deed."
Danilo Ilić and several of the accomplices were hanged for murder and treason,
but Princip, Čabrinović, Grabez, Cubrilović, and Popović were not yet twenty
years old and thus were spared. The first three did not survive long, dying of tuberculosis in prison. Austria-Hungary and the rest of Europe also died a slow
death over the next four years.

CHAPTER SEVEN

The Fatal Alliances

War did not break out immediately after the archduke's assassination, but followed with a time lag of about a month. In 1914 the great powers did not strike with the swiftness of a terrorist's revolver or a Japanese torpedo boat. Indeed war did not need to come at all. Franz Ferdinand was not a beloved figure in Austria-Hungary or anywhere else in Europe. Among the heads of state, only Kaiser Wilhelm of Germany genuinely mourned his passing. Underneath the veneer of official solemnity, many Austrian officials breathed a sigh of relief. The general public felt sorry for Sophie and her three small orphaned children and expressed more sympathy for the aged emperor, Franz Joseph, than for his murdered nephew. The emperor's chamberlain, Prince Alfred Montenuovo, arranged a "third-class funeral" for Franz Ferdinand and Sophie, and no head of state attended the obsequies in Vienna. This proved unfortunate, for kings and emperors, without the care of day-to-day affairs, could often take a longer view than presidents and premiers and through personal friendships help keep the peace. Europe missed this opportunity in 1914.

The government of Austria-Hungary initiated the war in July 1914 because it desired to teach Serbia a lesson. This took time, however, for the two-headed Habsburg monarchy could do nothing swiftly. Seven people made the decision in Vienna: Emperor Franz Joseph; the foreign minister of Austria-Hungary, Count Leopold Berchtold; the finance minister, Count Leon von Biliński; the war minister, General Alexander Krobatin; the chief of the General Staff, General Franz Conrad von Hötzendorf; the prime minister of the Austrian half of the empire, Karl Stürgkh; and the prime minister of the Hungarian half, Istvan Tisza. In the complicated Austro-Hungarian system, these individuals met together as the Common Ministerial Council (called a Crown Council when the emperor was personally present). There was no one designated as prime minister for the entire empire, but the foreign minister generally took the lead; and this certainly proved true during the war crisis of 1914, when Berchtold dominated the proceedings.

The decision for war makes sense only when viewed against the backdrop of previous years, for this was the fifth war crisis that Austria-Hungary had faced in the Balkans since 1908. When the Dual Monarchy annexed Bosnia in 1908, the Serbs wanted war, but the Russians, who had still not rebuilt their military forces after the Russo-Japanese War, pressured them to back down. General Conrad of Austria advocated a preventive strike against Serbia, but his was a lone voice at that time. Then in December 1912, as Serbia and its Balkan League allies were driving Turkey out of Europe, Count Berchtold again raised the question of an attack on the Serbs before they grew too powerful. The military argued that nothing would be gained by waiting, and this time the Archduke Franz Ferdinand agreed. However, Berchtold and the emperor decided to do nothing. In the aftermath of the Balkan Wars, first Montenegro then Serbia defied the consensus of the great powers by holding on to Albanian territory they had seized. In 1913, therefore, Austria-Hungary acted more decisively, delivering an ultimatum to Montenegro in May and to Serbia in October. On both occasions, their adversaries backed down and withdrew from the disputed territory.

Austria's actions in 1913 nearly foreclosed its options the following year. If it had risked war over a few Albanian villages, how could it back down when Serbs murdered the heir to the Austrian throne? As historian Samuel Williamson has said in the most recent account of Austria's decision for war, "prestige politics, that most dangerous and self-fulfilling of all diplomatic pursuits, had replaced interest politics." Members of the Austrian Crown Council worried about losing face if they did not confront Serbia.

The Austrians first mounted an investigation of the Sarajevo murder in order to prove the complicity of the Serbian government. In the meantime, Berchtold dispatched his chief aide, Count Alexander Hoyos, to Berlin to ensure that their German allies would support them in whatever they did. The kaiser and his ministers granted Austria a virtual "blank check" on July 5. Then on July 13 Friedrich von Wiesner, a foreign office official, summed up the assassination investigation in a report to his government. He could not trace Princip's "smoking gun" all the way back to the Serbian government and did not discover the role of Colonel Dimitrijevic and the Black Hand, but he did establish conclusively that the weapons had been made in the Serbian arsenal at Kragujevać and had been dispensed to the assassins by Major Voja Tankosić and an employee of the Serbian National Railways, Milan Ciganović.

Armed with this information, the Habsburg Crown Council decided to issue an ultimatum so stiff that Serbia would certainly reject it and thus give the

Dual Monarchy grounds for declaring war. Only the Hungarian prime minister, Istvan Tisza, resisted this decision. Hungary would have to provide money and manpower for the war and would not likely gain anything tangible in the process. However, Tisza's chief adviser, Count Istvan Burian, finally convinced him that if Serbia went unpunished, the Romanian minority within Hungary might increase its own agitation against Magyar dominance. So domestic considerations helped tip the balance towards war. Neither half of the Austro-Hungarian Empire knew what to do about its minority nationalities. Both sides finally chose a punitive war for lack of any better ideas.

Tisza agreed with the war decision on July 14, and five days later the council settled on the wording of an ultimatum. They could not act for another week however, for General Conrad had previously granted many of the empire's soldiers summer leave to help with the harvesting of crops. The Austrian minister in Belgrade, Vladimir Giesl, delivered the ultimatum at 6:00 P.M. on July 23 to the Serbian foreign ministry. It posed nine strongly worded, even insulting demands on Serbia, including the suppression of all anti-Austrian publications, the censorship of schoolbooks that criticized Austria, the disbanding of the *Narodna Odbrana* society, and the immediate arrest of Major Tankosić and Milan Ciganović. Points 5 and 6 contained the most difficult terms of the ultimatum. Austria-Hungary insisted that "Imperial and Royal officials [i.e., Austrians] assist in Serbia in the suppressing of the subversive movement directed against the territorial integrity of the Monarchy," and that the Serbian government should "have a judicial enquiry instituted against all those who took part in the plot of 28 June, if they are to be found on Serbian territory; the Imperial and Royal Government will delegate organs who will take an active part in these enquiries." In short, Austria-Hungary was demanding that Serbia allow officials of a foreign government to exercise police powers on their sovereign territory.

The Serbian government knew it was not ready for war, and thus they wrote as conciliatory a response as they could. Prime Minister Nikola Pašić delivered the answer personally to the Austrian minister just fifteen minutes before the forty-eight-hour deadline expired on July 25. The Serbian note contained three definite "yes" replies to Austrian demands, pledging to shut down the *Narodna Odbrana,* stop the flow of arms into Bosnia, and keep the Austrians fully informed of its investigations into the assassination plot. It also crafted five cleverly worded "maybes," couching these in conciliatory, even obsequious language. However, the Serbian government refused to allow the participation of Austrian officials in the inquiry on Serbian soil, as this would contravene the country's constitution. Essentially, Serbia conceded as much as it could without yielding its national sovereignty.

The Austrian minister Baron Giesl glanced at the document and declared it unacceptable. His superiors in Vienna had already decided on war; the exact wording of the ultimatum and the Serbian reply were irrelevant. On July 28, 1914, the first month's anniversary of the archduke's murder, Emperor Franz Joseph signed the declaration of war against Serbia.

The officials of Austria-Hungary did not make the decision for war hastily or in anger. They were all seasoned veterans of similar crises, and they took their time. Nonetheless, they were driven by simple, elemental emotions of fear and pride. They feared that Serbian nationalism would tear the empire apart and that the Serbs' Russian ally was slowly encircling them. Their pride drove them to try and control events rather than let them run their own course. Not accepting the fact that they were merely a convenient buffer between more powerful neighbors, the rulers of Austria-Hungary decided to act like a great power, because they still believed they were.

Franz Conrad, a desk general who had seen battle only briefly in the Bosnia campaign of 1878, believed unreflectively in the power of an offensive strategy to overcome all obstacles, even common sense. He had been calling for war since becoming chief of staff in 1906. Leopold Berchtold, foreign minister since 1912, viewed war as the last resort, and he had consistently pursued a diplomatic solution in the Balkans. Indeed, his patient diplomacy paid dividends even during the July crisis of 1914 by securing the neutrality of Romania, Bulgaria, and Italy. Yet his patience made him appear weak and vacillating to the rabid anti-Slavic press of Vienna, so he finally capitulated to the warmongers. The Archduke Franz Ferdinand might have swayed Berchtold to persist in his diplomacy, for he had assumed a less aggressive stance since the two Balkan Wars; but of course the archduke was dead. Ultimately, Franz Joseph's opinion was the only one that mattered. He had presided over a number of unsuccessful wars in his sixty year reign and was cautious by temperament. Yet if the empire really were in danger of being torn apart by ethnic strife as his counselors advised him, he would never preside over the end of the Habsburg dynasty without a fight.

Before we condemn these men too harshly, let us consider a simple comparison suggested by historian Joachim Remak. Assume, hypothetically, that the vice president of the United States was assassinated in Houston by Mexican terrorists with clear links to the government and military in Mexico City. How would Americans react? What would the U.S. government do? How violent a response would the American public support? Such an occurrence might well result in war.

As of July 25, 1914, the imbroglio between the Habsburg monarchy and the kingdom of Serbia remained just a local conflict, a third Balkan War, so to speak. It became a general conflagration, however, because of interlocking alliances that bound the great powers together and kicked in almost automatically in the summer of 1914.

Germany's dominant position in the center of Europe had called the alliance system into existence. In a series of lightning wars from 1864 to 1870, the kingdom of Prussia, under the leadership of Chancellor Otto von Bismarck, had defeated Denmark, Austria, and France. Bismarck had then united most of the smaller German states with Prussia and proclaimed the Second German Reich (Empire), in 1871. The rise of a united and heavily armed Germany decisively altered the balance of power in Europe, and within a generation Germany's economic growth outstripped that of its main continental rival. By 1910 Germany had a population of 65 million compared to only 39 million in France, and the Reich produced three times as much iron, four times as much steel, and seven times as much coal as the French Republic. The German military outspent the French two to one.

Immediately after German unification, however, Chancellor Bismarck followed a cautious policy, avoiding colonial adventures overseas and keeping alive the idea of a Concert of Europe that would meet at times of crisis to prevent a general war. Accordingly, when Austria-Hungary invaded Bosnia and Russia defeated the Turks in the 1870s, Bismarck called the great powers together in Berlin to divide up the spoils. Russia, however, resenting the edicts of the Congress of Berlin that limited her gains in the Balkans, became increasingly alienated from her powerful German neighbor. The Concert of Europe was never the same again. Slowly, the idea of great power cooperation eroded as the major nations of Europe coalesced into two blocs.

Germany initiated the search for permanent allies with the Austro-German Alliance of 1879. In 1882 Italy joined up, turning it into a Triple Alliance, a bloc of Central Powers in the heart of Europe. The kingdom of Italy, which achieved political unification of its peninsula the same year that Bismarck united Germany, was only an honorary great power, however, and its loyalty to the alliance remained suspect. Indeed, shortly before World War I broke out, the French politician Raymond Poincaré accurately predicted what Italy's role would be in the coming crisis: "the Italian Government will employ all its efforts to preserve the peace; and in case of war, it will begin by adopting a waiting attitude and will finally join the camp towards which victory will incline." The opportunism of the Italians was well known, so neither Germany nor Austria-Hungary placed much faith in their alleged ally. The Central Powers remained essentially a dual alliance.

After Kaiser Wilhelm II came to power and dismissed Chancellor Bismarck in 1890, German policy became less cautious. Wilhelm II, of the House of Hohenzollern, was born with an undersized, weak left arm, and he often overcompensated for his physical disability by striking militant poses. The kaiser was also the product of two cultures. A grandson of England's Queen Victoria on his mother's side, he both admired and envied England, then at the height of its power in the world. His biographer, Michael Balfour, has concluded: "He had two ideals held out to him, that of the Prussian Junker [member of the landed aristocracy] and that of the Liberal English gentleman. . . . The tension between the two, superimposed on his physical disability . . . is the ultimate key to his character." Though never as bellicose in deeds as in words, Wilhelm II was an unstable, unfocused leader who rarely followed a consistent course for very long.

The most important consequence of the kaiser's love-hate relationship with England was the building of a High Seas Fleet in the years after 1897 and the simultaneous bid for world power through the acquisition of colonies. Under the leadership of Admiral Alfred von Tirpitz, Germany planned a battleship fleet to rival that of the kaiser's grandmother. Following what he called a "risk theory," Tirpitz believed that a powerful German fleet could inflict so much damage on the British navy, even in a losing battle, that the English would not risk an engagement and would thus acquiesce in Germany's assertive role on the world stage. The fleet, projected at two-thirds the size of England's, was not really intended for battle, but for "diplomatic bullying" (in the words of German historian Volker Berghahn). Furthermore, the battle fleet was something of a personal plaything for the kaiser, who proclaimed grandiloquently, "Our future lies on the water."

Kaiser Wilhelm and Admiral Tirpitz desired a fleet for its own sake, but Chancellor Bernhard von Bülow and other civilian officials also sought domestic political benefits from their *Weltpolitik* (world policy). The buildup of the navy would provide profits for the industrialists and jobs for the working class, while rallying the whole nation in a nationalistic orgy of self-congratulation as Germany assumed her rightful place in the sun. Ultimately, this policy failed. Rather than uniting German society, the naval buildup divided it, and the Socialist Party increased its support in the Reichstag with a powerful anti-militarist appeal. Instead of cowing Germany's international rivals into submission, the aggressive policy of *Weltpolitik* prompted them to forge alliances and encircle the German Empire.

France and Russia, which lay on either side of Germany, came together in a defensive military alliance in the years 1892-94. The generals of the two countries signed a secret military convention on August 17, 1892, which the tsar confirmed the following year and the French government ratified in 1894. The crucial passage in the Franco-Russian Alliance stated, "If France is attacked by Germany, or by Italy supported by Germany, Russia shall employ all her available forces to attack Germany. If Russia is attacked by Germany, or by Austria supported by Germany, France shall employ all her available forces to fight Germany."

The forging of the Franco-Russian Alliance illustrates clearly how much Germany's neighbors feared her, for France and Russia had nothing else in common. Tsarist Russia remained the last autocracy in Europe, whereas France was a republic, heir to the great revolution of 1789. In the aftermath of that revolution, Napoleon had led his Grand Army into the heart of Russia and burned Moscow, before being finally defeated by the Russian winter. It must have aggravated the tsar immensely to stand at attention for the playing of his new ally's national anthem, the revolutionary hymn the *Marseillaise*. Yet the tsar endured this, and the French swallowed their dislike of Russian authoritarianism. As the French ambassador to Great Britain, Paul Cambon, remarked when the Franco-Russian Alliance was finalized: "If you cannot have what you like, you must like what you have." Financial ties helped seal this unlikely alliance, for France was a nation of savers and the Russians needed loans to further their industrialization and build up their army.

The two new allies feared Germany's growing power in Europe, but overseas, in Asia and Africa, their colonial interests more often collided with those of England than Germany. Eventually they had to decide which country posed the greater threat and then make up with the other. The French foreign minister, Théophile Delcassé, opened conversations with the English in 1903; then he signed an agreement with England on April 8, 1904, that became known as the Entente Cordiale, or "friendly understanding." The Entente settled all outstanding colonial differences between France and England. Most importantly, France granted England a free hand in consolidating its rule over Egypt and the English recognized the predominance of French influence in the kingdom of Morocco.

The Entente Cordiale was not a formal alliance, but a complicated series of winks and nudges whereby the two powers agreed to stay out of each other's way in North Africa and other parts of the world they were exploiting. The agreement never mentioned Germany, and neither side promised assistance in case of war. Yet the growing fear of Germany had been the driving force behind the agreement. England would never have signed if the kaiser had not issued his challenge to the Royal Navy. In the long run, the simple fact of a Franco-British understanding proved far more significant than the exact terms of the agreement.

The Germans could not believe that the French and the English would ever agree to anything, and they set out immediately to drive a wedge between the two before the Entente could solidify. In March 1905, the Kaiser sailed into the Moroccan port of Tangier on his imperial yacht and delivered one of his patented warlike speeches demanding the reduction of French influence in Morocco and equal treatment for German trade in that kingdom. The German government gambled that England would not publicly support France, and thus the Entente would be exposed as a straw man; but the gamble backfired. In the ensuing flurry of diplomacy, the full Concert of Europe met for the last time, at Algeciras in January 1906; but the great powers confirmed France's predominant colonial position in Morocco. The English backed France staunchly and the Germans appeared diplomatically isolated, with only their ally Austria-Hungary supporting them.

In the meantime, the threat of war which the Morocco crisis posed had caused the English and French military to begin joint planning discussions. After

General Henry Wilson became director of military operations in 1910, these talks intensified and became more detailed. The English even reduced their naval strength in the Mediterranean in return for a French withdrawal from the English Channel. This created an implicit promise by the English to protect the French channel ports in case of war. The informal Entente was beginning to look more like an alliance all the time.

The year after the Morocco crisis, England signed another colonial entente, this time with Russia. England and Russia had engaged in "the great game" of colonial warfare for over a century in the interior of Asia, as the Russian Empire expanded, and the English feared for the security of its major Asiatic possession, the Raj of India. In 1907 they brought this all to a close by mutually agreeing to stay out of Tibet, by granting Russia a free hand in Afghanistan, and dividing Persia into separate spheres of influence. As in the earlier agreement with France, the Anglo-Russian Entente dealt only with colonial matters; but just as in the former case, the very fact of the agreement proved significant.

Germany and its two weak allies were now surrounded by three loosely allied powers, and Europe was divided into two mutually antagonistic blocs. A cold war developed between the Triple Alliance (Germany, Austria-Hungary, Italy) and the Triple Entente (England, France, Russia), similar in many ways to the Cold War that later dominated the second half of the century. An arms race ensued. In particular, the naval buildup in Germany led England to increase spending for its navy and thus keep a numerical lead. The launching in 1906 of *HMS Dreadnought,* the largest battleship ever built and the first in a new class of warships, added a qualitative dimension to the rivalry. Both sides built up their land forces as well, with Germany increasing the size of its army in 1912 and the French matching this with the passage of a three-years conscription law in 1913, keeping soldiers in the service for three instead of two years, as previously.

The actual phrase "cold war" was not employed very frequently, but it accurately sums up the tense rivalry between the two alliances. Even as early as 1893, before the alliances had solidified, the German socialist intellectual, Edward Bernstein, had written: "This continual arming, compelling the others to keep up with Germany, is itself a kind of warfare. I do not know whether the expression has been used previously, but one could say it is a cold war. There is no shooting but there is bleeding."

The alliance system was defensive in intent. Quite simply, Germany sought allies to avoid encirclement, and the Triple Entente pursued a policy of containment aimed at German expansion. Yet the arms race took on a life of its own, as each side constantly raised the ante and in the process increased tensions. Historian James Joll perceptively points out: "Although governments claimed that their preparation for a defensive war was a sign of their wish for peace and their will to deter aggression, deterrents in fact often provoke as much as they deter."

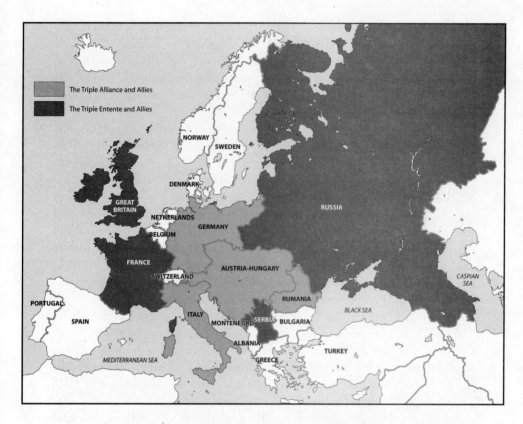

The Triple Alliance and the Triple Entente

And the French ambassador in Berlin, Jules Cambon, who worked unsuccessfully for peace between France and Germany, pointed out the danger inherent in containment: "By blocking up too many outlets of a boiler does one not cause it to explode?"

Furthermore, each alliance system developed a string of smaller client states, such as Romania, whose king secretly adhered to the Triple Alliance in 1883; and Serbia, which counted on the support of Russia, and thus the Triple Entente. These smaller states proved dangerous friends. When they engaged in military adventures on their own, they could drag their great power protectors along with them, and thus the tail wagged the dog.

The greatest danger of the alliance system, however, lay in the military plans that the generals of the two blocs formulated. These plans circumscribed the freedom of maneuver enjoyed by civilian officials and diplomats and sometimes became self-fulfilling prophecies. The famous Schlieffen plan of Germany, in particular, proved a time bomb that exploded in 1914.

As the kaiser quipped to the English statesman Arthur Balfour, "Whenever war occurs in any part of the world, we in Germany sit down and make a plan." Indeed, Count Alfred von Schlieffen, German chief of staff from 1891 to 1906, began planning for a two-front war as soon as he heard about the Franco-Russian Alliance. He left the final plan to his successor, General Helmuth von Moltke, in a memo dated December 31, 1905. Schlieffen knew that the Russians, though potentially the greater foe due to their vast manpower resources, would be slower to mobilize for an attack than France. Therefore, in the event of war, he planned to mount a passive defense in the East and march nearly the whole of the German army west to knock out France before the Russians could even get organized. He hoped to encircle the French defenders and force a surrender in less than six weeks. Neither Schlieffen nor anyone else before or during World War I used the term *Blitzkrieg*, but that in essence is what the plan amounted to, a "lightning war" on the western front.

The Schlieffen plan also required the Germans to march the right wing of their army through neutral Belgium, Luxemburg, and the Netherlands. Since the French had heavily fortified their common border with Germany in the lost provinces of Alsace and Lorraine, a swift strike could only succeed if the Germans outflanked the French fortresses. Schlieffen and the other generals considered the violation of Belgian and Dutch neutrality an unfortunate necessity of war, and in Wilhelm's Germany no one dared challenge this assumption.

Germany's war plan posed two great dangers to the peace of Europe. Since speed formed the essence of the plan, the generals would want to get moving as soon as war broke out. This drastically reduced the time available for diplomacy in any crisis. Schlieffen's successor added one complication to the plan which called for even greater haste. In 1911 Moltke decided not to invade Holland, as

Schlieffen had urged, but to restrict the sweep of the German right wing to Belgium and Luxemburg. This posed a stiff logistical problem, for the Germans would march through a narrow corridor around Liège, Belgium. To make this possible, Moltke planned a sneak attack on the fortresses of Liège on the third day of war mobilization. Now there was no time to waste with diplomacy. Only in Germany did the decision to mobilize amount to a virtual declaration of war.

The sweep through Belgium posed a second risk. Since all the great powers had guaranteed the neutrality of Belgium in 1839, when the Concert of Europe still ruled international relations, England would almost certainly react if Germany attacked Belgium. The Triple Entente did not require England to assist France or Russia if they were attacked, the way the Franco-Russian Alliance bound those two powers to help one another. Yet in the years since the Entente had been signed, the English had developed a moral commitment that the French were counting on. When General Henry Wilson asked Marshal Foch of France in 1909, "What would you say was the smallest British military force that would be of any practical assistance to you . . . ?", Foch replied without hesitation, "One single private soldier, and we would take good care that he was killed."

Still the government in Paris could never be sure the English would send even that one soldier. The invasion of Belgium, however, would likely settle the issue. Not only was England a guarantor of Belgian neutrality in international law, more importantly the coast of Belgium lay less than a hundred miles from London, across the English Channel. For centuries, no English government had ever ignored hostile armies in Belgium. The Schlieffen plan virtually dared the English to join France and Russia as a foe of Germany.

The alliance system and the Schlieffen plan dominated the thoughts of emperors, generals, and diplomats during the July crisis that followed the assassination of the archduke in 1914. Though the treaties and war plans of the rival blocs were secret, their general outlines were known by the governments, if not by the populace. Here is what happened from July 25, when Serbia rejected the ultimatum of Austria-Hungary, to August 5 when all five great powers found themselves at war: Austria-Hungary, sure of support from its German ally, declared war on Serbia; Russia, the traditional protector of the Slavs, mobilized its troops to threaten Austria-Hungary; Germany then declared war on Russia, but attacked France, Russia's ally, according to the Schlieffen plan; and, by marching through Belgium on the way to France, the Germans prompted the English to join the war. It all proceeded with machine-like momentum. On July 30, before Germany took the final steps towards mobilization, the German chancellor, Theobald von Bethmann Hollweg, remarked to his cabinet: "The great majority of the peoples are in themselves peaceful, but things are out of control and the stone has started to roll."

Let's inspect the events of the July crisis more closely. In both Russia and Germany, an even smaller circle of people made the crucial decisions than in Austria-Hungary. The foreign minister of Russia, Count Sergei Sazonov, received the text of the Austrian ultimatum to Serbia on July 24 and immediately "considered war inevitable." For the first time ever, he telephoned Tsar Nicholas II, rather than waiting for an audience. The tsar summoned the Council of Ministers to discuss the crisis that same day, and their initial responses seemed measured enough. They decided to ask Austria-Hungary to extend its time limit on the ultimatum and to urge Serbia to draft as conciliatory a response as possible. The council, however, also authorized a partial mobilization of troops at the discretion of the tsar. The next day, July 25, Tsar Nicholas declared the "period preparatory to mobilization," and thereafter he never recalled the council. He made subsequent decisions after consulting with Sazonov and with the war minister, General Vladimir Sukhomlinov.

The tsar acted in a partial vacuum since the leaders of his principal ally, France, were literally at sea. President of the French Republic Raymond Poincaré, and his prime minister, René Viviani, had just completed a state visit to St. Petersburg and had sailed across the Baltic to visit Sweden, Denmark, and Norway on the way home. The Austrians had intentionally waited until the French officials left Russia on July 23 to deliver their ultimatum to Serbia, thus making it impossible for the Russian tsar and French president to coordinate their response. Wireless telegraphy was not very reliable at that time, and most of the messages sent to the battleship *France* carrying Poincaré and Viviani became garbled. However, the French ambassador to Russia, Maurice Paléologue, assured Sazonov, just before the crucial Council of Ministers meeting on July 24, that the French would honor their alliance commitments. Much has been made of this unauthorized statement by Paléologue, but he was simply reiterating the consistent policy of his government for many years. Poincaré no doubt would have said the same thing had he been present. Throughout the July crisis, the Russians acted on the assumption that France would join in any war against Austria-Hungary and Germany. They knew that, in return, they had pledged to put 800,000 soldiers in the field by the sixteenth day of mobilization. In order to meet this commitment, the Russian generals did not want to delay unduly.

In the meantime, the English foreign minister, the Liberal Edward Grey, attempted to convene a modified version of the Concert of Europe. On July 26 he asked the ambassadors of France, Italy, and Germany, the great powers that were not yet involved in the Austria-Serbia-Russia triangle, to meet with him and mediate the crisis. Germany, however, refused. The kaiser, Chancellor Bethmann Hollweg, and the Chief of Staff, General Moltke, wished to avoid general war, but they did not want to prevent Austria-Hungary from punishing Serbia.

Accordingly, Austria-Hungary declared war on Serbia on July 28. Though their army was not yet fully mobilized and couldn't begin an invasion of Serbia for some weeks yet, Austrian batteries on the Danube bombarded Belgrade on

July 29. The Tsar hesitated between a partial mobilization aimed strictly at Austria-Hungary or a general mobilization to guard against a possible German attack. His military advisers convinced him that a partial mobilization would prove technically too difficult, so after more hesitation, Nicholas proclaimed a general mobilization on July 31. It didn't really matter whether Russia declared partial or general mobilization. When Kaiser Wilhelm discovered that the Russians had been preparing to mobilize as early as July 24, he became enraged at his cousin Nicky. He scrawled a note across one of the tsar's telegrams: "The Tsar — as is openly admitted by him here — instituted military measures . . . five days ago. Thus it is almost a *week ahead* of us. . . . I cannot agree to any more mediation, since the Tsar who requested it has at the same time secretly mobilized behind my back." The German generals were eager to trigger the Schlieffen plan. They mobilized on August 1, declaring war against Russia the same day.

Wilhelm, as usual, couldn't stick to one line of policy very long. When a confused message came in from the German ambassador to London suggesting that both England and France might remain neutral, he tried to short-circuit the Schlieffen Plan, cancel the attack on France, and just fight Russia in the East. General Moltke told him flatly this was impossible: "If His Majesty insisted on leading the whole army eastwards, he would not have an army ready to strike, he would have a confused mass of disorderly armed men without commissariat."

The Germans followed the plan. On August 2 they delivered an ultimatum to Belgium, stating their intent to march armies through the country and offering to pay damages if the Belgians did not resist. The next morning the government of Belgium rejected the ultimatum and mobilized their own meager forces. That same day Germany declared war on France, and that night the attack on Liège succeeded in opening a corridor for the right wing of the German army. On August 4 the British government demanded that Germany withdraw immediately from Belgium. When the British ultimatum expired at midnight without any reply, England finally declared war against Germany.

The blame game began even before the first shots were fired. In the frantic final days of July 1914, the German leaders seemed more intent on making sure that Russia mobilized first, and thus shifting the blame to them, than they were in preventing the conflict. The French generals were eager to mount an offensive of their own, but the civilian government ensured that Germany would be labeled the aggressor by decreeing that the mobilized troops remain at least ten kilometers back from the border and that no French soldiers enter Belgium before the Germans did. After the war, the victorious allies firmly saddled Germany with the war guilt. Article 231 of the Versailles Treaty stated that the war had been caused "by the aggression of Germany and her allies."

The Germans wailed for decades that the guilt was collective, shared by the tsar, who mobilized hastily and unnecessarily, and by the French "warmonger"

Poincaré. But with the publication of Fritz Fischer's blockbuster book, *Griff nach der Weltmacht* (Bid for World Power) in 1961, even German historians finally admitted that their country's recklessness had precipitated the war. A consensus has formed among historians, therefore, that Germany bears major responsibility for the origins of World War I.

It is still worthwhile, however, to analyze the critical decisions made by five great powers in the summer of 1914. Austria-Hungary obviously bears the immediate responsibility for starting a local war in the Balkans. The ultimatum to Serbia was high-handed and intended for only one purpose: to provoke a punitive war against the Serbs. Furthermore, the Austrians never would have taken this step if Kaiser Wilhelm and Bethmann Hollweg had not given them a "blank check" of complete support on July 5. The leaders of both countries hoped they could localize the conflict in the Balkans. Neither intentionally sought a general European war, but both knew very well that they were risking one.

Russia was the first power not immediately involved in the Austro-Serbian quarrel to mobilize its troops, and conversations between Sazonov and the tsar indicate that both understood the dreadful ramifications of this decision. Though the Russians only wanted to threaten Austria-Hungary and make it leave Serbia alone, they knew that mobilization made war with Germany nearly inevitable. Having backed down in similar crises over Bosnia in 1908 and during the Balkan Wars of 1912 and 1913, however, the Russians did not believe they could afford to abandon their Serbian clients once again. The immediate responsibility for war in 1914, then, lies on the three sides of the Eastern European triangle connecting Germany, Austria-Hungary, and Russia.

As soon as Russia mobilized, the Germans implemented the Schlieffen plan; and this, of course, was the most bizarre element in the race to war. Though the German quarrel lay with Serbia and Russia, they attacked France because the plan dictated this. By following the plan, Germany turned a local East European conflict into a general European war. Some of the more extreme disciples of historian Fritz Fischer affirm that Germany planned such a preventive war all along, and they compare the war aims of Wilhelm to those of Hitler. That is probably going too far. The tempered judgment of Joachim Remak seems better:

> Germany's responsibility, to reiterate the point, lies in the general foolishness with which the nation behaved in the quarter century before Sarajevo and, more immediately, in the panicky and pernicious decisions that Berlin made during the July crisis. These things were bad enough; there is no need to add imaginary guilt to real guilt.

For the most part, France and Britain appear to be innocent third parties, drawn into the conflict against their will. This is particularly true of France, which bore the brunt of Germany's aggressive war plan. It is true that France had woven the web of the Triple Entente around Germany, greatly increasing the Germans' sense of encirclement and insecurity. France had also experienced a nationalist revival in the decade before 1914; and with the election of Raymond Poincaré, a native of Lorraine, to the presidency in 1913, anti-German sentiment and a concern for the lost provinces reached new heights. Nevertheless, France did not attack Germany, and due to the circumstances of their state visit to Russia, the French leaders played a very passive role during the July crisis. Again, Joachim Remak provides an apt summary: "In 1914, the French entered the war because they had no alternative. The Germans had attacked them. It was that simple."

Finally, the English sanctimoniously declared their cause just and the actions of their enemies perfidious. Certainly, the English government did not intend to make war and did not decide to intervene until the final moment. The Liberal government in London contained a large radical, anti-war wing, and Prime Minster Herbert Asquith and Foreign Secretary Edward Grey were not sure until Germany invaded Belgium that they could carry the declaration of war in the Cabinet and the Parliament. The English went to war to protect the neutrality of Belgium and, more importantly, to ensure their own national security by preserving the balance of power. Their decision transformed a European war into a world-wide conflict.

Before closing this discussion of war guilt, we should probe beneath the surface and assess the deeper factors making for war. Consider the four "isms" that stalked the scene at the beginning of the century. Neither anarchism nor socialism played any direct role in fomenting World War I. The anarchists' propaganda by the deed served as a model for the assassination of the archduke, but the Bosnian assassins were not anarchists. The socialists utterly failed to stop the war, as their ideology would seem to require; indeed, they hardly even tried. Right up until July 1914, European governments took the threat of a socialist general strike upon the outbreak of war very seriously. On July 31, as war seemed imminent, a crazed nationalist assassinated the French Socialist leader Jean Jaurès to punish him for his supposed pacifism and anti-patriotism.

However, both the leaders and the rank and file of the socialist parties rallied to the defense of their own nations when war was finally declared. Jaurès would have done the same had he lived. The French government wisely chose not to arrest anyone from the list of socialist "troublemakers" they had meticulously assembled in previous years. In Germany the 111 Social Democratic deputies in the Reichstag voted unanimously for war credits on August 4. As Barbara Tuchman has so poignantly remarked: "Unhappily for world brotherhood, the worker felt he had a fatherland like anybody else. . . . The working class went to war willingly, even eagerly, like the middle class, like the upper class, like the species."

Acquiescence in war is not the same as provoking war, so we must look else-where for deeper causes. At first glance, imperialism seems unrelated to the origins of the war. The conflict broke out in Europe, not in the overseas possessions of any nation. As we have already seen, England, France, and Russia had resolved their colonial differences at the time they formed the Triple Entente. Even the Germans had begun to compromise with their European foes when colonial ambitions were at stake. Tsar Nicholas II had visited the kaiser at Potsdam in 1910, and the two leaders struck a deal to stay out of each other's way in Persia and co-operate in the building of the Baghdad railway through the Middle East. In the early months of 1914, the French and English also compromised with Germany over Middle Eastern questions and took a part in planning the Baghdad Railway. No issue outside Europe threatened the peace of the world in 1914.

The immediate cause of war, however, was Austria-Hungary's imperialist policy in the Balkans. Just because the colony of Bosnia lay on the edge of Europe, rather than in Africa and Asia, we should not avoid use of the word "imperial-ism." More importantly, the imperialist rivalry between England and Germany underlay a whole generation of international tensions. Historians rightly indict Germany for a blustering, imprudent policy of naval expansion and colonial ac-quisitions. The kaiser's biographer sums up the policy of *Weltpolitik* as "a natural product of the atmosphere of swagger and confusion prevailing in high German circles, an attitude which went beyond pride in one's own country to jealous con-tempt for others." The very vagueness of Germany's colonial ambitions made them especially threatening to England. The English could never be sure that spe-cific agreements and compromises would suffice to satisfy the Germans, because the kaiser and his followers never made clear just what they wanted. They spoke only of taking "their place in the sun."

However, if Germany was bidding for world power (whatever that might mean), it is important to remember that England already enjoyed world power, the largest empire the world had ever seen. Since the English consid-ered their empire an essential part of their national identity and literally a mat-ter of life and death, the German naval challenge prompted an uncompromis-ing attitude on their part. Eyre Crowe, a high official in the British Foreign Office, wrote in 1907: "A German maritime supremacy must be acknowledged to be incompatible with the existence of the British Empire." Once the kaiser set sail with his High Seas Fleet, a cold war became inevitable and a shooting war probable.

The ascendancy of social Darwinism in European thought justified the im-perialist rivalry. Applying Darwin's biological principle of the "survival of the fit-test" to individual human beings and to whole nations, social Darwinists believed that struggle was not only inevitable but desirable. It built character and ensured that the strongest and most advanced nations would survive. The struggle for national survival fueled the arms race and accustomed the peoples of Europe to the idea of violence as an arbiter in international affairs.

At the deepest level, however, nationalism impelled the Europeans to war. First of all, the clash of national ambitions in the Balkans set off the spark at Sarajevo. Secondly, an arrogant national pride drove the kaiser to compete with his cousins, the English. When, in his usual inconsistent fashion, he occasionally drew back from the belligerent implications of his policy, vocal German conservatives, organized in such groups as the Pan-German League, berated him. The kaiser felt intense pressure from German nationalists in 1914 because he and his country had been humiliated in the two Moroccan crises of 1905 and 1911, when Germany had failed to enlist any support for its positions in North Africa.

Finally, not just Germany but all the nations of Europe were bursting with national pride, antagonism towards others, and feelings of frustration owing to past national humiliations. The tsar felt a need to redeem his dynasty's honor after the defeat by Japan and the near overthrow of his regime in the revolution of 1905. Since his army was still rebuilding during the Bosnian crisis of 1908 and the Balkan Wars of 1912-13, he had followed a cautious policy and discouraged Serbian ambitions. But in 1914 he did not want to back down again. The conservative nationalist newspaper *Novoye Vremya,* which the tsar read daily, greeted the new year of 1914 with an editorial avowing that "the people's sense of pride and at the same time a feeling of patriotism, give such moral satisfaction that even if they are obtained at the price of great material sacrifices, these sacrifices are accepted calmly and without a murmur." With such advice passing for public opinion in tsarist Russia, it is not surprising that Nicholas risked war rather than national dishonor.

The French, as we have seen, had undergone a nationalist revival under the leadership of Raymond Poincaré. Though Poincaré's policy stopped well short of starting a war to recapture Alsace-Lorraine, the tide of nationalist fever made it impossible for him or any other French politician to de-escalate the arms race with Germany. The French ambassador to Berlin, Jules Cambon, pushed for a detente between the French and Germans for years, but French nationalism made such a detente political suicide in Paris.

The English, too, were swelling with national pride and prickly about their honor. Fearing that the Liberal Cabinet might not choose to intervene in the European war, Foreign Officer Eyre Crowe warned his minister, Edward Grey, on July 31, "The theory that England cannot engage in a big war means her abdication as an independent state." He need not have worried. Grey had already written to the German ambassador the day before, "For us to make this bargain with Germany [staying neutral in the conflict] at the expense of France would be a disgrace from which the good name of this country would never recover."

England, France, Germany, and Russia were fighting to prevent losing face, just as much as Austria-Hungary was. All the powers of Europe felt thoroughly frustrated after the generation-long series of crises that marked the cold war between Triple Entente and Triple Alliance. Leaders were determined to act more decisively and not to back down when yet another crisis struck in 1914, and the people were ready to follow them.

Ironically, the fact that Europe had not experienced a war between the great powers for forty-three years made war more likely in 1914. That period of time was long enough for intense national frustration to build up and too long for most adults to remember the horrors of war. When war came, most of Europe greeted it with enthusiasm and a sense of relief. As historian Eugen Weber sums up the mood: "It does indeed seem as if men did not go to war for the sake of Alsace or for the sake of Serbia; they went to war to clear the air. Because they had lived with the menace for so long, they were glad to see it face-to-face, tackle it, and get it over with." No less an authority on war than Adolf Hitler, who marched off to battle along with the rest of Europe's masses, wrote in his propagandistic autobiography, *Mein Kampf:* "One wanted at last to make an end to the general uncertainty."

CHAPTER EIGHT

The War of Exhaustion

In August 1914 Europeans marched off to war almost casually; no one expected a long struggle. General staffs planned swift, decisive battles, and common soldiers, inspired by the religious emotions of nationalism, believed their valor would carry all before them. The Schlieffen plan scheduled a victory over France within six weeks, and none of the military brass in any country projected a strategy or stockpiled munitions for more than six months. The kaiser cheerily promised his soldiers they would be home before Christmas.

An English journalist, Norman Angell, indirectly buttressed such opinions with his 1910 bestseller, *The Grand Illusion*. The world had become so economically interdependent, Angell argued, that both the victors and the vanquished would suffer equally in a general war, so modern war had become obsolete as an instrument of policy. If war did break out, however, it would disrupt trade and industry so greatly that the fighting would prove necessarily brief. Angell's viewpoint underestimated the productivity of modern industry and the tenacity of twentieth-century patriots.

The Schlieffen plan nearly achieved the swift, decisive victory the planners envisioned. After the high drama of July and the first four days of August, the gigantic armies took two full weeks to mobilize. Then from August 18 to the first week of September the Germans and the French threw themselves against each other. The French chief of staff, General Joseph Joffre, an inflexible believer in the supreme value of the offensive, did not wait passively for the Germans. Instead he mounted an attack in Alsace and Lorraine. Though the German lines held, this unexpected development so unnerved General Moltke, the German chief of staff, that he transferred some troops from his right wing in Belgium to help out in Lorraine, thus weakening the key forces of the Schlieffen plan. Nevertheless, two great armies of over 200,000 men each poured through Belgium on the German right wing.

The French did not remain back on their heels in this area either, but persistently counterattacked on the frontier between France and Belgium. The French generals did not yet understand that defenders armed with machine guns and artillery enjoyed a decisive advantage. They had learned little from the Anglo-Boer and Russo-Japanese wars. Had they remained on the defensive during the Battle of the Frontiers from August 20 to 24, they probably would have held the Germans back from French territory. Instead, the Germans mowed down the gallant French attackers, then pursued them over the frontier, constantly moving to the right toward the sea, seeking to outflank and eventually surround them.

In the meantime, the Russians surprised Germany by attacking within two weeks of mobilization, as they had promised their allies, even though they were by no means fully prepared. Two armies marched slowly into East Prussia, which was held by only one German army commanded by an aged, overweight court favorite of the kaiser's. After some initial encounters with the Russians, the unfortunate German general sounded retreat, preparing to abandon the whole of East Prussia; so Moltke swiftly replaced him.

General Erich Ludendorff, who had proved his audacity by the seizure of Liège in Belgium, took command in the east along with a prestigious retired general, Paul von Hindenburg. For the rest of the war, these two — Ludendorff the frenetic military gambler and Hindenburg the placid front man — directed key parts of the German military machine. In the last week of August 1914, they rallied the outnumbered Germans in East Prussia and defeated the poorly coordinated Russian offensive at Tannenberg. Moltke, however, not foreseeing this fortunate outcome, sent reinforcements from the western front to Ludendorff and Hindenburg. Twice before the end of August, therefore, the German general staff weakened the crucial right wing in Belgium, undermining the Schlieffen plan.

The First and Second German Armies kept pushing back the French and the small British Expeditionary Force in the west. Yet the retreating troops were never routed or disorganized; and as the Germans advanced, their own communications and supply lines stretched thin. The men, marching on foot, became bone-weary, and some of them were nearly starving. The French, in the meantime, enjoyed good interior railway lines on which they could transfer troops from Alsace and Lorraine to reinforce the defense.

The Germans had picked the one moment in history when an audacious flanking maneuver would not likely succeed. In earlier days, with both armies on foot, an envelopment might be engineered by the army with the largest numbers and the cleverest generals. Twenty years later, the addition of tanks and motorized transport made the German invasion in the Second World War a true *Blitzkrieg*, lightning attack. According to the Schlieffen plan, the First German Army

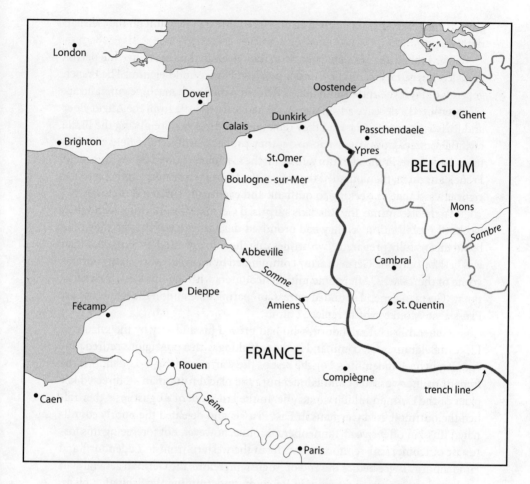

Front Lines on the Western Front at the end of 1914

would encircle Paris, cutting it off from the rest of France; but capture of the capital did not form an essential part of the plan. Destruction of the French armies remained the prime military goal. So when General Alexander von Kluck, commander of the First Army, realized his forces were stretched too thin, he decided on August 31 to wheel inwards to his left and continue his pursuit of the French troops north of Paris.

This presented a tantalizing opportunity to General Joseph Gallieni, directing the hastily improvised defense of the city. Commandeering six hundred Parisian taxicabs and their drivers, Gallieni ferried troops northward to attack von Kluck's right flank at the Marne River. For a brief, romantic, quintessentially French moment, the defenders possessed the advantage of motorized transport that the attackers lacked. At the same time, General Joffre turned the main French armies around and counterattacked. At the Battle of the Marne, raging from September 5 to 10, the German advance finally halted.

The armies of both sides now began a desperate "race for the sea" as each tried to outflank the other. They arrived at the English Channel about November 17, and the fighting tailed off. Both sides dug double and triple lines of trenches at the point of stalemate, 350 miles from Belgium across the north of France to the Swiss Alps.

In all but its deadlocked result, the four-month struggle in France and Belgium had been the tremendous battle both sides expected. No single battle for the rest of the war could match it in numbers of troops engaged or numbers of men killed and wounded. The French suffered over 800,000 casualties (dead, wounded, and prisoners) whereas the much smaller British force lost 85,000 men. The German attackers sustained losses of 677,000 men. The armies used up most of their six-months' supply of ammunition.

If decisive military victory were the object, the war on the western front should have ended in 1914. Had the French halted the German advance at the Belgian frontier, perhaps the short-war prophecies of Norman Angell might have been fulfilled and both sides, recognizing their exhaustion, would have negotiated a peace settlement. The Germans, however, held a sizeable chunk of French territory and lay entrenched within artillery range of Paris itself. National honor, which had brought on this horrible war, dictated a fight to the finish. No French citizen would dream of bargaining away the soil of the homeland; and the Germans, for their part, having come so close to total victory could not yet abandon the struggle. Like playground bullies, the two sides lay locked in a deadly embrace, neither daring to cry "Uncle."

At the end of 1914 the Allies and the Central Powers were deadlocked in every theater of the war, and despite four more years of slaughter neither side ever gained a strategic advantage. On the high seas, the German fleet, whose genesis had so provoked the English, stayed snug within its fortified harbors in the

Heligoland Bight, an inlet of the North Sea at the mouth of the Weser River. The kaiser knew that the English fleet outnumbered the German three to two, and the English ships possessed greater speed and larger guns.

The English admirals also had good reason for caution. Without firing a shot, the English already enjoyed control of the sea lanes around their home island and had imposed a blockade upon German trade. They would gain little more from a naval victory and could lose much from a defeat. Winston Churchill, who served as first lord of the Admiralty in the early part of the war, summed up the situation: "Sir John Jellicoe [the commander in chief of the British fleet] was the only man on either side who could lose the war in an afternoon." Accordingly, Jellicoe resisted plans to storm the German bases, keeping the fleet on alert at Scapa Flow in the Orkney Islands north of Scotland.

Segments of the German fleet periodically ventured into the North Sea for maneuvers or exploratory raids, and on December 10, 1914, a few cruisers bombarded two English seacoast cities, killing 137 civilians and injuring 592 others. The German ships, however, always raced for home when challenged; and for the most part the inhabitants of England were spared the horrors of bombardment.[1] On May 31, 1916, the two fleets nearly collided in a decisive battle off the coast of Jutland in Denmark. The battle cruiser squadrons sailing in advance of the two main fleets fought a furious artillery duel for two hours, but when the English dreadnoughts came in sight of the German High Seas Fleet, Admiral Jellicoe deployed his ships very carefully, and the two sides did not engage in all-out battle. When night fell, Admiral Scheer ordered the German ships to run for home base. Though Jellicoe might have cut him off had he made a concerted effort, he pursued cautiously, and the Germans escaped. The kaiser's fleet never came out again and played no significant part in the war.

The naval battle moved underseas. German U-boats attacked merchant ships in 1915, but the full force of unrestricted submarine warfare was not unleashed for two more years. Though submarines sank one in every four merchant ships approaching Britain for a few months in 1917, the English eventually found that convoys of ships protected by destroyers and armed patrol boats could minimize the danger and ensure control of the sea lanes. The naval war never witnessed a decisive breakthrough. Germany would have been better off, and the war might never have occurred, if the kaiser had not built his fleet.

Much more movement took place on the eastern front than on the high

---

1. German airplanes and zeppelins raided England from Christmas 1914 on but did relatively little damage. In all, about 100 air raids inflicted 5,000 casualties on the English population. By comparison, over 60,000 English died during the Blitz of the Second World War; and 600,000 civilians were killed in Germany by Allied bombing during the second war.

seas or in France. At the same time that Germany defeated the invading Russians at Tannenberg, other Russian forces were enjoying better luck against the hapless troops of Austria-Hungary. In a long series of engagements collectively called the Battle of Lemberg, the Russians took control of Austrian Galicia in September 1914. In addition, the Austrians, who had started the war to crush Serbia, found it difficult to accomplish this task. The Serbs successfully resisted all the Austrian assaults in 1914.

After the western front bogged down, however, Germany moved large numbers of troops eastward, and in 1915 they regained all the ground that Austria had lost to the Russians. Bulgaria then joined the war as an ally of Germany and Austria and helped in the conquest of Serbia. The Serbian army and government, along with many straggling refugees, retreated over the Albanian mountains in the dead of winter and were evacuated by their French and British allies. The Serbians found refuge in Greek territory on the island of Corfu and at the port of Salonika. Attempts to counterattack northward into the Balkans, however, proved unsuccessful until the last year of the war.

The Russians mounted one more successful offensive, under General Alexei Brusilov, in 1916. The unexpected vigor of this drive into Galicia convinced the Romanian government to abandon neutrality and attack Austria-Hungary, in hopes of "liberating" the Romanian populations of Transylvania. Angered at the Russian successes, however, the kaiser promoted Ludendorff and Hindenburg to the supreme command, and they moved more troops eastward, blunting General Brusilov's offensive and sweeping across Romania. This was the last year of fighting on the Russian front, for in 1917 the revolution overthrew the tsar, and the Russian armies abandoned the war. In sum, the war in the east saw a great deal of back-and-forth fighting, but no decisive strategic victories.

On the western front, which stalemated after the failure of the Schlieffen plan, soldiers dug for their lives. At Liège, Namur, and Antwerp in Belgium, German howitzers had blasted apart supposedly impregnable fortresses made of steel and concrete; but simple earth, with its natural give, absorbed the blows of artillery fire more effectively. Dugouts ten yards underground could sustain a direct hit. The opposing armies dug two and three lines of trenches, measuring altogether about 25,000 miles, enough to circle the earth. Tangles of barbed wire lined the fronts of these subterranean defenses.

Military orthodoxy lauded mobility and maneuver and prescribed flanking operations as the most desirable form of battle. In the words of Winston Churchill, "Battles are won by slaughter and manoeuvre. The greater the general, the more he contributes in manoeuvre, the less he demands in slaughter." But no flanks presented themselves on the western front, since the trench lines were anchored on the English Channel at one end and the Alps at the other; so a war of movement and maneuver became impossible. Only slaughter remained.

For the next four years, the British and French generals, still believing in the primacy of the offensive, constructed more temporary, shabby trenches than the Germans did and ordered their men to assault the enemy head on. In Churchill's words, they were "content to fight machine-gun battles with the breasts of gallant men, and think that was waging war." Generals were so out of touch with reality that they readied large regiments of cavalry to exploit any breakthrough. Some British soldiers absurdly advanced through no-man's land kicking a soccer ball.

The Allies mounted five great assaults: the French attempted to break through in Champagne, southeast of Paris, in the spring and again in the autumn of 1915; the British and the French mounted a massive assault on the Somme River from July to October of 1916; the two armies then tried again in a coordinated attack from April to July 1917; then finally the British and their colonial troops slogged through mud and rain in Belgium during the autumn of 1917.

The Germans, since they already held giant portions of France, dug elaborate, permanent trenches, made themselves relatively comfortable, and enjoyed the military advantages of a defensive stance. German troops, however, did mount one major offensive at Verdun in the spring of 1916; then during the final year of the war General Ludendorff made a last, desperate lunge for victory with five assaults on the trench lines during 1918.

None of these frontal assaults, by either side, gained more than a few miles of territory. Though massive artillery bombardments preceded offensives, these barrages simply highlighted the precise point of attack enabling the defenders to position their machine guns more effectively. Attackers sometimes used flame throwers and poison gas, but such horrendous devices won only local victories and increased the slaughter. Precious ground earned with human blood was often abandoned soon afterwards, for a salient of captured territory turned into a shooting gallery as the defenders raked it with machine gun and artillery fire from three sides.

Winston Churchill and others in both England and France realized early in the war that mechanical devices might protect the attacking troops. While serving at the Admiralty, Churchill reasoned that if heavy armored plate protected battleships from the long-range guns of the enemy's fleet, perhaps an armored vehicle could be built for land warfare. He originally called such contraptions "landships," but contractors building the prototypes disguised their work as steel plates for fuel tanks. When the first armored war vehicles appeared at the Battle of the Somme, therefore, the soldiers dubbed them "tanks."

Tanks could crunch barbed wire and roll right over trenches, but the Allies did not build enough of them or deploy them in sufficient force until very late in the war. Similarly, airplanes were not used to support offensives until the last year of war. Until then, aerial surveillance by planes and balloons helped the artillery aim their fire more accurately and thus made the trench soldier's life more dangerous. Throughout the war, the defense enjoyed an overwhelming advantage, with the attackers usually suffering twice as many casualties as the defenders. During the 1916 German assault on Verdun, casualties for both sides totaled more than a million men. "When all was over," Churchill wrote, "Torture and Cannibalism were the only two expedients that the civilized, scientific, Christian States had been able to deny themselves."

Alliances among the "civilized, scientific, Christian States" of Europe had prompted the outbreak of war, and most of the fighting took place in Europe, but the phrase "world war" was not merely a figure of speech. When Great Britain declared war on August 4, 1914, she engaged the great powers' imperial interests around the world and committed her own self-governing dominions to the struggle. Even the subject peoples of the British and French empires fought and died on various fronts. The British mobilized 1.3 million Indian soldiers and the French over half a million colonial subjects from Africa and Asia.

British and colonial troops immediately seized Germany's colonies in Africa, Asia, and the Pacific. A British army captain marched into the tiny colony of Togo in West Africa as soon as he heard of the war declaration, and the British and French jointly invaded the Cameroons. South African troops seized the lightly populated desert land of German Southwest Africa and held on to it for seventy-five years, until international pressure pried loose this territory (now called Namibia) towards the end of the century. Australian and New Zealand soldiers occupied German New Guinea and grabbed Samoa and other small islands in the Pacific. English and Indian troops sailed across the Indian Ocean to attack German East Africa, but they were repulsed by a tiny force of Germans and well-trained Africans, which then retreated to the interior and tied up 372,950 Allied soldiers for the duration of the war. (In the movie *The African Queen,* the fictional characters played by Humphrey Bogart and Katharine Hepburn unwittingly play a role in this East African struggle.)

England's Pacific ally, Japan, was not obligated to enter the war, but the rising nation of the rising sun jumped in eagerly for its own nationalist and imperialist reasons. On August 15, 1914, Japan sent an ultimatum to Germany demanding that it hand over the German naval base and sphere of influence on the Kiaochow (Jiaozhou) peninsula of China. Japanese leaders couched their demands in the exact phrases that the Germans and other Europeans had employed in the Triple Intervention of 1895, depriving Japan of its gains from the Sino-Japanese War. When Germany refused to surrender, Japanese troops fought their way into Kiaochow, winning sweet revenge. The following year the Japanese delivered their humiliating "Twenty-one Demands" to China, which would in effect make Japan the predominant power in that part of the world. In 1917 China declared war on Germany, hoping, in vain as it turned out, that the Allies would protect Chinese interests at the peace conference.

Neither Japan nor China sent troops to Europe. The government in Peking did send almost 100,000 laborers to France for dock work and construction, freeing up more Frenchmen for service in the trenches; and Japan dispatched a flotilla of destroyers to the Mediterranean in 1917, permitting more British ships to cruise the Atlantic on convoy duty. Despite the minimal role of the Pacific nations in the war, the epic struggle taking place on the other side of the world reverberated strongly in Asia. According to Chinese historian Jerome Ch'en, World War I marked a turning point in East-West relations, for Europeans lost confidence in themselves and the Chinese and Japanese discovered that Europe was not invincible. In Africa too the "war of the white tribes" tarnished Europe's image and encouraged anti-colonial movements.

Besides seizing German colonies, the British also hunted down German warships in all the oceans of the world. Though the High Seas Fleet remained sequestered in its North Sea bases, ten German ships were cruising on foreign stations when war broke out. The two ships in the Mediterranean, the *Goeben* and the *Breslau*, eluded the French and English navies and took refuge inside the Dardanelles Straits at Constantinople. Germany and Turkey had struck an alliance on August 2, just as war was breaking out, but the Turks proved hesitant to commit themselves. The arrival of these two German ships (especially the heavily armed *Goeben*) at the Turkish capital, however, tipped the balance, and Turkey joined the Central Powers on November 1. This effectively spread the fighting throughout the Middle East, as the Allies fought their way through the decaying Ottoman Empire.

The other scattered German warships were not so lucky as the *Goeben* and the *Breslau*. The British navy hunted down the *Dresden* in the West Indies and the *Emden* in the Indian Ocean, while blockading the *Königsberg* in port on the coast of East Africa. The *Karlsruhe* blew up in port in the West Indies. The two most powerful ships of the German China squadron, the *Scharnhorst* and the *Gneisenau*, under the command of Admiral Maximilian von Spee, proved the most dangerous and elusive of the German warships. Disappearing into the vastness of the Pacific when war broke out, von Spee's two cruisers led more than two dozen English ships on a four-month-long chase. The Germans destroyed two British cruisers at Coronel off the west coast of South America on November 1, 1914; but a month later, on December 8, British dreadnoughts sank the *Scharnhorst* and the *Gneisenau* at the Falkland Islands in the South Atlantic.

The Royal Navy cleared the high seas of German ships in just five months, yet the war still reached around the world as the white dominions of the British Empire and the former British colony, the United States, joined the fighting.

In Peter Weir's 1981 movie *Gallipoli*, two Australian youths are wandering through the outback on the way to enlist, when they encounter a grizzled old desert rat who hasn't heard about the European war. They proudly inform him that they're off to fight the kaiser, but he replies with a puzzled look on his face, "I didn't know we were mad at anyone over there." The oldtimer was wiser than he knew. What possible quarrel could a colonial people twelve thousand miles from Europe have with Germany and Austria? Indeed the only "natural enemy" of this continent-island in the Pacific, the only possible threat to its existence, Japan, became an ally in August 1914. Yet the two fictional Aussies — and 330,000 real Australian volunteers — actually did fight in World War I.

The six British colonies on the Australian continent had federated into a commonwealth in 1901, and its five million inhabitants clung to British institutions and a "whites only" immigration policy as badges of civilization at the farthest end of the world. When England declared war in 1914, Australia and all the other colonies of the British Empire were automatically engaged. No separate declaration of war was required. Indeed, the Australian government tendered the English a blank check, handing over its fledlging navy to British Admiralty control and offering a land force "of any suggested composition to any destination desired by the Home Government." Believing that an attack on the empire posed a threat to them, and longing for adventure, 42,561 young Aussies rushed to enlist before the end of 1914. Recruiters rejected anyone shorter than 5′ 6″, and the army doctors set high standards of physical fitness. The Aussie soldiers were young, overwhelmingly single, adept at riding and other outdoor skills, "the fittest, strongest, and most ardent in the land," in the words of historian Bill Gammage. Their only fear was that the war might end before they reached the western front.

As it turned out, their arrival in France was delayed by over a year. The first Australian Imperial Force (AIF) landed in Egypt on December 3, 1914, after a five-week passage of the Indian Ocean. The British war minister, General Horatio Herbert Kitchener, detained them there for further training and to guard the Suez Canal, joining them with a smaller New Zealand force as the Australia–New Zealand Army Corps (ANZAC). The Anzacs earned a reputation as hell-raisers during their enforced sojourn near the pyramids, unleashing two devastating riots on the brothel district of Cairo. A joke making the rounds of the army camps pointed up their irreverence:

> A sentry on guard duty challenges the soldiers returning from leave.
> "Halt, who goes there?"
> "Ceylon Planters Rifle Club."
> "Pass, friend. Halt, who goes there?"
> "Auckland Mounted Rifles."
> "Pass, friend. Halt, who goes there?"
> "What the f— has that got to do with you?"
> "Pass, Australians."

The Anzacs soon saw action in an out-of-the-way place that few of them had ever heard of, the fifty-two-mile-long Gallipoli Peninsula, Europe's south-easternmost projection, betweeen the Aegean Sea and the Dardanelles Straits. When the war had bogged down into a stalemate on the western front, a handful of British leaders with imagination, Winston Churchill chief among them, looked around for some place where a decisive flanking maneuver could be mounted. As first lord of the Admiralty, Churchill proposed a fleet bombardment of the Dardanelles fortresses, then an amphibious landing on the Gallipoli Peninsula to seize Constantinople, thus knocking Turkey out of the war and turning the right flank of the Central Powers.

This was a brilliant strategic concept in theory, and it almost worked in practice. Yet it posed enormous risks, as no one had ever mounted such a large amphibious operation before. Furthermore, the British and French generals opposed any diversion of men or materiel from the western front, so the Gallipoli-Dardanelles operation became a political football as its proponents had to fight for every army division, gun, and ship. Consequently, the campaign suffered frustrating delays and vacillating leadership that permitted Turkish reinforcements to reach Gallipoli. As Churchill remarked in retrospect: "History will pronounce that it was not upon the Gallipoli Peninsula that it was lost. . . . Instead the mistakes which were committed in Downing Street and Whitehall condemned us."

On February 19, 1915, the British and French fleets began bombarding the Turkish forts along the forty-mile-long passage of the Dardanelles. They made steady progress for several weeks, and the Allied governments optimistically promised Constantinople to the Russians. Then on March 18, while attacking the key Turkish position at the Narrows, the fleets ran into a hidden minefield, and several battleships were sunk or badly damaged. The British admiral called off the naval bombardment and asked for land forces to clear the Gallipoli Peninsula before proceeding.

Piecing together a landing force from the Anzac armies and a British and a French regular division, General Ian Hamilton, a protege of Kitchener's from the Boer War, directed an amphibious assault on the morning of April 25. The British and French landed at five points near Cape Hellas, the tip of the Gallipoli Peninsula, under heavy Turkish fire; whereas the Australian forces landed by mistake a mile north of their intended beachhead in a tiny cove faced by a desolate moonscape of sheer cliffs and precipitous ravines. The terrain at what became known as "Anzac Cove" was so forbidding that the Aussies and New Zealanders could not advance against the Turkish reserves, ably led by Mustafa Kemal, who later became the "father of his country" in a postwar revolution. The Anzac commanders thought about evacuating this tenuous beachhead, but General Hamilton ordered them to "dig, dig, dig" — and so they did, earning the nickname of Diggers, by which Australian soldiers were known thereafter.

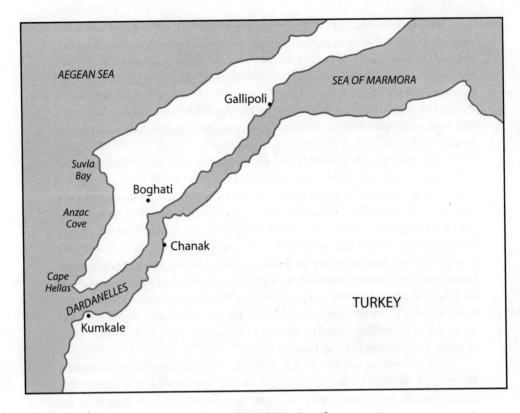

The Gallipoli Peninsula

The war of maneuver that Churchill had envisioned never materialized. Instead, the Gallipoli campaign, both at Cape Hellas and Anzac Cove, settled into the now-familiar pattern of trench warfare; only in the close quarters of Gallipoli the enemy trenches lay much closer together than in France, only ten yards apart in some places. The armies on both sides mounted senseless frontal assaults, resulting in general slaughter. When the Mediterranean summer arrived, the informal Aussies stripped to the waist and settled down to battle dust, flies, and dysentery.

After months of bureaucratic wrangling in London, the English sent out reinforcements and staged a second landing just north of Anzac Cove at Suvla Bay in the second week of August. English, Irish, and Indian troops landed successfully while the Anzacs mounted valiant and bloody feints to cover them, but the invaders failed to take the heights at the center of the peninsula from which they could have dominated the Dardanelles. The soldiers fell back into their trench routines and the fleet never moved. Finally, in the most brilliant operation of the whole campaign, 83,000 men, 5,000 animals, 2,000 vehicles, and 200 guns were secretly evacuated from the Anzac-Suvla beachhead on the nights of December 12-19, without the Turks realizing what was happening. Only two soldiers were wounded in the withdrawal. The British and French troops also withdrew successfully from Cape Hellas in January 1916.

Gallipoli marked a military failure for the Allies and a political disaster for Winston Churchill, who lost his place in the British government at the end of 1915 and labored under a cloud for a generation. Yet it fueled a nascent Australian nationalism. Young Captain F. B. Stanton wrote in his diary: "1915. Australia's entry into the Company of nations — no finer entry in all history . . . to have leapt into Nationhood, Brotherhood and Sacrifice at one bound."

Though Australian soldiers went on to fight in France (Captain Stanton died there in 1917, at age 23), Anzac Cove had been their own distinctive theater of war; 50,000 Australian soldiers fought there (1 percent of the total population of Australia) and more than half of them were killed or wounded, a casualty rate twice that of the whole British Expeditionary Force at Gallipoli. Australians took pride in their men's bravery and self-sacrifice, blaming British generals and politicians for the overall fiasco. The Australian government declared Anzac Day, April 25 (the anniversary of the first Gallipoli landing), a national holiday, which gradually replaced Empire Day, May 24, as the focus of patriotic loyalties. As Australian historian John Robertson concluded, "Anzac 'blooded' the young nation for its 'place in the sun.'" Ironically, the successful defense against Australian invaders also played a role in Turkey's emerging national identity after the war.

Before 1914 the Gallipoli campaign would have been considered a war in its own right. Indeed, it lasted about as long as the Russo-Japanese War of 1905, was fought over similar terrain on a narrow peninsula, and resulted in roughly twice as many casualties. In the context of world war, it was merely a sideshow. Yet like Japan in 1905, a Pacific island nation marked these battles as birthpangs of its twentieth-century national identity.

A month before the Anzac flotilla weighed anchor off western Australia in 1914, soldiers from the opposite end of the British Empire had set off for England. Canada, whose first contingent of troops landed at Plymouth on October 15, was an older, larger British dominion with a more developed sense of national identity than Australia. As early as the War of 1812, Canadian defense against invading Americans had furnished the "great deeds" and emotional symbols on which nationalism feeds. The British North American colonies had federated earlier (1867) than the Australians did (1901); indeed the very term "dominion," the label for a self-governing British colony, had been invented for Canada's confederation. By the time of the world war, the Canadian population had swelled to 8 million, compared to 5 million Aussies.

On the other hand, Canada's national unity remained far more fragile than Australia's. French-speaking and English-speaking Canadians formed "two solitudes" that shared little in common. Furthermore, English-Canadians were torn between loyalty to the old country and admiration for the wealthy, bustling Americans to the south. The duality of English and French Canada resembled, in some respects, the two-headed monster of Austria-Hungary, making swift, decisive action difficult.

Nevertheless, one portion of Canada responded to the outbreak of war enthusiastically. Automatically committed to Britain's cause, just as Australia was, the Canadian government pledged an overseas force of 25,000 men to be raised and maintained at Canadian expense. By September 4, 32,000 volunteers responded. Two-thirds of them had been born in Great Britain (by contrast, 72 percent of the first Aussie volunteers were native-born). Four battalions actually dressed in Scottish kilts. Economic hard times also pushed many Canadians to enlist; so a large proportion of volunteers were unemployed urban workers, in contrast to the backcountry origins of most Australian soldiers. Most noticeably, only 1,000 French-Canadians volunteered, a scant 4 percent of the first contingent, though the French comprised one-third of the country's population. Before the war ended, 619,636 Canadians entered the armed forces. A tiny minority of these came from Quebec.

The Canadians found their "Gallipoli" at the Ypres salient in West Flanders. When the Germans drove through Belgium in the autumn of 1914, they faced the retreating remnants of the Belgian army and the British Expeditionary Force. At the Yser River, King Albert of Belgium ordered the sluicegates opened, flooding the countryside ahead of the invaders. The Germans swung around the flooded bogs through the medieval cloth-making town of Ypres, but there the English and the Belgians halted them in the bloody First Battle of Ypres. More or less by accident, an awkward bulge, or salient, in the front lines projected outward from the town, forming a horrendous free-fire zone for German artillery on three sides of the defenders. Though it would have been militarily prudent to withdraw from the salient and fortify a more defensible position, the king of Belgium wished to retain this last remnant of his national territory, and the British believed that ground held with so much bloodshed should not be voluntarily yielded. So, for four more years, Ypres, or "bloody Wipers" as the British called it, became a killing ground.

Canadian troops arrived at Ypres just in time for the first use of poison gas in the war. On the afternoon of April 22, 1915 (three days before the Anzac invasion at Gallipoli), the Germans opened five thousand cylinders of chlorine gas, and a dense, green cloud drove two divisions of French troops into a panic. The Canadians, holding the town of St. Julien, found themselves alone with a four-mile gap in the line on their left. They fought grimly for three days, with only cotton cloth soaked in water for protection against the stinging gas, until reinforcements plugged the gap. Over six thousand Canadians were killed or wounded.

For the next two years, Canadians fought up and down the ninety miles of line held by the British, from Flanders to Picardy, losing 24,000 men at the Somme alone. By the middle of 1917, the Canadian government had voted conscription to shore up the dwindling pool of volunteers and had begun to act like an independent ally rather than an English colony. Four North American divisions united as the Canadian Army Corps, and in June 1917 Arthur Currie, a debt-ridden real estate promoter in peacetime, became its commander. In early October, Field Marshal Douglas Haig, the British commander in chief, ordered Currie's Canadians back into the Ypres salient for a battle that has lived in infamy. The poet Siegfried Sassoon summed it up tersely: "I died in hell — (They called it Passchendaele)."

Passchendaele was the name of both a town and a low ridge just beyond the edge of the salient. Marshal Haig planned a massive offensive to pin down large numbers of German troops, thus relieving pressure on the French, who had suffered defeat and troop mutinies farther down the line. He also hoped to break out of the narrow salient and capture German submarine bases at Ostend and Zeebrugge. Above all, Haig dreamed of a decisive victory that would overcome the war-weariness settling like a cloud along the western front.

The Third Battle of Ypres, as the ensuing actions are officially titled, began literally with a bang. On June 7, 1917, the British detonated nineteen huge land mines containing six hundred tons of explosives underneath the Messines Ridge on the right wing of the salient. The explosions were heard clearly on the English coast across the channel and rattled windows in London, more than a hundred miles away. British and Australian troops then stormed the ridge and secured it (the Canadians were about thirty miles away at this time, on another part of the front). Then a long delay followed as the field marshal wrangled with Prime Minister Lloyd George, who had grown weary of the bloodbaths on the western front and wanted to divert British soldiers to the defense of Italy.

Finally the offensive went forward on July 31, but by then torrential rains were falling. That August proved the wettest in forty years. Artillery pounding the terrain from both sides destroyed the drainage ditches of the low-lying bogland, increasing the flood. Often in the twentieth century, commentators describe an unsuccessful battle or war with the metaphor of a "quagmire." The ground between Ypres and Passchendaele became a literal quagmire, a "porridge of mud." Private C. Miles of the Royal Fusiliers recalled: "The moment you set off you felt that dreadful suction. It was forever pulling you down. . . . It was worse when the mud didn't suck you down . . . [then] you knew that it was a body you were treading on." The troops often marched up to their waists in water, holding their rifles overhead, while German artillery shells burst and machine-gun bullets whizzed by. Soldiers who took shelter in shell holes drowned. Bubbles burst at the surface of crater pools as the air escaped from bloated bodies.

The offensive resumed in better weather at the end of September, but the rains came again on October 4. Then Haig called on General Currie to relieve his exhausted troops. Both Currie and two of Haig's subordinate British commanders urged him to halt the deadly struggle, but Haig refused. The Canadian general later wrote: "I carried my protest to the extreme limit . . . which I believe would have resulted in my being sent home had I been other than the Canadian Corps Commander." Canadian soldiers found the salient even more terrifying than they remembered. Gunner J. J. Brown of the field artillery recalled: "We had been behind St. Julien in the gas attack in 1915. Now I wouldn't have recognized the place . . . just a few bits of foundations left. There was no trace of the farms or barns that were there in 1915, nothing but this ocean of mud." In fact, the picturesque villages and woods had first been wrecked and then transformed into fortresses. "Woods" were stark groves of denuded trunks, with reinforced concrete "pillboxes" housing machine gunners. Glencorse Wood changed hands eighteen times in a month.

The Canadians relieved Australian troops who had lost almost 60 percent of their soldiers in the fighting at the salient since July. On October 26 two Canadian divisions jumped off towards Passchendaele, then two fresh divisions relieved them a few days later. On November 6 they took the ruined village, and by November 10 they held the entire ridge. The Canadians suffered 15,564 casualties. A thousand of their bodies sank into the mud and were never recovered. Overall, the Passchendaele offensive took ninety-nine days and three hours to travel the five miles from Ypres, at a cost of 244,000 British casualties. When the Germans attacked again the following spring, the British withdrew from the ridge back to the narrow salient in front of Ypres.

Gallipoli and Passchendaele rank among the great fiascoes of warfare, but each stimulated the national feelings of a small nation striving for an independent place within the British Empire. After the war the Canadian government insisted that the dominions represent themselves at the peace conference. A Canadian veterans society briefly honored St. Julien's Day, April 22, the date of the first gas attack in the Ypres salient, but Armistice Day, November 11, soon overwhelmed it as a day of national observance. A Canadian army doctor, Lieutenant-Colonel John McCrae, penned a classic war poem that has ever after been associated with that day throughout the English-speaking world:

> In Flanders fields the poppies blow,
> Between the crosses, row on row,
> That mark our place; and in the sky
> The larks, still bravely singing, fly
> Scarce heard amid the guns below.
> We are the Dead. Short days ago
> We lived, felt dawn, saw sunset glow,
> Loved and were loved, and now we lie
> In Flanders fields.

Even at the end of the century, Canadians proudly wear a red paper poppy every November 11, for what they call Remembrance Day.

Canadians also remember that their contributions in blood and treasure equaled those of their far more populous American neighbor, and they complain that Americans take too much credit for winning the war. Indeed, the United States entered the war very late. In 1914 President Woodrow Wilson invoked the traditional American policy of avoiding European entanglements, imploring Americans to remain "neutral in thought as well as in deed." When a German submarine sank the English liner *Lusitania* on May 7, 1915, killing almost 1,200 passengers, including 128 Americans, Wilson still maintained that "there is such a thing as a man being too proud to fight." The following year, he obtained a pledge from the German government to restrict its submarine campaign and give ample warning before sinking merchant ships. As late as November 1916, Wilson campaigned for and won reelection on the slogan "He kept us out of war."

On February 1, 1917, however, the Germans rescinded their pledge to Wilson and declared unrestricted submarine warfare. Soon thereafter, one in every four American ships carrying supplies to Europe failed to return. The kaiser and Chancellor Bethmann Hollweg were gambling that they could starve England and France into submission before the United States made up its mind to intervene. Even if the Americans did enter the war, the Germans believed that their troops could not be recruited, trained, and transported overseas soon enough to make a difference. Adding insult to injury, German Foreign Secretary Arthur

Zimmermann instructed his diplomats in Mexico City to offer the Mexicans an alliance that would open a second front against the United States if it entered the war. The British intercepted Zimmermann's telegram and American newspapers printed it on March 1, 1917.

Woodrow Wilson found himself against a wall, virtually compelled to declare war and defend America's national honor. Yet he was a rigid moralist who might have resisted such pressure except for one deciding factor. From the very beginning of the war Wilson had wanted to mediate the conflict and bring about a just and lasting peace. By 1917 he had finally realized that the United States would enjoy no influence at the peace table unless the country participated in and helped win the war. On April 2 he asked Congress to declare war on Germany. Congressional response proved far from unanimous. The declaration carried the Senate by a vote of 82 to 6 on April 4, and the House followed by a margin of 373 to 50 on April 6, 1917.

The Germans almost won their gamble. Though the first contingent of Americans arrived in France in late June 1917, parading triumphally through Paris on the Fourth of July, General John J. Pershing insisted on thorough training and a period of seasoning in quiet sectors of the line. The American army did not suffer its first battle casualties until November. In 1918, however, over a million American troops helped blunt the final German offensives; then in late September the Americans took over a ninety-mile sector of the line from the Meuse River to the Argonne Forest, driving the Germans before them until the armistice on November 11.

A Canadian military historian, John Swettenham, has pointed out that in the final months of the war a mere 105,000 Canadian soldiers drove twice as far as the 650,000 Americans in the Meuse-Argonne sector, taking more than twice as many German prisoners at a cost of half the casualties. This is not an altogether fair comparison, for the Argonne Forest presented a much more formidable terrain than the low countries where the Canadians fought. Yet it does illustrate clearly how sensitive Canadians are about their powerful neighbor, and it makes the point that American troops did not "win the war" in any direct military sense. Winston Churchill aptly concluded, "The war ended long before the material power of the United States could be brought to bear as a decisive or even as a principal factor. . . . But if the physical power of the United States was not in fact applied in any serious degree . . . the moral consequence of the United States joining the Allies was indeed the deciding cause in the conflict." The availability of a vast new manpower pool meant that the Allies could hold out indefinitely, and Germany could not.

This "vast manpower pool," of course, consisted of individual young men. Why did they keep fighting? Canadian historians Desmond Morton and Jack Granatstein remind us:

Generals could draw objectives on maps and historians later would draw arrows to show how troops attacked, but the reality was tiny clumps of exhausted, frightened men. . . . The advance depended on a few men who found a way through the wire or who wormed their way within grenade-throwing range of a German machine-gun. If they had the luck to survive and the courage to go on, they and the handful of men who followed them were why battalions reached the goals marked out by staff officers' chinagraph pencils.

The word which leaps out of this and nearly every account of Great War fighting is "exhausted." All the nations, except the United States, nearly exhausted their manpower. Generals planned offensives in hopes of exhausting the enemy in a war of attrition. Individual soldiers marched to the front and fought until exhausted. Where did they find the "courage to go on"?

Some, of course, did not. In 1917 the peasant soldiers of Russia marched home in droves, prompting the Russian Revolution. The same thing nearly happened on the western front. After three years of useless offensives, bad food, and infrequent leave, whole battalions of French soldiers mutinied in the spring of 1917. Some simply refused to fight, others marched grudgingly back to the front *baa*-ing like sheep led to the slaughter. Marshal Henri Pétain suppressed the mutinies with a mixture of ruthless punishment for the ringleaders and timely concessions on food and home leave. Though some rebellious troops, both in Russia and France, sang the *Internationale* and waved the red flag, neither socialism nor anarchism but simply war-weariness spurred the mutinies.

However, with the major exception of Russia, most soldiers, on both sides, kept fighting for four long, seemingly hopeless years. What impelled them? In the first few weeks and months, a thirst for adventure, flight from boredom or unemployment, and unreflective patriotism prompted most of the soldiers. These motives died with the first recruits. For a long time thereafter, stern feelings of duty and honor, words which retained simple, unambiguous meanings early in this century, kept most soldiers in line.

National feelings ran high among all the troops. Frenchmen, of course, were defending their own soil, and the English their national security. The "colonial" generals, Arthur Currie from Canada, John Monash of Australia, and John Pershing from the United States, insisted that their soldiers fight together in national units, not be fed piecemeal into the meat-grinder as replacements for decimated French or English divisions. This decision harnessed the force of national pride to make soldiers fight harder and enhanced the nationalism of both soldiers and home-front civilians. Still, it is hard to believe that nationalism alone propelled men through the horror and the carnage.

Another "ism" entered the trenches of the western front about 1917: fatalism drove the soldiers to fight without hope, living only for the moment. Either a bullet had one's name on it or it did not. No amount of worry could change that. So the soldiers fought to the point of exhaustion in order to preserve their sanity and self-respect and not to let down their comrades. What Australian historian Bill Gammage has written about the Anzacs applies to all soldiers in the war of exhaustion:

> Their fatalism, their courage, their manhood, and their sheer dogged determination sustained [them]. . . . They fought for their own prestige because that would probably be their last cause, they took greatest comfort from their mates because their mates were all they had, they accepted the sight and spectre of death because they were themselves to die, they adjusted to the daily routine of war because they did not expect to know another. They lived in a world apart, a new world.

CHAPTER NINE

Peace and Consequences

Over 60 million men mobilized to fight in the First World War, and 8 million of them (15 percent of those mobilized) died in battle.[1] In addition, 7 million men were permanently disabled and about 15 million more were wounded less seriously. Serbia, whose assassins started the whole bloody business, suffered the greatest proportionate losses, with about 10 percent of the country's total population perishing. The French and Germans each lost 3 percent of their populations.

These battlefield casualties, however, only begin to plumb the depths of population loss during the war. Millions of civilians died from disease, famine, and privation, particularly in Russia and Austria-Hungary; and a whole generation of babies remained unborn due to wartime hardship and the absence of fathers at the front. The total population deficit for Europe due to the war — that is, the number of military and civilian casualties plus the number of people who would have been born under normal circumstances but were not — has been estimated at about 48 million. In addition, 15 million more were swept away in the postwar influenza epidemic, which was partly caused by the rundown condition of so many individuals in 1919.

So the total population loss for the period from 1914 to 1920 runs to about 60 million. This figure represents 7 percent of Europe's prewar population and equals the whole natural increase for the period. In short, the number of Europeans stood at the same level in 1920 as in 1914. The war froze the European population in the grip of death.

---

1. I follow Derek Aldcroft's discussion of the costs of war in *From Versailles to Wall Street*. I have cross-checked his figures with other sources, and find that the numbers vary. These should be used only to indicate the general magnitude of losses.

The impact of these deaths went further than the raw numbers might indicate, since most of those who died were in the prime of life and their potential productivity was lost forever. France, whose prewar leaders had been gravely worried by a low birthrate and a declining population, lost about 10 percent of its active male population in the war. Furthermore, the best and the brightest, the cream of their generation, were the first to enlist and the first to fall on the western front. In England, of the 14,561 Oxford men who served in the war, 2,680 (18 percent) died, twice the average proportion of deaths for all English males under age forty-five.

Property damage is much harder to estimate, but a figure of 30 billion dollars is sometimes put forward. This represents about one-thirtieth of the capital assets in Europe. The worst damage remained fairly localized, since there were no large-scale aerial bombing raids on civilian centers, as in the Second World War. Though the area of the trenches in northern France emerged from the war looking like a moonscape, this totaled only about 6 percent of France's geographical area. The armies wreaked the worst havoc in northern France, Serbia, Poland, and Russia. Great Britain and Germany remained almost totally untouched.

Amazingly, Belgium, whose invasion precipitated the war on the western front, suffered relatively little material damage. Germany occupied nearly all of Belgium, and after 1914 fighting was confined to a small corner of the country, around the Ypres salient. John Maynard Keynes, the eminent economist who served as an adviser at the peace conference after the war, estimated "I do not put the money value of the actual *physical* loss of Belgian property by destruction and loot above $750,000,000 *as a maximum*."

Keynes calculated that the total damage Germany inflicted on the western Allies would run somewhere between 8 and 15 billion dollars. Doubling this to include destruction in Germany, Austria-Hungary, and especially in Russia (which was devastated by world war, revolution, and then civil war) brings the total to the estimated 30 billion dollars. Summing up the work of various economic historians, Derek Aldcroft concludes that "in 1919 the world found itself with its physical capital in bad shape and in quantity no greater than in 1911."

The human mind does not easily grasp enormous numbers such as "a population deficit of 60 million" or "physical damage estimated at 30 billion dollars." The roll call of battlefield casualties on the Western Front usually causes the reader's eyes to glaze over. In an attempt to put these mind-numbing figures in comparative perspective, a Canadian geographer, Harold Foster at the University of Victoria, has devised a disaster magnitude scale, somewhat like the geologist's Richter scale which measures earthquakes. Bravely (or foolhardily), Foster has quantified the amount of human stress caused by natural and man-made disasters in order to compare events widely separated by time and place. He found that World War I ranks third in the worldwide list of disasters, exceeded only by the Black Death of the Middle Ages and by World War II in our own century.

I do not believe we should take the intellectual exercise of quantifying disasters very seriously, but it would be hard to quarrel with Foster's overall conclusion that World War I ranks up near the top of all-time catastrophes. However, the bubonic plague epidemics of the fourteenth century outrank the disaster of World War I, and more people were swept away by the influenza epidemic of 1919-20 than died in the trenches. At least until the invention of the atomic bomb, microscopic organisms could wipe out humans more swiftly than we could.

Aside from the death and destruction, World War I unleashed a host of political and social changes. Revolutions broke out all along the rim of the European war (as we shall see in great detail in part 3 of this book). Nations rose or fell as they faced the test of the first total war in modern times.

By the time the war ended, the government of the Russian tsar had fallen, and the whole of Russia was consumed in civil war and temporarily isolated from the rest of Europe. Four small nations subjected by Russia — Finland, Estonia, Latvia, and Lithuania — made good their independence while the Russians were distracted. Austria-Hungary, that two-headed giant whose internal problems had precipitated the war, simply dissolved during 1918 in a wave of strikes, food riots, army mutinies, and national uprisings. Emperor Franz Joseph had died in 1916, and his grandnephew Karl, who succeeded him, was forced to abdicate on November 11, 1918 (the day of the German armistice at Compiègne, France; Austria-Hungary had quit the war a week earlier, on November 3, when it negotiated an armistice with Italy at Padua). The sprawling empire shattered into its two constituent parts, Austria and Hungary, as well as three new countries, Czechoslovakia, Poland, and Yugoslavia.

Though new European nations were being born, the dominant position of Europe as a whole had eroded by 1918. Japan and the United States emerged from the struggle greatly strengthened, since both had suffered comparatively little from the war's death and destruction. Both nations became net creditors, rather than debtors, and both sat among the great powers at the peace conference. The white dominions of the British Empire — Canada, Australia, New Zealand, and South Africa — also benefited from increased industrial and agricultural production and a surge of national self-confidence. Submerged colonies in Asia and Africa bided their time but saw clearly that their imperial masters were no longer invincible. The independent but underdeveloped countries of South America drew closer economically to the United States as European investors proved unable to sustain their formerly dominant position on that continent. The world was turning upside down.

Social changes with long-range consequences broke out in all the major belligerent nations. In France and England the working classes, who proved their loyalty to the state by abandoning the anti-war precepts of socialism, won new respect and some concrete gains in wages and social legislation. A representative of the British Labour Party sat in the wartime coalition government, and Labour itself came to power for the first time during the 1920s. Women took over vital civilian jobs in all the warring nations while their men served at the front, and though they had to relinquish them when peace returned, this experience greatly augmented the self-confidence of feminists. To a lesser extent, the large black underclass in the United States enjoyed its first taste of well-paying industrial jobs and greater personal dignity.

Governments directed the economies of their nations and raised taxes to levels barely dreamed of before 1914. This economic mobilization for total war provided a powerful example that was followed later in the century. For instance, the United States, a latecomer to the war, raised and equipped an army from scratch then transported it thousands of miles across the ocean. A confusing medley of goverment boards and regulatory agencies cajoled, ordered, and guided both business and labor. This whole apparatus melted away as the country returned to a laissez-faire economy after the war, but politicians recalled this wartime experience a decade later when the Great Depression struck. Franklin D. Roosevelt modelled his New Deal quite closely on the wartime alphabet soup of government agencies. English historian Arthur Marwick, in his pioneering study of war and social change, has concluded that this powerful example of a thoroughly mobilized national society, what he calls "The Great Analogue of War," was one of the most important consequences of World War I.

The horrors of battle also caused enormous psychological changes, immense disturbances of the human spirit. Both those who fought and those who mourned at home suffered terrible tests of their religious faith and their human optimism. The literary critic Paul Fussell has provided a small but telling example. In the trenches of the western front, most attacks took place at either dawn or sunset, when the enemy was silhouetted against the sky. Consequently, all ranks mustered out for inspection and a heightened state of readiness at these two hours of the day. When a trench poet or diarist, therefore, wished to express irony, sarcasm, or horror he simply juxtaposed the usual romantic connotations of sunrise with the terror that the soldiers felt at that hour. Fussell concludes chillingly: "Dawn has never recovered from what the Great War did to it." The warriors in the trenches also feared that the war might never end, that one blood-soaked dawn would simply follow another. George Orwell's image of perpetual warfare as part of the human condition, expressed in his novel *1984*, came out of this World War I experience and has haunted the twentieth century ever since.

Soldiers who served in the war developed a twisted sort of esprit de corps, a solidarity of the trenches marked by bitterness toward and alienation from all civilians. It proved impossible to describe what life in the trenches had been like, so

141

as years passed old soldiers idealized and romanticized it. At the front all ranks and classes suffered a democracy of privation and terror; they became a new proletariat, marked not by economic status but by wartime experience. This brotherhood of war made ex-servicemen susceptible to demagogues who exploited their resentments. Adolf Hitler, himself a corporal in the German army during World War I, understood these confused emotions and played them like a virtuoso.

The solidarity of the trenches combined with the example of increased statism to produce the new "isms" of Nazism and Fascism which terrorized the world in the following decades. In this, as in other ways, the First World War led directly to the second.

The senseless slaughter of the trenches, however, led many others to recoil against war in general. "Pacifism" was a relatively new word, first used around 1902 to describe antiwar sentiment, but it had long held sway among certain Protestant sects, particularly the three historic peace churches, the Mennonites, the Church of the Brethren, and the Quakers. Taking literally the words of Jesus Christ in Matthew's Gospel account of the Sermon on the Mount, these radical Christians believed that they must always "obey God rather than men" and heed Jesus' invocations, "Blessed are the meek . . . ; Blessed are the peacemakers . . . ; Blessed are they that suffer persecution for justice' sake." About 16,000 dissenters in England and 4,000 in the United States declared themselves conscientious objectors during World War I. Most of them sat out the war in prison.

Mainstream Christians and most political leaders usually rationalized participation in warfare through "just war theory." According to this process of reasoning, a war could be considered just if it were declared by legitimate authority, were fought for a just cause, and employed just means. So, for example, all the nations of Europe that participated in World War I were led by indisputably legitimate government authorities, and most of these could easily declare their cause to be just. France was fighting in self-defense; England and Russia could rightly claim that they were intervening to protect an ally who had been attacked; and the United States proclaimed the most just cause of all: to make the world safe for democracy. Only Germany and Austria-Hungary would have difficulty justifying their war aims. Most of the warring powers also employed relatively just means of warfare. According to just war theory, soldiers carrying arms in battle may be freely killed, but no one else may be. In World War I, civilians remained largely immune from slaughter (unlike World War II), and prisoners of war were generally well treated. So, at first glance, it might seem that World War I could be justified, at least by the Allies.

Just war theory, however, contains one further condition that undermines its application to World War I — the principle of proportionality. Even if the cause is just and the means employed relatively clean, a war can be considered unjust if the evil it causes outweighs the good achieved. World War I accomplished some good ends: it saved Serbia and France from aggression, it liberated the subject nationalities of Eastern Europe, it unleashed refreshing winds of social change. Yet the cost was high, as we have already seen: 8 million battlefield deaths and a population deficit of 60 million overall. Such tremendous loss of life would seem to outweigh any possible good accomplished by the war. Paul Fussell states this case against World War I starkly: "Eight million people were destroyed [he speaks only of battlefield deaths] because two persons, the Archduke Francis Ferdinand and his Consort, had been shot." The means employed and their deadly consequences were totally disproportionate to the wrongs that were righted and the good ends that were achieved.

Many men and women of good will, in all the countries that participated in the war, shared this sense that World War I had been a disproportionately violent, irrational outbreak, even if they did not reason explicitly along these lines. Total pacifists, however, who now included people of no religious faith as well as members of the historic peace churches, went a step further. They argued that, at least in the twentieth century, all wars are unjust because the means of warmaking are necessarily disproportionate to any imaginable good end. Modern technology has rendered warfare so terrible that just war theory has become obsolete, if it ever was valid. Once soldiers mobilize with machine guns, artillery, flamethrowers, and poison gas, their ability to kill becomes so great that it can no longer be controlled by the finely tuned calculus of proportionality.

Bertrand Russell, the eminent English philosopher, outlined an alternative defense strategy during World War I, which was completely ignored at the time but which presents tantalizing possibilities for future conflicts. Russell's point of view, presented in an American magazine article entitled "War and Non-Resistance," posited two fundamental principles for victims of aggression: neither employ force, nor give in to it. He outlined his scenario this way:

> Let us imagine that England were to disband its army and navy, after a generation of instruction in the principles of passive resistance as a better defense than war. Let us suppose that England at the same time publicly announced that no armed opposition would be offered to an invader.... What would happen in this case?
>
> Suppose, to continue the argument, that the German government wished to take advantage of England's defenseless condition. It would be faced, at the outset, by the opposition of whatever was not utterly brutal in Germany, since no possible cloak could be found to hide the nakedness of aggression....
>
> But let us suppose all home opposition overcome, and a force dispatched to England to take possession of the country.... There would be no glory to be won, not even enough to earn one iron cross.... To the soldierly mind, the whole expedition would be ridiculous, causing disgust instead of pride....

However, we will suppose the invading army arrived in London, where they would evict the King from Buckingham Palace and the members from the House of Commons. . . .

But at this point, if the nation showed as much courage as it has always shown in fighting, difficulties would begin. All the existing officials would refuse to cooperate with the Germans. Some of the more prominent would be imprisoned, perhaps even shot, in order to encourage the others. But if the others held firm . . . the Germans would have to dismiss them all, even to the humblest postman, and call in German talent to fill the breach. . . .

Such a method of dealing with invasion would, of course, require fortitude and discipline. But fortitude and discipline are required in war. For ages past, education has been largely directed to producing these qualities for the sake of war. . . . The same courage and idealism which are now put into war could easily be directed by education into the channel of passive resistance.

Though Bertrand Russell uses the term "passive resistance," it is clear that pacifists are not really passive, they are active war resisters, albeit non-violent ones. The very word "pacifist" comes from the Latin *pacem facere,* to make peace, an active verb. Russell also emphasizes the importance of education, and with good reason. Citizens of the European nations did not march off to war out of some primal animal instinct; they had been instructed and socialized to defend their countries by a generation or more of compulsory public education. Some of the most ferocious, and certainly the most effective, nationalists in Europe were country and small-town schoolmasters.

In most wars before the eighteenth century, a small professional caste of soldiers did the fighting. Mobilizing the masses for warfare was a major, if dubious, achievement of modern nationalism. In the words of a Broadway musical, "They had to be carefully taught." Russell and other pacifists argue that if citizens can be taught, they can also be untaught. Education for nonviolence must precede resistance to war. Clearly this had not been done prior to World War I. Nonviolent resistance was then, and remains now, a minority position; yet it has been employed to good effect on several occasions in the twentieth century, most notably by Mohandas Gandhi in India and Martin Luther King Jr. in the United States.

The leaders of the victorious nations were as appalled as the pacifists by the slaughter they had unleashed, but they pursued a different approach to peacemaking. Believing that World War I had been largely an accidental war, caused by the alliance system and the arms race and precipitated by faulty diplomatic procedures among nations, they tried to build a better international system after the war. Woodrow Wilson of the United States placed himself at the head of these political peacemakers.

Thomas Woodrow Wilson had been a professor of history and the president of Princeton University before his election as governor of New Jersey in 1910. Campaigning for president in 1912 as a progressive Democrat, he trumpeted a program called the New Freedom that attacked big business monopolies and corrupt political bosses. Shortly before his inauguration, Wilson remarked to a friend: "It would be the irony of fate if my administration had to deal chiefly with foreign affairs." Lacking experience with other nations, but endowed with a firm Presbyterian sense of morality, Wilson pursued a course that his biographer, Arthur Link, has labelled "missionary diplomacy." After the war broke out in 1914, and especially after America's entry in 1917, Wilson viewed himself as a missionary bringing the blessings of American democracy and liberal capitalism to the rest of the world. As Winston Churchill tartly observed: "He saw himself for a prolonged period at the summit of the world, chastening the Allies, chastising the Germans and generally giving laws to mankind."

A desire to direct the peace negotiations had been a primary factor impelling Wilson to enter the war, and by 1917 the American president had placed himself at the head of an international movement for a liberal peace program. A group of peace advocates in England, composed of backbenchers from the ruling Liberal Party and members of the small Independent Labour Party, had organized the Union of Democratic Control shortly after the war broke out. They drew their peace proposals from an analysis of the war's causes. Since the system of alliances, intended to preserve a balance of power, had actually precipitated war, the liberal peace program called for an end to military alliances. Since the pre-war alliance system had encouraged a runaway arms race, the dissenting liberals advocated a drastic reduction of armaments. They further proposed an international council, or league of nations, to replace the discredited alliances and control the arms race. Finally, since the national aspirations of subject peoples had provided the immediate cause of war, liberals championed the self-determination of peoples in Europe and an end to colonialism throughout the world.

President Wilson adopted this program as his own. In a series of eloquent speeches, he transformed the war into a crusade to "make the world safe for democracy," a "war to end all war." In January 1917, even before U.S. entry into the struggle, Wilson exhorted the Allies to strive for a "peace without victory," i.e., not a vindictive, imposed settlement but a peace that would remove the causes of future wars. When the United States formally declared war in April 1917, the president kept his nation partially aloof, as an "associated power," not an ally. He knew that the Allies had signed secret treaties dividing up the spoils among themselves; he wanted to steer clear of these and preserve his freedom of action.

The Bolshevik Revolution at the end of 1917 forced Woodrow Wilson to elaborate his peace program more fully and disseminate it more widely. Lenin

145

and the Bolsheviks appealed over the heads of the "imperialist powers" to the war-weary masses of Europe, exhorting them to throw down their arms and make an immediate peace with no annexations and no indemnities. The Bolsheviks also published the secret treaties to which tsarist Russia had been a party, exposing the greedy and imperialist goals of the Allies. England, France, and Italy now needed President Wilson's moral leadership to counteract the Bolshevik propaganda and keep their troops fighting. Accordingly, on January 8, 1918, Wilson delivered his "Fourteen Points" address to a joint session of the American Congress, laying out his peace program in detail.

The Fourteen Points started with five general propositions, drawing on the liberal peace analysis: (1) "open covenants of peace, openly arrived at" — i.e., an end to secret treaties; (2) "absolute freedom of navigation upon the seas" — a specifically American grievance, reflecting traditional American concern for neutral shipping rights; (3) "the removal, so far as possible, of all economic barriers" — the dream of free trade, shared by liberals in both England and the United States; (4) "adequate guarantees . . . that national armaments will be reduced" — an end to the arms race; (5) "a free, open-minded, and absolutely impartial adjustment of all colonial claims" — an end to imperialism.

Points 6 through 13 became more specific, spelling out the territorial details for self-determination of peoples in Europe, such as the restoration of Belgium, the return of Alsace-Lorraine to France, the formation of an independent Poland, and satisfaction of the national claims of the subject peoples of Austria-Hungary. Finally, the fourteenth point, the most important of all in Wilson's opinion, demanded that "a general association of nations must be formed under specific covenants for the purpose of affording mutual guarantees of political independence and territorial integrity to great and small states alike."

Besides epitomizing the British peace program, Wilson's Fourteen Points also summed up traditional American foreign policy goals such as the dream of democracy for all peoples, the open door for trade, and the end of unjust European empires. They were the international counterpart of Wilson's New Freedom domestic policies, which attacked big business and political bosses. In the words of historian John Morton Blum, Wilson viewed the war "as a vast anti-trust action against Germany," to restore free enterprise and political democracy in the world.

Wilson was vying with Lenin to influence the hearts and minds of the world's people. Bolshevik socialism and American liberal democracy presented alternative paths away from the old diplomacy, imperialism, and the alliance system. In a sense, the ideological origins of the Cold War go back to 1918. In the short run, however, Wilson's influence overshadowed that of Lenin. Bolshevik Russia made a separate peace with Germany at the beginning of 1918 and was thereafter isolated from the main current of events, whereas the Fourteen Points provided the basis for the peace conference.

When Germany's military forces crumbled on the western front in October 1918, the kaiser instructed his relative, Prince Max of Baden, to take over the government and sue for peace. On October 5, Prince Max wrote President Wilson asking for an armistice based on the Fourteen Points. Though Germany was beaten, the Allied armies had not yet penetrated into German territory, so the vanquished nation hoped to salvage something by submitting to a "peace without victory." Wilson exchanged correspondence with the German government for several weeks, then the Allied and Associated Powers formally transmitted peace terms to the Germans on November 5. The armistice took effect at 11:00 A.M. on November 11.

The leaders of the victorious nations gathered in Paris from January through June 1919 to decide the fate of Germany and the new shape of the world. Twenty-seven nations, from all six inhabited continents, sent delegations to the first summit conference of the twentieth century. This number included all the countries (except Russia) that had borne the brunt of the fighting against Germany, as well as some smaller nations such as Liberia, Nicaragua, and Panama which had declared war near the end in order to be on the winning side. The five great powers (Great Britain, France, Italy, the United States, and Japan) each sent five delegates; most of the smaller nations were allotted just two. Prime Ministers David Lloyd George of England, Georges Clemenceau of France, Vittorio Orlando of Italy, and President Woodrow Wilson of the United States attended in person, whereas two career diplomats represented Japan.

The Paris Peace Conference delegates stayed far longer and worked more intensively than the "photo opportunity" summits later in the century. The leaders of the five major powers met in the Council of Ten (the prime minister or president and the foreign secretaries of each, except for Japan) for the first time on January 12, 1919, and this body functioned thereafter as an executive council for the whole conference. The American, French, and British delegations brought large numbers of experts who worked as the conference's bureaucratic staff. Finally, the delegates of all the nations participated in plenary sessions, ratifying the decisions taken by the ten. The first plenary session convened on January 18, but only five more were held during the six-month duration of the conference, and these consisted largely of talkfests and empty ceremonies.

President Woodrow Wilson received a triumphal reception when he toured the cities of Europe, but his Fourteen Points did not fare well in the Council of Ten. Before the conference even began, the English made it perfectly clear they would not abandon the right of naval blockade that had served them so well during the war, and therefore would not even discuss point 2, freedom of the seas. The principles of free trade and disarmament were deferred for later consideration. Though Germany was stripped of its colonies, no attempt was made to end colonialism by the Allied Powers. Indeed, the German colonies were parceled out, primarily to the white dominions and to Japan, as League of Nations "mandates," held in trust for the whole human community. This legal fiction fooled neither the colonists nor the colonized. Of all the Wilsonian Fourteen Points, only the founding of the League of Nations and the application of self-determination in Europe received serious attention at Paris.

Neither did the Allies pursue a "peace without victory." Germany had not surrendered unconditionally but had struck an armistice, a cease-fire, in order to negotiate peace under the terms of the Fourteen Points. Once the armistice went into effect, however, and the Allies realized how exhausted the German populace really was, they acted simply as victors, free to impose their own conditions. German representatives did not take part in the peace conference but were merely summoned at the end to sign the treaty. The Allies branded Kaiser Wilhelm a war criminal but could not bring him to trial since he took refuge in neutral Holland, whose government refused to extradite him. The victors imbedded a war guilt clause in the final treaty saddling Germany and its allies with sole responsibility for the loss and damage of the world war.

After four years of the most horrible warfare the world had yet witnessed, the ideals of Woodrow Wilson foundered on the rocks of vindictive public opinion in the victorious nations. Prime Minister Georges Clemenceau and the French delegation sought a peace settlement that would prevent Germany from ever again invading France. Italy had entered the war in 1915 only after the Allies promised it extensive new territory around the Adriatic Sea, and that country's delegates concerned themselves primarily with making good on those deals. Many of the English sympathized with Woodrow Wilson's peace program, for indeed the American President had largely stolen it from them. Yet Prime Minister Lloyd George had called a snap election immediately after the war, and the British electorate, while giving him a thumping majority, also clamored to "hang the kaiser" and "make the Germans pay the uttermost farthing." This infamous "khaki election," in which most victorious candidates had campaigned in uniform, constricted the British prime minister's freedom of maneuver.

The Paris Peace Conference also fell short of President Wilson's high expectations because of the sheer enormity of its tasks, to rearrange the whole world and prevent future wars. Harold Nicolson pointed out that "the trouble with the Paris Conference was not that there was too little information, but that there was too much." Highlighting this characteristically twentieth-century problem of information overload, Nicolson labeled his memoir of the conference "a study in fog." So, if World War I had been a war of exhaustion, the Paris Conference became a peace of confusion.

In another scene typical of this century, the confusion was compounded by five hundred newspaper reporters who descended on Paris, expecting that the first of Wilson's Fourteen Points, "open covenants of peace, openly arrived at," would be applied literally and they would be admitted to the deliberations of the peacemakers. The Council of Ten realized immediately, however, that nothing would be accomplished unless they met secretly and talked frankly. The reporters, therefore, were only admitted to the ceremonial plenary sessions. By the end of the conference, the Japanese and Italian delegates were frequently absent, so Lloyd George, Clemenceau, and Wilson dismissed their foreign ministers and staffs and hammered out the final decisions as a triumvirate, with only one secretary, Major Maurice Hankey of England, present.

The work of the conference fell into three stages. During the first month, from their initial meeting on January 12 until February 14, when President Wilson returned temporarily to Washington, the Council of Ten divided up the work among fifty-eight study commissions then wrangled interminably over general principles. During the second period, while Wilson was away, Prime Minister Lloyd George also returned to his home country, and the foreign ministers of the major powers drove the commissions to begin narrowing their options and preparing final recommendations. Finally, when Wilson and Lloyd George returned towards the end of March, the council whittled itself down to just five, then four, then only three, and then hammered out the final terms of peace.

On May 7, 1919, the Allies formally presented the treaty text to Germany. The eighty-year-old prime minister of France, Clemenceau, who vividly remembered the German occupation of Paris in 1871, stage-managed a triumphant ceremony at the Trianon Palace. With the delegates of twenty-seven nations arrayed like a jury, the triumvirate of Clemenceau, Lloyd George, and Wilson arraigned the Germans before the bar of humanity. The German delegates presented counterproposals on May 29, but nearly all of them were rejected. Minor functionaries from the defeated nation signed the treaty at the Versailles Palace on June 28, 1919.

The Treaty of Versailles stripped Germany of all her colonies, her navy, and most of her merchant ships and reduced her armed forces to only 100,000 men. Alsace-Lorraine was returned to France, a small strip of land was annexed by Belgium, some territory seized from Denmark in the nineteenth century was returned, and extensive lands in Poznania and West Prussia were ceded to the new state of Poland. This "Polish corridor" physically separated East Prussia, the historic homeland of Germany's ruling class, from the rest of Germany. The industrial areas of the Saar and Upper Silesia would later decide their ultimate disposition by plebiscites. The victors were unable to agree on a definite amount of reparations for war damages, but they set out in great detail the scope of the destruction that the Germans would have to pay for and added the cost of war pensions for soldiers and widows to the bill. They instituted a reparations commission to calculate the final totals, which finally presented Germany with a bill for 33 billion dollars. In sum, Germany lost about 13 percent of its territory, 10 percent of its population, and 15 percent of its economic capacity.

Winston Churchill wrote somewhat whimsically that Germany had been reduced to a state of utopia according to nineteenth-century British Liberal standards: a parliamentary form of government with universal suffrage, no colonies, no compulsory military service, and hardly any military at all. The Germans did not find this funny. They chafed at the burden of reparations, felt humiliated by the war guilt clause of the treaty, and believed that the Allies, and their own leaders, had betrayed them by holding out hopes of a "peace without victory" then imposing a "business as usual" treaty.

In fact the Versailles Treaty represented the worst of both worlds. The terms were not harsh enough to prevent Germany's revival, as Clemenceau and the French wished, but neither were they so benign as to remove all grievances. This "violence without energy" (in the words of an earlier American statesman, Alexander Hamilton) humiliated Germany but did not crush its ability to seek revenge. World War I and the Versailles Treaty did not end war for all time; they merely sowed the seeds for a new world war a generation later.

Woodrow Wilson knew he was abandoning many of his own principles in adhering to the Treaty of Versailles, but he placed great hope in the League of Nations as an instrument that would adjust and harmonize future conflicts. The British and American planners who fashioned a covenant for the League of Nations drew on four broad precedents from the nineteenth century. The first, the Concert of Europe, was the exclusive club of great powers which had met from time to time to settle European disputes. This served as a model for the executive council of the League, composed of "the principal Allied and Associated Powers" (Britain, France, the United States, Italy, and Japan) and four other member nations. The second series of precedents were the Hague Peace Conferences, convened in the capital of the Netherlands in 1899 and 1907, to discuss the laws of war. The 1907 Hague Conference included nearly all the independent nations of the world; so, following this precedent, the League Covenant established an Assembly open to all nations. The Hague Conferences had also discussed, and begun organizing, an international court of arbitration where nations could bring disputes for settlement. The League Covenant institutionalized this fledgling "world court" as the permanent Court of International Justice. Finally, a series of informal, non-governmental organizations, such as the Universal Postal Union and the International Telegraphic Union, organized in the nineteenth century for the practical tasks of coordinating international trade and communications, served as an example for the League Secretariat, the bureaucracy of the organization.

Though the basic structure of the League resembled that of a government, with an executive, a legislature, a judiciary, and a bureaucracy, it lacked the authority of a true world government. Each member state jealously guarded its individual sovereignty and retained the right to withdraw from the organization.

The League Covenant, which a plenary session of the conference approved on April 28, 1919, required member nations to bring all matters of dispute to the League and then to observe a three-months' "cooling off" period before resorting to war. Article 10 laid out the heart of the League's mandate, binding the members "to respect and preserve as against external aggression the territorial integrity and existing political independence of all members of the League." If taken literally, this article furnished a mutual guarantee against invasion for all League members. The covenant also contained a long labor and social welfare article (article 23) calling on member states to "secure and maintain fair and humane conditions of labour for men, women, and children" and to "undertake to secure just treatment of the native inhabitants of territories under their control." All in all, the founding document was a ringing manifesto for a new world order.

The League of Nations, however, did not live up to its promise. Some flaws were evident from the start. Since the organization was based on the "sovereign equality" of its members, most decisions required a unanimous vote, either in the council or the assembly, making controversial actions all but impossible. Furthermore, the Allies had rejected a Japanese proposal to write a racial equality clause into the founding charter. This rejection and the condescending language in which the League Covenant discussed the colonial mandates ("peoples not yet able to stand by themselves under the strenuous conditions of the modern world") indicated that in the new order not all nations were equal.

The fatal flaw in the League of Nations had nothing to do with its founding charter. It could not keep the peace of the world because several of the most important nations did not belong to it. The Allies rejected German pleas to let them join the League immediately after signing the peace treaty, and they refused to deal with Bolshevik Russia at all. Germany did not join the League until 1926, and then it withdrew shortly after Hitler took power in 1933. Russia was not admitted to membership until 1934. Amazingly, the United States, whose president had been the League's primary founder, refused to join. Wilson had insisted on inserting the Covenant of the League of Nations into the Versailles Peace Treaty so that the U.S. Senate would not be tempted to ratify just the peace treaty without the League Covenant. However, the Republican senators, led by Henry Cabot Lodge of Massachusetts, called Wilson's bluff by rejecting both the League and the treaty. (The United States later made a separate peace treaty with Germany.)

Wilson set out on a cross-country speaking tour in September 1919 to sell the League to the American people, but there was no national referendum to approve the treaty. The ratification battle would be decided in the Senate, not out on the streets, for U.S. senators enjoy six-year terms of office, and few would be up for reelection soon. Many crucial, undecided senators feared that article 10 of the League Covenant might automatically commit the U.S. military to action overseas. Out of sheer stubbornness Wilson refused to compromise with the Senate and ask for revisions in the treaty. Then on October 2, the president suffered a massive stroke and remained partially paralyzed for the rest of his term of office. On three separate occasions in late 1919 and early 1920, the U.S. Senate voted to reject the Treaty of Versailles and membership in the League of Nations. The League came into being at Geneva without its primary sponsor, the United States.

Besides the creation of the League, the other great achievement of the peace settlement after World War I was the rearranging of the map of Europe, the most massive shuffling of territories and boundaries since the Congress of Vienna one hundred years previously.[2] The dominant "ism" of nationalism, more precisely the principle of "national self-determination," guided the peacemakers as seven new countries — Finland, Estonia, Latvia, Lithuania, Poland, Czechoslovakia, and Yugoslavia — rose out of the wreckage of the German, Austro-Hungarian, and Russian empires.

The creation of these "successor states," rising like phoenixes from the conflagration in Eastern Europe, followed a standard script, a common scenario that helps make sense of the unfamiliar names and organizations in each country. First, the world war and the collapse of the multinational empires formed an essential precondition for the independence of these new nations. Second, the idealistic propaganda of Woodrow Wilson accelerated the process by making self-determination an explicit war aim of the Allies. However, the Poles, the Czechs, and the other subject nationalities largely liberated themselves in a complicated triangular process. Emigré leaders from Eastern Europe fled to the Allied capitals shortly after the war broke out and formed organizations to lobby for their nations' independence. These organizations received crucial financial aid and moral support from the masses of East European immigrants who had settled in the United States in preceding decades. The votes of these immigrants also figured in the calculations of President Wilson and increased his sympathy for the new nationalities. Finally, as the war wound down, leaders who remained in Eastern Europe with bands of armed men at their disposal, created faits accomplis that were ratified by the Paris Peace Conference.

Poland, the largest of the new nations, can serve as an example. Ignace Jan Paderewski, an internationally renowned pianist, fled to the United States in the fall of 1915 and exercised decisive influence on Woodrow Wilson through his foreign policy advisor, Colonel Edward House, whom Paderewski charmed and flattered. The charismatic Paderewski also rallied the Polish immigrant community,

2. The borders of Germany with its neighbors were delimited by the Treaty of Versailles, but most of the map of Europe was rearranged by the separate treaties imposed on the other defeated countries: Treaty of Saint Germain with Austria, September 10, 1919; Treaty of Neuilly with Bulgaria, November 27, 1919; and Treaty of Trianon with Hungary, June 4, 1920.

which numbered at least three million, raising millions of dollars and thousands of volunteers for a Polish army to fight on the Allied side in France.

Meanwhile, Józef Piłsudski, a colonel in the Austrian army, stayed behind in Poland when war broke out, organizing legions of volunteers who fought on the side of Austria-Hungary against Russia, but with independence as the ultimate goal. Piłsudski understood the value of "propaganda by the deed," which he called "agitating by means of war." In 1917 he abandoned the Austrian cause and was jailed for the remainder of the war. Upon his release from Magdeburg prison on November 10, 1918, he returned to Warsaw and assumed the title chief of state.

Ignace Paderewski joined Piłsudski as prime minister in a government of national unity. The Allies recognized Poland's independence and granted it a corridor of territory linking it with the Baltic Sea, but the Poles themselves had to fight the Bolsheviks and some of their other new neighbors to define the boundaries on the east and south. The new Polish state embraced large Ukrainian and German minorities, and the country remained poised uneasily between Germany and Russia.

Winston Churchill wrote in 1929: "It is by the territorial settlements in Europe that the treaties of 1919 and 1920 will finally be judged." Since then, many historians have judged these settlements critically, pointing out the numerous minorities remaining in the new states and the many frictions which led to another world war. Yet Woodrow Wilson and the other peacemakers followed the lines of ethnicity quite closely while erasing the old "Alsaces" and "Irelands" from the map. In particularly abrasive cases, such as Upper Silesia, the Allies supervised plebiscites and partitioned the territories according to the popular will.

The major problem with the successor states proved to be that they were both too big and too small. They were too big in one sense, for they tried to act like centralized national states, on the Western European model, while denying cultural autonomy and self-government to their ethnic minorities. In the long run, a federal structure might have proven more just and durable. Yet the new nations were also too small to stand alone against their larger neighbors Germany and Russia when those two states emerged strengthened and reconstructed. Only a federal superstate, or at least an economic union, in Eastern Europe would have been large enough to survive the rest of the century. This is not just a theoretical proposition endowed with hindsight. East European leaders, inspired by American sociologist Herbert A. Miller, and with some encouragement from the American government, moved tentatively in this direction just before the war ended. Thomas Masaryk, the Czech leader, became president of the Mid-European Union, organized in New York on September 16, 1918, to negotiate territorial disputes between the emerging nations and to work towards some form of federal union or economic alliance. Though the committee met a number of times before the end of the war, the armistice diverted all attention to more immediate

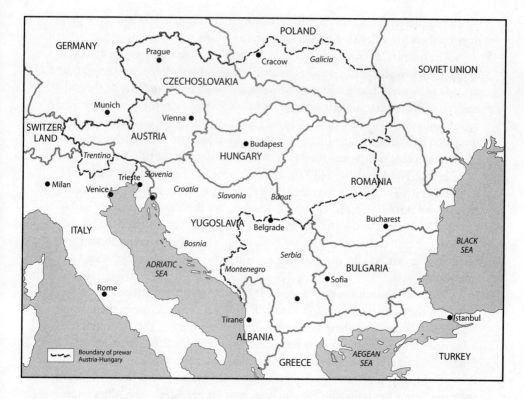

New States of Eastern Europe, 1920

problems and the Mid-European Union proved to be stillborn. Still, it provides a tantalizing glimpse of what might have been.

Woodrow Wilson has often been criticized as a naive or impractical visionary, yet his twin ideas of national self-determination and a league of nations have resonated throughout the twentieth century, an enduring legacy from World War I and the Paris Peace Conference. Combining small autonomous national communities into a larger economic or political entity — whether that takes the form of a Mid-European Union, a European Common Market, or a United Nations — still holds out the best prospect for world peace.

PART THREE

REVOLUTIONS ON THE RIM OF WAR

The first total war of the twentieth century tested the participant countries. France and England bent but did not break, and though Germany suffered military defeat and its imperial dynasty fell, the German economy and social structure survived. The United States and Japan, farther away from the hurricane winds of war, felt little strain. The multinational empires of Russia, Austria-Hungary, and the Ottoman Turks failed the test. Austria-Hungary, as we have already seen, crumbled into its constituent national pieces, and the Turks likewise lost their dominance over other peoples of the Middle East. The Turkish heartland in Asia Minor, however, underwent a nationalist revolution that ultimately strengthened it, and the Arabs and the Jews of the Middle East also experienced national revivals. At the other end of Europe, Irish nationalists challenged their English overlords in the moment of their world war victory and won independence.

Russia alone of the belligerent powers suffered a triple revolution — political, socioeconomic, and territorial. Russia's war-weary peasant armies quit fighting in 1917, and the tsar abdicated. Conditions of perfect liberty approaching the dreams of the anarchists prevailed for a time throughout Russia, but the working classes of the city, led by a ruthless, well-organized party of socialists, overthrew the provisional government and forced a social revolution. After a fierce three-year civil war, the Communist government consolidated its power on a slightly smaller territorial base than the tsarist empire.

The revolt in Russia threatened to spread throughout war-torn Europe. Local communists briefly seized power in parts of Germany and in Budapest, the capital of Hungary; and newly liberated nationalities throughout Central and Eastern Europe took up arms to resist them and to carve out broader borders for their newly born states. Cynics remarked that Woodrow Wilson came to the Paris Peace Conference with fourteen points and Europe greeted him with fourteen small wars, one for each point. Ultimately, nationalism in Eastern Europe checked the spread of communism for a generation.

The crisis of war and revolution finally ended with anarchism eclipsed and imperialism wounded. Nationalism and socialism (now renamed communism) emerged as the strongest ideological forces.

On the other side of the world, Mexico experienced a series of political and social revolutions that started before the world war, but became indirectly involved in it. After a generation of fighting, Mexican nationalism emerged greatly strengthened and Mexico's politicians institutionalized the results of their revolution in a one-party state far different from the Bolshevik dictatorship in Russia.

158

CHAPTER TEN

Revolutions in Red, White, and Black

Revolution in Russia had been long expected. The Romanov tsar was the last functioning autocrat in Europe, but the abortive revolution of 1905 had undermined his legitimacy. The small middle class of businessmen, professionals, and intellectuals desired a Western European parliamentary style of government; the factory workers demanded an eight-hour workday, better wages, and improved working conditions; the peasants wanted land of their own. Tsarist Russia produced a bumper crop of professional revolutionaries, driven underground by the secret police and schooled in the tactics of conspiracy and terror. Like the early Christians of the catacombs, the Russian revolutionaries divided and subdivided into numerous "heretical" sects and parties, each with its own leaders and ideology. For a long time, they seemed more dangerous to each other than to established authority.

Then in 1917, the third year of unsuccessful warfare against Germany, the terrible "isms" collided, with socialists denouncing the tsar's imperialist war and the resulting revolts unleashing new energies of nationalism and anarchism. Yet the Russian Revolution was not the inevitable result of historical forces. More than most historical events, it flowed from profoundly personal, individual actions. Tsar Nicholas II, his wife, Alexandra, their hemophiliac son Alexei, and the infamous monk Rasputin who advised the tsar and tsarina estranged all of Russian society, including their own imperial relatives. So central was Alexei's hemophilia to the tsar's erratic behavior, that Robert K. Massie, biographer of Nicholas and Alexandra, exaggerated only a little when he stated, "Imperial Russia was toppled by a tiny defect in the body of a little boy."

The revolution finally arrived when hungry women workers tired of standing in line to buy bread. Their hunger marches snowballed, individual soldiers refused to shoot them, and the tsar, left alone and friendless, abdicated. Then one man, Lenin, almost singlehandedly shaped and directed the revolution toward a communist dictatorship. In fact, two Russian revolutions took place in 1917: a spontaneous revolt in February that overthrew the tsar, then a tightly organized coup in October[1] that brought the Bolsheviks to power.

The February Revolution unfolded more on the anarchist model than the socialist, though avowed anarchists did not play a prominent role in it. Revolt exploded spontaneously when suffering and oppression were ignited by a spark, just as the anarchists had long predicted. Few of the professsional revolutionaries took part in the February Revolution. Lenin lived in Switzerland, and most of his followers were scattered in exile or imprisoned in Siberia. As late as January 1917, Lenin had remarked in a speech, "We of the older generation may not live to see the decisive battles of the Revolution." Yet, a month later the tsarist regime collapsed. There is no other word for it; it simply collapsed.

The alienation of the tsar from his people went back a long way. The assassination of Alexander II in 1881 revealed the deep contempt in which the intellectuals held their ruler; then the events of Bloody Sunday in 1905, when Nicholas II's police fired on unarmed protesters, decisively separated the tsar from the masses. Ever after, the tsar was known around the world, and deep within Russia, as "Nicholas the Bloody."

Less than six months before Bloody Sunday, Empress Alexandra had given birth to her only son, the Tsarevich Alexei, heir to the throne. What should have been a joyous event turned to deep gloom, for the boy suffered from hemophilia, frequent, uncontrolled bleeding that threatened his life. Alexei's malady, often called the "disease of royalty" since it was passed down in the female line from the descendants of Queen Victoria, was kept secret from the public. Secrecy led to fantastic rumors as the tsar became reclusive and protective of his family.

Toward the end of 1905 Alexandra's best friend, Anna Vyrubova, introduced the tsarina to a peasant monk, Gregory Rasputin, who showed a nearly hypnotic ability to calm the hemophiliac Alexei, thus slowing his hemorrhages. The tsar appointed Rasputin *lampadnik,* or lamplighter, charged with the task of keeping the flames lit in front of the many religious icons in the palace. The monk

---

1. Russia still followed the Old Style Julian calendar in 1917, which was thirteen days behind the Gregorian calendar. Therefore, the February Revolution actually occurred in March and the October Revolution in November. Since the dramatic events of 1917 in Russia have long been described by the months of their occurrence, it seems important to retain the Old Style dates in describing them. Therefore, in this chapter I have adopted the following dating policy: (1) all events of the two 1917 revolutions in Russia are given Old Style dates; (2) when Russians interacted with other countries during 1917, I have given both the Old Style and New Style dates, separated by a slash; and (3) all dates after February 10, 1918, when the Bolsheviks converted to the Gregorian calendar, are given in standard, New Style format.

drew Alexandra and her retainers closer into his circle of mystics, and rumors of holy orgies circulated around the court. Rasputin's twisted brand of Christianity taught that personal redemption was necessary for salvation, but one could not be redeemed until one had sinned profoundly. He thus satisfied his own enormous lusts, then offered his victims, and himself, redemption and salvation.

The tsar would not have tolerated or condoned Rasputin unless the monk had proven his ability to control Alexei's hemophilia. Though this mystical healing may seem incredible, Robert K. Massie's biography proves conclusively that such psychosomatic medical tactics could have worked. In any case, Nicholas and Alexandra believed that the monk was their son's only hope, and they became increasingly dependent upon him for both personal and political advice. Accordingly, Rasputin secured high positions in the government for his followers, a narrow circle of corrupt yes-men who isolated the tsar from the rest of the country.

The Russian war declaration of 1914 cannot be blamed on Rasputin, for he was seriously wounded in an assassination attempt just before war broke out and was still recovering when the battles began. Furthermore, he opposed the war, instinctively sensing that it could only lead to disaster for the peasants of Russia, who would bear the brunt of fighting. Nicholas II wanted to lead the troops personally but was talked out of this temporarily in 1914. A year later, however, the tsar assumed the role of commander in chief at the front and left Alexandra alone with Rasputin to tend the government in Petrograd. (The capital was renamed from the German *Petersburg* to the Russian *Petrograd* at the beginning of the war.) Nicholas's assumption of direct command coincided with severe defeats and retreats in 1915, further wounding his reputation.

In the tsar's absence, intrigues surrounding the court became so intense that people openly grumbled about the "German empress" (Alexandra had been born in Hesse-Darmstadt) and blamed her for military setbacks. In December 1916, a wealthy young nobleman assassinated Rasputin. The "Mad Monk" possessed such amazing vitality that poison, a number of gunshots, and repeated ax blows to his head didn't kill him; he drowned after his unconscious body was tossed through the ice of a river. After Rasputin's murder, other members of the nobility conspired with the tsar's uncles and cousins to depose Nicholas and Alexandra and send them into exile.

Before the nobility could act, however, the war-weary common people of Petrograd took matters into their own hands. A tsarist police report in January 1917 summed up the popular mood:

> The proletariat in the capital is on the verge of despair. It is believed that the slightest disturbance, on the smallest pretext, will lead to uncontrollable riots with thousands of victims. In fact, the condition of the masses, in spite of large raises in wages, is near the point of distress. . . . Even if wages are doubled, the

cost of living has trebled. The impossibility of obtaining goods, the loss of time queuing up in front of stores, the increasing mortality rate because of poor housing conditions, the cold and dampness resulting from lack of coal . . . all these conditions have created such a situation that the mass of industrial workers is ready to break out in the most savage of hunger riots.

Driven by hunger, the women of the capital took the lead. On Thursday, February 23, celebrated by Russian socialists as International Women's Day, female industrial workers and the wives of male workers marched throughout the capital demanding bread. The police looked on passively. The next day, the women, reinforced by numerous striking male workers, demonstrated again. On Saturday, February 25, the police opened fire, killing several demonstrators, and on Sunday the authorities called in the military, who killed or wounded over 150 demonstrators. Yet Sunday marked a turning point. Disgusted by their shoot-to-kill orders, many ordinary soldiers refused to obey and began fraternizing with the workers. This remarkable event reversed and avenged Bloody Sunday of 1905.

On Monday, February 27, 1917, regiment after regiment of troops defected, joining the demonstrators and distributing their weapons among them. At the end of the Five Days of February, workers and soldiers had seized the entire city of Petrograd, and the tsar's ministers had fled. When the mob approached the Tauride Palace, a magnificent edifice erected by Catherine the Great, where the Duma, or parliament, was meeting, the delegates panicked, uncertain whether the crowd would lynch them or hail them as leaders. Alexander Kerensky,[2] a silver-tongued lawyer associated with the Socialist Revolutionary Party, saved the situation by grandiosely welcoming the demonstrators. The Duma then appointed a provisional committee to restore order in the city, and the same day the various socialist factions joined together in the Soviet of Workers' and Soldiers' Deputies. Kerensky served as a key liaison between the two newly formed bodies.

Striking railway workers halted troops sent from the front to put down the revolt in the capital, so on March 2 Tsar Nicholas II abdicated in favor of his brother Michael. That same day the Duma committee declared itself a provisional government for Russia. Michael Romanov wanted no part of the unfolding tragedy, so he declined the throne his brother offered him and also abdicated on March 3. In just nine days, the centuries-old Romanov autocracy had collapsed. The February Revolution was a spontaneous conflagration, fueled by decades of

2. Russians, Ukrainians, and other Slavic people who belong to the Eastern Orthodox faith write their languages in the Cyrillic alphabet. Many different systems of transliteration into the Latin alphabet exist, producing variant spellings of Russian names in English. I have chosen to use the most familiar spellings, the ones closest to ordinary English usage, such as Alexander instead of Aleksandr and Kerensky instead of Kerenskii.

alienation between the ruler and the masses and three years of grinding war-weariness, then ignited by the spark of food riots and demonstrations in the capital. It was swift, sudden, and nearly bloodless.

The immediate result of the February Revolution was anarchy, in the literal sense of the word, no effective government. People throughout Russia followed the example of Petrograd and organized local *soviets* (elected governmental councils); if anyone objected to the decisions of these newly minted authorities, they simply seceded and formed another soviet. The day before the tsar abdicated, the Petrograd Soviet issued "Order No. 1," proclaiming democracy in the army. Soldiers were freed from petty signs of rank, such as the duty to salute officers even when off duty, and they soon formed committees to debate and question all military orders. Russia became, for a brief moment, what even the Bolshevik Lenin admitted was "the freest country in the world."

The provisional government and the soviet worked in uneasy tandem, eventually forming a coalition government in May when some moderate socialists accepted cabinet posts. The government, however, postponed most major decisions until a constituent assembly could be elected to write a new constitution for Russia. Groups and individuals from across the sprawling landmass of Eurasia sent thousands of telegrams, formal motions, and letters to Petrograd. Historian Marc Ferro, who has studied this first open outburst of public opinion in Russia, concluded that "suddenly the dream of liberty was turned into the reality of 130 million individual enthusiasts, who became so many specialized reformers, each with his plan for reforming the country." The reform plans of the workers were surprisingly modest at first. A group of women demanded the eight-hour day and a few fundamental gestures of human respect such as "boiling water for meals, installation of canteen and toilet facilities, improved ventilation in the factory," and politeness on the part of management toward workers.

Yet more urgent demands and actions soon followed. The peasants, who formed an overwhelming majority of the populace, demanded land, and by early summer they had begun seizing it themselves, expropriating farms from the large landowners. Soldiers resisted the harsh discipline of their officers, and tens of thousands voted with their feet by deserting the front and returning to their homes in the countryside. Factory committees of workers seized their workplaces and imposed the eight-hour day. Anarchists felt a great exhilaration as they raised their black flag amid the revolutionary chaos. An anarchist tract published on March 23, 1917, proclaimed, "The liberation of the workers can only be accomplished by a social revolution. . . . The Russian Revolution must have a free hand and it must decentralize itself. . . . All of Russia must be made into a network of sovereign revolutionary communes, which by occupying the land and factories will expropriate the bourgeoisie, abolishing private property."

One voice, however, rose above the clamor and pushed the revolution in a new direction. Vladimir Ilyich Ulanov led the Bolshevik faction of the Social Democratic Workers' Party. Born in 1870 in the Volga region of central Russia, the son of a provincial school inspector, Vladimir Ilyich became a revolutionary after his older brother Alexander was hanged for terrorism in 1887. Arrested and sentenced to three years' internal exile in 1897, he assumed his revolutionary nickname, Lenin, from the river Lena, though he was not actually sent that far into Siberia. After his release in 1900, he and his wife, Nadezhda Krupskaya, spent most of the following years exiled in Western Europe.

Lenin possessed a sharp but dogmatic intellect. The only bourgeois institution he respected was the public library; indeed, historian Adam Ulam has jocularly suggested that the Guild of Librarians should adopt Vladimir Ilyich Ulanov as their patron saint. For all his bookishness, however, Lenin was a ruthless fighter in the internecine battles of the socialist parties, always adopting the hardest line, rejecting collaboration with bourgeois politicians, and following a strict policy of the end justifying the means. He could never belong to any party that he didn't lead. When the Social Democratic Workers' Party split in 1903, he grabbed the name Bolshevik, which means "majority," for his faction.

Yet the Bolsheviks, despite their name, formed only a tiny splinter of the Russian left wing. When the February Revolution broke out, the two largest groups in the Petrograd Soviet were the peasant-based Socialist Revolutionaries and the Menshevik (minority) faction of the Social Democratic Workers' Party. The Bolsheviks of Petrograd played little role in the February Revolution, and with Lenin and most of their other leaders still absent in March, they acted timidly, collaborating with more moderate socialists in the Soviet. If anyone had suggested in March that the Bolsheviks would seize power seven months later, no one, even among the Bolsheviks, would have given the prediction any credence whatsoever.

All this changed when Lenin returned to Russia on April 3. The German military, still at war with Russia in 1917, let Lenin and his companions cross Germany in a "sealed train" — that is, the train was declared extraterritorial and was not permitted to stop. The Germans injected Lenin like a virus into the Russian body politic, accurately guessing that he would stir up trouble and reduce the threat of a renewed offensive by Russian troops. Shortly after arriving at the Finland Station in Petrograd, Lenin published his April Theses, rejecting all cooperation with the provisional government, calling for a swift end to the war, advocating the seizure of landed estates and their distribution to the peasants, and finally, urging the Bolsheviks to break with other socialists and change their name to Communists.

Lenin's theses were amazingly uncompromising, and they experienced strong opposition before the Bolshevik Party conference adopted them on April 27. Lenin got his way through sheer force of willpower, like a military general who makes his men more afraid of kindling his wrath than of facing the enemy's bullets.

Yet despite their controversial nature, the April Theses embodied a penetrating analysis of the revolutionary situation. By denouncing the provisional government and avoiding the other socialist parties, Lenin preserved his freedom of maneuver and enjoyed the luxury of criticizing everybody. He realized that, with the fall of tsarism, *all* authority remained suspect in Russia. Therefore, he kept his party free of any cooperation with the new rulers. His policy of land confiscation made a direct appeal to the peasant majority of Russia, and his call for peace capitalized on the war-weariness that had started the revolution in the first place. All his positions could be summarized easily in two popular slogans: "Peace, Bread, Land," and "All Power to the Soviets." Lenin seemed to be the only leader in Russia who knew what he wanted.

He did not remain alone however. Lev Davidovich Bronstein (with the revolutionary nickname of Trotsky) arrived in Petrograd on May 4 and soon endorsed Lenin's policy of noncooperation with the revolutionary regime. A member of a small socialist faction, Trotsky had earned fame as president of the short-lived St. Petersburg Soviet during the Revolution of 1905. Lenin recognized that Trotsky brought oratorical and organizational abilities to the hardline resistance that he himself lacked, so he collaborated closely with him, though Trotsky did not formally join the Bolshevik Party until later in the year.

In the Bolshevik slogan "Peace, Bread, Land," peace proved most important. As long as the war continued, so too would war-weariness, food shortages, desertions, strikes, and riots. Lenin did not initially advocate unilateral withdrawal from the war, but rather a concerted push for a general peace with "no annexations and no indemnities." This struck such a popular nerve that the provisional government adopted the "no annexations" policy in May. Yet the government also assured the nervous Allies, France and Great Britain, that they would not unilaterally quit the war. Alexander Kerensky, who had become war minister, made a grand tour of the front lines and used his prodigious oratorical ability to rally the soldiers. On June 18/July 1 he ordered an offensive on the Austrian front in Galicia. After a few days of forward momentum, the offensive stalled, and the Russian front simply melted away as the Germans counterattacked and the peasant soldiers deserted. This ill-fated attempt to revive the Russian war effort marked the beginning of the end for the provisional government.

In the wake of the failed offensive, intense unrest broke out in Petrograd. From July 3 to 5 mobs of workers, soldiers, and sailors, with anarchists and rank-and-file Bolsheviks prominent among them, raged around the capital. The Bolshevik leaders did not instigate this uprising, but they joined it once it had broken out and tried to seize power. They failed. The provisional government and the Soviet acted in unison, calling in loyal troops to suppress the insurrection. After the July Days, the Bolshevik Party was temporarily discredited, and some of its leaders were arrested while the rest went into hiding. Lenin again fled into exile, but this time to nearby Finland, which was ruled by Russia but enjoyed substantial freedom and autonomy.

The tottering provisional regime survived another attack in August, when General Lar Kornilov, appointed commander in chief of the Russian army by Kerensky, marched on the capital. Kerensky (who by this time had been named prime minister) thought he was using Kornilov to smash the Bolsheviks, but the general intended to eliminate the government. At the last moment, Kerensky discovered the plot and armed the workers for the defense of the capital. Despite its amateurish nature, the attempted Kornilov coup proved significant, for it convinced everyone in the provisional government that the real threat to their regime came from the right, from the proverbial "man on horseback" that had haunted revolutionaries ever since Napoleon. So when the Bolsheviks staged their final coup in October, it surprised the government.

In fact, it surprised nearly everyone, including most Bolsheviks who felt that time was on their side and they should simply wait for Kerensky's regime to collapse as the tsar's had. Lenin, however, urged an armed uprising. He had learned from the Revolution of 1905 that there comes a moment in every revolutionary situation when one must strike, before it is too late. If revolutionaries hesitate then, the moment may pass and not come again for another generation. Lenin returned to Petrograd in disguise in early October and badgered, harangued, and pushed his fellow Bolsheviks to revolt. Yet he himself remained in hiding, and Trotsky took the lead in organizing the uprising. In the words of historian Theodore Von Laue, "If Lenin may be called the Grand Strategist of Revolution, Trotsky in these weeks was the Grand Stage Manager."

The workers of Petrograd had remained armed after the Kornilov affair, ready to resist any further right-wing coup, and the Petrograd Soviet, by this time dominated by Bolsheviks, formed the Military Revolutionary Committee. Still, the Soviet and most of the workers were arming for *defense* of the revolution against counterrevolution. Only Lenin kept pushing for an offensive rising.

The Kerensky government inadvertently triggered the insurrection against itself. John Reed, the dashing young American journalist who witnessed the October Revolution and wrote the classic account *Ten Days That Shook the World*, summed up Kerensky's predicament: "In the relations of a weak government and a rebellious people there comes a time when every act of the authorities exasperates the masses, and every refusal to act excites their contempt." Damned if they failed to act, doomed if they chose to act. In the early morning hours of October 24, Kerensky sent troops to close the Bolshevik newspaper offices. This goaded the Bolsheviks into action.

In the name of the Military Revolutionary Committee, Trotsky ordered workers, soldiers, and sailors to seize the key points of the city — the bridges, the telegraph office, the post office. Lenin arrived at Bolshevik headquarters in the Smolny Institute (formerly an elite girls' school) about midnight and made it clear that the Military Revolutionary Committee was not just defending against counterrevolution but taking over. Kerensky fled Petrograd the next day, October 25, and the rest of the provisional government, holed up in the tsar's old Winter Palace, surrendered at about 2 A.M. the following morning.

The October Revolution took place before most residents of Petrograd even knew it had started. Stores, schools, and theaters remained open throughout. Anarchy had made this revolution possible. Central authority was so weak and the situation so confused that, as Adam Ulam has pointed out, any determined band of people could have seized power. In the days and years that followed, however, the Bolsheviks proved they were not just any band of people, but rather were ruthless, pragmatic, and opportunistic enough to defend and consolidate their revolution.

The Second All-Russian Congress of Soviets of Workers' and Soldiers' Deputies, the most representative body in revolutionary Russia, opened the evening after the Bolshevik coup. On October 26 it officially dissolved the provisional government and issued three proclamations proposing immediate peace negotiations among all belligerents in the world war, nationalizing all farmland for distribution among the peasants, and setting up the Council of People's Commissars to serve as a new provisional government. The Bolsheviks dominated the Congress of Soviets and the Council of Commissars; and when the long-planned Constituent Assembly assembled in the Tauride Palace on January 18, 1918, Bolshevik Red Guards surrounded the palace. The delegates talked long into the night, but when they adjourned the Guards padlocked the building and declared the assembly dissolved after only one day. The Bolsheviks proclaimed their own constitution later in the year.

On March 8, 1918 (New Style), the Bolshevik Party congress officially changed its name from the Russian Social Democratic Workers' Party to the Russian Communist Party, and two days later, on March 10, it moved the seat of government from Petrograd to Moscow, deeper in the interior of Russia. Then the party moved to crack down on the anarchists, who had enthusiastically joined in overthrowing Kerensky's government in October but now posed a threat to one-party rule. Though always acting in the name of the workers, Lenin and the Communists believed that they, the revolutionary elite, the intelligentsia, should guide the workers into the right path. What they called the "dictatorship of the proletariat" was really a dictatorship of the party leadership. Theodore Von Laue has concluded that "by his own theory, Lenin was cast into the role of a counter tsar."

The freewheeling anarchists fared no better under Lenin than they had under Nicholas the Bloody. On April 11 the Soviet secret police, the Cheka, mounted midnight raids on twenty-six anarchist cells in Moscow, killing or wounding forty individuals and arresting more than five hundred. The black flag of anarchy rarely flew over Moscow or Petrograd after this.

The most important measure that ensured the survival of the new Communist regime, however, was the treaty of Brest-Litovsk, whereby Russia abandoned its allies and formally made peace with Germany. In the revolutionary chaos of 1917-18, the Russian masses grabbed bread and land for themselves. Groups of peasants expropriated the landowners' estates, and armed bands of workers ranged out into the countryside to confiscate grain for the starving masses of the cities. Yet only a government could make terms with Germany and end the war.

The German military occupied most of western Russia, but throughout 1917, as this territory dissolved in chaos and hence posed a diminished threat, large numbers of German troops were transferred to the western front in France. The Germans were confident that they could advance deeply into Russia at any time if necessary, sweeping the Bolsheviks from power and ending the Communist experiment in Russia.

Aware of this potential, Lenin overcame opposition within the party and sought a separate peace with Germany, however humiliating it might prove. Talks began at Brest-Litovsk, in German-occupied Russia, in December 1917; but Trotsky, the Commissar for Foreign Relations in the Communist government, stalled the negotiations with his propaganda and oratory. Not so convinced as Lenin that a separate peace was necessary, he tried to follow a policy of "No War, No Peace." This simply meant that the Russians would cease fighting but they would not sign a treaty.

The Germans rejected this nonsense and mounted a major attack on February 18, driving deeper into Russia. Lenin exploded at Trotsky: "It is a question of signing the terms now or of signing the death sentence of the Soviet Government three weeks later." On March 3, 1918, Trotsky returned to Brest-Litovsk and signed the terms dictated by the Germans. It was a harsh treaty in which Russia ceded about one-third of its land and population. Yet Lenin's decision to swallow the humiliation of peace at any price saved his revolutionary government.

Though Brest-Litovsk freed the Communists from the German threat, they still faced widespread internal opposition that flared into full-scale civil war in 1918 and raged for three more years. Russia's former allies, the British, French, Americans, and Japanese, and their former enemies, Czech soldiers from the Habsburg monarchy and an army from the newly revived nation of Poland, also intervened in the civil war.

General Kornilov and four other generals had been imprisoned to await trial for their attempted coup in August, but they escaped after the October Revolution and made their way in disguise to the Don River in the south of Russia.

Raising the standard of counterrevolution, the Whites (as they were called) conspired with the Don Cossacks, a privileged band of cavalry that had traditionally supported the monarchy. Bolshevik forces, however, drove the disorganized plotters further south to the Kuban River area east of the Black Sea in the deadly Ice March of February 1918, temporarily checking this threat.

Far to the north, above the Arctic Circle, a band of British marines landed at Murmansk to guard the vast horde of military stores that had accumulated there during the war. Later in the year, the Allies reinforced this frozen beachhead and mounted an offensive in league with White troops. At the other end of Russia, Japanese and British troops seized the terminus of the Trans-Siberian Railway at Vladivostok. Meanwhile, the Czech Legion, about 35,000 soldiers who had fought in the Austrian army, been captured by the Russians, then liberated by the revolution, were proceeding along the Trans-Siberian in the summer of 1918, trying to reach Vladivostok for transfer to the western front. The Allies, however, encouraged them to dally along the way and link up with White forces commanded by a former tsarist admiral, Alexander Kolchak. Inadvertently, the counterrevolutionary activities of the Czech Legion led to the death of the former tsar and his family.

After Nicholas II's abdication, the provisional government had tried to convince the British to grant him and his family asylum, but the reputation of Nicholas the Bloody and his German empress was so unsavory among the trade union workers and the Labour Party politicians of Britain that this proved impossible. During the July Days of 1917, when the Bolsheviks first tried to seize power, Kerensky had transferred the Romanov captives to a secure area in western Siberia for their own protection. There they stayed under house arrest for a year as the October Revolution unfolded and the civil war began. In July 1918, as the Czechs advanced toward the mining city of Ekaterinburg in the Ural Mountains, where Nicholas and his family were held, the local city soviet ordered an evacuation. Before they left, however, the Communists executed the Romanovs on the night of July 16-17, 1918.

The Czechs finally moved eastward where the Allies had landed a force of about 100,000 soldiers from England, France, the United States, Japan, Poland, China, Serbia, Italy, and Canada. The Japanese greatly outnumbered the other Allied contingents, with the Americans running a distant second. Twenty years previously, a similar international force had fought its way to Peking and lifted the siege of the legations in the Chinese capital. But Moscow was over 6,000 miles distant from Vladivostok, and the Allies lacked the unity of purpose they had possessed when trying to rescue their own citizens in China. The Czechs mainly wanted to get out of Russia, the Japanese wanted to carve out a sphere of influence on the mainland of Asia, and the Americans spent most of their time watching the Japanese. None of the Allied commanders planned to march on Moscow.

Admiral Kolchak's White forces continued fighting for another year in Siberia, with sporadic aid from the Allies, but they were finally defeated. The Czechs handed Kolchak over to a provisional socialist government in Irkutsk that soon abdicated in favor of the Communists, who executed him on February 7, 1920.

The White forces in the south of Russia mounted their own major offensive under command of General Anton Denikin in the summer of 1919. With World War I finally over in the West, Britain and France both landed troops and supplies in the Black Sea ports to support the Whites. Denikin's soldiers then swept up from the Don and Kuban valleys through Ukraine and threatened Moscow itself. At the same time, another White force under command of General Nicholas Yudenich threatened Petrograd from the west. However, both White commanders overextended themselves and suffered defeats in the fall of 1919. The Western Allies, overcome by their own war-weariness, then withdrew their support.

Another year of fighting began in April 1920, when the Polish army commanded by Marshal Piłsudski pushed eastward into territories long ago part of Poland but largely inhabited by Ukrainians, Belorussians, Russians, and Jews. After initial successes, the Poles were pushed back almost to the gates of Warsaw, where a spectacular battle, dubbed the "Miracle of the Vistula," blunted the Reds' advance.

A final push from the south by General Peter Wrangel in 1920 fell short, and the Red Army finally swept the Whites down into the Crimean Peninsula. Like the British and Australians at Gallipoli, the most successful operation of the Whites was their evacuation. In the middle of November 1920 General Wrangel transported about 150,000 officers, soldiers, and other refugees from the Crimea to Constantinople. For the rest of the decade, Dr. Fridtjof Nansen, the Norwegian Arctic explorer, worked tirelessly for the League of Nations to resettle the White Russians, even issuing them special "international passports" when necessary.

In the course of the civil war the Red Army, founded by the Communists in March 1918, grew from a ragtag bunch of workers, sailors, and criminals into a disciplined mobile force of over 5 million men. War Commissar Trotsky recruited the military expertise of former tsarist officers to train his men. As the ranks swelled, so too did the number of officers, about 70 percent of whom had formerly fought for the tsar. In order to ensure their loyalty, Trotsky paired each officer with a Communist commissar.

Though at the start of the civil war the Communists controlled only Moscow, Petrograd, and the central heartland of Russia, they skillfully used the railways that emanated from the capital to blunt the uncoordinated attacks of the Whites. Trotsky and the other commanders sped across the countryside in armored trains with red flags flying. Much more than the fragile tanks of the western front, these armored trains fought like land-bound battleships. When they had secured an area, they were replaced by propaganda trains emblazoned with slogans and carrying books, pamphlets, and films to indoctrinate the populace.

The Whites, for their part, made enormous territorial advances, but they never consolidated their gains or struck the Bolsheviks a death blow. The Whites could not rally resistance to the Reds because they represented the discredited old regime, and the peasant majority of Russia did not wish to return their former masters to power. The Communists later proved destructive to the interests of the peasants; but for the time being, the peasants resisted the devils they knew, the White soldiers and officials.

The Whites also alienated their potentially greatest source of support, the non-Russian, subject nationalities. Russians formed a little more than half the population of the former Russian Empire, with the other half comprising dozens of nationalities. Belorussians and Ukrainians lived along the western and southern borders of the realm, and numerous small nationalities such as Armenians, Georgians, and Azerbaijanis inhabited the mountain region of the Caucasus, between the Black and Caspian Seas. Nearly 14 million Turkic peoples, more Turks than could be found in the Ottoman Empire, roamed along the Central Asian frontier with China. The Whites held no appeal for these diverse nations. General Denikin and the other White commanders still believed in "Great Russia, One and Indivisible" so they did not encourage separatist tendencies among the subject nationalities. This proved fatal to their cause.

The Communists, though intending to centralize authority, officially championed the right of national self-determination. Lenin conveniently advocated self-determination as a general democratic right, like the right to divorce, but that didn't mean he actually favored either divorce or national separatism. Before this became clear, however, he and the Communists skillfully propagandized among the subject nations. The Cheka, or secret police, under Felix Dzerzhinsky, harnessed the power of national hatred to their terrible work. Non-Russians, particularly Latvians, outnumbered Russians in the highest ranks of the Cheka, and Dzerzhinsky assigned a disproportionate number of Jewish agents to work in the anti-Semitic Ukraine. The Communists thus coopted some of the subject nationalities and used divide-and-conquer tactics against others.

In the end, the White counterrevolution and the half-hearted foreign intervention were classic cases of "violence without energy." Too uncoordinated to topple the revolutionary government in Moscow, they proved sufficiently disruptive to spread misery among the populace, which led to grudging support for the Communists, thus legitimizing their regime.

In the maelstrom of the civil war, however, an alternate form of revolutionary society made a fleeting appearance on the Ukrainian steppes; and for a few brief years the Black forces of anarchism held off both Reds and Whites. The course of the revolution and civil war in Ukraine provides a complicated but instructive case study of the terrible "isms" — nationalism, socialism, and anarchism — locked in mortal combat under the most extreme circumstances.

Ukraine is an ill-defined territory that sprawls from the Dniester River to the Don River along the north shore of the Black Sea. The fertile but largely treeless Ukrainian prairies, or steppes, had been separated from Russia proper by centuries of invasion, first by Mongols then by the Poles. Throughout its history, this territory harbored numerous fugitives from Russia, either runaway serfs, political prisoners, or simply criminals. These renegades formed themselves into self-governing companies of Cossacks (a Turkish word meaning freebooter) to defend their lands and rights. Catherine the Great finally annexed the greater part of Ukraine in the late eighteenth century and reduced much of the population to serfdom. She coopted the Cossacks, however, by offering privileges in return for military service, and these proud horsemen became a strong prop holding up the autocracy. Their free-wheeling traditions, however, lived on in memory and predisposed the Ukrainian peasants toward anarchism.

Ukraine became the breadbasket of the Russian Empire, and it also developed important coal-mining and iron-making industries in the Donets Basin (or Donbas). Furthermore, the major rail lines connecting Moscow with the Black Sea and the Caucasus ran through the region. Inevitably, therefore, this territory became a major arena of combat in the civil war; as historian Bruce Lincoln has pointed out, "No region of the Russian Empire witnessed more violence, more destruction, and more unvarnished cruelty."

Shortly after the February Revolution of 1917, a group of Ukrainian intellectuals and moderate socialists in Kiev, the traditional capital of Ukraine, organized the Ukrainian Central Rada (council). These Nationalists enjoyed support from the small class of educated professionals and the wealthier landowning peasants, particularly in Kiev itself and on the right bank (or western shore) of the Dnieper River, which bisects the territory. The population of the other major Ukrainian cities, however, was largely Russian or Jewish, and these workers generally supported the Bolsheviks. Ukrainian Nationalists and Russian Bolsheviks worked uneasily together to overthrow the Provisional Government in October, but once this was accomplished, they turned on each other.

The Rada proclaimed Ukrainian independence on January 9, 1918, but almost immediately lost Kiev to the Red Army. The desperate Nationalists, therefore, made a separate peace with the Germans, who installed a puppet regime in Ukraine under the military leader, Hetman Paul Skoropadski. After the Germans withdrew at the end of 1918, civil war broke out in earnest, and Kiev was quickly won and lost by Nationalists, Reds, and Whites. Altogether, nine different governments briefly set up shop in the Ukrainian capital between 1917 and 1920. The rest of the country was left in a condition of total anarchy, virtually a state of nature.

In this power vacuum, a guerrilla leader, Nestor Makhno, briefly applied the principles of anarchism to a peasant society.

Nestor Ivanovych Makhno was born in 1889, the son of a poor peasant, in the market town of Guliai Pole, on the left bank (eastern shore) of the Dnieper in southern Ukraine. He joined an anarchist group in 1905 and was arrested for treason three years later. Sentenced to death in 1910, he escaped execution since he had been under age twenty-one when arrested (just like the young Bosnian, Gavrilo Princip, who assassinated the Austrian archduke). Makhno served seven years in a Moscow prison, where he fell under the influence of a well-educated anarchist, Peter Arshinov.

Liberated on March 2, 1917, Makhno returned to Guliai Pole and immediately organized a peasant union. During the heady days of freedom after the February Revolution, he led a Robin Hood existence, seizing large estates and distributing the land among the peasants. While most peasants were simply land-hungry, a number of anarchists among them founded voluntary self-governing communes, one of which Makhno joined. When Austrian troops supporting the puppet regime took over his town, Makhno fled to Moscow, but found the anarchists there under attack by the Bolsheviks and more inclined to talk than action. So he returned to Ukraine in July 1918 and began a partisan, guerrilla war against the occupiers. A brilliant victory over a much larger Austrian force in October 1918 established his reputation as a military tactician and earned him the name Batko, or father to his people.

Throughout 1919, Makhno maneuvered between the contending forces of Ukrainian Nationalists, Communists, and Whites. He generally remained aloof from the Nationalists, who operated largely on the right bank of the Dnieper, away from his territory, but he fought the Whites implacably. Therefore, according to the principle that the enemy of my enemy is my friend, he often allied with the Communists, though he did not trust them. When General Denikin mounted his major offensive toward Moscow, Makhno's partisans checked him with a counterattack at the town of Perehonivka on September 26, 1919. This setback enabled the Red Army to regroup and force Denikin to retreat.

During the autumn months after Denikin's defeat, Makhno reached the height of his power, commanding about 40,000 troops. He employed guerrilla hit-and-run tactics, aided by his innovative use of Ukrainian *tachanky,* carriages on sprung wheels with a machine gun mounted at the back. Makhno used these carriages the way later armies employed armored personnel carriers, to carry infantry swiftly over long distances, as much as fifty miles in a single day. The lead *tachanka* flew the black flag of anarchy, emblazoned with the slogan "Liberty or Death" in silver letters.

The outlines of an anarchist society emerged in southern Ukraine during 1919. A series of peasant congresses decreed the equal distribution of all land.

173

Anyone who would actually till the soil, including former landlords, was allotted as much land as he and his family could cultivate without hired help. Political power would be wielded by free soviets, elected by each local commune or town and federated together at the regional level. Makhno attempted to apply anarchist principles to the cities that he briefly occupied in 1919, but the workers were cool to his ideas and his movement remained confined to the countryside, where Cossack traditions and land hunger predisposed the peasants to follow him.

After a final alliance between Batko Makhno and the Red Army defeated General Wrangel in November 1920, the Communists turned decisively against the anarchist leader. Weakened by an epidemic of typhus, an infectious disease spread by lice, Makhno and his followers fled the Red Army and finally escaped across the border to Romania on August 28, 1921. He lived out his life as an unhappy exile in Paris, meagerly supported by anarchists around the world.

The total disruption of society caused by world war, revolution, and civil war permitted the limited application of anarchist ideas to Ukrainian peasant society in 1919. Yet these very conditions doomed the experiment to failure, for Makhno never enjoyed a long enough period of peace to develop the anarchist communes. After Makhno's flight, the Communists exterminated all remaining manifestations of anarchism and completed their conquest of Ukraine and other subject nations.

Having shown utter ruthlessness during the civil war, the Bolsheviks compromised and offered concessions after the conflict's conclusion. In March 1921 Lenin decreed his New Economic Policy that postponed the collectivization of agriculture and allowed peasants to keep their land and market surplus crops. This introduced capitalist, free-market agriculture into the Communist countryside, ending the famines that had prevailed during the civil war.

Then the regime made formal concessions to the principle of nationalism by creating the Union of Soviet Socialist Republics, in theory a federal state. Joseph Stalin, who served as commissar of nationalities and was rapidly rising in influence as Lenin's health failed, worked out the details of federalization at the end of 1922. A union of four republics, Russia, Belorussia, Ukraine, and the Transcaucasian Federation, was proclaimed in December 1922. Later the Transcaucasian group divided into three separate republics, and five more republics were added in Central Asia. On January 31, 1924, the Congress of Soviets formally ratified the constitution of the USSR.

Federalism was largely a sham in the Soviet Union. The Communist Party retained ultimate power in the government, and it remained highly centralized and Russian dominated. In 1922, over 70 percent of the party's members were of Russian nationality. However, the USSR did permit far more use of Ukrainian and other non-Russian languages in its constituent republics than the tsarist government ever had, and the national-territorial principle was symbolically enshrined in the constitution. Since language and territory form key ingredients of nationalism, the national consciousness of Ukrainians and others survived during the long rule of the Communists. Unlike the anarchists, who were totally crushed in Russia, nationalists emerged again at the end of the century when Soviet rule collapsed.

Lenin suffered a series of strokes in 1923 and finally died on January 24, 1924, just days before the proclamation of the Soviet constitution; but he had lived long enough to see his revolution consolidated. His combination of utter ruthlessness with tactical flexibility had enabled the Communist regime to survive.

CHAPTER ELEVEN

Gray Wolf on the Prowl

In Turkish legend, a gray steppe wolf led the first Turks out of Central Asia when the rains failed in their Eden-like home. Fanning out like the rays of the sun, Turkish warriors then brought civilization to China, the Middle East, and Europe.

This bit of nationalist mythology would have been incomprehensible to the leaders and people of the Turkish Ottoman Empire for most of its six-hundred-year history. The Turks, like many nomadic warriors who conquer a more sedentary population, adopted the religion and customs of the subject people, in this case the Arabic culture of Islam. From the first incursion of Turks into the Middle East about a thousand years ago, through the founding of the Ottoman dynasty in the early 1300s, and right up to the present century, the Ottomans wrote their Turkish language in the Arabic script and worshiped Allah according to the teachings of the Prophet Muhammad. Little of the pre-Islamic past, such as the gray wolf legend, survived, until nationalist scholars began recovering and inventing it in the late nineteenth and early twentieth centuries. Indeed, the very word "Turk" generally carried a negative connotation, meaning something like peasant, yokel, or country bumpkin. The cultured classes called themselves *Osmanli*, people loyal to the dynasty, not Turks.

The Ottomans, like the Habsburgs of Austria-Hungary, ruled a multi-national empire. At its greatest extent in the seventeenth century, their domain stretched from Algeria in the west, across North Africa to Egypt, Arabia, and the Persian Gulf, through the Middle East and the Anatolian Peninsula into Europe, where it encompassed all of the Balkans. Even after Greece and Serbia won their independence in the nineteenth century, the Ottoman Empire still counted numerous Serbs, Greeks, Romanians, Bulgarians, Jews, Armenians, Kurds, and Arabs among its 24 million subjects.

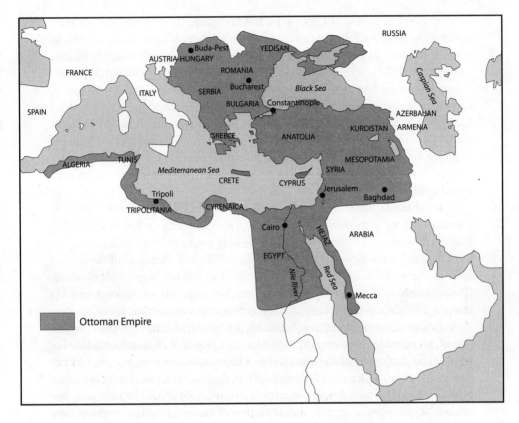

The Ottoman Empire at the Time of Its Greatest Extent c. 1700

The ruling House of Osman did not recognize these subjects as separate nations, but dealt with them according to their religion. Muslim Arabs and Turks stood at the head of the social structure, for the empire was a thoroughly Islamic country. In theory, all Muslims waged holy war against nonbelievers (polytheists), but they had always made exceptions for People of the Book, that is, Christians and Jews, who possessed part of the truth revealed more fully to Muhammad. They viewed them, therefore, as forerunners, much as "New Testament" Christians deemed "Old Testament" Jews their precursors. The Ottomans continued and elaborated this system of tolerance, offering Christians and Jews a choice between conversion or a circumscribed, second-class position as protected minorities. Most chose the latter.

Ottoman Muslims afforded both Christians and Jews better treatment than Jews experienced in medieval Europe. The various minority groups — Greek Orthodox, Armenian Christian, and Jewish — were organized into *millets,* or communities, under the supervision of their religious leaders. Members of the subject *millets* were not liable for conscription into the army but paid a special tax instead. Christians and Jews were second-class citizens, to be sure, but while the empire remained strong, they enjoyed a reasonably secure and autonomous status.

By the nineteenth century, however, the Ottoman Empire was no longer strong. As nomadic warriors, the Turks had swept out of Asia and invaded Europe, threatening the Habsburg capital of Vienna as late as 1683; but once its expansion ended, the Ottoman Empire began to decline, by its own standards, as a military power. Bernard Lewis, the premier historian of the Middle East, has concluded: "The Ottoman armies, once the terror of Europe, ceased to frighten anyone but their own sovereigns and their own civil populations. . . ." At the same time, the empire's rulers remained blithely unconcerned with any external threats. Profoundly convinced of Islam's superiority, the Ottoman sultans resembled the Chinese emperors in their self-satisfied isolation.

The occupation of Egypt by Napoleon in 1798 shook the Ottomans out of their complacency. Just as the British would take Peking with only a few thousand soldiers during the Opium Wars, fewer than thirty thousand French troops overran Egypt. When they were defeated three years later, it was the English who expelled them, not the Ottomans. For the next century, therefore, the Ottoman rulers embarked upon a series of reforms similar to the "self-strengthening" movement in China, adopting European innovations in military training and equipment and modernizing the transportation and communications of the empire. The sultan opened permanent embassies in European capitals in 1834, and thereafter the most vigorous reform leaders served their apprenticeships in these missions, studying European ideas and practices firsthand.

Yet the Ottoman rulers did not adopt a European scheme of government; instead they used technical innovations to bolster and increase the autocratic power of the sultan. Turkish liberals induced Sultan Abdulhamid II to introduce a European-style constitution in 1876, but he dismissed the first parliament after less than a year and suspended the constitution. Abdulhamid then ruled as an autocrat for the next thirty years, using the newly introduced telegraph to control provincial governors throughout the empire and draw them more tightly into a centralized despotism. Like the Ch'ing emperors in China, the Ottoman sultan bought a new bottle — railroads, telegraphs, military discipline — but kept the same old wine of Islamic law and centralized autocracy. It didn't work any better in Turkey than it did in China.

By the end of the nineteenth century, the Ottoman Empire was widely considered "the sick man of Europe." Like China, it faced a growing threat from the extraterritorial status of foreigners living and working within the empire. Sultan Suleiman the Magnificent had granted the first of the so-called "capitulations," or foreigners' privileges, to the French in 1535. This exempted French merchants living and trading in Constantinople (Istanbul)[1] from Islamic law and allowed them to control their own affairs, much as the minority religious *millets* did. The other European powers soon demanded and received the same special treatment. Unlike China, which granted extraterritorial status only under duress in the nineteenth century, the Ottoman Empire had conceded these privileges while at the height of its power. For centuries, the capitulations usefully greased the wheels of trade between Turkey and Europe; but when the empire's might waned, the Europeans steadily extended their privileges and took advantage of them.

The growing weakness of the Ottomans threatened the security of the religious minorities. Since the government often failed to keep order within its domains, some of the merchants among the Greek, Jewish, and Armenian minorities sought protection from the foreign powers and were brought under the umbrella of extraterritoriality. This increased Muslim resentment of the minorities. Abdulhamid II, attempting to regain control throughout the country, fanned the flames of hatred against the Christians. He organized special cavalry regiments of Kurds, a Muslim minority people in eastern Anatolia, modeling these new military detachments on the Russian Cossacks and naming them *Hamidiye* after himself.

As the Russian tsar employed Cossacks to mount pogroms against the Jews,

---

1. Many cities of the Ottoman Empire originally had Greek names, which Europeans continued to use long after the Turks conquered the Byzantine Empire in 1453. I have generally followed this practice, choosing the place name that was most commonly used among English-speakers and giving the Turkish name in parentheses the first time I mention a city. The word Istanbul, or Stamboul, was most likely a corruption of Constantinople. Though in common use for centuries, it did not become the official name of the Turkish capital until after World War I.

Sultan Abdulhamid sent the *Hamidiye* against the Christians. In 1894 a detachment of Kurds attacked Armenian villagers in the central Anatolian district of Sosun, murdering several thousand. C. M. Hallward, a British vice consul who investigated the atrocities, reported "that all the local officials, high and low, are penetrated with the idea that any act of oppression or injustice towards Armenians will be overlooked, if not actually rewarded by their superiors. . . ." Over the next two years, Abdulhamid unleashed more massacres in town after town until 50,000 to 100,000 Armenians lay dead.

European governments protested these massacres of the sultan's Christian subjects, but took little effective action. As the twentieth century approached, none of the great powers wanted the tottering Ottoman Empire to fall over, for fear that a rival power would occupy the lion's share of the sultan's domains. Yet the power of nationalism finally tore the empire apart, freeing parts of it from Ottoman rule and reinvigorating the Turks themselves.

Among the various peoples of the Ottoman Empire, Turks and Arabs were both slow to feel the force of nationalism. In European parts of the empire, Greeks, Serbs, Romanians, Bulgarians, and Albanians all revolted and won their independence before World War I, yet the growth of Turkish nationalism remained slow (we shall consider Arab nationalism in the next chapter). Indeed, it was "outside Turks" — Turkic-speaking intellectuals in Russia, and Ottoman exiles living in Western Europe — who first developed the idea of a separate Turkish national consciousness. Then in 1908 a revolution broke out which eventually destroyed the Ottoman Empire and created a purely Turkish state out of its wreckage.

The "Young Turks" who revolted against Abdulhamid's despotism were products of the sultan's own military reforms. Primarily young army or navy officers who had studied at one of the elite new military schools and knew at least one European language, the rebels belonged to a secret society known as the Committee of Union and Progress *(Ittihad ve Terakki),* founded in 1889 (the centennial year of the French Revolution) by four students at the army medical school. Growing particularly strong in Macedonia, the only part of Europe that still remained under firm Ottoman control, the Unionists gradually drew in most of the younger civil servants and army officers. Members of the committee worked for what their name proclaimed, union of all the various nationalities of the empire into a community of citizens with equal rights and duties, and progress towards constitutional government along European lines. Modeling their organization on the secret societies that had revolted against European monarchies in 1848, the "Young Turks" added a phrase to the English language. Henceforth, throughout the twentieth century, "Young Turks" has served as a name for upstarts impatient with the system of government under which they live.

The revolution began almost accidentally, as a defensive reaction to

Abdulhamid's internal espionage network. A military chaplain in Monastir, an outpost in Macedonia, discovered a Unionist cell led by an army major, Niyazi.[2] On July 3, 1908, the major led about two hundred of his followers into the hills with arms, ammunition, and money they had looted from their military base. Other junior officers throughout Macedonia followed suit, and the Committee of Union and Progress then issued a manifesto, demanding that the sultan reinstate the constitution of 1876. When the government transported more troops from the Asian part of the empire to quell the revolt, their officers fraternized with the rebels. Recognizing the weakness of his position, Sultan Abdulhamid II capitulated and restored the constitution on July 24, 1908.

Having come to power in the Ottoman Empire, the Young Turks did not know quite what to do with it. Rising from the lower ranks of the social order, they were without government experience. They had looked upon constitutional government as an end in itself, and after achieving it so easily, they were unsure how to proceed; so they left the older elite in positions of authority and acted as watchdogs of the constitution. They easily survived a counterrevolution by religious leaders and some segments of the army in April 1909. After about a week of turmoil, an "Action Army" from Salonika, a hotbed of Unionist activity, marched on the capital of Constantinople and routed the counterrevolutionaries, deposed Abdulhamid II, and installed his brother, Mehmed V, as sultan. For the next several years, the Unionists, the old ruling elite, and the army struggled for control of the government, with the sultan reigning only as figurehead.

The Young Turk revolution stimulated much favorable comment among liberal opinion in Europe, but the governments of the great powers greeted it more cynically. Austria-Hungary seized the occasion to proclaim its formal annexation of Bosnia-Hercegovina in October 1908, a highhanded act we have already analyzed (in chapter 6) as a major step toward world war. Great Britain then rebuffed the Young Turks when they requested a military alliance in November 1908. The Ottoman revolutionaries were acutely aware that their empire could end up partitioned by foreign powers, as China was. They hoped instead to follow the Meiji of Japan, modernizing their country rapidly enough to earn respect from the European powers. When they asked the British for support they invoked the example of the Anglo-Japanese Alliance of 1902 and called their country the "Japan of the Near East." The British, however, remained unconvinced and refused to upset the precarious balance of alliances by tying themselves to the new Ottoman leadership.

The breakup of the empire accelerated rapidly thereafter. In September 1911 Italy invaded the weakly held Ottoman province of Tripoli in North Africa (pres-

---

2. Turks did not generally use surnames before 1934. A single name would sometimes be followed by a nickname or by an honorific title such as Bey, Pasha, or Effendi.

ent-day Libya). In the meantime, dissatisfaction with the Committee of Union and Progress came to a head at the capital and the Unionists lost much of their influence over the government. Then in 1912 the small Balkan states of Greece, Serbia, Montenegro, and Bulgaria united to throw the Ottomans out of their remaining territories in Europe. As 1912 came to a close, the troops of the Balkan League besieged Adrianople (Edirne) on the road to Constantinople itself.

The Young Turks seized this moment to regain power. Charging that the weak Ottoman government was planning to surrender Adrianople (which it probably was), Major Enver, a leading Unionist, stormed into the legislative chamber and forced the prime minister to resign at gunpoint. Enver rallied the troops and defended Adrianople bravely, but it fell anyway on March 26, 1913. However, the Balkan allies failed to take Constantinople and soon started fighting each other. During the Second Balkan War of 1913, the Young Turks recaptured Adrianople on the fifth anniversary of their revolution, in July 1913.

Finally in firm control of the Ottoman government, the Committee of Union and Progress had by 1913 degenerated from its earlier idealism into a political machine wedded to a military dictatorship. A virtual triumvirate, composed of Enver, Talat, and Jemal,[3] ruled the country. Enver, the youngest of the Young Turks, born in 1881 and graduated from military school in 1903, became minister of war at the beginning of 1914. Having served as military attaché in Berlin shortly after the revolution, Enver was enamored of German military methods, and he welcomed a German training mission led by General Otto Liman von Sanders to Constantinople.[4] Jemal, an older and more cautious officer, born in 1872, became military governor of the capital, essentially the policeman in charge of preserving the regime. He later became minister of the marine during World War I. Talat, a former postal clerk born at Adrianople in 1874, served as minister of the interior. Although the constitution remained nominally in effect and a figurehead served as grand vizier, or prime minister, these three and their Unionist colleagues ran the Ottoman government until the end of World War I.

The most fateful event in the history of the Young Turk revolution was the loss of the European provinces in the Balkan Wars of 1912-13. Rumelia, as the

---

3. Ottoman Turkish was written in Arabic script and transliterated into English in a variety of confusing ways. After World War I, the Turkish government officially adopted the Latin script used in Western Europe. There are a few variants, however, most notably the letter *c*, which is pronounced like *j*; *ç*, which is pronounced like *ch*; and *ş*, which is pronounced like *sh*. For simplicity, I have simply adopted the phonetic spelling — thus, *Jemal Pasha* rather than *Cemal Paşa*.

4. Most European historians who trace the events leading to World War I assign at least a minor role to the so-called "Liman von Sanders incident." Members of the Triple Entente, particularly the Russians, were sensitive to any increase of German influence in Turkey, and the Liman von Sanders appointment was clearly provocative.

Turks called the Balkans, had always been the most prosperous and most important part of the empire, and furthermore it was the cradle of the Young Turks.
The loss of all but a tiny foothold in Europe reduced the population of the empire
from 24 to about 19 million and made it much more homogeneous, consisting
primarily of Arabs in the Middle East and Turks in the Anatolian peninsula. The
remaining Greek, Jewish, and Armenian minorities became more vulnerable, for
the Young Turks were now vociferously nationalistic. Though a liberal opposition, led by Prince Sabaheddin of the Ottoman ruling family, championed a decentralized form of government that would grant toleration and autonomy to
the religious and national minorities, the Committee of Union and Progress insisted on centralization and Turkish dominance. The despotism of Sultan
Abdulhamid had given way to a more dangerous, national despotism of the
Young Turks.

Indeed, Enver, the most energetic and impulsive of the ruling triumvirate,
embraced an expansive pan-Turkish form of nationalism (sometimes called pan-
Turanianism). Since Europe was lost and the Arabs might soon go their own way
as well, Turkey should unite the Turkish heartland in Anatolia with Turkic-
speaking peoples in Russia and Central Asia, creating a Greater Turkey, or Turan.
Chasing after the gray wolf of Central Asia, Enver pursued his nationalist dreams
and dragged his country into World War I, where it committed the greatest atrocities of that horrible conflict, then ultimately went down to defeat.

In retrospect, it appears that the Ottoman Empire should have remained
neutral during World War I. The Turks learned this lesson well and kept a strict
neutrality during the Second World War until the very end, when it became clear
which side would win. In 1914, however, the Ottoman leaders believed that neutrality would only result in partition of their empire by the imperialist victors of
the war. Yet they remained uncertain which side to choose. Intellectuals in the
Committee of Union and Progress, former exiles in Paris or London, generally
leaned toward the Triple Entente, for they admired the ideals of the French Revolution and the practices of English constitutional government. The army officers,
however, respected the German military machine, and German influence grew
after Liman von Sanders arrived in Constantinople.

Enver, the Ottoman minister of war, struck a secret treaty with the Germans on August 2, 1914, as the armies of Europe mobilized. Only three other
members of his government knew about this treaty. Yet even then the Turks
played for time, hoping to avoid the conflict altogether if Germany won a swift
victory. When the war on the western front bogged down, however, the Germans
wanted active assistance from their new ally, and they demanded it in dramatic
fashion, with two armed cruisers, and some unintentional assistance from the
British.

The Turkish navy had literally rotted at anchor during the long reign of

Abdulhamid II, but the Young Turks realized how foolish this policy was for a country that straddled the straits separating Europe from Asia. During the Balkan Wars, the Ottomans purchased a modern cruiser, the *Hamidieh,* from the United States, and a young naval officer named Rauf made daring sorties around the Balkan coasts in this vessel. Then the government contracted with a British naval yard to build them two modern dreadnought battleships, mounting a popular subscription campaign to pay the cost. Women sold their jewelry and children offered their small pittances in this remarkable outpouring of national spirit. During the diplomatic crisis of July 1914, however, Winston Churchill, first lord of the Admiralty in Britain, seized the newly completed Turkish vessels in the shipyards, before the Turks had decided which side to join. This highhanded snub built popular support in Turkey for Enver's pro-German policy.

The Germans, by chance and good seamanship, replaced the lost warships and forced the Ottoman Empire into the war. In August 1914, two modern German cruisers, the *Goeben* and the *Breslau,* were patrolling the Mediterranean. Rather than dive for cover at the Austrian seaport of Pola, as the British and French expected them to, the German ships sailed east to the Dardanelles, narrowly avoiding their Allied pursuers. Enver persuaded his colleagues in the government to raise the defenses in the straits and welcome their German allies. Two months later, the *Goeben* and *Breslau,* manned by Turkish crews, set out with the *Hamidieh* to bombard Russian targets along the Black Sea coast. Russia and her Allies responded with a war declaration on November 1.

Enver took direct command of the Ottoman army in eastern Anatolia and mounted an offensive against Russia on December 25, 1914. Blizzards and freezing temperatures inflicted more damage than Russian guns, and within a matter of weeks 80 percent of the Turkish soldiers had been wiped out. Defeated by the Russian winter, like Napoleon before him, Enver raced back to the capital as if nothing had happened. Then in February and March of 1915, British and French warships tried to force their way through the Dardanelles; failing that, they landed their own and the Australian troops on the Gallipoli Peninsula.

When the Aussies charged ashore at Anzac Cove on April 25, they faced a Turkish commander who would later redirect the faltering Turkish revolution and bring it to a successful conclusion. On that fateful day, Mustafa Kemal was simply a young colonel, the same age as Enver, but a bitter rival who had labored in the shadow of that Young Turk leader. Liman von Sanders commanded the Ottoman forces defending Gallipoli, and he assigned one of his six divisions to Mustafa as a floating reserve unit, ready to move wherever it was needed most.

Realizing the importance of the Anzac landing before Liman von Sanders did, Mustafa Kemal committed his troops to battle on his own authority, and despite a lingering case of malaria that he had contracted in North Africa, he fought like a man possessed. Though the Ottoman troops had suffered a long string of de-

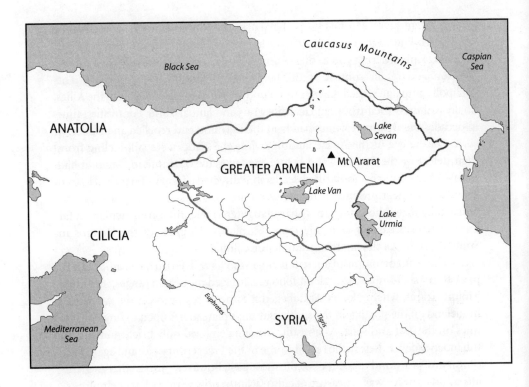

Historic Armenia

feats in recent years, Mustafa knew that Turkish soldiers would fight tenaciously when defending their own country, so he harangued them: "I am not ordering you to attack. I am ordering you to die." Enough Turks took him literally to blunt the invasion and retain control of the heights commanding the peninsula. The Gallipoli campaign settled down into a bloody, year-long stalemate until the Allies finally withdrew their troops in December 1915 and January 1916. For the first time in decades the Ottoman armies had held their ground and repelled an invader.

On the eve of the Anzac landing, while the Turks were still reeling from their defeat by the Russians and before the favorable outcome in Gallipoli had unfolded, the insecure Young Turk leadership directed a frenzy of national hatred against their most prominent minority group, the Armenians. Proceeding systematically throughout 1915, the Turks slaughtered one million Armenians, a far more extensive case of genocide than Germany's slaughter of the Hereros in South West Africa during the scramble for colonies.

The Armenians are an ancient people who have lived on a volcanic plateau in eastern Asia Minor since at least 1000 B.C. Rugged mountain ranges, including Mount Ararat, where Noah's Ark allegedly came to rest, protect the Armenian homeland on the north and the south, but their plateau lies open to invading armies on the east and west. As a result, Armenia enjoyed only brief moments of full independence, before the rise of Rome in the first century B.C. and again for a century or so around 1000 A.D. For the most part, however, the best that Armenians could hope for was a measure of cultural autonomy within a larger empire.

The Armenians accepted Christianity in 301 A.D.; but cut off from the early church councils that defined the major Christian dogmas, they adhered to a "heretical" interpretation of the nature of Christ called Monophysitism. The Armenian Apostolic Church, separated both from Rome and Constantinople, nevertheless clung fiercely to its Christian faith. Ironically, medieval Armenians found the Muslim yoke of the Ottomans more permissive than rule by the Greek Orthodox Catholics of the Byzantine Empire. For centuries Armenians were considered the most loyal of the non-Muslim *millets* in the Ottoman state.

When the Russian tsars conquered the Caucasus region between the Black and Caspian Seas in the early nineteenth century, Armenia found itself partitioned between the Russians and the Turks. Most of the Ottoman Armenians lived in six *vilayets* (provinces) at the eastern end of Asia Minor, separated by a purely artificial boundary from their countrymen in Russia. On the eve of World War I there were about 4.5 million Armenians in the world. About 1.75 million lived in Russia and a nearly equal amount in Turkey, with the remaining million scattered as emigrants, mainly in the United States.

The Russians allowed Armenians their customary autonomy, but as the Ottoman Empire decayed, the status of Turkish Armenia became more insecure. Though most Armenians were peasants in agricultural villages, a small number

186

lived at the capital of Constantinople as prosperous merchants or professionals, and others kept shop or peddled goods in small towns throughout the empire. The urban Armenians suffered second-class citizenship but overcompensated and prospered through hard work, as a result becoming targets for Turkish persecution.

The massacres perpetrated by the sultan in 1894-96 were horrifying but would not qualify as genocide. Abdulhamid did not try to exterminate the Armenians; he merely wanted to put them in their place. The Young Turks, however, nurtured a more highly developed nationalist ideology, and they practiced statecraft more ruthlessly than the sultan. When their revolution seemed threatened in the early days of World War I, they lashed out at the most visible, vulnerable enemy.

On April 24, 1915, a day ever after commemorated as the start of the Armenian genocide, the police arrested hundreds of the most prominent Armenians in Constantinople, then took them out to the hinterlands and shot them. These *amiras*, as the wealthy Armenians of the capital were known, were the most conservative, assimilated, pro-Ottoman individuals in the Armenian community. Their massacre made no sense ideologically or economically.

The Young Turks then spread their terror through the six *vilayets* of Turkish Armenia. Enver spearheaded the slaughters with his "Special Organization," an elite corps of soldiers organized before the war to spread pan-Turkish propaganda in Russia and Asia, now supplemented by common criminals released from the jails. They followed a common pattern. All able-bodied men were summoned to the *konak*, or government building, in a village or town and summarily arrested. Soldiers would then march them outside of town, where they were shot, bayoneted, or pushed over cliffs. Old men, women, and children suffered longer. The Turks deported them on foot from their villages to the Syrian deserts south of Aleppo. Most did not survive the hunger, thirst, and nomadic deprivations of their forced marches, and many who did arrive in Syria perished in the brutal concentration camps set up to receive them. Of the 1.75 million Armenians in Turkey at the start of the war, about a quarter million fled as refugees to Russia, and a million of the rest died in the massacres.

The other large non-Turkish community of Eastern Anatolia, the Kurds, willingly cooperated in the genocide of the Armenians. The Kurdish Hamidíye corps, officially disbanded after the Young Turk revolution, persisted as irregular troops, willing to do the Empire's dirty work. Ironically, once the Armenian population was largely eliminated, the Turks planned a campaign of "ethnic cleansing" against the Kurds. Turks had never admitted that Kurds formed a separate ethnic group, calling them "mountain Turks" instead. Rather than exterminate them, like the Armenians, various governments of the Ottoman Empire attempted to assimilate the Kurds. In 1917 the Young Turk government decreed their forcible resettlement into areas where they would not exceed 5 percent of the population. Only the unfavorable outcome of the war prevented the full execution of this policy.

The Turks have always denied any intent of genocide, pleading the necessities of war to justify their actions. Certainly, the Armenians hoped for an Allied victory in the war that would liberate them from the Turks and unite them with their brethren in Russia, and they lived in a strategically vital region directly between the Turks and their ancient enemy, the Russians. This might explain, though it would not justify, internment of "suspicious" Armenians or even deportations. After all, the United States cleared the West Coast of Japanese during World War II and herded them into concentration camps. Nations at war often take hasty actions and trample on human rights in the name of national security. Yet none of this justifies or explains the slaughter of a million people, including noncombatant women and children. And, of course, the Kurds were mainly loyal to the Ottoman Empire throughout the war. Turkish leaders were clearly trying to solve their Armenian and Kurdish problems once and for all, clearing eastern Asia Minor of all non-Turkish populations and making it possible to link up with Turkic-speaking peoples in the Caucasus and in Central Asia.

Historians of anti-immigrant movements in the United States have demonstrated that nativism peaks at times of national stress and insecurity. Experiencing even greater stress during World War I, the Turkish revolutionary leadership took ethnocentrism to murderous extremes. Robert Melson, a political scientist who survived World War II in Germany as a Jewish child, has written the best account of the Armenian genocide, comparing it astutely to the Jewish Holocaust. He notes that in both instances revolutionary regimes whose very existence was threatened by total war tried to eliminate a highly visible, successful minority with seemingly dangerous foreign connections. Melson sums up his argument thus: "Total domestic genocide . . . is likely to occur only under circumstances of revolutions that lead to war. . . ." Rostom Zorian, a leader of the *Dashnaks,* an Armenian nationalist party in Russia, made the same point: "Revolution during time of war! That is death for the Armenian people."

World War I also brought death to the Young Turks, for neither they nor the Ottoman Empire survived it. The British and their Arab allies swept through the Middle East from Suez (as we shall see in the next chapter) and pushed the Ottoman armies back to the mountainous borders of Asia Minor. Still pursuing his pan-Turkish dreams in Asia, Enver deprived the Ottoman forces in the Middle East of necessary reinforcements and concentrated for another atttack in the Caucasus. After the Russian Revolution, resistance collapsed on that front so the Turks swept forward, all the way to Baku on the Caspian Sea in September 1918. Yet despite this brief success, the war was coming to an end for the Central Powers. On October 30, 1918, Turkish delegates signed an armistice aboard a British warship off the island of Lemnos in the Aegean Sea.

Two days later, on November 1, Enver, Talat, Jemal, and the other Young Turks escaped Constantinople on a German cruiser; but the Armenian *Dashnaks* formed a secret death squad, named Nemesis, to hunt them down and avenge the genocide. One of them shot Talat on a streetcorner in Berlin on March 15, 1921. After the captured gunman narrated the story of the Armenian genocide on the witness stand, the German jury swiftly acquitted him. Enver, Jemal, and several other Young Turks moved on from Germany to Soviet Russia, hoping eventually to work their way back to Turkey through the Caucasus. Two Nemesis operatives assassinated Jemal in Tiflis, Georgia, on July 25, 1922. Finally, Enver died a more romantic death in the heart of Central Asia, the legendary home of the gray wolf. The Soviet government had sent him to Turkestan to put down a rebellion of nomadic tribesmen, but Enver swiftly changed sides and became a warlord in Buhkara. In August 1922, he was killed in battle by the Red Army.

Back in Constantinople, an Allied fleet had sailed through the Dardanelles after the armistice and dropped anchor at the Turkish capital. On February 8, 1919, French troops disembarked, and General Franchet d'Esperey humiliated the Turks by riding a white horse through the streets, as the conquering sultan had done five hundred years before. Still pursuing their old imperialist dreams, the Allies now proceeded to carve up what was left of Turkey. Secret treaties during the war had granted spheres of influence to the French and the Italians in Anatolia, so both powers moved in troops to claim what was theirs. A new sultan, Mehmed VI, desperately tried to save his throne by organizing a puppet government and accommodating the Allies in every possible way. Reluctantly, he accepted the terms of the Treaty of Sèvres, which partitioned the empire among the victorious powers and, in a nod to Wilsonian self-determination, recognized an independent Armenia and an autonomous region of Kurdistan. Under this treaty, the sultan was left with little more than the environs of Constantinople, and even there the straits were to be internationalized and patrolled by the powers.

Before this treaty went into effect, however, the Allies committed a major blunder which stirred up ferocious Turkish resistance. On May 15, 1919, a division of Greek troops landed at Smyrna (Izmir) on the southwest coast of Anatolia. Smyrna had a large Greek population, and much of the surrounding coast and the Aegean islands had been inhabited by Greeks since antiquity. Greek Prime Minister Eleutherios Venizelos, a charismatic leader who had belatedly brought his country into the war on the side of the Allies after sending the pro-German King Constantine into exile, was now pursuing his "Grand Idea" of a Greater Greece surrounding the Aegean. When the other powers moved into Turkey after the war, he demanded a share of the spoils. Since the British and French were exhausted, they unwisely consented, hoping the fresh Greek troops would serve as their surrogates in pacifying Turkey.

Winston Churchill, who opposed the move at the time, wrote years later: "Here then we have reached a new turning point in the history of the peoples of the Middle East." Historian Arnold Toynbee concurred: "I remain convinced that the crucial event in the tragedy was the landing of Greek troops at Smyrna on the 15th of May 1919." They did not exaggerate. Turkey was a thoroughly defeated and demoralized country, willing to accept almost any terms from the victorious Allies. The Greeks, however, were a former subject people of the Ottoman Empire and a historic enemy; their invasion galvanized Turkish resistance.

Coincidentally, as the Greeks were disembarking at Smyrna, a new Turkish leader was moving into the interior of Anatolia, positioned in the right place at the right time to mount a nationalist revival. Mustafa Kemal, the hero of Gallipoli, having wangled an appointment as military inspector general, had landed at Samsun on the Black Sea coast on May 19, 1919. The sultan instructed him to quell any resistance to the Allies, but he actually intended to fan the flames.

Mustafa had been born in 1881 at Salonika, a port city in what was then European Turkey but is now a part of Greece. He earned his nickname, Kemal ("perfect") because of his quick mind and his arrogant ways as a schoolboy. He graduated from the military staff college in 1905, and, like most bright young officers, joined the secret Committee of Union and Progress. Yet due to his rivalry with Enver, he never played a major role in the Young Turk revolution. The Committee kept sending him on farflung assignments at crucial moments of the revolution. It was only by sheer luck that he found himself at Gallipoli when the Aussies landed, and then again in Anatolia at the time of the Greek invasion.

Anatolia is an arid, rugged plateau stretching from Mount Ararat in Armenia nearly to the coast of the Black, Aegean, and Mediterranean Seas which surround it on three sides. The birthplace of the Ottoman dynasty and the home of sturdy Turkish peasants, it had nevertheless been neglected by the sultans, who lavished their attention on the richer provinces of Europe and Syria. Now Kemal planned to build a new nation-state in Anatolia. Like the Young Turks, he would reorganize his country on the basis of Turkish nationalism; but unlike them, he renounced any dreams of pan-Turkism in Asia and limited his ambitions to the Turkish heartland.

Mustafa Kemal toured the rugged countryside of Anatolia with a small band of like-minded military men, making contact with local "Defense of Rights" associations that had sprung up spontaneously to resist the Greeks and the Allies. He chaired a congress at Erzurum, in what had been the Armenian provinces but was now firmly under Turkish control, and another at Sivas in the summer of 1919 and proclaimed the National Pact. This manifesto claimed the right of self-determination for the Turks and declared a willingness to defend the borders of indisputably Turkish territory. At Sivas, near the geographical center of Anatolia, Kemal spent hour after hour on the telegraph wire recruiting provincial governors and military commanders to his cause. At the end of 1919 he moved into Angora (Ankara), a sleepy town of about 20,000 people, previously noted only for its long-haired sheep, planning to transform it into a new Turkish capital, far away from the cosmopolitan, corrupting influence of Constantinople. He then organized elections and convened the Grand National Assembly, a de facto government for the new Turkey, on April 23, 1920.

In the meantime he had won his first military victory over an Allied power, driving the French and their Armenian auxiliaries off the southeastern portion of the Anatolian plateau. As the French retreated in brutal winter weather, the Turkish soldiers massacred any remaining Armenians, burning some of them alive in their homes, schools, and churches. Later that year he sent troops eastward and raced the Red Army to carve up what remained of Armenia. The treaty of Moscow in 1921 earned Kemal's Nationalists their first formal international recognition and partitioned Armenia between Russia and Turkey along a line that still stands today.

The Greek invasion still posed the greatest threat to the reviving fortunes of the Turks. Kemal's closest military aide, General Ismet, checked the Greek forces at the First Battle of Inonu in January 1921. A few months later, Ismet defeated them again at the same town, and though the Greeks remained numerically superior it was becoming clear that Turkish strategy and staff work outclassed them. King Constantine, who had returned from exile after Venizelos lost an election in Greece, took personal command of the Greek troops, the first Christian king to land in Asia since the Crusades. Yet Mustafa Kemal, obtaining dictatorial powers from the Grand National Assembly, mounted a national crusade of his own and mobilized his country for total war. As the Greeks advanced on Ankara in August 1921, Kemal's troops stopped them at the Sakarya River, in a battle that raged for twenty-two days. A year later, the Turkish forces drove the Greek army all the way back to the coast at Smyrna, where they were hastily evacuated by Allied ships. Then, a final atrocity took place in September 1922.

The Greek soldiers had burned and pillaged all the way back to the coast, and now at the approach of the Turkish army the local Christian population in Smyrna feared reprisals. Indeed, Turkish soldiers looted homes and shops in the city and killed at least two thousand Greeks and Armenians. Then while they were trying to burn out a band of Christians, the fire raged out of control and swept through the city. Smyrna burned to the ground. After some hesitation, Allied warships evacuated as many homeless refugees as they could. The British Lord Kinross, a usually sympathetic biographer of Mustafa Kemal, concluded coldly: "Kemal . . . was not unduly perturbed by the fire. . . . For Smyrna was a foreign city. . . . Thus, whether or not the Turks had a major hand in the burning of Smyrna, it represented in their hearts a fitting culmination to the Nationalist victory."

The Turkish Grand National Assembly deposed the last sultan and on November 16, 1922, a British warship spirited Mehmed VI away from Constantinople. Then the Allies finally agreed to renegotiate the Treaty of Sèvres. Kemal sent his trusted lieutenant, Ismet, to confer at Lausanne, Switzerland, and after much hard bargaining he managed to strike a peace among equals. Turkey preserved its territorial integrity and won recognition as a sovereign state from the European powers, who then swiftly evacuated their last troops from the country.

A separate agreement with Greece prescribed a compulsory exchange of populations between the two countries. Almost a million Greek inhabitants of Turkey had fled or been driven out during the Greco-Turkish war, and Kemal's government not only refused to take them back but expelled the 300,000 or so remaining Greeks from their territory. In return about 400,000 Turkish Muslims were removed from Greece to Turkey. This forced emigration was based entirely on religious affiliation. Ironically, most of the Orthodox Christians "repatriated" to Greece had never before set foot in their "homeland," and some of them did not even speak Greek; likewise, some "returning" Muslims were seeing Asia Minor for the first time. The League of Nations collaborated with the Greek government on the Refugee Settlement Commission, which labored from 1923 to 1930 to help resettle those uprooted by the agreement. This exchange of populations, what would later in the century come to be known as "ethnic cleansing," increased the population of Greece by about 10 percent. It also complemented the work of the earlier genocide in Turkey, making that country a nearly homogeneous nation-state.

The success of the Nationalist revolution marked the end of any hopes for an independent Armenia. No European power was willing to commit troops to the Armenian cause or accept a League of Nations mandate for that fledgling country. The peace conference in Paris asked the United States to accept an Armenian mandate. Woodrow Wilson sent two commissions to the Middle East to investigate and he ultimately proposed a fair-minded map for the borders of an independent Armenia. Yet all this proved academic, for the U.S. Senate voted to refuse an Armenian mandate. The only remnant of Armenia that survived was a small, landlocked Soviet republic, devastated by war and massacre and crammed with refugees.

Turkey's Grand National Assembly proclaimed the country a republic on October 29, 1923, but for the rest of Mustafa Kemal's life and during the presidency of his hand-picked successor, Ismet, it was really a one-party dictatorship. Kemal made few apologies for his one-man rule. His biographer Kinross has styled him "a democrat by conviction but an autocrat by temperament." Nor did the Turkish president try to hide his personal habits of womanizing and heavy drinking. Once when a French journalist wrote that Turkey was governed by one drunkard (Kemal), one deaf man (Ismet), and three hundred deaf-mutes (the deputies in the assembly), Kemal retorted, "The man is mistaken. Turkey is governed by one drunkard."

Yet unlike the fascist dictators who came to power in Europe a decade later, Kemal retained a sense of limits. Firmly renouncing any expansionist plans, he concentrated on the modernization of the Turkish heartland. Though he had always resented the imperialist powers' domination of his country, Mustafa Kemal greatly admired the civilization of Western Europe and the United States. So as president of the republic in the late 1920s and early 1930s, he demanded, cajoled, and bullied a cascade of Westernizing reforms from the Grand National Assembly.

On March 3, 1924, shortly after the proclamation of the republic, the assembly abolished the position of caliph, or spiritual leader of the Muslims, and banished all members of the Ottoman imperial family from the country. At Kemal's urging they thoroughly secularized the state, abolishing religious courts, shutting down Islamic schools and shrines, and seizing the property of the so-called dervishes, mystical religious brotherhoods popular in the countryside. In 1926 a new legal code, modelled on that of Switzerland, was adopted. Among its many innovations it abolished polygamy and established equality between men and women in the divorce regulations. Ironically, Kemal divorced his wife, Latife, in the old Islamic fashion, by simply dismissing her, shortly before the new law code took effect.

The Turkish president followed the other reforms more consistently. He helped devise a new Latin script in which to write the Turkish language, and after it was adopted in November 1928 he toured the country with blackboard in hand, tutoring the populace like a schoolmaster. He also forbade the wearing of the Turkish fez, the turban, or other "Oriental" headgear, which he felt unworthy of a civilized populace. On a journey through a conservative rural district in 1925, Kemal wore a Western business suit, a shirt and tie, and carried a Panama hat in his hand. While addressing the crowds, he held his stylish headgear aloft and shouted, "The name of this is hat." When he returned to Ankara, the crowd that greeted him all wore home-made Western hats. Even Kemal, however, did not feel strong enough to ban the Islamic veil which women customarily wore to hide their faces in public, though he discouraged its use whenever possible. Toward the end of the reform period, on December 5, 1934, the government did grant women the right to vote and run for office. In the general election of February, 1935, seventeen women were elected to the assembly.

At the same time that he was working to Westernize and secularize his country, however, Kemal also sought to "Turkify" it. The assembly officially designated Ankara, in the heart of Turkish Anatolia, as the capital and adopted the Turkish name Istanbul for the old capital city of Constantinople. Kemal appointed commissions to purify the Turkish language by discarding words borrowed from Arabic or Persian, and he encouraged the writing of an extremely nationalistic history. A popular text of the 1930s not only enshrined the gray wolf legend but argued that Turks were the original inhabitants of Anatolia and the progenitors of all major civilizations. A 1934 law revived the Young Turk plan to hasten assimilation of non-Turkish populations (mainly Kurds) by uprooting and resettling them in areas where they would constitute no more than five percent of the population. Though not carried out systematically, this version of ethnic cleansing caused considerable hardship and bitterness.

The last of the great reforms decreed that all citizens of Turkey had to adopt a surname by January 1, 1935. At the same time, the assembly banned the use of the old Turkish honorific titles, such as Pasha, Effendi, and Bey. Many Turks adopted their father's name, with the suffix *oglu* (son of), as their surname. Kemal amused himself by dreaming up names for his cabinet ministers and aides. He bestowed the last name of Inonu on his prime minister Ismet, in honor of the two victories he had won over the Greeks at that town. For himself, President Kemal dropped the Arabic-sounding Mustafa, which he had been given at birth, and adopted the surname Ataturk, or Father of the Turks.

Kemal Ataturk, "the Perfect One, Father of the Turks," died on November 10, 1938, and was succeeded as president by Ismet Inonu. Their People's Republican Party continued to rule Turkey through the Second World War and up to 1950. Together they had created a modern nation-state, with strong Turkish roots, out of the wreckage of a multinational empire. At the turn of the century, the Ottoman Empire seemed to be going the way of China, breaking up under the onslaught of Western European imperialism. Yet the Young Turks and Kemal's Nationalists sought to imitate the Japanese by modernizing and strengthening their nation. They ended up somewhere halfway between the Chinese and the Japanese experience, with a stable but economically weak nation-state. This achievement, the creation of the first modern, secular state in an Islamic nation, has been much admired by leaders of the Third World struggling to repeat its success in the second half of the century. Yet the Turkish revolution was bloody and brutal, and during its Young Turk phase the revolutionaries committed genocide.

It remains an open question whether Kemal himself would have committed genocide. We will never know for sure since he was busy fighting in Gallipoli in 1915 when the atrocities took place, and by the time he came to power in the 1920s most of the Armenians had fled or been killed. The massacres by Nationalist troops in southeastern Anatolia, the burning of Smyrna, and the population transfers of Greeks and Kurds are not reassuring signs. Yet Ataturk was a pragmatic and realistic leader, ruthless when opposed but not inclined to brutality for its own sake. Thus it is not quite fair to say, as one Armenian historian has, that "The *Aghed* [the Armenian word for *catastrophe*] is an essential part of Kemalist Turkey's birth certificate." Kemal inherited a land cleared of Armenians; he did not perpetrate the catastrophe himself.

Yet massacre, genocide, and ethnic cleansing form an essential part of the Turkish revolution in its broadest sweep from Abdulhamid's despotism through the Young Turk nightmare up through Kemal's consolidation of the Turkish nation-state. Lacking the homogeneity and isolation of Japan's island nation, the Turks, in the maelstrom of a world war, brutally created a homogeneous national homeland for themselves.

CHAPTER TWELVE

A Tangle of Promises

After the Ottoman Empire lost its European provinces in the Balkan Wars of 1912-13, Arabs outnumbered Turks by a ratio of about three to two in the empire's remaining territories, 10.5 million Arabs to 7.5 million Turks. National consciousness had developed slowly among the Arabic-speaking people, but it surged when the Young Turks came to power in 1908 with their repressive anti-minority policies. During the First World War, the Arabs revolted and allied with Great Britain against Turkey and Germany. After the war, however, they found themselves enmeshed in a tangle of British promises, ultimately swapping one set of imperial masters for another.

Originally, the term "Arab" applied to the nomadic camel herders who roamed the desert spaces of the Arabian Peninsula between the Persian Gulf and the Red Sea. In their constant struggle to secure food and water, they often spilled over into more settled areas to the north in Syria and Mesopotamia, but their effect on history was slight until the seventh century A.D. when the prophet Muhammad[1] converted them to his new monotheistic religion of Islam. Stressing the unity of God, Muhammad also applied the principle of harmony to politics, uniting many quarrelsome Arab tribes behind him.

After Muhammad's death in 632, the caliphs of Islam (the word *khalifa*, or caliph, means successor) led the mounted Arab tribesmen out of the desert peninsula, spreading the new religion through the Middle East and North Africa. The Arab ar-

---

1. There are numerous ways of rendering the Arabic name of the Prophet into English — Mohammed, Mehemet, Mahomet, Mehmed, etc. In this case as with other Arabic names I have tried to choose the most familiar and accessible form, without worrying too much about academic consistency.

mies also crossed the Straits of Gibraltar and conquered Spain in the early eighth century. At its height under the Umayyad Dynasty, which established its capital at Damascus, Arab rule extended from the Pyrenees Mountains that separate France from Spain, along the southern shore of the Mediterranean Sea through the Middle East, beyond the Tigris and Euphrates Rivers to Persia and parts of Central Asia.

The Arabic language (a Semitic tongue, related to Hebrew) accompanied the conquerors and their new religion, for the sacred book of the Muslims, the Koran, was written in Arabic and was believed to contain the literal words of God. Thus the term "Arab" took on a new meaning, embracing all the peoples who spoke Arabic and shared in the developing Arabic culture. (Ultimately the religion of Islam spread farther than the Arabic language, so there are today many Muslim peoples who do not speak Arabic.)

Though Arabic language and culture left a permanent imprint on North Africa and the Middle East, Arab political control eventually deteriorated. The Umayyad caliph was overthrown in 750 by a group of military officers, the Abbasids, who were more Persian than Arab, and who moved the capital to Baghdad on the Tigris River. There the legendary caliph Haroun al-Rashid ruled in the late eighth century, and his court poet wrote the enchanting tales *The Thousand and One Nights,* contributing the stories of Aladdin and his lamp, Ali Baba and the forty thieves, and Sinbad the sailor to world literature.

Abbasid rule in Baghdad lasted five hundred years, but eventually Mongol and Turkish nomads from Central Asia overthrew it. From the mid-thirteenth until the early twentieth century, one or another Turkish dynasty ruled the Arabic-speaking masses. The Ottoman Turks conquered nearly all the Arab lands in the early sixteenth century, stretching their domain from Algeria in the west to the Euphrates River in the east. Since the Turks had converted to Islam, the Arabs accepted their rule relatively peacefully, for Islam preaches utter submission to God and strict obedience to earthly authority. Though Turkish predominated in government, Arabic remained the language of religion and education. Furthermore, Ottoman Turkish was written in Arabic script, and many Arabic words infiltrated into the language as well.

Napoleon's temporary conquest of Egypt in 1798 first loosened the hold of the Ottoman sultan on his Arab domains. An Albanian commander, Muhammad Ali, sent to Egypt to restore order after Napoleon's withdrawal in 1801, built a virtually independent kingdom for himself and his descendants. First he drove out an upstart Arab tribe, the house of Saud, from the Islamic holy cities of Mecca and Medina, then he conquered the Sudan on the Upper Nile and sent his son Ibrahim into Syria to take Damascus. Muhammad Ali conquered in the name of the sultan, but he ruled by his own power. In the 1830s, he and his family controlled the Nile Valley, the Red Sea, and the eastern Mediterranean. Though Muhammad Ali never learned Arabic, his son Ibrahim had grown up in Egypt, identified strongly with Arabic culture, and dreamed of building an Arab empire independent of the Turks.

Yet this all proved premature, for the conquests of Muhammad Ali and Ibrahim alarmed the European powers, who preferred a weak Ottoman sultan in the Middle East to a strong, expansionist Egyptian ruler. So in 1841 the Treaty of London forced Muhammad Ali to relinquish some territory, affirm his allegiance to the sultan, and drastically reduce his army. As a consolation prize, his family obtained the hereditary right to rule as *khedive* (viceroy) of Egypt under the Ottomans. Muhammad Ali died in 1849, but his subdynasty remained in Cairo until the last of the line, King Farouk, was forced to abdicate over a hundred years later, in 1952.

After putting Muhammad Ali in his place, Europeans nibbled away at the Arab provinces of the Ottomans. French troops first landed in Algeria in 1830, but they did not suppress all resistance against imperialist rule until 1880. About the same time, in 1878, the French also seized control of Tunisia. In the meantime, a French engineer, Ferdinand de Lesseps, had completed the Suez Canal in 1869, and both the French and the English exercised considerable influence over Muhammad Ali's successors in Egypt. Finally, just before the First World War, in 1911, Italy jumped into the imperialist race for colonies by grabbing Libya.

All of North Africa, therefore, came under European rule, but Egypt's status remained unusually complicated. With their hands full elsewhere, the French bowed out of Egypt, and England gained the upper hand. The Suez Canal was a vital link on the most direct route to India, England's most valuable colony. Yet the English did not annex Egypt, nor even formally declare it a protectorate. Instead, they propped up the weak rule of the khedive in an arrangement often referred to as a "veiled protectorate." Each Egyptian cabinet minister worked under the watchful gaze of an English advisor (a sort of commissar, to use a loaded twentieth-century term). The British agent and consul-general in Cairo, despite his innocuous-sounding title, exercised ultimate authority in the country. From 1882 to 1906, Sir Evelyn Baring, later named Lord Cromer, held this post as de facto English ruler of Egypt. Though still technically under the suzerainty of the Ottoman Empire and the rule of the Egyptian khedive, Egypt was in fact, though not in name, one of the most important British colonies.

To recapitulate, on the eve of World War I, the Ottoman Empire had lost its European provinces (except the immediate vicinity of Constantinople) and all of north Africa. It still exercised direct control over Anatolia (present-day Turkey), Syria, Lebanon, Mesopotamia (present-day Iraq), and Palestine. By completing the Hejaz Railway from Damascus to Medina in 1908, the Ottomans had taken a firm grip on the holy places of Islam on the western side of the Arabian Peninsula, but its authority over the rest of the peninsula was merely nominal. The nomadic tribes of the Arabian desert, most notably the Saudis, remained virtually independent of the sultan, and the more settled people along the rim of the Persian Gulf and the Indian Ocean all signed treaties of protection with the British. All the Arabs, except for a few nomads, remained subjects of either the Turks or the European empires.

Imperialism finally produced a nationalist reaction in the Arab lands. In cities such as Damascus, Beirut, Aleppo, and Baghdad, the traditional urban notables — landowners, merchants, bureaucrats — joined with army officers and an emerging middle class of teachers, journalists, and other intellectuals in literary and cultural associations. Language and history formed the twin pillars of Arab nationalism. Arabic had produced a rich poetic literature and Arabs firmly believed that "the beauty of man lies in the eloquence of his tongue." Moreover, history revealed that the Arabs were a great people when the Turks still roamed the steppes and the English and French lived in mud huts and dank stone castles. Pride in the Islamic religion generally reinforced national feeling, for Muslims believed that Arabic was the language in which God revealed himself; but Arab nationalism was not limited to Muslims. Many Christian intellectuals, encountering European nationalism at missionary schools, also contributed to the Arab national revival.

After the Young Turk revolution, Arab nationalist associations became more overtly political. The new rulers in Constantinople pressed the use of Turkish language in education and dismissed many urban notables from previously secure positions as local officeholders. Furthermore, the Young Turks barely disguised their contempt for Arabs, calling them "the dogs of the Turkish nation."

The impact of Europe proved even more important than Turkish repression in arousing nationalist feelings. Arab notables and middle class intellectuals felt acutely ashamed at their weakness before European military power, political dominance, and economic penetration. History spurred their emotions and pointed a way out of their present pitiable state. Arab nationalists reasoned in a sort of syllogism: Europe is strong and the East is weak; but, in ages past, when the Arabs dominated the Middle East, Europe was weak and the East was strong; therefore, the East will be strong once again when it regains its Arab identity. The classic definition of nationalism, "a feeling we have done great things together in the past," fits perfectly this Arab national revival of the early twentieth century.

In 1909 Aziz Ali al-Masri, a major in the Ottoman army, founded a secret nationalist society called al-Qahtaniya (the descendants of Qahtan), which aimed at complete autonomy for the Arab provinces. Al-Masri hoped to transform the Ottoman Empire into a dual monarchy, like the Austro-Hungarian Empire. A few years later, the major formed a more tightly organized secret society, al-Ahd (the Covenant), composed entirely of army officers, most of them from Iraq. Reportedly, 315 of the 490 army officers stationed in Constantinople at the outbreak of war belonged to al-Ahd.

Arab exiles in Paris hatched another secret society in 1911, al-Fatat (the Young Arab Society), which later moved its headquarters to Beirut and eventually to Damascus. Al-Fatat went beyond the dual monarchy idea and championed complete independence for the Arabs. Finally, a group of Syrian exiles in British Cairo organized the Administrative Decentralization Party, working, as their name implied, for Arab autonomy within the Ottoman Empire. Representatives of all these groups convened an Arab Congress in Paris during July of 1913 to state their demands before the world.

Throughout the twentieth century, so many deadly national quarrels have broken out in the Balkans and the Middle East that it's possible to feel nostalgia for the old Ottoman and Austro-Hungarian Empires. If either empire had evolved in a decentralized, federal direction, as the Arab nationalists and some of the Balkan revolutionaries desired, such nostalgia would be justified. Yet the rulers of both empires rejected this course, trying instead to suppress the nationalist movements and eventually provoking a devastating war. They thus failed the ultimate test of any government, to provide peace and security for their inhabitants.

At the outbreak of World War I, the urban areas populated by Arabs were seething with nationalist frustration at both the Turks and the Europeans. Arab nationalism, however, did not yet form a mass movement, but was largely a product of the urban elite. With the exception of al-Fatat, moreover, few of the nationalists foresaw complete independence from the Ottoman Empire. They hoped merely to reform it into decentralized provinces with national autonomy. The fortunes of war, however, triggered an Arab revolt which finally overthrew Turkish rule. Ironically, the leadership of this revolt came from a seemingly unlikely source, the Sherif Hussein,[2] religious ruler of Islam's holiest shrines in the Hejaz region of western Arabia.

Hussein ibn Ali was born in 1853 into one of the noblest Arab families, the Hashim, or Hashemites, who traced their lineage directly back to the Prophet Muhammad and traditionally ruled the holy places as emir or sherif of Mecca (the honorific title *sherif* is applied to all Arabs descended from the Prophet; *emir* means "commander" or "prince"). Hussein's father died when he was very young, and he therefore grew up amid the family intrigues that placed four of his uncles in the emirate and witnessed three of them deposed or assassinated. Then in 1893 Sultan Abdulhamid II, fearing potential rivals in the outposts of the Ottoman Empire, "invited" Hussein and his family to live in Constantinople where his spies could keep an eye on him. So the thirty-nine-year-old Hussein moved to the

---

2. Hussein was not related to the infamous Saddam Hussein of Iraq against whom the United States fought the Persian Gulf War much later in the century. Hussein is a very common name among Muslims. One of the prophet Muhammad's grandsons was named Hussein.

capital with his wife and his sons, Ali, Abdullah, and Feisal, living there in luxurious house arrest for fifteen years. In 1908 the Young Turk revolution freed him and sent him home to Hejaz as grand sherif of Mecca.

Hejaz in Arabic means "barrier," and the region on the western coast of the Arabian Peninsula took this name from the steep ridge of hills that runs parallel to the shoreline. In one sense, the Hejaz was the center of the Muslim universe, for believers all over the world turned towards Mecca when they prayed five times each day. Furthermore, pilgrims gathered there annually, for Islam enjoined Muslims to visit Mecca once in their lifetime if their health and financial means permitted. Yet despite its religious significance, this parched coastal plain of the Red Sea remained an impoverished backwater in a backward empire. Unable to produce enough food for its inhabitants, the Hejaz depended on annual subsidies from the Ottoman authorities and grain from Egypt. Most of the population made their living, either directly or indirectly, off the pilgrim trade. The region contained few of the middle-class intellectuals who fueled the nationalist movement in cities such as Damascus; and since inhabitants of the Hejaz enjoyed an exemption from military service, there were no rising young army officers to scheme and conspire.

Nevertheless, war catapulted Hussein and the Hejaz into leadership of an Arab revolt. Like other urban notables, the grand sherif's position had been threatened before the war by the centralizing policies of the Young Turks, particularly the completion of the Hejaz Railway to Medina and its proposed extension to Mecca. Looking for leverage to preserve their local autonomy, the Hashemites had consulted with nationalists in Damascus and opened discreet conversations with the British in Cairo. When the war broke out, Hussein's position became critical. The British blockaded the Red Sea and stopped grain shipments from Egypt, threatening the Hejaz with famine. Then the Turks proclaimed a *jihad* against Christian invaders and demanded that Hussein, as a prominent religious leader, ratify their proclamation of holy war.

Hussein stalled for time and considered his options. He could support the Turks and then demand substantial autonomy in Hejaz as his reward after the war. His third son, Feisal, who had visited the Arab nationalists in Syria and seen how weak and disorganized they were, initially counselled this course. Yet his second son, Abdullah, who had conducted the prewar discussions in Cairo, urged a British alliance to destroy the Ottoman Empire and win Arab independence. The Turks finally forced the issue and helped Hussein make up his mind. Jemal Pasha, one of the ruling triumvirate of Young Turks, took command in Syria and Palestine during the war. His attacks on British Egypt failed, but behind his own lines he unleashed a savage repression of the Arab nationalist leadership.

Sherif Hussein, therefore, initiated negotiations with the British, sending a letter to Sir Henry McMahon, the high commissioner in Cairo, on July 14, 1915.

The McMahon-Hussein correspondence, continuing until January 1916, laid out the terms of an alliance between Great Britain and the Arab leader. Hussein's demands had been formulated by his son Feisal and the nationalists in Damascus, specifically, recognition by the British of an independent Arab state (or confederation) in the territory between the Mediterranean on the west, the Persian border on the east, the Taurus Mountains in the north, and the Indian Ocean on the south.

McMahon's second note to the sherif, on October 14, 1915, contained the meat of the bargain. McMahon wrote that "Great Britain is prepared to recognise and uphold the independence of the Arabs in all the regions lying within the frontiers proposed by the Sharif of Mecca." In return, Hussein would raise a revolt against the Turks and use all his religious influence and material resources to defeat them.

The McMahon promises, however, contained several crucial reservations which caused endless controversy after the war. In defining the limits of the Arab territories, McMahon reserved Iraq, which the British were already invading with Indian troops, for "special administrative arrangements," i.e., English occupation. Hussein protested this but deferred a final decision, tacitly accepting a fait accompli he had little hope of reversing. McMahon also excluded from the promised Arab state "the portions of Syria lying to west of the districts of Damascus, Homs, Hama and Aleppo." These regions, the present-day state of Lebanon, formed a traditional sphere of influence for the French, and the British intended to protect the interests of their principal ally. After the war, the British tried to argue that this reservation also applied to Palestine, but a glance at a map shows the contention to be spurious. Palestine lies well south of all four towns mentioned in the correspondence.

McMahon also stated a more far-reaching reservation, hedging all his pledges to Hussein with the qualification "[insofar as] Great Britain is free to act without detriment to the interest of her ally France. . . ." In short, the British left themselves wiggle-room to redefine the agreement with the Arabs if great-power politics demanded it. In the building of their empire, they had consistently "played it by ear," and the McMahon-Hussein correspondence was no exception.

In the short term, the alliance between Britain and the sherif of Mecca proved mutually advantageous. A holy war, supported by the keeper of the holy places, could seriously affect all the Allies. Britain had 70 million Muslim subjects in India and 16 million more, much closer to the fighting, in Egypt. The French and the Russians also ruled substantial Muslim populations. Hussein's allegiance to the Allied cause neutralized religious disaffection. Furthermore, alliance with the Hejaz cemented British control of the Red Sea and protected the sea route to India. In return, of course, the Arabs slipped out of the Turkish yoke, and Hussein and his sons gained, at least temporarily, a preeminent position in the Arab lands.

The origins of the Arab revolt, therefore, lay more in imperial and dynastic interests than nationalist fervor, but it drew strength from and reinforced the power of Arab nationalism.

Hussein did not begin fighting immediately after concluding his correspondence with McMahon. Without an army of his own, he had first to convince the Bedouin nomads to follow him and then obtain weapons from the British. Again the enemy forced his hand, by sending a strong German and Turkish force down the Hejaz Railway to reinforce the Ottoman position in Yemen, at the southern end of the Arabian Peninsula. Hussein suspected these troops were really aimed at him, so he raised the banner of revolt on June 5, 1916. The sherif's Bedouin followers seized Mecca and most of the surrounding towns by the end of September, but Medina, the terminus of the railway, held out. The last three months of 1916 petered out as the Arabs haggled with the British for more weapons and supplies.

The chief hagglers on the British side belonged to the Arab Bureau in Cairo, a think-tank established by the Foreign Office at the beginning of 1916. England has always produced a bumper crop of romantics and adventurers who test themselves against nature and exotic cultures. The deserts of Arabia particularly attracted them, perhaps because of the total contrast to England's damp and dreary climate. Among those who fell under the spell of Arabia were a man named William Shakespear and at least one woman, Gertrude Bell. The most famous of the "Arabists" or "Orientalists," however, was Thomas Edward Lawrence. Born in 1888 to an Anglo-Irish nobleman and the governess he had run off with, T. E. Lawrence was about the same age as Hussein's son Feisal (born in 1885) and seems to have impressed him when they first met in October 1916. Lawrence had taken a short leave from the Arab Bureau that month and accompanied a British mission to the Hejaz; thereafter he served as a British liaison officer with the Arab revolt for the remainder of the war.

At the beginning of 1917 the Arab forces moved up the east coast of the Red Sea, with British naval support. Then in July 1917 a Bedouin sheikh named Auda Abu Tayeh conceived and executed a bold flanking maneuver through inhospitable desert to seize the key port of Aqaba from behind. Lawrence accompanied the Bedouin on this trek and earned their respect with his powers of physical endurance.

The seizure of Aqaba transformed the Arab revolt. Having cleared all of the Hejaz except Medina of enemy troops, Hussein now left his two oldest sons, Ali and Abdullah, to bottle up the Turks in that city and instructed Feisal to recruit new forces for a drive on Damascus. With Lawrence acting as liaison and dispensing hundreds of thousands of British pounds, the Arab forces served as the right wing of General Edmund Allenby's army when it captured Jerusalem in December 1917. After a lull in the fighting the Allies advanced north through Palestine and into Syria, with the Arabs east of the Jordan and the British to the west. The combined forces reached Damascus on September 30, 1918, then two days later both Allenby and Feisal entered the city in triumph. Arab nationalists had already set up a local administration. For the first time in centuries, Arabs controlled their first capital, the seat of the ancient Umayyad empire.

The Arab revolt proved an important asset to the Allied war effort in the Middle East. Hussein's defection from the Turks blunted their use of the religious weapon and his rebellion in the Hejaz prevented Turkish and German troops from linking up with German forces across the Red Sea in East Africa and thus threatening the sea lanes to India. On the road to Jerusalem and Damascus, Arab participation encouraged the local populace to support the invaders. All in all, the Arab Legion either killed, captured or kept under siege about 35,000 Turkish troops, greatly easing Allenby's advance.

After four years of stalemate on the western front, the rapid march of the Arabs and British through Palestine and Syria captured the attention of the Allied public, hungry for clearcut victory and dashing heroes. An American war correspondent, Lowell Thomas, romanticized T. E. Lawrence, whom he dubbed "Lawrence of Arabia," into a great white demigod commanding savage hordes. Actually, Lawrence was in no sense the commander of the Arab Legion as Thomas's dispatches and the later film, *Lawrence of Arabia* (1962), suggested. He did lead daring commando raids on the Hejaz Railway and accompanied the Bedouin on the crucial march to Aqaba, but his primary mission remained liaison between Allenby and Feisal. When the British journalist David Holden asked an elderly sheikh about Lawrence many years later, the Arab replied: "Laurens? He was the man with the gold." In short, Lawrence of Arabia served the Arab revolt as messenger and bagman.

By the time of Allenby's march, the Arab Legion was no longer so undisciplined and picturesque as the Lawrence myth implied. The Bedouin from the Arabian Peninsula remained with Ali and Abdullah besieging Medina while Feisal raised new troops among the nomads and the settled population of Palestine and Syria. Besides the irregular cavalry which had previously been his mainstay, Feisal also commanded a detachment of about eight thousand well-trained regular troops, mainly deserters or prisoners of war from the Ottoman army. Most of the officers in this column were secret members of al-Ahd. General Allenby treated them with respect and let them lead the ceremonies when liberating major cities.

Unfortunately, not all the British leaders acted so forthrightly. Before the revolt even began, England had started weaving the tangle of promises that ultimately ensnared the Arabs and robbed them of their victories. While the high commissioner in Egypt was promising Sherif Hussein Arab independence, the British Foreign Office was negotiating a partition of the Middle East with its principal ally, France.

In the closing weeks of 1915, Sir Mark Sykes, another of those wandering Englishmen fascinated by the mysterious East, met secretly with François Georges-Picot, a former consul in Beirut, at the French embassy in London. Born to a Yorkshire baron with a penchant for travel and a mother who baptized him a Catholic at age three, Sykes grew up an outsider in upper-class Britain but an expert on the Middle East. His father first took him abroad in 1886, when he was only seven years old. Sykes attended Jesus College at Oxford, coincidentally the same college as T. E. Lawrence, but unlike Lawrence he never graduated. Historian Ronald Sanders has remarked that travel was Sykes's university. In subsequent years, he wrote travel books enlivened by his own cartoons. When war broke out he signed on as assistant secretary to the British War Cabinet, overseeing foreign policy toward Muslim countries.

In his negotiation with Sykes, Picot claimed the traditional French dominance in all of Syria, an area that then embraced all of modern-day Lebanon, Syria, Israel, and Jordan. After much hard bargaining, he settled for a compromise with Sykes, dividing the Middle East into five zones, each marked by a color or a letter on an accompanying map. According to the exchange of secret diplomatic notes, which were cleared with the Russians in April 1916, then made final in May 1916, the French reserved the right to stake out a colony in the "Blue Area," encompassing Turkish Armenia and the coastal regions of Syria and Lebanon. Likewise the English claimed a free hand to colonize the "Red Area," Iraq from Baghdad to the Persian Gulf. In between these two zones, the powers pledged to recognize independent Arab states in Areas A and B, comprising most of inland Syria and what is now Jordan. However, the agreement stipulated that France would hold primary economic and political influence in Syria and British power would dominate in the trans-Jordan region. Finally, the "Brown Area," embracing the Christian, Jewish, and Muslim Holy Land of Palestine (which is now the state of Israel), was designated somewhat vaguely as a zone of "international administration."

In sum, the Sykes-Picot Agreement of 1916 carved the Arab territories of the Ottoman Empire into two colonies and two protectorates, reserving Palestine for special treatment. Needless to say, these secret arrangements conflicted with the Arabs' understanding of the British promises to Sherif Hussein. The first Arab historian to chronicle these events, George Antonius, has branded the Sykes-Picot Agreement "a shocking document" and "a startling piece of double-dealing." British journalist and historian Peter Mansfield has stated it a bit more mildly: "Britain's Arab policy evolved in a way that the British considered pragmatic but which the Arabs came to regard as unprincipled." Sykes himself was an optimist who probably believed he could juggle both French and Arab interests, somehow satisfying both parties after the war. He and other British leaders would make any promises necessary to keep their allies fighting.

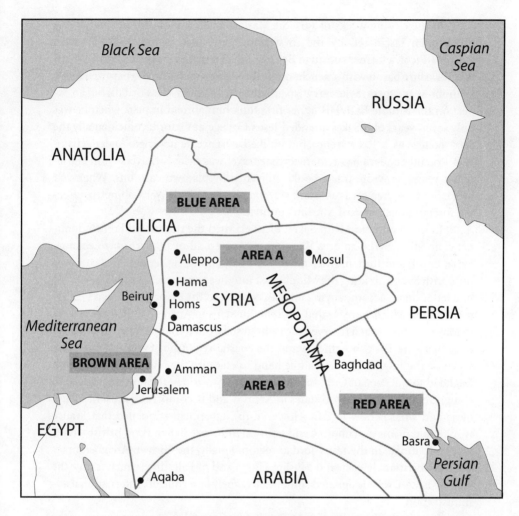

The Sykes-Picot Agreement, 1916

Hussein heard rumors of the Anglo-French deal early in 1917, so the Foreign Office sent Sykes himself to reassure the sherif. Sykes equivocated and did not reveal the exact nature of the agreement he had signed. Hussein finally learned the details at the end of 1917 when the Bolsheviks overthrew the Russian government, discovered the Allies' secret treaties, and published them to the world.

The Arab leaders received another nasty shock at this time. On November 2, 1917, the British foreign secretary, Arthur James Balfour, sent a letter to the English financier Lionel Rothschild. This letter, ever after known as the Balfour Declaration, was released to the public a week later. It read:

> His Majesty's Government view with favour the establishment in Palestine of a national home for the Jewish people and will use their best endeavours to facilitate the achievement of this object, it being clearly understood that nothing shall be done which may prejudice the civil and religious rights of existing non-Jewish communities in Palestine, or the rights and political status enjoyed by Jews in any other country.

The British government had added yet another promise to the McMahon-Hussein correspondence and the Sykes-Picot Agreement, the promise to establish a national homeland for Jews from around the world in the center of Arab territory.

The Jews, of course, had lived in the land of Israel from the time of the patriarch Abraham until after the death of Jesus Christ. The Romans, however, had defeated and dispersed them in 71 A.D. and thereafter they scattered throughout Europe and the Mediterranean world, carefully preserving their religion and their national identity though living among and often suffering persecution by Christians and Muslims. In the nineteenth century, Jews in England, France, and Germany were emancipated from the discriminatory laws that had held sway in the Middle Ages. A larger number of European Jews, however, lived in the Russian Empire and still suffered under crippling restrictions limiting where they could live and the kinds of jobs they could take.

Many Jews of Western Europe considered themselves fully assimilated into the nation-states where they lived. In England, for example, the Rothschilds and other wealthy Jews called themselves Englishmen of the Mosaic religion. Others dropped their religion entirely, converted to Christianity and intermarried with Christians. Yet most Gentiles still considered Jews different. Karl Marx, for instance, had been baptized a Christian by his parents but was a lifelong atheist; yet the readers who rubbed elbows with him daily at the British Museum called him a Jew.

Toward the end of the nineteenth century, new pseudo-scientific theories of race ascribed ethnic traits to genetic inheritance. According to racial nationalism, Jews could convert and try to assimilate, but they could not change their racial heritage any more than a leopard can change its spots. In this unhealthy atmosphere of anti-Semitism, the notion of Zionism, that is, a return of the Jews to their ancient homeland in the Middle East, emerged. Zionism, like most nationalisms, developed in reaction to the hostility of others. Just as the Arabs became nationalistic under the impact of European imperialism and Turkish oppression, Jewish nationalism grew as a response to anti-Semitism.

After the assassination of Tsar Alexander II in 1881, the Russian masses, encouraged by the government and the military, turned on the Jews as scapegoats. Pogroms, or massacres (from the Russian verb *pogromit,* to destroy), broke out across Russia and set the Jews in motion, seeking refuge in other countries. The majority of those who left Russia emigrated to the United States, but smaller numbers moved to Western Europe, and a few filtered into the ancient homeland. Associations promoting emigration to Palestine, known as the *Hovevei Zion* (Lovers of Zion), sprang up across Russia, and over the next two decades a few thousand settlers joined the handful of religious pilgrims who already lived in the Middle East. The Lovers of Zion were people seeking refuge, not a nationalist movement. Political Zionism was launched in the last decade of the nineteenth century by Theodor Herzl.

Born in 1860 in Budapest, Herzl studied law in Vienna but pursued a career as a writer, an aesthete, and a dandy. In 1891 the *Neue Freie Presse* of Vienna, one of Europe's leading newspapers, assigned the young Herzl to report from Paris, where he witnessed the Dreyfus affair, in which a Jewish army officer was sentenced to a penal colony for a crime of treason he had not in fact committed. The fierce expressions of anti-Semitism that Dreyfus's case evoked in France shocked Herzl and turned his thinking toward a remedy. He concluded that only a Jewish homeland, a nation-state of their own where Jews could "live as free men on their own soil, to die peacefully in their own homes," could restore and protect the dignity and self-respect of Jews.

In 1896 Herzl published a brief book called *Der Judenstaat* (The Jewish State), and a year later he convened the First Zionist Congress in Basel, Switzerland. The Basel Congress proclaimed that "the aim of Zionism is to create for the Jewish people a home in Palestine secured by public law." One of Herzl's followers, Max Nordau, coined the German phrase *Heimstatte* (home or homestead) instead of the word "state" in order not to provoke unnecessary opposition. Still, Herzl's goal remained avowedly political. He disdained the slow emigration of settlers into Palestine sponsored by the Lovers of Zion, scornfully calling it "infiltration," and advocated instead a grand political stroke, an agreement with the Ottoman Empire to grant the Jews a charter for mass settlement.

A new outbreak of pogroms at Kishinev in south Russia in 1903 gave greater urgency to Herzl's efforts, but ultimately his desperate diplomacy failed. The Ottomans had declared a firm policy towards Jewish immigration in 1881: "Immigrants will be able to settle as scattered groups throughout the Ottoman Empire, excluding Palestine. They must submit to all the laws of the empire and become Ottoman subjects." Such a policy precluded a deal with Herzl; but, in practice, it was openly evaded, and the numbers of Jews in Palestine grew slowly until the First World War. Herzl died in 1904, no closer to his goal than when he wrote *Der Judenstaat.* Yet he had succeeded in building a nationalist movement.

The Zionists received a relatively friendly reception in Great Britain. Protestant England was a country steeped in the Bible. As the Welsh-born politician David Lloyd George once remarked, "I was brought up in a school where I was taught far more about the history of the Jews than about the history of my own land." Evangelicals, who read the Bible literally, believed that the Jews must return to Israel before the Second Coming of the Lord and the end of the world would arrive. In addition, Jewish immigration from Russia had swelled the working-class ghettoes of Whitechapel in London and Cheetham Hill in Manchester, so British politicans were open to any scheme that might induce the Jews to move elsewhere.

Accordingly, the British government in 1903 offered Herzl a colony in East Africa (present-day Kenya), and the Zionist organization considered the matter at its 1904 and 1905 congresses before rejecting it. If refuge from persecution were the main goal, East Africa, Argentina, the United States or anywhere else would do; but the Zionists desired a "national" homeland, steeped in their own history and religion. Only Palestine, or *Eretz Israel,* the land of Israel, could satisfy this requirement.

When World War I broke out, about 85,000 Jews lived in Palestine amidst a total population between 600,000 and 800,000. This represented a larger percentage of Jews in one country than anywhere else in the world, yet it still measured only about 14 percent. The largest number of Jews resided in Jerusalem, which had a Jewish majority, but many of these were Orthodox pilgrims who had come to Israel for religious reasons and possessed little national or political consciousness. The true Zionists formed a minority within a minority, living mostly in the cities of Jaffa and Haifa, the new, entirely Jewish town of Tel Aviv, or in agricultural colonies. Jemal Pasha tried to deport the Jews of Palestine, for few of them had taken out Ottoman citizenship, but the Turks' German allies pressured him to stop before the Jews suffered the fate of the Armenians. Nevertheless, war, deportation, and emigration reduced the Jewish population of Palestine to only 56,000 in 1918, about 8 percent of the country.

At the beginning of the war, the only Jewish member of the British Cabinet, Herbert Samuel, suggested that Britain proclaim a Jewish homeland in the Middle East as one of the country's war aims. His memorandum eloquently predicted the main effect of a Jewish nation-state: "Insensibly, but inevitably, the character

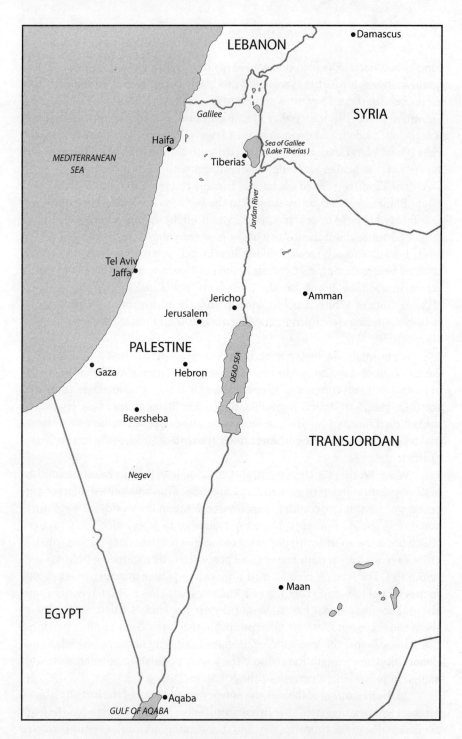

Palestine at the Time of the Balfour Declaration

of the individual Jew, wherever he might be, would be ennobled. The sordid associations which have attached to the Jewish name would be sloughed off. . . ." The prime minister, Herbert Asquith, and the rest of the Cabinet rejected this advice for the time being. However, an English Zionist leader, Chaim Weizmann, a chemist by training who was working on explosives for the wartime government, kept the issue alive. After his first meeting with Weizmann, the Bible-reading Lloyd George commented that "he kept bringing up place names which were more familiar to me than those on the Western Front."

As the Allies' wartime situation grew more desperate, the British government looked for new ways to sway world opinion. Many members of the British upper class held an exaggerated view of the Jews' international influence. Some believed that a Zionist declaration might convince American Jews to work for U.S. intervention in the war or that Russian Jewish pressure might keep the Russians fighting. Yet strategic calculations proved more important. Despite their agreements with Hussein and Picot, the British did not want either the Arabs or the French to control Palestine. The route to India represented Britain's most significant interest in the Middle East. The British intended to keep a firm hold on Egypt and the Suez Canal, and at the same time they wanted to open a land route from the Mediterranean to the head of the Persian Gulf in Iraq. This required possession of Palestine. Yet the British had promised an Arab state in the region and had agreed with France to internationalize the "Brown Area." Zionism seemingly offered a way out of these promises.

Mark Sykes took the lead in forging a Zionist policy for the British government. As a Catholic, he believed that Palestine might become a Jewish equivalent to the Vatican State, a spiritual center for Judaism, but not a politically signficant nation-state. If Britain protected the Zionists in Palestine, the empire could enjoy the best of both worlds, a strategic bastion in the Middle East ratified by spiritual authority. Ever the optimist, Sykes thought he could reconcile all this with Arab aspirations and French designs. When a coalition government took office in Britain in December 1916, with David Lloyd George as prime minister and Arthur Balfour as foreign secretary, Sykes found a sympathetic reception. After much discussion and delay, the War Cabinet finally approved the Zionist policy at its meeting on October 31, 1917. Rushing outside the Cabinet room to a waiting Chaim Weizmann, Sykes declared, "Dr. Weizmann, it's a boy."

The Balfour Declaration signified that the British would control Palestine themselves, with the championship of the Jewish national cause as an idealistic rationalization. Individual members of the British Cabinet undoubtedly believed that Zionism would right a historical wrong toward the Jewish people. As historian Barbara Tuchman has pointed out: "To be effective it had to be meant, and in 1917 it was meant." Yet the strategic goal was paramount. An Israeli historian, Mayir Verete, has concluded: "The sympathy alone of Balfour and Lloyd George for the Zionist cause would not have convinced the Cabinet to accept the Declaration. And had there been on their part sympathy alone without interests . . . it is nearly certain that the Zionist question would not have been raised by them at all in the Cabinet."

Verete makes a telling comparison to buttress his argument. The British advocated Armenian independence in reparation for the Turkish genocide against these people, but no important British interests were at stake. So in the hard bargaining after the war, the English dumped the Armenians. Sympathy without interests did not count for much in the Armenian cause, but Britain's imperial interests supported the sentimental attachment to Zionism.

Neither the Zionists nor the British seriously considered the impact of a Jewish national home upon the Arabs in Palestine. A nineteenth-century British enthusiast for Zionism, Laurence Oliphant, proposed in 1880 that the Bedouin could be driven out and the peasant Arabs settled on reservations, like the American Indians. The earliest Lovers of Zions, who emigrated from Russia after the pogroms, were sometimes surprised to discover how many Arabs lived in Palestine. They had thought they were resettling an empty land. Arthur Balfour himself wrote in 1919: "Zionism, be it right or wrong, good or bad, is rooted in age-long tradition, in present needs, in future hopes, of far profounder import than the desires and prejudices of the 700,000 Arabs who now inhabit that ancient land."

Though the British officials who took over in Palestine were far less committed to Zionism than Balfour, Arab-Zionist reconciliation proved a hopeless task, for two national revivals were clashing within the boundaries of one very small region, "a country the size of Wales, much of it barren mountain and a part of it waterless," as Herbert Samuel once phrased it. The Jewish historian Walter Laqueur concluded in his history of Zionism, "There was a basic clash between two national movements. . . . It is impossible even with the benefit of hindsight to point with any degree of conviction to an alternative Zionist policy . . . which might have prevented conflict."

This was not immediately clear after the war, for the ambiguous phraseology of the Balfour Declaration did not specify that a Jewish national home would necessarily lead to a national state with a Jewish majority. The British and French mollified Arab feelings with a joint declaration on November 7, 1918, promising that new governments in the Middle East would "derive their authority from the free exercise of the initiative and choice of the indigenous populations." Trusting this new promise, Feisal, who attended the Paris Peace Conference as his father's delegate, signed an agreement with Chaim Weizmann accepting the Balfour Declaration and permitting large-scale Jewish immigration into Palestine. Yet Feisal was no innocent straight from the desert. He had grown up in the capital of intrigues, Constantinople, and served in the Ottoman parliament. He did not trust anyone unconditionally, so in an addendum to the agreement he stipulated that its provisions would only take effect "provided the Arabs obtain their independence as demanded."

As it turned out, the Arab revolt did not result in full independence for all the Arab lands. Instead the victorious Allies imposed the Sykes-Picot Agreement, with some substantial modifications in favor of Great Britain.

The French had taken little part in the Middle Eastern fighting, but when General Allenby drove to Jerusalem he was accompanied by none other than François Georges-Picot, assigned as French consul to the liberated territories. Allenby, however, declared martial law in Palestine and politely but firmly froze the French out of the country's governance. Prospects for an "international administration" of Palestine disappeared forever. The British military also kept a firm hold on Iraq, largely with Indian troops. Lest they lose any more influence, therefore, the French hastily landed soldiers in Beirut right after the war to prop up their interests in Lebanon and Syria. An Arab administration remained in Damascus, for the time being, with British support.

Feisal proved unable to win recognition for Arab independence at the Paris Peace Conference. The powers instead were planning to take over the newly conquered countries in the guise of "mandates" from the League of Nations. In the meantime, Mark Sykes, working feverishly behind the scenes in Syria and Palestine, finally discovered how deep-rooted Arab nationalism had become and how hopelessly it conflicted with Jewish, French, and British interests. He returned to Paris exhausted in February 1919 and was felled by the flu epidemic raging throughout the postwar world. He died within two days, at the age of forty.

Disgusted by the barely concealed imperialism of the great powers, the survivors of the Arab nationalist society al-Fatat held elections and convened the General Syrian Congress on July 2, 1919, in Damascus. The congress demanded independence for all of Syria, including Lebanon and Palestine, with Feisal ruling as a constitutional monarch. The Syrian resolutions protested the notion of big power mandates, acidly remarking that "the Arab inhabitants of Syria are not less fitted or gifted than were certain other nations (such as Bulgarians, Serbs, Greeks, and Rumanians) when granted independence. . . ." The congress also rejected "the claims of the Zionists for a Jewish commonwealth. . . ."

Feisal was willing to compromise and save at least some form of Arab self-rule and his prospects for a throne, but the Syrian General Congress rejected all deals and declared independence. The French then issued an ultimatum to the Syrians, which Feisal accepted; but like the Austro-Hungarians when the Serbs accepted their ultimatum in 1914, French troops invaded anyway and took Damascus on July 25, 1919. The British felt embarrassed by this but they accepted it, since the French had something they wanted, potential oil fields in northern Syria around Mosul.

One of those intrepid English adventurers had discovered the first Middle

Eastern oil in 1908 in Persia, and the British navy had converted its ships from coal furnaces to oil burners just before the war. Oil was also known to exist in Iraq and the Mosul region, and the British were determined to control it. They therefore acquiesced in France's control over Lebanon and Syria in exchange for Mosul, which was subtracted from the French mandate and added to British-controlled Iraq.

The Allies ratified this deal at the Italian resort town of San Remo in April 1920, where they formally assigned France the mandate for Lebanon and Syria, and the British assumed control over Iraq and Palestine. The San Remo agreement affirmed the Balfour Declaration, and the British spent the next twenty years unsuccessfully trying to reconcile Jewish and Arab interests in Palestine. Still hoping to wiggle out of their tangle of promises, the British made one more attempt at an overall Middle East accord. Winston Churchill, the colonial secretary, convened a conference at Cairo in March 1921 and offered a face-saving deal to the family of Hussein. Feisal, whom the French had kicked out of Damascus, was named king of Iraq. Then the British detached the lightly populated Arab regions of Palestine lying east of the Jordan River and created a new kingdom of Transjordan with Abdullah as ruler. The final postwar settlement in the Middle East, therefore, created five new nations: Lebanon and Syria under French control, and Palestine, Transjordan, and Iraq under British mandate. Arbitrary lines through the desert which the British and the French drew in the 1920s still outline the frontiers of these countries today.

Two of the Hashemites who had led the Arab revolt made their peace with the British and garnered uneasy thrones in Arab lands. Under Feisal Iraq eventually gained full independence from Britain and was admitted to the League of Nations in 1932. The other states waited until after World War II to win their freedom. The military eventually deposed Feisal's successor in Iraq but a Hashemite, the great-grandson of Hussein, grand sherif of Mecca, still rules today as King Hussein of Jordan.

The original Hussein was less fortunate than his sons. He badgered the British to honor their promises of complete Arab independence, yet at the same time he needed British aid to fend off a stronger rival in the Arabian Peninsula, the warlike ruler of central Arabia, Abdul Aziz al Saud (usually called Ibn Saud by Europeans). The House of Saud had long ago allied itself with a fundamentalist Muslim sect called the Wahhabis and had gradually consolidated its position in the desert center of the peninsula. At British insistence, the Saudis had sat out the war against Turkey, but after the war they pressured Hussein's meager forces in the Hejaz. Britain discouraged them for a time, but when Hussein refused to ratify the imposition of the mandates, the British left him to his fate. Ibn Saud conquered the Hejaz in 1924-25, sending Hussein into a bitter exile on the island of Cyprus. He died in 1931 at his son Abdullah's court in Amman, Transjordan, after persuading the British to let him die in an Arab land. The Saudis, meanwhile,

214

earned recognition as the dominant power in Arabia at the Treaty of Jedda, signed by the British in 1927.

Those Arabs who raised the banner of revolt against the Turks during World War I, therefore, received relatively little reward for their military exploits. Arab nationalism clashed with the imperialism of two European powers and jostled for room with the Jewish national revival and the dynastic power of the Saudis. The British, entering their final generation of world power, had wrapped the Middle East in a tangle of promises, which the rest of the century could not fully unwind.[3]

3. To cynical readers looking for hidden motives, I should point out that oil played no role in the conflicts over the Arabian Peninsula or Palestine. The British had oil in mind when they seized Iraq and dealt for Mosul, but oil was not discovered in Saudi Arabia until 1938 and has never been found in Palestine.

CHAPTER THIRTEEN

The Beginning of the End

The British had stimulated Arab nationalism for their own ends during World War I, then frustrated it at war's end with the barely disguised imperialism of the mandate system. Yet a more fully developed nationalism, at England's own back door, successfully challenged the British during and after the war. The Easter Rising and the war of independence in Ireland signaled the beginning of the end for the world's most formidable empire.

Ireland was Great Britain's first overseas colony. In 1169, just a century after the Normans conquered England itself, Anglo-Norman knights landed on the smaller, green island to the west and carved out a sphere of influence around Dublin called the English Pale. Yet for several hundred years they lacked the will to complete the conquest and were partly assimilated by the native Irish, just as earlier Viking conquerors had been. Only after the Protestant Reformation, in the last years of Queen Elizabeth I's reign, did the English throw their full military power against Ireland. In 1603, a few days after Elizabeth had died, the Earl of Mountjoy crushed the last independent Irish chieftain, Hugh O'Neill, earl of Tyrone, in the northern province of Ulster. Four years later, in the "flight of the earls," O'Neill and over a hundred chieftains left for the Continent. In the leadership vacuum they left behind, England staked out its first overseas colony.

The English considered the "wild Irish" as little different from the Indians of North America, where they were also planting colonies at this time (the first permanent English colony was settled at Jamestown in 1607). In fact, the English had developed their conquest ideology while trying to colonize Ireland in previous centuries. The essential first step was to think of the Irish (or the Indians or the Africans) as "savages," as a lower form of life. If this were true, then conquest was good for the peoples conquered; it was a process of civilizing the savages. All

European imperialists justified their conquests around the world in this fashion. The English did it first in Ireland.

After the flight of the earls, Elizabeth's successor, King James I, seized all the land abandoned by them in six northern Irish counties — Armagh, Cavan, Donegal, Fermanagh, Derry, and Tyrone — and leased it to "undertakers," entrepreneurs who undertook to bring in colonists. The City of London claimed the largest lease, renaming Derry in northern Ireland Londonderry. More Scottish Presbyterians than Englishmen took up land in the government-sponsored Plantation of Ulster, and many more Scots came across independently, settling in the two easternmost counties of Down and Antrim. At its narrowest point, the north channel of the Irish Sea, which separates Scotland from Ireland, is only twelve miles wide.

Despite its closeness, Ireland seemed a wilderness to the new Protestant settlers, both Scottish and English, and the conquered natives remained decidedly hostile. The colonists built fortified farmhouses, or bawns, and erected stout walls around the market towns. Historian A. T. Q. Stewart has pointed out that the first Presbyterians in Ulster "had to struggle to survive the first winter, as the Puritan fathers were to do in New Plymouth a few years later. . . ." The Bible-reading Ulster Scots, like the Puritans in America, compared themselves to the ancient Israelites, settling amid hostile tribes in the land of Canaan.

By the end of the seventeenth century, after King William of Orange put down the last serious Irish rebellion at the Battle of the Boyne in 1690, Ireland had become home to three distinct religious and national groups. English Protestants, who belonged to the established Anglican Church, formed the ruling class with a monopoly on political power, though they were only a tiny minority throughout the island. Scots Presbyterians comprised a more formidable minority in Ulster, but their numbers were insignificant elsewhere. The majority of Irish Catholics lost ownership of the land and were pushed to the margins of society. Historian Donald Akenson has discovered that land ownership in Ulster can be determined by simply measuring a farm's distance above sea level. If the land lies more than fifty meters above the nearest market town, it must be owned by Catholics. Protestant settlers seized the fertile valleys in the seventeenth century and have remained there.

For a century after the British settlement of Ireland, the Anglo-Protestant ascendancy imposed the Penal Laws upon both Irish Catholics and Scots Presbyterians. The Test Act of 1704, for example, required the taking of communion in the Anglican Church as a prerequisite for all officeholders. The Penal Laws came down more heavily on Catholics than Presbyterians, however; and at the first sign of Catholic rebelliousness, Presbyterians closed ranks with the Anglo-Protestants. The Penal Laws exiled Catholic bishops, outlawed religious orders, forbade the importation of priests from the Continent, and heavily regu-

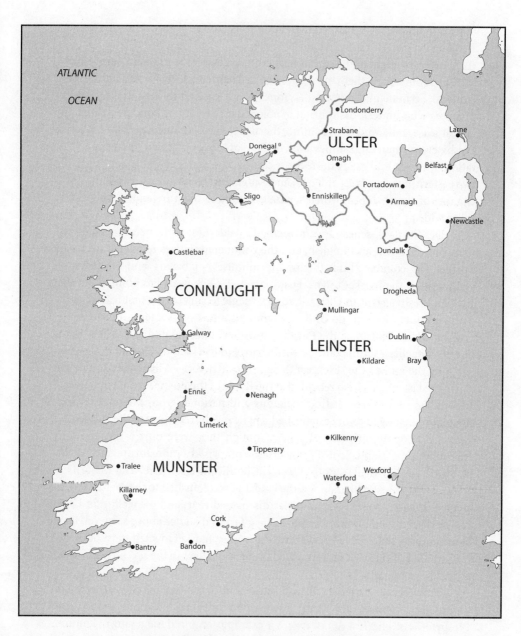

The Historic Four Provinces of Ireland

lated the remaining Catholic clergy. Catholics could not vote, hold office, practice law, establish their own schools, or purchase land. They paid taxes to support the established Anglican Church.

The Penal Laws were not always rigorously enforced, and most of them were repealed by the end of the eighteenth century, but they clearly stamped the Irish Catholics as a subject nation. On paper, the status of Catholics (and Presbyterians) in Ireland looked far worse than the condition of Christians and Jews in the Ottoman Empire. In practice, their conditions may have been just about the same. Yet Muslims did not openly ridicule minority religions the way Englishmen defamed Catholicism. Furthermore, the Protestant Anglo-Irish enjoyed more political rights in their own country than the ruling class of Ottomans did in Turkey, so the contrast between rulers and ruled stood out more starkly. This history of humiliation became the seedbed of Irish nationalism.

Few Irish at this time extolled the glories of their own language, as Arab nationalists did. In fact, by 1800 Gaelic was in full retreat before the onslaught of English and was spoken only in isolated rural districts. The Irish instead nurtured their nationalism on the resentments of conquest and poverty and the beliefs of their Catholic religion. Had the English treated the Catholic religion with respect and tolerance, they would probably have annexed Ireland successfully, just as they pacified Scotland and Wales. Yet, even though the British Parliament declared Ireland a part of the United Kingdom in 1800, the Irish never ceased their resistance.

As the nineteenth century unfolded, two separate nationalist movements developed among Irish Catholics: a political struggle to change the constitution and win greater freedom for Ireland, and a romantic, revolutionary movement of physical force and cultural revival. Daniel O'Connell led a successful campaign for Irish emancipation, that is, an end to the remaining Penal Laws. O'Connell's Catholic Association, formed in 1823, mobilized the Irish masses for the first time and won them the right to vote in 1829. The "Great Emancipator" led another mass movement in the 1840s to repeal the union with England and gain a form of Home Rule (a subordinate status similar to that of an American state), but the movement failed and O'Connell died in 1847.

Daniel O'Connell was the father of Irish nationalism, yet he admired English government and culture. A native speaker of Irish in his youth, he abandoned the language and assumed that an autonomous or independent Ireland would be an English-speaking country. Yet another mid-nineteenth century group of nationalists, collectively known as Young Ireland, taught themselves Gaelic, recovered some of the poetry and legends of the distant Irish past, and idealized the simple country folk of the *Gaeltacht,* the increasingly smaller area in the west of Ireland where Gaelic remained the native tongue. Young Irelanders mounted an armed uprising against the British in 1848, a year when revolutions broke out across Europe, but they failed miserably. The country people of Ireland

219

had no energy to revolt, for they were in the grips of the terrible potato famine which raged from 1846 to 1848. When the potato crops failed, over a million Irish died and millions more emigrated to America. The population, which had stood at 8 million in the early 1840s, finally stabilized at about 4 million and remained there for over a century, through a policy of late marriage and frequent emigration.

Though Young Irelanders failed in their own time, their cultural romanticism and their dedication to revolutionary violence established a second current within Irish nationalism. Just as importantly, they carried on an old tradition of suffering and martyrdom. Laying down one's life for the people held a powerful religious appeal for devoutly Catholic nationalists who contemplated the image of their crucified Savior, Jesus Christ, in every church. Irish nationalism possessed tremendous staying power because it believed in "the triumph of failure."

The twin nationalist movements of constitutional struggle and physical force continued in counterpoint for the rest of the nineteenth century. On St. Patrick's Day in 1858, James Stephens organized the Irish Republican Brotherhood, a secret society often known as Fenians. The English easily suppressed a Fenian rising in 1867, but again they provided martyrs for the cause, three rebels executed after trying to stage a jail break in Manchester, England.

Shortly after the failure of the Fenian rising, a Dublin lawyer, Isaac Butt, formed the Home Rule Party to win political autonomy for Ireland within the United Kingdom. In the 1874 general election, the first conducted via secret ballot, the Home Rulers secured 59 of the 103 Irish seats in the British Parliament. A year later, Charles Stewart Parnell, a landlord in County Wicklow, won a by-election as a Home Ruler and soon took over the movement.

Parnell proved a true successor to Daniel O'Connell in Irish politics, mobilizing the resentments of Irish Catholics and tapping the funds of Irish-Americans. He forged an alliance with the Irish Land League, a radical movement of tenant farmers demanding the reduction of rents and an end to forced evictions. By joining with the often violent Land Leaguers, Parnell combined a hint of physical force with his own political movement. The two strains of Irish nationalism proved most effective when they worked in tandem.

Parnell realized that his Irish Parliamentary Party could hold the balance of power between the two major parties in Great Britain and bring down governments that displeased him. In 1885 he denied a majority to the Conservatives and supported the Liberal William Gladstone for prime minister. Gladstone introduced the Home Rule bill in 1886, offering a limited form of political autonomy to Ireland, but the bill was defeated in the House of Commons, with many Liberals defecting from Gladstone. The Commons passed a second Home Rule bill in 1893, but the Conservative House of Lords rejected it. In the meantime, Parnell had been driven from politics in a nasty sex scandal (he was openly living with

Kitty O'Shea, a married woman) and had died of tuberculosis in 1891. By the turn of the twentieth century, both revolutionary violence and political action had failed to secure either Home Rule or independence for Ireland.

The British, meanwhile, with Conservatives back in power for most of the 1890s and the first few years of the new century, pursued a policy of law and order combined with economic reforms in Ireland. Arthur Balfour (later the author of the Zionist Balfour Declaration) served as chief secretary for Ireland from 1887 to 1891, earning the nickname "Bloody Balfour" for his firm coercion of nationalist agitation. Yet he also established the Congested Districts Board in 1891 that targeted relief aid and economic stimulus at the most depressed portions of the country. Historian Lawrence McCaffrey has characterized the Congested Districts Board as "the most intelligent, successful, and humane product of British rule in Ireland."

Balfour's successors also went a long way toward solving the problems of tenant farmers, by loaning them money to buy out their landlords and become independent farmers. Under the land acts of 1903 and 1909, Irish Catholic peasants took over about half the arable land in Ireland. The British also extended a system of national schools throughout the country, producing a literacy rate of nearly 100 percent. In sum, British policy in Ireland at the turn of the century has been characterized as "killing Home Rule with kindness." Nevertheless, the British did not kill the Home Rule movement, or the spirit of Irish revolt, either with kindness or coercion. Reforms had come too late, after Irish nationalism had already blossomed out of history, humiliation, and religion.

Around the turn of the century, Ireland experienced a remarkable cultural revival that further stimulated the growth of nationalism. In 1893 Douglas Hyde, Eoin MacNeill, and other intellectuals organized the Gaelic League to preserve the threatened Gaelic language where it still was spoken and to extend its use to a new generation. League members wrote poetry and prose in Gaelic and translated Irish classics into English for those who had irrevocably lost the old language. Though generally non-political, they lobbied for the teaching of Gaelic in the national schools. The revival of Gaelic never caught on with the masses, but it did provide an advanced group of nationalists with a new reason for national pride.

The Gaelic League was an elite movement that appealed to the educated middle class in towns and cities, but the growing pride in Irish customs percolated down to the masses through the work of the Gaelic Athletic Association. The GAA tried to recapture the soul of Ireland by de-Anglicizing everyday life. The association promoted ancient Irish games such as hurling in place of cricket or rugby. Though the GAA was non-political at first, its emphasis on physical fitness made it a natural recruiting ground for revolutionaries.

A third movement, the Irish literary revival, is often listed along with the

Gaelic League and the Gaelic Athletic Association as a sign of Irish cultural re-birth at this time. This literary revival, associated with the poetry of William Butler Yeats and the theatrical productions of the Abbey Theatre in Dublin, made a permanent mark on world literature, and it did draw on ancient Irish sources and romantic Irish emotions. Yet the majority of its writers were Protestant Anglo-Irish and they produced their literary output almost exclusively in the English language. So it is a related movement, not part of the mainstream of Irish cultural nationalism at the turn of the century.

The old Fenians, most of whom had been on the run in America since their unsuccessful rising of the 1860s, recognized the revolutionary potential of the Irish cultural revival. In 1907 they sent Tom Clarke, a bitter man of about fifty whose health but not his spirit had been broken by fifteen years in English jails, back to Ireland to reinvigorate the Irish Republican Brotherhood. While running a tobacco shop in Dublin, Clarke quietly recruited eager young men and infiltrated them into the Gaelic League, the GAA, and other organizations. By 1914 this revolutionary cabal had forced Douglas Hyde, the Protestant founder of the Gaelic League, to resign from its presidency in protest against its increasingly political activities.

Another new organization that the IRB infiltrated offered a middle ground between the legal political action of the home rulers and the revolutionary plotting of the Fenians. Arthur Griffith, a Dublin journalist, wrote a book called *The Resurrection of Hungary* in 1904, proposing the Dual Monarchy of Austria-Hungary as a model for Ireland's relationship with England. Griffith advocated far more autonomy than the Home Rulers did; in fact his ideal would be a republic in all but name, preserving only a tenuous tie to Britain through recognition of a common monarch. Griffith also proposed a new non-violent strategy, similar to that being worked out by Mohandas Gandhi of India, for attaining this quasi-independent status. He argued that when Irishmen were elected to the Parliament of Great Britain they should refuse to take their seats, withdrawing to Ireland to set up a shadow government, complete with informal arbitration panels so Irish citizens could avoid litigation in British courts. In addition, Ireland would develop its economic independence by boycotting British goods and adopting a "buy Irish" consumer policy. Through moral, political, and economic pressure, therefore, Irish policy would force England to recognize a fait accompli. Griffith adopted the name *Sinn Fein* ("ourselves alone") for the organization he founded in 1908. Though it offered Irish nationalists a new goal and a new strategy, Sinn Fein remained for the moment a small fringe group.

While poets dreamed, Griffith argued, and Tom Clarke schemed, the Irish Parliamentary Party, under the leadership of Parnell's successor, John Redmond, continued its political quest for Home Rule. The Liberal Party returned to power in 1906 with such a huge majority that it didn't need any Irish votes, but after their majority in the House of Commons dwindled they again tried to satisfy the Home Rulers. Foreseeing continued obstruction by the House of Lords, Liberal Prime Minister Herbert Asquith forced through a Parliament bill in 1911 that reduced the power of the Lords to veto legislation. Henceforth, the upper house could delay passage of a bill until it was passed in three successive years, but they could not veto it outright. The Liberals then passed a Home Rule bill in 1912, the Lords suspended it, but everyone knew that it would finally pass in 1914.

Considering the ruckus which the Home Rule bill caused, it is worth considering how little autonomy it would have granted to Ireland. The British Parliament retained control not only over foreign affairs and defense, but also revenue, coinage, the post office, and, for a number of years, the police. Home Rulers hoped to obtain about the same powers that an American state enjoyed in the United States, but Asquith's bill granted them much less than that.

Nevertheless, the near certainty of Home Rule took Irish nationalism out of the realm of theory and forced serious decisions on Irish leaders. The first to react were the Protestant Unionists of Ulster. Hypothetically, all residents of Ireland might have become Irish nationalists and welcomed Home Rule, regardless of their religion or ethnic origin. Ireland, after all, was a separate island, ruled from overseas for centuries, and any Irish man or woman might reflect on this history and opt for fuller autonomy. In the past, some of the most important Irish nationalist leaders, such as Charles Stewart Parnell, had been Protestants, and the founder of the Gaelic League, Douglas Hyde, was also a Protestant.

Yet Parnell and Hyde remained exceptions, for religion divided the Irish like a chasm. In particular, the Scots Presbyterians had lived with a siege mentality since their settlement of Ulster in the seventeenth century. Though originally discriminated against by the Anglicans, they had increasingly thrown in their lot with the English in a united front against Catholic pretensions. Industrialization of the Belfast region in the nineteenth century drew Ulster closer to England and emphasized its separateness from rural Ireland. Therefore, the Ulster Scots overwhelmingly rejected Home Rule and vowed to fight for the union with England.

Sir Edward Carson, an Anglo-Irish lawyer from Dublin, and James Craig, an Ulster Presbyterian from Belfast, led the Unionist resistance. After the passage of the 1911 Parliament bill which reduced the power of the Lords and rendered Home Rule possible, the Unionists staged a massive rally on the grounds of Craig's estate (he was the son of a wealthy industrialist) outside Belfast. The following year, in September 1912, Craig and Carson organized simultaneous mass meetings throughout Ulster at which over 200,000 men (practically the whole male Protestant population of Ulster) signed the Solemn League and Covenant. They pledged themselves to use "all means which may be found necessary to defeat the present conspiracy to set up a Home Rule Parliament in Ireland." The "conspiracy," of course, was no conspiracy at all, but an act of the British Parliament. By pledging to resist its authority, the Unionists were actually vowing to commit treason. Nor were they bluffing. In January 1913, the Unionists organized a military force called the Ulster Volunteers that openly drilled in the streets of Belfast. On the night of April 24-25, 1914, the Volunteers smuggled in a massive shipment of rifles and ammunition they had purchased from Germany. Ulster was armed and ready.

Irish Catholic nationalists swiftly followed suit, organizing the Irish Volunteers in 1913 to defend Home Rule. Though they too smuggled in weapons from Germany on July 26, 1914, the guns they obtained were inferior in number and quality to those the well-financed Ulster Volunteers had purchased.

Thus, the Liberal Government of England faced two private armies in Ireland, and it soon discovered that its own military forces were neither impartial nor reliable. Both the chief of staff, Lord Roberts, and the director of military operations, Sir Henry Wilson, openly counseled Craig and Carson on their resistance to Parliament. Then in March 1914 the British officers at the Curragh military camp in Ireland, when put on alert for possible duty against the Ulster Volunteers in the north, pledged to resign their commissions rather than obey such orders. Though not technically a "mutiny," such open resistance by the military showed the British government that they could not force Home Rule on Ulster. Therefore, Asquith began exploring various schemes of partition, whereby Southern Ireland would be granted Home Rule but Northern Ireland would remain in the United Kingdom.

Yet Protestants and Catholics could not agree whether the exclusion of Ulster should be temporary or permanent or on how big a territory should be excluded. As the passage of Home Rule in September 1914 approached, Ireland teetered on the brink of civil war. Only the assassination of the archduke in Sarajevo and the outbreak of World War I prevented this. The Asquith government passed the Home Rule Act, but immediately suspended it until the end of the war. The Irish question had been deferred, not solved.

John Redmond and the Irish Parliamentary Party supported the war effort and encouraged Irishmen to enlist in the British army. Redmond found himself in a difficult position. Irish nationalists had long been battling to shed their reputation as "wild Irish" and prove they were capable of self-government. By defending Britain in its moment of peril, Redmond hoped to put all doubts to rest and prove the loyalty and capability of the Irish nation; yet he risked the appearance of selling out. In September 1914, however, most Europeans still expected the struggle against Germany to last only a few months, so Redmond took the risk of urging the Irish to enlist. About 43,000 Irishmen signed up immediately and another 37,000 enlisted in the first half of 1915. Yet most of these were Protestant Unionists or working-class Catholics who were fighting poverty more than the Germans. As the war dragged on, Irish enlistment fell off drastically.

Redmond's gamble also split the Irish Volunteer Organization. The great majority, about 170,000 men, remained loyal to Redmond and renamed themselves the National Volunteers. Some of them enlisted as individuals in the British army, fighting and dying at Gallipoli and in the trenches of the western front. Yet about 11,000 dissidents retained the original name of Irish Volunteers and elected Eoin MacNeill as their chief of staff. MacNeill's cadets drilled and paraded openly but pursued a cautious strategy. They intended to defend Home Rule, whenever it was granted, against any challenge from Ulster, and they determined to resist conscription into the British army if the English should attempt it; but they were not plotting a revolution. However, the Irish Republican Brotherhood, who had infiltrated the Volunteers, was hatching a revolt. Following the old adage, "England's difficulty is Ireland's opportunity," the leaders of the IRB hoped that circumstances would permit a successful rebellion sometime before the First World War ended. They determined to mount such a revolt only after a democratic process of debate within the organization.

A tiny group of IRB conspirators, however, led by Tom Clarke and his young national organizer, Sean MacDermott, proved more impatient. They organized a secret military council in May 1915 and actively plotted an uprising, which finally took place on Easter Monday, April 24, 1916. The Easter Rising, like the Bolshevik Revolution the following year, was a secret conspiracy, hatched by an undemocratic process that surprised nearly everyone, including many of its supposed leaders. Irish historian Mark Tierney has accurately labeled it "an artificial phenomenon, deliberately contrived by a minority within a minority."

Clarke and MacDermott were not Bolsheviks themselves. No dreams of class conflict or social revolution motivated them, only simple hatred of England. James Connolly, however, whom Clarke and MacDermott coopted onto the military council in January 1916, was a dedicated socialist. He and James Larkin had founded the Irish Transportation and General Workers' Union, led a Dublin general strike in 1913, and organized the Irish Citizen Army of about two hundred workers to resist reprisals by employers. The failure of English trade unions to support his general strike convinced Connolly to set aside his socialist dreams for a time and concentrate on the nationalist struggle for independence. When he met with Clarke and MacDermott, therefore, he pledged the Irish Citizen Army to aid the forces of the Irish Volunteers. Four other nationalist leaders — Patrick Pearse, Thomas MacDonagh, Joseph Mary Plunkett, and Edmund Kent[1] — filled out the roster of the secret military council.

Though Clarke and MacDermott were the chief instigators of the rising,

---

1. I have consistently used the more familiar English version of most Irish names, even though some nationalists adopted Gaelic forms — thus, Sean MacDermott for Sean MacDiarmida, and Edmund Kent for Eamonn Ceannt.

and Connolly proved its most gifted military leader, Patrick Pearse best typified the spirit of the rebellion. According to his biographer, Ruth Dudley Edwards, Pearse "usually dressed in black, and this, combined with his natural earnestness of expression and his high smooth forehead, made him look like a young clergyman." In fact, Pearse was the most religious of the rebels, a daily Mass-goer who neither smoked nor drank and had no time for social or sexual relations with women. As a kind of secular priest, he gave the Easter Rising a decidedly Catholic twist with his thirst for martyrdom and Christ-like self-sacrifice.

Pearse was a Gaelic poet and educator who did not join the revolutionary IRB until December 1913; but as early as 1908, when he was organizing the private school of St. Enda's, he wrote in the school's prospectus: "It will be attempted to inculcate in them [the schoolboys] the desire to spend their lives working hard and zealously for their fatherland and, if it should ever be necessary, to die for it." Pearse held romantic views about violence. In 1913 he proclaimed that "bloodshed is a cleansing and sanctifying thing, and the nation which regards it as the final horror has lost its manhood. There are many things more horrible than bloodshed; and slavery is one of them." Many young Europeans marched off to war in 1914 sharing these views, but Pearse added a uniquely Catholic, religious dimension. In his last political testament, he wrote:

> Like a divine religion, national freedom bears the marks of unity, of sanctity, of catholicity, of apostolic succession. Of unity, for it contemplates the nation as one; of sanctity, for it is holy in itself and in those who serve it; of catholicity, for it embraces all the men and women of the nation; of apostolic succession, for it, or the aspiration after it, passes down from generation to generation from the nation's fathers.

In this spirit of sublime self-sacrifice for church and nation, both of which were one, holy, catholic, and apostolic, Pearse and those who thought like him mounted a hopeless and unsuccessful revolt against the English in 1916.

The Easter Rising almost fizzled before it began. The original plan scheduled a landing of arms from Germany on Saturday, April 22, and then a rising of all 10,000 or more Volunteers throughout the country the next day, Easter Sunday. The British navy, however, intercepted the German merchant ship, whose captain scuttled the vessel, sending the weapons to the bottom. Roger Casement, a nationalist who had accompanied the arms ship in a German submarine, was captured shortly after landing. Then the legal head of the Irish Volunteers, Eoin MacNeill, finally discovered the plans for a rising and countermanded the orders. Clarke, Pearse, and the other members of the military council, however, had come too far to stop now; so they scaled down their plans to a Dublin-only rising and mustered out about 1,000 Volunteers on Easter Monday, April 24, a spring holiday when many British troops were on leave or attending the horse races.

At noon on Monday, Pearse, styling himself president of the provisional government and "Commandant-General, Commanding in Chief, Army of the Irish Republic," and James Connolly, commandant of the Dublin Brigade of the Volunteers, seized the General Post Office from a group of startled civil servants. The GPO, a massive classical hulk on Sackville Street (now renamed O'Connell Street), was the symbolic heart of Dublin, the landmark around which shops and businesses clustered. Outside the post office, Pearse read a declaration signed by the seven members of the military council, proclaiming "the Irish Republic as a Sovereign Independent State."

James Connolly directed the defense of the General Post Office and its surrounding buildings, while Pearse, in the words of his biographer, "was to spend most of the week doing what he always did — writing, talking, and thinking." One comrade at the GPO recalled that he and Pearse endlessly discussed the theological arguments that justify revolution. Three other members of the military council, Tom Clarke, Sean MacDermott, and Joseph Mary Plunkett, were also present in the GPO, as was a detachment of female nurses and cooks from the *Cumann na mBan* (League of Women).

Meanwhile, other battalions of the Dublin Brigade seized the Four Courts in the center of Dublin on the north bank of the Liffey River, and Jacob's Biscuit Factory, Boland's Flour Mill, and the South Dublin Union (a poorhouse complex), all south of the Liffey. The Irish Citizen Army, made up of unionized workers under the command of Michael Mallin and the radical Countess Constance Markiewicz (an Anglo-Irishwoman married to a Polish count), marched into St. Stephen's Green, a central square of Dublin; but British rifle fire drove them back to the College of Surgeons on the west side of the square. The Irish Republicans followed the same strategy as the Bolsheviks in Petrograd a year later. They seized a number of strong points in the city and declared themselves in charge. Unfortunately for them, the legitimate government did not collapse as Kerensky's regime did in Russia.

The British authorities had been pursuing a lenient policy to keep Ireland quiet during the world war. They did not arrest known leaders of the IRB nor extend conscription to Ireland when it took effect in England in 1916, and they had gotten accustomed to what they considered the comical parades and drills of Irish Volunteers. So the rising took the British by surprise. Yet they reacted swiftly to crush it, immediately labeling it a German plot, though, in fact, the abortive arms shipment was the only German involvement.

The British military took advantage of the rebels' immobility and applied a strategy of slow strangulation. Soldiers cordoned off the inner city of Dublin, then brought in artillery and a gunboat on the Liffey to bombard the Irish positions. By Friday, April 28, when General John G. Maxwell took over the British command, the heavy shelling had destroyed block after block of working-class Dublin, with heavy civilian casualties, and fires were raging in the vicinity of the General Post Office and elsewhere throughout the city. Dublin endured a small-scale version of the Blitz which devastated London in the next war.

James Connolly had suffered a bullet wound in his ankle on Thursday and was writhing in agony on a cot at the GPO. Then on Friday a British shell registered a direct hit and the building caught fire. Pearse released the prisoners he had been holding and sent the women away, then he and his compatriots evacuated the burning building, taking shelter on Friday night in surrounding homes and shops. Pearse surrendered unconditionally on Saturday, signing a surrender order at 3:45 P.M., April 29. Elizabeth O'Farrell, an Irish nurse, carried Pearse's order to the other commandants still holding out, and by Sunday all had surrendered.

The Easter Rising lasted just six days and ended in failure. About 450 people, mostly civilians, had died in the fighting and much of downtown Dublin lay in ruins. Yet, as one historian has styled it, consciously imitating John Reed's classic description of the Bolshevik Revolution, it was "six days to shake an empire." Pearse's declaration of independence on Easter Monday marked the beginning of the end for English rule in Ireland, though the struggle took seven more years to complete.

The British themselves pushed the Irish along toward independence by their bumbling policies during and after the rising. In retrospect, it is easy to see that the British military should have held their fire during the rising, simply cordoning off the affected areas and waiting the rebels out. Had they done so, they might have won Irish public opinion to their side. Wives of soldiers at the western front, for example, could not pick up their welfare checks at the GPO and would have turned on the rebels had the siege continued longer. Still, this is asking for more restraint than soldiers can be expected to show during wartime.

It is harder to understand the politically inept policy of reprisals that General Maxwell carried out after the rising. He tried nearly 200 rebel leaders in secret courts-martial lasting no more than five minutes each, and simply interned about 2,000 others without trials of any kind. Maxwell's troops began executing the ringleaders on Wednesday, May 3, just three days after the surrender. A firing squad dispatched Patrick Pearse, Tom Clarke, and Thomas MacDonagh that day, and Joseph Plunkett and three others died the next. Pearse had been courting martyrdom openly, Clarke was an old man, and Plunkett was already dying of tuberculosis, but MacDonagh was an eminent professor with a wife and children and a full life to look forward to. The British shot a few more rebels each day until Friday, May 12, when James Connolly and Sean MacDermott died.

Connolly's execution seemed particularly humiliating. His ankle wound was so severe that he could not stand to meet the firing squad, so the British strapped him into a chair and shot him sitting down. By the time the authorities came to their senses and commuted the remaining sentences to life imprisonment, they had executed fifteen rebels. Roger Casement's treason trial in England later that year also seemed outrageous, for he was prosecuted by F. E. Smith, a notorious Ulster Protestant leader, and the government leaked copious hints of Casement's homosexuality to the press. The British executed Casement, bringing the number of those killed to sixteen. Public opinion in Ireland, which had initially greeted the rising with disbelief and ambivalence, turned decisively against the British as the roster of martyrs grew. Pearse's blood sacrifice, however romantic and mystical it may seem, had worked.

The British Parliament compounded the public relations disaster by voting to extend conscription to Ireland in April 1918. As it turned out, the government backed off and didn't draft any Irishmen, but they did send Field Marshal Lord John French, former commander at the western front, to crack down on anti-conscription demonstrations in Ireland. The British were rapidly turning their military victory over the Easter Rising into a defeat in the battle for the minds and hearts of the people. As Irish historian Joseph J. Lee has remarked playfully, "The British lost the propaganda war with a spectacular series of own goals." (An "own goal" is a soccer term referring to the accidental kicking of the ball into a player's own goal, thereby scoring a point for the opposition.)

The British performed another curious service for the Irish rebels by misnaming them all "Sinn Feiners." In fact, Arthur Griffith, the founder of Sinn Fein, opposed violence and had played no role in the Easter Rising, but the misunderstanding gave his movement a new impetus. The Home Rule Party of John Redmond had lost its gamble by collaborating with the British war effort and condemning the Easter Rising, so Griffith's Sinn Fein replaced it as the political wing of the independence movement. Griffith himself, however, was soon overshadowed by the only surviving commandant from the rising, Eamon de Valera, whose life was spared because he was an American by birth.

De Valera was originally named Edward when he was born in New York City in 1882 to a Spanish immigrant father and an Irish mother. His father abandoned the family two years later and soon died of tuberculosis, so Mrs. de Valera sent her son back to Ireland to be raised by relatives in rural County Limerick. De Valera's grandmother often left him in the parish church while she ran her errands, and he developed a lifelong habit of talking alone to God, and eventually talking for God as well. He became a mathematics teacher and developed a love for Gaelic, marrying his language teacher in 1910. About this time he adopted Eamon (technically, it means Edmund) as his first name. De Valera joined the Irish Volunteers and commanded the battalion which seized Boland's Mill during the Easter Rising. He inherited Pearse's priest-like leadership of Irish nationalism, but he was more politically savvy and less suicidal than Pearse. An old joke asks, "Why is it that no street in Dublin has been named for de Valera?" Answer: "Because no street exists which is long enough, narrow enough, or crooked enough."

When de Valera was released from prison in 1917, he stood for a by-election in County Clare and was triumphantly elected. Following Sinn Fein strategy, however, he refused to take his seat in the British Parliament. Later that year, he was elected president both of Sinn Fein and the Irish Volunteers (who now more frequently called themselves the Irish Republican Army, or IRA).

Sinn Fein's strategy paid off in the general election right after the end of World War I. In England, Prime Minister David Lloyd George's victorious coalition swept to victory, but Sinn Fein carried seventy-three Irish seats, reducing the Home Rulers to a tiny rump of six. The Sinn Fein members of Parliament refused their seats at Westminster and convened instead in Dublin on January 21, 1919, calling themselves the *Dail Eireann* (Assembly of Ireland). Only twenty-seven delegates were present, for most of the rest remained in prison; but these Irish representatives ratified Pearse's 1916 declaration of independence and addressed a "Message to the Free Nations of the World." Ominously, however, on this same day a detachment of the IRA operating on their own captured a cartload of high explosives at Soloheadbeg near Tipperary, killing two policemen in the process. For the next three years, Sinn Fein and the IRA would work in uneasy tandem in a war for independence from England. As in the days of Parnell, shrewd politics and a threat of force got results.

The Dail named de Valera president of the republic, but he had been rearrested by the British in 1918. The IRA staged a spectacular jailbreak to liberate him, but he then left for the United States where he remained until December 1920. In his absence, Arthur Griffith stood in as acting president. The Dail applied Griffith's Sinn Fein strategy of presenting England with a fait accompli. They took over many local municipal administrations and set up their own courts wherever possible. The British still possessed power in Ireland but they had lost legitimacy. The Irish people did not recognize their authority any longer. This was nearly the same scenario that Gandhi's Congress Party followed in India a generation later, after the Second World War.

Like Gandhi also, the Sinn Fein leaders experienced problems exercising their authority, for they could barely control their military wing, the Irish Republican Army. Beginning in August 1919, the Dail required IRA members to swear an oath of allegiance to the civilian government, but most local units still operated independently. Violent resistance to British occupation started slowly in 1919 but rose in frequency and ferocity the next two years. An incident at Fermoy, County Cork, on September 7, 1919, set a pattern that continued throughout the war for independence. An IRA brigade attacked a party of British infantry, killing one and wounding four more. A coroner's jury refused to indict the rebels for murder, calling their action an act of war. In revenge, therefore, the British troops rampaged from their barracks and wrecked the shops of the town.

The British inadvertently assisted the rebel cause yet again by recruiting a force of demobilized soldiers in England and sending them over as reinforcements for the regular police force of Ireland, the Royal Irish Constabulary. These undisciplined troops, hardened to slaughter in the trenches of France, rampaged virtually out of control from the time of their recruitment in early 1920. The Constabulary had insufficient numbers of uniforms for the new recruits, so they initially wore an odd melange of their old army khaki and the dark green of the RIC. When they went on a spree in County Limerick in April 1920, their odd garb earned them the nickname "Black and Tans," after a local band of foxhunting hounds. The British had blundered into an unwinnable situation where they were applying "violence without energy." The Black and Tans outraged Irish and Irish-American public opinion and even began to concern the English themselves, but they never attacked in sufficient force to crush the IRA.

The Republicans, for their part, escalated guerrilla warfare in the summer of 1920 with the organization of "flying columns" that roamed the countryside on bicycles or country carts, mounting ambushes against patrolling troops of Black and Tans. The violence culminated on "Bloody Sunday," November 21, 1920. Michael Collins, head of IRA intelligence in Dublin, ordered a squad of commandoes to murder twelve British counterintelligence officers. In reprisal, the Black and Tans swept through a crowded soccer stadium, firing their rifles randomly and stampeding the crowd. Twelve died and eleven were seriously wounded. Such massacres continued on both sides, and the British even began burning farmhouses and whole villages in reprisal for IRA attacks. Finally, British public opinion forced the government to call a truce on July 11, 1921, and begin negotiations for Irish self-rule.

The Irish won their independence but they could not gain the status of a republic through negotiations with the British. Lloyd George set forth two non-negotiable conditions: that Ireland must remain part of the British Empire, and that Protestant Ulster must not be forced to join Catholic Ireland. De Valera, back from America, proposed a hair-splitting formula he called "external association," whereby Ireland's government would not take an oath of allegiance to the King of England and would not remain part of the British Empire, but it would voluntarily form an alliance with England. This formula was later adopted by some members of the British Commonwealth after World War II, but it was ahead of its time in 1921. Lloyd George flatly refused to grant anything more than dominion status to Ireland. After months of fruitless debate, the English prime minister finally threatened the Irish delegates with "war in three days," if they failed to sign a peace treaty on his terms. To de Valera's distress, the delegation, led by Michael Collins, signed the treaty and the Dail narrowly approved it on January 7, 1922.

The Anglo-Irish Treaty declared that "Ireland shall have the same constitutional status in the community of nations known as the British Empire as the Dominion of Canada, the Commonwealth of Australia, the Dominion of New Zealand, and the Union of South Africa . . . and shall be styled the Irish Free State." Since all those former colonies had evolved considerably during the First World War, this meant effective independence. Michael Collins sensibly concluded that such status "gives us freedom, not the ultimate freedom that all nations desire and develop to, but the freedom to achieve it."

De Valera, however, choked at the oath of allegiance to the king, resigned from the Dail, and backed renegade IRA gunmen in a civil war against the pro-treaty Irish. William T. Cosgrave now headed the Dail government after de Valera resigned, Arthur Griffith died, and Michael Collins was killed by an IRA ambush in the summer of 1922. Cosgrave's government raised a new army to replace and oppose the runaway IRA, and the result was never in doubt after the capture of Cork and other major cities in August 1922. Still, the IRA "Legion of the Rearguard" continued a bitter guerrilla resistance until the spring of 1923. Over five thousand people died in the civil war, more than had fallen in the war for independence against the English.

In the meantime, on December 6, 1922, the king of England signed a proclamation officially recognizing the Irish Free State. Just a day later, the six counties of Ulster opted out of the Free State, as provided in the treaty, to remain within the United Kingdom. The last British troops left Southern Ireland on December 17, 1922, ending over seven centuries of occupation.

Eamon de Valera had chosen the wrong side in the civil war, and he wandered in the political wilderness for a few more years, refusing to take the oath of office even when elected to the Dail. However, in 1927 he produced another hair-splitting distinction that allowed him to take office with a mental reservation, styling the oath "an empty political formula." Five years later, at the head of a new political party, *Fianna Fail* (The Warriors of Ireland), he became prime minister.

De Valera dominated Irish politics thereafter, somewhat like Ataturk in Turkey, but without the military trappings. "The Chief," as he was affectionately called, served as prime minister for twenty-three of the years between 1932 and 1959, then another fourteen years in the ceremonial post of president. He died in 1975 at age ninety-three. He outlawed the remnants of the IRA in 1936, then a year later introduced a new constitution ending all attachment to Great Britain and abolishing the hated oath of allegiance to the King. England was too preoccupied by the Depression, the rise of Hitler, and the abdication of its own king to do anything about this.

The Irish government finally proclaimed the country a republic in 1949. By this time, the British Empire had evolved into a loose commonwealth, and other nations had adopted de Valera's external association with England. However, to quote historian Desmond Williams, "by the time the British found the answer, the Irish had lost interest in the question."

The Liberal governments of Great Britain had tried to solve the Irish question through Home Rule. Most Catholic Irish before the First World War would have accepted this, but sentimental attachment to the union within England and the violent rejection by Protestant Ulster torpedoed this solution. The Easter Rising of 1916 changed the terms of debate. Most Irish nationalists thereafter sought a republic, but they finally settled for dominion status in the Irish Free State. This evolved naturally, and for once peacefully, into a republic.

General Henry Wilson, an Ulster Unionist and no friend of Catholic Ireland, remarked astutely in 1920 that if English policy in Ireland should fail, "the Empire would be lost." In the long run, he was correct. England's oldest colony became the second, after the United States, to win independence through revolution. Other subject nations of the British Empire followed their example later in the century.

Ireland's subsequent history, however, has been happier than that of most other newly liberated nations in the twentieth century. It inherited governmental, economic, and educational institutions that worked, and its colonial masters had already solved the land ownership question that bedevils so many new nations today. Over a century of nationalist agitation had provided the Irish with valuable experience in democratic government and had given their national sentiments a larger base of support than the top-down nationalism of the Young Turks or the Arab urban notables. Furthermore, partition of the country, though bitterly disappointing to nationalists, made independent Ireland even more homogeneous than modern Turkey, without the horrors of genocide.

The rebels of the Easter Rising died for an independent, republican, Gaelic, and united Ireland. The country never successfully revived Gaelic, and it is still not united, but it has remained independent and republican. This marked a partial, though substantial, success for the Irish nationalists. Before World War I, Europe was riddled with "Irelands" and "Alsaces," subject nations and fragments of nations. Though the world cataclysm did not win self-determination for all small nations, as Woodrow Wilson had preached, Alsace was reunited with France and Ireland won its independence. This signaled the beginning of the end for European imperialism.

CHAPTER FOURTEEN

Revolutions, Constitutions, and Institutions

Four years before World War I, a series of revolutionary upheavals broke out in Mexico. The Mexican Revolution, which lasted a generation, became entwined in the diplomacy of the world war and the politics of Mexico's dominant neighbor, the United States; but it ultimately ran an independent course. At the end of the struggle, Mexican leaders institutionalized the results of their revolution in a unique constitutional and political order.

Mexico had won its independence from Spain nearly a century before, while the mother country was embroiled in the Napoleanic Wars. Yet its first decades of freedom had been marked by political instability, frequent civil wars, an invasion by the United States in 1847 that resulted in the loss of half its territory, and another invasion by French troops in the 1860s. In the midst of this turmoil, Benito Juarez and other political leaders who emulated the representative democracies of Europe and the United States wrote the Constitution of 1857 and a series of Reform Laws later incorporated into the constitution. These measures attacked the privileges of the landed aristocracy, the Catholic Church, and the military, but did not break their power. Nevertheless, the Constitution and Reform Laws provided an agenda for future revolutionaries. As Adolfo Gilly, a Mexican political scientist, points out: "The juridical principles of the 1857 Constitution were those of an imaginary country. It was a dream to which reality might one day correspond. . . ."

For thirty-four years, however, Mexico's reality remained the dictatorship of General Porfirio Diaz. A full-blooded Indian who had risen to prominence fighting the French invasion of the 1860s, Diaz never abolished the Constitution of 1857, but he amended the clause forbidding presidential reelection and ignored numerous other provisions of the fundamental law. Serving a first term from 1876 to 1880, then five consecutive four-year terms and a final six-year term from 1884 until 1910, Diaz allowed a token candidate to run against him in each election but suppressed any serious opposition.

President Diaz surrounded himself with European-trained intellectuals, the so-called *cientificos,* who tried to stimulate the economic development of the nation. In the process, however, they granted lucrative economic concessions to European and American business interests. Foreign investment grew from 110 million pesos in 1884 (when the peso held the same value as the American dollar) to 3.4 billion pesos (with the peso devalued to half a dollar in value) by 1911. The building of railroads between the major cities of Mexico and the American border towns in Texas, Arizona, New Mexico, and California linked the Mexican economy firmly to the American.

At the same time that foreigners were grabbing valuable mining, ranching, railroad-building, and oil-drilling rights, Mexican landowners were depriving the peasant masses of their land. Since before the Spanish Conquest, most Mexican Indians had lived in villages holding much of their land as common property, called *ejidos.* Yet the Diaz regime encouraged the formation of large capitalist haciendas that swallowed up the best land for commercial crops such as wheat, cotton, and sugar cane. By 1910 some 57,000 villages had lost their land and only 13,000 remained independent.

Porfirio Diaz also relaxed the laws separating church from state, and he cultivated army officers with jobs, favors, and lucrative moneymaking opportunities. As a result, the church hierarchy, the military, and domestic and foreign business interests strongly supported his perpetual reelection.

In the first decade of the twentieth century, the tiny industrial labor force began organizing strikes against foreign business interests, but Diaz crushed these disturbances. In June 1906, for example, workers walked out at the Cananea copper mines in Sonora, but the federal troops invited American rangers across the border to help suppress them. These early stirrings of revolutionary unrest were stimulated by the anarchist writings of Ricardo Flores Magon, who began publishing the journal *Regeneracion* in 1900 and helped found the misleadingly named Mexican Liberal Party a year later. Magon and his followers spent most of their time in exile, or in prison, in the United States, but their journal exercised a wide influence on working-class and peasant leaders. The Mexican labor movement adopted the red-and-black flag of the Spanish anarchists as their own banner.

Yet the revolution was finally touched off not by a peasant or a worker, an anarchist or a socialist, but by a rich hacienda owner, dissatisfied with the political stagnation of the Diaz regime. Francisco Indalecio Madero had been born in

1873 to a landowning family of Coahuila state in northern Mexico, and educated first at a Jesuit school, then in France and at the University of California at Berkeley. His family grew wealthy from investments in banking and mining, but they lost influence and status to the *nouveaux riches* gathered around President Diaz.

Madero was a bookish, idealistic man who dreamed of restoring his family's prominence and democratizing Mexico's political system. He echoed the progressive reformers in the United States, such as Theodore Roosevelt and Woodrow Wilson, who attacked the entrenched power of big business and political bosses. In ideas and temperament, Madero closely resembled the scholarly, moralistic Woodrow Wilson. Yet Wilson and the progressives were working in a well-established representative framework, avowing that the "cure for democracy is more democracy." Mexico had yet to establish a democratic political system, and when Madero attempted to do so he unleashed revolutionary forces he could not control.

Like Woodrow Wilson, Madero was easy to underestimate. When he wrote a book entitled *La sucesion presidencial en 1910*, advocating "effective suffrage and no re-election," Diaz ignored this seemingly insignificant little man and allowed him to press his candidacy for the presidency. Yet Madero stumped the country in an American-style barnstorming campaign, hammering home the theme that Diaz must go. Finally, the police arrested him on the eve of the election, and Diaz was duly reelected in July 1910. Released on bail, Madero fled to San Antonio, Texas, and denounced the Mexican presidential election as a fraud.

Seeing no other alternative, Madero issued his Plan of San Luis Potosí (the city where he had been imprisoned), calling for a revolution to take place at 6:00 P.M. on November 20, 1910. The reluctant revolutionary hoped to topple Diaz, establish the principle of a one-term presidency, institutionalize democratic practices throughout Mexico, and decentralize power from the central government to the states. Like the American progressives, he envisioned local and state governments as "laboratories for democracy." The Plan of San Luis Potosí advocated just one social reform, the return of land illegally seized from the peasants.

Madero's revolution did not proceed on his precise schedule, but it did move forward. Scattered groups across Mexico, especially in the northern tier of states near the American border, responded to his call and formed armed bands of insurrectionists. Foreign investment in the desert states of northern Mexico had attracted large numbers of job-seekers during the Diaz years, uprooting them from their ancestral communities. These rootless and underemployed workers formed the backbone of the various revolutionary armies for the next decade.

Ricardo Flores Magon sent a motley troop of radical miners and soldiers of fortune into Baja California, dreaming of an anarchist commonwealth. Ranchers such as Abraham Gonzalez and Pascual Orozco, joined by the soon-to-be-

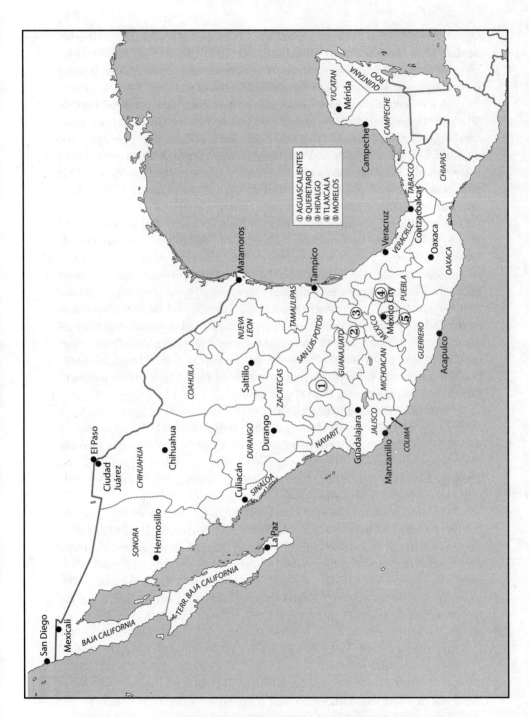

Mexico in the Twentieth Century

legendary bandit Pancho Villa, rebelled in Chihuahua across the Texas border. Madero himself crossed into Chihuahua in March 1911; then in April and May his insurgents captured the border towns of Agua Prieta and Ciudad Juarez, making it easy to import weapons from the United States.

In a purely military sense, Madero's revolution had barely dented Porfirio Diaz's control of Mexico. Many rural Mexicans did not even know that a revolution had broken out. Yet the Diaz clique decided that the eighty-year-old president had become a liability and that they should bargain with Madero before more radical revolutionaries came to the fore. So Diaz vanished from Mexico, his dictatorship exposed as a hollow bluff. He resigned the presidency on May 25, 1911, and went quietly into European exile aboard the steamship *Ypiranga*.

A provisional president took office for the rest of 1911. Madero rode triumphantly into Mexico City on June 7, then in the freest elections Mexico had known, was elected president on October 1. Madero's strength had been his single-minded attack on the Diaz dictatorship. This united disparate groups behind him: other wealthy landowners like himself who had been left out of the Diaz clique; rising middle-class ranchers and businessmen who desired a freer economic and political system; trade unionists and uprooted migrant workers aspiring to a better life; and the vast mass of peasantry who took seriously the vague promise of land redistribution. Once elected, however, Madero's unstable coalition fell apart, and some of his followers refused to put down their weapons. Mexico was swarming with local revolutions.

After less than a year and a half of tumult, the Mexican military overthrew Madero. On the morning of February 9, 1913, garrison troops and military cadets converged on the center of Mexico City, freed a number of dissident generals from prison, and attacked the Citadel, where troops loyal to Madero held out. The siege lasted for "Ten Tragic Days," with much careless artillery fire from both sides setting fire to homes and shops.

Madero appointed General Victoriano Huerta to put down the uprising, but Huerta betrayed his president. The American ambassador Henry Lane Wilson (no relative to Woodrow Wilson, who had been recently elected U.S. president but had not yet taken office) told Huerta that the United States would recognize "any government capable of establishing peace and order in place of the government of Señor Madero." Huerta took the hint and arrested Madero and his vice president on February 18, bringing the Ten Tragic Days to a close. After obtaining the president's and vice president's resignation, Huerta had them shot on February 21, staging it to look like a jailbreak. Consulted beforehand, the American ambassador told Huerta he should do "whatever he thought best for the country." General Huerta became president, and Madero, the dreamy liberal who could not master Mexico in life, became a martyr after his tragic death.

Great Britain and other European countries, worried about their investments, swiftly recognized Huerta; and most state governors of Mexico swore allegiance to him. Yet newly inaugurated President Wilson recalled the ambassador who had lent support to Huerta's coup and refused to recognize the military strongman. Then, on March 26, 1913, the governor of Madero's home state of Coahuila, Venustiano Carranza, rejected Huerta's presidency as unconstitutional and declared himself first chief of a Constitutionalist movement dedicated to his overthrow.

Carranza and Wilson, though they distrusted each other and did not work in concert, eventually toppled the Huerta dictatorship. Wilson stubbornly refused American recognition, and in 1914 he sent U.S. Marines to occupy the port of Vera Cruz and block the import of weapons for Huerta. Carranza just as stubbornly rallied the scattered forces loyal to the martyred Madero and continued the revolution in Mexico. Peasant leaders Emiliano Zapata, in the state of Morelos south of Mexico City, and Pancho Villa in the north rallied to the Constitutionalist cause, as did a young rancher from Sonora, Alvaro Obregon, who showed natural military gifts of patience and good timing. With Carranza's forces bearing down on Mexico City, Huerta resigned on July 15, 1914, and fled Mexico on the German cruiser *Dresden* (which would be hunted down by the British navy in a matter of months after World War I broke out). Obregon marched his troops into the capital on August 15, 1914 (just as the Germans were putting the Schlieffen plan into gear in Europe).

Carranza could not control the forces he had unleashed much better than Madero had. He particularly feared Francisco "Pancho" Villa. Born Doroteo Arango to a family of Durango sharecroppers in 1878, the future rebel leader had fled to the hills after killing a man at the age of sixteen. Adopting a new name, he lived as a cattle rustler for nearly two decades before the revolution. A flamboyant horseman who kept a hundred *dorados* ("golden boys") about him for protection and married at least twenty-four wives in his lifetime, Villa disliked the fastidious Carranza, whom he dismissed as a *chocolatero perfumado* ("perfumed chocolate-drinker"). For his part, the first chief intentionally deprived Villa of ammunition on the drive to Mexico City so that Obregon would reach the capital first.

When Carranza called a junta of military chiefs to consolidate his victory, Villa and his supporters dominated the discussions and forged a tentative alliance with the southern peasant leader Zapata. The Convention of Aguascalientes, meeting in October 1914, deposed Carranza and proclaimed a social revolution. Obregon and Carranza fled to the port city of Vera Cruz, only recently evacuated by the Americans, and Villa and Zapata rode into Mexico City for a memorable meeting in December 1914. Had the two peasant leaders remained in the capital they might have defeated Carranza. Yet neither Villa nor Zapata felt comfortable in the city. Villa relied on long supply lines from the American border through his northern strongholds and felt vulnerable and cut off. "This place is too big for us;

it's better out there," he told Zapata. The leaders, therefore, returned to their home bases, allowing Carranza time to regroup.

The wily first chief cleverly appealed to all segments of Mexican society. He issued a decree on January 6, 1915, promising land to the peasants, and Obregon forged an alliance with the labor union leadership, recruiting four "red battalions" to fight against Villa. Both men appealed to the lowest common denominator of the revolutionary movement, anticlericalism, by seizing church property and humiliating the bishops and clergy.

While Carranza and Obregon played for time, Zapata returned to Morelos and fought few battles. Villa fought too many, dispersing his troops' energies in small skirmishes throughout the northern tier of states. Obregon, on the other hand, concentrated his forces and began a systematic drive northward against his most dangerous foe, Pancho Villa. Descending from the high plateau around Mexico City into the central Mexican lowlands, Obregon imitated the European powers on the western front by digging a line of trenches and daring Villa's horsemen to assault it. In two furious battles at Celaya in April 1915, thousands of Villistas were mowed down by machine guns. In a follow-up battle in June, a hand grenade shattered Obregon's right arm. In intense pain, he tried to commit suicide but his aide had forgotten to load his revolver, so the general survived, having lost an arm but gained another victory. Pancho Villa retreated to the mountains of Durango and Chihuahua. On October 19, 1915, President Wilson, who had withheld U.S. recognition from either side after the overthrow of Huerta, finally recognized the Carranza regime.

Villa feared that Carranza had sold out Mexico to the Yankees. Indeed, U.S. State Department officials had discussed a plan to grant Carranza loans in exchange for economic concesssions and increased U.S. political influence. President Wilson had not approved this plan, and Carranza would never have agreed to it, but Villa did not know this. Enraged by the imagined treason of his opponents, the rebel leader staged a desperate raid on American territory, attacking the tiny border town of Columbus, New Mexico, on March 9, 1916. The United States, as Villa expected, sent a punitive expedition of 10,000 troops under command of General John J. Pershing (who would soon lead the American Expeditionary Force in France) into Mexico to chase the "bandit" leader.

Anti-Americanism united all Mexican factions even more than anticlericalism, so the American invasion cancelled any conspiratorial plans Carranza or anyone else might be hatching. Villa led the Americans on a merry chase, eluding them for over a year, until they withdrew their troops in February, 1917 (in order to send them to France). This episode restored Villa's prestige, allowing him to remain at large in northern Mexico until the end of the revolution. The central government finally bought him off in July 1920 with a spacious hacienda and a large bodyguard.

Throughout 1915, while Carranza's troops were battering Villa, the other outstanding peasant leader, Zapata, was creating a social revolution. The battles in the north created a breathing space in Zapata's home state of Morelos, and the Zapatistas made good use of this opportunity to create a commonwealth of villages, similar to what Ricardo Flores Magon and the anarchists had been advocating. Flores Magon did not leave Los Angeles during the revolution and thus missed his chance to practice anarchism in Baja California. He eventually died of diabetes in the U.S. prison of Leavenworth. Yet Zapata adopted his slogan of "Land and Liberty" and implemented many of his ideas in Morelos.

Emiliano Zapata was born in 1879 to a peasant family of Anenecuilco in Morelos. Inheriting a little land and livestock, Emiliano was neither rich nor poor, but he identified with the downtrodden peasantry and was elected president of his village council in 1909, just before the revolution. Porfirio Diaz's capitalist friends had exploited Morelos systematically, since it lay conveniently close to the national capital. Large landowners converted their plantations from beans and corn to the cash crops of sugar cane and rice. By the end of Diaz's regime, the thirty-six largest haciendas had gobbled up all the best land, comprising over 25 percent of the state's total area.

Some villages held on to a little marginal land, and individual peasants often worked as sharecroppers on the hacienda, but they inevitably fell into debt to the company store and became virtual slaves of the landowner to work off their debts. Many peasants simply abandoned all hope of cultivating their own land, moved into the hacienda compound, and worked as wage laborers. The dispossession of peasants from their *ejidos* had been not only a land-grab but a ruthless ploy to create a pool of cheap labor. The plantations of Morelos produced more sugar than any other region in the world, except Hawaii and Puerto Rico, and they functioned more like factories than medieval manors.

Zapata contacted Francisco Madero shortly after he raised the banner of revolution in November 1910, and in spring of the following year he captured the two major cities of the state, Cuautla and Cuernavaca, then challenged Madero to make good his promise of land to the peasants. At a face-to-face meeting in Mexico City, Madero temporized and promised to study the question. Zapata impulsively grabbed the other man's watch and demanded: "If I keep this, won't you try to get it back?" When Madero replied, "Of course," Zapata spat out, "that's exactly what has happened to us in Morelos, where a few planters have taken over by force the villages' lands."

Zapata returned to Morelos, and with the aid of a local schoolteacher, Ottilio Montaño, he drafted the Plan of Ayala, which he and his rebel colleagues signed on November 25, 1911. The Ayala Plan projected a thoroughgoing agrarian reform for Morelos and all of Mexico. Peasant villagers whose lands had been illegally seized and who still retained old deeds proving their ownership were authorized to "im-

241

mediately enter into possession" of this property. Madero and Carranza both promised the return of such illegally seized lands, but only after lengthy legal proceedings. Zapata's plan reversed the burden of proof, encouraging the peasants to take the land first, maintaining possession "with arms in hand," and let the former owners try to prove their rights in court. In addition, the Ayala Plan decreed that anyone who opposed the revolution would have his property confiscated outright and that one-third of all other industrial and agricultural properties would be expropriated, with compensation, for the benefit of the common good.

The movement of the revolutionary civil war to the north in 1915 left Morelos free of federal troops, so Zapata's rebels implemented the Ayala Plan. In January 1915, forty-one graduates from the National School of Agriculture volunteered to serve on agrarian commissions. These eager, young agronomists surveyed the boundaries of disputed properties and allotted each village its landed entitlement. The village councils freely decided whether to hold the lands in common or divide them into individual farms. The Morelos revolutionaries also confiscated the sugar mills and rum distilleries of the large haciendas, and Zapata hoped to develop these into a cash-earning trade. However, most of the farm factories had been ruined by war, and the peasants preferred to grow subsistence crops of corn and beans rather than sugarcane.

Morelos, therefore, reverted to an economically primitive, but independent commonwealth of villages. Theoretically, the Zapatistas recognized the Convention of Aguascalientes as the national government of Mexico, but its leaders were constantly on the run from Carranza and Obregon and exercised little effective authority. In Morelos itself, Zapata and his chieftains rendered a rough-and-ready revolutionary justice in various disputes, but they zealously respected the rights of individual villages. The revolutionaries and villagers drew more on their communal Indian traditions than on anarchist theory, but the results came remarkably close to what anarchists advocated. Enrique Flores Magon, Ricardo's brother, later remarked: "Thanks to our tribal traditions; thanks to us being mostly Indians and, therefore, close to nature . . . it should not be surprising to find that other rebels under different banners are more or less inclined towards anarchism. . . ." For more than a year, the Morelos Commune, this quasi-anarchist utopia, had more freedom to implement anarchist ideas than Nestor Makhno ever enjoyed in Ukraine after the Russian Revolution.

After Villa's defeats in the north, however, Carranza ordered Pablo Gonzalez, widely derided as the "general who never won a battle," to pacify Morelos. With overwhelming firepower, he recaptured the cities, drove Zapata's guerrillas back into the hills, terrorized the villagers, and shot hundreds of prisoners. Other prisoners were sent as virtual slave laborers to the henequen (a form of hemp, used for making rope) plantations of the remote Yucatan peninsula. Still Gonzalez could not win a battle, and after a year of fighting evacuated Morelos.

Yet Zapata remained under constant military pressure and was no longer able to protect the peasants and their communal lands. When the worldwide influenza epidemic struck Mexico towards the end of 1918, General Gonzalez invaded Morelos once again and drove off the flu-weakened rebels. The state lost a quarter of its population in 1918 to disease, government guns, and panicked emigration.

With his back against the wall militarily, Zapata tried to convince one of Gonzalez's cavalry officers, Colonel Jesus Guajardo, to join the rebel cause. Guajardo feigned cooperation, luring Zapata into a trap at the Chinameca hacienda, close to Emiliano's home village. Shortly after noon on April 10, 1919, Zapata entered the hacienda with an honor guard of ten soldiers and was shot down by Guajardo's federal troops. Though the soldiers displayed his corpse publicly and invited photographers to record his burial, many peasants believed that Zapata had somehow escaped and was haunting the mountains. His legend has inspired peasant leaders throughout the century. As recently as January 1994, a peasant revolt in the far-southern state of Chiapas was led by a group calling itself the Zapatista Liberation Front.

While Villa was riding for his life across the northern deserts and Zapata still roamed the mountains of Morelos, Mexico nearly got sucked into the maelstrom of World War I. Since the onset of the war, German foreign officers and spies had been trying to keep the United States out of the European struggle by stirring up trouble in her own backyard. When the Germans decided at the beginning of 1917 to declare unrestricted submarine warfare, they knew this might precipitate an American war declaration, so they simultaneously launched a plot to deflect American anger against Mexico. German Foreign Secretary Arthur Zimmermann sent a coded cable to his ambassador in Mexico City offering Carranza an alliance. If Mexico would attack the United States, the Germans would deliver arms and munitions and help the nation recover its lost territories of Texas, New Mexico, and Arizona at the successful conclusion of the war. In addition, Zimmermann requested the Mexicans, who had been buying munitions from Japan during their revolution, to try and detach Japan from the Western Allies and induce her to join the prospective German-Mexican alliance.

With America's Punitive Expedition fresh in his memory, Carranza must have been tempted to wreak revenge. However, he realized that Germany could not produce enough surplus arms for Mexico while engaged in its own deadly struggle, and that the promise of recovering territory from the United States was a pipe dream. Even if Germany won the war, it would be impossible to enforce such a penalty a hemisphere away. So Carranza politely refused Germany's offer. As it turned out, the Zimmermann Telegram was intercepted and decoded by the British and the plot backfired. Instead of tying America down in the Western Hemisphere, the proposed Mexican alliance, when publicly revealed by the Wilson administration, enraged public opinion and hastened the American war declaration.

Having avoided the German trap, Venustiano Carranza consolidated his hold on Mexico and made a first attempt to institutionalize his vision of the revolution by calling a constitutional convention. Carranza had clung tenaciously to the name "Constitutionalist" throughout the revolution, to emphasize his legitimacy as defender of the Constitution of 1857; and he had carefully retained his title as "first chief," not provisional president. The concept of "no reelection" remained so sacred to all who had opposed Porfirio Diaz that even the acceptance of a provisional presidency might have prejudiced Carranza's chances for a regular term as president once the political order stabilized.

On October 22, 1916, constitutional delegates were elected in all the areas under Carranza's control, and they convened at the central Mexican city of Queretaro on November 20. Carranza's lawyers presented a draft incorporating most of the 1857 Constitution, with only a few changes. The presidency was strengthened at the expense of the legislature, but the principle of no reelection was enshrined prominently. For the rest of the century, this remained a noteworthy result of the Mexican Revolution, a strong president limited to just one term.

The delegates, who were mostly soldiers of the revolution, accepted much of Carranza's draft, but they pushed the lawyers aside and went far beyond the political reforms dear to the first chief. Led by General Francisco Mugica from the state of Michoacan, the Queretaro delegates wrote education, religion, land, and labor reforms into the Constitution of 1917. It is worth emphasizing that the Mexican revolution took place *before* the Bolsheviks seized power in Russia. The radical reforms of the 1917 Constitution were an independent Mexican creation. The Queretaro delegates had never heard of Lenin, and he did not know they existed.

Article 3 decreed that all primary education must be carried out in public, secular schools, and it forbade the clergy to conduct any schools of their own. The Queretaro constitution tried to ensure that succeeding generations would imbibe the religion of nationalism, not Christianity. As historian Robert Quirk has phrased it: "The rural teacher was to be a priest without a cassock, carrying the banner of the Revolution, instead of the cross of Christ."

Article 130 placed further restrictions on the Catholic Church. The old constitution had already separated church from state and deprived the church of all its landed property, but some ambiguity remained as to whether the bishops and priests still owned the church buildings. Article 130 removed this ambiguity, nationalizing all church edifices and authorizing the government to decide how many such buildings would be leased to the clergy for church services. In addition, the corporate existence of the church was dissolved, and clergymen were considered simply as individual professionals, like lawyers or doctors. Unlike other professionals, however, clergy were banned from voting, holding office, or publicly criticizing the constitution. State governments were empowered to decide how many religious professionals to license in their own territories. Clearly the Constitution of 1917 went far beyond separation of church and state to a clear subordination of church to the state. The convention narrowly turned down a proposal that would have forced all priests to marry.

The constitution not only wrote a secular charter for the church but also a labor charter for industrial workers and an agrarian charter for the peasants. Article 123 contained the most advanced labor code in the world at the time it was written, with detailed provisions banning child labor and regulating hours and wages. Carranza's emergency declaration of 1915, promising the return of agricultural land seized illegally from the peasants, was also enshrined in the constitution.

Finally, article 27 declared categorically: "The property of lands and waters included in the limits of the national territory belongs originally to the nation, which has had and has the right to transmit the domain in them to individuals, thus constituting private property. . . ." According to the Mexican constitution, private property became a conditional right, subject to change at any time in the national interest. If the government chose to seize landed property and divide it among the peasant villages, it had the constitutional right to do so. Furthermore, the minerals below the surface of the soil were declared the perpetual property of the state. Individuals could sell their land, but not the right to drill for oil or prospect for other minerals beneath that land. This provision proved to be a time bomb in relations between Mexico and the foreign oil companies that had been drilling there.

Carranza disliked the radicalism of the Queretaro constitution, but he promulgated it on February 5, 1917, and called a presidential election for March 11. To no one's surpise, the first chief was elected overwhelmingly and inaugurated as president of Mexico on May 1, 1917. Though his victorious army had forced him to accept more social reforms than he wished, President Carranza made no effort to enforce them and did not ask Congress for enabling legislation to implement them. The Catholic Church, therefore, remained in a kind of limbo, with no legal rights but with church buildings and schools still functioning unofficially. Labor leaders found themselves without influence, and peasants who expected their land to be returned were disappointed. The Mexican Revolution had reached a point of equilibrium under Carranza, but many who had fought in it felt unsatisfied.

Carranza had seemed an unlikely revolutionary all along. A large landowner, like Madero, he was nearly two decades older than the other rebel chiefs, a tall but harmless-looking individual with a bushy beard and obviously weak eyesight. Yet he had shrewdly identified himself with all the popular causes while keeping the reins of power firmly in his own hands. Historian Douglas Richmond has dubbed Carranza an "authoritarian populist." He was, in effect, Francisco Madero with an iron will.

Yet when Carranza faced the problem of presidential succession, the very issue that had begun the revolution, his political instincts failed him. He knew he could not violate the "no reelection" principle when his term of office expired in 1920, but he unwisely promoted the candidacy of a nonentity, Ignacio Bonillas, who had not even been in Mexico during most of the revolution, instead of a popular general such as Obregon. The army, therefore, turned against Carranza, who fled the capital toward his old base in Vera Cruz. On the night of May 21, 1920, his own bodyguard murdered him at the village of Tlaxcalantongo. A provisional president was installed, and Obregon was elected at the end of 1920. His four-year presidency represented another point of equilibrium for the revolution.

Alvaro Obregon (the name is derived from O'Brien, an Irish soldier who settled in Mexico in the nineteenth century), born in 1880, was an ambitious young rancher in Sonora when the revolution broke out. As Carranza's best general, he was primarily responsible for the Constitutionalist victories over Huerta and then Pancho Villa. An irreverent jokester, he sometimes staged mock executions to terrify and humiliate priests who fell into his hands. Noting how many revolutionary officers had enriched themselves with the property of the old landowning class, he coined a memorable phrase: "There is no general capable of resisting a cannon blast of 50 thousand pesos." He could turn his sharp humor upon himself in engaging fashion. He often told political rallies that he found his missing arm on the battlefield when he tossed a golden coin over the carnage and his arm leaped up to grab it.

As president, Obregon attempted to balance all of the competing forces let loose by the revolution. He negotiated a settlement of oil rights with the American companies and government, assuring them that the Mexican claim to subsoil minerals would not be applied retroactively. Despite his anticlericalism, he continued Carranza's detente with the Catholic Church and did not enforce the antireligious clauses of the constitution. Most importantly, Obregon made peace with the successors of Zapata in Morelos, distributing a considerable amount of land to the villages of that state, and incorporating Zapatistas into his cabinet. He also forged an alliance with the largest labor confederation in the country, and under his patronage union membership swelled from a minuscule fifty thousand to over a million. Finally, he bound all the special interests together with the glue of cultural nationalism. His minister of education glorified Mexico's Indian past and encouraged the painting of giant, patriotic murals by such artists as Diego Rivera.

This politics of patriotism and accommodation was buttressed by force once again when some elements of the military rebelled against Obregon in the final months of his term. Labor and business both backed the president and the United States allowed him to import arms freely and thus crush the rebellion. In addition, Pancho Villa was murdered on July 20, 1923, probably at the president's instigation. Obregon passed on the presidency to a close associate, General Plutarco Elias Calles, who was elected in 1924.

Calles shattered Obregon's political truce by agitating the religious issue, thus touching off the last great revolt against the revolution. In June 1926, by executive decree, the president issued regulations implementing the antireligious clauses of the 1917 Constitution. Some of these restrictions were nuisances for the church, but not critical to religious activities. For example, priests and nuns were forbidden to wear religious garb in public, and all church services were confined to the insides of buildings, effectively banning the popular outdoor processions. Other provisions proved more serious, such as the expulsion of foreign priests, the banning of monastic vows, and the nationalization of church property. Still, Catholics could live with these as well.

The three most serious religious "reforms" of the constitution and the Calles Law, however, were the ban on religious education, the power of state governors to limit the number of priests, and the law of civil registration requiring all priests to apply for a government license. In some states, the suppression of religion had already proceeded very far. In the remote southern state of Tabasco, where an avowedly socialist governor, Tomas Garrido Canabal, held sway, only married priests were permitted, which meant in effect that no Catholic priests could practice their celibate ministry. Civil registration of the clergy threatened to extend such measures to the whole nation.

Both the bishops and the Catholic laity resisted the Calles Law. The Mexican hierarchy declared a clerical strike, beginning on July 30, 1926, shutting down all church services until the offensive laws were repealed. This might seem a curious strategy, but a few years previously a similar ploy in the state of Jalisco had forced the governor to lift his restrictions on the number of priests. The bishops hoped to repeat this success nationally. The laity took even stronger action, organizing an economic boycott of all non-essential goods, to buttress the clerical strike, and eventually mounting a violent rebellion. As in Ireland, innovative non-violent strategies proceeded in parallel with armed violence.

A young middle class of socially minded Catholics had grown up in the early years of the twentieth century in the staunchly Catholic states of Jalisco, Colima, and Michoacan to the west of Mexico City. Ironically, the anti-religious fury of the revolution fell upon the Mexican church when it had already lost most of its old privileges and was trying to transform itself into an agent of progressive social change in its own right. Anacleto Gonzalez Flores, from the high plains region of Los Altos in Jalisco, was the outstanding intellectual leader of the younger Catholic militants. He abhorred secularism and exhorted his followers to build a more just, Christian social order. Though he opposed violence, he finally consented to join the armed rebellion that broke out at the end of 1926, realizing it was going to proceed anyway. Like Patrick Pearse in Ireland, Gonzalez Flores openly courted martyrdom. When he finally consented to the rebellion, he warned his followers: "I know only too well that what is beginning now for us is a Calvary. We must be ready to take up and carry our crosses. . . ." He got his wish, for on April 1, 1927, he was arrested, tortured, and shot. He died proclaiming: "God does not die. *Viva Cristo Rey!*"

In the meantime, the Cristero Rebellion, as it came to be called, had broken out in at least ten states and had risen to serious proportions in Jalisco, Colima, and Michoacan. Middle-class laypeople led the revolt, but many peasants took up arms, and several priests, including two outstanding military leaders in Jalisco, joined them. The bishops neither condemned nor approved the uprising, but their public statements assuring that church doctrine permitted revolt against tyrants amounted to tacit approval.

The Cristero Rebellion raged on for three years and claimed 90,000 lives, but it never seriously threatened the government of Calles. The rebels controlled the countryside of the Catholic states and often raided the railways and the cities, but they could never hold any large population center or strike a crushing blow. The federal army employed "reconcentration" tactics, much like the British had done during the Boer War. Forcibly relocating peasants to the larger towns, they then declared the countryside a free-fire zone. This increased the ferocity of the struggle, but did not defeat the Cristeros, who found shelter in the mountains, just as Zapata's rebels had in Morelos.

Finally, in June 1929, the American ambassador, the Vatican, and a number of American Catholic priests worked out a compromise with the Mexican government restoring the status quo of the Carranza and Obregon years. The government affirmed that the civil registration of clergy was a mere administrative formality and that it would not interfere with the bishops' right to appoint priests, and it promised that religious education would be permitted freely within church buildings, though not in schools. In return, the bishops called off the clerical strike and restored normal church services. The Cristero Rebellion melted away without a formal surrender. Though some of its leaders were hunted down and a few bishops were exiled, most Catholics were left in peace.

Nevertheless, the agreements of 1929 marked a sharp defeat for the Catholic Church and an important victory for the revolution. The church was allowed to survive, but all the anti-religious clauses of the constitution remained on the books and could be enforced at any time. In the mid-1930s, church-state relations worsened, and limits on clergy were implemented again, before easing finally at the end of the decade. The government of Mexico went far beyond separation of church and state; it outlawed the church as an institution, but grudgingly tolerated private worship.

If the Mexican Revolution had ended in the 1920s, this subjugation of the church would have marked its only unqualified victory. Land redistribution had not gone very far except in a few isolated instances, such as Morelos. Instead, the revolutionary army officers gobbled up the best land confiscated from the old landowning class. Though the constitution decreed national ownership of subsoil minerals, U.S. and European companies still pumped nearly all of the country's oil.

The political succession problem remained as muddled as ever. Obregon obtained a constitutional amendment allowing him to run again in 1928, since he had already been out of office for one full term, and extending the presidential term from the traditional four years to six. He was easily elected, but a Cristero militant assassinated him before he took office. A series of weak provisional presidents served out his six-year term, with Calles, calling himself the *Jefe Maximo* ("Supreme Chief"), manipulating them behind the scenes. Mexico seemed as addicted to one-man rule as in the days of Diaz. A character in Carlos Fuentes's novel *The Death of Artemio Cruz* summed up the situation poignantly: "I don't know if you remember the beginning. It was only a short time ago, but it seems so far away. . . . When the leaders didn't matter. When we weren't doing this to raise up one man but raise up all men."

President Lazaro Cardenas, however, who served from 1934 to 1940, reinvigorated the revolution and finally institutionalized the results in a stable political system. Born in 1895 in a small village of Michoacan, Lazaro was only a boy when he ran off to join the revolution. He worked his way up to the rank of general, serving primarily under Calles in Sonora, and earned a reputation as one of the few revolutionary officers who committed no atrocities. Though his patron Calles engineered his election as president in 1934, Cardenas resisted his efforts to manipulate him and eventually sent the supreme chief into exile. This action, plus his own retirement at the end of his term when he was only forty-five, validated the no-reelection principle in practice.

His most important contribution to the revolution, however, was his vigorous promotion of land reform. The classic Cardenas anecdote captures his reputation as a champion of the peasants: One day President Cardenas found a stack of urgent matters waiting his action — Bank reserves low, Tell the Treasurer; Agricultural production falling, Tell the Minister of Agriculture; Railways bankrupt, Tell the Minister of Communications; Serious message from Washington, Tell Foreign Affairs. Then he opened a telegram — "My corn dried, my burro died, my sow was stolen, my baby is sick. Signed Pedro Juan, village of Huitzlipituzco." Cardenas thundered, "Order the presidential train at once. I'm leaving for Huitzlipituzco."

During his six years in office, Cardenas visited all twenty-eight Mexican states and spent about one-third of his time away from the capital, usually in remote Indian villages. He distributed nearly 50 million acres of nationalized agricultural property to peasants, as *ejidos,* or village community lands, more than twice as much as all his predecessors combined. In 1930, despite the revolution, Mexico's village communities controlled only about 13 percent of the country's cropland. After Cardenas's reforms, that total rose to 47 percent. This poses a classic "half-full or half-empty" interpretive problem. Should one emphasize the fact that Mexico's peasantry had obtained nearly half the land, or the equally true statement that they failed to gain the other half? Dana Markiewicz, a Marxist social scientist who emphasizes the half-empty interpretation, still concludes accurately that "*cardenismo* went to the very limits of what was possible under capitalism."

President Cardenas also tested the limits of anti-Americanism for a country often described as "so far from God, so close to the United States." In 1938 seventeen foreign-owned oil companies rejected a Mexican Labor Board order to raise their workers' wages. In retaliation, Cardenas activated the national subsoil mineral rights claimed in the 1917 constitution and expropriated the oil companies' property. The U.S. government used diplomatic and economic pressure to change his mind but did not invade as in the days of Woodrow Wilson. Eventually, the Mexican government negotiated compensation payments to the oil companies. Yet the oil expropriation crisis capped a generation of revolutionary nationalism with a triumph over the Yankees. At the demonstrations backing Cardenas's strong stand, an American professor, William Cameron Townsend, noted that the black-and-red anarcho-syndicalist flags had been largely supplanted by Mexico's national colors of green, white, and red.

Cardenas achieved a new, more permanent equilibrium than his predecessors by institutionalizing the gains of the Mexican Revolution in a political party. Calles had first thought of this in 1929, when he founded the *Partido Nacional Revolucionario* (National Revolutionary Party) or PNR, but Cardenas fine-tuned the idea. In December 1937 he reorganized the party, renaming it the *Partido de la Revolucion Mexicana,* or PRM. Four functional sectors supported the party — labor unions, peasant associations, a middle-class sector composed mainly of businessmen and professionals, and a military sector. These functional groupings cut across the regional factions that had previously supported local revolts.

With four major interests dealt in, and the Catholic Church excluded, the revolutionary party enjoyed a stable monopoly on political power. The president chosen by the party exercised nearly absolute authority, but he was restricted to just one term. Thus the Mexican Revolution produced a one-party dictatorship free of the one-man rule that has marked Soviet communism. Ex-presidents, from Cardenas onwards, functioned as elder statesmen, like the *genro* in Japan, further stabilizing the system. In 1946 the ruling party changed its name a final time to the PRI — *Partido Revolucionario Institucional* (Institutionalized Revolutionary Party). It has governed Mexico ever since, with no presidential candidate before the 1980s receiving less than 75 percent of the votes.

Judged by its own goals, the Mexican Revolution was one of the most successful of the twentieth century. Francisco Madero championed the principle of no reelection, no one-man rule in 1910; and thirty years later Lazaro Cardenas made this principle stick. Revolutionaries of all stripes opposed the large landowners, foreign business interests, and the Catholic Church, and the revolution either eliminated or reduced the power of all three. Zapata's slogan of "land and liberty" bore fruit for at least half the peasants, and the peasantry possesses an organized voice in the future of the country. Finally, Mexico experienced a cultural renaissance in art and literature during the revolutionary years.

Success came at a high cost. Between one and two million Mexicans died from bullets, influenza, or typhus during the decade 1910-20. This figure represented about 12 percent of Mexico's population, nearly double the death rate suffered by Europe during World War I. The governing party that institutionalized the revolution is not democratic, by American or Western European standards. Yet the Mexican revolutionaries preserved more individual liberty than the Bolsheviks did and have not slipped into one-man dictatorship like Soviet Russia or Mustafa Kemal's Turkey. They fulfilled their goals far more completely than the Arabs, the Zionists, or the Irish.

Mexico remains a relatively impoverished country with a corrupt ruling party. The revolution did not bring utopia. Yet it did reach its own goals and stimulated a burst of national pride. Near the end of Elia Kazan's 1952 film, *Viva Zapata*, Zapata's wife laments that so little has changed in Mexico. Zapata, played by a very young Marlon Brando, replies, gesturing towards the peasants: "They've changed." Far from Hollywood, the Marxist Adolfo Gilly made the same point: "The Mexican people . . . burst onto the historical stage and lived for a time as its main protagonists. . . . They stored up a wealth of experience and consciousness which altered the whole country as it is *lived* by its inhabitants." The Mexican Revolution has provided an alternative to the Soviet (ideological) or the Turkish (strongman) model for emerging nations.

PART FOUR

EUROPEAN CIVILIZATION
JUMPS THE TRACKS

World War I struck a hammer blow at European civilization, which had spread around the world during the previous century. The revolutions spawned by the world catastrophe eventually petered out, and Europe had largely rebuilt by 1925, when the leaders of France, Belgium, and Germany signed the Treaty of Locarno, ratifying and guaranteeing each other's postwar borders. Yet Europeans never regained full confidence. Historian Bentley Gilbert's comment about Great Britain applies equally well to all the great powers: "The First World War not only had decimated the manhood of the nation but it had stunned the survivors."

Economic preeminence shifted towards the United States, which had gone from the world's largest debtor nation to its largest creditor during the war years. By the end of the 1920s the United States produced 40 percent of the world's manufactured goods, more than Britain and Germany combined, and accounted for 12 percent of world imports, mostly from raw material producing countries.

America had become the engine that drove the global economy, yet the engineer — the president and other politicians, the businessmen and bankers — seemed intoxicated or asleep. Americans were neither prepared for nor eager to assume world leadership in the 1920s. They plunged instead into a consumer spending frenzy that culminated in a wild stock market boom and its inevitable bust in 1929. Thereafter, American business and government ceased lending to the rest of the world, raised high tariff barriers against imports, and made the economic downturn worse by trying to balance the budget. With its engine out of control, the world economy careened into the worst depression of the industrial era.

At the onset of hard times, mutants of nationalism and socialism, named Nazism and Fascism, flourished in the depressed countries of Germany and Italy. The Communists in Russia largely avoided the depression by uncoupling from the careening locomotive at the head of the world economy. Shunting themselves off on a siding, they mounted a heroic campaign to build their formerly backward economy into an industrial giant. Under Stalin's dictatorship, however, Soviet Russia suffered horrors even greater than those of the economically depressed nations.

The bloody civil war that broke out in Spain in the mid-1930s was a sideshow in the wider struggle between the "isms" of Europe. The three major dictators of the thirties — Mussolini, Hitler, and Stalin — meddled in Spain, sending troops and arms that prolonged and intensified the conflict. Yet they gained very little in return and when the Second World War broke out, exhausted Spain remained neutral. Despite the wide attention that the Spanish Civil War attracted, it is best understood as a local, national tragedy.

Fascism in Italy, Nazism in Germany, Stalinism in Russia, civil war in Spain, economic catastrophe in all the industrialized nations. From Siberia to San Francisco, it seemed that all the world touched by European civilization had gone mad.

CHAPTER FIFTEEN

The Intoxicated Engineers

In October 1929 the New York stock market crashed, marking the beginning of the Great Depression in the United States and throughout the world. A spirit of reckless confidence, a psychological force without rational explanation, had fueled the market boom on Wall Street that led to the inevitable bust. The eminent and irreverent economist, John Kenneth Galbraith, has best summed up the mood of the late 1920s:

> We do not know why a great speculative orgy occurred in 1928 and 1929. The long accepted explanation that credit was easy and so people were impelled to borrow money to buy common stocks is obviously nonsense. On numerous occasions before and since, credit has been easy and there has been no speculation whatsoever. Far more important than rate of interest and the supply of credit is the mood. Speculation on a large scale requires a pervasive sense of confidence and optimism and a conviction that ordinary people were meant to be rich.

The get-rich-quick spirit was deeply ingrained in the American psyche, but what had previously been just a tendency turned into a fetish.

Everything about the Roaring Twenties in America encouraged this fetish. Human energy, which earlier in the century had fueled political reform movements and then Woodrow Wilson's great crusade to make the world safe for democracy, found no other outlet in the twenties except acquisition. The country consciously rejected idealism. Novelist F. Scott Fitzgerald whined: "We have paid back Lafayette [by fighting in France], now who the hell else do we owe?" Business ideas and ideals dominated the decade, and Republican President Calvin

Coolidge (who served from 1923 until 1929) summed up the general mood with his succinct pronouncement that "the business of America is business." The stock market, which took off in 1924 after some initial postwar uncertainty and then climbed for the rest of the decade, symbolized for most people America's rising standard of living; and it seemed to offer an effortless means of acquiring personal wealth.

Casual accounts of the 1920s give the impression that everyone in America was playing the market and that it rocketed to dizzying heights. Supposedly, messenger boys overheard stock tips from their employers, invested their meager savings, and became millionaires overnight. Obviously such tales were not literally true, but stock ownership was more widespread than ever before in the 1920s. Still, only a few million Americans out of a population of 120 million played the market. Nor were stocks as overvalued as has been previously thought. In the light of later economic experience, the sharp rise in stock prices does not seem so remarkable as it did in the 1920s.

The important point is not how high stock prices rose nor how many people speculated in the market, but how Wall Street became central to American culture in the twenties. Whether they played the market or not, nearly all Americans watched and discussed it. Like that other new passion of the twenties, major league baseball, the stock market provided statistics to memorize and sensational careers to marvel at. When a reporter asked Babe Ruth how he could justify earning more money than the president of the United States, he responded, "I had a better year than he did." Many a Wall Street speculator felt the same way, and the American public applauded. In the folklore of the times, a market speculator was not a shifty capitalist but a shrewd go-getter.

Then the market crashed and the mood of optimism disappeared. Yet the crash didn't occur all at once, on one date, but rather in a long, protracted agony. Other great public disasters, such as the Japanese attack on Pearl Harbor or the assassination of President John F. Kennedy, are irrevocably associated with a specific date (December 7, 1941; November 22, 1963), and most everyone who was alive then can remember vividly what he or she was doing at the time. The market crash, however, stretched out over several weeks, and this long duration intensified the tragedy.

The market had been rising steadily since 1924, culminating in a spectacular runup from 1927 through the summer of 1929. In just three months, for example, from June to August 1928, the Dow Jones industrial index of stocks increased by 25 percent. A heavy volume of trading indicated that speculators were constantly buying and selling to gain an advantage. Whereas 237 million shares of stock had changed hands in 1923, over a billion shares were traded in 1929. Even the price of a seat on the stock exchange increased spectacularly, from $175,000 in 1926 to $310,000 in 1927.

The market seemed unsteady throughout September and October of 1929, but brief downturns had punctuated the progress before and the market had always rallied, so investors paid little attention. Then on October 24, 1929, a day henceforth known as Black Thursday, prices fell sharply on a huge volume of sales. Over 12 million shares were traded on this one day, whereas previously a turnover of 5 million shares would have been considered a heavy trading day. Panic set in among stock owners and the public gallery of the New York Stock Exchange was closed at 11:00 A.M. to prevent a riot. New York's leading bankers met around noon and deputized Richard Whitney, the vice president of the exchange, to spend about 20 to 30 million dollars ostentatiously buying stocks in order to stop the panic and reinstate investor confidence. It worked for awhile. That day and the next, the fall in prices halted.

Yet stocks closed lower again the following Monday; then on Black Tuesday, October 29, 1929, the bottom fell out (this is the day usually commemorated as the date of the Great Crash). In the first hour of trading, 3.26 million shares were sold, and by the end of the day over 16 million shares had changed hands. Neither record for volume of trading was surpassed until the 1960s. Among the visitors in the gallery was Winston Churchill, out of office and on an American tour. He personally lost about $50,000 that day. Over the next two weeks, feeble rallies were followed swiftly by new declines, until the market finally hit its low for the year on November 13. By that time industrial stocks had lost half their value since September.

According to popular mythology, the stock market crash led to a wave of suicides. Allegedly, hotel clerks in New York asked their patrons whether they wanted a room for sleeping or for jumping. Actually, no rise in suicides can be detected in police reports, but there was an increase in embezzlements, as hard-pressed speculators desperately tried to raise cash to pay their debts.

Yet the crash, though immensely damaging to individuals who lost everything in it, did not make a depression inevitable. Republican President Herbert Hoover, an engineer by profession who had earned an international reputation for his relief missions after World War I, had just succeeded Calvin Coolidge as president in 1929, and he rushed to reassure Americans, proclaiming that "the fundamental business of the country . . . is on a sound and prosperous basis." In March 1930 he soothingly predicted that the crisis would be over in sixty days. Had Hoover's major premise been correct — if the economy had been fundamentally sound — perhaps his conclusion might have proven true also and the crisis would have blown over quickly. There is no absolute necessity for a market panic to lead to an economic depression. A similar catastrophic drop in stock prices in 1987, for example, led to few econominc consequences. Yet the American economy was *not* fundamentally sound in 1929. The much-vaunted prosperity of the 1920s was built on a shaky basis.

The mass consumption society beckoned Americans for the first time during the 1920s. Henry Ford had perfected the process of mass production for automobiles and with low prices and installment credit plans had made it possible for ordinary working people to buy them. Automobile production and related enterprises, such as petroleum refining, road building, and the manufacture of rubber tires, boomed. Electric power production also surged, and advertisers used the new mass medium of radio to hawk their wares, shiny new labor-saving devices both for industry and for homeowners. American business, however, overbuilt its productive capacity during the 1920s. Once it had satisfied the pent-up housing demand left over from the war years and had sold all the autos and electric appliances that people could buy on credit, industry began to slow down. In fact, the top of the business cyle and the subsequent downturn had actually come *before* the stock market crash, in June 1929, but few had noticed it in the midst of the Great Bull Market.

Personal income was not distributed widely enough among the population to provide sufficient purchasing power for a truly mass consumption society. This was the basic economic problem of the 1920s. Farmers, for example, experienced little of 1920s prosperity. Farm acreage and production had expanded greatly during the war to feed the fighting nations, but with the resumption of normal agricultural yields in Europe after the war, the world was awash with surplus foodstuffs and prices plummeted. Workers in the cities fared better, but their wages didn't rise sufficiently for them to afford all the newfangled goods they were producing in their factories. Few industrialists saw as clearly as Henry Ford the close connection between good wages and increased purchasing power. From 1918 to 1928, American productivity increased about 40 percent, but wages rose only 26 percent. As economic historian Robert Sobel has concluded: "In the end, the fatal flaw of low wages in an economy of high productivity would haunt the nation."

About 5 percent of the American population received one-third of all personal income in the 1920s. Despite the foretaste of a mass consumption society, much of the purchasing power in the decade flowed into luxury goods. That top 5 percent of the population, however, was precisely the group most affected by the stock market crash. After October 1929, they abruptly stopped purchasing consumer goods and investing in productive enterprises. The American economy faced a chronic condition of overproduction, underinvestment, and underconsumption. Some sort of recession or depression was inevitable, given the flawed fundamentals; but the market crash intensified it by replacing the optimism of the 1920s with a psychology of gloom and excess caution. In short, people stopped buying anything except bare essentials, and factories shut down, further reducing personal income and purchasing power. The nation entered a downward spiral.

Since the American engine drove the world economy, when it put on the brakes the entire train slowed down. Before the war, Britain, France, and Germany had produced about 60 percent of the world's manufactured goods; but by 1929 European production had dwindled below that of the United States, whose share had risen to 40 percent. When American factories closed during the depression, they no longer bought raw materials from the countries of Asia, Africa, and Latin America. The United States had also become the predominant world lender, and when it abruptly stopped investing overseas, the banks and industries of Europe, particularly Germany, suffered severe strains. It had become a truism (changing the metaphor from transportation to medicine) that "when America sneezes the rest of the world catches pneumonia."

The world economy, like that of the United States, was not fundamentally sound in the 1920s. The world war had disrupted long-standing economic relationships and distorted world trade. What economists call primary products, that is, foodstuffs and minerals, provide a good example. Primary products loomed large in the world economy of the time. Nearly two-thirds of the world's population labored in agriculture or related industries, and about half of world trade conveyed food or minerals from the so-called underdeveloped world to the industrial countries of Europe and America. Just as American farmers had geared up to overproduce during World War I, the numerous countries throughout the world that relied on agriculture or raw materials also increased production during the conflict. Australia grew more wheat, Chile mined more copper, and the Dutch East Indies (today's Indonesia) tapped more rubber trees. When the war ended, a glut ensued and prices slumped. European nations aggravated the problem by protecting their reviving farm economies with high tariffs that reduced their imports of food. Furthermore, the growth industries of the 1920s produced synthetic substitutes for some of the basic raw materials, such as rubber, further reducing demand.

From 1925 to 1929, while the industrial world was booming, nearly every farm or mineral product fell in price. Wheat, sugar, coffee, and rubber were particularly hard hit. When the U.S. economy crashed, Americans imported less food and needed few raw materials, since they were manufacturing very little. The prices of primary products in international trade collapsed completely. From 1929 to 1933, world food prices dropped 55 percent and raw material prices fell 60 percent. The countries of Latin America, Asia, and Africa were drawn into the depression and eventually defaulted on the foreign loans extended to them in the 1920s.

The world war had disrupted and distorted the economies of the industrial nations as well. European manufacturing as a whole did not reach prewar levels until 1925. It then picked up, but still grew more slowly than the United States and Japan. Great Britain, which relied on foreign trade more heavily than most nations, lost many of its accustomed markets for textiles, coal, iron and steel, and ships during the war. Cut off from their usual supply of cheap British textiles, for example, other nations had begun buying from the United States and Japan or even manufacturing their own textiles in a process economists label "import substitution." Oddly enough, for a major industrial nation, British trade had also relied heavily on the export of a basic primary product, coal; yet after the war, industries accelerated their conversion to oil as a primary fuel, depressing demand for English coal. Therefore, the north and west of Great Britain, the areas that had witnessed the first Industrial Revolution, fell into a permanent slump that dragged on the whole economy. Even in the 1920s, before depression hit elsewhere, British unemployment never fell below 10 percent, about a million men and women out of work.

Most important for British pride and British economic well-being, London banks had ceased to be the center of world investing and money management. Instead of a lender to the world, Britain became a debtor, borrowing billions of dollars from the United States to carry on the war. Though British banks resumed some lending overseas after the war, the United States had captured the lion's share of traditional British investment markets in Latin America and Europe. From 1924 to 1929, the United States loaned 6.4 billion dollars abroad, whereas English bankers invested about half that amount.

The German reparations problem created the most obvious distortion in the new pattern of international finance. France and England had insisted that Germany pay the major cost of European reconstruction as a penance for starting the war. The Germans could only pay, however, if their economy were vigorous, and they needed new infusions of capital to gear up. American bankers filled the need and became Germany's primary creditors. This created a vicious circle. The United States loaned money to Germany, which then paid reparations to France and England, who in turn paid installments on their war loans to the United States. If the United States ever stopped lending, the circle would cease revolving.

In 1928, before the crash and depression, American lenders had already pulled back from international investments, preferring to pump their capital into the booming New York stock market. Then after the 1929 crash, they ceased investing altogether, at the same time that American industries stopped buying goods abroad. In 1929, the last year of the boom, the United States had poured 7.4 billion dollars into the world economy through the import of goods and services and the lending of capital, but by 1932 their economic impact on the rest of the world had fallen to just 2.4 billion dollars.

The world's leaders should have heeded the advice of English economist John Maynard Keynes, who in his 1919 book, *The Economic Consequences of the Peace,* had recommended that all the war loans be cancelled and Germany's reparations set at a moderate figure it could easily pay. This would have wiped the slate clean after the war and removed one major distortion from the world economy. Yet the victorious nations refused this advice, and the reparations issue exploded ten years later, when the United States ceased lending to Germany and the German economy collapsed.

In trying to recapture its former preeminence at the head of the world's banking systems, England harmed itself with a return to the gold standard in 1925. The gold standard simply meant that English pounds sterling (and any other currencies tied to gold) were readily convertible into gold. A foreign bank holding pounds could, if it wished, present them to the Bank of England and receive gold at a fixed ratio of so many grains to the pound. So long as Britannia ruled the waves and her economy remained strong, few holders of British pounds availed themselves of this privilege. The world's monetary system before the war, therefore, was based on confidence in the British pound and the British economy.

England ceased converting pounds to gold during the war and the postwar reconstruction period; but when Winston Churchill became Chancellor of the Exchequer in a Conservative government in 1925, he took the advice of the principal London bankers and returned the country to the gold standard at the prewar ratio of 123.27 fine grains of gold and $4.86 to the pound. The problem with this action is that it overvalued the pound by about 10 percent. In a free market exchange, an English pound would purchase somewhat less than $4.86.

Overvaluation of England's currency meant overpricing of its exports by about 10 percent. Thus, the largely symbolic attempt to restore the gold standard and the prewar currency exchange ratio further hindered the already limping English export industries. Protecting the overvalued pound exchange rate also required high interest rates in Britain, which discouraged investment in new plants and equipment and kept unemployment high. John Maynard Keynes published another polemic, entitled *The Economic Consequences of Mister Churchill*, denouncing this action as folly. John Kenneth Galbraith, who, like his hero Keynes, never minces words, has termed Churchill's actions "the most dramatically disastrous error by a government in modern economic history."

America had become the world's lender of last resort in the 1920s, but the nation's bankers lacked experience. Before the war, English investors had pumped money into their own economy when it was booming, and when it slowed down they directed their investment funds overseas. This influx of capital into other countries helped them increase their imports from England, thus reviving the slowed English industries. English capital, therefore, had performed a countercyclical function and kept the world economy moving like a perpetual motion machine. When the United States assumed world financial leadership, however, American banks invested heavily both overseas and at home. They pulled back from foreign loans in 1928 and then, when the crash hit the following year, they ceased lending altogether. Like intoxicated engineers, the inexperienced American bankers opened the throttle too wide in good times and hit the brakes recklessly when danger loomed.

England tried to take up the slack again in 1930 and 1931, lending to Germany and other distressed nations, but it no longer possessed the financial strength to keep the system working. When the Austrian central bank, the Kredit Anstalt, suspended payments on its debts in May 1931, an international banking crisis hit. First the Austrian and German banks closed, unable to pay their creditors, then the British banks came under pressure. Holders of British currency no longer felt confidence in the solidity of the British economy as they had in the prewar era, and thus they exchanged their pounds for gold. Finally, to stop the run on its banks, the English government abandoned the gold standard on September 21, 1931, ceased converting pounds into gold, and permitted its currency to float and find its own level against the dollar. This effectively devalued the pound by about 30 percent and made English exports cheaper. The English had saved their own economy from falling further, but the world banking and credit system had lost its engineer.

To sum up, the Great Depression began in the United States, the world's leading economic power. At the end of the 1920s, the American market for housing, automobiles, and other consumer durables became saturated and thus investment in manufacturing slowed to a halt. When the stock market crashed in October 1929, investor and consumer confidence crashed with it, preventing any upturn in economic activity. As Americans stopped lending money overseas and halted their purchases of both primary products and industrial goods, they transmitted the depression to the rest of the world. Agriculture, industry, and finance all slumped simultaneously.

President Herbert Hoover, nicknamed the Great Engineer, was as sober and serious as any politician could possibly be. Yet his attempts to deal with the depression proved as useless and damaging as if he were intoxicated or asleep at the throttle. In short, Hoover followed the conventional wisdom that an economy must simply ride out a depression and wait patiently for an upturn. He attempted to balance the budget and cut spending, just as the leaders of business and industry were doing. In fact, the balanced budget now became as much of a fetish as stock market speculation had been before the crash. The result was a massive deflation of the economy. Farm prices plummeted by 60 percent, industrial production was cut in half, and the gross national product contracted by 30 percent. By the end of Hoover's term in office in 1933, the American unemployment rate had reached 25 percent, with 13 million workers out of jobs. Perhaps an equal number found themselves underemployed, in insecure or part-time jobs.

Hoover's counterparts in other nations, from Chile to Germany, reacted similarly, with belt-tightening and budget balancing. A national coalition government in Great Britain, dominated by the Conservatives, accompanied the abandonment of the gold standard with massive cuts in government expenditures. Britain slashed unemployment payments by 10 percent and reduced the salaries of school teachers, the police, and the military.

Nations around the world turned inwards to protect what little economic activity they still maintained. The United States again led the way with the Smoot-Hawley Tariff Act of 1930 which raised the tariff on industrial goods so high as to virtually exclude their import. Similarly, and more surprisingly, the British abandoned nearly a century of free trade by instituting protective tariffs in 1932 and then striking agreements with Canada, Australia, and the other dominions for imperial preference. This meant that the British Commonwealth became a closed trading bloc, with relatively free trade inside but high tariffs and inconvertible currencies raised against the rest of the world. With walls going up everywhere, world trade withered even more.

By 1933 about 30 million workers were unemployed throughout the world. Two-thirds of these jobless could be found in just three countries: the United States and Germany, where the economic downturn was most severe, and Great Britain, where it formed a dreary extension of the depressed twenties. The International Labor Organization of the League of Nations published an index showing that in 1932 world unemployment stood at nearly three times its level of 1929. Assessing the leadership of the Great Engineer and his counterparts in other countries, historian John Garraty has concluded: "The leaders of most nations were blissfully ignorant of economics (which was not necessarily a handicap) and (far more serious) short on insight, imagination, and political courage."

The Great Depression posed not just an economic problem but a crisis of leadership. Dictatorships sprang up to exploit the grievances of the unemployed masses. Adolf Hitler came to power as Germany's economy touched bottom in 1933. Mussolini had already ruled Italy for a decade but his handling of the depression convinced many that he could indeed "make the trains run on time." Two leaders of "insight and imagination," however, John Maynard Keynes in England and Franklin Delano Roosevelt in the United States, provided alternatives to the dictators. Keynes fashioned the intellectual tools to comprehend the causes of the depression, and he proposed a bold, effective remedy. Roosevelt never thoroughly understood, nor consistently applied, the Keynesian economic prescription, but he captured the mood of the American people and lifted their spirits out of the slough of depression, restoring the national self-confidence which the crash had wounded.

John Maynard Keynes (pronounced "canes") was born in 1883, the year that Karl Marx died. His life work eventually saved and transformed the capitalist system that Marxism attempted to overthrow. Maynard, as his family and friends always called him, grew up in the comfortable environment of Cambridge, England, a clever, pampered son of devoutly religious, academic parents. Educated at the best schools — Eton and Trinity College, Cambridge — he became a civil servant in 1905 but spent much of his time with the Bloomsbury Group of writers, artists, and intellectuals in London. He served at the Treasury during the First World War and attended the Paris Peace Conference, where he was appalled at the vindictiveness of the French and the economic stupidity of all the victors. Nearly suffering a breakdown at the conference, he returned to England and poured out his feelings in *The Economic Consequences of the Peace*, a bestselling book that denounced the Versailles settlement.

Keynes had broken the rules of the English establishment by airing his grievances publicly, so he became an outsider for the rest of his life. Yet his book made him famous, and he remained an outsider with influence, and with multiple "networks of persuasion" for making his ideas known. In the 1920s and 1930s he divided his time between King's College at Cambridge, where he lectured and supervised students; the Bloomsbury set in London, which included Virginia Woolf and other unconventional writers; and the corridors of government, where he assumed many tasks as a consultant. On the side he wrote extensively for newspapers and journals of opinion, served as chairman of an insurance company, and speculated on the currency exchange, commodities markets, and the stock market. He made and lost large sums of money in the twenties, then succeeded in earning a fortune during the depression through conservative investments. In 1925 Keynes, a homosexual, married the Russian ballerina Lydia Lopokova. His biographer Robert Skidelsky argues convincingly that this was not just a marriage of convenience but a true love match; Maynard remained devoted to Lydia until his death in 1946.

The chronic unemployment in England, which began long before the Great Depression and persisted throughout the twenties and thirties, pushed Keynes's economic analysis in new directions. Classical economists taught that an economy ordinarily rests in a state of stable equilibrium at the level of full employment. Unemployment, then, was merely a temporary aberration, usually caused by labor unions holding out for too high a wage. When a depression hit, therefore, the proper remedy was to ride it out, let wages and prices fall and the job market rise naturally to its equilibrium state of full employment. Keynes, however, observing the slack performance of the British job market throughout the twenties, realized that it was perfectly possible for an economy to reach an equilibrium state at less than full employment. Furthermore, there was no natural, self-adjusting mechanism that would snap a country out of this sluggish state. As Keynes's biographer Skidelsky has phrased it, "the revolutionary thought was that people could be unemployed due to a 'lack of effective demand,' and not because they had 'priced themselves out of jobs.'" It might prove necessary for governments to stimulate demand, thus breaking up the "underemployment equilibrium" of a depressed economy.

Keynes initially hoped that monetary adjustments by the central bank might pump new life into the economy. He proposed low interest rates to make borrowing and the creation of new money easy. Yet in the psychological slump of the depression, even low interest rates could not induce capitalists to borrow and invest. Keynes concluded "that the duty of ordering the current volume of investment cannot safely be left in private hands." Therefore, he recommended that the government directly stimulate effective demand by embarking on a large-scale program of public works.

Shortly before the 1929 general election in Great Britain, he converted the old war leader, David Lloyd George, to the concept of public works as a remedy for unemployment; but Lloyd George's Liberals were being slowly squeezed by the Labour Party on its left and the Conservatives on the right. Keynes considered the Conservatives the party of stupidity and Labour the party of silliness; yet they overwhelmed the Liberals, who elected only fifty-nine members in 1929, coming in a distant third. Within a few years, the party had virtually ceased to exist. Only one member of the new Labour government, Oswald Mosley, accepted Keynes's public works policy, and he soon left the Cabinet and formed the Union of British Fascists. Politically, Keynes was a prophet without honor in his own country.

Keynes, therefore, withdrew for a time to develop his ideas, publishing them in final form as *The General Theory of Employment, Interest and Money* in 1935. By then he had discovered the secret to restarting the economic engine in the concept of the "investment multiplier," developed by one of his students, Richard Kahn, in a 1931 article. Kahn and Keynes reasoned that any new investment in the economy, whether by government or private industry, set off a chain reaction. A million dollars worth of public works, for example, provided much more than a million dollars worth of economic stimulus, because the newly hired workers spent nearly all their wages on goods and services, and the providers of those goods and services, therefore, hired new workers, who spent their wages, and so on. If workers spent none of their new wages at all but simply put them in an old sock, there would be no multiplier effect, but in the real world the multiplier would increase the economic stimulus by a factor that could be mathematically determined.

The Keynesian remedy for the depression, therefore, was a program of government-sponsored public works. The government should not balance its budget in the short run but rather run a deficit, borrow money, and create public jobs for the unemployed workers. Through the multiplier effect, this would jump start the economy and eventually create enough new taxable wealth for the government to pay off its debt and balance the budget somewhere down the line. Keynes didn't shrink from the standard criticism that government-sponsored public works would be wasteful, that the workers would simply dig holes one day and fill them in the next. With his usual irreverent wit, he concluded:

If the Treasury were to fill old bottles with banknotes, bury them at suitable depths in disused coal-mines which are then filled up to the surface with town rubbish . . . there need be no unemployment. . . . It would indeed be more sensible to build houses and the like; but if there are political and practical difficulties in the way of this, the above would be better than nothing.

Despite the political resistance to his ideas, he remained hopeful for he had a profound belief in the effectiveness of ideas. At the end of the *General Theory* he concluded:

The ideas of economists and political philosophers, both when they are right and when they are wrong, are more powerful than is commonly understood. Indeed the world is ruled by little else. Practical men, who believe themselves to be quite exempt from any intellectual influences, are usually the slaves of some defunct economist. Madmen in authority, who hear voices in the air, are distilling their frenzy from some academic scribbler of a few years back.

Ironically, the foremost madman of the age, Adolf Hitler, was unconsciously and instinctively applying the recommendations of this particular academic scribbler. Hitler conscripted the manpower of Germany in a vast program of public works and rearmament, a Keynesian solution without Keynes. Yet the leaders of England and the United States still resisted such ideas, and not until the rearmament for World War II did those countries recover fully. In the *General Theory,* Keynes had cynically remarked that "pyramid-building, earthquakes, even wars may serve to increase wealth, if the education of our statesmen . . . stands in the way of anything better." Tragically, this assessment proved correct. Only war pushed the drunken engineers of England and the United States to rev their engines fully. In the meantime, however, a new president in the United States, Franklin Delano Roosevelt, who defeated Herbert Hoover in 1932, gave the American people a wild ride, picking up Keynes along the way.

FDR (the new president and all his programs were labeled in an alphabet soup of initials) came from a privileged background, somewhat similar to that of Maynard Keynes in England but without Keynes's academic connections. The Roosevelts were a family of country gentry who had been socially prominent in the Hudson River valley of New York since Dutch colonial times. James Roosevelt married Sara Delano, a woman half his age, and the couple had only one child, Franklin Delano, who was born in 1882 (just a year before Keynes). Young Franklin was a pampered mama's boy who attended the elite prep school of Groton, then Harvard University and Columbia Law School, without distinguishing himself at any of them. When he married his cousin Eleanor in 1905 and began practicing law in New York City, Sara Roosevelt, by then a widow, moved in with the young couple.

Though Franklin's distant cousin, the Republican Theodore Roosevelt, was residing in the White House, and most of the Roosevelts were devoted Republicans, Franklin's branch of the family had always been Democrats. So Franklin entered politics in league with the Tammany Hall Democrats of New York, who saw this dashing young aristocrat as a good front man. After a number of terms in the state legislature, he secured a post as assistant secretary of the navy in Washington during World War I, and then was chosen vice presidential candidate in 1920, going down to defeat with his presidential running mate, Governor James M. Cox of Ohio. Had Cox and Roosevelt been elected in 1920, their administration would probably have proven as forgettable as that of the Republicans, Harding and Coolidge, who defeated them.

In 1921, while swimming in the icy waters of the Bay of Fundy at Campobello, his summer home in Maine, Roosevelt contracted a severe case of polio which left his legs permanently crippled. This physical crisis changed his life, the way World War I, the Paris Peace Conference, and the British unemployment slump redirected the life of John Maynard Keynes. Whereas Keynes changed from a clever aesthete to an applied theorist on a mission to save society, Roosevelt transformed himself from a lightweight playboy to a man with a steely nerve and a twofold ambition in life, to walk unassisted and to make his mark in politics. He never achieved the first goal (though he never stopped trying), but he kept a "rendezvous with destiny" as Governor of New York from 1928 to 1932, and then as the only president elected to four straight terms in office.

Roosevelt sensibly focused his 1932 presidential campaign on the do-nothing policies of the incumbent, Herbert Hoover. The public needed little encouragement to reject the austere Hoover; they had already dubbed the shanty-towns of the homeless unemployed "Hoovervilles." Yet Roosevelt did not present any coherent plan, Keynesian or otherwise, to cure the economic downturn. Instead, he sounded the keynote that would characterize his approach to the depression: "The country needs and the country demands bold, persistent experimentation. It is common sense to take a method and try it, if it fails, admit it frankly and try another. But above all, try something."

Common sense and bold, persistent experimentation were what Roosevelt promised and what he delivered. This is very similar to Keynes's point of view when he moved from the realm of theory to the arena of politics. At the end of a pamphlet he wrote for the Liberal Party in 1929, Keynes had counseled, "There is no reason why we should not feel ourselves free to be bold, to be open, to experiment, to take action, to try the possibilities of things." Yet this attitude disappointed doctrinaire Liberals who wanted a clear outline for the future. The columnist Walter Lippmann, writing in the *New Republic,* concluded just before the election that Roosevelt was "a man who, without any important qualifications for the office, wants very much to be President."

Roosevelt didn't worry about his critics, however. He was angling for political support and public confidence, and he stage-managed his campaign and the first few months in office to give the public an impression of vigorous action and determination. He attacked the listless economy of the United States the way he exercised his lifeless legs: he wasn't sure how, or even whether, he could budge them, but he would never stop trying.

When the Democratic National Convention nominated Roosevelt in the summer of 1932, he flew to Chicago to accept the nomination in person, a sharp break from past party practice.He thus symbolized his intent to shatter traditions whenever the crisis demanded it. The closing line of his acceptance speech, "I pledge myself to a new deal for the American people," captured the public mood perfectly, without outlining what the new deal might consist of. Then in his inaugural address, on March 4, 1933, Roosevelt again caught and led the public mood when he proclaimed, "The only thing we have to fear is fear itself."

The newly installed president called Congress into special session and kept it working for over three months, or roughly one hundred days. During this period FDR pushed through fifteen major pieces of legislation. They did not add up to a consistent policy; some of them contradicted and neutralized each other, and they did not cure the depression. Yet they did provide some relief — welfare checks or public works jobs — to the unemployed, and they created a sense of momentum that gave the public hope and confidence. Just a week into his term as president, Roosevelt conducted his first "fireside chat" with the nation via radio. His jaunty, reassuring tone of voice soothed the fears of his listeners. The comedian Will Rogers quipped that "the President took a complicated subject like banking and made everyone understand it, even the bankers."

Roosevelt's policies fell roughly into two acts. During the First New Deal, from 1933 to 1935, the president governed as a nonpartisan leader, a broker between competing special interests. The National Recovery Administration (NRA) brought business, labor, and government together to set prices and allocate markets, whereas the Agricultural Adjustment Administration (AAA) paid farmers to restrict their output and thus raise prices. None of this had much economic effect, but it did rally the American people and create the illusion of national purpose. At the same time, the president appointed Harry Hopkins, a hard-drinking, poker-playing social worker from New York, as his relief administrator; and Hopkins cut through bureaucratic red tape, funneling money to the unemployed as quickly as possible. When conservatives criticized such welfare spending and urged the administration to invest in projects that might have more value in the long run, Hopkins scornfully replied, "People don't eat in the long run, they eat every day." Without knowing it, Hopkins was echoing one of Keynes's most famous dicta, "In the long run we are all dead."

Yet despite the seeming profligacy of the New Deal's relief programs, Roosevelt actually believed in a balanced budget every bit as much as Hoover did. At the same time he was unleashing Harry Hopkins to dole out relief, he also slashed federal workers' wages and pensions and tried to economize elsewhere. Keynes addressed an open letter to President Roosevelt at the end of 1933, urging him to abandon such contradictory measures; and he met briefly with FDR in Washington on May 28, 1934. After this confab, the president commented that he had conducted a "grand talk with Keynes and liked him immensely." This was how Roosevelt typically treated visitors, and it signified nothing. Franklin Roosevelt liked to follow his instincts and keep his options open, and Keynes could not convince him to follow a consistent, large-scale policy of public works. FDR eventually wound up with a Keynesian solution, but only towards the end of his second term.

The First New Deal failed to end the depression, and it drew increasing attacks from conservatives, so as Roosevelt prepared for his reelection campaign he embarked on a more class-conscious, reformist Second New Deal in 1935 and 1936. He convinced Congress to raise taxes on the rich and establish the largest public works program in American history, the Works Progress Administration (WPA), directed by Harry Hopkins. The Wagner Act, introduced by New York Senator Robert F. Wagner, guaranteed the rights of labor unions to bargain collectively with employers and established the National Labor Relations Board (NLRB) to adjudicate labor disputes. Most importantly, Congress in 1935 passed the Social Security Act, establishing a nation-wide system of old-age pensions for American workers. In the short run, this measure probably aggravated the depression by imposing a payroll tax on workers and thus reducing their purchasing power, but it created a permanent "entitlement" which has become the cornerstone of the American welfare state.

Despite the twists and turns and the inconsistencies of policy, the economy did pick up moderately by 1936, and the New Deal had lightened the public mood considerably. Roosevelt won the confidence game that his predecessor, Hoover, and many European leaders had lost. He carried all but two states in his decisive reelection campaign of 1936.

Then during his second term, President Roosevelt miscalculated badly and almost destroyed all his accomplishments. Angered that the Supreme Court had overturned some of his New Deal legislation, he requested authority from Congress to "pack" the Court with supporters, by enlarging its size from nine to fifteen justices. Public opinion reacted negatively and the court-packing bill failed. Then FDR again indulged his old-fashioned penchant for a balanced budget, reducing expenditures sharply. The 1936 federal budget had run a deficit of 3.6 billion dollars, but Roosevelt pared this down to only 358 million dollars in 1937. As a result, the economic recovery halted and unemployment figures soared again. Pundits dubbed this 1937 downturn the "Roosevelt Recession."

269

By this time Keynes had published the *General Theory* and had won many converts at Harvard and other American universities. Many of these academics took jobs in Roosevelt's so-called brain trust in Washington, and now they urged the president to adopt a Keynesian policy of massive federal spending. After some initial resistance, FDR finally capitulated in March 1938 and increased spending on welfare and public works. This reversed the recessionary trend, but by the end of 1938 eight million Americans still remained unemployed. Only with the outbreak of World War II did the Roosevelt administration finally abandon all inhibitions about deficit spending. Total federal outlays jumped from 8.9 billion dollars in 1939 to 34 billion dollars in 1941. It seems a melancholy fact that governments are more willing to waste money on warfare than invest it in peacetime jobs and public works.

As engineer of America's economic recovery, Franklin Delano Roosevelt sometimes seemed as intoxicated as any other political leader of the 1930s. For example, in 1933 he cavalierly torpedoed a world economic conference with a hasty cable sent overseas from his vacation yacht. Roosevelt, like most national political leaders, intended to focus on the home front rather than exercise world economic leadership. Before following England off the gold standard, FDR tinkered with the gold content of the dollar, meeting every morning, while still in his pajamas, with the secretary of the treasury to arbitrarily fix that day's dollar exchange value. As we have already seen, Roosevelt's budget balancing often conflicted with his welfare and works spending, effectively canceling it out as an economic stimulus.

Yet if the engineer seemed intoxicated, the train ride often proved intoxicating. Roosevelt's flexible temperament, his experimental approach, and his willingness to try anything transformed the mood in America from gloom and a threat of revolt to confidence and a shared sense of purpose. By way of comparison, the economic performance of England's politicians was no worse than Roosevelt's, and in some ways better, yet they received little credit for it. A building boom in housing throughout the 1930s reduced unemployment more quickly than the New Deal did in America, and England's welfare policies provided a more dependable social safety net than the ad hoc programs administered by Harry Hopkins. Yet neither the Labour Party leader, Ramsay MacDonald, nor the Conservative Stanley Baldwin, who governed together for much of the thirties in a national coalition government, captured the public's imagination the way Roosevelt did. The "Great Slump," as it's called in England, is remembered as a gray, lifeless time, with the people more depressed psychologically than in America.

Franklin Roosevelt, despite the fact that his New Deal did not end the Great Depression, is recalled as one of the greatest presidents in American history. Not a great thinker like Keynes, Roosevelt possessed, in the words of one admirer, "a second-rate intellect but a first-class temperament." He transmitted his confidence and determination to ordinary Americans. The political effect proved similar to the intellectual effect of Keynes upon his listeners. D. M. Bensusan-Butt, one of Keynes's disciples at Cambridge, recalled that "what we got was joyful revelation in dark times . . . less a work of economics theory than a Manifesto for Reason and Cheerfulness." Keynes and Roosevelt shared more in common than appears at first glance. Skidelsky asserts that "Keynes was an applied economist who turned to inventing theory because the theory he had inherited could not properly explain what was happening." Roosevelt resisted theory as long as he could, but he eventually adopted Keynesian ideas because nothing else worked.

The leadership of Maynard Keynes and Franklin Roosevelt proved vitally important, for the two decades between the world wars witnessed a worldwide crisis of leadership. Both searched for and found a middle way between communism, which appealed to many intellectuals in England and America during the depression, and fascism, with its frightening grip on the masses. Keynes clearly set out to save the economic system from itself. He wrote in the *General Theory:* "The authoritarian state systems of to-day seem to solve the problem of unemployment at the expense of efficiency and of freedom . . . but it may be possible by a right analysis of the problem to cure the disease whilst preserving efficiency and freedom." The effectiveness of his remedies was demonstrated during World War II, and policymakers insitutionalized his methods and techniques on a regular and permanent basis after the war.

Many historians believe that Franklin Roosevelt's performance as president saved the United States from radical disorders or even a revolution. During his first inaugural address, FDR had warned that if Congress failed to act, "I shall not evade the clear course of duty that will then confront me. I shall ask Congress for the one remaining instrument to meet the crisis — broad Executive power to wage a war against the emergency." Eleanor Roosevelt, who often acted as her crippled husband's eyes and ears, shuddered when the crowd reacted more enthusiastically to this hint of dictatorship than to anything else the president said in his speech. Fortunately, rule by executive decree proved unnecessary in the United States, but in other countries, where no Roosevelt stepped forward to massage the public mood, and where Keynes was unknown or unheeded, more ominous leaders filled the vacuum.

CHAPTER SIXTEEN

Italy's "New Deal"

Benito Mussolini's Fascist movement came to power in Italy on October 31, 1922, seven years before the Wall Street stock market crash and a full decade before Franklin Roosevelt's New Deal in the United States. Mussolini's dictatorship provided an alternative to Roosevelt and Keynes for countries in crisis after World War I and during the Great Depression. Many political leaders between the two world wars viewed Italian fascism as another possible "third way" between capitalist democracy and Marxist socialism.

Yet the term "fascism" is one of the most abused and abusive words of the twentieth century, often employed carelessly as a political epithet. In 1934, in the depths of the depression, the young Eric Sevareid, who would later become a noted television journalist, witnessed the violent suppression of a truckers' strike in Minneapolis and exclaimed passionately: "Suddenly I knew, I understood deep in my bones and blood what fascism was." Much later, American student radicals in the 1960s casually labeled all policemen "fascist pigs." Throughout the century, leftists and liberals in many countries consistently branded their conservative opponents "fascists"; communists even dismissed moderate socialists as "social fascists."

Used this way, to lump together the Minnesota National Guard, the Chicago Police Department, and the German Social Democrats, the word becomes meaningless. Yet the employment of the term "fascism" by historians, philosophers, and political scientists can be almost as misleading. Most scholars agree that fascism was a distinctive development in European politics springing from the chaos of World War I, and they often link together such movements as Italian Fascism, German National Socialism, the Spanish Falange, and the Romanian Iron Guard. Definitions break down quickly, however, and common elements are

272

Italy after World War I

hard to isolate when such disparate movements are compared closely. It is advisable, therefore, to focus initially on Mussolini's Italian Fascists, the political party which provided the name and example for all similar movements, leaving the fine points of analysis and comparison for later.

The term "fascism" comes from the Italian word *fascio,* which simply means a bundle, or group. In ancient Rome, the *lictor,* one of the officers of the Roman Republic, carried the *fasces,* a bundle of sticks or rods with an axe embedded in them, as his symbol of authority. In modern times, various Italian protest movements adopted the word *fascio* for their political groups and employed the ancient *fasces* as a symbol. Mussolini followed this usage when he established his own political movement right after World War I.

Italian Fascism was an anti-movement, more easily defined by its enemies than its ideas. Fascists violently opposed Marxist socialism and parliamentary liberal democracy, both of which seemed to have failed in Italy by the time of the First World War. In order to make this clear, we must set the career of Mussolini and the rise of fascism against the history of modern Italy. Only then will the definitions and distinctions begin to make sense.

Italy was one of the youngest nation-states of Europe, united politically only in 1871. The tiny kingdom of Piedmont, at the foot of the Alps, formed the spearhead of the *Risorgimento,* the political movement for Italian unification. Count Camillo di Cavour, serving as prime minister of Piedmont under the Savoy dynasty, skillfully played the great powers of France, England, and Prussia against one another to create political space for a united Italy. When the nationalist adventurer Giuseppe Garibaldi led a motley volunteer army into Sicily in 1860, Cavour persuaded him to recognize the authority of King Victor Emmanuel II of Piedmont and then proclaimed the new Kingdom of Italy in 1861. Venice and its surrounding area still remained under Austrian rule and the pope still ruled Rome and parts of central Italy as a secular monarch, but the new kingdom embraced the rest of the peninsula as well as the islands of Sardinia and Sicily.

During this same decade of the 1860s, Bismarck's drive to unite Germany under the Hohenzollern monarch of Prussia assisted the Italian *Risorgimento.* Prussia defeated Austria in 1866 and dictated the cession of Venice to Italy. Then the Franco-Prussian War of 1870-71 forced the French emperor to withdraw his troops from the Papal States which they had been protecting. Garibaldi marched into Rome virtually unopposed in 1871, acquiring the ancient capital for the new Kingdom of Italy. The *Risorgimento* proved remarkably bloodless, claiming only about six thousand lives in battle between 1848 and 1870. It owed more to Germany's armies, and a favorable international situation, than to Italian efforts.

Though united politically after 1871, Italy remained a deeply divided and incomplete nation-state. Its natural boundaries were more clearly defined than those of most European states, for the peninsula was surrounded by water on three sides and bounded by the summits of the Alps to the north. Yet a sharp economic divide cut the peninsula in two. The northern part of the kingdom, including the urban triangle of Genoa, Turin, and Milan, and the fertile Po River valley, was the more prosperous and politically conscious region, the home of the *Risorgimento*'s leaders. All the territory south of Rome, including the huge island of Sicily, remained poverty-stricken. Rome itself, despite its legacy of beautiful ruins, was an unhealthful, poor southern city. King Victor Emmanuel II died in 1878 of the deadly malaria endemic in the marshes surrounding his newly acquired capital. The south of Italy resembled Ireland, a region of large landowners and rebellious peasants, governed absent-mindedly by a distant, virtually foreign ruling class. Like Ireland, impoverished southern Italy constantly threatened the central government with rebellion.

Ordinary Italians cherished a regional *campanilismo,* that is, loyalty to the countryside lying within sight of the local church steeple or campanile, rather than a national feeling. Furthermore, rural Italians, the vast majority of the peninsula's inhabitants, lavished most of their love and devotion on their extended families. A twentieth-century sociologist, Edward Banfield, has christened this phenomenon "amoral familism." Nothing mattered to many Italians except the fate of their family.

With a rich history that includes the ancient Roman Empire and the artistic flowering of the Renaissance, Italians possessed some of the building blocks of national consciousness. Nearly all shared a heritage of Catholic religion, and they could glory in a beautiful literary language crafted by the Renaissance poet Dante. Yet the *Risorgimento* was fiercely anticlerical, since the pope's temporal power stood in the way of Italy's reunification. Thus the new Kingdom of Italy was divided between believing Catholics and wholly secular liberals. Indeed, Pope Pius IX forbade Catholic participation in the political life of the new kingdom. Furthermore, the majority of Italians did not speak the literary language, but one of a dozen or so local dialects. Ironically, the Savoy kings and their ministers, such as Cavour, felt more at home speaking French than Italian, for the heartland of Piedmont lay on the French side of the Alps.

In sum, the newly unified Italian state lacked legitimacy. To most Italians it was a distant, hostile force of tax collectors and military police, tolerated but not venerated. One of the leaders of the *Risorgimento,* Massimo D'Azeglio, summed up the sorry state of national spirit in the peninsula: "We have made Italy, now we must make some Italians."

Italy's political system earned little respect for the new state. A small, educated elite of landowners, businessmen, and professionals had led the *Risorgimento,* and this same class ruled the kingdom with a remarkable disdain for the masses. The majority of Italians remained illiterate and disfranchised until after the turn of the century. Parliamentary deputies were local notables who bribed the tiny electorate of their districts with jobs and favors and then represented the strongest vested interests within their constituencies. No broad ideological parties crystallized to formulate and execute national policies. In parliament, therefore, cliques of deputies formed and re-formed temporary coalitions, a process that a prime minister of the 1880s, Agostino Depretis, named *trasformismo*, transformism. Political opponents of yesterday might transform themselves into political allies today, especially if their votes were bought with graft and patronage. The lack of a two-party system and the pervasive corruption brought Italian parliamentary politics into increasing disrepute. A vast gulf separated "legal Italy," the tiny class of Italians politically active, from "real Italy."

The disfranchised masses of "real Italy" began to find their voice during the 1890s. The Italian Socialist Party, founded in 1892, glorified and exploited the spontaneous uprisings of peasants and miners in Sicily and the south. The bourgeois national government savagely repressed these southern risings in 1893, but discontent still simmered. Then in 1898 a series of "bread and work" riots spread throughout the peninsula, climaxing with street fighting in Milan, the industrial metropolis of the kingdom, from May 7 to 10. The army proclaimed martial law and pacified Milan at the price of 80 civilians killed and 450 wounded. Finally, on July 29, 1900, Gaetano Bresci, an anarchist who had been living and working in Paterson, New Jersey, returned to Italy and assassinated King Humbert in retaliation for the martial law outrages of Milan.

Italian politics calmed down in the relatively prosperous years of the new century's first decade. A skillful political manipulator, Giovanni Giolitti, raised transformism to a new level of perfection, ruling Italy directly as prime minister or indirectly through a handpicked lieutenant for all but 219 days between 1903 and 1914. Giolitti appeased the working class with piecemeal economic reforms and he tried, unsuccessfully, to convince the socialist leaders to join his governments. When the socialists of Milan declared a general strike in September 1904, he kept the troops in reserve should serious trouble break out but refused to confront or suppress the workers. The strike petered out on its own in just four days. Giolitti's restraint was undoubtedly wise, as it avoided unnecessary bloodshed, but it created an unfortunate image of weakness on his part that further eroded public confidence in parliamentary politicians.

In the last years before World War I, Giolitti attempted a triple-play of transformism to consolidate his political control. He persuaded Pope Pius X to ease the papal ban on Catholic voting, and he nearly convinced the moderate socialists to support him as well. He pandered to extreme nationalist sentiments by an imperialist attack on Turkish Libya in 1911. Had he continued in power a few more years, he might have united most of "real Italy" behind him; but in a routine parliamentary maneuver, he resigned in March 1914, expecting to regain power shortly. World War I broke out that summer, preventing his return. Giolitti's administration had brought political stability to Italy, but his incessant maneuvering in parliament offended the sensibilities of both principled conservatives and leftist radicals. The Italian public felt that Giolitti lacked poetry and vision; in ten years of power he had failed "to make a single chord of the nation vibrate."

The outbreak of war posed a thorny dilemma to Italian politicians. Since 1882, Italy had been a member of the Triple Alliance with Germany and Austria-Hungary, but most Italians feared the Germans and resented the continuance of Austrian rule over Italian-speaking areas around Trent and Trieste. Italy owed its very existence as a united nation to the uneasy balance of power north of the Alps, so it remained reluctant to commit itself in 1914. Since the Triple Alliance was a defensive agreement, Italy could and did remain neutral when Germany attacked France and Austria-Hungary attacked Serbia. The government that succeeded Giolitti's, with Antonio Salandra as prime minister and Sidney Sonnino as minister of foreign affairs, tried to win concessions from Austria as a price for remaining neutral. At the same time they negotiated with the Triple Entente — England, France, and Russia — to see what gains might be made by declaring war on their side. They finally signed the secret Treaty of London on April 26, 1915, committing Italy to the Entente in return for territorial gains at Trent, Trieste, and the Dalmatian coast on the eastern shore of the Adriatic Sea.

The majority of Italians would have preferred neutrality. Giolitti, as an opposition member of parliament, opposed the declaration of war. The Italian socialists, unlike their comrades in France and Germany, remained true to their pacifist principles and did not rally to the flag. Pope Benedict XV worked tirelessly for a negotiated peace, and Italian Catholics generally opposed a war against Catholic Austria.

Yet a noisy minority of interventionists saw the war as a golden opportunity for Italy to gain territory and acquire the influence of a great power. Throughout the month of May 1915 they staged demonstrations urging the government to join the struggle. Salandra finally secured the backing of both king and parliament for a war against Austria, which was declared on May 24.[1] In an unfortunate turn of phrase, he exhorted the staff of the foreign ministry to cast aside any doubts and devote themselves to a *sacro egoismo* ("sacred egoism") for Italy. This expression sums up the mystical nationalism which was both cause and consequence of World War I, and which contributed to the rise of fascism.

Italy fought a grueling trench war against Austria on the plains and foothills between Venice and Trieste, in the northeastern corner of the peninsula. The socialists remained opposed throughout the struggle, and most workers avoided military service since they labored in essential industries. The peasantry provided the majority of the cannon fodder for the trenches. Though initially short of guns

1. Italy did not declare war on Germany until over a year later, on August 28, 1916.

and supplies, Italian soldiers fought as doggedly and fatalistically as the other conscript armies of Europe. They suffered a stunning defeat at Caporetto in October 1917, followed by a humiliating retreat; yet they avenged this tragedy the following year at the battle of Vittorio Veneto, knocking Austria out of the war and then capturing Trieste.

Italy fell into turmoil and disillusion immediately after the war. In just three years of combat, the government had spent twice as much money as it had for the entire period from the *Risorgimento* onwards. In all, 5.75 million Italians mobilized, and 600,000 of them died; another half million were permanently disabled. Over 100,000 deserters remained at large after the war, raising the threat of renewed banditry in the countryside.

The peace treaty did not bestow all the territorial gains that Italian sacred egoism desired. The American president Woodrow Wilson opposed the Allies' secret treaties; in particular, he judged Italian claims in the Treaty of London unjust to the newly formed country of Yugoslavia. The Italian prime minister at war's end, Vittorio Orlando, secured Wilson's consent to the annexation of Trent and South Tyrol from Austria but proved unable to change Wilson's mind about the Slavic territory in Yugoslavia. Orlando's government fell right after the peace conference adjourned in June 1919. The Italian poet Gabriele D'Annunzio, who had led a swashbuckling life as an aviator during the war, coined the phrase "mutilated victory" to describe the frustration of Italy's territorial ambitions.

D'Annunzio brought these postwar frustrations to a boil when he seized the port of Fiume on September 12, 1919. Fiume was a largely Italian city about forty miles southeast of Trieste, surrounded by Croatian inhabitants in the countryside. It had not been included in the spoils of war promised Italy in the Treaty of London, but the Italians had tried unsuccessfully to obtain it at the peace conference. D'Annunzio marched into the port at the head of a legion of discontented war veterans and established an independent government that lasted over a year, until the Italian army expelled him at the end of 1920. Italy eventually gained control of Fiume by diplomatic means, but D'Annunzio's expedition provided an important model for Mussolini, pioneering many of the more flamboyant aspects of fascism.

Meanwhile, during the *Biennio Rosso* ("two Red years") of 1919 and 1920, the urban socialists struck repeatedly for higher wages, and radical peasant leagues organized a virtual monopoly of farm labor in the northern country districts. In 1919 1,663 industrial strikes involved over a million workers; 208 agricultural strikes embraced about half a million peasants. Rapid demobilization of soldiers pushed the number of unemployed over the two million mark. In the national elections of November 1919, the socialists polled about a third of the popular vote, becoming the largest single party in parliament, with 156 seats. Local socialist administrations controlled 2,162 of the 8,059 communes and 25 of the 69 provinces in Italy. Anarchists were active as well, for the radical seamen's union had smuggled Enrico Malatesta, a legendary anarchist leader, back into the country in December 1919; he was greeted by his followers as "the Lenin of Italy."

Then in August 1920 the metal workers at the Alfa Romeo plant in Milan seized control of their factory and prevented the owners from locking them out in a labor dispute. On August 31 the metalworkers union occupied 280 other factories in sympathy. Emboldened by the Bolshevik Revolution in Russia, some of the Milanese socialists called the workers' councils in these occupied factories *soviets*. Giovanni Giolitti, who had again become prime minister, followed the same cautious strategy he had pursued in 1904, and the socialist uprising in Milan fizzled.

The factory seizure of 1920 marked a significant turning point in Italian history. The middle classes feared a Bolshevik Revolution and roundly condemned Giolitti's restraint. Many working-class leaders, however, took the opposite lesson from the collapse of the factory movement. They believed that organized socialism had failed. Both left and right, however, agreed that parliamentary politicians, such as Giolitti, had become irrelevant. In this crisis atmosphere of frustration, disappointment, and fear, Italian Fascism took shape.

The ideas of fascism were a hybrid of two other "isms" — the brand of socialism known as syndicalism, and an extreme version of Italian nationalism. Syndicalists believed that the labor union (*syndicat* in French; *sindicato* in Italian) should be the spearhead of the socialist revolution, not the political party. Workers' syndicates would teach revolutionary values and class-consciousness to the masses; and with the solidarity and camaraderie they fostered, they would provide a model for the classless society of the future. Rather than politics, the syndicalists used the general strike as their major weapon, and it was socialists of a syndicalist bent who had mounted the Milan general strike of September 1904. Syndicalists in both France and Spain had forged close ties with the masses through disciplined labor unions, but Italian syndicalism remained largely an intellectual movement, unsuccessful when it actually tried to organize the workers.[2]

The unhappy experiences of Italian immigrants in the United States disenchanted many syndicalists with working-class solidarity. Paolo Orana, a syn-

---

2. This variety of socialism is often referred to as anarcho-syndicalism, stressing the anti-government, anti-political nature of syndicalist ideology. Some anarchists did indeed view the revolutionary syndicate, or labor union, as a spearhead of the new society they were aiming at. Yet Italian syndicalists firmly dissociated themselves from the individualism of the anarchists. Sergio Panunzio, a leading syndicalist theorist, wrote a book in 1908 entitled *Una Nuova Aritocrazia* ("A New Aristocracy") that advocated the leadership of a vanguard revolutionary elite, a new aristocracy, who would guide the masses in a disciplined, authoritarian movement. This is the antithesis of anarchism.

dicalist leader, concluded cynically that in America "the sons of Abruzzi and of Sicily empty the garbage and wash the dirty clothes of the American workers." Then World War I completely reoriented Italian syndicalist thought. Sergio Panunzio, a leading theorist, concluded that the nation-state had surpassed the labor syndicate as an object of mass loyalty. A solidarity of the trenches had transcended class barriers and transformed all the soldiers fighting for their country into brothers. Therefore, he proclaimed a "national syndicalism" that would draw on the experience of war to create a united, disciplined, and productive nation. Since Italy remained underdeveloped economically, redistributing income from one class to another as orthodox socialists advocated made little sense. Instead, national syndicalism proposed to discipline the masses and foster increased production and national wealth.

The intellectual course of syndicalism in Italy paralleled the development of extreme Italian nationalism. In 1903 Enrico Corradini, a literary figure from Florence, founded a political journal named *Il Regno* (The Kingdom), giving voice to young nationalists frightened by the socialist upsurge of the 1890s. Corradini and his followers championed a strident expansionist policy that would seek colonies in Africa as a safety valve for national frustrations and a destination for Italian emigrants. These nationalists hoped that the working class would thus contribute to Italian national greatness rather than stage rebellions or leave for America.

In 1910 a congress in Florence launched the Italian Nationalist Association as an organized pressure group. About the same time, Corradini made the decisive intellectual contribution of the new nationalism to Italian politics. He declared that Italy was a "proletarian nation," that is, an impoverished newcomer to statehood and industrialization, contending on the world stage against "plutocratic nations" such as England, France, or Germany. The nationalists, therefore, replaced the socialists' class struggle of proletariat against bourgeoisie with an international struggle of proletariat nations against plutocratic nations.

Though they started from different premises and continued as separate movements until after World War I, Italian syndicalism and nationalism shared much in common. Both movements addressed the fundamental Italian problems of economic underdevelopment, political immaturity, and incomplete national integration. Both rejected the parliamentary maneuvers of Giolitti and the transformists as irrelevant to these serious national concerns. The twin movements were elitist and authoritarian, and they emphasized the need for greater economic productivity if Italy were to catch up with more advanced nations.

Then World War I brought them even closer together. Since both groups advocated struggle and violence, they actively campaigned for Italian intervention and drew on wartime experience to refine their thinking. By 1919 both the Italian Nationalist Association and the syndicalist leadership were using the same term, "national syndicalism," to describe their policies. They both rejected the artificial distinction between bourgeoisie and proletariat and emphasized instead the conflict between productive and nonproductive groups. Any productive Italian, whether a factory worker, a technician, or a business entrepreneur, could join the new elite that would unite the nation. The demobilized veterans of the First World War, whose shared sufferings had created a new kind of classlessness, would form the vanguard of this elite. Nationalists and syndicalists aimed to sweep away the parliamentary system, replacing it with a government of producers that would move at the pace of modern machines.

Benito Mussolini was neither a syndicalist nor a member of the Nationalist Association, but as a socialist journalist he had encountered both currents of thought and been influenced particularly by syndicalism. On March 23, 1919, in a hall on the Piazza San Sepolcro in Milan, he launched his own movement, the *Fascio di Combattimento* (Group of Combatants). Over the next three and a half years, while maneuvering to gain power, he effectively fused the ideas of syndicalists and nationalists into a new amalgam, Italian Fascism. All the fermenting "isms" of the early twentieth century blended together in the creation of fascism; for Mussolini's movement combined nationalism and one variety of socialism (syndicalism) in opposition to mainstream socialism and anarchism. It also charted an imperialist future for Italy.

Benito Mussolini was born on July 29, 1883, in the rural commune of Predappio in the Romagna, a central Italian region of barren hills and rebellious peasants. His father, Alessandro, was a blacksmith and self-taught Marxist, who named his first son Benito Andrea Amilcare after Benito Juarez, the Mexican revolutionary, and two Italian radicals, Andrea Costa and Amilcare Cipriani. Alessandro's wife, Rosa, a devout Catholic, worked as the local schoolteacher and provided the financial support for the family. Young Benito proved a bright but rebellious student and was kicked out of a Catholic boarding academy before earning his teacher's certificate at a government normal school. In 1901, at age eighteen, he struggled as a poorly paid schoolteacher before taking off for Switzerland to evade the draft. Mussolini, therefore, came from the social class that would later provide him consistent political support, the rootless lower middle class — more precisely, the underpaid, underemployed intellectual proletariat.

In Switzerland, Mussolini wandered from one odd job to another, agitating among the Italian migrant workers who labored in Swiss tourist resorts. He took advantage of the excellent Swiss public libraries to increase his knowledge of Marxist literature, just as Lenin was doing at about the same time. He returned to Italy in January 1905 to get his military service out of the way, then took another teaching post for a short time. In 1909 he moved to the Italian-speaking but Austrian-ruled region of Trent, and began his real career, editing a socialist newspaper for the local chamber of labor. Though he remained a member of the Socialist

Party and read widely in syndicalist literature, the subject condition of Italians at Trent (one of Italy's "Alsaces") aroused his nationalist feelings. Like many other emigrants, Mussolini discovered his national identity after leaving his nation-state.

Returning to his home village in Italy once again, Benito set up housekeeping with his future wife, Rachelle, who was the daughter of his father's mistress. Though he married her in 1915 and fathered five children by her, Mussolini continued to consort with numerous mistresses. His biographer, Ivone Kirkpatrick, has summed up Benito's relationship with Rachelle: "He was fond of her as one might be of any familiar piece of furniture."

Mussolini made a name for himself within the socialist ranks as a vigorous organizer and a vivid journalist. He faithfully followed the anti-imperialist line during the Libyan War and was imprisoned for his protest activities. When released from prison in early 1912, a comrade hailed him as "the Duce of all revolutionary Socialists in Italy," probably the first time that the word *Duce* ("leader") was applied to him. Later that year, at the socialist congress in Reggio Emilia he indeed became a leader of the party, sponsoring a successful resolution to expel the moderate socialists who advocated cooperation with Giolitti's government. He was rewarded with the editorship of the daily newspaper, *Avanti!*, the second most important position in the Socialist Party.

When World War I broke out, he initially toed the party line of absolute neutrality but found that the more interesting and active elements in the nation were clamoring for combat. After the greatest intellectual and emotional crisis of his life, he renounced Italian neutrality on October 18, 1914, in the pages of *Avanti!* and was swiftly fired from his editorship and drummed out of the party. He soon started a new daily, *Il Popolo d'Italia*, partly financed by the Entente powers who were cultivating Italian interventionist sentiment, and joined the first *fascio*, a group of like-minded interventionists, which he eventually took over.

Mussolini was conscripted into the Italian infantry in September 1915 and served in the trenches on the Austrian front for a year and a half. In February 1917 a mortar he was operating in a training exercise exploded, and he was invalided out of the service later that year, returning to his editorship of *Il Popolo d'Italia*. He still considered himself a socialist of sorts, viewing the war as a struggle against the imperialist pretensions of Germany; yet he became completely estranged from the Socialist Party leadership, which held firmly to its neutralist policy.

The war experience profoundly altered Mussolini's thinking. His service at the front lines had exposed him to the exhilaration of danger and combat and had revealed a classless, fully national sentiment among the soldiers. He now advocated a *trincerocrazia*, or aristocracy of the trenches, to lead the nation after the war. In July 1918 he changed the subtitle of his paper from "A Socialist Daily" to "the newspaper of combatants and producers." The socialist journalist, Mussolini, had embarked on the same intellectual journey as the syndicalists and nationalists during wartime, arriving at roughly the same policy, which political scientist A. James Gregor has styled "military national socialism" or "barracks socialism." He advocated a union of all who had fought for Italy and all who could make her more productive.

In this spirit Mussolini convoked a meeting of 119 war veterans at the Piazza San Sepolcro on March 23, 1919. The newly organized Fascists failed miserably in the first postwar elections of November 1919. Running in Milan, they garnered only 5,000 votes, compared to 170,000 for the Socialists, and elected not a single deputy. Yet amidst the upheavals of the *Biennio Rosso,* Fascists in the streets seized the leadership of the forces opposed to socialism. As early as April 15, 1919, less than a month after the party's founding, the Milanese Fascists attacked the office of Mussolini's former newspaper, the socialist *Avanti!,* completely destroying the printing presses and the subscriber lists.

Over the next two years, local Fascist squads sprang up in numerous towns and cities across northern and central Italy, terrorizing the Socialists and peasant rebels in violent punitive expeditions. These *squadristi,* only loosely allied with Mussolini's organization in Milan, were led by local war veterans such as Italo Balbo in Ferrara, Dino Grandi in Bologna, and Roberto Farinacci in Cremona. They beat the Socialist leaders with heavy truncheons and forced them to drink enormous doses of castor oil. Through the violent efforts of these Fascist squads and similar groups organized by the Nationalist Association, the number of socialist strikes declined precipitously from 1920 to 1921. Respectable businessmen and landowners looked the other way, and the police usually absented themselves while the Fascists performed the dirty work of repressing the working-class in Italy.

During these years between the organization of the Fascist movement and its seizure of national power in October 1922, Mussolini showed remarkable political astuteness. D'Annunzio's seizure of Fiume provided him models for mobilizing the masses. The *arditi,* veterans of the wartime special forces who wore black shirts and carried long knives, formed the shock troops of D'Annunzio's legionnaires. They pioneered use of the extended-arm Roman salute and the singing of the youth hymn, *Giovinezza,* which Mussolini adopted. Acknowledging D'Annunzio's notoriety as an aviator, Mussolini took flying lessons in 1920 and cultivated an image of youthful modernism and activism. Though publicly supporting the adventure at Fiume, he felt relief when the occupation of that city collapsed, removing D'Annunzio as a rival for national leadership.

Mussolini's primary tasks before seizing power were to unite his loosely organized supporters and convert as many of his opponents as possible to present a national front and rescue the nation from its postwar crisis. Consequently, he

283

bobbed from left to right, picking up supporters along the way and forever confusing historians, many of whom have concluded that he had no principles at all but was merely a power-hungry opportunist.

His firmest support came from the lower-middle-class strata from which he had arisen — schoolteachers, journalists, low-level civil servants, artisans, and craftsmen. In the turbulent postwar years, these petty bourgeois saw themselves ground between the power of big business and the rebelliousness of the Socialist workers. Many found themselves at loose ends after demobilization from the war. The Fascist squads drew from the same restless, unemployed class of war veterans that volunteered for the Black and Tans in England's struggle against Irish independence.

Big business interests and the traditional politicians thought they could use Mussolini to crush the socialist menace, but he wound up using them instead. When Giolitti called national elections in May 1921 he invited the Fascists to join his electoral bloc, hoping to exploit their aura of youthful activism and draw them into yet another transformist coalition. With Giolitti's support, therefore, the Fascists won thirty-five seats and entered parliament for the first time. Parliamentary status bestowed on Mussolini and the other Fascist deputies immunity from arrest.

After veering to the right to earn respectability, Mussolini tried to gain support from a segment of the working class, forging a "Pacification Pact" with the moderate Socialists in August 1921. The regional *squadristi*, however, protested so vigorously against this pact with the enemy that Mussolini backed off and even threatened to resign from leadership of the movement. The following summer, in August 1922, the Socialists unwisely launched another general strike, providing Mussolini the opportunity to pose as savior of the country. The Fascists brutally broke the strike, and after three days of street fighting in Milan they again sacked the offices of *Avanti!*.

The Fascists still enjoyed only minimal representation in parliament but they effectively controlled many cities and towns in northern and central Italy. Giolitti's government had been replaced by a series of even weaker prime ministers, and Italian public opinion seemed ready to welcome a strong man who would end the postwar chaos. At a meeting on October 16, 1922, the Fascist leaders discussed a "march on Rome" to seize power, on the model of D'Annunzio's expedition to Fiume. Mussolini postponed the march until the previously scheduled Fascist congress in Naples on October 24; but after the congress adjourned, 14,000 Blackshirt volunteers concentrated in three columns, ready to assault the capital.

Strong leadership in the central government could have prevented a Fascist takeover, for the army still remained loyal to the king and vastly outnumbered the poorly armed Blackshirts. Indeed, the prime minister, Luigi Facta, prepared a decree of martial law in Rome, but when he presented the proclamation to King Victor Emmanuel III on the morning of October 28, the king refused to sign. Victor Emmanuel feared that if he opposed the popular Mussolini he might lose his throne to his adventurous cousin, the Duke of Aosta. Furthermore, most of the politicians wanted to invite Mussolini into the government anyway, so it seemed pointless to shed blood.

Accordingly, Facta, Salandra, and all the other conservative parliamentary leaders tried to forge a coalition government with Mussolini, who was prudently waiting in Milan to see how the Blackshirt expedition turned out. When it became clear, however, that the army would not oppose him, Mussolini realized he held all the cards and steadfastly refused to join any government that he did not lead. Consequently, the king sent Mussolini a telegram formally requesting him to form a government.

When Mussolini entered the train station at Milan on the evening of October 29, he stage-managed his ride to Rome for maximum effect. He instructed the stationmaster, "I want to leave exactly on time. From now on everything has got to function perfectly." The wife of the British ambassador, who overheard this comment, reported it to the world and thus launched the myth that Mussolini made the trains run on time. After being sworn in as the youngest prime minister in Italian history (age thirty-nine) on October 31, Mussolini afforded his Blackshirt supporters the satisfaction of marching into Rome. He subsequently glorified the "march on Rome" and pretended that he had seized power in a military operation, but in fact he had assumed government office perfectly legally the day before the Blackshirts arrived. His assumption of power was a superb example of successful psychological warfare.

The Fascist government did not become a dictatorship all at once; indeed, it took Mussolini about four and a half years to consolidate his authority and crush the opposition. Parliament did, however, vote him plenary powers for the first year of his rule and he soon became accustomed to governing by decree rather than by legislation. He swiftly coopted other movements and power centers that were sympathetic to his rule, formally fusing the Fascist Party with the Nationalist Association early in 1923 and appeasing the Catholic Church with concessions that allowed religious education and the display of crucifixes in the public schools. In the meantime, Fascist squads continued their brutal campaigns against the working class in the provinces.

In order to win an unassailable political majority, Mussolini pushed though a new electoral law in 1923 that granted the leading party in the national elections (so long as it gained at least 25 percent of the vote) a full two-thirds of parliamentary delegates. Through fraud and violence, and much genuine enthusiasm for the "new deal," the Fascists actually won close to two-thirds of the vote outright in the April 1924 elections. Thereafter, the subsequent elections in 1929 and 1934 became complete shams. The Fascist Party presented a single list of delegates to the voters, who could only accept or reject them. Mussolini scornfully remarked that "supermen elect themselves."

The last crisis that might have toppled Mussolini occurred after the election of 1924, when a courageous Socialist deputy, Giacomo Matteoti, denounced the Fascists' rigging of the polls. On June 10, 1924, Matteoti disappeared. Though his body was not discovered for several months, no one doubted that the Fascists had murdered him. Mussolini's government was thrown on the defensive, and the Duce considered resigning. Yet the violent *squadristi* from the provinces convinced him to stand firm; so on January 3, 1925, Mussolini delivered a decisive speech assuming full responsibility for the Matteoti affair and daring his opponents to depose him.

The opposition remained divided, however, and both big business and the Catholic Church still considered the Fascists a lesser evil than the Socialists. No one, therefore, called the Duce's bluff. Four attempts to assassinate him between November 1925 and October 1926 provided convenient pretexts for full-scale repression. Within the next two years, Mussolini banned all political parties except the Fascists, drove the remaining opposition leaders into exile, and thoroughly censored the press. By the end of 1926 the Fascist regime in Italy ruled unchallenged.

Mussolini came to power in Italy because he offered the nation a "new deal" in the economic, political, and spiritual crisis of the postwar years. He proposed an alternative, a third way, between the discredited status quo of parliamentary politics and laissez-faire economics and the revolutionary threat of socialism.

In employing the term "new deal" to describe Italian Fascism, I do not intend to draw too close a comparison between the administrations of Mussolini in Italy and Franklin Roosevelt in the United States a decade later. No two men could have been more dissimilar in background and temperament. Nor were their policies alike. Roosevelt rescued the free-enterprise system with a dose of Keynesian economics, but Mussolini imposed an authoritarian form of state capitalism. Most important, Roosevelt never made good on his threat to assume "broad executive authority," and he did not rely on violence as Mussolini did.

Yet each possessed superb political instincts and a keen sense of the public mood. Both Roosevelt and Mussolini could confound their opponents by weaving from left to right in order to pick up support, changing direction abruptly when a government policy failed. Mussolini's biographer, Ivone Kirkpatrick, has confessed that "nothing can be said of him which is completely true or which cannot be immediately disproved from some reliable source, or even from his own mouth." Political philosopher Ernst Nolte has concluded that "Mussolini was not the man with the deepest thoughts but he was probably the one with the most thoughts." Both statements apply equally well to FDR. What some historians label cynical opportunism on the part of Mussolini or Roosevelt can be better understood as political flexibility and superb timing.

The metaphor of a "new deal" for the Fascist regime is also useful in explaining Mussolini's appeal. English-language histories of fascism too often condescend to the Italians, branding them incomparably stupid for following Mussolini. The negative image of a scowling buffoon in Charlie Chaplin's silent film classic *The Great Dictator* has remained vivid. Yet one need not admire Mussolini to understand his appeal. The sense of crisis in Italy after World War I was very real, and the political system enjoyed far less legitimacy than the long-existing democracies of England and the United States. In such circumstances, Mussolini's forcefulness and decisiveness seemed refreshing, a new deal, a breath of fresh air. Mussolini denounced the tired old politicians, such as Giolitti or Facta, the way Franklin Roosevelt later excoriated Herbert Hoover. In both cases, postwar Italy and Depression-era America, a new leader came to power because the populace felt desperate for vigorous leadership.

There is a final similarity between Mussolini and Roosevelt worth emphasizing. Though the two leaders were often dismissed as mere pragmatists and opportunists, each remained faithful to a core of values he believed in, and both eventually adopted a systematic economic policy developed by others. This similarity, however, only highlights an essential difference between fascism and democracy, for their core values and economic policies contrast sharply.

FDR was a country squire raised with the values of noblesse oblige, an aristocratic duty to help out the less fortunate. Furthermore, since he built his political base in the Democratic Party among the unemployed of the working class, his New Deal aimed to relieve individual suffering and provide for the public welfare. The Keynesian policy of public works and increased purchasing power perfectly suited his upbringing and values.

Mussolini's background, however, was less secure and stable than Roosevelt's, and he harbored a deep personal and national inferiority complex. Believing Italy a proletarian nation in competition with better-endowed enemies, he stressed the core values of national sacrifice and increased production. Shortly before seizing power, he exclaimed that Italy must become a nation of producers, not balladiers and tour guides. Therefore he adopted the long-range plans of the Italian Nationalist Association, written mainly by Alfredo Rocco, for a three-stage development of Italy: first, intensive capital investment, the building of a modern infrastructure, and the development of heavy industry; second, a drive for national self-sufficiency in key industries and food production; and finally, territorial expansion to fulfill Italy's destiny as a great power.

The policies of the Mussolini regime in pursuit of these goals illustrate clearly the difference between Italian Fascism and the Roosevelt New Deal. The earliest measures of the Fascist government suppressed the independent labor unions and revised the tax laws to encourage capital formation and investment. Whereas Fascism trampled the rights of labor and favored industrialists, the American New Deal passed the Wagner Act in 1935, guaranteeing the right of collective bargaining and establishing the National Labor Relations Board to ensure fair play between employers and employees.

After suppressing labor and encouraging investment, Mussolini's government entered the next phase of its national development policy in 1927, when it set the *quota 90* for the Italian currency. Since the British had returned to the gold standard at an artificially high exchange rate, Mussolini followed suit, pegging the exchange at ninety lire to the British pound. This high exchange rate automatically made Italian exports more expensive and thus threw Italians out of work. Yet Mussolini believed a high rate essential for national prestige and a useful first step in withdrawing Italy from the international trading system. He had previously declared a "Battle for Grain," aiming at self-sufficiency in food production. High tariffs on foodstuffs raised farmers' incomes and nearly doubled production of wheat in Italy, but it lowered the working-class standard of living by raising the price of bread. The *quota 90* and the "Battle for Grain," therefore, hit the Italian masses with increased unemployment and higher prices, even before the Great Depression. These policies purchased national prestige and economic self-sufficiency at the cost of Italians' living standards.

Along the same lines, Mussolini encouraged industrialists to hold down the wages of their workers in order to increase profits and productivity. Despite a growth in gross national product of over 16 percent from 1920 to 1939, the average wages of Italian workers remained just marginally above the pre-war level. Such ruthless control of the economy inspired awe and admiration among British industrialists, who were unable to lower wage costs throughout the 1920s due to the power of labor unions. This factor probably explains the strength of British admiration for Mussolini, almost up to the outbreak of World War II.

All of these economic policies differed significantly from Roosevelt's New Deal, which aimed at increased purchasing power for the masses through higher wages, public works, and liberal welfare payments. Keynes and Roosevelt sought individual welfare and a high standard of living, Mussolini pursued national economic development and self-sufficiency at all costs.

The Duce moved into the third stage of his plan for national greatness, foreign expansion, in the mid-1930s. His troops invaded the independent African state of Ethiopia in 1935, brutally suppressing opposition, and proclaiming it a part of the Italian Empire in May 1936. Economic penetration of the Balkan Peninsula in southeastern Europe produced relatively meager results, but Italy did reduce the tiny state of Albania to a virtual satellite, then finally annexed it in April 1939. These bellicose aspects of Italian policy contrasted sharply with the isolationism of the United States during the 1930s.

Mussolini's "new deal" for Italy, therefore, was far different from the Roosevelt program. Indeed, the Duce believed that "the Fascist State is unique; it is an original creation." In his infamous Matteoti speech of January 1925, he coined a new word to describe it, calling Italy a *totalitarian* regime. Totalitarianism implies the complete dominance of the state over the individual — "everything in the state, nothing outside the state, nothing against the state." Mussolini cleverly argued that "in the Fascist State the individual is not suppressed, but rather multiplied, just as in a regiment a soldier is not weakened but multiplied by the number of his comrades." This dictum shows how important the wartime trench experience was in the formation of fascism, but it glosses over the extent of repression in Italy.

Though the Catholic Church, the army, and big business retained a certain amount of autonomy that Mussolini could never quite reduce, he worked to suppress as many independent institutions as he could, replacing them with separate Fascist organizations, such as the youth groups or the *dopolavoro*, after-work societies. This is the first mark of totalitarianism — the elimination of every independent power center between the State and the individual. Mussolini did not completely attain this goal, but he worked assiduously toward it.

The second mark of totalitarianism is the cultivation of popular enthusiasm for the political regime. A traditional authoritarian dictatorship, such as tsarist Russia or Kemal Ataturk's Turkey, cowed the populace into passivity. When discontent bubbled up, the army would clear the streets with a cavalry charge or an artillery barrage. Nothing was demanded of the people except obedience and order. Yet a totalitarian regime requires popular support and participation, not passivity. Mussolini told an interviewer in the 1930s that to "control the masses, it is necessary to employ two levers: enthusiasm and interest." It was not sufficient to appeal to the self-interest of the middle classes for order and economic development; he also aroused the enthusiasm of all classes for the greatness of Italy.

Mussolini proved a master manipulator of the masses. He used his journalistic experience and an innate actor's mentality to propagandize and even mesmerize the Italian people. He referred to the balcony of the Palazzo Venezia, from which he harangued the crowds at the height of his power, as "my stage." He made a fetish of youthfulness and subsidized both spectator sports and a program of physical fitness. The *dopolavoro* sent actors in thespian cars and a traveling cinema into remote areas of the country. Since Mussolini's economic policies reduced consumption, cutting down on the masses' bread, he substituted circuses instead. A combination of totalitarian repression and mass enthusiasm kept Benito Mussolini in power for twenty-three years.

Having surveyed the major features of the Duce's regime, we can now draw a definition of fascism from the actual history of the movement in Italy, not from

289

abstract reasoning: Fascism was an authoritarian system of government based on the "leader principle" (one-man rule), and marked by —

- extreme nationalism, that is, excessive glorification of the nation or race;
- central direction and mobilization of the economy;
- violence as an ordinary political practice;
- glorification of military values; and
- expansionist foreign policies.

Political scientist James Gregor has summed up this terrifying new form of government as a "mass-mobilizing, totalitarian, developmental dictatorship." This definition and summary characterization of fascism provide us a baseline for judging the other dictators and mass movements of the 1930s.

CHAPTER SEVENTEEN

A Delayed-Action Fuse

In the aftermath of World War I, defeated Germany experienced a series of up-heavals that gave birth to Adolf Hitler's National Socialist (Nazi) movement. Indeed, it's surprising that Hitler did not come to power shortly after the war, as Mussolini did in Italy, for Germany had been defeated and humiliated by the Allies, had suffered far greater casualties than Italy, and had undergone a socialist revolution that transformed the country from a monarchy to a republic. Yet the opposition of the German army defeated his first attempt to seize power. The Nazi movement, however, smoldered like a delayed-action fuse and finally ex-ploded after the onset of the Great Depression in the 1930s.

The German High Command of Generals Hindenburg and Ludendorff had realized that the war was lost at the end of September 1918, so they abruptly recommended the formation of a new government in Berlin. The generals were placing responsibility for defeat on the shoulders of civilian politicians. As histo-rian A. J. Nicholls has phrased it, "an invitation to enter the Government at that stage was an invitation to share in the greatest humiliation ever inflicted on Ger-many." The Social Democratic Party, the mainstream socialists in Germany's Reichstag who had faithfully supported the war effort, combined with moderate parties of the middle class to form a ministry under the chancellorship of Prince Max of Baden, who made peace overtures to the Allies.

Before the armistice of November 11 could be concluded, however, the pent-up discontent of war-weary Germans broke out. A mutiny of sailors at the Kiel naval base on October 28 inspired mass marches and demonstrations by sol-diers and workers across the country. The mainstream socialists now in the gov-ernment lost control of these demonstrations to more radical agitators who orga-nized workers' and soldiers' soviets, on the Russian model, in many towns and

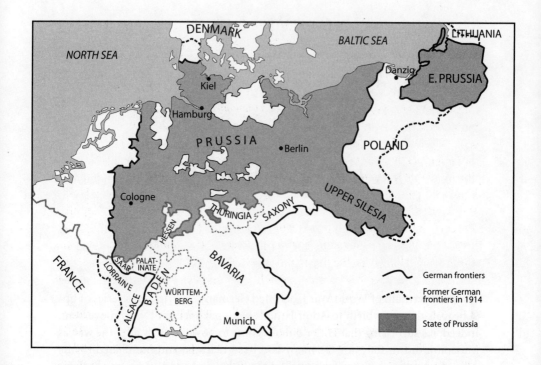

Germany c. 1920

cities. On November 7, in the south German kingdom of Bavaria,[1] the revolutionaries chased King Ludwig III from his palace and proclaimed Bavaria a republic, under the leadership of a maverick socialist, Kurt Eisner. The mainstream socialists in Berlin, therefore, demanded that the kaiser and his son, the crown prince, abdicate, which they did on November 9. Friedrich Ebert, the leader of the Social Democrats, was proclaimed chancellor, and Germany became a republic two days before the armistice was signed.

Germany, therefore, experienced a socialist revolution at the end of the war, but attempts by Bolsheviks to mount a second revolt, as in Russia, failed. Unlike the moderate Russian government of Kerensky in 1917, the new German republic mustered enough force to preserve itself. The defense minister, Gustav Noske, employed volunteer units of demobilized soldiers, called *Freikorps*, to suppress the soviets and put down further revolts. It is ironic that a socialist-republican regime consolidated its revolution with the power of the military, but in Germany the army had long been the most loyal support of the state. Since the new government had come to power in an ostensibly legal manner, army tradition dictated an impartial loyalty to it.

After restoring some semblance of public order, the government conducted elections to the Constituent National Assembly on January 19, 1919. The Social Democrats, the Center Party (which was the Catholic party in Germany), and the moderate middle-class Democratic Party elected enough delegates to dominate this assembly. They convened at Weimar, a small city about 150 miles southwest of Berlin, since the capital still seemed revolutionary and unsafe. This gathering produced a republican constitution and gave its name to the new regime, ever after known as the Weimar Republic.

The new republican government had to swallow the humiliation of the Versailles Treaty which the Allies imposed on Germany in June 1919. Besides the heavy reparations that Germany was required to pay, the most objectionable feature of the treaty was the article acknowledging Germany's war guilt. The Weimar Republic, therefore, was born under a black cloud of national shame.

The two groups supporting the republic most fervently, the socialists and the Catholics, were suspect minorities in Germany. Bismarck had suppressed them both at various times during his long rule in the nineteenth century, and the two groups were still considered "unpatriotic" by many members of the Protestant nobility and middle class. Furthermore, the Catholics and the socialists distrusted each other. The so-called Weimar coalition, therefore, composed of

---

1. The German Reich created by Bismarck in 1871 and ruled by Kaiser Wilhelm II until the end of World War I was actually a federal empire, composed of twenty-two kingdoms or principalities and three city-states. The individual federal states retained their hereditary princes or kings, who were subordinate to the kaiser.

Social Democrats, the Center Party, and Democrats, remained highly unstable. So insecure was it that the first President of the Republic, Friedrich Ebert, took office on August 21, 1919, without the benefit of a popular election, and the Constituent Assembly postponed new Reichstag (parliamentary) elections for nearly a year. When those elections were held in June 1920, the three parties most loyal to the Weimar constitution lost their combined majority. The German republic had come into being with too few republicans to make it legitimate in the minds of most Germans.

In this atmosphere of national humiliation, revolutionary unrest, and political intrigue, Adolf Hitler developed his ultra-nationalist ideas and entered politics for the first time, though he was not yet a German citizen. Born on April 20, 1889, in Braunau, a small town on the Austrian side of the border between Austria and Germany, Adolf Hitler was the son of a Habsburg customs officer. His father, Alois, had been born out of wedlock to a peasant girl named Maria Anna Schicklgruber and bore her last name until about age forty, when his birth was formally legitimized and he took the name of his presumed father, a wanderer named Johann Hiedler (or Hitler, as it was usually written).

Alois Hitler became reasonably prosperous as a low-level civil servant, but he was unlucky in love. His first wife, Anna Glass, was older than himself, frequently ailing, and childless. A month after her death in 1883 he married a young servant girl, Franziska Matzelberger, who had already borne him a child out of wedlock and who gave birth to another child before her premature death from tuberculosis. He finally married a third wife, Klara Polzl, his second cousin, in 1885, and she gave birth to Adolf and four other children, only one of whom lived. Adolf Hitler thus grew up in a family with a younger sister, Paula, and a half-brother, Alois, and a half-sister, Angela, from his father's previous marriage. The father retired from the civil service in 1895 and moved to a village outside of Linz, Austria, where he supported his family on a government pension until he died in 1903. His widow still lived comfortably on this pension after his death.

Young Adolf, who was raised a Catholic and attended state schools in Austria, proved a bright but lazy student, who did well in subjects that stirred his interest (mainly history and art) but refused to study anything that bored him. He left school in 1905 at age sixteen, without earning a high school certificate, and for the next two years lived in his mother's home and dreamed of becoming an artist. In 1907 he moved to Vienna to study, but the Academy of Arts refused him admission due to his lack of a diploma. His mother died at the end of 1907, and Adolf remained in Vienna for the next six years. He still had some financial resources — a small legacy from his father, an orphan's pension that he drew fraudulently by pretending to be enrolled as an art student, and later a small bequest from an aunt — but he eventually spent them all and lived in a homeless men's shelter. He supported himself by painting copies of popular postcards and selling them on the streets. Though he occasionally took odd jobs as a manual laborer, he was never a house painter or a paperhanger, as later myth claimed. He was, instead, a starving artist, a bohemian.

Hitler hated Vienna, and the six years he spent there were the hardest of his life; but these years crystallized his political ideas. He conceived a great hatred for socialists, who tried to muscle him into joining a union on one of his odd jobs, and he expressed contempt for the politicians who talked endlessly in the Austrian parliament. Nevertheless, he greatly admired one Austrian politician, Vienna's mayor Karl Lueger of the Christian Social Party, who pioneered techniques of rabble-rousing politics; and he grudgingly admitted that the Social Democrats too were skillful in mobilizing the masses.

The young drifter in Vienna concluded that life was a difficult struggle and only iron willpower could ensure survival. The German word, *kampf*, meaning "struggle," appears over and over again in his later writings and speeches. He wrote in his autobiography, entitled *Mein Kampf* ("My Struggle"), "I owe much to the time in which I had learned to become hard." Hitler may have never heard the term "social Darwinism," but that sociological concept, embodying a life-and-death struggle for the survival of the fittest, aptly sums up his attitude.

Above all, however, Hitler's years in Vienna reinforced his ultra-nationalist German racial feelings. The Austrian capital was a city of two million people, encompassing all the ethnic groups of the Habsburg Empire, including about 200,000 Jews. Hitler later wrote: "I detested the conglomerate of races that the realm's capital manifested." In particular, he demonized the Jews, blaming them for both the socialism and the parliamentary democracy which he abhorred. One of Hitler's biographers, Joachim Fest, affirms that "we may never be able to trace Hitler's overwhelming Jewish phobia down to its roots. But on the whole we may say that an ambitious and desperate loner was finding a formula for politicizing his personal problems." Certainly, the son of a respectable civil servant found it humiliating to be thrown among the working class and the destitute street people of Vienna and may have found a twisted explanation for his plight in the economic success that Viennese Jews enjoyed. The extreme nature of his anti-Semitism and the sexual charge he infused into it call to mind the racist ravings of the American Ku Klux Klan. In both cases, insecure individuals bolstered their self-esteem by trying to drive down a member of another racial or ethnic group.

The monstrous deeds that Adolf Hitler later committed cry out for some sort of psychological explanation of his twisted personality, and numerous historians and social scientists have produced "psychohistories" of the Nazi leader. Yet any attempt to psychoanalyze a historical figure is fraught with perils. A competent analyst requires many hours of conversation with the patient, which is, of course, impossible when the person is dead. Furthermore, psychohistory is usually attempted with people who seem abnormal, so most psychohistorians start with preconceived notions, such as "Hitler was a neurotic psychopath." They then marshal superficial evidence "proving" this diagnosis.

The uncomfortable conclusion from studying Hitler's youth is that it seems rather normal. He did not have a deprived childhood, and no evidence indicates major conflicts with his parents or siblings. The profile of a brilliant but lazy student could fit millions of indifferent adolescents from any period of history, and his bohemian drifting in Vienna is hardly unprecedented either. Even his anti-Semitism was common in many parts of Europe before World War I. Hannah Arendt, one of the earliest analysts of totalitarianism, has coined the chilling phrase "banality of evil," which aptly fits Hitler's early years. From banal, provincial, middle-class roots, a monstrous evil sprang.

Without too much psychologizing, however, we can conclude that his Austrian Catholic background helped shape his later career. As an Austrian subject, separated from the fatherland of his ethnic group, he grew up more German than the Germans. He also inherited a prickly status consciousness from his Austrian bourgeois family. His Catholic upbringing instilled some unusual lessons for his political career. He admired the atmosphere of drama and mystery surrounding Catholic church services and believed that the church's rigid refusal to change its dogmas represented a sound strategy. Once his own beliefs were formed, he never deviated from them.

As Hitler's racial nationalism increased, he found the multicultural character of the Dual Monarchy intolerable. Finally, in 1913, in order to avoid military service for this empire he detested, he moved to Munich in German Bavaria. He later wrote glowingly of his immigration: "A *German* town! What a difference as compared with Vienna!" Yet, he continued selling pictures in the streets and arguing politics in the cafes, and his life did not change significantly until the outbreak of World War I.

Like so many other Europeans, Adolf Hitler volunteered for service in August 1914 with great enthusiasm, enlisting in a Bavarian regiment even though he was not a German citizen. He survived the entire four years of war on the western front, serving in the dangerous capacity of runner, or messenger, between headquarters and the front lines. The discipline and danger of the trenches exhilarated him. His biographer, Fest, declares that "in no man's land he felt at home." He was wounded twice and decorated for bravery three times, yet never received promotion any higher than a lance corporal. Since he had neither a family nor a job to return to, he remained in the army for over a year after the war, indoctrinating new recruits with patriotic ideas and spying on radical groups in his adopted city of Munich. In the course of this work, he developed a natural talent as a speaker and discovered a small political party that he decided to take over.

Karl Harrer, a sports journalist, and Anton Drexler, a machinist, had founded a Political Workers' Circle just before the war ended, renaming it the

Deutsche Arbeitspartei (German Workers' Party) in January 1919. The DAP didn't amount to much when Hitler discovered it in September 1919. Joachim Fest has characterized it as "a combination . . . of secret society and locals gathering at the pub for their evening pint." The party was so insignificant that an unknown like Hitler could join up and dominate it, using his skill as a speaker and propagandist to bring in new members and make himself indispensable.

Small though it was, the German Workers' Party espoused a significant idea, the merger of nationalism with socialism. Several parties in both Germany and Austria had proposed a national socialism before the war; and, of course, Mussolini fused his early socialism with Italian nationalism as he rose to power in 1922. Unlike Mussolini, Hitler had never been a socialist, but he shrewdly guessed that a facade of working-class solidarity might make his extreme nationalist views more politically palatable. He therefore included a number of working-class planks in the twenty-five-point program promulgated in 1920. Shortly thereafter the party changed its name to the *Nationalsozialistiche Deutsche Arbeitspartei,* NSDAP (National Socialist German Workers' Party), from which the acronym NAZI derives.

Devoting himself full-time to party organizing, Hitler soon muscled the founders out of power. As early as 1921 local followers began calling him their *Führer* ("leader"), and he often boasted that he was the "king of Munich." He devised a distinctive Nazi flag, employing the red, white, and black colors of the former German imperial banner rather than the red, white, and gold of the Weimar Republic. He also incorporated the swastika into the new flag. This twisted cross was a common symbol in German mythology, representing the "fire whisk" that had twirled the primal substance of creation into the visible universe.

Hitler's personality fitted the times. He had himself experienced downward mobility and humiliation, just as the German nation did after the war, and he had already singled out scapegoats, the Jews and the socialists. Hitler and other ultra-nationalists blamed these two groups, whom they collectively dubbed the "November criminals," for a "stab in the back" that caused Germany's defeat. Like Italy after the war, Germany seemed poised for a takeover by a charismatic individual.

Events in 1923 appeared to play into Hitler's hand. The German government had been dragging its feet over the payment of reparations to the Allies, so in January 1923 French troops occupied the industrialized Ruhr valley of western Germany. The German government declared a policy of passive resistance, instructing its civil servants and other essential workers to withdraw their services in the Ruhr. The subsidies paid to these striking workers exaggerated an already virulent inflation of the German currency, which raged out of control for the rest of the year.

The origins of the German hyperinflation of 1923 go back to the war years.

Germany, like all the other fighting nations, financed her war effort by heavy borrowing. The country spent 164 billion marks during World War I but took in only 121 billion in revenue. The 40 billion mark deficit was covered by war bonds, which German citizens could freely cash in for currency. As a result, the war ended with five times as much money in circulation as before the war, but each mark was worth only about half as much. Heavy spending for reconstruction and war reparations increased pressure on the currency, as the new government in Berlin felt too insecure to raise taxes and cover its expenditures.

The declining value of the mark is best measured against the American dollar, which remained stable. In 1914 a dollar would purchase 4.2 marks on the international currency exchanges, but by war's end, it was valued at 8.5 marks. A year after the war, in February 1920, the German currency had so diminished in value that a dollar would buy 100 marks. The next two years saw the mark fluctuate with the fortunes of the unstable German government, but when Foreign Minister Walter Rathenau was assassinated on June 24, 1922, and the French invaded the Ruhr six months later, confidence in the government plummeted and inflation soared. On November 13, 1923, one dollar was exchanged for 840 billion marks; a week later, on November 20, the inflation reached its fantastic peak, with a dollar worth 4 trillion, 200 billion marks.

A few examples illustrate what these incredible numbers meant. A German student dropped into a cafe for a cup of coffee priced at 5,000 marks. After he had read his paper and drained his cup, the waiter demanded 8,000 marks. The dollar exchange rate had gone up 60 percent during the hour he had idled away in the cafe. Another German recalled that he had stashed away 68,000 marks, which he considered a fortune, in a bank before the war; but in 1923 a banker wrote him that the firm could no longer bother with such tiny sums. Since they didn't have any small (!) thousand-mark bills, they rounded up his deposit and sent him a million mark note. The stamp on the letter cost five million marks.

Obviously, money had become worthless. Many citizens resorted to barter, and the rest carted around baskets of marks to buy a simple loaf of bread. Much of the middle class, especially those on pensions or other fixed incomes, and many civil servants and military officers who had supplemented their meager salaries with supposedly conservative investments, were wiped out.

The German hyper-inflation was not a natural disaster or an act of God; it was not inevitable. As economic historian Steven Webb has commented, "the inflation did not happen because the Reichsbank's printing press had a faulty tachometer." Political decisions and a lack of public confidence in the politicians making them produced the catastrophe. The German government could have snuffed out inflation at any point by stopping the printing presses, raising taxes, and producing a budgetary surplus to reassure the nervous public. Eventually this is what they did, in November 1923, when they created a whole new currency, the *Rentenmark* ("mortgage mark"), backed by the land and industrial plant of the entire country, and then refused to print any more currency until the mark had stabilized.

In the immediate postwar years, however, the Weimar government refused to raise taxes and deflate the economy for fear of massive unemployment and a revolutionary upheaval. Furthermore, the Germans believed, rightly, that any budgetary surpluses would simply go to the Allies as reparations payments, so they felt little incentive to put their finances in order. Finally, the government and other debtors were able to pay off their accumulated debts very cheaply with depreciated marks. So, inflation was really a disguised, indirect form of taxation. As historian Derek Aldcroft explains: "It was relatively easy to administer and held attractions for governments which were weak, inexperienced and disorganized."

Though the inflationary policies of the Weimar government are thus understandable in political and economic terms, they proved disastrous psychologically. The German people who saw their savings wiped out in 1923 blamed the Weimar Republic for their misfortunes, and they harbored a deep sense of insecurity for the rest of the decade. When the depression hit in 1929, they unleashed their fury against the government. More than any other event, the great inflation of 1923 kept the fuse of Hitler's revolt burning.

The Nazi leader tried to capitalize on the economic discontent of 1923 by staging a *putsch* (revolt) in Munich and then mounting a "march on Berlin," like Mussolini's victorious march on Rome the previous year. Hitler believed that the Bavarian authorities, who were hostile to the Weimar Republic, might assist him. The Bavarian government had declared a state of emergency to deal with the unrest surrounding hyper-inflation, declaring Gustav von Kahr "general state commissioner." Von Kahr shared his dictatorial power in a triumvirate with Colonel Hans von Seisser, head of the state police, and General Otto von Lossow, commander of the local army detachment.

On the night of November 8, 1923, von Kahr was delivering a speech to the elite of Munich in the three-thousand-seat auditorium of the Bürgerbräukeller, when Hitler's armed followers surrounded the beer hall. The Nazis muscled their way into the auditorium and Hitler fired his revolver at the ceiling, hushing the crowd. He then proclaimed a revolution and hustled Kahr, Seisser, and Lossow into a sideroom, urging them to join his revolt. Erich Ludendorff, the legendary World War I general, appeared by prearrangement and broke down the resistance of the government leaders, who reluctantly promised their support. When Hitler left the beer hall to direct the revolt elsewhere in the city, however, the Munich triumvirate slipped away. Their subordinates in the military and the police persuaded them to resist the putsch.

By the morning of November 9, Hitler's men had captured the war ministry and police headquarters in Munich, but other key points in the city eluded them. Ludendorff and Hitler realized they could not seize control by force, so they embarked instead on a protest march through the city, hoping to convince the authorities that the populace supported them. Linked arm in arm, about two thousand men paraded through the main streets to the cheers of the crowd, but the police blocked them at the Odeonsplatz.

Shortly after noon shots rang out, and in a minute-long firefight fourteen rebels and four policemen were killed. A Nazi in the front rank was killed instantly, and his dead weight pulled Hitler down, dislocating his shoulder. The "king of Munich" and other party leaders scrambled away, with only Ludendorff marching unperturbed across the square until arrested. Hitler took refuge at a friend's house forty miles outside Munich and nearly committed suicide. The police picked him up two days later.

The Beer Hall Putsch was not so hopeless as Dublin's Easter Rising of 1916, but it did not succeed as Lenin's coup of October 1917 had. The populace of Munich and the ruling triumvirate sympathized with the ultra-nationalist cause and would not have minded overthrowing the Weimar Republic. Yet the majority of military and police officers in Munich honored their apolitical code and resisted the putsch. In Berlin, too, the government and the military stood firm. President Ebert signed an emergency decree under article 48 of the Weimar constitution, vesting full authority in the hands of General Hans von Seeckt, the army commander in chief. Von Seeckt himself felt little sympathy for the republic, but he did his duty. The German government and military did not roll over and play dead as the Italian authorities had in the face of Mussolini's challenge the previous year. The Weimar Republic survived for nearly another decade.

Hitler and his associates were tried in April 1924, but the Nazi leader turned the trial into a propaganda triumph. He accepted full responsibility for the putsch, haughtily demanding: "How can I be considered guilty of high treason when there is no such crime as an act of treason against the traitors of November 1918?" The court found him guilty but sentenced him to a relatively light term of five years imprisonment. He served less than a year. The national hero, General Ludendorff, was acquitted.

Hitler made good use of his time in prison, writing his autobiography and political testament, *Mein Kampf.* Yet more important, he learned a lesson from the unsuccessful Beer Hall Putsch. He realized that an old-fashioned street revolution had become nearly impossible in the twentieth century, for the state controlled too much firepower. Lenin succeeded in Russia because government authority had simply collapsed, but this was unlikely to happen in Germany. If Hitler were to take power, he decided, he would have to use the power of the state itself to overthrow the state. He spent the rest of the 1920s planning for a legal takeover of the government.

The Beer Hall Putsch trial had earned Hitler some notoriety, but his movement remained small. When the Nazis backed General Ludendorff in the presidential election to succeed Friedrich Ebert in 1925, he won only 211,000 votes out of 27 million cast. Field Marshal Paul von Hindenburg, Ludendorff's wartime partner who had held himself above politics in the postwar period, was elected president instead. In 1928 the National Socialists won only twelve seats in the Reichstag, and until the end of that year Hitler himself was banned from speaking in public throughout much of Germany. At the same time, the Weimar Republic, sustained by large American loans, enjoyed its period of greatest prosperity and stability from 1924 until 1929. A Hitler biographer, Alan Bullock, concludes: "At the end of 1928 Hitler was still a small-time politician, little known outside the south and even there regarded as part of the lunatic-fringe of Bavarian politics."

Yet anyone who read *Mein Kampf* at this time should have feared for the future of Germany and Europe. Published in two volumes in 1925 and 1927, Hitler's testament sold moderately well and, along with speaker's fees and probably some secret subsidies from wealthy admirers, supported him for the rest of the decade. The books ramble on, but many passages, particularly those dealing with advertising and propaganda, are brilliant. He makes his hatreds vividly clear. He hates socialists and communists, he harbors only contempt for the "prattlers" in parliaments, and above all he blames the Jews for everything.

Hitler's racism was common throughout Europe and North America in the late nineteenth and early twentieth century. Under the influence of social Darwinism, scientists and sociologists divided the world into separate races and posited a struggle for survival among them. Even the white race was marked by subdivisions into so-called "Nordics" or "Aryans," who were tall, blond-haired, and blue-eyed and were a natural fighting race; "Alpines," a stocky peasant people with strong backs and weak minds; and "Mediterraneans," a swarthy race, brilliantly artistic but unstable. The United States based its restrictive immigration policy of the 1920s on such racial stereotypes, and serious scholars throughout Europe spoke apprehensively about the dangers of race mixing and "mongrelization."

Hitler enjoyed plenty of company, therefore, when he wrote in *Mein Kampf* that "all great cultures of the past perished only because the originally creative race died off through blood-poisoning" or "every race-crossing leads necessarily sooner or later to the decline of the mixed product." His hatred of the Jews was based on such racial thinking, not religious animosities. He believed it irrelevant whether Jews converted or not. "A splash of baptismal water" made no difference and could not change the inferior blood of the race. Hitler concluded: "All that is not race in this world is trash." He never deviated from this doctrine.

In *Mein Kampf,* Hitler also showed a perceptive if amoral sense of geopolitics. He derided the kaiser's policy of *Weltpolitik,* that is, his attempt to rival Great

Britain by building a navy and acquiring colonies. Rather than challenge the strength of the British, Germany should seek to keep England friendly or neutral and then pursue a continental strategy, acquiring *Lebensraum* ("living-space") in Europe at the expense of Russia. Germany would truly become a great power only if it imitated the United States and dominated a continent, pushing the indigenous population aside.

Joachim Fest has aptly summarized Hitler's ideology: "Nationalism, anti-Bolshevism, and anti-Semitism, linked by a Darwinistic theory of struggle, formed the pillars of his world view and shaped his utterances from the very first to the very last." None of his views were original. What made them unusual was his sheer consistency and tenacity. As A. J. Nicholls has pointed out: "If a party leader were only to be judged by the extent to which he carried out his promises, Hitler would have to be put in the highest class."

Though consistent in his prejudices and his strategy, Hitler could be crafty and flexible in his choice of tactics. Once he had abandoned the route of open revolt after 1923, he pursued an infinite variety of legal, semi-legal, and illegal means to acquire power and pursue his goals. His greatest strength as a politician was his seemingly mystical bond with the masses as an orator and a stage manager of spectacles. Hitler referred to the masses as a "woman" and his "only bride," and biographer Fest has pointed out that the recordings of his rallies sound like collective orgasms. Hitler's personality fed off the mass audience. In private, he appeared quite unimpressive, lazy, even apathetic, but he would work himself up into a frenzy when delivering a speech and then feel totally drained afterwards. The party rallies he staged at Nuremberg every summer from 1927 on were masterpieces of choreography, inducing mass hysteria in the audience. The march-by of brown-shirted "storm troopers" at these rallies created an aura of danger and violence. A mixture of the ceremonial and the terroristic characterized Nazi techniques.

Yet none of this would have mattered if Germany had remained prosperous. The Great Depression, however, struck the Germans especially hard. The Wall Street crash of 1929 led to a withdrawal of the foreign loans which had artificially propped up the Weimar economy; and unemployment reached a high of 6 million, nearly 30 percent of the working population. Germany suffered a greater psychological shock than other countries with high unemployment, such as Great Britain and the United States, because of its previous experience with hyper-inflation. Though the causes of the two economic catastrophes were different, many Germans blamed both on the Weimar government, the socialist unions, and the Treaty of Versailles. The Nazi delayed-action fuse burned very short.

As the depression worsened Social Democrats and conservatives argued in the Reichstag over a raise in the unemployment compensation tax. The government of Social Democrat Hermann Müller, therefore, fell on March 27, 1930. This was the last government under the Weimar constitution which had been able to forge a majority coalition in the parliament. Though Hitler would not come to power for almost three more years, the fall of the Müller ministry marked the end of ordinary democracy in Weimar Germany. Müller's successor as chancellor, Heinrich Brüning from the Center Party, wished to balance the budget by cutting expenditures and slashing wages, just as politicians throughout Europe and America were doing in the face of the depression; but he could not obtain a parliamentary majority. He therefore obtained an emergency decree from President Hindenburg to ram through his austerity policies and then called new elections for September 14, 1930.

The long-burning fuse of Nazi agitation finally exploded in the 1930 Reichstag elections, surprising everyone, even Hitler. The Nazis had expected to pick up about 50 or 60 seats, but instead they polled over 6 million votes, 18 percent of the total, and gained 107 seats. This made them the second largest party, behind the Social Democrats. Most of the unemployed continued to vote for the socialists or the communists, but the National Socialists attracted those voting for the first time and voters who had previously been apathetic. They appealed mainly to the middle class, who dreaded the revolutionary potential of the working-class unemployed and feared that they too might lose their jobs. The paramilitary *Sturmabteilung* ("storm detachment"), or SA, swelled in numbers as young, unemployed workers poured into it.

Brüning grimly clung to office after the elections, without a parliamentary majority but with the support of President Hindenburg, who allowed him to rule by emergency decree. The Depression only grew worse, however, and the unfortunate Center Party leader came to be known as the "hunger chancellor." Hindenburg finally dismissed him on May 30, 1932, replacing him first with another Center Party politician, Franz von Papen, then later with General Kurt von Schleicher.

In 1932 Germans endured five separate elections — two rounds of voting for the presidency in March and April; then local elections in Prussia and several other states, which together encompassed about 80 percent of Germany at the end of April; and finally two successive Reichstag elections in July and November. The incessant voting failed to break the political deadlock in the country but ultimately paved the way for Hitler's rise to power.

Hitler ran for president against Hindenburg and several other candidates, hastily acquiring citizenship in a small German state in order to qualify. He picked up 31 percent of the votes in the first round and 36 percent in the runoff, but the eighty-five-year-old Hindenburg won a second term with a 53 percent majority. In the Prussian elections the same month, the National Socialists again polled about 36 percent of the votes. Then in the Reichstag elections of July 31, 1932, the Nazis reached 37 percent of the vote, gaining 230 seats to become the largest single party in the parliament. A clear majority still eluded them, however; and when the unpopular chancellor, von Papen, dissolved the Reichstag almost immediately, calling new elections for November, the Nazi vote fell off slightly to about 33 percent.

The electoral marathon of 1932 appeared increasingly meaningless, for chancellors continued to rule by presidential decree. Weimar democracy was effectively dead by this time. The socialists and communists held on to about 30 percent of the vote between them, but the conservative politicians had no intention of letting them back into the government. Meanwhile, a small clique of landowners and military officers surrounding the president were scheming to make the "emergency" regime of presidential decrees permanent and bring back the monarchy after Hindenburg's death. The problem these schemers faced was unpopularity. Only the National Socialist Party possessed the mass backing to make their plans practical, but the proud conservatives considered the Nazis vulgar upstarts. Hindenburg interviewed Hitler in August 1932, after the Nazis became the largest party in the Reichstag, but the conversation went badly, and he refused to name him chancellor.

Hitler, for his part, faced three options at the end of 1932. He could unleash his growing number of storm troopers and attempt a violent seizure of power, or alternatively, he could accept minor office in a coalition cabinet and try to take over gradually from within the government. He rejected both alternatives, however, and held out for the chancellorship. He was determined to take power legally, at the request of the president, and he wanted the full power of the state at his back when he came to office. It required tremendous willpower for him to maintain this position, for the storm troopers were eager to fight, and his political operatives, such as Gregor Strasser, wanted to enter a coalition immediately.

Finally, at the beginning of 1933, the conservative clique around Hindenburg solved Hitler's dilemma. On January 4, 1933, Franz von Papen met secretly with Hitler and proposed a deal. He would use his influence with Hindenburg to have the Nazi named chancellor, but Papen himself would become vice-chancellor and other conservatives would hold the majority of cabinet posts. After several more negotiating sessions, Hitler accepted and the president swore him in as chancellor on January 30, 1933.[2]

Adolf Hitler came to power in Germany by legal means, but not democratically through the will of the majority. At none of the last elections under the Weimar constitution did the Nazis gain much more than a third of the votes, and in the snap election Hitler called after becoming chancellor his party still fell short of a majority with about 44 percent. This point is often misunderstood. As recently as 1994 the president of the American Historical Association wrote, "We

2. Less than five weeks later, on March 4, 1933, Franklin D. Roosevelt was inaugurated president of the United States.

might also reflect on the fact that Hitler came to power via majority rule." He did not. Germany had already become an executive dictatorship, governed for almost three years by emergency decrees, and Hindenburg simply changed dictators in 1933. Hitler's biographer, Alan Bullock, makes the point emphatically: "Hitler . . . was jobbed into office by a backstairs intrigue."

Franz von Papen thought he had been clever, enlisting Hitler's mass following behind the conservative program but hemming in the chancellor with non-Nazi advisors. Yet Hitler swiftly outmaneuvered him. When the massive old Reichstag building mysteriously burned down on February 27, 1933,[3] Hitler blamed the communists and immediately obtained an emergency decree from President Hindenburg granting him extraordinary powers to round up agitators. Then after elections in March that failed to provide a clear Nazi majority but elected enough sympathetic fellow-travelers for Hitler to have his way, on March 23 the Reichstag passed the Enabling Act, which became the foundation of the Nazi dictatorship. This law allowed the chancellor himself, without the president's approval, to rule by decree. Using this power ruthlessly, Hitler banned trade unions and all political parties other than the National Socialists, arrested communist and socialist leaders, burned books by Jewish authors, and dismissed Jews from positions in the civil service. By the summer of 1933, just six months after taking office, he had consolidated his authority, a feat that had taken Mussolini four and a half years to accomplish.

Only two power centers remained that might challenge Hitler's control, the German army and his own storm troopers, the SA. The army officers had acquiesced in the Nazi takeover because they believed Hitler would grant them their fondest wish, rearmament in defiance of the Versailles Treaty. Yet the army resented the growth of the paramilitary SA, which also worried Hitler because of its recklessness and its independence. The *Führer* solved both problems on the "Night of the Long Knives," June 30, 1934. Hitler's elite guard, the *Stosstrupp* (shock troop), or SS, brutally murdered the leaders of the SA, including Ernst Röhm, one of Hitler's oldest supporters from Munich days. They also eliminated other possible rivals such as Gregor Strasser and General von Schleicher.

The elimination of the SA as an independent power source strengthened Hitler's personal rule, and the acquiescence of the army in the murder of one of their own showed that they no longer posed a threat either. The Nazi *Führer* put the final seal on his absolute power when President Hindenburg died on August 2, 1934, and Hitler combined the office of presidency with the chancellorship.

---

3. It was widely believed, both in 1933 and later, that the Nazis themselves set the Reichstag fire to provide a pretext for dictatorship. Much probing by historians, however, has left the matter an open question. No one knows for sure who set the fire. In any case, the Nazis made the most of the opportunity.

Hitler's National Socialism in Germany and Mussolini's Fascist Party in Italy shared enough similarities that we may consider them variants of a generic ideology of fascism. Both movements traced their origins to the social and economic tensions of pre-war Europe and were crystallized by the shock of World War I. Both Hitler and Mussolini emerged from the trenches with a vision of a new society that would transcend class divisions and instill discipline into the masses. They embraced violence and struggle as hard facts of life and espoused one-man rule, the leader principle. All varieties of fascism trumpeted an extreme nationalism and opposed both parliamentary democracy and Marxist socialism. Both Mussolini and Hitler took power through semi-legal means in the midst of national crises, Mussolini in the postwar turmoil of 1922 and Hitler a decade later during the Great Depression.

Nazism, however, differed in some significant respects from Italian Fascism. Though Hitler's movement was named National Socialism, the *Führer* himself never advocated a true fusion of socialism with nationalism as Mussolini did. The only socialism he favored was the "socialism of the trenches" where discipline and danger broke down all class distinctions, but this remained far from the Marxist or any other economic definition of socialism. The earliest Nazis, such as Anton Drexler and the economist Gottfried Feder, did espouse a vague anti-capitalist, anti-big business philosophy which found its way into the initial twenty-five-point program of the party, but Hitler viewed this merely as tactical window-dressing. Gregor Strasser, the Nazis' most gifted organizer, shared Mussolini's vision of uniting the "proletarian nations" against the "plutocratic nations," but he abandoned most of his semi-socialist views upon Hitler's insistence in the mid-1920s. Therefore, Italian Fascism represented a more genuinely national socialism than the National Socialist Workers' Party of Germany.

Italian Fascism operated in an economically underdeveloped country and took as its primary tasks the building of a modern infrastructure and the increasing of production. Germany, on the other hand, had been a leading industrial power since the late nineteenth century and already enjoyed an efficient transportation system and a skilled work force. Though weakened by war and depression, Germany possessed a modern economy comparable to that of England or the United States. Hitler's task, therefore, was not to develop the economy virtually from scratch, as Mussolini and other developmental dictators did, but to get it going again, as Roosevelt was doing in the United States. Without any master plan, he employed Keynesian and Rooseveltian methods of public works and increased spending. German unemployment, therefore, dropped drastically every year after 1932 until full employment and even a labor shortage appeared by 1938.

Both Hitler and Mussolini aimed for totalitarian control of their countries, but Hitler approached the ideal of eliminating opposition and stirring up enthusiasm for his regime more closely than Mussolini did. The church remained a strong alternative source of authority in Italy, but Hitler bought off the German Catholic leaders by striking a concordat with the Vatican in 1933, and Protestant pastors and laity remained among his most enthusiastic supporters. Resistance cropped up from individual Christians of both persuasions, but they remained isolated cases. In Italy, the Savoy monarchy retained some prestige and symbolic weight, but the German kaiser had abdicated after World War I, and the death of President Hindenburg in 1934 removed the last authority figure outside the Nazi Party.

Mussolini could be ruthless when necessary. He drove his political opponents into exile or kept them in internal quarantine on remote islands off the Italian coast, but his police state was neither efficient nor consistent. Hitler's lieutenant, Hermann Göring, however, organized a secret police force as soon as the Nazis came to power, reorganizing a small counterintelligence office at Berlin police headquarters into the dreaded *Geheime Staatspolizei* (Secret State Police), better known by its acronym, the Gestapo. Along with the SS, directed by Heinrich Himmler, the secret police began interning political enemies in concentration camps as early as 1933.

The Third Reich was built on force from the very beginning, but it also aroused popular enthusiasm. Though Mussolini proved a gifted actor in his frequent harangues from the balcony of the Palazzo Venezia, Hitler's party rallies at Nuremberg, attended by half a million faithful, outshone the Italian Fascists, with searchlights scraping the sky and Hitler's oratory mesmerizing the masses. The Nazis also organized youth groups to indoctrinate the younger generation and a "Strength through Joy" movement that occupied the free time of adults after work.

The most important difference between Nazism and Fascism, however, was the racial anti-Semitism of the Nazi leader. Italy had few Jews, and Mussolini's movement remained nearly free of anti-Semitism until the late 1930s, fifteen years after taking power. Hatred for the Jews and plans to eliminate them, however, obsessed Hitler from his earliest years. Racial nationalism so pervades the Nazi movement that it strains the definition of a common fascism embracing both Hitler and Mussolini. The two leaders both emerged as fascists from the crucible of total war; they shared many ideas and admired each other. Yet Hitler's racism set him apart. Mussolini wished to develop his nation and expand its influence by war, but Hitler remained truly single-minded in his plans for dominating Europe and eliminating the Jews. He took the generic sense of fascism to new extremes.

Hitler's anti-Semitism and his imperialist dream of *Lebensraum,* surprisingly, played little role in his rise to power. In 1932 the frightened middle classes of Germany resented the Versailles Treaty but thought little about future foreign policy; and though they might share common prejudices against Jews, they did not pay much attention to Hitler's racial theories. The Nazis' main appeal in the early 1930s was their opposition to the discredited "socialist" republic and their trumpeting of a national revival that would restore Germany's place in the world and set the economy back in motion. If these appeals seem vague, they were intentionally so. Like Roosevelt in America and Mussolini in Italy, Hitler promised a lot but didn't get too specific.

Finally, despite the monstrous evils Hitler eventually perpetrated, he was not crazy, nor were the German people irrational in supporting him. Though obsessed with his twin ideas of anti-Semitism and continental imperialism, Hitler remained quite flexible and pragmatic in his choice of political tactics. He would work himself into a frenzy to deliver his speeches but appear perfectly normal at other times. As we have already seen, his background and upbringing were unremarkable, even banal, in their ordinariness. He proved to be one of the most evil figures of the twentieth century, but calling him a madman simply dodges the issue.

The majority of Germans never voted for Hitler, but many, if not most, eventually welcomed his regime. Even the working class appreciated his job creation programs during the depression. Above all, Hitler restored German national pride after the humiliation of wartime defeat and the economic troubles of the Weimar Republic. If he had died in 1938, before sparking World War II and perpetrating the Holocaust, he would still have been a ruthless dictator, but he would probably be remembered as one of the greatest leaders in German history.

CHAPTER EIGHTEEN

Socialism in One Country

Lenin and the Bolsheviks believed in 1917 that the Russian Revolution would spark a widespread upheaval among the working classes of the warring European nations. In fact, they counted on it. Orthodox Marxism held out little hope for the survival of a socialist revolution in such a backward country as Russia unless it were aided by the proletariat of more advanced, industrial nations. Socialists did revolt in defeated Germany and Hungary, and (as we saw in section 3) revolutions broke out on the rim of war in countries as diverse as Ireland and Arabia. Yet these latter revolts were nationalist uprisings against colonial powers, not class struggles, and the truly socialist outbreaks in Europe failed. At the end of their own civil war in Russia, the Bolsheviks found themselves victorious, but alone. They would have to build "socialism in one country," leaving the goal of worldwide revolution for the distant future.

Lenin adapted swiftly and proclaimed the New Economic Policy (NEP), easing the most draconian features of communism, at the party congress of March 1921. During the civil war, the Communists had expropriated grain by force of arms and tried to herd the peasants into collective farms. Under the NEP collectivization ceased. The peasants had to deliver a "tax in kind," a set proportion of their harvest, to the state; but they were then free to sell the rest on the open market. This allowed wealthier peasants, often called *kulaks,* to lease or buy more land, hire laborers, and become small-scale capitalists. A terrible famine fell upon Russia in 1921, but after that the peasants produced a large surplus of grain to feed the cities and to export for profit.

The Communists had nationalized most of Russia's manufacturing establishments immediately after the revolution, and they retained control of what Lenin called the "commanding heights" of industry under the NEP. Yet they exempted small-scale enterprises from the nationalization program and even allowed larger factories to be leased out to individual entrepreneurs. These private industrialists and the sharp merchants who sold on the free market became known as "Nepmen," capitalists within a socialist state.

The New Economic Policy allowed Russia to recover from the ravages of war, revolution, and civil war; yet the industrial workers and the party faithful viewed it as a sellout of Communist ideas. Lenin never made clear how permanent the NEP would be. He described the policy as merely a tactical maneuver, "a retreat — for a new attack." One of his Bolshevik colleagues called it a "peasant Brest," that is, a humiliating but temporary capitulation like the Treaty of Brest-Litovsk, whereby Russia withdrew from the First World War. Yet Lenin also proclaimed that the NEP should be pursued "seriously, and for a long time." The Bolshevik leader suffered a series of crippling strokes in 1922 and 1923 and died on January 21, 1924, before he could resolve these policy contradictions.

Like most great founders in business or politics, Lenin never adequately settled the succession problem. Through the power of his intellect and will he had made a great revolution and lived long enough to consolidate it, but he became more and more dictatorial as time went on. He did not believe any of his Bolshevik colleagues could carry on his one-man rule, so he suggested a period of collective management would best serve Russia after he died.

On December 25, 1922, after his second stroke, Lenin dictated a letter to the upcoming party congress which became known as his "testament." He exhorted the party leaders to remain united and avoid internal factions. He identified six members of the Central Committee — Gregory Zinoviev, Lev Trotsky, Joseph Stalin, Gregory Pyatakov, Lev Kamenev, and Nicholas Bukharin — as the heart of the collective leadership he envisioned and proceeded to outline the strengths and weaknesses of each. He called Trotsky "the most able man" but faulted him for his "excessive self-assurance." He labeled Bukharin, widely reputed as the best ideologue of the bunch, too "scholastic" in his thought processes. He wondered whether Stalin would "manage to use this power with sufficient caution."

Of the six Bolshevik leaders that Lenin singled out, Stalin was probably the least well known among the general populace. He had held the post of general secretary of the party since April 3, 1922, but this was considered a routine, bureaucratic position, and few took much notice of his appointment. Stalin appeared to be a hardworking, but unimaginative, party hack. Lenin, however, realized that the general secretary might run roughshod over his colleagues; so on January 4, 1923, he added a postscript to his testament, declaring that "Stalin is too rude. . . . Therefore I propose to the comrades to find a way to transfer Stalin from that office and appoint another man more tolerant, more loyal, more polite and more considerate of comrades." Lenin suffered his final stroke two months later, and his letter was not read at the party congress, though it did circulate privately. The Bolsheviks ignored their leader's advice to avoid factionalism and embarked on a Byzantine struggle for power after his death, a struggle that the "rude" general secretary ultimately won.

Stalin was not his real name, but a revolutionary nickname meaning "man of steel." He had been born Joseph Vissarionovich Djugashvili in the small town of Gori in the Caucasus Mountain region of Georgia on December 9, 1879. He was an ethnic Georgian, did not learn to speak the Russian language until his teens, and though he became quite fluent in Russian he never spoke it without an accent. Both his parents, Vissarion and Catherine, were peasants who had been born into serfdom. The father worked as an independent shoemaker after emancipation but later became merely a laborer in a shoe factory. He was a drunken, abusive husband and father who died in a brawl in 1890. Since Catherine's other children had died in infancy, she devoted herself to her only surviving child, known affectionately as Soso, and supported him by work as a domestic.

Joseph attended the local elementary school, which was conducted by the Orthodox Church, and then in 1894 he enrolled at the theological seminary in Tiflis (or Tbilisi), the capital of the province of Georgia. His mother devoutly hoped he would become a priest. She had obtained a small stipend from an Orthodox priest for whom she worked and paid the rest of her son's board and tuition out of her meager earnings. Joseph's own hopes at this time are unrecorded, but it's quite possible he never intended to become a priest. Georgia had no local university and the theological seminary provided the best education available. Not only Djugashvili but many of his seminary classmates became fervent believers in socialism rather than Christianity.

Joseph Djugashvili attended Marxist circles in Tiflis and he read voraciously in forbidden secular literature. He did well at the seminary for a time, but as his subversive activities became more time consuming he neglected his studies and was finally expelled in 1899. He took a clerical job in Tiflis, but worked primarily as a professional revolutionary, propagandizing and organizing in the major towns and cities of the Caucasus region. He adopted the first of several revolutionary nicknames, calling himself "Koba," after the Robin Hood–like hero of a Georgian novel.

"Koba" was arrested for the first time in 1902 during an oil refinery strike in Batum on the Black Sea and was exiled to Siberia, from which he escaped in 1904. For the next ten years he rotated in and out of prison and exile. He married Catherine Semyonovna Svanidze in 1907, who gave birth to a son, Jacob, in 1908; but his wife died in 1910, and the boy then lived with his Svanidze relatives.

During the long factional wrangles that marked the course of socialism before the revolution, Djugashvili always took the hard, uncompromising line of Lenin and the Bolsheviks. This made him something of an oddity in Georgia, for most of the local socialists were Mensheviks. Lenin adopted Koba as a promising

311

Bolshevik with a truly proletarian background, unlike himself and most of his colleagues, who had come from the middle-class intelligentsia. When the split within the Russian Socialist Party became final and irrevocable in 1912, Lenin co-opted Stalin (who had begun calling himself by this new name about that time) onto the Central Committee of the Bolshevik faction.

The Bolshevik leader also sent Stalin to Vienna in January 1913 to research and write a tract on the nationality problem, which appeared later in the year under the title, "The National Question and the Social Democratic Party." He concluded that the right of national self-determination could be a useful tool for undermining capitalist countries but would have little relevance under a socialist state. These conclusions, and his later actions, indicate that Stalin had rejected his Georgian background and become thoroughly Russian in his outlook, ready to impose a Great Russian primacy on the subject nations of the empire. Lenin, who never recognized how nationalistic he himself remained, later remarked about Stalin: "It is well known that Russified aliens always overdo things when they try to show themselves authentic Russians by adoption."

Upon his return to Russia in February 1913, Stalin was arrested again and exiled to the deepest, coldest reaches of the Siberian Arctic, the Yenisei-Turukhan region, from which escape was impossible. He remained in exile for four years, until the February 1917 Revolution freed all political prisoners. Stalin's extended banishment in Siberia seems to have exercised a decisive impact on his personality, making him truly a "man of steel." Unlike most of the tsarist political prisoners who spent their time reading, debating points of doctrine with fellow exiles, and writing arcane contributions to Marxist literature, Stalin kept to himself and apparently wrote nothing at all. Hunting and fishing on the tundra, he developed a lonely austerity that stayed with him. His daughter, Svetlana Alliluyeva, later wrote that "he loved Siberia, with its stark beauty and its rough, silent people."

In 1916 Stalin was called up from the tsarist prison camp for military service in the First World War, but he failed his physical examination at the Siberian city of Krasnoyarsk. A deformed left arm that was longer than the other and slightly fused at the elbow disqualified him. The authorities, however, allowed him to remain near Krasnoyarsk; so when the February Revolution broke out, he was near the Trans-Siberian Railway and reached Petrograd in just a few days. He did not, however, play an especially prominent role in the revolutionary events. Lacking the flash and dash of Lenin and Trotsky, devoid of oratorical ability or debating skills, he remained a hardworking backroom organizer, grinding out party literature and managing the paper flow. Some authors have suggested that Stalin and a few other Bolsheviks intentionally stayed in the background to avoid arrest so they could pick up the pieces if the revolution failed.

Despite his near invisibility when the Bolsheviks stormed the Winter Palace, Stalin was named to a high government post, commissar of nationalities, after the revolution. He also served on numerous party committees where his bureaucratic skill and dogged patience paid dividends. His most noteworthy revolutionary service came during the civil war in June 1918. As political commissar for the Red Army in the Volga River city of Tsaritsyn, he ruthlessly extracted grain from the peasants and drove the soldiers on to defeat the White armies. Seven years later, after he had assumed the party post of general secretary, the city of Tsaritsyn was renamed Stalingrad.

In the meantime, he had married a seventeen-year-old secretary in his commissariat, Nadezhda Alliluyeva, in 1918, and they had taken over a *dacha* (country house) outside Moscow that had formerly belonged to an oil baron from Baku. A son, Vasily, was born in 1920 and a daughter, Svetlana, in 1926. The 1920s marked the only period of domestic happiness in Stalin's life, a brief respite from Siberian loneliness and the whirlwind of revolution.

Yet while both the Russian people and Joseph Stalin enjoyed a period of "normality" in the twenties, the general secretary was scheming to accumulate absolute power over Russia. Trotsky seemed to many, including himself, Lenin's heir apparent; but for all his oratorical skill he lacked common sense and a feel for political strategy. He also underestimated Stalin, thinking him a lightweight, useful for bureaucratic drudgery but no leader. On the contrary, as Stalin's biographer Adam Ulam has stated, "Stalin was a man of uncommonly good sense and unusually vile as well as brooding temper." Exercising patience and brooding slowly until the time was right, he outmaneuvered his rivals in the collective leadership of the party.

Policy differences played a relatively minor role in the jockeying for power after Lenin's death. Stalin formulated the phrase "socialism in one country" and fulminated against Trotsky's theory of "permanent revolution," but most of this was mere shadow-boxing. Stalin still believed in the ultimate overthrow of capitalism worldwide, but sensibly realized that this goal had receded into the distant future. Trotsky, though more impatient than Stalin, was not such a fool that he opposed the strengthening of Russia as the motherland of the revolution.

Differences over the New Economic Policy were more marked. The right wing of the party favored an indefinite continuation of the policy, and Bukharin even remarked incautiously that the peasants should "enrich themselves." Trotsky and the party leftists opposed the NEP and advocated a return to nationalization and collectivization as soon as possible. Stalin, not wishing to repudiate a policy begun by Lenin, at first backed a continuation of the NEP but ultimately chose to scuttle it. His real differences with both the left and right, however, had more to do with power than policy.

Stalin used his control of the party organization and his common man image among the rank and file to consolidate his authority. Just before Lenin's death, the party had expanded its membership by enrolling 200,000 new members, mostly from the working class. This "Lenin levy" of new Communists over-whelmingly supported the general secretary in his factional struggles. Trotsky's oratory could move a crowd, but Stalin held the "inside track" to power.

The Central Committee removed Trotsky from command of the Red Army a year after Lenin's death. Unwisely, Zinoviev and Kamenev backed Stalin in this maneuver, for they too underestimated the general secretary and believed Trotsky posed the greater threat. The following year, 1926, Stalin turned against Zinoviev and Kamenev, stripping them of their most important positions. He did not yet possess absolute power, so he moved cautiously, allowing the opposition leaders to remain within the party for a time. Adam Ulam has called this a "purge by installments." The other installments eventually came due, however. The Central Committee terminated Kamenev's membership on the committee and expelled Trotsky, Zinoviev, and Bukharin from the party altogether. Stalin exiled Trotsky to Alma Ata in Central Asia for a year, then in 1929 deported him from the country. Trotsky's exile took him first to Turkey, then Norway, and finally to Mexico, where one of Stalin's agents murdered him with a mountaineer's ice ax in 1940.

Long before Trotsky's death, Stalin ruled supreme in Russia. On the occasion of his fiftieth birthday in 1929, the party congress showered him with personal praise. Seven years after Il Duce took power in Italy and four years before der Führer's ascent in Germany, Stalin's "cult of personality" had transformed the gray bureaucratic general secretary into a new tsar of Russia.

Once in full control of the party and the government, Stalin gave a fuller meaning to the slogan "socialism in one country" by abandoning the New Economic Policy and mounting a drive to industrialize the nation and collectivize its agricultural production. Obsessed with industrialization, he spurred his countrymen on to heroic deeds with appeals to their national pride. In 1929, the same year that the party nearly deified him, Stalin proclaimed, in a rare burst of lyricism:

> We are going full steam along the road of industrialization to socialism, leaving behind our age-long "Russian" backwardness. We are becoming a country of metal, a country of the automobile, a country of the tractor. And when we have seated the USSR in an automobile, and the peasant on a tractor, then let the honourable capitalists . . . try to catch us up. . . . We have lagged 50 or 100 years behind the advanced countries. We must close this gap in ten years. Either we shall do it, or they will crush us.

Though industrialization remained the primary goal, Stalin also reorganized Soviet agriculture. The Communists required a secure grain surplus to feed the increasing numbers of workers who would flood into cities as industrialization proceeded and they hoped to export some of this surplus to earn hard capital for investment in industry. Beyond these economic considerations, however, the peasantry posed a political problem. Still comprising a large majority of the Russian population, the peasants had flourished under the New Economic Policy, and capitalism remained alive and well in the countryside, mocking the ideals of socialism. With his characteristic ruthlessness, Stalin waged war upon the peasantry from 1928 to 1933, destroying the independent capitalist farmers and forcing the rest on to collective farms.

The war against the peasantry began with the 1927 harvest. Low prices and a brief international war scare prompted the peasants to hoard their grain that year rather than sell it. This temporary crisis could have been surmounted by tinkering with the prices. Instead, Stalin personally descended upon the farm areas of western Siberia, near the slopes of the Ural Mountains, in January 1928, driving his commissars to requisition grain by force, just as he had during the civil war near Tsaritsyn. This worked so well that he applied the "Ural-Siberian method" — forced requisitions — throughout Russia after the next harvest. The peasants reacted, however, by reducing production and hiding what they did grow.

At the end of 1929, therefore, Stalin decreed the "liquidation of the kulaks as a class." *Kulak*, which literally means "fist" in Russian, was a derisive term for a village moneylender, a Shylock who exploited the peasants. Long before the Revolution, Lenin and the Bolsheviks had applied it to any wealthy peasant who hired other peasants to work for him, and thus, by Marxist definition, exploited them. The term always remained fuzzy and unclear. Like the U.S. Supreme Court justice who said he could not define pornography but he knew it when he saw it, Lenin stated that "they will know on the spot who is a kulak." Therefore, when Stalin pushed for "dekulakization," the Communists attacked not only rich peasants but any peasant who resisted or displeased the local Communist authorities.

After the 1929 harvest 25,000 workers from the city volunteered for the dekulakization drive, descending upon the villages like a plague and evicting so-called kulaks from their land. The evicted peasants, along with their families, were exiled to remote Arctic areas and forced to work for the state. Over the next few years, between 10 and 15 million peasants were uprooted in this way. About 6.5 million of them, primarily children and the elderly, perished in the process. This wave of dekulakization hit hardest in Ukraine, the richest grain growing area of the Soviet Union, and Stalin used the occasion to cripple Ukrainian nationalism by also arresting the intelligentsia and the church leaders.

While exterminating the wealthier peasants, the Communists also herded the landless and the peasants with small holdings into collective farms. In the winter of 1929-30 roughly half of all peasant households were collectivized. The process proved immensely disruptive. Some peasants resisted forcibly; many more engaged in sabotage, killing their cattle and burning their houses and equipment. Therefore, Stalin called an abrupt tactical retreat in March 1930, allowing peasants to leave the collectives if they wished. Even though they faced an uncertain future by leaving, for the government would not return their land to them, nearly 9 million peasants voted with their feet against socialized agriculture in the summer of 1930. After this brief respite, however, the Communist cadres returned to the countryside and completed the job. By the end of 1934, 90 percent of the cropland in the Soviet Union was collectivized. Twenty-five million peasant holdings had been consolidated into 240,000 collective farms.

Before agricultural reorganization was completed, one more horror descended upon the countryside, the terror-famine of 1932-33. The main reason for collectivizing agriculture in the first place was to obtain a secure surplus of grain for state purposes, to feed the cities and to gain export earnings. Yet the terrorized peasants had reduced their sowing, killed their cattle, and hoarded what little grain they did produce, so the harvests of the early 1930s were greatly reduced. Nevertheless, the Communists insisted on requisitioning the same or larger amounts of grain, no matter how small the harvest. If there wasn't enough left over after meeting the state quota, the peasants starved. For example, in 1930 the state claimed 22 million tons of grain out of a total harvest of 83.5 million tons. The following year, the harvest produced only 70 million tons, but the state still extracted 22.8 million tons.

This government-induced famine proved most severe in two of the Soviet republics, Kazakhstan and Ukraine. Kazakhstan in Central Asia posed a special case for collectivization, since two-thirds of the population were semi-nomadic herders. The Communists forced the pace of history by transforming the Kazakhs in one fell swoop into settled farmers, and socialized farmers at that. The results proved devastating. Without their accustomed herds, a million of the four million Kazakhs died of starvation in 1932.

The Kazahkstan catastrophe was probably not intentional, but rather the result of stupid and impatient policies, like the forcing of the American Indians onto reservations in the western United States. The terror-famine in Ukraine the following year, however, represented a more calculated atrocity. The major brunt of both dekulakization and collectivization had hit the rich grain areas of Ukraine, and Stalin had attacked the cultural and political leadership of the region as well. Then in 1932 the Communists set unrealistic grain quotas for that year's harvest. By the end of the year only 70 percent of the plan had been fulfilled, so the government refused to release surplus grain stocks to feed the peasants. They even sealed the border between Ukraine and Russia so that peasants could not escape and food could not be smuggled in. During the winter and spring of 1932 and 1933, about 5 million Ukrainian peasants died, representing between 20 and 25 percent of the total population of that region. Robert Conquest, the historian of the terror-famine, has stated without exaggeration that "the Ukraine . . .

was like one vast Belsen" (a Nazi concentration camp). Enthusiastic Communists ripped apart farm huts looking for hidden grain and watchtowers towered over the fields to spy on the peasants.

The casualty total from Stalin's war on the peasants is staggering. Conquest, who has made the most thorough study, estimates that between 1930 and 1937, 14.5 million Soviet peasants died, 6.5 million in the "liquidation of the kulaks as a class" and 8 million in the terror-famine. Both the Kazakhs and the Ukrainians lost nearly a quarter of their populations. It could be argued that this represented an unintentional by-product of economic policies gone wrong. This argument is more plausible in the case of the Kazakhs than the Ukrainians, for Stalin was clearly trying to kill two birds with one stone in Ukraine, the rich peasants and Ukrainian nationalism. The attack on the kulaks, however, was clear-cut and openly acknowledged.[1]

The word genocide is often used too casually, but I would argue that it applies here. The official United Nations definition of genocide, adopted in 1948, refers to "acts committed with intent to destroy, in whole or in part, a national, ethnical, racial or religious group." This could reasonably be extended to the destruction of a social class. In fact, the original draft of the UN definition included classes, but this phrase was removed at the insistence of Stalin's representatives, for obvious reasons. The crucial element in any case of genocide is the killing of individuals and their families, not because of anything they have done, but simply because they belong to a particular category (an ethnic group or a social class). A character in a Soviet novel about the kulaks makes this glaringly clear: "Not one of them was guilty of anything; but they belonged to a class that was guilty of everything."

Tragically, all this slaughter produced an inefficient, unproductive system of agriculture. Though the peasants lavished time and care on the small personal farm plots they were allowed to retain, they felt no incentive to work hard or take initiative on the collective farms. As a result, Russia, which had exported substantial amounts of grain in tsarist times and under the New Economic Policy, has had trouble feeding itself since the 1930s. Yet in one way, collectivization proved successful. It eliminated private property in land and the class of capitalist farmers, thus removing those threats to the regime. It produced a cowed, controlled populace in the countryside. To Stalin's mind, this political result probably outweighed any economic shortcomings.

1. The agricultural revolution also cost Stalin his family life. His wife, Nadezhda, a sensitive and independent woman who had already threatened to leave him before, heard of the atrocities in Ukraine from classmates at the Industrial Academy. Distraught by these revelations, she committed suicide on November 8, 1932. It was officially announced that she died of appendicitis. Stalin's daughter, Svetlana, six years old at the time, did not find out the truth about her mother's death until ten years later.

317

If agriculture is universally acknowledged as the most signal failure of Soviet Communism, Stalin's industrialization drive has often been lauded (and not just by Communists) as a great success. It made a particularly strong impact on world opinion in the 1930s because the so-called advanced industrial nations were suffering from the Great Depression. While millions of workers languished without jobs in capitalist Britain, Germany, and the United States, Stalinist Russia was building gigantic factories and power plants and experiencing a labor shortage.

Stalin attempted to compress the Industrial Revolution into a single decade or less. The engineers and economists who formulated the first Five-Year Plan in 1928 presented the Communist leaders with both "optimum" estimates of what could be accomplished and a "basic," more realistic, estimate. The Politburo cavalierly adopted the optimum plan; Stalin later demanded its completion in four years rather than five. The timid engineers, most of whom were "bourgeois specialists" trained under the tsarist regime, were arrested as "saboteurs and wreckers" and executed after a series of show trials in 1929 and 1930.

Needless to say, the official plan set hopelessly unrealistic goals. Adam Ulam has called them "a propaganda broadside in figures." Steel production, for example, was projected to increase from 4 million tons annually in 1928 to 10.4 million tons by 1933. Actual production came to about 6 million tons. At the end of the 1930s, the Communists claimed their gross national product had multiplied five times during the decade. Recent, more accurate figures indicate that it only increased about 150 percent. Still, this represented a remarkable leap forward, particularly at a time when the European and American economies lay crippled.

More striking than economic statistics were the gigantic mega-projects constructed under Stalin's Five-Year Plans. The three most monumental were the hydroelectric power dam on the Dnieper River in Ukraine, the Magnitogorsk steelmaking complex east of the Ural Mountains, and a canal linking the Baltic with the White Sea in the Russian Arctic.

The *Dneprostroi* (Dnieper construction project) had been projected by Gosplan, the state planning agency, shortly after the revolution; for Lenin dreamed that *energetika*, electrical energy, would power the Soviet future. Stalin's Five-Year Plan made the dream a reality, building the world's largest dam to power the coal mines of the Donbas region, plus new iron, steel, and aluminum factories. The Communists also planned a new city, Magnitogorsk, as the site of gigantic steel mills near the "Magnetic Mountain," one of the richest iron ore deposits in the world. Stalin believed that Magnitogorsk, tucked behind the Ural Mountains, as far east of Moscow as Berlin was to the west, would be safe from German invaders in the case of war, and this proved correct. However, the best source of coal power for the steel mills lay another fifteen hundred miles to the east, at Kuznetsk in Siberia. Therefore, the Magnitogorsk mills proved enormously expensive to operate.

Dneprostroi was a useful, though environmentally damaging, hydro dam, and Magnitogorsk a productive, though inefficient, steel town; but the third mega-project, the White Sea Canal, was a pure boondoggle. Built almost entirely with prison labor, the canal was rushed to completion in a mere eighteen months without the use of any heavy machinery. The head of the secret police, who assigned manpower for the canal, took Stalin for a steamboat cruise upon completion in May 1933; yet the canal was a white elephant. It remained frozen much of the year and was far too shallow for oceangoing ships.

The Soviet industrialization drive, therefore, yielded mixed results. By emphasizing heavy industry, the Communists built an enormous capacity for steelmaking and electrical production that served them well when World War II broke out. Eventually Russia became a superpower. They purchased industrial progress, however, at the expense of consumer comfort. Not only did millions of peasants starve, but industrial workers saw their already low standard of living plummet by about one-third during the period of the first Five-Year Plan.

Much of Soviet industry was constructed hastily and shoddily, with no thought for the damage it inflicted on the environment. An American historian of technology, Loren Graham, has concluded that "standard Soviet industrialization policy . . . emphasized gigantic projects over smaller ones, centralized plans over locally sensitive ones, output above safety, technology above human beings, closed decision making to the detriment of critical debate, and, above all, a madly rushed tempo." In short, Stalin's Five-Year Plan was inhuman and in a hurry. Yet the era of the Five-Year Plan seemed heroic to many at the time, both inside and outside the Soviet Union. Adam Ulam has shrewdly remarked that "Stalin was a great teacher," that is, a propagandist. Much that seems puzzling about his rule can best be understood from the viewpoint of the young, who found his regime challenging but exhilarating.

In 1932 a twenty-year-old American named John Scott, the son of radical parents Scott Nearing and Nellie Seeds, went to live and work in Magnitogorsk. Scott remained in Russia for eight years, married a Russian woman, then later wrote a book, *Behind the Urals*, which has been called the "classic firsthand account of the daily life of Stalinism." Scott thought he was visiting the future. "Something seemed to be wrong with America," he wrote. "I decided to go to Russia to work, study, and to lend a hand in the construction of a society which seemed to be at least one step ahead of the American."

Suffering and sacrifice inspired many young Russians so long as the goal, a productive, classless society, remained clear and unsullied. Yet Scott discovered what dissident Marxist Milovan Djilas would later call "the new class" in Communist Russia. The technical specialists and party bigwigs enjoyed a separate suburb of single-family homes outside Magnitogorsk, while most of the workers lived in barracks or in the poorly planned model city, directly downwind from the steel mills. Perhaps a quarter of the workers were prisoners, either common criminals or so-called dispossessed kulaks, living in tents or huts under constant supervision of the secret police. Disillusioned, Scott returned to America in 1940 with his Russian wife and children. The future didn't work quite so well as casual visitors thought. Fifty years later, satellite photos would reveal that the open-hearth mills of Magnitogorsk had poisoned a strip of earth 120 miles long and 40 miles wide, downwind from the "Magnetic Mountain."

John Scott also viewed firsthand the most terrifying, and puzzling, feature of Stalin's Russia, the great party purges of the late 1930s. The elimination of rich peasants, the execution of bourgeois specialists, and the suppression of Ukrainian nationalists possessed a brutal logic. If one grants the premise that these people were all "class enemies," then their liquidation makes sense, as long as one has no moral scruples. Stalin, however, went one step further. He murdered not only his supposed enemies but also his closest friends and followers.

High-level Communists expelled from the party before the mid-1930s lost their jobs, but they were not killed. This changed, however, after the murder of Sergei Kirov on December 1, 1934. Kirov was probably Stalin's closest friend, but he possessed a mind of his own and a devoted following in the Leningrad party apparatus, which he headed. As the best Communist orator since Trotsky and a supposed "moderate" in policy matters, he could possibly have threatened Stalin's position as general secretary had he been willing to form a conspiracy. He never had the chance, and there is no evidence he would have. A lone gunman, Leonid Nikolayev, put a bullet in Kirov's back as he was walking down the corridor to his office at the Smolny Institute (the same building Lenin had used as headquarters in October 1917). To this day, no one knows for sure who put Nikolaycv up to the assassination, but many historians believe Stalin's police organized it. In any case, the Kirov murder played a role in Stalin's career similar to that of the Reichstag fire in Hitler's. It provided the pretext for repression. Whether Stalin engineered the crime or not, he certainly seized the opportunity.

The very day of Kirov's death Stalin issued a decree expediting the arrest and execution of oppositionists. Thirty to forty thousand members of the Leningrad party organization were deported to prison camps in the Arctic; Nikolayev and a group of alleged conspirators were summarily tried and shot on December 29, 1934. Then Zinoviev, Kamenev, and several other prominent Communists were tried for "moral complicity" in the crime. Supposedly, their long-standing opposition to Stalin's leadership had given the assassin bad ideas. Stalin's former rivals received five or ten year prison sentences.

The Kirov affair, however, was just beginning. The unfortunate prisoners were tortured and broken down until they were willing to confess a more active role in Kirov's murder. On August 19, 1936, the first of the great Moscow show trials opened with an audience of 150 Russians, mostly secret police agents, and about 30 foreign diplomats and journalists. Zinoviev, Kamenev, and fourteen others confessed profusely in open court that they had conspired with the exiled Trotsky to murder Kirov and Stalin, and thus overthrow the government. They were all shot less than twenty-four hours after the guilty verdict was pronounced.

Two more show trials and a more secret purge of the top military leadership followed over the next two years. On September 30, 1936, Stalin named Nicholas Yezhov head of the People's Commissariat for Internal Affairs (NKVD), and he unleashed a reign of terror ever after known as the *Yezhovshchina,* "the Yezhov time." Yet Stalin himself was directly responsible. During the eighteen months of Yezhov's administration, he sent the general secretary 383 lists of prominent Communists marked for death. Stalin and his closest lieutenant, V. M. Molotov, meticulously perused them, checking off those they aproved for execution.

On January 23, 1937, the second show trial assembled in Moscow. Gregory Pyatakov, one of the six leaders singled out by Lenin in his final testament, was the lead defendant. As chief assistant to Sergo Ordzhonikidze in the Commissariat for Heavy Industry, he had been one of the driving forces behind the industrialization program. Yet now he confessed to sabotage of the economy and conspiracy with both the Germans and the Japanese. He and his cohorts were duly convicted and executed. Ordzhonikidze himself, a Georgian like Stalin and an old friend of the general secretary's, was found dead in his apartment on February 18, 1937. Historians now believe that Stalin either murdered him or induced him to commit suicide to avoid arrest and torture.

The last public trial, on March 2, 1938, claimed Nicholas Bukharin, another member of the fated six that Lenin discussed in his testament. Robert Conquest has termed this final spectacle "little more than a victory parade" for Stalin. All the supposed plots against Kirov, the general secretary himself, the collectivization and industrialization drives, and the like were wrapped together and blamed on the hapless defendants. Yet this trial almost went wrong. One defendant retracted his confession, until further torture brought him around. Bukharin himself, as always the scholastic ideologue, played a subtle game in court. He admitted general responsibility for treason as the head of a so-called "Bloc of Rights and Trotskyites" but denied most of the specific acts brought forward as evidence. However, the controlled Soviet press simply reported that he had confessed. He and the others were shot.

All in all, fifty-four Communist leaders "confessed" their crimes publicly during the three show trials, and their performances were convincing enough to persuade many of the foreign observers. Teams of interrogators had systematically broken them down over long periods of time in prison, with the liberal use of physical beatings. Apparently they were not drugged while on trial, as sometimes thought at the time, but were kept in line by fear of more torture and the threat to arrest other members of their families. Forty-seven of the fifty-four defendants were executed; the seven others disappeared into prison camps.

These public trials, however, represented merely the tip of the iceberg. On June 11, 1937, Marshal Michael Tukachevsky and other high military officers were arrested, tried in secret, and summarily shot. Within little more than a week, almost a thousand officers were arrested. By the end of the military purge, three of the five Soviet marshals, thirteen of the fifteen commanding generals, and eight out of nine top admirals in the fleet had been either killed or imprisoned. Less prominent Communists suffered as well. The secret police greeted nearly all relatives or close associates of those convicted with the dreaded middle-of-the-night knock on the door, sending them off to remote prison camps in the Gulag (main prison camp administration). Troikas, or three-man tribunals, spread out through the provinces, banishing Communist Party members who were denounced by their comrades. Anyone who had ever met a foreigner became immediately suspect. After John Scott returned to Magnitogorsk from a family visit in America in 1937, people were afraid to talk to him and he couldn't get a job.

Though much higher estimates have been given, researchers in newly opened Russian archives have judged that about 2.5 million Soviet citizens were arrested during the Yezhov years of 1937-38, and nearly 700,000 of these were executed. Hundreds of thousands more perished in the prison camps. Many more had died during the genocidal attacks on the peasantry, but the great terror of the late 1930s was more pervasive and indiscriminate. No one felt safe. Adam Ulam has termed it a "democracy of fear." Yezhov himself lost his job at the end of 1938 and was arrested and shot the following year. His successor, Laurenti Beria, institutionalized and systematized the reign of terror. No more show trials were mounted until after World War II, but fear of the police remained a fact of life in Soviet Russia.

The great purges have fascinated and perplexed historians. Walter Laqueur has called them "an event unique in world history." Mussolini never purged his Fascist Party membership and only executed a few dozen political prisoners. Hitler mounted just one party purge, the Night of the Long Knives on June 30, 1934, which destroyed Ernst Röhm and the SA storm trooper organization. Stalin's reign of terror, on the other hand, seems extravagant and unnecessary. In 1934, 1,966 delegates attended the party congress. By the time the next congress convened in 1939, 1,108 of them had been arrested. Only 59 veterans of the 1934 gathering attended in 1939.

These figures provide a clue to Stalin's motives. He wanted to forge a totally new organization, completely under his own control. The new men he appointed were qualitatively different from their predecessors. They were younger, had played little or no part in the revolution, and did not know Stalin as anything other than the supreme leader. Moreover, they had risen to the top as faithful instruments of terror. Stalin had created a new party in his image and likeness, a party of denouncers and torturers.

As in the case of Hitler, the enormity of Stalin's deeds seems to cry out for psychological analysis. Certainly the bare facts of Stalin's life provide plenty of opportunities for psychologizing. He was a short man, standing no more than five feet four inches tall, thus a perfect candidate for a "Napoleon complex," that is, an over-achiever compensating for his lack of physical stature. His deformed left arm and pockmarked face, his Georgian accent and peasant background might further feed a sense of inferiority and prompt him to get even with those who mocked him. As a child he endured the beatings of a violent, alcoholic father, and like not a few other abused children he repeated this abusive behavior as an adult.

The material available for psychoanalysis of Stalin, however, is even scantier than in the case of Hitler. Very little is known about his early childhood or his private life and thoughts. Furthermore, Alan Bullock, who has written a dual biography of Hitler and Stalin, sensibly points out that both men functioned perfectly normally and enjoyed unparalleled success as political leaders. They may have possessed unusual personalities, but whatever disorders they suffered did not render them dysfunctional. In the twentieth century, many find it easier to embrace the concept of mental illness than to admit the existence of evil. In the final analysis, I would suggest that Stalin and Hitler were not sick; they were evil. The Yugoslav Communist Milovan Djilas called Stalin "the greatest criminal in history."

Stalin's bloody rise to totalitarian leadership is best explained by a combination of three factors: psychology, strategy, and circumstances. Whether we judge him psychopathic or not, he clearly possessed a hard-driving but controlled personality, prone to vengeance against real or supposed enemies. Nearly everyone who encountered him remarked upon his intense suspiciousness. In the words of the old cliché, he didn't get mad, he got even.

The strategy Stalin employed may be described, in a comparison that would have outraged the Communist leader, as an amoral version of office politics. Think of Stalin as the head of a giant corporation. Having clawed his way to the top, he fires anyone with independent ideas, anyone who might possibly threaten his control. He also settles old grudges with former colleagues who crossed him on his way up. Remembering how the previous CEO (Lenin) suffered a crippling stroke and was ignored by the board of directors (the Politburo), he packs the board with yes men who owe their careers to him alone. This happens all the time in capitalist countries. Stalin, however, didn't just fire his subordinates; he killed them. Stalinist psychology and strategy created a new category of leader, the terror-bureaucrat.

323

In addition, however, two sets of circumstances eased Stalin's decision to rule through terror. First of all, while creating socialism in one country, he rightly judged that Soviet Russia was surrounded by capitalist enemies, an international pariah that other nations would gladly destroy. When he unleashed his party purges in 1936, he feared the imminent outbreak of a two-front war. The Japanese military had occupied Manchuria, right on the border of Siberia, in 1931; and by the mid-1930s, Hitler's Germany had thrown off the last restraints of the Versailles Treaty and was frantically rearming. One can argue that it was dangerous to execute the bourgeois specialist engineers, the most productive peasants, and the top military commanders in a time of danger. Yet from Stalin's perspective, it made sense to eliminate any potential for sabotage, rebellions, or coups and to fill the ranks with young cadres of unquestioned loyalty. In any case, Stalin was not crazy to fear Hitler or the Japanese. Paranoia is defined as a fear of imaginary enemies; Stalin's enemies were real enough.

A second, and more fundamental, circumstance predisposing Stalin to terror was the nature and history of the Communist Party. The Communists came from a violently conspiratorial tradition of Russian radicalism. Lenin had created the first Soviet secret police force, the Cheka (Extraordinary Commission),[2] on December 17, 1917, and up to the time of his death, the police executed at least 200,000 Russians. Stalin's great rival, Trotsky, even wrote a tract called *The Defense of Terrorism* in 1920. John Scott, the American in Magnitogorsk, best summed up how the revolutionary circumstances of Communist history led to Stalinism:

> Twenty years of underground activity under the despotic conditions of Czarist Russia, the arrests, the *agents provocateurs* were dominant factors. . . . In the Bolshevik Party there is no appeal after a decision has been reached. There is no protesting, no resigning. The only chance of the opposition, after they have been voted down, is conspiracy. This method of dealing with opposition sowed the seeds of purges.

Whether we emphasize Stalin's psychology, his strategy, or the circumstances of his revolutionary inheritance and international situation is a matter of interpretation. The results of Stalin's actions, however, are clear: the closest approximation to a totalitarian state that had been achieved up to that time. Stalin, like Hitler and Mussolini, followed the leader principle and created a cult of per-

---

2. The Soviet secret police were known as the Cheka from 1917 to 1922, GPU (State Political Administration) from 1922 to 1924, OGPU (Unified State Political Administration) from 1924 to 1934, and NKVD (People's Commissariat of Internal Affairs) from 1934 to 1941. After the Second World War, they became known as the KGB (Committee of State Security).

sonality. More than either of the other two he erected a true police state. The Soviet secret police wielded more power than either the government or the Communist Party and ruled an empire of misery in the Gulag. Stalin also fostered a new class of political bureaucrats who managed the state economy.

Like Mussolini, but more successfully, Stalin was a developmental dictator, forcing his countrymen into startling feats of economic development. Many party cadres, especially the young, devoutly believed they were building a freer, classless socialist society; but the masses were motivated by older, deeper impulses of Russian nationalism. When Milovan Djilas met Stalin during World War II, he noted to his horror that the Communist "pope" never mentioned defense of communism or the Soviet Union, but spoke only of *Russia*. Stalin, much more than Hitler or Mussolini, fused the terrible "isms" of socialism and nationalism into a dreadful new amalgam. "Socialism in one country," a truly national socialism, packed more power than any religion. In the words of Djilas, Stalin was "one of those rare terrible dogmatists capable of destroying nine tenths of the human race to 'make happy' the one tenth."

CHAPTER NINETEEN

The Spanish Tragedy

The word "tragedy" is commonly used to describe all manner of horrible events, from floods and earthquakes to mass murders. Yet as originally conceived by the ancient Greek playwrights Aeschylus, Sophocles, and Euripides, tragedy has a more precise meaning, useful for describing the Spanish civil war.

In tragic drama, circumstances, or fate, predetermine men and women to commit terrible deeds. Yet free will still exists, and the dramatist presents options which reasonable human beings might choose to avoid the horrible consequences. Due to a tragic flaw, usually pride (*hubris* in Greek), the hero or heroine of Greek tragedy fails to seize these options and thus seals his or her fate. Human choice, therefore, is essential to tragedy. Cattle led to the slaughterhouse, or whole villages destroyed by a volcano are not tragic events, as they could not be foreseen or avoided by the victims. True tragedy is more horrible than a natural disaster for it turns upon human folly. Aristotle said that tragic drama evokes pity and fear in the viewers. So do tragic historical events.

The Spanish civil war was a classic case of tragedy, in the ancient Greek sense. The history and geography of Spain predisposed the country to fall apart when its centuries-old monarchy ended in the 1930s and the nation became a republic. The Spanish Republic produced outstanding leaders who could have made choices to avert the tragedy. Yet, in a country where "courage is a second fatherland," as the novelist André Malraux has phrased it, pride and *machismo* foreclosed these options and Spaniard fought Spaniard for three terrible years.

As the twentieth century began, Spain's recent history paralleled that of Italy in a number of respects. Both countries had enjoyed a glorious imperial past but were mired in a shabby, underdeveloped present. Both suffered from strong regional divisions. Unlike Italy, Spain had long been united politically under one monarch, but its geography led to intense localism. Mountain ranges criss-cross the Iberian peninsula, cutting it into a checkerboard of distinct environments. Generally speaking, the north is cool and rainy, with numerous small peasant farms, whereas the south, the region of Andalusia, is extremely dry, almost desert, filled with large estates worked by landless laborers. The coastal regions along the Mediterranean enjoy a semi-tropical climate, but only a few dozen miles inland, bitter winters coat the mountains with snow. The central plateau around Madrid, the Spanish heartland of Castile where the fictional Don Quixote chased windmills, bakes in summer and shivers under icy winter blasts.

Language, history, and culture created a separate country, Portugal, on the western edge of the Iberian peninsula, and two other regions also developed their own national consciousness. The Basques, an ancient people with a language unrelated to any other in Europe, have lived for thousands of years on the north coast of the peninsula at the foot of the Pyrenees Mountains. In the extreme northeast along the Mediterranean coast lies Catalonia, a formerly independent kingdom centered around the port city of Barcelona, the second largest city of Spain. The Catalans speak a Romance language derived from Latin and closely related to Spanish and French. Both Catalonia and the Basque provinces formed "Irelands" within the Spanish realm, resenting the rule of Castile. Spain resembled the multi-ethnic empire of Austria-Hungary more than consolidated national states such as France.

Traditionally, the monarchy and the Catholic Church were the only forces of unity in Spain, with the regions, the village communes, and the towns retaining strong local traditions. Gerald Brenan, whose *Spanish Labyrinth* is the best single book on Spain in the English language, has concluded that "Spain is a collection of small, mutually hostile or indifferent republics held together in a loose federation."

During the nineteenth century, both the crown and the church became weaker, accentuating the country's disunity. The Bourbon royal family fled ignominiously when Napoleon invaded Spain after the French Revolution, and their dynasty never enjoyed much popularity or legitimacy after it was restored to power. Of all the monarchs who sat on the Spanish throne in the nineteenth century, four were compelled to abdicate, one was kept in power only by foreign (French) support, and one died young from consumption. In the first half of the century, the army decided which politicians would exercise power under the monarchy, staging *pronunciamentoes* (military coups) on an average of one every twenty months or so. After 1885, however, the Liberal and Conservative parties lessened the influence of the military by agreeing to a "pacific rotation" in office. This practice of *Turnismo*, alternating power in extremely corrupt, controlled elections, resembled the contemporary Italian practice of transformism.

At the same time, the Catholic Church, though legally established, lost its extensive landholdings to state confiscation. Without their own land, the bishops, priests, and religious orders curried favor from the rich landowners and rising industrialists and became alienated from the masses. By the twentieth century, as few as 10 percent of Spaniards attended church regularly in some areas. The twin forces of Spanish unity had declined drastically.

Spain remained neutral during the First World War and prospered selling food and war materials to both sides, but this bubble of prosperity floated prices out of sight for the workers and farmers. Socialists and anarchists had been organizing among the masses, and in the immediate postwar years Spain suffered a wave of strikes, general strikes, and lockouts similar to those in Italy at the same time. Barcelona witnessed open class war as workers and employers both hired gangsters, or *pistoleros,* who claimed about nine hundred lives.

One of Spain's leading philosophers, José Ortega y Gasset,[1] wrote *España Invertebrada,* analyzing Spain's social pathology in the early 1920s. The country was invertebrate, Ortega argued, without a skeleton holding it together. The church, the monarchy, and the army, which had previously been national institutions, had degenerated into special interests or cliques, looking out only for themselves. Meanwhile, the country was divided into quarreling regions and warring social classes. Certainly national consciousness existed, especially in Castile. Spain's history of "great deeds" in the past — expelling the Moslems from Europe, conquering most of the Western Hemisphere in the sixteenth century — ensured that. Yet Spain lacked great deeds in the present and a program for the future. Its head, Castile, thought and felt nationally, but its body, without a spine, was fractured both vertically and horizontally.

In Italy the postwar strike wave had prompted Mussolini's seizure of power, and Spain too soon succumbed to a dictatorship. General Miguel Primo de Rivera y Orbaneja "pronounced" against all the political parties on September 13, 1923, with the consent of King Alfonso XIII, and ruled by decree for the rest of the decade. Primo de Rivera, however, was no fascist, but rather an old-fashioned military dictator who merely wanted to suppress disorder. His rule coincided with the economic boom of the twenties when Spanish agriculture enjoyed high prices for its exports, and he increased the nation's well-being by borrowing lavishly and constructing numerous public works. The worldwide

---

1. Spaniards commonly use both their parents' last names. The first surname is the father's and the second the mother's. In some cases, as in this example, the two are connected by the conjunction *y,* which means "and," but generally this is absent. An individual frequently uses just his father's name for short, but if it is a very common name, he will use both, or even just the mother's. So, for example, the playwright Federico Garcia Lorca was known as Garcia Lorca or even Lorca, but never Garcia.

depression and Spanish weariness with the general's dictatorship, however, brought about his resignation in January 1930. The king appointed another general to succeed him, but when local elections in April 1931 showed a strong surge of support for republicans and socialists, King Alfonso left the country and Spain became a republic.

The political extremes of left and right rejected the Spanish Republic from the very start. Anarchists, who were more numerous in Spain than in any other country, opposed participation in government and mounted a "cycle of insurrections" throughout the country that left 400 dead and 3,000 injured. In the most notorious rising, at the small village of Casas Viejas in southern Spain, the republican government retaliated as brutally as any dictatorship, burning the rebels alive in their besieged dwellings and leaving the charred corpses on display to deter further revolts.

Two brands of monarchists, supporters of Alfonso XIII and the Carlists, who backed one of his Bourbon relatives, also wanted to overthrow the republic. General José Sanjurjo Sacanell mounted a military coup in August 1932, but it failed miserably. The Spanish Republic enjoyed enough political support and military strength to suppress revolts from both the extreme right and the extreme left, but quarrels between the Socialists and the Catholics, both of whom accepted the republic provisionally, gradually tore it apart.

The first governments of the republic, from April 1931 to November 1933, were dominated by republican leaders from the so-called "generation of '98." Spain's loss of her last New World colonies (Cuba, Puerto Rico, and the Philippines) in the Spanish-American War of 1898 had jolted the nation profoundly, but it also stimulated a generation of intellectuals to bring Spain into line with the liberal-democratic practices of other European nations. The Constituent Cortes, or parliament, elected in 1931 to write a constitution for the republic, formed a virtual "assembly of notables," mostly lawyers, writers, and other professionals from this generation. The large Socialist party, led by Francisco Largo Caballero and Indalecio Prieto y Tuero, supported the republic and accepted cabinet posts in center-left coalition governments. The moderate, non-monarchist Catholics were initially disorganized, but they too supported the republic at first.

The two most controversial issues facing the Constituent Cortes, which threatened to tear the nation apart, were the separation of church and state and agrarian reform.

Moderate Catholics might have accepted a benign separation of church and state, such as in the United States; but the leading republicans, particularly Manuel Azaña Diaz who swayed the Cortes on this issue, were extremely anticlerical. Article 26 of the new constitution ended all state subsidies to the church (such subsidies had been granted as compensation for the seizure of church lands in the nineteenth century) over a two-year period, forbade outdoor religious processions, banned religious orders from teaching, closed all *conventos*[2] (houses of religious orders) and completely dissolved any religious order that took an additional vow besides poverty, chastity, and obedience. This last provision applied only to the Society of Jesus (Jesuits) who adopted a fourth vow of complete obedience to the pope. Anticlericals particularly resented the Jesuits since they had long cultivated the "movers and shakers," the wealthy and influential. They and other religious orders dominated secondary school education in Spain, intending to train the elite in Catholic values.

The anticlerical attack on the Catholic Church marked the first tragic decision of the Spanish republican politicians. A more moderate measure of disestablishment might have retained the loyalty of many Catholics, but the bitterness of the republicans towards the church blinded them.

Manuel Azaña, who became prime minister shortly after Article 26 passed, had been born in 1880 in Alcala de Henares, hometown of Cervantes, the author of *Don Quixote*. An outstanding member of the generation of '98, he worked as a writer and journalist and became president of the Madrid literary club, the *Ateneo*. Another member of the same intellectual generation, Salvador de Madariaga y Rojo, described Azaña as "a Castilian tree, rather solitary, deep-rooted, rough-barked, many-branched. . . . But no birds."

Azaña had been educated in a secondary school conducted by the Augustinian religious order, and in 1927 he published a nasty little book called *El jardin de los frailes* (The Garden of the Monks), in which he poured out his bitterness at his former teachers. Then in 1931, while discussing the constitution, he proclaimed categorically that "Spain has ceased to be Catholic" and that banning the clergy from education was a matter of "public mental health." This fatal flaw produced the first tragic mistake of the Spanish Republic. Catholics who might have supported the new regime were alienated, and those who would have rejected it anyway could now justify their conduct by claiming to defend religion.

The republican politicians compounded their problems by failing to bring about land reform. The depression had destroyed markets for Spanish agriculture and had cut off the safety valve of emigration, driving landless farm laborers to the brink of starvation. The Socialist party, previously limited to city workers, expanded its membership among these farm laborers, particularly in Andalusia. Only the confiscation of large landed estates and their division into individual peasant plots or communal village farms would satisfy them. After long debates, the Cortes passed an agrarian law in the summer of 1932, setting up the Institute

---

2. In Spain, the residences of both male and female religious orders were called *conventos*.

of Agrarian Reform to study the land question and decide which estates to expropriate; but it worked at a snail's pace and accomplished little. The republican government had alienated the landowners without satisfying the landless peasants, its second tragic mistake.

In the national elections of November 1933 a new Catholic party campaigned vigorously against the excesses of Azaña's government. José Maria Gil Robles y Quiñunas had organized the *Confederacion Espanola de Derechas Autonomas* (Spanish Confederation of Autonomous Right Wing Parties), usually known by its acronym of CEDA, on March 4, 1933. Gil Robles and his intellectual adviser, Angel Herrera Oria, editor of the Catholic daily newspaper, *El Debate*, considered themselves "Social Catholics," that is, advocates of the social encyclicals written by Popes Leo XIII and Pius XI. Pius's 1931 encyclical, *Quadragesimo Anno*, had rejected both socialism and unbridled capitalism and tried to mark out a "third way." This quest for a third way dominated the intellectual history of the thirties, for the Great Depression rendered capitalism a failure and socialism a threat. Both Keynes in England and Mussolini in Italy were also exploring alternatives in political economy.

The papal social ideas resembled Mussolini's more than those of Keynes. Pius rejected individualism as the basis of society and called for a social order composed of "vocational groups." Thus, businessmen, manual workers, farmers, intellectuals and other vocational groups would organize in their own interest and negotiate with other groups, or "corporations." The government would represent these corporations rather than individual voters. Mussolini and the fascists also aimed to replace liberal democracy with a "corporate state," but what distinguished the Catholic vision from fascism was the papal "principle of subsidiarity." Subsidiarity means that higher forms of government should not do anything that lower forms of government or social organization can accomplish for themselves. It is essentially a principle of federalism and decentralization, the exact opposite of Mussolini's all-embracing state.

In the United States, liberal Catholics welcomed the papal encylicals' support for labor unions and a living wage, but few understood the political economy the popes were advocating, for the democratic system of "one man-one vote" was firmly established. In a Catholic country such as Spain, however, the papal ideas became the ideology of a political party, the CEDA, which aimed at transforming the system of government.

Gil Robles pursued a policy of "accidentalism." The term comes straight from the medieval philosophy of St. Thomas Aquinas. According to Aquinas, all matter is composed of "substance," the essence of a thing, and "accidents," the outward appearances. In the most famous application of this theory, he reasoned that the substance of the Holy Eucharist was the body and blood of Christ while its accidents remained the appearances of bread and wine. To use a modern scientific example of the same idea, we could say that H_2O (two molecules of hydrogen bonded with one molecule of oxygen) remains the substance of water, even when its accidents change from liquid to solid ice or to steam.

In Spanish politics, this Catholic philosophical idea of accidentalism meant that the CEDA considered forms of government, such as monarchy, a republic, or a dictatorship, mere appearances, accidents, relatively unimportant matters. Since Spain was currently a republic, they would work within it, but they might eventually change the form of government, depending on circumstances. What they cared about was the substance of legislative policy, specifically, repeal of anticlerical laws, resistance to land confiscation and socialism, passage of milder labor and agricultural reforms for the workers, and in the long run the formation of vocational groupings to reorganize society.

Though the socialists were "accidentalists" in their own right, adhering to the bourgeois republic for the moment but aiming at a socialist state in the long run, they mistrusted Gil Robles and considered the CEDA merely a front for landowning interests, monarchists, and fascists. They had good reasons for their fears. Large landowners dominated the CEDA, and Gil Robles had a hard time convincing them to back any reforms in favor of their laborers. Furthermore, many CEDA backers were really monarchists in disguise; and José Antonio Primo de Rivera y Sáenz de Heredia, the intellectual son of the former dictator, had recently founded an authentically fascist organization, the Falange, and was openly courting Catholic votes. Gil Robles himself, though he firmly rejected violence, mimicked some of the more outlandish mannerisms of Mussolini; and his youthful followers chanted *Jefé! Jefé! Jefé!* (Chief! Chief! Chief!) at his rallies.

The right won an astounding electoral victory in 1933. The center-left coalition that had supported Azaña's government elected only 99 deputies (58 of them socialists) to the 470-seat Cortes, whereas the right and the center-right elected the rest. The CEDA formed the largest single party, with 110 deputies, but was far from a majority. In fact, the popular support of the left and the right were fairly evenly balanced. What made the difference in 1933 was the abstention of the anarchists, who actively discouraged their followers from voting and thus ensured a right-wing victory.

CEDA did not organize the government in 1933 but backed a coalition of conservative republicans led by Alejandro Lerroux Garcia, a reputedly corrupt politician. This center-right coalition repealed most of the anticlerical legislation and let the workers' and peasants' reforms of the previous government lapse. It did not, however, substitute any reforms of its own, a third tragic flaw, alienating moderate, centrist voters.

In October 1934 a government reorganization brought three members of CEDA into the cabinet. The entire left — anarchists, socialists, Catalan separatists, even left republicans — reacted belligerently. A group of separatists in Barcelona, with anarchist support, declared Catalonia independent, the socialists declared a general strike in Madrid, and the coal miners of Asturias in northern Spain seized control of the main towns of their region. This seeming overreaction to a government reshuffle owed its vehemence to events elsewhere in Europe. Socialists had watched in horror as Hitler eliminated their German comrades in 1933, and now in 1934 a Catholic premier in Austria, Engelbert Dollfuss, had also repressed the socialists. In the polarized atmosphere of Spain and Europe, Gil Robles seemed another Dollfuss, if not another Hitler.

The government easily put down the Barcelona and Madrid risings, but the tough Asturias miners, using dynamite instead of artillery, held out for two weeks. Finally, General Francisco Franco Bahamonde brought in the Foreign Legion and a Moorish regiment from Spain's North African colony of Morocco to crush the miners. The use of Moorish soldiers in Asturias, one of the few regions of Spain that had never been ruled by the Moslems in previous centuries, shocked public opinion. From this point on, October 1934, polarization between left and right in Spain was nearly complete and civil war seemingly inevitable.

Yet two more years of politics unrolled. A series of financial scandals disgraced Lerroux's government in October 1935; Gil Robles assumed that he and the CEDA would then take over, but the president of the republic did not ask him to form a government, calling new elections instead. Verbal abuse between the socialist Largo Caballero, who had begun calling himself the "Spanish Lenin," and Gil Robles dominated the election campaign of February 1936. All the left-wing parties, including the socialists, the small communist party, and several left republican parties, formed the Popular Front to resist the CEDA. The anarchists did not formally join the Popular Front but fewer abstained from voting than in 1933, and this made the difference. The Popular Front won an overwhelming victory, electing 278 deputies. Actually, the right also picked up votes in this election, but the center was wiped out. The Popular Front polled 4,176,156 votes in February 1936 to 3,783,601 for the right-wing parties. The country was almost evenly divided and rapidly falling apart.

One slim hope remained that politics might yet triumph over violence. In May 1936, the Cortes elected Manuel Azaña president of the republic, a largely ceremonial post that suited him well as the living emodiment of the constitution. He invited Indalecio Prieto, the most moderate and able of the socialist leaders, to serve as prime minister. Possibly, Azaña and Prieto, who feared the coming violence, might have fashioned a grand coalition of moderate left, center, and moderate right to save the republic. But Prieto's rival in the socialist party, Largo Caballero, vetoed his candidacy, and a weak caretaker government was fashioned instead. This was the final tragic mistake that fated the Spanish Republic. Salvador de Madariaga concluded: "What made the Spanish Civil War inevitable was the civil war within the Socialist Party."

The Spanish Republic perished for lack of republicans who backed it wholeheartedly. Anarchists, monarchists, and fascists rejected the republic completely, but the government always controlled enough force and popular support to repress them. The socialists and the Catholics both played politics within the republican framework, but neither considered a republic their ideal form of government. Both deemed it provisional, temporary, "accidental." The socialist leaders, victorious in the Popular Front elections of 1936, continued backing the republic to the very end, but the Catholics did not. After the 1936 elections, Gil Robles rapidly lost influence and many of his followers joined a military conspiracy against the Popular Front government.

By the middle of 1936 Spain's leading generals were ready to assume their traditional role as the final arbiters in politics and to "pronounce" against the republic. General Emilio Mola Vidal headed the conspiracy, with General Sanjurjo, leader of the earlier unsuccessful coup, backing it from exile in Portugal. General Franco, who was banished to a remote outpost in the Canary Islands by the Popular Front government, kept abreast of their plans.

A violent incident in Madrid precipitated the rising. The fascist Falange, still a fringe group, assassinated a lieutenant in the elite Assault Guards at the capital on July 12, 1936. The guards ran amok, kidnapping and murdering José Calvo Sotelo, an extreme right-wing politician, in the early morning hours of July 13. This "Spanish Sarajevo" gave the military conspirators the excuse they needed. On July 17 a garrison of troops at Melilla in Morocco rebelled against the government. General Mola issued a proclamation calling on all the army units in Spain to renounce allegiance to the republic. A British airplane, a Dragon Rapide, rented by the conspirators, ferried General Franco from the Canaries to North Africa on July 18 and 19, where he assumed command of the Foreign Legion and the Moorish regiments.

On the first two days of the uprising, July 17 and 18, 1936, both sides missed opportunities to strike a decisive blow. Not all the army garrisons rose simultaneously. Had they done so they might have quelled all opposition before it could get organized. On the other side, the government of the republic, fearful of its own supporters, refused to arm the populace. Had they taken this measure immediately, the militants of the socialist and anarchist trade unions might have overwhelmed the rebel garrisons. The government in Madrid finally decided to release arms to the people on July 19, but by this time the revolt was well underway. As a result, the military uprising succeeded in roughly half the country, drawing a line through the center of Spain from northeast to southwest.

Nearly all of Spain to the south and east of this line, including the large cities of Madrid and Barcelona and the turbulent agrarian districts of Andalusia, remained republican, fiercely defended by their working-class populations. The more prosperous and traditionally Catholic agricultural districts to the north

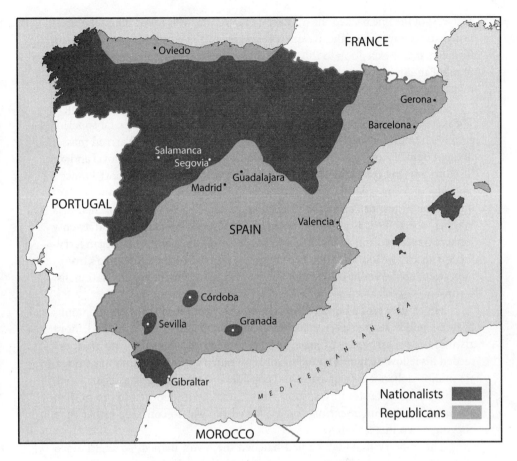

The Division of Spain in July 1936

and west of the line backed the military conspirators, who called themselves Nationalists. Asturias and the Basque provinces on the northern coast of Spain formed a major exception to this north-south division by remaining loyal to the republican government, even though they were physically separated from the main body of the republic.[3]

Very early in the war, foreign intervention proved decisive in prolonging it. The Nationalist rebels included most of the officers and commanded far superior equipment, but they lacked sufficient manpower to overcome the armed masses of the republic. Furthermore, the small Spanish navy had remained loyal and refused to join the rebellion; therefore the generals could not transport Franco's columns in Morocco, their best troops, to the mainland. Franco, however, requested air transport from the German government. Hitler, approached at a Wagner opera festival in Bayreuth, decided almost casually to send twenty Junkers transports and a half-dozen fighter escorts. On July 29 they began ferrying Spanish and Moorish soldiers across the Straits of Gibraltar. Franco's troops then swept up the western edge of Spain, greatly enlarging the area of Nationalist control.

Hitler later sent a battalion of fighters, bombers, and tanks, the infamous Legion Condor, named after the wide-winged South American bird, and about 215 million dollars worth of arms and equipment. Mussolini, for his part, exceeded his fellow dictator's contributions to Franco with 72,000 infantry troops, 354 million dollars worth of arms, and considerable air and naval assistance. Yet, the first Nazi assistance, air transport from Africa, proved more important than any other foreign intervention, for it allowed the war to continue rather than bogging down in a stalemate.

The military junta which had hatched the revolt named General Franco "Generalissimo of the National Forces" and "Head of State" of a new Spanish government on October 1, 1936, at the city of Burgos in northern Spain. Franco had not been the original leader of the revolt, but he was an obvious choice. General Sanjurjo was killed at the very beginning of the uprising when the plane bringing him home from exile in Portugal crashed on takeoff. Franco outranked Mola and the remaining rebel generals. He had earned fame fighting Moslems in Morocco during the early years of his career and had served as both chief of the general staff and director of the military academy during the republic.

3. The Asturias mining region had long been a socialist stronghold, but the adherence of the Basques to the republican cause seems curious at first sight, for the Basques were the most fiercely traditional Catholics in Spain. However, they also desired greater linguistic and cultural autonomy and the right wing Catholic parties, such as the CEDA, had been unwilling to grant this, whereas the republican parties passed statutes of autonomy for both the Basque and Catalan provinces. Therefore, both minorities, Basques and Catalans, defended the republic, even though one was Catholic and the other secularist.

Born in 1892 at El Ferrol, in the extreme northwestern corner of Spain, Francisco Franco was a cautious soldier, more a leader of men than a brilliant strategist. He was a believing Catholic and nursed an obsessive fear of communism, but he had been largely apolitical most of his life. Though he adopted the Falange as the only legal political party in Nationalist Spain, he was not an authentic fascist. He admired Mussolini and adopted some superficial fascist trappings; but he was ill-suited to demagogy or charismatic leadership, for he was excessively short and fat with a weak, high-pitched voice. Like Primo de Rivera, or Chiang Kai-Shek in China, his deepest values were those of the barracks and the military academy. His political goals were limited to restoring order, suppressing communist revolution, and protecting religion.

Hitler and Mussolini supported Franco for opportunistic reasons. They wished to stir up trouble for France by promoting turmoil in France's southern neighbor, and they enjoyed posing as defenders of order against communism. They hoped to gain some diplomatic, economic, or propaganda advantages from the civil war, but neither considered Franco an ideological soul mate or expected Spain to become a thoroughly fascist state. The German ambassador to the Nationalists sized up Franco perfectly when he called him a "clerical reactionary." Hitler himself later summed up his policy in Spain: "Our interest lay in a continuation of the war and in keeping up the tension in the Mediterranean."

In the closing months of 1936 and the beginning days of 1937, Franco's troops laid siege to Madrid, hoping to end the war by capturing the Spanish capital. Foreign intervention again proved decisive, but this time on the other side, and the Nationalist assault fell short.

Socialist trade union militias had taken the lead in the defense of Madrid, and their anarchist counterparts played the same role in Barcelona and throughout Catalonia. The Communist Party of Spain was tiny and without influence before the war broke out. So despite Franco's obsession with the red peril, the Spanish Republic had in no sense been dominated by communists before the civil war. However, communist influence increased astronomically after the war started. The republican government had been reluctant to arm the workers of Madrid in July 1936 because they knew that such a move by the Russian Kerensky in August 1917 had led to a Bolshevik takeover. Much the same thing happened in Spain, primarily because Soviet Russia proved to be the only reliable source of arms and assistance available to the republic.

The major powers of Europe had declared a policy of non-intervention as soon as the war broke out, forming the Non-Intervention Committee to enforce arms embargoes against both sides. This was a sensible policy since the issues in Spain seemed obscure and no one wished to see the civil conflict spread into a new world war. Yet when Italy and Germany flouted the non-intervention edicts, Soviet Russia followed suit.

A Russian military entourage arrived in Madrid at the end of August 1936, and eventually Stalin provided about 400 million dollars in arms and equipment, more than either the German or Italian aid to Franco but less than their combined total. The Comintern, or Communist International, recruited volunteers to serve in International Brigades for the defense of the Spanish Republic. The first volunteers came mainly from exiled German and Italian socialists and communists, driven from their homelands by the dictators. One Italian volunteer summed up his own motivation succinctly: *Oggi in Spagna, domani in Italia* ("Today in Spain, tomorrow in Italy"). Later recruits poured in from France, governed at the time by a Popular Front government of its own, and from the United States, Great Britain, and Canada. Altogether about 40,000 foreigners served in the International Brigades. The North American volunteers were more naive than the Europeans, believing they were defending democracy and sometimes unaware of the communist sponsorship of the brigades.

The first International Brigade arrived in Madrid on November 8, 1936, just in time to blunt the attack of Franco's columns at the western edge of the city. The republican government had fled to safety in Valencia two days previously, and the city was defended by a communist-dominated junta that used the International Brigades as shock troops. The Spanish communist Dolores Ibarruri, nicknamed *La Pasionara,* inspired the volunteers with her slogan, *¡No pasarán!,* a Spanish translation of *Ils ne passeront pas* ("They shall not pass"), which the French used at Verdun during the First World War. Like the defenders of Verdun, excessive numbers of Internationals (30-40 percent) paid with their lives; but Franco never did capture Madrid, which remained in republican hands until the final surrender in 1939.

After the failure of the Madrid offensive, the struggle became a war of attrition as Franco systematically conquered region after region of Spain. His troops captured all the north coastal areas, Asturias and the Basque provinces, during 1937. In the midst of this campaign, Germany's Condor Legion bombed the ancient Basque capital of Guernica on April 26, 1937. Incendiary bombs ignited the wooden houses of the town, sowing panic among the populace, one of the earliest examples of terror bombing by aircraft. Pablo Picasso's famous painting of this attack, with its fractured human and animal torsoes, symbolizes the horror of this war, or of any war in this terrible century.

The Spanish Republic still held Madrid, Barcelona, and much of the south in 1938, but Barcelona suffered systematic bombing raids more deadly than the famed Guernica attack. The Nationalists drove southeast towards the Mediterranean in the summer of 1938, capturing Valencia at the end of July, thus cutting the remaining Republican territory in two. A final offensive swept through Catalonia with the Nationalists reaching Barcelona in January 1939. About 300,000 refugees streamed across the border into France. The communists wanted to fight on in

Madrid, but republican army officers began negotiations with Franco, and the city surrendered on April 1, 1939, ending the struggle.

It served the propaganda purposes of both sides to trumpet a final toll of "one million dead." The likely casualty figures are less than this, but still horrendous. Hugh Thomas, who has written the most comprehensive history of the struggle, estimates that battle deaths, civilian casualties, and political executions on both sides totaled 400,000.

The dictatorship of Francisco Franco arrested Spanish political development for the next forty years. The regime imprisoned over 300,000 opponents in the years immediately after the civil war, and at least 10 percent of these were shot. Franco did permit a group of technocrats to loosen up the economy in the 1950s and 60s, bringing Spain into the booming free market of Europe; but he firmly suppressed all political debate or opposition until his death in 1975. Though calling himself a Nationalist, Franco enjoyed support initially from only the wealthy and religious faithful. Over the decades of his rule, however, the economic prosperity fostered by his regime earned him grudging acceptance from large numbers of Spaniards. By the time of his death, his regime had brutally but effectively consolidated Spanish national unity, and post-Franco Spain has remained a largely prosperous and peaceful national state, with moderate socialist governments.

Franco long outlived the two dictators who aided him during the civil war. Hitler gained some economic and military benefits from his assistance to the Nationalists. Spanish wool and hides clothed and shod the rearming German military in the 1930s; and the Germans signed long-term contracts granting them access to iron ore, copper, and more exotic minerals vital to their chemical and armaments industries. By the end of the civil war, Germany had become Spain's most important trading partner, taking 50 percent of Spanish exports. Hitler's generals also learned some valuable military lessons from the fighting in Spain. In particular, they observed the effectiveness of concentrated tank formations coordinated with massive aerial bombing, the basis of the famous Blitzkrieg.

Still, Hitler never made a massive commitment of troops in Spain, and he did not expect much in return. Franco declared Spain neutral in World War II, and neither side pressed him too hard to reconsider, for the country was exhausted and far from the main theaters of battle. Franco did send a division of Spanish volunteers to fight alongside the Germans on the Russian front and continued to trade important minerals to Germany, but these contributions did not prove vital to the Nazi war machine.

Neither Mussolini nor Stalin gained much for their efforts in Spain. Stalin, of course, assisted the losing side, and he was preoccupied much of the time with staging purge trials in Moscow. Some of the communists who fought most heroically for the Spanish Republic were killed when they returned to Russia. The Italians made the largest contribution in men and materials but received virtually no payback. The economies of Spain and Italy were too similar for much mutual trade to develop, for each needed what the other lacked. The Italian military learned few lessons from its performance in Spain and did not even replace or upgrade all the equipment it lost in that struggle.

Probably the greatest losers of the Spanish civil war were the anarchists, who had done much to provoke the conflict and played a major role in its battles. Anarchism had come to Spain at an early date, even before Marxist socialism, and had put down deep roots. In October 1868, the Italian Giuseppe Fanelli, a tall, bearded disciple of Mikhail Bakunin, arrived in Spain. According to legend, Fanelli spoke not a word of Spanish but his flashing eyes and flamboyant gestures conveyed his ideas to the entranced workers of Madrid and Barcelona. This story sounds highly embellished, but it does illustrate an important point: anarchism suited Spain well.

The decentralization of Spanish society, its "invertebrate" quality, matched the anarchist ideal of self-governing communes. Indeed, in the isolated backwaters of rural Andalusia whole villages caught the anarchist spirit; every strike became a general strike, as even craftsmen and shopkeepers supported the farm laborers. Robin Hood-type bandits had long roamed the rural districts, so it took only a short leap to convert such banditry into "propaganda by the deed." Finally, the condition of peasants and workers remained more desperate in Spain than in any other country of Europe. Barcelona became an anarchist stronghold because the country people from Murcia, Aragon, and Andalusia, who streamed into the city looking for work, were the wretched of the earth. Prosperous Catalans referred to these desperate migrants with the demeaning epithet "Murcianos."

Anarchists rocked Barcelona with a series of spectacular bombings during the 1890s; then in July 1909, a general strike to protest the call-up of military reserves for a colonial venture in North Africa swiftly turned into an orgy of rioting, known ever after as Tragic Week. Actually, anarchists played only a small role in the events of Tragic Week for socialist labor unions and demagogic politicians had taken the lead. Yet the anarchist reputation for violence was so widespread that most of those arrested were anarchists, including Francisco Ferrer y Guardia, who had organized a string of secular schools in Catalonia. Ferrer's execution became a cause-célèbre throughout Europe.

The aftermath of Tragic Week impelled leading anarchists to move away from individual violence and to organize their own trade union, the *Confederacion Nacional del Trabajo* (National Confederation of Work), in October 1910. The CNT pursued a syndicalist policy, working not for incremental gains, but for a social revolution, with the trade union, not the political party, in the vanguard. It employed few paid secretaries, accumulated no strike funds, and counted on the daring and dedication of its members to escalate any strike into a general strike. Not all anarchists, however, became syndicalists, and the strain of individual violence remained strong. The most militant of the anarchists, who mistrusted the CNT's tendency to collaborate with other unions, formed their own organization, the *Federacion Anarquista Iberica* in Valencia in 1927. Both CNT and FAI employed a distinctive anarchist flag, with black and red triangles separated diagonally — black for the poor's misery and red for revolution.

The class warfare of the immediate post-World War I years radicalized a young socialist, Buenaventura Durruti, and transformed him into the leading anarchist militant in Spain. Durruti had been born in 1896 in the central Spanish region of Leon. On the run after a violent strike at the Rio Tinto copper mines in 1918, Durruti met a number of anarchists, including Francisco Ascaso, who became his closest friend. These two formed an anarchist action group called the "Solidarios" that roamed Spain assassinating politicians, robbing banks, and attacking trains. Durruti and Ascaso slipped over the border into France during Primo de Rivera's dictatorship; and while they lived in Paris, the exiled Ukrainian anarchist, Nestor Makhno, tutored them in the strategy and tactics of partisan warfare.

Durruti and Ascaso then wandered through Latin America and Europe until the dictatorship ended, robbing and plundering to support themselves and their movement. They lived a freewheeling, Butch Cassidy and Sundance Kid existence; nevertheless, they were serious revolutionaries. When the civil war broke out in 1936, they and other anarchists daringly attacked the barracks of Barcelona on July 18 and 19, forcing the surrender of the military the next day and delivering the city over to the Anti-Fascist Militia Committee. Ascaso was killed in the street battles of July 19, but Durruti survived to lead the anarchist militias on the Aragon front for the rest of 1936.

In the early months of the civil war, Catalonia and its neighboring region of Aragon became anarchist commonwealths. Anarchists had always felt more comfortable in separatist, freedom-loving Catalonia whereas centralizing Castile proved more congenial to authoritarian Marxists. Workers' councils took over Barcelona's industries, and control patrols replaced police on the streets, dispensing revolutionary justice. In the countryside, villagers seized the landed estates and operated them as communes. Three-quarters of the farmland in Aragon and about half that in Catalonia became peoples' collectives. The militia which held the Aragon front between Barcelona and Saragossa organized itself along libertarian lines. Soldiers elected their own officers and sent delegates to the Council of Workers and Soldiers to plan strategy. Durruti led these militias through bravery and charisma, not rank.

Anarchist control of Catalonia and Aragon, however, posed sharp dilemmas. The communists and socialists in Madrid, who controlled the flow of weapons from Russia, starved the anarchists for supplies and urged them to organize in more centralized, orthodox military fashion. In September 1936, the socialist Largo Caballero invited the anarchists to join his Popular Front government. They refused at first, but they had already begun to rationalize that Spanish revolutionary bodies formed a "de-politicized" government. They substituted the word "committee" for "bureau" or "government agency" whenever possible. Finally, on November 4, 1936, the merged CNT/FAI accepted four cabinet posts in the republic, the first and only time that anarchists had participated in a national government. Juan Garcia Oliver, an old associate of Durruti, became minister of justice and Federica Montseny, a feminist journalist, took over the Health Ministry, the first female cabinet officer in Spanish history.

Anarchist influence, however, swiftly waned as the war dragged on. The Popular Front transferred Durruti to the Madrid front on November 7, 1936, and two weeks later he was killed by a sniper's bullet. Many anarchists believed the communists had murdered him, but no conclusive evidence has been discovered. In any case, his passing removed the most dynamic of the anarchist leaders. Thereafter, the government sytematically integrated the anarchist militias into a disciplined, centralized, communist-dominated army. Though this increased efficiency in an orthodox military sense, it foreclosed the option of guerrilla warfare and diminished morale.

Then in the first week of May 1937, government troops tried to oust the CNT from its control of Barcelona's central telephone exchange. The anarchists resisted and a new week of street fighting ensued. In the aftermath, the anarchists were disarmed, and the communists, socialists, and authoritarian republicans took total control of the republic. The anarchists' dreams of voluntary, self-governing institutions were killed not by Franco's Nationalists but by their Marxist comrades. Catalonia in 1936-37 marked the last stand for international anarchism. Never again in the twentieth century did it step forward as a dynamic movement.

Perhaps the most distinctive aspect of Spanish anarchism, throughout its seventy-year history, was its extreme anticlericalism and hatred of religion. Anarchists everywhere, of course, rejected the church as they rejected property and government, but Spanish anarchists were unusually incendiary, in the literal sense of that word. Spanish anarchists burned churches.

During Tragic Week of 1909, twelve churches and forty *conventos* of Barcelona went up in flames. Shortly after the republic was proclaimed, on May 11 and 12, 1931, bands of workers torched eleven religious buildings in Madrid, forty-one in Malaga, twenty-one in Valencia, and thirty-four more in other cities and towns. Few priests or nuns were killed during these two outbreaks of incendiarism; the mobs attacked convents as symbols of the established order, as "Bastilles" of the working class. Yet, when the miners of Asturias rose up in October 1934, they murdered 34 priests, brothers, and seminarians.

The early days of the civil war witnessed a savage attack against the Catholic Church. In all, 4,184 diocesan priests and 2,365 religious order priests were killed. This represented about 25 percent of all the male clergy living in republic-controlled territory. Though 283 nuns were also murdered, apparently few if any were raped. Anarchist "uncontrollables" were responsible for most of the church burnings and killings. Their anticlerical fury was fueled by indignation, ignorance, inertia, and idealism.

All over Europe in the nineteenth century, the Catholic Church lost touch with the working class as it relied on the wealthy for its support. In Spain, although most priests and nuns came from the lower-middle class, they identified with those above them on the social scale rather than those below. While workers and their families benefited from church-sponsored education and charity, they resented the priests and nuns and grew increasingly indignant at their condescending attitudes.

A remarkable ignorance also marked the anarchist anticlericals. Rumors of fabulous church wealth circulated widely, often repeated by demagogic politicians trying to divert lower-class wrath away from themselves. Workers showed a morbid fascination with the penitential practices of nuns and monks, believing that they tortured unfortunate women or children who fell into their clutches. Such fantastic stories had been common for centuries in Protestant countries, such as England and the United States, but their currency in Spain illustrates how alienated from religion the masses had become. They could no longer separate fact from fiction.

Church-burning also owed its frequency to a kind of inertia. Whenever trouble broke out in Spain, it had become traditional to burn churches, just as looting stores became a commonplace during American race riots later in the century. This traditional practice also provided protection and cover to the workers. If they were seen dancing around a church inferno, they would not be suspected of fascist or pro-Franco sentiments.

Finally, the anarchists approached the burning of churches with a strange idealistic, even spiritual, motivation. Gerald Brenan has suggested that Spanish anarchism was a belated form of Protestant revolt against the corruption of the Catholic Church. Spain had missed the original Protestant Reformation, but the anarchists, with their idealistic belief in human freedom, made up for it in the nineteenth and twentieth centuries. Brenan writes that church burning "can only, I think, be explained as the hatred of heretics for the Church from which they have sprung." A contemporary Catalan Catholic, Maurici Serrahima, agreed: "I have always maintained that, deep down, these burnings were an act of faith. That's to say an act of protest because the church was not, in the people's eyes, what it should be." Anarchists everywhere were moralists, concerned with the rightness or wrongness of human acts; but Spanish anarchists were more spiritually motivated than most. Spanish philosopher Miguel de Unamuno Jugo summed it up succinctly: "Here in Spain, we are all Catholics, even the atheists."

In the final analysis, the Spanish civil war was a war of religion. Even the Moorish legions wore Sacred Heart badges as talismans; and behind Franco's lines, the Nationalists executed as many as the anarchists did on the republican side. The hierarchy of the Catholic Church did not acknowledge or speak out against this until long afterwards, in 1971. The Spanish conflict of the 1930s was a religious tragedy, in which followers of different creeds, Catholics on one side, anarchists and Marxists on the other, went into battle blinded by bitterness and hate.

PART FIVE

THE SECOND
WORLD CATASTROPHE

The First World War began within a short space of time in the summer of 1914. A flurry of diplomatic activity at the European chancelleries in July, then the clockwork maneuvers of Europe's mobilized mass armies in August precipitated the conflict. By the end of August 1914 most of the major countries of the world found themselves at war. World War II, however, broke out in fits and starts at widely scattered points around the globe over a long period of time. A number of dates could qualify for the beginning of the second world catastrophe.

As early as 1931 in East Asia Japan had attacked China; within less than a year, the Japanese occupied all three provinces of Manchuria. On July 7, 1937, an incident at the Marco Polo Bridge near Peking escalated into a full-scale East Asian war, which raged for eight years.

Meanwhile, in a Europe whose civilization had jumped the tracks, the totalitarian dictators, Mussolini, Hitler, and Stalin, stocked their arsenals with new weapons. In 1938 and 1939, the German führer, Adolf Hitler, executed a series of step-by-step annexations in Central Europe through a policy of bluffs and threats. Then on September 1, 1939, he sent his armies crashing into Poland, subduing that country in less than a month. After a fearful period of waiting in the winter of 1939-40, Hitler then turned his armies westward, attacking and subduing Norway in April 1940 and totally defeating France within six weeks in May and June 1940. Mussolini's Italy jumped in at the very end of the attack on France. Hitler's air force bombarded England from the summer of 1940 onward but his army and navy never invaded the British Isles. Instead, the Germans attacked Soviet Russia in June 1941, turning a series of regional wars into a general European conflict.

Hostilities in Europe created a power vacuum in Asia that Japan determined to fill. At the end of 1941 Japanese naval airplanes launched a sneak attack on the American base at Pearl Harbor, securing the flanks for an invasion of Southeast Asia. The already existing East Asian war merged into an all-out Pacific War.

The conventional date for the beginning of World War II is September 1, 1939, when Hitler invaded Poland. However, in Asia fighting had commenced in 1931, and Hitler had been conducting a cold war of nerves at least since 1935 in Europe. The two struggles merged into a world war in 1941.

CHAPTER TWENTY

Incidents and Accidents in East Asia

In the early decades of the twentieth century, China and Japan, both emerging from traumatic encounters with imperialist powers, followed separate paths of national development, paths that often intersected and finally collided. Secure in its alliance with Great Britain, Japan functioned as a junior-level great power in East Asia, annexing Korea in 1910, gradually extending its influence over Manchuria, and sharing the other imperial powers' rights and privileges in China. Since Japan had emerged from its isolation in a period of intense European and American imperialism, it adopted the spirit and practice of imperialism as part of its accommodation to the modern world. China, on the other hand, remained a *victim* of imperialism. After the republican revolt that chased the Manchus off the throne in 1911, the country disintegrated into a number of feuding warlord regimes. The warlord who controlled Peking maintained the fiction of a unified Chinese Republic, but in fact the country had dissolved.

This political dissolution and the preoccupation of the European powers with the World War of 1914-18 created a vacuum in East Asia that the Japanese eagerly filled. Japanese troops, with some help from British colonial soldiers, ousted the Germans from their leasehold on the Kiaochow Peninsula in Shantung province shortly after the beginning of the war; and the imperial navy swiftly seized a number of German islands in the Pacific. Then Japan presented China with the infamous Twenty-one Demands.

On January 18, 1915, the Japanese foreign minister transmitted sixteen "demands" and five "desires," grouped into five separate categories, to the struggling government of Yuan Shih-kai in Peking. The first four categories of demands largely reiterated or extended imperialist privileges the Japanese already enjoyed. For example, the Chinese were asked to ratify the Japanese seizure of German interests in Shantung and to extend the present Japanese leasehold in Manchuria to ninety-nine years. The final group of "desires," however, proposed that "influential Japanese" be hired as political, financial, and military advisers to the Chinese government and that much of China be placed under joint Chinese-Japanese police protection. Acceptance of these provisions would have rendered China a protectorate of Japan. Chinese students and merchants protested vigorously against the Twenty-one Demands, launching the first of many boycotts against Japanese goods. Influential elder statesmen in Japan finally convinced the foreign minister to withdraw the five desires.

The immediate result of the Twenty-one Demands incident, therefore, was the inflammation of Chinese nationalism and the imparting of an anti-Japanese cast to nationalist opinion. However, the Japanese government had laid out for the first time a vague but ominous long-range vision of "co-existence and co-prosperity" in East Asia which it would pursue more vigorously in ensuing decades. The Japanese believed they were destined to replace the European and American imperialists as leaders of the region.

Chinese nationalism flared up again at the end of the First World War, when the Chinese discovered a secret treaty between the European Allies and Japan, supporting Japanese retention of Germany's economic and military privileges in Shantung. The Japanese had also bribed the weak warlord government of Tuan Ch'i-jui (Duan Qirui) in Peking to recognize their assumption of Germany's privileges. When Wilson, Lloyd George, and Clemenceau ratified these secret dealings at Versailles, students in Peking and other cities of China erupted in protest on May 4, 1919. These demonstrations imparted a new name, the May Fourth Movement, to a wide-ranging national upheaval already in progress.

The May Fourth Movement gave intellectual substance to the confused elements of revolution unleashed in China since 1911. Academics at Peking University called on all Chinese writers to adopt the simpler, vernacular language of the people rather than the stylized, literary language inherited from the empire. A magazine entitled *New Youth,* written in the new popular style, explored all manner of European liberal and radical ideas. Most of all, the May Fourth Movement severed the bonds of authority that held together the Confucian world-view — the subordination of subjects to the government, of sons to fathers, and of wives to husbands; and it attacked old customs restraining the individual, such as arranged marriages and the binding of women's feet. Unlike the Ch'ing reformers of the nineteenth century, who clung to traditional culture while adopting some European inventions, the May Fourth intellectuals rejected China's cultural past in order to liberate the nation for a more prosperous future. They denounced European imperialism, but still wished to adopt European ideas.

Amid the welter of such ideas, the writings of Marx and Lenin enjoyed new prestige due to the success of the Russian Revolution. Though the Bolsheviks imposed their own imperial grasp on the subject nationalities of the former Russian Empire, they still trumpeted the notion of anti-imperialism worldwide. At the very moment when the May Fourth Movement was flourishing in China, Lenin's government renounced the rights the Russian tsars had claimed in Manchuria and other border areas and dispatched agents of the Commmunist International to China. Under their direction, Ch'en Tu-hsiu (Chen Duxiu), the editor of *New Youth*, was elected head of the Central Committee at the founding convention of the Chinese Communist Party (CCP) in July 1921. Mao Tse-tung (Mao Zedong), born in 1893 in Hunan province, was a member of the party from the start, but did not lead it until more than a decade later.

Intellectually, adherents of the May Fourth Movement moved constantly to the left, so Marxist communism became the leading current of ideas in China. Yet politically the CCP remained small and weak and constantly subservient to the party line laid down by Stalin and the Comintern in Moscow. The immediate future of government in China belonged to less radical nationalists.

Sun Yat-sen had never ceased writing, fundraising, and organizing conspiracies, even after the failure of the 1911 revolution. He still hoped Japan might serve as a model for China and did not even protest against the Twenty-one Demands, but he eventually became disillusioned with the arrogant Japanese and looked for help elsewhere. Moving in and out of Canton and Shanghai, he tried to recruit warlords and mercenaries for his republican cause; but as late as 1922 he remained a failure.

Then in January 1923, Sun signed an agreement with Adolf Joffe, a diplomat from Soviet Russia, that marked the first international recognition of his movement. This written accord declared that China was not yet ready for communism, but individual communists might join Sun's nationalist party, the Kuomintang (Guomindang), and the Soviet Union would cooperate closely with Sun's movement for the liberation of China. The Russian Communists pursued a united front with bourgeois reformists, rather than relying on the tiny Chinese Communist Party, because they valued Sun Yat-sen's revolutionary prestige and believed they could easily dominate the disorganized Kuomintang. Yet Sun Yat-sen was no fool. As his biographer, Harold Z. Schiffrin, has stated, "nothing . . . was more characteristic of Sun's style than its fluidity; any alliance was possible and none was exclusive." Each party — the Russian Communists and the Chinese Kuomintang — hoped to use the other for its own purposes.

As it turned out, Sun's Nationalists gained the most. The Communists showed Sun how to organize a tightly controlled party apparatus and how to win mass support. They helped him establish the Whampoa Military Academy on an island in Canton harbor, under the command of Chiang Kai-shek (Jiang Jieshi), one of Sun's military disciples, and with Chou En-lai (Zhou Enlai), a young Chinese Communist, as political commissar. Sun had always been a gadfly, inspiring in speech and skilled at fundraising, but disorganized and inconsistent. Now under Soviet influence he developed his Three Principles of the People more systematically, in a series of lectures delivered between January and August 1924, and built an authoritarian party structure.

Sun Yat-sen hoped to unite the whole country under Kuomintang rule, either through force of arms or by negotiation with the warlords. On his way to Peking for crucial talks in January 1925, however, his doctors discovered inoperable liver cancer. Sun died on March 12, 1925, at the age of fifty-eight. Historian Jonathan Spence has summed up his final years: "Indigenous nationalism could now call on Soviet organizational expertise to build for meaningful political action. Perhaps this was Sun Yat-sen's true legacy."

The commandant of Whampoa Military Academy, Chiang Kai-shek, seized Sun Yat-sen's mantle by mounting a northern expedition in the summer of 1926 to unite the country militarily. Born in 1887 (a full generation later than Sun Yat-sen, but just six years before Mao Tse-Tung) in Chekiang (Zhejiang) province, Chiang[1] came from a moderately prosperous family that had marked him out for the study of law. Chiang wished to emulate the military strength of the Japanese, however, and become a professional soldier, so he studied first at a military academy near Peking then in 1907 was accepted for advanced training at the staff college in Japan. After his graduation in 1909, he served two tough years of apprenticeship as a private in the Japanese artillery.

Chiang had joined Sun Yat-sen's Revolutionary Alliance while studying in Japan. When the revolution broke out in 1911, he returned to lead the rebel forces in his home province. During the chaos of the warlord years, Chiang made money and contacts with the underworld gangs that dominated Shanghai's financial district, rejoining his hero Sun Yat-sen in 1923 when the latter asked him to command the new military academy. Whampoa's commandant studied in Moscow for several months before assuming his duties, but he did not like what he saw. Inheriting a pro-Soviet policy from Sun, he cooperated with the Communists for a time, but turned upon them at the first opportunity.

As Chiang's troops approached the central Chinese coastal city of Shanghai during the northern expedition, the Communist-organized labor unions declared a general strike. The workers then seized the city on March 21, 1927, delivering it to the Nationalist troops. Chiang arrived in Shanghai on March 27 and began recruiting his former colleagues in the so-called Green Gang for a preventive

---

1. Chiang answered to at least three different names in his lifetime. As a child, he was called Chiang Chou-tai; then upon his first, arranged marriage he assumed the name Chiang Chung-cheng. His most formal, ceremonial name was Chiang Chieh-shih. This was translated in the dialect of Canton into Chiang Kai-shek, and he always wrote his name in this form in European languages.

coup against the Communist workers. On April 12, the Society for Common Progress, an alliance of underworld and business leaders, attacked union headquarters throughout Shanghai, beating and murdering men, women, and children. The reign of terror lasted about three weeks. Then Chiang outlawed unions and strikes and shook down the business interests to raise money for the next step in the northern expedition.

A new Nationalist government now established itself, under Chiang's direction, at Nanking (Nanjing), a former imperial capital up the Yangtze (Yangzi) River from Shanghai. The left wing of the Kuomintang, which had remained faithful to the Soviet alliance, finally sent the Comintern representatives back to Moscow in July 1927 and made peace with Chiang. The remnants of the Chinese Communist Party, including Mao, went into hiding, either in Shanghai or among the peasants.

Chiang Kai-shek formed a marriage alliance that strengthened his position even further. Charles Soong had been one of the first Chinese to study in the United States, under the Ch'ing Empire, and had converted to the Methodist Church while in Massachusetts. When he returned to China he became wealthy as a comprador, or middleman, betweeen Chinese and American merchants in Shanghai. He also developed a profitable sideline printing and selling Bibles. Soong fathered three attractive and intelligent daughters who studied at Wellesley College in the United States. The eldest, Ai-ling (Friendly Life), served as secretary to Sun Yat-sen for a time then married a prominent Chinese businessman, H. H. Kung. The second daughter, Ch'ing-ling (Glorious Life), succeeded her sister as Sun's secretary and married the Kuomintang leader in 1915, even though both were Christians and Sun had not yet attained a divorce from his first wife. Madame Sun remained loyal to her husband's memory and to his pro-Soviet policy after his death, withdrawing to Moscow with the retreating Comintern agents in 1927. Later in that same year, Chiang Kai-shek married the third Soong daughter, Mei-ling (Beautiful Life).

In a second phase of the northern expedition, the Nationalists fought their way to Peking in the summer of 1928. On July 6 Chiang and his principal generals visited the tomb of Sun Yat-sen at Western Hills outside the city, ceremonially marking the fulfillment of Sun's dreams for a unified, republican China. The Nationalists retained the capital at Nanking and renamed Peking, which means "northern capital," Peiping, or "northern peace." Chiang Kai-shek had triumphed over his communist, warlord, and Kuomintang rivals because of his military skill, his ability to raise large sums of money in Shanghai, and his skillful negotiations with rival warlords. Whenever possible, he won his battles with "silver bullets," that is, bribes to induce defections from warlord armies.

The Nationalist government in Nanking from 1928 until 1937 was authoritarian but far from totalitarian. Sun Yat-sen had prescribed a three-stage progression of revolutionary government: first a period of martial law, then a "tutelary period" in which the party would educate the masses in the practices of democracy, then a final stage of full constitutional government. Chiang never got beyond the tutelary stage, and some of his followers from the military academy organized a secret society of Blueshirts, in imitation of the Italian Fascists. Yet the government remained too inefficient and lacking in a mass base to be considered truly fascist in nature.

Chiang's rule probably resembled that of Kemal Ataturk in Turkey more than it did the regimes of the totalitarian dictators. Like Ataturk, Chiang encouraged respect for the national past, prescribing the reading of Confucius and declaring that sage's birthday a national holiday. He also encouraged modernization of industry but neglected the much larger agricultural segment of the economy, just as the Turkish leader did. Above all, both Chiang and Ataturk relied heavily on the military as a power base. Chiang Kai-shek was dubbed the "super-warlord" by the Chinese press, and his ultimate model for a modern society was not fascism, nazism, or communism but the barracks discipline he had endured in the Japanese military academy.

Nationalist China during the "Nanking decade" of 1928 to 1937 enjoyed greater unity than the country had experienced in a half century. National unification marked Chiang Kai-shek's greatest, and basically his only, achievement. The country remained poor and weak, ravaged by the effects of the Great Depression, which lowered agricultural prices as it did the world over, and a series of horrendous floods and poor harvests. In the end, however, Chiang's Nationalist revolution was cut short by the increasing intrusion of Japanese ambitions on the mainland.

While China had been struggling with the chaos of revolution and civil war, strong and prosperous Japan had been undergoing its own crisis of confidence. The Meiji emperor died on July 30, 1912, and his successor, Yoshihito, who assumed the reign name of Taisho (Great Righteousness), was mentally retarded. The emperor's death held great symbolic significance, and it coincided with the passing of many elder statesmen, the *genro* who had guided Japan since the 1867 restoration. The country's society and economy also experienced new strains and challenges. The Russo-Japanese War had been financed by massive borrowing, and it took nearly a decade of retrenchment to pay this off. The population, which had remained stable during the centuries of isolation under the Tokugawa, was now growing rapidly, and the country needed to import food. Socialists agitated among the discontented urban masses, despite severe government censorship and repression.

For the first time since the Meiji Restoration, significant segments of public opinion questioned the wisdom of imitating Europe and America. Just as conservative Americans felt alienated during the economic scramble and popular lawlessness of the Roaring Twenties, many Japanese rejected the era of *ero, guro, nansensu* ("eroticism, grotesqueness, and nonsense"). Hundreds of nationalist societies sprang up to counteract corrupt foreign influences. When the Taisho emperor died on December 25, 1926, his son, Hirohito, adopted the reign name of

Showa[2] (Universal Peace). Many nationalists hoped for a Showa Restoration, that is, a conservative return to older models of morality and politics. In short, modernizing Japan was undergoing severe growing pains.

Like so many nations before, Japan sought relief from its ills in overseas expansion. The Meiji generation had exercised great restraint in its foreign policy, but as the *genro* passed away Japanese foreign policy lost its sense of limits. Imperialism, after all, represented the way of the world. The European and American powers that Japan imitated all pursued expansionist policies and engaged in sharp imperial rivalries in the early twentieth century. So in the simplest sense, there isn't much to explain about the roots of Japanese imperialism. As historian W. G. Beasley has remarked, "Japanese imperialism becomes the illegitimate child of *Western* capitalism, with international rivalry as midwife." If Japan wished to be fully modern, it had to play the game.

Yet Japanese imperialists were not just blind imitators, for elements in Japanese culture predisposed them to a policy of imperialism. The governing class of the nation were descendants of the samurai, either literally or ideologically, with a respected code of military valor. Furthermore, the Meiji reformers had fostered a more extreme form of emperor-worship than that of other Asian cultures. The Chinese, for example, revered their emperor as a representative of heaven, but did not consider him divine. The Japanese not only deemed the *tenno,* or "Heavenly Ruler," a god, but since they formed one family with him, they too shared a divine superiority over other peoples. This nourished a popular Japanese sense of mission, an Asian version of the "white man's burden."

Japanese imperialists looked to the mainland of East Asia as the obvious field for overseas expansion. Korea lay a few miles across the Straits of Tsushima and Manchuria loomed just beyond that, bordering on the Russian Empire (and later the Soviet Union). Strategic considerations, therefore, dictated control of these regions, as a defense in depth for the home islands. In the first three decades of the twentieth century, they also took on considerable economic importance, particularly as suppliers of food for the Japanese masses. Japan, therefore, formally annexed Korea in 1910 and began to build up economic interests in the Kwantung[3] Leased Territory of Manchuria, conquered from Russia in 1905. The Kwantung Army and the South Manchuria Railway corporation (which also con-

2. The emperor's given name, Hirohito, though commonly used by foreigners, was hardly even known to ordinary Japanese, who referred to him as Tenno Showa.

3. This should not be confused with the province of Kwangtung in southern China. Kwantung was an alternative name for the Liaotung Peninsula, where the battles of the Russo-Japanese War took place, and which Japan retained as a leasehold. Kwantung means "east of the barrier," that is, east of the Shanhaikuan mountain pass that connects Manchuria with China proper.

trolled important mining interests) became nearly independent forces, increasingly hard to control from Tokyo.

Japanese leaders felt uncertain of their position in the world after the First World War. New trade opportunities made the nation increasingly prosperous, and the system of international cooperation symbolized by the League of Nations held out the prospect of universal peace. The Japanese, therefore, withdrew from the Shantung leasehold in China in 1922. That same year they signed the Treaty of Washington, limiting Japanese battleships to three-fifths the tonnage allowed to Great Britain and the United States. In 1925 the size of the Japanese army was reduced by the elimination of four divisions and the retirement of about two thousand officers.

Yet a number of foreign insults rankled the Japanese. The Versailles Treaty conspicuously omitted the "racial equality" clause that Japanese diplomats had advocated. Then, in 1924 the United States passed a restrictive law completely banning immigration from Japan and China. Furthermore, Great Britain declined to renew its alliance with Japan in 1922, replacing it with the weaker Four-Power Treaty that called for consultation between Great Britain, France, the United States, and Japan. Many Japanese felt insulted and isolated in international affairs.

A sharp debate over foreign policy, therefore, raged within Japan during the 1920s. The Foreign Ministry, usually headed by Shidehara Kijuro, a former Japanese ambassador to the United States who had family ties to the Mitsubishi business conglomerate, counseled a policy of restraint in China and cooperation with the other great powers. A military faction, particularly younger officers in the Kwantung Army, favored what they called a "positive policy," that is, complete control of Manchuria, for strategic and economic reasons, and more aggressive actions in China proper. Both sides in this foreign policy debate championed a policy of imperialism in China (it was not a quarrel between "good guys" and "bad guys"). The civilian wing of the Japanese government favored informal, economic empire, whereas the military urged outright annexations. Yet neither believed that China and Japan could relate to each other as equals. Both believed Japan should guide and direct the Chinese in their efforts to modernize, avowing a vague pan-Asianism. They differed largely over means, not ends.

The success of Chiang Kai-shek in unifying China at the end of the 1920s imparted a new urgency to this Japanese policy debate. Two examples show how easy it was for incidents and accidents to break out when Chinese nationalism clashed with Japanese imperialism.

As Chiang's soldiers streamed north towards Peking in 1928, a nervous Japanese government landed troops on the Shantung Peninsula to protect Japanese nationals living there. Prime Minister Tanaka Giichi, though a general identified with the "positive policy" wing, intended this as a purely precautionary and defensive measure; but General Fukuda Hikosuke, commanding the expeditionary force, occupied the provincial capital of Tsinan (Ji'nan) on his own authority. Japanese officers prided themselves on their exercise of independent judgment in the field, believing it had given them a decisive advantage over the tsarist generals in 1905. When the Nationalists arrived in Tsinan, clashes broke out between individual soldiers and civilians, which escalated to full-scale battle. An over-eager general and a weak chain of command caused the Tsinan incident of May 1928, not a conscious policy decision.

An even more outrageous incident occurred later the same year. When the warlord, Chang Tso-lin (Zhang Zuolin), who had controlled north China for a number of years, finally evacuated Peking in the summer of 1928, the Japanese military offered him and his army safe passage to Manchuria. An impatient colonel in the Kwantung Army, Komoto Daisaku, planned to assassinate Chang, thus creating a pretext for greater Japanese control of Manchuria. On June 4, 1928, Chang's train was blown off the tracks near Mukden and the warlord died two weeks later. Yet neither the Japanese military nor the government exploited the opportunity. The Tsinan incident and the murder of Chang Tso-lin held awesome portents for the future, as they were the first instances of unilateral action by Japanese field officers, but as yet the government still restrained them.

The onset of the Great Depression, however, tipped the balance against the civilians in the Japanese government. Over a third of Japan's exports had been going to the United States, and much of the trade consisted of raw silk. The depression wiped out American demand for this luxury product and plunged the silk-making districts northeast of Tokyo into economic disaster. This increased popular discontent and greatly disturbed the younger military officers, who retained close ties to the rural districts of their origins and feared a communist upheaval there. At the same time, the depression discredited civilian politicians, such as Shidehara, with their links to big business and further damaged the prestige of the other great powers. As a result of this ferment, some junior officers hatched plots to overthrow the government and institute direct military rule. Though they didn't succeed until late in the 1930s, their attempted assassinations and conspiracies terrorized civilian politicians and made them reluctant to challenge the military. Other soldiers concentrated on building a sphere of "co-prosperity" in Manchuria and China proper. Since all the depression-wracked powers were closing in upon themselves and building regional economic blocs, the Japanese military believed they must do likewise in East Asia.

On September 18, 1931, a clique of staff officers surrounding Ishiwara Kanji and Itagaki Seishiro in the Kwantung Army blew up the rail line south of Mukden, blamed it on nearby Chinese troops, and used this excuse to seize the city. The plotters had obtained at least tacit approval from superiors in Tokyo, and when the operation was completed the government consented to aggressive

The Japanese Empire after the Manchurian Incident, 1931

measures extending Japanese control over nearly all of Manchuria. Unlike 1928, popular opinion in depression-era Japan favored the exploiting of the "Manchurian incident." The debate had largely been settled in favor of a "positive policy."

The other powers, weakened and preoccupied by the depression, did little more than protest. The League of Nations investigated the incident and voted not to recognize the Japanese occupation of Manchuria, but Japan ignored the condemnation and left the League in 1933. In the meantime, the Japanese army had convinced the last Manchu emperor of China, Pu-Yi, to serve as chief executive of a puppet state called Manchukuo, "land of the Manchus."

It is tempting to ascribe the Manchurian incident and its aftermath to an individual army unit out of control, much like the Tsinan incident of 1928. The Kwantung Army, which had enjoyed semi-independent status since the Russo-Japanese War, was taken over by junior staff officers who provoked an incident and exploited it. Yet the general staff and the army ministry in Tokyo largely shared the aims of Ishiwara and the other junior officers in the Kwantung Army. They differed over tactical matters in Manchuria, but not over fundamental policy goals. As historian Akira Iriye has pointed out, the Kwantung Army never defied or disobeyed a direct order from Tokyo during the Manchurian incident. On several occasions, they slowed or postponed their advances under orders from the General Staff. The Kwantung Army was not out of control; it was leading its more cautious superiors toward a commonly shared goal.

By 1931 the "positive policy" of the Kwantung Army enjoyed great popularity in Japan. Nationalist organizations whipped up popular emotions; and the civilian government ministers felt powerless to resist. The Meiji constitution contained an unresolved conflict over the right of military command. One article placed military operations outside civilian government control, but another article assigned responsibility for military organization to the cabinet ministers. It was never clear where military organization ended and command responsibility began, so in 1931 civilians in the cabinet, fearing assassination by fanatical nationalists, decided to leave the military alone. The last genro, or elder statesman, Prince Saionji Kimmochi, opposed the expansionist policy, but he was largely ignored. Even the emperor himself felt uneasy; but exploiting the ambiguities of the constitution, military leaders used his divine prestige to sanction policies he himself opposed. Not just the military, but the whole Meiji experiment in orderly government and controlled modernization was spinning out of control.

The Japanese militarists fiercely opposed communism, and they admired the policies of Mussolini and Hitler. Yet they represented both more and less than a fascist movement. On the one hand, they were more ultra-nationalist than any fascists, "double patriots" in the phrase of one Japanese journalist; for Japan already possessed a cohesive national identity, complete with historical myths and a divine ruler. Ordinary Japanese showed heartfelt devotion to their nation and their emperor without the need for mass manipulation such as the European fascists practiced. On the other hand, the notion of one-man rule, the leader principle, that lay at the heart of Mussolini's and Hitler's versions of fascism, seemed alien to the Japanese. They worshiped the emperor, but did not accord him any political power. The military cliques dominating Japanese politics in the 1930s remained a collective leadership, riven by intense factionalism. Imperialist Japan, therefore, possessed a cultural nationalism that European fascists could only dream of, but not the single-minded leadership of the totalitarian dictators. Policy remained confused, subject to incidents and accidents.

The Japanese militarists most closely resembled the Young Turks of the pre-war Ottoman Empire. Historian Marius B. Jansen has described them as "young enough to be unchastened by the Meiji memory of weakness, educated enough to be convinced of the need for sweeping technological and institutional change . . . [and] insular enough to be wholeheartedly committed to the doctrines of national purity and distinctiveness."

After their seizure of Manchuria, the Japanese army continually probed south of the Great Wall of China, striving to build a security buffer zone for their new conquest. The Chinese public felt thoroughly outraged and were ready to fight, but Chiang Kai-shek reacted cautiously to the Japanese incursions. He refused to recognize the puppet state of Manchukuo, but he avoided encounters with the Japanese military and even suppressed anti-Japanese demonstrations within China. Chiang wanted to complete his task of national unification by wiping out the Chinese Communists before turning full attention to the Japanese challenge. "The Japanese are like a disease of the skin," the Chinese leader instructed his impatient followers in the Kuomintang, "but the Communists are like a disease of the heart."

After Chiang's initial anti-Communist coup in 1927, the Communist leadership had gone underground in Shanghai, and still following the party line from Moscow, had tried to organize the working class clandestinely. Mao Tse-tung and many other Communist cadres, however, withdrew into mountainous regions between provinces, where governmental authority had always been weak, and built up base areas among the peasants. From time to time the Twenty-eight Bolsheviks, as the orthodox Marxist leadership in Shanghai was called, ordered him and his followers to mount suicidal attacks on the cities. By about 1930, Mao began ignoring these orders and devoted himself to organizing the peasants, an unorthodox but effective revolutionary strategy in a country as overwhelmingly rural as China. He was joined by a gifted military leader, Chu-Teh (Zhu De), who defected from Chiang's Nationalist army, and together they built a stronghold in Kiangsi (Jiangxi) province. The local peasants referred to the Kiangsi Communists as "Chu-Mao."

The Nationalist troops slowly eliminated the other Communist base areas in what Chiang Kai-shek referred to as "bandit extermination campaigns"; but Mao and Chu employed skillful guerrilla tactics, luring their enemies into traps, then performing the extermination themselves. In the fifth extermination campaign of 1933-34, however, Chiang systematically blockaded Kiangsi, preventing any food or supplies from reaching the Communists. The Nationalist leader employed over 800,000 of his best soldiers, built 1,500 miles of new roads to deploy them, and constructed 14,000 fortified blockhouses, about two-thirds of a mile apart, ringing the entire province. This resembles the strategy of General Kitchener against the Boers of South Africa, but Chiang was actually following an indigenous model, a nineteenth-century Chinese general who had suppressed a rebellion in similar fashion.

By the autumn of 1934 the Communists' prospects in Kiangsi had become hopeless, so they decided on a daring break-out and a strategic retreat. On October 16, 1934, about 80,000 men marched out of Kiangsi toward the southwest, where the blockhouse system had not yet been completed. Only the top leadership, including Mao, took their wives with them (thirty-five women in all); the other women, children, and wounded remained behind, where most were massacred by Chiang's forces.

The Chinese Communist retreat, ever after known as the Long March, lasted just over a year (370 days). The Communists trekked six thousand miles, passing over twelve mountain ranges and crossing two dozen rivers, often under fire from the pursuing Nationalist troops. According to historian Lucien Bianco, they fought "a skirmish every day and a full-dress battle every two weeks." In the midst of the march, Mao Tse-tung was elected chairman of the Revolutionary Military Council; from then on he remained the unchallenged leader of the Chinese Communists. Mao directed the marchers toward a remote base area in northwestern China, in the hills of Shensi (Shaanxi) province. In order to get there, they had to swing over a river gorge on chains, with their enemies firing from the opposite bank, survive the frigid cold of the Snowy Mountains, and inch their way across the bogs and swamps of the Grasslands on their bellies. Only 8,000-9,000 of the original 80,000 Communists arrived in Shensi on October 20, 1935.

Though reduced in numbers and isolated in a remote area, Mao's Communists took advantage of the anti-Japanese frenzy growing in China. After burrowing into caves for rest and recuperation during the winter of 1935-36, the Communists attacked Japanese troops in the neighboring province of Shansi (Shanxi). The local Chinese warlord, Chang Hsueh-liang (Zhang Xueliang), son of Chang Tso-lin, who had been assassinated by the Japanese in Manchuria, was impressed by the national valor of the Communists. So he took it upon itself to reconcile Chiang Kai-shek's Nationalists with Mao's Communists in order to present a united front against the Japanese.

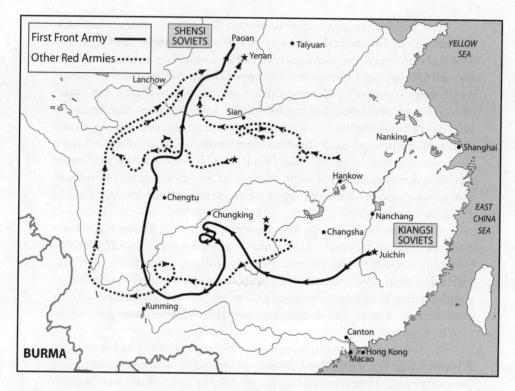

The Chinese Communists' Long March, 1934-35

Chang Hsueh-liang created an outrageous incident of his own to accomplish his united front. He invited Chiang Kai-shek to a meeting in Shensi's provincial capital of Sian (Xi'an) in December 1936, and at dawn on the twelfth his soldiers stormed Chiang's headquarters and kidnapped the general. Then he summoned the Communist Chou En-lai to negotiate with the captured Nationalist leader. Chiang courageously refused to commit himself in writing to any deals with the Communists; but eventually on Christmas Day, he offered Chang and Chou a verbal agreement to suspend the "bandit extermination campaigns" and concentrate his energies against the Japanese. Chiang flew back to Nanking and received a hero's welcome. The Sian incident proved decisive, for when the Japanese renewed their pressure against China they found the country united in resistance.

The incident that ignited full-scale war between Japan and China occurred the summer after the Sian affair. On the evening of July 7, 1937, a company from the Japanese Garrison Army, still patrolling the Peking area under the Boxer Protocol of 1900, practiced routine maneuvers near the ancient and historic Marco Polo Bridge eight miles west of Peking. It appears that the momentous events of that evening were truly an accident, not a planned provocation such as the Manchurian incident of 1931. About 10:30 P.M., Chinese troops, possibly spooked by the flares and blanks shot off by the maneuvering Japanese, fired several rounds of artillery shells into the Japanese company. No one was killed, but one soldier appeared to be missing, so the Japanese commander ordered an attack on the Chinese garrison, which the Chinese repelled. The missing soldier reappeared in the confusion twenty minutes later, but his unfortunate absence had touched off the first battle of World War II.[4]

The Marco Polo Bridge incident was inherently no more serious than numerous other local skirmishes between Chinese and Japanese troops from 1931 to 1937. This time, however, following Chiang's new policy, the Chinese fought back. Local commanders and authorities nearly settled the affair by the end of July, but Chiang realized that if the regional authorities reached an agreement with Japan, it might lead to an autonomous North China protectorate, akin to Manchukuo. So he moved several army divisions northwards to threaten the Japanese positions. The Japanese in turn poured in reinforcements and consolidated control over the entire Peking-Tientsin area.

On August 7, 1937, Chiang declared war against the Japanese invaders, and he decided to engage them not in the north, where they were entrenched, but in Shanghai where their numbers were fewer and where international observers would witness the battles. As Nationalist troops streamed into Shanghai, the Japanese navy bombarded the Chinese sector of the city, setting whole neighbor-

4. The soldier has since been identified as Private Shimura Kikujiro from Tokyo. He died fighting in Burma in 1943.

hoods ablaze. On August 13 the Japanese cabinet sent two army divisions to reinforce the navy and marines. At this point, the Marco Polo Bridge incident became the Sino-Japanese War. It raged for eight more years.

Chinese soldiers impressed the diplomats and businessmen of Shanghai's International Settlement with their valiant defense through the months of September and October 1937, but eventually they retreated up the Yangtze River to Nanking. Chiang Kai-shek's army had suffered 250,000 casualties (killed and wounded), perhaps 60 percent of their effective strength, whereas the better-equipped Japanese lost 40,000 men. The Japanese army then captured Chiang's capital of Nanking on December 13. Just as in 1900, when the expeditionary force of the imperialist powers sacked Peking after relieving the Boxers' siege of the legations, the conquering Japanese ran wild in Nanking. For the next seven weeks the soldiers killed, looted, and raped without restraint. Foreign observers estimated that 42,000 Chinese, soldiers and civilians, were murdered, and 20,000 women were sexually assaulted in the "Rape of Nanking." More recent studies present much higher numbers for both types of atrocities. One estimate suggests that 350,000 were killed in Nanking over a period of six weeks. Japanese frustration at the unexpectedly stiff Chinese resistance, which was largely responsible for the horrors in Nanking, only increased when Chiang refused to capitulate after the loss of his capital.

Chiang Kai-shek followed a strategy of "trading space for time." He retreated up the Yangtze and tried to defend the three industrial cities collectively known as Wuhan. His Communist allies, fighting under nominal command of the Nationalists as the Eighth Route Army, even secured Russian airplanes from Stalin to slow the Japanese advance. Nonetheless, Wuhan fell at the end of 1938 and Chiang retreated again, beyond the Yangtze gorges to the remote capital of Szechwan (Sichuan) province, Chungking (Chongqing). Here he regrouped his rump government in relative safety and waited for international aid, which he assumed would come eventually if the Japanese overreached themselves.

By the end of 1938, the Japanese military controlled the coastline of East Asia, the major cities of north and central China, and the roads and rail routes into the interior. Yet they could not penetrate very far into the countryside or beyond the mountain ranges of western China. The Japanese had been sucked into a quagmire in China, with thirty-four army divisions bogged down, denuding the army of reserves and ammunition. Government in the occupied territory followed the Manchukuo model of puppet states under the direction of the military. The Chinese Republic, which Chiang Kai-shek had united in the previous decade, was fragmented into ten semi-autonomous states, six of them controlled by Japan.

The outstanding feature of Japanese imperialist policy during the decade of the 1930s is its indecisiveness and lack of direction. After chasing Chiang Kai-shek westwards in 1938, the Japanese government and military proclaimed a new order in East Asia. By 1940 they settled on the term "co-prosperity sphere," which had been used as early as 1915, for the conquered areas of China. In reality, however, they were making it up as they went along. The Japanese were not pursuing consistent, long-range goals, such as those Hitler laid out in *Mein Kampf*. In the 1920s, the Chinese had published the so-called Tanaka Memorial, which purported to be a master plan of empire submitted by General Tanaka Giichi to the emperor; but historians have since proven this a forgery, concocted by Chinese patriots for propaganda purposes. Fired by ultra-nationalist sentiments, the Japanese army wanted to build a strategic and economic bloc in East Asia, but they blundered their way through its construction in a series of incidents and accidents.

The closest approach to a master plan the Japanese military ever concocted was the work of Ishiwara Kanji, one of the staff officers who planned the Manchurian incident of 1931. Ishiwara combined military history with an apocalyptic form of Japanese Buddhism to fashion a breathtaking vision of a coming final war between Japan and the United States. At the peak of his influence in 1936, Ishiwara and his associates on the General Staff planned to wage war in a series of stages: first, the elimination of Russia as a power in Asia, then the expulsion of the British from their colonial holdings, then finally all-out war against the United States. They hoped to avoid war with China through a policy of pan-Asian solidarity which would unite Japan, Manchukuo, and China against the Europeans and Americans. The ultimate goal in this scenario was world peace through the elimination of Western imperialism and its replacement by a superior, more spiritual, Asian culture, presided over by Japan's divine emperor. In order to reach the goal, Ishiwara projected a national defense state, free of party politics, with the economy totally mobilized for warfare.

Ishiwara Kanji did not convert more than a small clique of military planners to his sweeping vision, and he was removed from the General Staff in 1937 after opposing the full-scale invasion of China. He was finally retired from the army in 1941 and played no part in the war against the United States when it finally came.

The Japanese army remained divided into factions. One faction, which included Ishiwara himself, favored the use of Manchuria as a fortified bastion from which to attack the historic Russian enemy and seize large portions of Siberia and the Soviet Pacific coast. Others, however, urged a drive into China to build a pan-Asian co-prosperity sphere. The navy felt lukewarm toward each of these scenarios, wishing to expand into the islands and mainland colonies of Southeast Asia, where they could obtain supplies of oil and other strategic commodities. No firm decision was reached before 1941. In the meantime, local incidents, often engineered by impatient junior officers, drove the Japanese to war with China without much planning or foresight.

Had the Japanese halted at any point in their conquests before 1941, they probably would have avoided a world war. Manchuria, for example, had long been a sphere of special interest to Japan. When the Kwantung Army seized it in 1931, the international community protested but did nothing. In fact, if the Japanese had used Manchuria as a base to attack the Russian Communists, the other major powers would probably have applauded. Even the conquest of China did not provoke intervention from the other powers. The Japanese air force, approaching Nanking in December 1937, recklessly bombed both a British and an American gunboat in the Yangtze, but the incidents were swiftly patched over. Preoccupied with the totalitarian dictators in Europe, Great Britain, France, and the United States would have conceded control of China to the Japanese so long as they respected trading rights of other nations. What eventually transformed the Sino-Japanese struggle into a world war in the Pacific (as we shall see in chapter 22) was the Japanese decision to follow the navy policy of expansion into Southeast Asia, and to stage a final, shocking incident at the American base of Pearl Harbor.

CHAPTER TWENTY-ONE

The Onset of Hitler's War

The onset of World War II in Europe can be explained in a single, brief sentence: Hitler caused the war. Many historians, of course, hate such simplicity; it gives them little to analyze or elaborate. Ever since 1961, when the English historian A. J. P. Taylor published his controversial book *The Origins of the Second World War,* the road to war in the 1930s has looked more complicated. However, as another English historian, Norman Rich, has underlined, World War II would not have taken place if the German chancellor of the 1930s were named Müller or Schmidt, or Schmendermann. Hitler caused the war.

Actually, the origins of World War II in Europe require three or four sentences for a complete explanation. Hitler caused the war. But German frustration with the Versailles Peace Treaty and with the economic hardships of the Great Depression caused Hitler, that is, brought him to power. And, of course, World War I led to the infamous peace treaty and contributed to the coming of the Great Depression. Therefore, in the final analysis, World War I caused World War II. Many observers, from Winston Churchill onward, have considered both catastrophes merely two stages in a thirty-year war. Having already considered the importance of the first war in causing the depression (chapter 15) and the depression in bringing Hitler to power (chapter 17), we shall now concentrate on the final stage in this circle of horror, examining how Hitler brought war to Europe in the 1930s.

At the outset, we must clarify one aspect of our simple proposition that the German führer caused the war. Adolf Hitler, long before he came to power, articulated a clear and chilling vision of his expansionist goals. In a terrifyingly literal-minded way, he never deviated from his vision. Yet, he did not follow a detailed blueprint or timetable for expansion, but reacted opportunistically to unfolding events. Hitler's foreign policy, therefore, combined a consistent strategy with infinitely flexible tactics. One of his disillusioned followers, Hermann Rauschning, described him as a "master tactician with a daemon."

Hitler's overall strategy, laid out in *Mein Kampf* and elaborated in numerous speeches and conversations, encompassed three stages. First, Germany would dominate Europe and invade Russia, thereby securing *Lebensraum* ("living space") in the East. Hitler proposed that the existing populations of Poland and Russia be "ruthlessly Germanized," but not through cultural or linguistic assimilation. Even if a Slav learned German, his blood remained Slavic and inferior. Therefore he aimed to Germanize the soil, pushing aside or enslaving the Slavic population, exterminating the Jews, and resettling Eastern Europe with German colonists.

Throughout this first stage of conquest in the East, Hitler would ally with Italy and England, thus protecting his rear and avoiding a two-front war (he did not consider France alone, without either the English or the Italians as allies, much of a threat). Since Italy was governed by a Fascist dictator with expansionist aims of his own, an Italian alliance was obvious; but the idea of Nazi Germany allying with England seems startling at first glance. Like the kaiser before him, Hitler nurtured a love/hate relationship with the English. He felt racial kinship with his fellow Aryans and admired the ruthlessness that had won them a worldwide empire. Yet he resented their opposition to German dominance of the Continent and believed that much of their old vigor had been sapped by Jews in commerce and industry. Nevertheless, he considered the kaiser foolish to have antagonized England by building a navy and acquiring colonies. He deemphasized naval power and overseas colonies, therefore, concentrating on expansion in Eastern Europe, hoping for England's agreement or at least acquiescence. He scorned competition with England on its own ground of overseas imperialism: "a territorial policy . . . cannot find its fulfilment in the Cameroons . . . but almost exclusively in Europe."

Hitler considered the first stage of Nazi policy, the conquest of Russia and the acquisition of *Lebensraum,* his life's work; but he did not expect to carry out the second stage personally. In this second, future phase, he envisioned a world struggle between Germany, dominant in Europe, and the United States, supreme in the Western Hemisphere. Again, he hoped the English would join the Germans in this struggle, or at least remain neutral; but if the English-speaking peoples united against Germany, they would both be crushed. In a final, third stage, Germans would racially purify the world by eliminating all Jews and subjugating other inferior peoples. The maintenance of racial purity by the governing Aryan race would ensure permanent German world dominance.

Hitler's war aims resonated powerfully with the German people. If they had not, he could never have enlisted the loyalty of millions. When we state categorically that Hitler caused the war we are not saying that he acted alone. German nationalists had long championed the goal of *Lebensraum* in the East. During the First World War the government of Kaiser Wilhelm II formulated expansive war aims, envisioning German dominance of Central Europe, annexations of key territories in the West, such as Alsace-Lorraine, Luxemburg, and parts of Belgium, and in the East huge slices of Poland, Ukraine, and Russia. The Treaty of Brest-Litovsk, imposed on Soviet Russia in 1918 when German military power reached its height, embodied the goal of *Lebensraum* quite literally. For the most part, Hitler only dusted off these old plans when he formulated his first stage of foreign policy.

Despite such precedents, however, the führer's goals did exceed those of previous German leaders, such as Bismarck, Bethmann Hollweg, or Kaiser Wilhelm. German historian Klaus Hildebrand emphasizes the point: "This order to conquer *Lebensraum* and simultaneously exterminate Bolsheviks and Jewry in order to create a 'pure-bred' world . . . lent the war a new character which European and German history had previously known only in colonial wars." Hitler's goals were familiar to the German people, but his exterminationist methods had previously been employed only in colonial conflicts, such as the Herero revolt in South West Africa. The Nazis brought the atrocities of the old imperialism into the heart of Europe, intensified them, and made them official policy.

The most terrifying aspect of Hitler's rule was the literal-minded way that he pursued his policies. Many Europeans after World War I believed democracy had failed. Millions in Central Europe were anti-Semitic, blaming Jews for all the ills of the time. Nearly all patriotic Germans believed their nation deserved a larger role in world affairs. Most men and women, in Germany and throughout Europe, just parroted the conventional wisdom in a thoughtless manner. Hitler, however, took all these ideas seriously and literally. He would crush democracy, exterminate Jews, and conquer Russia.

The führer never deviated from his long-range aims, but his tactics showed an astonishing craftiness, flexibility, and amorality. For the first two years after he took power, from 1933 to 1935, he rarely mentioned long-range goals and concentrated instead on universally popular themes, such as revising the Versailles Treaty and ending the depression. Though secretly beginning the rearmament of Germany during this period, he avoided foreign policy risks and drew on his World War I battle experience to highlight the horrors of war and pose as an advocate of peace.

From 1935 to 1939, as Germany emerged from the depression and rearmed more vigorously, Hitler became more aggressive. He waged a war of nerves with France and England, slowly gobbling up the smaller states of Central Europe through a policy of undeclared, largely bloodless, lightning wars of bluff. Then from 1939 to 1941 he waged lightning wars of action, conquering Poland, Denmark, Norway, the Netherlands, Belgium, France, Yugoslavia, and Greece in turn.

Every step of the way, Hitler's actions remained opportunistic, tentative, capable of reversal if they did not succeed. Like a boxer in the early rounds of a fight, he bobbed and weaved, jabbed and sparred, seeking a weak point for a knockout.

The concept of *blitzkrieg,* or lightning war, was central to Hitler's foreign policy. As we shall see later in this chapter, blitzkrieg usually refers to a battle strategy employing massed concentrations of tanks and aircraft to cause a breakthrough in a defensive line. The German army used this strategy most effectively in France in 1940, but the idea of a lightning quick victory underlay everything Hitler did in foreign affairs during the 1930s. Before 1939, his blitzkriegs were largely diplomatic coups, executed with brutally frank threats of military action. After 1939, they became literal, lightning-swift wars. Hitler's pose as a battle-scarred veteran of the World War I trenches was partly based on fact. He wished to avoid the long-drawn out, static, meatgrinder warfare of 1914 to 1918 and win quick, cheap victories, by bluff, bluster, or surprise attack.

Actually the führer's fellow dictator, Benito Mussolini, made the first military conquest of the 1930s when Italian troops invaded Ethiopia (also called Abyssinia) in 1935. Yet Mussolini's alliance with Hitler, despite their ideological affinities, had not yet been sealed at the time of the Ethiopian invasion. Hitler praised Mussolini as early as 1925 in *Mein Kampf,* but the Italian duce did not return the admiration until much later. Mussolini had come to power a decade earlier than Hitler and considered the new dictator an upstart. Furthermore, Germans and Italians had been enemies and rivals for centuries, most recently in World War I. Mussolini had a strong strategic interest in preserving an independent Austria as a buffer between Italy and Germany, yet the Nazis made no secret of their desire to annex Austria, creating a common border with Italy. Most Italians feared this eventuality.

Hitler and Mussolini met in person for the first time on June 14, 1934, in Venice. The two dictators did not get on well; for Hitler talked constantly and did not defer to his senior colleague. Then, just a month later, the Austrian Nazi Party assassinated Chancellor Engelbert Dollfuss in an unsuccesful bid for power. Dollfuss had been scheduled for a trip to Italy on the very day of his murder, July 25, 1934, and Mussolini himself broke the news of the chancellor's death to his widow in Rome. The duce concentrated troops on the Brenner Pass, at the border with Austria, and assured the Austrian government of his support for its independence. Hitler backed off, reining in the local Nazis for the moment.

The following year, however, Mussolini moved closer to Nazi Germany in the wake of the Ethiopian invasion. The Italians had tried to conquer Ethiopia in the 1890s, at the height of the "scramble for Africa" but had been rebuffed at the battle of Adowa in 1896. Mussolini hoped to avenge the Adowa humiliation, but he had other reasons for the African invasion as well. He had long envisioned an expansionist foreign policy as soon as Italy developed enough economic and military power. Now with Hitler rearming, the duce grew jealous and impatient. Dreaming of a new Roman Empire to challenge Britain at Suez and Gibraltar and the French in North Africa, he believed Ethiopia would complement existing Italian colonies in Somaliland and Libya.

Playing up a border incident with Ethiopian soldiers, Mussolini sent large numbers of troops to Somaliland in early 1935. These crossed into Ethiopia on October 2, 1935, and within three days captured the infamous town of Adowa. The campaign bogged down about eighty miles inside the border, but Mussolini replaced the Italian commander and ordered a drive to the capital, Addis Ababa, which was captured on May 5, 1936. The Ethiopian emperor, Haile Selassie, fled the country, and Mussolini declared the Italian king, Victor Emmanuel, emperor of Abyssinia.

The British and French governments condemned the Ethiopian invasion at the League of Nations, and the League duly voted for economic sanctions against Italy. Neither Britain nor France, however, wished a fight with Mussolini, so they did not push for an embargo on oil, which would have halted the invading troops. Nor did Britain close the Suez Canal to Italian vessels. The sanctions policy, therefore, represented the worst of both worlds — harsh enough to enrage Mussolini and inconvenience the Italian people but not so strong as to stop the aggression.

Mussolini had not consulted Hitler or coordinated his plans with him, and the German government remained correctly aloof from the struggle, observing the sanctions but continuing vital exports of coal to Italy. In the aftermath of the sanctions debacle, however, Mussolini turned away from France and Britain and grew closer to Germany. In October 1936 Italy's foreign secretary, Mussolini's son-in-law Count Galeazzo Ciano, traveled to Hitler's private lair at Berchtesgaden, high in the Alps, and signed a vague but wide-reaching protocol of friendship. This fell short of a binding alliance, but Mussolini could not resist the temptation to embellish it rhetorically. On November 1, 1936, at Milan, he orated: "The Berlin conversations have resulted in an understanding between our two countries . . . an axis, around which can revolve all those European states with a will to collaboration and peace." A year later, in September 1937, the Rome-Berlin Axis acquired a personal dimension when Hitler charmed Mussolini on a five-day visit to Germany. Before the end of the year, Italy formally withdrew from the League of Nations and joined Germany and Japan in signing the Anti-Comintern (anti-Russian) Pact. Mussolini fell increasingly under Hitler's influence, as evidenced by his introduction of discriminatory measures against Italian Jews for the first time in September 1938.

In the meantime Hitler had taken his first risky steps towards revising the Versailles Treaty and challenging British and French dominance of Europe. In March 1935 he decreed conscription for the army and announced publicly what everyone already knew, that Germany was building an air force, the Luftwaffe.

Changes in Europe, 1935-39

Both measures violated the Versailles restrictions on German armed forces; so representatives of France, Britain, and even Italy duly met and condemned the moves, but they took no action. In fact, the British compounded the felony by striking a private bargain with Germany in June 1935. Ever fearful of any challenge on the seas, the British signed an Anglo-German naval agreement limiting German shipbuilding to one-third that of England. This reassured the British Admiralty but ignored the fact that Versailles prohibited Germany from building *any* navy. England winked at the violation in order to put a cap on it. The Germans, however, were not planning a huge navy at this time so they gave away nothing.

Encouraged by the complacency of the English and taking advantage of European preoccupation with the Ethiopian incident, Hitler then violated one of the most important restrictions of the Versailles Treaty, the de-militarization of the Rhineland. The west bank of the Rhine, between the river and the German border with France, Luxemburg, and Belgium, had been the staging area for the Schlieffen plan in 1914. The victors in 1919, therefore, declared this territory, and a strip on the east bank of the Rhine as well, a de-militarized zone. By the Locarno Treaty of 1925 France, Britain, and Germany ratified this provision.

On Sunday, March 7, 1936, Hitler repudiated the Locarno Treaty by sending troops into the Rhineland. The German inhabitants welcomed the soldiers with flowers and cheers. Again, France and Britain (but this time not Italy) protested, but took no action. Thereafter, the German army fortified the Rhineland border, thus closing the western door to Germany and preventing punitive action by France. By the end of 1936, both Hitler and Mussolini had defied the European democracies and gotten away with it.

Throughout the 1930s, the leaders of Britain and France met the challenge of the totalitarian dictators with a policy of appeasement. The word was originally used in its literal, dictionary sense — to pacify, to make peace, to soothe and ease tensions — without any negative or ironic connotations; but it has since come to imply a cowardly policy of unnecessary concessions or even abject surrender. This is not altogether fair. Appeasement represented a consistent policy that was neither passive nor cowardly; unfortunately, however, it proved unsuccessful.

The main architect of appeasement was Neville Chamberlain, who became prime minister of Britain on May 28, 1937. For six years previous to this, however, Chamberlain had served as chancellor of the exchequer, distinguishing himself as the strongest member of various British cabinets. His influence, therefore, pervaded British foreign policy throughout the decade.

Neville Chamberlain was born on March 18, 1869, to a wealthy shopkeeping family in Birmingham, England. His father, Joseph, served as colonial secretary during the height of the "scramble for Africa" and was widely considered the

371

main spokesman for British imperialism. His older half-brother, Austen, was a long-time power in the Conservative Party, holding a variety of Cabinet posts. Neville cut a quieter, less flamboyant figure than either his father or brother, impressing the public with his hardheaded, shopkeeper's steadiness and his typically English avocations of fishing, gardening, and birdwatching. Historian R. A. C. Parker has summed up his image perfectly: "His dark clothes and his stand-up starched Edwardian collars suggested the prudence of the managing director of an old-established bank or the senior partner of a large firm of solicitors, perhaps, in family settlements."

As "senior partner" of the British government, Chamberlain pursued a two-fold policy towards Germany. First of all, he placated Hitler with territorial concessions in Europe, provided they were carried out peacefully. Second, after satisfying Hitler's reasonable demands, he endeavored to draw Germany into a wide-ranging, multilateral pact with all the powers of Europe that would limit armaments and ensure peace. Chamberlain's concessions, since recalled as shameful acts of surrender, were intended only as first steps to a general settlement in Europe. Far from being passive or defeatist, appeasement actually represented an active, optimistic, even arrogant policy of great risks for high stakes.

Chamberlain carried the British public and the French government along with his policy because of the general recoil from war that followed the horrors of World War I. His goals, to limit armaments and prevent war, won general agreement. His tactical concessions to Hitler, which now seem so foolish and shortsighted, made sense in the context of the times. Hitler cleverly featured only his short-range goals, the revision of the Versailles Treaty restrictions, and downplayed the drive for *Lebensraum*. Since many in England believed the Versailles Treaty had been unduly harsh (blaming the French for this) they judged Hitler's desires reasonable. The reoccupation of the Rhineland, for instance, merely reclaimed full sovereignty over clearly German territory. Hitler also confused the English with his continuing "peace offensive," offering negotiations to limit air forces and armaments. Since Hitler wanted England as an ally or a neutral, these offers were not completely insincere.

The fatal weakness of the appeasement policy lay in its misjudgment of Hitler's goals. If Hitler simply wanted to reclaim Germany's rightful place in Europe, throw off restrictions from the Versailles Treaty, and readjust some inconvenient boundaries in Central Europe, Britain and France would agree, so long as he proceeded peacefully. If he wished to dominate Europe and build a self-sufficient empire in the East, however, not even Chamberlain would tolerate this. Chamberlain's appeasement policy never embraced "peace at any price." It simply misjudged how far Hitler intended to go and how high the price would be.

From another point of view, Chamberlain's appeasement policy may be judged as too little too late. To have any hope of success, the long-range goal of banishing war from Europe should have been pursued more radically and much earlier, before anyone had ever heard of Adolf Hitler. Timing is everything in politics; and the right time for a thoroughgoing policy of appeasement, in its literal sense, came at the end of the First World War. Europe was exhausted and its people literally or figuratively shell-shocked in 1919. Woodrow Wilson's idealistic rhetoric was gaining momentum and pacifist sentiments were growing as never before. That was the time to attempt a policy of great risks for high stakes.

Hindsight isn't necessary to construct such a possible postwar policy, for it would encompass primarily ideas and proposals current at the time. First, the Allies should have heeded Wilson's call for a "peace without victory" and held a true peace conference, not a congress of victors imposing terms on the defeated. Capitalizing on the immense war-weariness in Europe, the leaders of England, France, and the United States should have declared a policy of "no more war; war never again" and invited the defeated Germans to help construct a more peaceful order. Pope Benedict XV, who had condemned the war vehemently, should have been invited, along with other religious leaders, to participate in the conference. If he were not invited, the Pope should have called an ecumenical council to trumpet the ideals of peace and put pressure on the great powers.

Second, the victors should have imposed the same terms on themselves that they did on the Germans. Specifically, if they limited Germany's army to 100,000 men, they should have reduced their own to the same numbers, and declared complete disarmament as the long-range goal. Also, when they stripped Germany of its colonies and declared them League of Nations mandates, they should also have assigned their own colonies to the League and started a vigorous policy of decolonization for all of Africa and Asia. Third, the Allies should have listened to John Maynard Keynes and cancelled both the war debts owed by Britain and France to the United States and the reparations owed by Germany to Britain and France. Having wiped the economic slate clean, the major powers could then cooperate in the reconstruction of Europe.

Decolonization and the economic reconstruction of Europe were both pursued after the Second World War. Had they been adopted a generation earlier the German grievances which Adolf Hitler manipulated might never have developed, and the second catastrophe might have been avoided. By the mid-1930s, however, the favorable moment for such a far-sighted policy had passed, and Hitler's moment had arrived.

After the reoccupation of the Rhineland in 1936 Hitler continued rearmament, cultivated Mussolini, and offered limited aid to General Franco's side in the Spanish civil war. Then in 1938 and 1939, he pursued an undeclared war of nerves in Central Europe, annexing territory at six-months intervals. This created the impression of a precise timetable, but in fact the timing was completely coincidental. Hitler had begun his drive to the East, but his motives were still disguised and his tactics opportunistic.

Adolf Hitler was an Austrian by birth, and he had announced his intention to annex Austria to the German Reich on the very first page of *Mein Kampf:* "German Austria must return to the great German motherland, and not because of economic considerations of any sort. . . . *Common blood belongs in a common Reich*" (Hitler's italics). Many Germans, on both sides of the Austro-German border, shared this belief; but the Treaty of Versailles explicitly prohibited the *Anschluss,* or annexation, of the smaller German state by the larger. Italy had also blocked any step in this direction for strategic reasons. By the end of 1937, however, Mussolini had thrown in his lot with Hitler, informing both the Austrian and the German governments that he no longer opposed the *Anschluss.*

Hitler invited the Austrian chancellor, Kurt von Schuschnigg, to his mountain home at Berchtesgaden, overlooking the Austrian border, and harangued him mercilessly on February 12, 1938. This illustrates his standard technique throughout the war of nerves in Europe: first isolate a victim diplomatically then humiliate or terrorize him. The führer presented ten demands, including the appointment of an Austrian Nazi, Arthur Seyss-Inquart, as minister of the interior; Schuschnigg agreed. Yet a month later, the Austrian leader decided to strengthen his bargaining position by announcing a plebiscite on the question of preserving Austria's independence. Hitler demanded on March 11 that the plebiscite be cancelled, and Schuschnigg caved in. The whole Austrian cabinet, except Interior Minister Seyss-Inquart, then resigned. At Seyss-Inquart's invitation, the German army crossed the border and marched peacefully to Vienna, with Austrians cheering and showering them with flowers. Hitler declared Austria part of the German Reich on March 13. The takeover was not altogether peaceful, though, for SS guards followed the German army into Vienna, harassing and humiliating the Jews that had so agitated Hitler as a youth in that city. Many were deported to concentration camps and never returned.

Germany's annexation of Austria posed a direct threat to Czechoslovakia; for after the *Anschluss,* German territory surrounded this small country on three sides, like the jaws of a pincer. Ruled by the Austro-Hungarian empire before 1914, the lands of Bohemia, Moravia, Sudetenland, Slovakia, and sub-Carpathian Ruthenia had been assembled together in the single state of Czechoslovakia, one of the more curious and least viable entities created by the peacemakers of 1919. The primary nationalities of the state, the Czechs and the Slovaks, did not get along well together, and the state also contained 3.5 million Germans in the Sudetenland, as well as smaller minorities of Poles, Ruthenians (Ukrainians), and Hungarians. The Czechs, who firmly controlled the government, formed barely more than 50 percent of the population. Rather than an ethnically homogeneous nation, Czechoslovakia was a miniature version of the old Habsburg state.

The German minority in the Sudetenland posed the greatest threat to Czechoslovakia's stability due to their large numbers, assertive cultural nationalism, and strategic location. The Sudetenland wrapped around the western border of Czechoslovakia like a German glove. If the Czechs ever ceded control of this province, they would give up their best defensive positions in the mountains separating Sudetenland from Germany. For a time after World War I, the Sudeten Germans suffered cultural and political discrimination from the ruling Czechs; but by the mid-1930s they had organized a formidable political party to protect their interests and had enlisted public opinion in Germany to support them. The Czechs, therefore, became far more conciliatory.

Hitler, however, exploited the Sudeten Germans for his own annexationist ends. He fully intended to erase Czechoslovakia from the map; but publicly he emphasized the minority grievances of the Sudeten Germans. Konrad Henlein, the leader of the Sudeten German party in Czechoslovakia, agreed with Hitler in March 1938: "We must always demand so much that we can never be satisfied."

The Czech president, Edvard Beneš, expressed his willingness to grant substantial autonomy to Sudeten Germans in early September 1938; but rather than negotiate in good faith, Henlein provoked a riot and appealed for German aid. At the annual Nazi Party rally in Nuremberg on September 12, Hitler denounced Beneš and the Czechs, threatening war. On September 15 Henlein fled to Germany when the Czech police restored order in Sudetenland.

At this point, Prime Minister Chamberlain mounted an audacious last-ditch effort to solve the Czech crisis and build a more durable framework for peace. Though he was sixty-nine years old and had never flown in an airplane before, Chamberlain flew from London to Munich on September 15, 1938, then continued on by train to Hitler's home at Berchtesgaden. Such personal summit meetings were far less common than they are now and this one caused a sensation. Hitler greeted Chamberlain warmly, flattered him, and played on his vanity, seemingly building a personal bond of understanding between the two leaders.

After returning from Germany, Chamberlain continued his summitry, summoning Prime Minister Édouard Daladier and Foreign Minister Georges Bonnet of France to London for consultations on September 18. Both the English and French leaders assumed that Czechoslovakia should cede the Sudetenland to Germany, though they had not yet consulted the Czechs. They fashioned an agreement calling for a peaceful transfer of territory, supervised by an international body. Through heavy diplomatic pressure they wrung agreement from the Czech government on September 21. Chamberlain then flew to Bad Godesberg, in the German Rhineland, to obtain Hitler's approval.

The führer refused the Anglo-French-Czech proposal, though it granted the Sudeten Germans what they had always said they wanted, union with Germany. Hitler actually desired the annexation of all Czechoslovakia, and he probably wanted to accomplish it by war in order to test and harden his armed forces. Accordingly, he demanded even more territory than the Chamberlain proposal granted and announced that his troops would march on September 28 if he was not satisfied. War was averted when Mussolini, who had played no role in this drama so far, proposed a conference of the four major powers. Though Hitler felt thwarted, he decided not to risk war against Czechoslovakia, France, and Britain without Italy's aid. So he accepted the conference proposal and met with Chamberlain, Daladier, and Mussolini at Munich on September 29. Neither the Czechs, the subjects of discussion, nor the Russians, highly interested bystanders, were invited.

At Munich the four powers arranged the peaceful transfer of Sudetenland to German rule and offered an international guarantee of the continued existence of the remainder of Czech territory. The day after the formal conference, Chamberlain conferred privately with Hitler and pressed his wider scheme for a general peace agreement. He drafted a joint statement pledging Britain and Germany to work for the elimination of bomber aircraft, the reduction of other armaments, and peace through "the method of consultation." Hitler signed without protest, and Chamberlain returned to London triumphantly. When he waved the piece of paper to the crowds at 10 Downing Street, he hailed the agreement as "peace with honour. I believe it is peace for our time."

The Munich Conference sealed Czechoslovakia's fate, for without the border fortresses of Sudetenland the country was indefensible. However, its actual demise, like the annexation of Austria, came about somewhat unexpectedly. In March 1939 the president of Czechoslovakia, Emil Hacha (Beneš had resigned after Munich) made a final effort to preserve the country's unity by dismissing the provincial governments of Ruthenia and Slovakia and declaring martial law. Hitler decided to act. On March 15 German forces occupied the Czech heartland of Bohemia and Moravia. Slovakia declared independence, but in fact became a German protectorate. Hitler permitted Hungary to grab the province of Ruthenia, and Poland took a small piece of territory around Teschen that they had long disputed with the Czechs. Though Britain and France had guaranteed the existence of Czechoslovakia at the Munich Conference, they realized they could do nothing effective at this time, so they pretended the country had spontaneously fallen apart. This was the last time, however, that Hitler's bluffs worked and he gained territory without war.

Chamberlain had never pursued peace at any price. He believed Hitler would be satisfied when the last vestiges of the Versailles Treaty were erased and all German inhabitants of Europe had been gathered into the Reich. The partition of Czechoslovakia and the absorption of millions of Czechs into Germany, however, revealed far more ambitious aims. For centuries, British policy had thwarted any power that threatened to dominate the whole European continent

— whether it was Louis XIV of France in the eighteenth century, Napoleon in the early nineteenth, or the kaiser's Germany in the early twentieth. When it became clear that Hitler held similar goals, British policy stiffened.

On March 31, 1939, the British and French governments delivered a public guarantee of Poland's independence, in the case of further aggression. On April 7, Mussolini's troops occupied Albania, which was already a virtual protectorate of Italy. This marked a frantic effort by the duce to keep up with his more ruthless partner. After the German takeover of Czechoslovakia, Mussolini fretted: "The Italians will laugh at me. Every time Hitler occupies a country he sends me a message." Yet it looked like a coordinated offensive by the two dictators; therefore, Britain and France extended their guarantees to Greece and Romania on April 13. On May 22, Mussolini and Hitler did coordinate their plans, signing the Pact of Steel, which transformed the earlier "Axis" agreements into a full military alliance. War seemed imminent in the summer of 1939.

In fact, Hitler had already instructed his generals to devise an operational plan for the invasion of Poland. He believed neither Britain nor France would honor their guarantee but would simply contrive another "Munich Agreement." To complete Poland's isolation he needed the neutrality of Soviet Russia. So on August 23 the Nazi foreign minister, Joachim von Ribbentrop, signed a non-aggression pact with his Soviet counterpart, V. M. Molotov.

No other Nazi action demonstrates more clearly Hitler's amazing tactical flexibility. Hitler detested Communism, and was working towards the conquest of Soviet Russia as his long-range goal, yet he made a pact with the Russians to facilitate his short-run aims. Stalin, for his part, held no ideological objections, for all capitalist governments were considered equally hostile, but defense of Russia sometimes required deals with them. His recent purges had demoralized the military leadership of the Soviet Union, so Stalin needed to buy time. Furthermore, the Molotov-Ribbentrop Pact ruthlessly partitioned Poland between Russia and Germany, promising Stalin lucrative spoils.

In the early morning of September 1, 1939, the Luftwaffe destroyed much of the Polish air force on the ground and sent five German armies crashing across the border in a gigantic pincer movement. The Poles resisted fiercely, but fighting lasted only about nineteen days. Within a month, the Polish armies were destroyed and the government had fled into exile in Great Britain. Not everything worked out perfectly for the Germans. To Hitler's surprise, both Britain and France did declare war against Germany on September 3; and much to Hitler's disgust, Mussolini evaded the Pact of Steel and remained neutral for the moment. None of this made any difference, however, for neither France nor Britain sent troops to Poland, and Mussolini's help proved unnecessary.

Though a state of war existed, Europe lapsed into an uneasy quiet after the Polish conquest. Neville Chamberlain called this period the "twilight war," whereas American observers across the ocean dubbed it the "phony war." Hitler actually intended to turn west immediately and deal France a knockout blow, but insufficient planning and bad winter weather delayed this for six months. In the meantime, Hitler and Stalin divided up Poland and the Nazis initiated their Germanization of the East. Under the direction of Heinrich Himmler, 80,000 Poles were forcibly evacuated from regions near the former border with Germany to make room for German settlers. Meanwhile, the SS systematically murdered the local Polish leadership, wiping out aristocrats, priests, schoolteachers, and politicians. The exiled Polish general, Władysław Anders, accurately labeled this "beheading the community" in order to create a leaderless mass of drone laborers for the Nazis. Although Jews were also herded up and confined in urban ghettoes, at this time the Polish nation was the prime target for repression.

An astonished world press labeled the conquest of Poland blitzkrieg, and it was certainly a "lightning war" in the swiftness of its outcome. Yet the German army had employed the conventional military strategy of a double envelopment, in which massive armies encircle enemy troops and destroy or capture them. This classic strategy worked so well in Poland because the Germans had mobilized secretly and not formally declared war, thus surprising the Poles, and had then gained total command of the air. Though the Germans' new panzer divisions[1] took part in the campaign, they did not employ any startling new techniques; and 90 percent of the German soldiers marched on foot and were supplied by horse-drawn wagons, like their counterparts in the previous war.

Initial planning for the invasion of France manifested equally conventional military thinking. In the winter of 1939-40, German generals dusted off the Schlieffen plan for a massive sweep through Belgium to envelop the left wing of the French armies. The only significant change came at the insistence of the Luftwaffe, who coveted bases right across the channel from England. The air force, therefore, persuaded the generals to sweep through Belgium *and* Holland this time, instead of avoiding Holland as they had in 1914.

Hitler instinctively realized that "you cannot get away with an operation like that twice," and he searched for some way to win a quick victory that would not bog down into trench warfare. As early as 1929, a German officer, Heinz Guderian, had worked out a revolutionary new method of attack, first suggested by the British soldier-historian, Basil Liddell Hart, but neglected by the British military. Liddell Hart, Guderian, and other advocates of "the armored idea" rejected the static use of tanks as artillery support for the infantry. They proposed

---

1. Panzer divisions were armored, motorized divisions — that is, tanks and mobile infantry — with specialized groups of highly trained combat engineers. The German word for tank is *Panzerkampfwagen*, literally, "armored fighting vehicle."

instead to concentrate tanks and aircraft for a breakthrough at the weakest point in an enemy line, then direct the tanks to avoid enemy troops and strike swiftly in the rear at communications and command facilities, sowing panic along the way. This indirect approach would avoid the slogging matches of the first war and ensure a relatively cheap victory.

In October 1939 General Erich von Manstein, chief of staff for one of the army groups on the French border, saw the recycled Schlieffen plan and realized its hopelessness. He proposed instead that Guderian's panzers concentrate in the Ardennes Forest at the center of the French line and spring a surprise attack. Once through the mountainous Ardennes and across the Meuse River, the panzers could race across flat ground to the sea, demoralizing the French and cutting their defense in two. The German General Staff rejected Manstein's impertinent advice and transferred him to the other side of Germany; but before taking up his new post he lunched with Hitler on February 17, 1940, and persuaded him to try the blitzkrieg strategy. The strongest of the ten German panzer divisions, commanded by Guderian and General Erwin Rommel, took up positions opposite the Ardennes.

French defensive strategy played right into the Germans' hands. Appalled by their losses in the First World War and aware of their numerical inferiority to the Germans, the French had constructed an enormous series of underground fortresses and concrete blockhouses (the Maginot line) along their border with Germany. They had not continued the line across the Ardennes, however, believing it impassable, or along the border with Belgium.

Neglecting the Belgian border seems astonishing, since the Germans had come that way in 1914; but up until 1936 Belgium and France were allies, and the French could hardly seal off their border, thus signaling their abandonment of Belgium to German attack. After Belgium renounced its alliance and resumed neutrality in 1936, France might have continued the Maginot line; but the low, waterlogged terrain of the Belgian frontier would make underground fortifications incredibly expensive, and the fortress line would cut right through France's industrial heartland, exposing it to enemy bombardment. Therefore, the French planned to sprint forward toward a defensible river line in Belgium as soon as war with Germany broke out. The Ardennes, still considered impassable, would be held with only light covering troops.

The phony war lasted six months. Then on April 9 the Germans mounted a surprise attack on Norway with airborne paratroopers and sea-transported regular troops. This prevented the British navy from controlling the Norwegian coast and protected Germany's supplies of iron ore from neutral Sweden. The Norwegians were subdued in a few weeks through an unprecedented combination of sea, land, and air action. Winston Churchill later hailed it grudgingly as a masterpiece of "surprise, ruthlessness, and precision."

Finally, with equal inventiveness, the Germans invaded France and the Low Countries on May 10, 1940. The move into Holland and Belgium employed tricks and ruses, such as soldiers disguised in Dutch military uniforms, glider troops landing on the concrete roof of a Belgian fortress, and paratroops and float planes descending on the center of Rotterdam. The bulk of the French troops, along with ten divisions of the British Expeditionary Force, moved forward to counter these moves, as planned. Then the panzers struck in the rear of the advancing French and British.

The first two days of the advance through the Ardennes consisted of traffic control, not battle, as the tanks and trucks made their way along narrow, twisting mountain roads, finally reaching the Meuse River on May 12. After herculean efforts by the combat engineers, and terrifying attacks by dive-bombing German Stukas, both Guderian's and Rommel's panzer divisions crossed the Meuse on the 14th and began racing toward the English Channel. The French generals reacted slowly and tentatively, uncertain what was happening. On the morning of May 15, however, the French prime minister awakened Winston Churchill (who had just taken over the British government from Neville Chamberlain) with a frantic phone call: "We are beaten, we have lost the battle."

The Germans had torn a hole in the French defense line fifty miles wide and were pouring troops through it. In a week, the panzer spearheads raced two hundred miles. In one record-breaking day, Rommel's division covered fifty-two miles, driving all through the night. On May 20, Guderian's division reached the English Channel at Abbeville, then turned north to attack the rear of the demoralized French, English, and Belgians. As British writer Len Deighton has pointed out: "A modern army attacked from the rear is as good as defeated. It simply seizes up into a traffic jam of monumental confusion."

The British, however, gained a moral victory in the midst of the confusion by successfully evacuating nearly 340,000 soldiers, including 110,000 French, from the port and beaches of Dunkirk on the French side of the English Channel. The German generals had nervously followed the sprint of their panzer divisions and attempted to slow or halt them at several points. Then on May 24 Hitler ordered a definite stop for regrouping. This provided just enough time for the British evacuation. Between May 27 and June 4, 1940, 850 boats, from yachts to destroyers, descended on the channel coast under a relentless bombardment by the Luftwaffe, plucking French and English soldiers from the beaches.

The Dunkirk "miracle" allowed the British to fight another day, but the French were thoroughly beaten and demoralized. The French government asked for an armistice on June 17; and on June 22 Hitler arranged a capitulation ceremony at the same place, in the same railroad car, where Germany surrendered after the First World War. The next day he fulfilled a lifelong ambition by touring Paris and its architectural treasures. In the meantime, Mussolini had finally joined in, declaring war on June 10, when France was already beaten; but his troops barely got across the border before the armistice.

Hitler was now master of the European continent, and he expected Britain to abandon the struggle, finally granting him the free hand in the East he had always desired. He underestimated British stubbornness. Winston Churchill had taken over as prime minister and minister of defense the very day Germany attacked France, May 10, 1940; and he publicly vowed, "we shall fight on the beaches, . . . we shall never surrender."

Winston Spencer Churchill was born on November 30, 1874, at Blenheim Palace, the splendid country house of his uncle, the duke of Marlborough. His father, Randolph, was the younger son of an aristocratic family, his mother, Jennie Jerome, an American heiress. Five years younger than Neville Chamberlain and nearly a generation older than Adolf Hitler, Churchill was raised in the same warlike, imperialist culture that produced Kaiser Wilhelm II in Germany and Teddy Roosevelt in the United States. He fought colonial wars in India, the Sudan, and South Africa, sending home dispatches to newspapers and magazines at the same time. He served as first lord of the Admiralty at the beginning of World War I and chancellor of the exchequer in the 1920s. Though retaining a seat in the Commons throughout the 1930s, he did not hold Cabinet office, and earned his living primarily through his writings. Since he dictated his books orally, he once remarked that he "lived from mouth to hand."

Churchill was an annoying gadfly to British governments throughout the 1930s, speaking out on two big issues, India and Germany. The British Parliament passed the Government of India Act in August 1935, granting self-government to the various Indian provinces and holding out fully autonomous dominion status as a future goal for India as a whole. Churchill, however, opposed this bill advanced by his own party, arguing vehemently that the Indians were too immature and divided to rule themselves. He also fought Chamberlain's appeasement of Germany, calling instead for rearmament and a firm policy of collective security against Hitler. When he came to write his memoirs, Churchill named the Second World War "The Unnecessary War," and proclaimed as the theme of his first volume, *The Gathering Storm*: "How the English-speaking peoples through their unwisdom, carelessness, and good nature allowed the wicked to rearm." The book was a 667-page "I told you so."

Churchill's views had been too militarist and imperialist for the British public in the 1930s, but he proved an ideal choice to rally the nation in wartime. Speaking to the House of Commons on June 18, 1940, the day after France sued for peace, he orated:

> The Battle of France is over. I expect that the Battle of Britain is about to begin. Upon this battle depends the survival of Christian civilisation. . . . If the British

Empire and its Commonwealth last for a thousand years, men will say, "This was their finest hour."

He followed this rhetoric with deeds. On July 3 he ordered all warships belonging to the defeated French interned or destroyed, lest they fall into German hands. When the powerful French fleet at Oran in North Africa resisted, the British navy bombarded them, sinking or beaching three large battleships. Churchill later boasted: "Here was this Britain which so many had counted down and out ... striking ruthlessly at her dearest friends of yesterday. ... It was made plain that the British War Cabinet feared nothing and would stop at nothing."

The Battle of Britain opened with a barrage of air attacks, for the Germans needed to win command of the air before they could mount an invasion of the British Isles. Beginning on July 10, 1940, the Luftwaffe attacked English coastal shipping, airfields, industrial centers, and cities. The heaviest attacks came on August 15 and September 15, and London was bombed continually from September 7 to November 3. The German blitz killed 23,002 English civilians in 1940, far fewer than alarmists had feared. A previous prime minister, Stanley Baldwin, had predicted in 1934 that "the bomber must always get through." This did not prove to be the case. Aided by radar, which the British had been developing secretly, the Royal Air Force shot down nearly twice as many German planes as they themselves lost. After September 15, German losses became so heavy that the Luftwaffe abandoned daytime bombing and continued the blitz only at night.

Though it was not apparent at the time, the Battle of Britain had been won by this date. Referring to the RAF fighter pilots, Churchill pronounced that "never ... has so much been owed by so many to so few." On September 17, Hitler indefinitely postponed the British invasion and turned his attention to the East again. German forces overran both Yugoslavia and Greece in early 1941, after Mussolini's armies botched their own Greek invasion.

In two years of bluff, March 1938 to September 1939, and two years of battle, September 1939 to June 1941, Hitler had gained control of Europe west of the Russian border. Germany annexed Austria, the Sudetenland, a portion of Poland, Alsace-Lorraine, Luxemburg, and a slice of Belgium. The German army exercised occupational authority over Bohemia-Moravia, the rest of Poland, Yugoslavia, Greece, Belgium, Holland, Norway, and two-thirds of France. Sweden, Switzerland, Ireland, Spain, and Portugal remained neutral; but Slovakia, Denmark, Finland, Hungary, Romania, Bulgaria, and the unoccupied portion of France ("Vichy France") had become German satellites. In winning these victories one at a time, the German military avoided a two-front war and suffered fewer casualties than in a single battle of the First World War.

Had Hitler been satisfied with these gains, he could have retained them indefinitely. Neither Russia nor England were strong enough to attack Germany and the United States would have remained aloof as it had throughout the 1930s. Yet Hitler's long-range goal had always been the elimination of Soviet Russia and the winning of *Lebensraum* in the East. Flush from his lightning victory in France, he grew overconfident. He wanted to act quickly, for he had a premonition of an early death. Therefore, he directed his generals to plan a blitzkrieg of Russia, expecting it to go as quickly and easily as the conquest of Poland and France. On June 22, 1941, the German army crossed the Russian border. This attack, along with the Japanese raid on Pearl Harbor, transformed a European war into the Second World War.

CHAPTER TWENTY-TWO

The Coming of the Greater East Asia War[1]

Japan's warlike expansion in East Asia lacked the obsessive drive and clear sense of purpose that Hitler's will imparted to German expansionism. Japanese leaders, civilian and military alike, shared a common worldview. They felt themselves encircled by hostile imperialists, and thus they wished to expel Europeans and Americans from Asia and become the dominant power in the region. Yet their proposed New Order or Greater East Asia Co-Prosperity Sphere, as they variously called it, remained a vague concept. The Japanese often acted with arrogant contempt for other Asian peoples, but they did not exterminate or push them aside in their drive for *Lebensraum*. When all-out war ensued between Japan and the United States, it came as a result of mutual misunderstandings and blunders, rather than a blueprint for conquest. Until 1941 the Japanese had not even decided in which direction to mount their major expansionist drive.

Russia was Japan's traditional rival in East Asia; and ever since the Russo-Japanese War of 1904-5, the Japanese army had been preparing for a rematch. In 1936 the Japanese signed an Anti-Comintern Pact with Nazi Germany (joined by

---

1. The Japanese used the term "Greater East Asia War" as their official designation for World War II; but the term became so closely identified with wartime propaganda and the idea of Japanese dominance in Asia that postwar governments dropped it, substituting the more neutral phrase "Pacific War." This term accurately describes the battles against the United States, which were fought primarily on islands in the Pacific; but the majority of Japanese troops remained engaged on the continent of Asia, in China, Burma, and other countries. Therefore, I employ the term Greater East Asia War in a simple geographic sense as the best descriptive title for Japan's portion of World War II.

Mussolini's Italy the following year), as a signal of their continued hostility to Russia and communism; but this fell short of a formal alliance and did not obligate the parties to any specific action. Japan, Germany, and Italy felt a vague kinship as "have-not" nations, but the European and Asiatic partners did not coordinate their military activities. In fact, during the early years of Japan's invasion of China, Germany furnished supplies and advice to Chiang Kai-shek. The Nazis shocked their Asiatic partner more severely in 1939. Despite the Anti-Comintern Pact, Hitler struck a nonaggression deal with Stalin to facilitate his invasion of Poland. He neither consulted nor informed the Japanese in advance of this turnabout.

At nearly the same time, the Russians sent the Japanese army reeling in ferocious border fighting. From the time Japan created the puppet state of Manchukuo, an arms race had ensued between the Japanese Kwantung Army and the Soviet Far Eastern forces. In 1937 and 1938 adventurous Japanese officers had probed the Soviet defenses, leading to sharp but short-lived border incidents. When they advanced again in May 1939 on the frontier between Manchukuo and Outer Mongolia, they found the Russians alert and well supplied with tanks and artillery. In August 1939, at virtually the same time that Stalin and Molotov were signing their pact with Hitler and Ribbentrop, the Soviet army mounted a major offensive in the Nomonhan region of Mongolia, virtually annihilating the Japanese troops, who suffered over 18,000 fatalities. Snubbed by their "ally," Nazi Germany, defeated by their arch-enemy, the Soviet Union, and still tied down by the endless war in China, the Japanese army began reassessing its options.

Hitler's lightning victories in May and June 1940 presented the Japanese with a golden opportunity they did not want to miss. Since the Germans had conquered both France and the Netherlands and were pressing Great Britain to the limit, the colonial possessions of these three nations seemed ripe for the picking. The Japanese, therefore, looked southward to the islands of the East Indies and the mainland of Southeast Asia.

Japan had first shown interest in a "southern advance" as early as August 1936, when the cabinet issued an official document including economic expansion into Southeast Asia in its "fundamentals of national policy." However, the military struggle against the Chinese Nationalists absorbed so much attention thereafter, that when Prime Minister Konoe Fumimaro proclaimed the New Order in East Asia on November 3, 1938, he limited its extent to Japan, Manchukuo, and China. Konoe himself, a popular prince from a prominent family, resigned soon after this, having failed to secure even this much territory for Japan's New Order. Not until Hitler knocked out the European powers one by one in 1940 and Konoe returned to office in July 1940 did the Japanese take up the idea of a southern advance once more.

The navy had traditionally been the strongest advocate of a southern policy. Yet the first actual troop movement, into northern Indochina in September 1940, was spearheaded by the army, which hoped to outflank Chiang Kai-shek and cut off his supplies. The Japanese pressured the government of Vichy France, which still ruled in Indochina (encompassing today's Vietnam, Cambodia, and Laos), to grant them basing rights. The occupation of northern Indochina remained technically voluntary and legal, but adventurous Japanese officers did provoke a number of violent incidents.

Just prior to this occupation, in a press conference on August 1, 1940, Prince Konoe and his activist foreign minister, Matsuoka Yosuke, had broadcast a new title for Japan's ambitions in Asia: the Greater East Asia Co-Prosperity Sphere. They envisioned the sphere as a self-sufficient economic entity, inhabited by peaceful Asian peoples, free from European colonialism but guided by their advanced Japanese brothers.

The Japanese never clearly defined the extent of the co-prosperity sphere. In the most ambitious version, the sphere might sweep from Sakhalin Island and Siberia in the north, east to include Hawaii and all the intervening Pacific islands, south to Australia and New Zealand, then westward through Southeast Asia, perhaps even including India. Practically speaking though, policy makers never made specific plans to conquer Australia or India, confining their activities to the islands of the Dutch East Indies (today's Indonesia) and the Southeast Asian countries of Indochina, Thailand, Malaya, and Burma.

During his year in office as foreign minister, from mid-1940 to mid-1941, Matsuoka assisted the southern advance by forging closer ties with the Nazis and Fascists in Europe and neutralizing the threat of opposition from the Russians. He negotiated a formal treaty of alliance with the German ambassador in Tokyo, and the resulting Tripartite Pact between Germany, Italy, and Japan was signed in Berlin on September 27, 1940. This treaty obligated each nation to aid the others if they were attacked by a non-treaty member. Hitler neither wanted nor needed any military aid in Europe at this time, when he was at the height of his power; but he hoped the Tripartite Pact would warn off the United States from joining in. Matsuoka, for his part, believed that German pressure on its puppet states of Holland and Vichy France would ease the Japanese advance into Indochina and the Dutch East Indies.

Then Matsuoka imitated the Nazis by making a pact with the Soviet Union. He toured Europe in the spring of 1941, first consulting with Hitler in Berlin at the end of March, then paying a courtesy visit to Mussolini from March 31 to April 3. He arrived in Moscow on April 7 and hammered out a neutrality treaty with Molotov. Stalin made an unprecedented appearance at the railway station to wish Matsuoka farewell on his long journey home via the Trans-Siberian Railway.

Supported by the so-called "renovationist" faction in the Japanese foreign service, Matsuoka Yosuke harbored grandiose plans of world politics. By allying

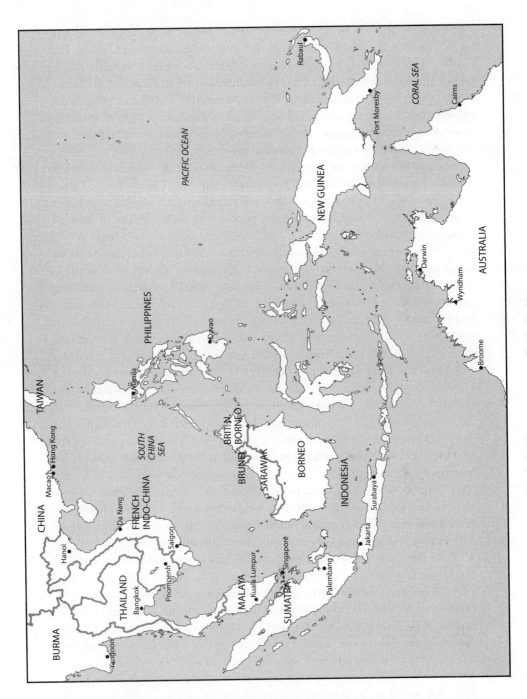

Japan's Greater East Asia Co-Prosperity Sphere

with the Nazis and Fascists and neutralizing the Soviets, he dreamed of dividing up the world into spheres of influence. Germany would dominate Europe and much of Africa, granting its junior partner Italy its own sphere around the Mediterranean. Meanwhile, Japan would reign supreme in East Asia, and the Soviet Union would direct its expansionist aims southward in Central Asia towards Afghanistan and India. Britain would be gradually squeezed out of its empire, but the U.S. sphere of influence in the Western Hemisphere would remain untouched. Matsuoka's four-power entente, dividing up Europe, Asia, and Africa into self-sufficient regions, represented the most extreme version of an anti-Anglo-American policy developed by Japan.

The incipient entente lasted barely two months, for on June 22, 1941, Hitler double-crossed his Asiatic partner again by attacking the Soviet Union. Foreign Minister Ribbentrop had given the Japanese ambassador copious hints of this move beforehand, so the Japanese military were not so surprised as they had been by the nonaggression pact in August 1939; but Matsuoka himself, fresh from his triumphal procession through Europe, was deeply shocked. For the second time in two years, Hitler's Germany had forced the Japanese to drastically rethink the assumptions of their foreign policy. In 1939 they had planned war against Russia, but Hitler made peace with Stalin. Then in 1941 Japan tried to follow suit with the Russo-Japanese Neutrality Pact, but Hitler attacked the Soviet Union. Historian Akira Iriye has accurately pointed out: "While it is quite possible to discuss the origins of the European war without paying much attention to Asian factors, the obverse is not the case." When Hitler sneezed, the Japanese caught a cold.

Konoe reorganized his cabinet on July 16, 1941, eliminating Matsuoka in the process; but even before that the military and the cabinet had begun to rethink their foreign policy once again. The first, and seemingly most obvious option, would be to attack Russia through Manchukuo, thus assisting their German ally and forcing Stalin to fight a two-front war. Hitler and Ribbentrop requested this Japanese assistance on June 30, 1941; and a strongly pro-Axis faction on the Japanese General Staff advocated compliance. They called this the "strategy of the green persimmon" — to pick persimmons one shakes the tree while the fruit is still green.

Yet the stinging defeat at Nomonhan in 1939 made the Japanese cautious. Furthermore, a war in the north would consume great amounts of military supplies and petroleum with no prospect of capturing any new resources in the bleak expanses of Siberia. A southern advance, on the other hand, promised to deliver copious supplies of oil, rubber, tin, and aluminum from the Dutch East Indies. Therefore, the liaison conferences held between the army, navy, and cabinet[2]

2. Shortly after the China incident in 1937, the Japanese established these liaison conferences to coordinate policy between the army and navy general staffs, which traditionally enjoyed the prerogative of command independence, and the government cabi-

adopted instead the "strategy of the ripe persimmon." That is, they would wait for the Soviet fruit to ripen while remaining on the defensive in the northern sector. When and if the Soviets drastically reduced their military forces in the Far East, moving them west to meet the German invasion, then the Japanese would invade. In the meantime, they would pluck riper fruit in the South Seas and Southeast Asia.

Pursuing the ripe persimmon, the Japanese again pressured Vichy France, and in the last few days of July 1941 they moved troops into the southern portion of Indochina, intending to use it as a staging area for further advances into British Malaya and the Dutch East Indies. In so doing, the Japanese crossed an invisible line which brought forth a strong response from the United States and led within six months to a wider, Greater East Asia War. For the first, but unfortunately not the last time, American policymakers decided that the status of southern Vietnam was worth fighting for. In order to understand why, we must pause and reflect on larger trends in Japanese and American policy before resuming the narrative of events.

Briefly, we can say that Japan and the United States went to war against each other in 1941 because they held conflicting views of the world and their own roles in it. The leaders of both countries were deeply ethnocentric, and they neither understood nor respected the other's worldview.

The Japanese remained divided on foreign policy matters throughout the incidents and accidents of the 1930s and early 1940s. The navy and the army held different priorities, and both branches of the military were internally divided into a bewildering group of cliques and factions. Relatively junior, middle-echelon officers on the army and navy general staffs, as well as enterprising field officers, frequently exercised more influence on policy than their nominal superiors, in a process the Japanese called *gekokujo*, meaning "the low oppress the high." Furthermore, the military as a whole often disagreed with, and tacitly threatened, the civilian government ministers in the cabinet.

Many observers have ascribed Japan's warlike actions to a rogue military class lording it over helpless, passive civilians. This is the view that dominated the war crimes trials after the war, in which over forty Japanese "militarists" were indicted and seven were executed. Others blame the "system," a faction-ridden, out-of-control governmental machinery, for the war decisions. Both views contain some truth, but they are incomplete and misleading. Despite the factional-

---

net ministers. The practice lapsed for awhile after 1938, but was reinstituted in November 1940. Seventy-five liaison conferences were held between this time and December 4, 1941. When the conferences reached important decisions, these were ratified formally at an imperial conference in the presence of the emperor, who usually said nothing but affixed his seal to the policy documents.

ism and creaky machinery of government, most Japanese leaders held a common worldview and formulated their policies accordingly. Their admittedly important and fierce disagreements dealt with means not ends.

The Japanese of the 1930s viewed themselves, correctly, as a relatively weak, poor, and disadvantaged people, a have-not nation and a junior-grade great power. Their home islands, which lacked the natural resources necessary for an industrial economy, groaned under the burden of supporting a growing population. The Meiji Restoration had opened a gap between a modern urban sector of the economy and a larger, traditional farm sector. The Great Depression widened this gap and placed additional strains on both sectors.

Despite these problems, Japanese leaders swelled with pride over what they had already accomplished since the Meiji era. They had witnessed the seeming invincibility of European imperial powers crack during the First World War and the depression. They believed that over the centuries Japan had absorbed and assimilated the best of both Asiatic and Euro-American cultures and thus could forge a more satisfying synthesis. Above all, the generation of soldiers, sailors, and government bureaucrats that came of age in the 1920s and 1930s lacked the sense of limits that the Meiji had possessed.

Self-confident, yet fearful for the future, the Showa generation believed the time had come to displace the Europeans and Americans in Asia, impose a new order, and build a self-sufficient pan-Asian sphere of influence. Amid the muddle and blunders of actual policy decisions, nearly all Japanese leaders, military and civilian, agreed on these goals derived from their worldview. At the very least, as a lowest common denominator, they were resolved to keep control of Manchuria and to prevent China from becoming communist.

Many Japanese pan-Asianists were sincerely idealistic in their hopes and dreams. Ishiwara Kanji, the architect of the Manchurian incident of 1931, treated the Chinese and other Asians as partners in progress. He hoped to build a multicultural society of Japanese, Chinese, Manchus, and Koreans in Manchukuo which would serve as a model for an East Asian League. When he returned to Manchukuo in 1937 he felt disgust at Japanese manipulation of the puppet state.

Another Japanese colonel, Suzuki Keiji, adopted a Burmese name, Bo Mogyo; and like an Asiatic "Lawrence of Arabia," he organized a Burmese independence army which not only fought the British but resisted Japanese domination as well. At first, many Asians welcomed the Japanese as liberators from colonialism. Even those who feared Japanese imperialism might prove as oppressive as the European variety could not stifle their emotional pan-Asianism. One civil servant in Malaya stated that "although his reason utterly rebelled against it, his sympathies instinctively ranged themselves with the Japanese in their fight against Anglo-America."

Too often, however, the Japanese squandered this latent goodwill by highhanded, even brutal, behavior. In China, particularly, the Japanese showed contempt for their fellow Asians by referring to them with the demeaning epithet *chankoro*. Matsuoka Yosuke, a number of years before he became foreign minister, summed up the typical Japanese attitude towards China in a press interview:

> China and Japan are two brothers who have inherited a great mansion called Eastern Asia. . . . The ne'er-do-well elder brother turned a dope fiend and a rogue, but the younger, lean, but rugged and ambitious, ever dreamed of bringing back past glories to the old House. . . . The younger in a towering rage beat up the elder — trying to beat into him some sense of shame and awaken some pride in the noble traditions of the great house.

Most Japanese, formed by an educational system that encouraged conformism, considered the Japanese way of life spiritually superior to that of Europe and America. Forming one family with their divine emperor, they believed they possessed a heaven-sent mission to bring this culture to all of Asia, and perhaps someday to the whole world. They proved as ethnocentric as any European imperialists.

The United States of America also cherished a sense of national mission, a manifest destiny to spread its own superior culture and economy worldwide. Franklin Roosevelt's secretary of state, Cordell Hull, summed up America's worldview at this time in four principles which he communicated to the Japanese ambassador in 1941. Hull was a former senator from Tennessee, a disciple of Woodrow Wilson, and a devoted advocate of free trade. His four principles were:

1. Respect for the territorial integrity and the sovereignty of each and all nations.
2. Support of the principle of noninterference in the internal affairs of other nations.
3. Support of the principle of equality, including equality of commercial opportunity.
4. Nondisturbance of the status quo in the Pacific except as the status quo might be altered by peaceful means.

Most Americans, now as then, would consider Hull's four principles simple truisms, like "motherhood and apple pie." Yet the American government had frequently violated the first two in the past. In the early decades of the twentieth century, the United States sent troops into Latin American countries on numerous occasions, seizing the Panama Canal zone from Colombia, toppling unfriendly governments in Santo Domingo, Nicaragua, and Haiti. During the Mexican Revolution, General Pershing's legions roamed the northern Mexican deserts hunting for Pancho Villa. Japanese intellectuals claimed that the Monroe Doctrine, staking out North and South America as a U.S. sphere of influence, differed little from Japan's goal of a co-prosperity sphere in Asia. They were correct.

The United States had also intervened outside its own hemisphere, particularly in Asia which it considered a natural extension of its western frontier. America became a Pacific Ocean power by violating Hull's fourth principle, altering the status quo with decidedly non-peaceful means. In 1898 the United States had seized the Philippine Islands from Spain, then fought a bloody war of repression against Filipino independence. The American government proclaimed the Open Door Policy in China to forestall European imperialists, but it also enforced extraterritorial status for its business interests in China with troops and gunboats. The Japanese, therefore, accused Cordell Hull and the Americans of hypocrisy.

Though protecting their home market with high tariffs, the American government tried to impose the third of Hull's four principles, equality of commercial opportunity, in Asia; and this clashed head-on with the autarchic, closed nature of Japan's co-prosperity sphere. American businessmen had always sought to trade with everyone, worldwide; thus they advocated the Open Door Policy. That, after all, is why Commodore Perry forced open the Japanese market in the first place. Now the Japanese, the Nazis, and the Italians, as well as the British and the Americans' own high tariff advocates at home, were trying to divide up the world into closed blocs. This challenged the very heart of the Open Door Policy, championed most eloquently by Woodrow Wilson. The United States had grown great on free trade and would fight to maintain it.

The American ambassador in Tokyo, Joseph Grew, accurately represented his country's position when he told a group of important Japanese civilians in 1939 that the United States would not go to war over the violation of human rights in China or the violation of a treaty or two. "The important factor," Grew concluded, "the factor that would transform dislike for Japan into action against Japan, was the Japanese assault on the liberal commercial world order. . . ."

The way Grew stated U.S. aims made it sound as if American policy were motivated by narrowly economic interests. This was not the case. In the eyes of most Americans, free trade and capitalist enterprise went hand in hand with political freedom. What was good for American trade was good for the world, since democracy and a better way of life inevitably followed. In addition, in the late 1930s and early 1940s, most world leaders, Americans included, felt they were playing for higher-than-average stakes. Since Hitler clearly wanted to dominate the world, other leaders with aggressive, expansionist plans, such as the Italians and Japanese, were presumed to have similar designs. Therefore, when Cordell Hull and Franklin Roosevelt drew a line in Southeast Asia, they believed they were protecting free trade, democracy, and the future of the world against a terrible, multi-headed tyranny. The Japanese, for their part, viewed the

Americans as economic imperialists, trying to replace the older, European imperialists.

We can assess this ethnocentric clash of worldviews according to the four criteria developed in chapter 3. First, as an island nation, Japan's environment was more constricted and its resources more limited than those of the United States or other continental nations. The Japanese, therefore, felt an acute need for expansion onto the continent of Asia. The United States, on the other hand, blessed with enormous resources, could confidently champion a world of free trade and open economic competition for its leaders believed they would come out ahead in such a contest.

Second, employing a functional approach, it seems clear that Japan's attempt to build a pan-Asian league of co-prosperity made sense in the specific circumstances of the time. A pan-Asian sphere could serve the function of economic survival in a hostile world that was fragmenting into self-contained economic blocs. On the other hand, the Wilson-Hull-Roosevelt dream of an Open Door World would probably produce a higher level of economic prosperity in a benign, free-trading world. The Japanese approach was the more realistic in the 1930s. Japanese diplomats occasionally emphasized this, offering to open their economic sphere if the rest of the world followed suit. There was no chance of this happening.

Third, judged by their own standards, both the Japanese and the American approaches to world politics failed in the years between the two world wars. Because of the highhanded methods of the Japanese military, their co-prosperity sphere, intended to bring peace, brotherhood, and prosperity, led to resistance and resentment on the part of other Asians and finally resulted in world war. The American free trade approach had already failed in the Great Depression and had been largely abandoned by most of the world.

Finally, neither the Japanese nor the American worldview could lay claim to moral high ground. Whatever abuses Japanese imperialists committed were paralleled by the abuses of European and American imperialism. Though American leaders had long believed that their seizure of the Philippines had been a mistake and were planning to grant independence in the near future, they were still defending the British and French empires in Southeast Asia against Japanese advances. Ishiwara Kanji lashed out bitterly at the war crimes trials after the war: "And so for its own defense it [Japan] took your own country as its teacher and set about learning how to be aggressive. You might say we became your disciples. Why don't you subpoena [Commodore] Perry from the other world and try *him* as a war criminal?"

In any case, the free-trade obsession of Cordell Hull, Franklin Roosevelt, and many other Americans clashed with Japan's drive for pan-Asian self-sufficiency in the 1940s. At the deepest level, this conflict, and the mutual misunderstandings it promoted, was the cause of the Greater East Asia War. Historian John Toland summarized the causes brilliantly:

> A war that need not have been fought was about to be fought because of mutual misunderstandings, language difficulties, and mistranslations as well as Japanese opportunism, *gekokujo,* irrationality, honor, pride and fear — and American racial prejudice, distrust, ignorance of the Orient, rigidity, self-righteousness, honor, national pride and fear. Perhaps these were essentially the answers to Handel's question: "Why do the nations rage so furiously together?"

For several years before 1941, the United States and Japan had been engaged in a cold war of words in East Asia. Cordell Hull presided over a State Department almost as faction-ridden as the Japanese military. His chief Asian advisor, Stanley Hornbeck, advocated a tough policy to stop Japan's dominance of China; but his European specialists counseled that America's economic interests in Asia were not worth fighting for. Hull followed a middle course. He tried not to offend or confront the Japanese unnecessarily, but he refused to withdraw or abandon American interests in Asia. Since Hull was a disciple of Woodrow Wilson, a phrase describing the former president can aptly be applied to him as well: "He would do anything in the world for you except get off your back."[3]

President Roosevelt was preoccupied with domestic politics and with his attempts to aid Great Britain against Hitler, so he intervened in Asian affairs only sporadically. For example, after the "Rape of Nanking," FDR toyed with the idea of a long-distance blockade of Japan, with American ships lined up from the Aleutians to the Philippines and British ships forming a picket line from the Philippines to Singapore. He sent a naval planner to England in 1938 to discuss this idea, but nothing came of it. For the most part, he left Cordell Hull in charge of U.S.-Japanese relations.

The secretary of state followed a policy of slowly escalating economic pressure against Japan; he proceeded cautiously but tenaciously. On July 26, 1939, the United States gave the required six months' notice to abrogate its 1911 Treaty of Trade and Commerce with Japan; but when the treaty lapsed on January 26, 1940, commercial relations continued on an ad hoc basis. Then in the summer of 1940, Roosevelt made one of his occasional interventions, ordering the American fleet to remain at Pearl Harbor after its annual maneuvers in the Pacific instead of returning to the California coast. Hull agreed with this as a sensible middle course. Some wanted to withdraw the fleet from the Pacific to aid British convoys against

---

3. Social worker Raymond Robins said this of Wilson at the time of the Punitive Expedition in Mexico.

submarines in the Atlantic; others wished to send it all the way to the British Asian base in Singapore to threaten the Japanese. Hull and Roosevelt left it halfway between, in the middle of the Pacific.

On July 2, 1940, the U.S. Congress passed a National Defense Act giving the executive branch authority to embargo the export of strategic materials. The primary aim of this law was to stockpile war materials the United States would need if attacked, but the State Department also used it as a weapon of economic warfare against Japan, slowly increasing the number of items that could be exported only to "friendly nations." Japan was not listed in that category. Aviation-grade gasoline was added to the embargo list on July 26, 1940, but Japan continued to buy lower grades of petroleum and enhance them for use in its aircraft. The export of scrap iron which could be used for making steel was banned after Japan moved into northern Indochina in September 1940.

Nearly a year later, when the Japanese military landed in southern Indochina, the United States imposed its most stringent sanctions. On July 25, 1941, the American government froze all Japanese assets in the United States. Japanese purchases of American goods would require a license from the Export Control Commission, releasing just enough funds to pay for these approved transactions. Also, on August 1, the export of gasoline to Japan was totally prohibited. This was a crucial blow, since Japan relied on the United States for about half its petroleum supplies. Its only other major sources of oil were on Sakhalin Island to the north and the Dutch East Indies to the south. Heavy pressure on the Dutch colonial government had increased the amount of oil the Japanese could purchase in the Indies, but they still needed American supplies. This accounts for much of Japan's feeling of encirclement and its fear of American economic imperialism.

Amazingly, neither Hull nor Roosevelt had ordered the total oil embargo. Government policy after the freeze still permitted the Japanese to import the average amount of low-grade petroleum it had bought in the years before the China War began. In theory, this would allow normal civilian activities in Japan but would hamper the military. Export Control calculated the permitted amount and notified the joint State-Treasury-Justice Department Foreign Funds Control Committee to "unfreeze" sufficient funds. However, Assistant Secretary of State Dean Acheson, who chaired the Foreign Funds Control Committee, kept the oil export funds frozen on his own authority. The Japanese were not the only ones with a *gekokujo* problem. Hull didn't discover the total embargo for over a month, but by that time it was too late to change it. If the United States relaxed the ban then, they would seem to be backing down from a tough policy and might encourage the Japanese rather than deter them.

The freezing of Japanese funds in the U.S. and the total oil embargo made war with Japan almost certain. The Japanese had stockpiled about two years' worth of oil supplies, but if war broke out this would last only about one year. Thus the Japanese had to obtain more oil from Southeast Asia or else back down completely from their earlier conquests in China in order to appease the United States and reopen the oil spigots. It was unlikely that proud nationalists in Japan would back down.

Nevertheless, both sides kept talking, since neither wanted war with the other. Since April 1941, Secretary Hull had conducted extensive negotiations with the Japanese ambassador, Nomura Kichisaburo, one of a dying breed of pro-American Japanese leaders. Hull stuck rigidly to his four principles and demanded Japanese troop withdrawals from both China and Manchuria before making any significant American concessions. The Japanese insisted that the status of Manchukuo was final and that they needed to keep troops in China to prevent Communist dominance of the Asian continent. This left little room for compromise on either side. After the oil embargo, the best that could be hoped for was what diplomats call a modus vivendi — that is, a minor, tactical compromise that settles little but buys time for more negotiations. Yet Hull continued pushing for a comprehensive solution of all outstanding problems.

In August and September 1941, Prime Minister Konoe mounted a final, desperate effort to prevent war with the United States. He proposed a summit meeting between himself and President Roosevelt on U.S. territory. To guard against military sabotage of his plans, he schemed with Imperial Palace officials to cable any agreement reached at the summit directly to the emperor, who would then announce it as a fait accompli. It's surprising that Roosevelt did not seize this opportunity, for he enjoyed personal diplomacy; but Cordell Hull opposed the summit meeting, and Roosevelt himself did not want to do anything that smacked of a Munich agreement, so he refused the offer.

Failure to negotiate with Konoe marked a major tactical mistake by the U.S. government. A modus vivendi reached at the summit would have bought at least six months' worth of time; and the United States needed time in the fall of 1941. At the very least, it would have allowed for an American military buildup. At best, it might have prevented war altogether, for by the spring of 1942 the German invasion of Russia had gone sour and the Japanese might have decided to avoid further risks in Asia. All this is speculation. What actually happened is that the Konoe government fell in October and Japan prepared for war.

General Tojo Hideki formed a cabinet on October 18, 1941, with himself as prime minister, war minister, and home minister. American wartime propaganda, not unnaturally, painted Tojo as a fascist dictator in the mold of Mussolini or Hitler, and he was hanged as a war criminal after the war. This is an overly simplified and largely erroneous view. His American biographer, Robert Butow, has concluded: "Tojo did not himself indulge in the sputterings of a Hitler or a Mussolini. . . . [He] remained adamant toward the American and British enemy, but he did not treat Japan's foes with contempt or subject them to fanatical abuse."

Born in 1884, Tojo Hideki was the son of a lieutenant general and had become a career military officer himself. A rigidly honest soldier who believed in firm discipline, he rose through the ranks in mostly administrative posts. Konoe named him war minister in 1940, then he succeeded the prince as prime minister in the crucial days of October 1941. His holding of multiple offices was not a power grab on his part. The emperor had ordered him to "return to blank paper" after the failure of the Konoe initiative, that is, make a final reexamination of Japanese-U.S. relations before deciding on war or peace. To the surprise of his colleagues, Tojo took this order very seriously, abandoning his narrowly pro-army viewpoint and trying hard to speak for the national interest. He retained the war minister post so that he could control the military, whatever decision was reached; and he took on the Home Ministry temporarily to suppress civilian disorder if a decision for peace led to riots.

Tojo's government held intensive liaison conferences from October 23 to November 1. They considered three alternatives: (1) do nothing; (2) go to war immediately; or (3) mount further diplomatic efforts while preparing for war. On November 5, 1941, an imperial conference chose the third option, even though there seemed little chance for successful negotiations. The American and Japanese positions were too polarized by this time, with the Americans demanding a withdrawal from China and Manchuria, and the Japanese insisting on recognition of Manchukuo as a separate state and the continued garrisoning of troops in China to guard against communism. The Japanese made a final decision to continue diplomatic negotiations in Washington, but to make war if no settlement was reached by December 1.

Cordell Hull, who could read the Japanese dispatches from Tokyo to its embassies since the American military had broken the Japanese diplomatic code,[4] also realized that negotiations held out little hope. So on November 26, he handed Ambassador Nomura a strongly worded note, restating the maximum American position for the record. The Japanese considered this final Hull note an ultimatum and thus decided to make war on December 8 (Tokyo time) with simultaneous attacks on the Philippines, Malaya, and the Hawaiian Islands.

Japanese military leaders were not optimistic about war with the United States. The Navy knew it could win immediate victories but was not sanguine about the long-range prospects. General Tojo, however, proclaimed: "There are times when we must have the courage to do extraordinary things — like jumping, with eyes closed, off the veranda of the Kiyomizu Temple!" As historian Nobutaka Ike has pointed out, the Japanese leaders may have been thinking of the Russo-Japanese War. In 1904-5 Japan's military scored astounding successes,

---

4. The Japanese diplomatic code was nicknamed "Purple," and the system that American intelligence used to crack it was known as "Magic."

but they soon strained the country's resources to the breaking point. Only the early peace negotiated by Theodore Roosevelt saved them from disaster. "One suspects that either consciously or unconsciously the Japanese leaders in 1941 were hoping for a more or less similar sequence of events." Japan went to war fatalistically, as a desperate gamble, largely to break the tension and uncertainty.

In a final, humiliating comedy of errors, the Japanese government sent its Washington embassy a long message informing the United States that it was breaking off diplomatic relations, with instructions to deliver it at 1:00 P.M. December 7 (Washington time), an hour before the attack on Pearl Harbor was scheduled. Unable to decode and translate the message in time, the Japanese envoys delivered it *after* the attack had taken place. Cordell Hull could barely contain his rage as he snatched the missive from the abashed Japanese diplomats. The following day, President Roosevelt told Congress and the American people that December 7 was "a date which will live in infamy."

The Japanese military had not originally planned an attack on Pearl Harbor at the onset of war. Their goal was the capture of natural resources in the Dutch East Indies and Southeast Asia, so the main military advance would go south. According to the naval war plan, if the American fleet intervened it would be lured west into Japanese waters, harassed along the way by submarines, and then destroyed in "one big battle," like Tsushima in 1905. However, the commander of the Japanese Combined Fleet, Admiral Yamamoto Isoroku, convinced his superiors to stage an attack on the American fleet at its base in Pearl Harbor, thus knocking it out at the beginning of the war and securing the navy's flank for the main advance into Southeast Asia.

Born the same year as General Tojo (1884), Yamamoto had fought in the "great all-out battle" of Tsushima, losing two fingers of his left hand to shell fragments. Yet he was one of the few battleship admirals who understood how air power had transformed naval strategy since then. He had studied English at Harvard and had served as naval attaché at the Japanese embassy in Washington during the 1920s. Ironically, he belonged to the more pro-American faction in the navy that would have preferred avoiding war with the United States, but he patriotically did more than was expected of him as war loomed on the horizon.

Yamamoto had begun thinking about an attack on Pearl Harbor as early as March or April 1940, but systematic planning did not begin at his Combined Fleet headquarters until the end of 1940. The Pearl Harbor plan represented yet another example of *gekokujo,* incubated and hatched at the fleet level, rather than in the War Ministry or the Naval General Staff. Yamamoto did not gain final approval for the operation until October 19, 1941, and it remained a closely guarded secret until it was executed on December 7.

The Pearl Harbor task force, commanded by Admiral Nagumo Chuichi, rendezvoused at remote Hitokappu Bay in the Kurile Islands north of Japan, while Yamamoto remained on his flagship *Nagato* in home waters. Nagumo's flotilla of six aircraft carriers, three battleships, two heavy cruisers and a light cruiser, flanked by destroyers and submarines, maintained strict radio silence while cruising towards the Hawaiian Islands from the north. Yamamoto could send them instructions securely, since the Americans had not broken the admiralty codes as they had the diplomatic cyphers.

The Japanese task force paused about 220 miles north of the island of Oahu to launch its dive bombers, torpedo bombers, horizontal bombers, and fighters. Two waves, 350 planes in all, took off at approximately 6:00 A.M. and 7:00 A.M. on December 7 (Hawaii time). As the first wave reached Oahu, Commander Fuchida Mutsuo signaled the task force that complete surprise had been achieved with the code words, *Tora! Tora! Tora!* ("Tiger! Tiger! Tiger!"). The attack on American ships lying at anchor in Pearl Harbor began at 7:53 A.M.

A lucky hit from a high-altitude horizontal bomber sank the battleship *Arizona* in a spectacular explosion; but Japanese torpedo bombers, swooping in almost at sea level, caused the greatest destruction along "battleship row." The British navy had shown how devastating a torpedo attack could be when they destroyed half the Italian fleet at anchor in Taranto the previous year (November 12, 1940), but few believed Pearl Harbor was deep enough for air-launched torpedoes. The American fleet, therefore, was not protected by torpedo nets. However, Yamamoto's air advisor, Genda Minoru, had modified the torpedoes with special fins to keep them from burrowing into the mud of shallow waters.

All in all the Japanese sunk or seriously damaged 8 battleships, 3 light cruisers, 3 destroyers, and 4 auxiliary craft. They also destroyed 87 naval airplanes and 77 army aircraft, while damaging 128 additional planes. Incredibly, the army commander, General Walter Short, had lined up all the planes wingtip to wingtip on the landing strip, making them easy targets. As a result of the attack on Pearl Harbor, 2,403 Americans died and 1,178 were injured. The Japanese attackers lost only 29 airplanes and 45 airmen.

Surprise had been so total that many Americans demanded an explanation and began looking for scapegoats. Over the years a conspiracy theory has developed, alleging that President Franklin Roosevelt deliberately exposed the fleet to attack in order to bring the United States into the war. Though he had been gradually increasing aid to Great Britain in the European struggle, Roosevelt faced isolationist opposition every step of the way. He did not dare ask for a declaration of war, against either Germany or Japan, because he knew that Congress would not pass it. Thus, the intentional unpreparedness of the fleet in Hawaii, so the conspiracy theory goes, constituted a "back door to war." Once the Japanese attacked U.S. territory and killed Americans, a war declaration would follow easily.

There is plenty of circumstantial evidence to support this conspiracy theory. Roosevelt did breathe a sigh of relief, once the shock of Pearl Harbor wore off, for it did solve his political problems. He obtained a unanimous war declaration against Japan on December 8, and the country responded with nationalistic fury.

General Walter Short and Admiral Husband Kimmel, the army and navy commanders on Oahu, had received several warnings and hints of the impending attack, so their lack of preparedness does look suspicious. Both the Army Chief of Staff, General George Marshall, and the Chief of Naval Operations, Admiral Harold Stark, sent "war warnings" to Hawaii and other American naval bases on November 27, after the Hull-Nomura negotiations in Washington broke off. Then on the morning of December 7 itself, two Japanese scout planes flew right over Pearl Harbor without anyone noticing them. An American destroyer sank a Japanese submarine off Oahu that morning, but the top brass did not increase the state of alertness. Two naval radar operators spotted the first wave of planes 130 miles out shortly after 7:00 A.M., but the lieutenant in charge told them not to worry about it.

Despite such tantalizing clues, however, no conclusive evidence has ever been found that Roosevelt or anyone else knew of the attack beforehand and ordered this knowledge suppressed. Roosevelt, Marshall, and the secretaries of army and navy believed the Japanese attack would fall upon the Philippines and Southeast Asia, and were not especially concerned about Hawaii. The failure to prepare properly at Pearl Harbor seems due to horrible snafus, rather than conspiracy.

General Short and Admiral Kimmel, for example, did heed the November 27 warnings from Washington, but only according to their own preconceptions. Short believed the greatest danger in Hawaii would come from "fifth column" sabotage by the 160,000 Japanese-Americans resident in the islands. So he lined up his planes together, where they could be guarded easily, and locked most of the ammunition safely away from saboteurs. This was a rational response to a threat of sabotage, but disastrous when attack came from the air. Similarly, Admiral Kimmel believed that submarines posed the major threat to his fleet; so after the November 27 war warning, he issued a shoot-on-sight order for any unidentified submarine. Again, a rational but inadequate response. Finally, Lieutenant Kermit Tyler told his radar operators not to worry about the blip on their screens because he was expecting a flight of American B-17s from the mainland about the same time. Sure enough, these arrived as the attack was in progress, and some were destroyed after landing. Bad luck and poor analysis of intelligence, not conspiracy, doomed Pearl Harbor. Appropriately, Gordon Prange titled his definitive book about the attack *At Dawn We Slept*.

The Japanese caught Pearl Harbor sleeping because the Americans underestimated them. When Admiral Kimmel's behavior on December 7 came under investigation by Congress after the war, the chief investigator asked him privately why he hadn't sent the whole fleet out of the harbor for safety's sake. He replied: "I never thought those little yellow sons-of-bitches could pull off such an attack. . . ." Ethnocentrism to the point of racism lay at the roots of the tragedy.

Probably the best refutation of the conspiracy thesis lies in the background and psychology of President Roosevelt. FDR was a navy man through and through. An avid sailor before he was stricken with polio, he cherished a nearly mystical passion for ships. He had served as assistant secretary of the navy during World War I, and even after he became president he called his former superior Josephus Daniels "Chief." General Marshall once begged him to quit calling the U.S. Army "them" and the U.S. Navy "us." Roosevelt was a slick political operator, capable of many devious maneuvers; but he was simply incapable of setting up a fleet of ships with thousands of sailors as sitting ducks. Hitler certainly could have done something like this; possibly even Churchill; but not FDR.

Pearl Harbor marked a great humiliation for the United States, but it turned into a Pyrrhic victory for the Japanese. Though the Pacific Fleet was knocked out for six months, most of the ships sunk in the shallow waters of Pearl Harbor were eventually refloated, salvaged, and returned to action. Furthermore, the three aircraft carriers assigned to Kimmel's fleet had been out at sea on December 7 and thus survived unharmed. The Japanese did not follow up the Pearl Harbor raid with an invasion of Hawaii, as Yamamoto desired. Most importantly, though there was no Roosevelt conspiracy, the Japanese attack did serve the purpose alleged by the conspiracy thesis: it brought the United States into World War II.

There is no certainty that the United States would have declared war if it had not been attacked. Roosevelt had stretched neutrality to the breaking point throughout 1940 and 1941 with the passage of the Lend-Lease Act that funneled aid to Great Britain and Russia, and the arming of American merchant ships in the Atlantic. In one of his most memorable speeches, FDR christened America the "arsenal of democracy." Congress had passed the first peacetime military draft in its history in June 1940. Yet the president knew that neither Congress nor the public was ready for war. When the draft law came up for renewal in June 1941, it passed by only a single vote. Roosevelt had done all he could to aid the Allies short of war and, as one of his advisors remarked, "he had run out of tricks."

The Japanese solved Roosevelt's political problem and brought the full weight of American manpower and resources down upon themselves. Had the Japanese navy stuck to its original plans and overruled Yamamoto, invading the East Indies and Southeast Asia, but avoiding Hawaii and the Philippines, they might have avoided war with the United States. Ultimately, the attack on Pearl Harbor proved just as disastrous for the Japanese as Hitler's panzer attack on Russia was for the Germans.

The onset of World War II in Asia, the Greater East Asia War, resembles in many ways the coming of World War I. In both cases, no one wanted war, but everyone was making plans to wage a war. Once tension reached a high point, a relatively weak aggressor decided to fight, despite poor prospects for success. In 1914 Austria-Hungary attacked Serbia out of desperation, fearing it might otherwise cease to be a great power. In 1941 Japan opted for war, lest it decline to the status of a third-rate power. Both the European and the Asian nation fought primarily to save face, and both relied on a more powerful German nation to assist them. Once the decision for war was taken, the dominant emotion all around was a blessed sense of relief from uncertainty.

In Europe in 1914 and the Pacific Ocean in 1941, war plans kicked in nearly automatically. Both the German Schlieffen plan and Yamamoto's Pearl Harbor attack nearly succeeded, but fell just short of their ultimate goals. As a result, in both cases, a long, protracted war that no one felt prepared for ensued. For the second time in twenty-five years, but now on an even greater scale, the world blundered into a catastrophic war.

CHAPTER TWENTY-THREE

Coalition Warfare, Unconditional Surrender

With the entry of the Soviet Union, Japan, and the United States, the Second World War reached around the globe. The catastrophic struggle that raged from 1941 to 1945 was more truly a world war than the 1914-18 conflict. President Franklin D. Roosevelt coined the term "United Nations" for his country and its allies, and twenty-six nations signed the original United Nations Declaration on January 1, 1942. Others joined later.

Opposing armies fought on the continents of Europe, Africa, and Asia and on numerous islands in the Pacific, while the navies dueled above, below, and on the surface of all the world's oceans. Japanese airplanes rained bombs on the Australian city of Darwin and their submarines lobbed a few shells at the West Coast of the United States. Late in the war, balloons carried incendiary bombs across the Pacific, igniting forest fires in Canada and the United States.

South America remained wholly free of warfare, though naval battles and submarine raids took place off her coast. Nevertheless, all the Latin American countries eventually declared war against the Axis, except Argentina with its pro-Fascist government headed by Juan Peron. Few South Americans took an active part in the fighting, but Brazil did send troops against Italy in the Mediterranean, and Mexican airmen fought Japan in the Pacific.

Only five countries of Europe remained neutral throughout the struggle. All of the British Dominions — Canada, Australia, New Zealand, and South Africa — and the colony of India declared war almost immediately after Great Britain did. China had been fighting Japan since 1931, and the colonial dependencies of France and Holland in southeast Asia were swept up in Japan's drive to the south. France's African colonies became involved in a tug-of-war between Free French and pro-Axis Vichy French soldiers.

The global conflict was a coalition war, but primarily on one side. The Axis powers of Germany, Italy, and Japan were bound by a formal, Tripartite Pact, but they cooperated very little. The wars in the Pacific and in Europe remained almost wholly separate. In 1942 the Western Allies feared a possible linkup between German and Japanese forces in the Middle East, if Hitler knocked out Russia and the Japanese gained control of the Indian Ocean; but this was never a very real possibility.

Italy also tried to wage a "parallel war" to Germany's, confining most of its belligerence to the shores of the Mediterranean, where Mussolini hoped to construct a new Roman Empire. Yet when Italian troops faltered against British forces in North Africa, Hitler sent General Erwin Rommel with German reinforcements to take over this theater. For most of the war, until Mussolini was deposed by the Fascist Grand Council in July 1943, Italy functioned as a very junior partner of Germany. Thereafter, the German army simply flooded Italy, continuing the war on their own. Similarly, the other Axis partners — Finland, Romania, Hungary, and Bulgaria — served mainly as cannon fodder for the German war machine.

The Big Three Allied Powers — Britain, the United States, and Russia — worked together more closely than the Axis nations. Winston Churchill forged a very close relationship with Franklin D. Roosevelt. The two leaders appealed to different, but complementary constituencies, in both countries — Churchill to conservatives and FDR to trade unionists and liberals. The British prime minister crossed the Atlantic five times after the United States entered the war, staying at the White House while in Washington, just across the hall from FDR's chief adviser and troubleshooter, Harry Hopkins. When the two met in Casablanca in January 1943 to concert strategy, Churchill insisted after the conference that the president drive with him 150 miles across the desert to share a villa in Marrakech and "see the sunset on the snows of the Atlas Mountains."

British and American military chiefs had been meeting secretly since the beginning of 1941, long before the Americans entered the war. At the first Roosevelt-Churchill conference after Pearl Harbor, they formalized the arrangement by establishing a Combined Chiefs of Staff. Whenever the two nations' armies fought together during the war, FDR and Churchill agreed upon a single supreme commander for that particular theater. Historian Keith Sainsbury has concluded: "Roosevelt and Churchill achieved probably the closest planning relationship between allies in history."

Both found their dealings with the Soviet dictator more rocky. Churchill and Stalin, as warriors, realists, and survivors, had much in common, but did not get on well. Roosevelt, who viewed himself as a mediator between his blunt and contentious colleagues, tried harder to charm and conciliate the Russian leader. Stalin once remarked to the Yugoslav communist Milovan Djilas, "Churchill is the kind who, if you don't watch him, will slip a kopeck out of your pocket. . . . Roosevelt is not like that. He dips in his hand only for bigger coins. But Churchill? . . . even for a kopeck."

The British prime minister flew to Moscow twice during the war, and all three leaders met on two occasions: at Teheran, the capital of Persia, in November 1943 and at the Russian city of Yalta in February 1945. Yet the Anglo-Americans and the Russians never really trusted each other. Soviet generals did not exchange plans with the Combined Chiefs, and for most of the war Stalin refused to let Allied planes land on Russian airfields after their bombing missions over Germany. The British and Americans pooled their knowledge and resources to produce the atomic bomb, under the code name "tube alloys," but they told the Russians nothing about it. (Stalin found out anyway, through his espionage agents.)

The partnership between the Anglo-American powers and the Soviet Union was a "shotgun marriage," an alliance of necessity. Churchill summed it up best, in a remark to his private secretary: "I have only one purpose, the destruction of Hitler, and my life is much simplified thereby. If Hitler invaded Hell I would make at least a favourable reference to the Devil in the House of Commons."

The other United Nations contributed much to the struggle. Many of the "British" soldiers who fought against Rommel in North Africa, for example, actually came from Australia, New Zealand, and India. Canadians took their place on the western front after the invasion of Normandy in 1944, just as they had in 1914. That epic invasion also included contingents of Poles and Frenchmen, whose countries had been conquered earlier by the Nazis.

Yet these other Allies were essentially pawns manipulated by the Big Three, as two striking examples illustrate. Russia had cooperated with Germany in the 1939 partition of Poland, arresting many of the Polish Army's officers and soldiers, and murdering fourteen thousand of them in the Katyn Forest. After Hitler's invasion of the Soviet Union, Stalin released most of the remaining Polish soldiers and permitted them to organize their own army of liberation. In 1942, however, he sent the Polish divisions to reinforce the British in the Middle East, wanting them as far away from the scene of the crime (the Katyn Massacre) as possible. Eventually, these Poles fought their way up through Italy and re-entered their country from the south, not the east.

In the other example, the British mounted a small-scale dress rehearsal for the Normandy invasion that turned into a suicide mission. On August 19, 1942, nearly five thousand Canadian troops, along with a smaller number of British soldiers and a handful of American observers, stormed the German-occupied channel port of Dieppe on the French coast. Withering machine-gun fire cut down the Canadians, their boats and tanks were destroyed, and the shocked survivors surrendered. The Canadians suffered a two-thirds casualty rate, with about a thousand killed and nearly two thousand taken prisoner. Military historians emphasize that valuable lessons were learned at Dieppe. Yet one of the best military analysts, John Keegan, concludes: "Dieppe, in retrospect, looks so recklessly hare-brained an enterprise that it is difficult to reconstruct the official state of mind which gave it birth and drove it forward."

The Big Three held different war aims and strategic points of view. Churchill worked primarily for the survival of Great Britain and the total defeat of Nazism, but he also wanted to keep Britain's colonial empire intact. In the midst of a speech on November 17, 1942, he stated unequivocally: "I have not become the King's First Minister in order to preside over the liquidation of the British Empire." Churchill and the British generals, with long memories of the trench battles in the First War, wanted to pursue more indirect strategies this time around and nibble at the "soft underbelly" of Europe. Churchill even illustrated the principle for Stalin by drawing a picture of a crocodile, poked from beneath. The British and Americans, therefore, invaded Morocco and Algeria in 1942, following up in Sicily and Italy the following year. At British urging, they kept pushing back the date for the direct cross-channel invasion against Germany.

Stalin was also fighting for his country's survival and for the total defeat of Nazism, but he too, like Churchill, had ulterior motives. He wanted to prevent any future German invasions of his country by constructing a buffer zone of "friendly" neighboring states in Eastern Europe. Strategically, he disagreed bluntly with Churchill's indirect approach, and constantly demanded "a Second Front now."

Roosevelt enjoyed the luxury of a more Olympian viewpoint since his country was not directly threatened. He certainly aimed at the total defeat of Nazism before it could pose a threat to America's existence, but he also wanted to diminish colonialism and reconstruct a new world order. Strategically, he agreed with Churchill in the short run, consenting to the North African and Italian campaigns while the United States was building up its manpower and material strength, but he also believed that a cross-channel invasion should be mounted as soon as possible to face Germany with an unwinnable two-front war.

Obviously, the only firm point of agreement between the three great allies was their desire for the total defeat of Nazism. The principle of "unconditional surrender," therefore, became the glue which held the alliance together. Roosevelt first enunciated this war aim at the news conference ending the Casablanca Conference on January 24, 1943. He surprised Churchill with the announcement, though the two had discussed the idea previously, but the prime minister immediately concurred with the president.

Roosevelt pushed for unconditional surrender to avoid the political mixup that followed the First World War. In 1918 Germany sued for peace on the basis of Woodrow Wilson's Fourteen Points, but the Versailles Treaty proved much harsher. This fostered the "stab in the back" myth in Germany that helped bring Hitler to power. Roosevelt, Churchill, and Stalin agreed that this time the Germans should have no illusions and no excuses. The Allies would demand unconditional surrender and would enjoy a free hand to impose any terms they felt necessary. In addition, the unconditional surrender formula made great wartime propaganda on the home front, whipping up the populace for a supreme effort. Most importantly, however, it knit the alliance together, for it was one of the few things all three agreed upon wholeheartedly.

The Big Three also agreed that the battle against Germany would hold first priority. Churchill and Roosevelt adopted a "Germany first" policy at their first conference after Pearl Harbor. Although the American public would have preferred immediate revenge in the Pacific, the president correctly judged that Germany was the more dangerous enemy. Japan had neither the manpower, the resources, nor probably the desire, to go much beyond its initial conquests; but if Hitler conquered Britain and Russia he would have more than enough of everything to bid for world power. Stalin followed a "Germany only" policy, not joining the battle against Japan until the very last days of the war.

Aside from the unconditional surrender formula and some vital supplies of airplanes and trucks, Britain and the United States could do little for Russia in the short run. Despite the Anglo-American efforts in North Africa, the Russians did most of the fighting against Germany until the middle of 1944.

The German army's lightning victories in the West made Hitler overconfident when he attacked the Soviet Union in June 1941. He believed that the Russian army, demoralized by the Communist system and decapitated by Stalin's purges, would collapse under the blows of his panzers. "You have only to kick in the door and the whole rotten structure will come crashing down." Once the German blitzkrieg had defeated the Soviet army, Hitler planned to resettle vast reaches of Russia with German colonists and govern his new empire cheaply and easily. "Let's learn from the English," he told his generals, "who with 250,000 men in all . . . govern 400 million Indians."

The early weeks of the Russian campaign seemingly vindicated Hitler's confidence. The Luftwaffe, numbering about 5,000 airplanes, caught most of the Russian air force on the ground, destroying at least 4,000 planes. Then Hitler launched a force of 3.2 million soldiers, with 3,500 tanks, 7,000 pieces of artillery, and 600,000 horses. Three great army groups thrust forward towards Leningrad in the north, Moscow in the center, and Kiev in the south; but their immediate goal was to encircle as many Soviet soldiers as possible.

Stalin had ignored repeated warnings, from around the world, dismissing them as capitalist provocations. Up to the day before the invasion, he kept sending supplies to Germany in accord with the Molotov-Ribbentrop Nonaggression Pact. When the blow finally fell, Stalin suffered some sort of breakdown and withdrew to his villa outside Moscow, apparently expecting a rebellion by the army or the party. At the end of June, when he realized his subordinates were as dazed as he was, he snapped out of it, appealed on the radio to the national patriotism of the Russian people, and assumed direct command of the defense.

The Germans paused at the end of July to regroup and to argue over their next moves. The panzer generals wanted a direct push on Moscow; but Hitler insisted on mopping up whole armies first. So on August 23 the main German attack thrust southeastward, capturing Kiev on September 18 and sweeping up another half million Russians.

Finally, on October 2 the Germans advanced towards Moscow, creating a panic in the city. The Soviet government evacuated to Kuibyshev, six hundred miles east on the Volga River, but Stalin remained in the capital and recalled his best general, Georgi Zhukov, to organize the defense. Meanwhile, Hitler had destroyed his best chance of toppling the Soviet regime by his brutal treatment of Russian prisoners. Many were shot outright; more perished from mistreatment and neglect. Out of 4 million Russian prisoners taken in the first year's campaign, almost 3 million died. This outraged the Russians and stimulated their national patriotism. As the Germans approached Moscow in October 1941, hundreds of thousands of Muscovites, the majority of them women, dug anti-tank trenches and strung barbed wire. A similar desperate effort saved Leningrad from the thrusts of the northern German army.

The Germans made their final lunge towards Moscow in the winter snow and freezing fog of late November. Some panzer groups got within twenty miles of the city, but by December 5 the attack petered out. The Russians immediately launched a counterattack, driving the Germans back to a line about sixty miles from the city. Hitler's unbroken string of one-campaign victories was broken on the icy plains of Russia. Too much space, and too little time.

The Russians continued their counterattacks throughout the winter, making the freezing Germans even more miserable, but regaining little territory. When the spring thaw halted all activity in March, Hitler reinforced his troops and prepared for a new summer offensive. The Germans still had about the same number of planes as the year before, but fewer tanks and only about half as many soldiers. So Hitler supplemented the depleted German ranks with substantial numbers from Hungary, Romania, and Italy, and several divisions of volunteers from Franco's Spain. The Axis coalition concentrated for attack on just one portion of the front. The northern armies besieged Leningrad, for a total of nine hundred days, starving over a million civilians; and the center army held a static front before Moscow. The main attack came in the south, towards the rich agricultural lands and industrial cities of Ukraine and the oilfields of the Caucasus Mountains.

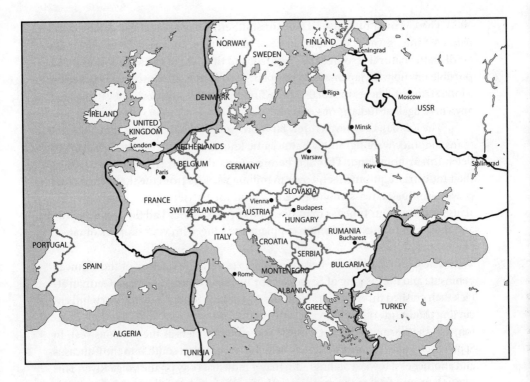

The Greatest Extent of Hitler's Conquests

The German offensive of 1942 in southern Russia was the supreme campaign of Hitler's war. If he captured Ukraine and the Caucasus he would be master of all the natural resources he required, and the road to the Middle East and a possible linkup with Japan would be open. At this time, the British were suffering a long string of defeats in North Africa, and the Americans were not yet engaged anywhere against Italians or Germans.

The Russians, however, threw far more troops into the battles than the Germans did; they were fighting what became known as the Great Patriotic War to defend their homeland. Through heroic efforts they had transported much of their industrial equipment and over 10 million workers from the threatened areas in western Russia, reassembling them behind the barrier of the Urals. The Russians produced four times as many weapons in 1942 as they had the previous year, and the United States and Britain supplemented this with vital supplies of tanks, planes, and trucks.

The German offensive began in May 1942 with the clearing of the Crimean peninsula and the blasting of Sevastopol by huge siege guns. The main German attack then crashed through Ukraine at the end of July, gobbling up territory and encircling thousands of defenders. The Russians, however, retreated in orderly fashion, and the Germans did not capture so many prisoners as the previous year. In September, Hitler divided his forces, sending one portion south into the Caucasus and another east toward Stalingrad, a major industrial city on the Volga River. This division proved fatal to the campaign. The southern thrust fell just short of the vital oilfields, and the Russians determined to hold Stalingrad at all costs. The battle for this city, site of the Soviet leader's earliest military activities in the 1919 Russian civil war, marked the turning-point of the Russo-German war.

The German Sixth Army attacked Stalingrad on September 13. The Luftwaffe leveled the wooden buildings on the outskirts and the army pushed the defenders back into the industrial district along the Volga. In October, the struggle turned into a street-by-street, house-by-house, floor-by-floor battle of attrition. As one German officer described it, "The front is a corridor between burnt-out rooms; it is the thin ceiling between two floors." By the middle of November, the Germans split the Russian perimeter in the factory district and actually reached the Volga in places. They had left the defense of their flanks, however, to their lightly armed and poorly motivated Romanian allies. So on November 19 the Russians crashed into these flanks behind Stalingrad in a giant pincer attack. On November 23 the pincers closed and the German Sixth Army was cut off in the city of rubble they had nearly conquered.

Hitler had assumed direct command of the German army after the failure of 1941 and had moved his headquarters forward into Ukraine for the 1942 campaign. Now his dictatorial ways doomed the encircled Germans in Stalingrad. He refused permission for a breakout from the pocket, ordering the Sixth Army to

410

stand and fight where they were. The Luftwaffe tried to supply them by air, and a relief force under General Manstein thrust toward the city, but fell short. From December into January the isolated Germans starved and froze as they fended off Russian attacks. Finally on February 2, 1943, the remnants of the 250,000 Germans cut off in Stalingrad surrendered. About 150,000 had died and the rest were taken prisoner and paraded through the streets of Moscow on their way to camps in Siberia. Hitler had turned the battle for Stalin's own city into a supreme test of wills, and had lost.

As in the previous year, the Russians counterattacked during the winter all along the front. By the time of the spring thaw in March 1943, they had pushed the Germans back to their summer 1942 starting point. On July 5, 1943, Hitler launched his last offensive in Russia, crashing into a huge exposed salient in the Russian lines around the city of Kursk. This turned into a week-long slugging match of heavy armored divisions, the largest tank battle in history. No longer mobile enough to employ their panzers in lightning thrusts, the Germans found themselves outgunned by the larger and better Soviet tanks. By July 13 the Russians regained the initiative. Previously on this front, the Germans had attacked in summer and fall, with the Russians counterattacking in winter. From July 1943 onwards, however, the Russians pushed the Germans back slowly and methodically. By the middle of the following year, they had cleared nearly all their territory of the German invaders.

The Germans and Russians waged war on a scale never before seen. More soldiers died on the eastern front of World War II than in all the fronts and battles of the First World War. Stalin rightly believed his nation had held off Hitler single-handedly, and he felt intense anger and frustration at his Allies' slowness in opening a second front in the West.

The Big Three had been arguing about the second front since the invasion of Russia in June 1941. Though the British admitted in principle that an invasion of Western Europe would probably prove necessary, they were haunted by memories of the trenches in the first war, where "the British soldiers fought like lions, but were led by donkeys." Churchill also harbored a personal fear of the amphibious operations required to re-enter the Continent, because of the Gallipoli fiasco for which he had been responsible. British strategy, therefore, envisioned prolonged bombing and blockade of Germany, coupled with propaganda to encourage uprisings by the subject nations of Europe. They then added a policy of "attrition by overstretch," forcing the diversion of German manpower and resources to peripheral campaigns in the Mediterranean. Needless to say, Stalin did not find this policy of indirection very useful.

The American military, on the other hand, wanted a direct, massive blow in Western Europe, as soon as possible. Two fairly junior staff officers, Albert C. Wedemeyer and Dwight D. Eisenhower, had separately prepared elaborate plans for an "offensive operation in one theater and concurrently defensive operations in all others." General George C. Marshall, the Army Chief of Staff, adopted this scenario in March 1942. President Roosevelt greeted the plan, now dubbed the Marshall Memorandum, enthusiastically, sent the general off to London to confer with the British, and promised Soviet Foreign Minister Molotov that the Western Allies would open a second front before the end of 1942.

It proved impossible to train the troops and assemble enough shipping for a large-scale invasion in 1942. Theoretically, the best course of action would have been a methodical, systematic buildup of resources in Britain, then a massive assault in 1943. Both coalition politics and domestic politics, however, made it impossible for American troops to sit idle while the Russians fought Hitler and the British dueled with Rommel in the desert. Therefore, FDR agreed to the small-scale invasion of northwest Africa (Operation Torch) in November 1942, so he could at least tell Stalin and the American public that he was doing something. The unexpected difficulty of clearing out North Africa, however, meant that the cross-channel invasion would be postponed until 1944, maybe even longer.

The Americans pinned down the British, however, in May 1943 at the Trident Conference in Washington, D.C. The British chiefs of staff agreed to a May 1, 1944, deadline for the European invasion, now code-named Overlord. Churchill still hatched new schemes for the Mediterranean theater; but when the Big Three met together personally for the first time, at Teheran in November 1943, Stalin put a stop to such diversions. The Soviet leader demanded the immediate appointment of a supreme commander for the invasion. A week later, Roosevelt and Churchill named General Eisenhower to overall command of the operation, assisted by the British General Bernard Montgomery, who would direct the ground forces on the spot.

Montgomery was a famous fighting general, who had earned his reputation by defeating Rommel in North Africa, but he had a prickly personality. Eisenhower, on the other hand, was the perfect leader for a coalition war, a staff officer with an even temperament and a commonsense manner. He insisted that everyone under his command put aside nationalistic quarrels: "I don't mind if one officer refers to another as that son of a bitch . . . but the instant I hear of any American officer referring to a brother officer as that *British* son of a bitch, out he goes." Not only was this good advice for coalition warfare, but an excellent prescription for overcoming the rage of nations.

Amphibious invasions posed two thorny dilemmas for military planners. First of all, if the attackers preceded the invasion with a massive air and naval bombardment, they would destroy the element of surprise. However, Dieppe and various island landings in the Pacific had shown that invasion without bombardment was suicidal. So the Allies decided on a massive air campaign weeks ahead of time and a daylight landing so that naval gunners could see what they were doing. The second dilemma weighed the advantages of seizing a port, for immediate supply and reinforcement, against the value of a surprise landing on isolated beaches. Dieppe also settled this question. Overlord's warriors landed on beaches, supplied by ingeniously designed landing craft and two artificial harbors.

The remaining questions before D-day were "Where?" and "When?" The shortest route across the English Channel lay between Dover and Calais, and the Germans were expecting the major landing there. The Allies created a fictitious army group near the Pas de Calais and fed the Germans phony intelligence about it while actually planning to land at the opposite end of the channel on the beaches of Normandy. Last minute delays in assembling landing craft let the May 1 deadline slip by, but the next combination of moonlight for the paratroopers and tides for the landing craft would come on June 4, 5, and 6. The weather proved horrible on the first two days, but a brief break in the clouds and rain enabled Eisenhower to trigger the assault on D-day, June 6, 1944.

The Germans had posted a dozen first-class infantry divisions along the French coast, backed by six panzer divisions; and General Erwin Rommel had strewn formidable obstacles along the shores, hoping to stop the invaders at the waterline. Yet Rommel did not enjoy complete authority over the battlefield. He only controlled three of the panzer divisions himself, with the others held in reserve under the direct command of Hitler. Furthermore, the Allies gained the advantage of surprise after all, due to the weather. Since the Germans no longer controlled the skies, they could not patrol over the Atlantic for advanced weather forecasting, and they remained unaware of the approaching clear skies on June 6. Rommel himself had gone on vacation to Germany, and other commanders were attending war games. Hitler lay sound asleep at his hideout of Berchtesgaden, far away in the Alps. It was almost like Pearl Harbor in reverse — at dawn they slept. The invaders therefore enjoyed the best of all worlds — decent weather, a fierce prelanding bombardment, and nearly total surprise.

One British and two American paratrooper divisions jumped into Normandy after midnight on June 6. Though many missed their drop zones and thousands were killed or got lost, the very messiness of this preliminary assault confused the defenders. Then at first light, an armada of four thousand landing craft dropped five infantry divisions on the Normandy beaches, code-named Utah and Omaha (American), Gold (British), Juno (Canadian), and Sword (British). The surprised and outnumbered defenders raked the beaches, but on all but one (Omaha Beach) the invaders quickly gained a secure foothold. Allied control of the air hindered the counterattack of the panzers; and Hitler still believed the Normandy invasion was a feint, so he would not release the infantry divisions holding the Pas de Calais. By the time a great spring storm blew up on June 18, the Allies had reinforced their beachhead and were on the Continent to stay. Stalin finally had his second front.

In return, the Soviet leader ordered a renewed offensive on June 22, thus preventing the transfer of German troops from the eastern front. The Germans still resisted fiercely in Normandy. Sheltered by the *bocage* ("hedgerows"), which made the rural landscape ideal for anti-tank defense, they prevented a breakout from the beachhead until the end of July. By late August, however, the invading troops had just about reached their projected destinations. It had taken them longer in the beginning, but they moved more rapidly than expected after the breakout.

British and Canadians raced north along the channel coast, seizing the vital Belgian port of Antwerp in early September. Meanwhile, the mass of German defenders narrowly avoided encirclement in what became known as the Falaise pocket. Over 300,000 Germans escaped eastward across the Seine, but 200,000 were captured and 50,000 killed in the first ten weeks after D-day. In a fitting gesture of coalition harmony, General Eisenhower had included a division of Free French soldiers in the Normandy invasion force. On August 26, when the German general holding Paris disregarded the führer's orders to destroy the city, Eisenhower allowed General Charles de Gaulle and his followers the privilege of entering the French capital first.

The Allied advance slowed in the autumn as it approached the pre-war borders of Germany. The Germans rapidly refurbished the old Siegfried line, and they could possibly have held it indefinitely, but Hitler hated the First World War's defensive stalemate every bit as much as the British did. So he planned one last offensive surprise for the invaders. The Ardennes Mountains had been the scene of the blitzkrieg that knocked out France in May 1940. On December 16, 1944, the German army tried to duplicate this success, by driving their last reserves of tanks and motorized troops through the Ardennes, across the Meuse, and onwards to the vital Allied supply port of Antwerp. The attack caught the Americans, who were holding this sector, by surprise; and the Germans drove a large salient, or bulge, in the defenders' lines. Swift counterattacks, however, stopped the advance before the Germans could cross the Meuse. Both sides lost about equal numbers of men and tanks, but the Germans could ill afford such losses, whereas the Allied forces were still growing. The Battle of the Bulge, as it became known in the United States, marked Hitler's last desperate bid for victory. Its failure sealed his fate.

When Churchill, Roosevelt, and Stalin met for the second and last time, at Yalta from February 4 to 11, 1945, the Western armies stood poised to cross the Rhine and the Soviets had advanced to the Oder River, only about fifty miles from Berlin. Much hard fighting remained in Germany over the next three months, but the two advancing armies, one from the east and the other from the west, finally met on the Elbe River on April 25. The Red Army then took Berlin in street-to-street fighting reminiscent of Stalingrad; on April 30 Adolf Hitler committed suicide along with Eva Braun, his longtime mistress, whom he had married the previous night. The war in Europe ended when representatives of Admiral Dönitz, Hitler's designated successor, surrendered to the Western Allies on May 7 in Rheims and to the Russians in Berlin the next day.

Meanwhile, as the Big Three Allies were focusing on "Germany first," Japan's Admiral Yamamoto had, as he predicted, "run wild for six months" through the Pacific Ocean, the China Sea, and the Indian Ocean, filling out the Greater East Asia Co-Prosperity Sphere. On the same morning as the Pearl Harbor attack, a Japanese task force had bombarded the coast of British Malaya and then landed troops at three different spots on the peninsula. Ten hours after Pearl Harbor, Japanese planes from Formosa destroyed the formidable B-17 Flying Fortress bombers stationed at Clark airfield in the Philippines. American fighters had been alerted and were flying reconnaissance all morning, but through a combination of bad luck and poor planning, all the planes were on the ground refueling when the Japanese struck.

Two days later, on December 10 west of the International Date Line, Japanese torpedo planes sank the most powerful British ships in Asian waters, the *Prince of Wales* and the *Repulse,* off the coast of Malaya. Winston Churchill later recalled that "in all the war I never received a more direct shock." It was the British equivalent of Pearl Harbor. During three days in December 1941, the Japanese won control, temporarily, of the air and the sea in the Pacific. By the end of the year they had captured the British colony of Hong Kong and occupied America's Pacific bases on Wake Island and Guam.

In the early months of 1942 Japanese army troops fought their way down the Malay Peninsula towards Singapore and penned up American defenders of the Philippines on the Bataan Peninsula and the island of Corregidor. Singapore, the major British naval base in Asia, was defended against sea attack, but had neglected its land defenses. The British garrison of 130,000 troops surrendered Singapore on February 15, 1942, the greatest British defeat in history. Meanwhile in the Philippines, the American military ordered General Douglas MacArthur to leave his troops on Bataan and fly to Australia. The remaining Americans surrendered Bataan on April 9 and Corregidor on May 5. The loss of these twin bastions in East Asia marked the low point of Anglo-American fortunes.

The Japanese had earlier rounded out their East Asian sphere with the capture of the long-coveted Dutch East Indies[1] in February and March. A motley assortment of British, American, Australian, and Dutch ships challenged the Japanese in the Java Sea, but only four American destroyers escaped destruc-

1. After the Germans conquered Holland in May 1940, Queen Wilhelmina and her government took refuge in England. Officials of the Dutch government-in-exile retained control of the East Indies until the Japanese attack.

tion. Japanese troops then occupied Java virtually unopposed. Another desperate sea encounter, in the Coral Sea on May 7, 1942, resulted in heavy American losses but did block Japanese troops from landing on the east end of New Guinea. The Battle of the Coral Sea also marked the first naval battle in which the opposing ships never fired upon or even saw each other. Carrier-borne aircraft did all the fighting.

The American navy finally stopped the Japanese advance with another all-aerial "naval battle," the Battle of Midway on June 4, 1942. Admiral Yamamoto tried to duplicate his Pearl Harbor success with a similar attack on Midway Island. This time, however, the Americans were better prepared. The intelligence service had finally cracked the Japanese naval code, so they knew Yamamoto was coming. The fleet put out to sea looking for the Japanese, and American fighters did not remain on the ground at Midway. So when Japanese planes struck the American base, they did not register a knockout blow. In the meantime, American planes sank four Japanese aircraft carriers, losing only one of their own. Historian John Toland concludes: "In every battle luck plays a part. At Midway it went against the Japanese."

Admiral Yamamoto's[2] six-month rampage through the Pacific had ended and the Japanese sphere had reached its greatest limits, stretching through the mid-Pacific, south to the Solomon Islands, New Guinea, Java, and Sumatra, then west to the Burma-India border. It's impossible to know exactly how Japan would have ultimately governed this sphere, since the demands of wartime overwhelmed it. Burma declared independence, under Japanese tutelage in August 1943, and the Philippines followed suit in October. In November of that year, representatives from all of Japan's new client states met in Tokyo for a Greater East Asia Conference that issued a highminded declaration of co-prosperity principles. In practice, however, the Japanese military remained in control of the sphere and funneled its natural resources into the war effort.

In the meantime, the Americans mounted their first counterattack with a landing on the large jungle island of Guadalcanal in the Solomons on August 6, 1942. A few thousand U.S. Marines held out against desperate Japanese charges, then in November the U.S. Navy blocked the final attempt to retake the island. American marines equated Guadalcanal with hell. Like the Europeans under siege at the turn of the century in China and South Africa, they suffered from disease and a sense of abandonment. Yet, in fact the Japanese soldiers besieging them were far worse off, due to inadequate supplies. They calculated their chances of survival thus: "He who can rise to his feet — 30 days left to live. He

---

2. The admiral who had planned the Pearl Harbor attack lost his life over Bougainville in the Solomon Islands. Having intercepted and decoded messages giving Yamamoto's itinerary on an inspection trip, American fighters ambushed his plane on April 18, 1943.

who can sit up — 20 days left to live. He who must urinate while lying down — 3 days left to live. He who cannot speak — 2 days left to live. He who cannot blink his eyes — dead at dawn."

November 1942 marked the turning point of the war, not just in the Pacific at Guadalcanal, but also in North Africa, where Montgomery defeated Rommel, and in Europe, where the Russians closed the Stalingrad trap. In one of his most famous phrases, Churchill remarked at the time: "Now, this is not the end. It is not even the beginning of the end. But it is, perhaps, the end of the beginning."

For the next two years, the Americans followed a two-pronged strategy in the Pacific. General MacArthur and Admiral William Halsey slowly retook the Solomon and Bismarck Islands one by one, then began crawling up the coast of New Guinea toward the Philippines, which MacArthur had vowed to liberate with his dramatic phrase, "I shall return." MacArthur's theater of command had to compete for resources, however, with the "island-hopping" operations commanded by Admiral Chester Nimitz in the central Pacific. Developing the art of amphibious warfare as they advanced, the navy and marines, with some army troops as well, fought brutal batttles on the Gilberts, Marshalls, and Marianas, island groups that Japan had either inherited as mandates after World War I or had seized in the first six months of this war. These island battles served two purposes: they gradually brought the United States within strategic bomber range of the Japanese home islands, and they forced the Japanese navy to come out and fight. By the middle of June 1944, after the Battle of the Philippine Sea, which was nicknamed the "Great Marianas Turkey Shoot," the United States had decisively recaptured control of the sea and the air from Japan.

In theory, there was not much chance for surprise when assaulting a small island in the middle of the ocean, where the few suitable landing beaches were obvious to attackers and defenders. Yet Admiral Nimitz devised a strategy of leapfrogging beyond obvious island targets and taking another island by surprise. As a result, a number of Japanese garrisons in the Pacific were never captured at all, but simply left to rot. Some survivors on isolated islets did not surrender until years after the war ended. When attacked, Japanese forces fought with unprecedented persistence. The samurai military code forbade surrender, so repeatedly, on islands such as Tarawa in the Gilberts, Kwajalein in the Marshalls, and Saipan in the Marianas, the Japanese fought to the last man, often mounting suicide charges at the end. The last commanders remaining, and often many civilians as well, committed individual acts of suicide. The Americans rooted out any stragglers hiding in caves with grenades and flamethrowers. So, for example, on Saipan, an island about twice the size of Manhattan, the entire Japanese garrison of at least 25,000 perished, along with 22,000 civilians, many of whom threw themselves into the sea. The American attackers suffered 14,000 casualties (3,000 killed and 11,000 wounded).

With the capture of the Marianas (Saipan, Guam, and Tinian) in the summer of 1944, the newest U.S. bombers, the B-29 Superfortresses, could reach Japan itself, about 1,400 miles away. At the end of the year, massive bombing raids began. By that time, the other prong of the American advance had reached the Philippines. On October 20, 1944, General MacArthur scrambled ashore behind his troops on the island of Leyte, broadcasting over the radio, "People of the Philippines, I have returned." Over the next few days, the Pacific Fleet destroyed the last important elements of the Japanese navy in the Battle of Leyte Gulf. By the end of the year, American troops had secured Leyte and seized several other Philippine islands. In January 1945 MacArthur's forces invaded the main island of Luzon, retaking Manila, Bataan, and Corregidor. Japanese troops held out on parts of Luzon, but MacArthur controlled the vital population centers and air bases.

At the beginning of 1945, the Second World War should have ended. Both Japan and Germany were decisively beaten by this time. Yet war follows its own law of inertia, similar to a Newtonian law of physics. As the American journalist Walter Lippmann once remarked, a people at peace, like a physical body at rest, tends to remain at peace. This helps explain the long period of appeasement in the 1930s. Yet once pushed into motion, a body acquires momentum and so does a war. When a twentieth-century nation-state has fully mobilized, propagandizing its people with modern communications, it fights to the bitter end. The irrational resistance of Japan and Germany and the Allies' unconditional surrender formula are both expressions of this law.

More Japanese soldiers than usual had surrendered or deserted during the battles for the Philippines, but most still fought tenaciously, even while subsisting on beetles, frogs, and snails. Furthermore, the Japanese had embarked on a final suicide strategy, crashing kamikaze[3] planes on American naval vessels. An invasion of Japan's home islands, therefore, seemed necessary to end the war. Yet Nimitz's island-hopping, leapfrog strategy had shown that invasion was often unnecessary and that amphibious assaults were always extremely bloody. So the chief of naval operations, Admiral Ernest King, advocated a strategy of blockade and bombing to force a surrender or else starve the Japanese out.

The Joint Chiefs of Staff, however, decided that American forces should approach still closer to the home islands. American troops mounted enormous assaults on Iwo Jima in February and Okinawa in April 1945. Both islands — the former a small volcanic cone in the Bonin chain, the latter, a large fertile farming plot in the Ryukyus with almost a half million permanent residents — were part of Japan proper, not recently conquered territories. The Japanese dug immense

---

3. *Kamikaze* means "divine wind." The name commemorates the typhoon that destroyed a Chinese fleet invading Japan in 1570.

418

labyrinths of underground defenses on these islands to repel attack, and the fighting proved the most bloody in the Pacific struggle. The famous flag-raising on Iwo Jima's Mount Suribachi, commemorated in a statue at Arlington Cemetery, was actually a reenactment for the press of an earlier event with a smaller flag. The photo by Joe Rosenthal of the Associated Press appeared on the front page of nearly every Sunday paper in the United States, feeding the national war frenzy for final, decisive, unconditional victory. The bloody battles on Iwo Jima and Okinawa, the defeat of Germany, and the stubborn resistance of the Japanese military set the stage for the final act of World War II.

Warfare in the East Asia theater had been far less a coalition affair than in Europe. Russia remained neutral vis-à-vis Japan; and China, Great Britain, and the United States fought largely separate campaigns. Now with the final battles in Asia impending the leadership of the Big Three changed. Franklin D. Roosevelt died on April 12, 1945, just two weeks before Hitler's suicide. Harry S. Truman, a former senator from Missouri who had earned his post as vice president with a vigorous investigation of war production and profiteering, succeeded the legendary four-term president. Truman has since acquired folk-hero status as a feisty leader unafraid of tough decisions, yet in 1945 he was simply a small-state politician devoid of international experience.

In mid-July Truman met Churchill and Stalin for another Big Three conference in the Berlin suburb of Potsdam. Halfway through the meeting, on July 26, the leaders were shocked by the news that Winston Churchill's Conservative Party had been turned out of office in the British postwar election. Churchill was not a man for all seasons, but rather a leader for one season only, wartime. The British voters, sensing hard times and painful changes ahead, elected the socialist Labour Party led by Clement Attlee, who now joined Truman and Stalin at Potsdam.

As early as the Teheran Conference of 1943, Stalin had promised to join the struggle against Japan as soon as Hitler was defeated. Anticipating fanatical resistance on the part of Japan, the British and American Combined Chiefs of Staff desperately wanted Russian assistance for the final battles. Stalin confirmed the commitment both at Yalta and Potsdam, making it more specific by promising to declare war within three months of victory in Europe. He kept his promise to the day.

American military planners were projecting two successive invasions of Japan, one on the southern island of Kyushu in November 1945 and the other on Honshu, near Tokyo, in March 1946. British naval forces would participate in the assault. Russia would not take part in these invasions, but would attack in Manchuria and Korea, tying up large numbers of Japanese troops and preventing their transfer to the main islands. With the experience of Iwo Jima and Okinawa fresh in their minds, the Americans expected massive resistance and heavy casualties, perhaps 63,000 in the initial assault on Kyushu alone.

The unconditional surrender formula complicated efforts to avoid these horrors through a negotiated peace. Hitler had fought to the end, as everyone expected he would, so the Allies' formula caused no problems on the German fronts. However, when Mussolini had been overthrown in July 1943, the Allies had negotiated with King Victor Emmanuel and let him remain on the throne, until the Italian people could freely choose their form of government after the war. The Americans could have, and indeed should have, made a similar offer to Japan's Emperor Hirohito.

In fact, the number-two man in the State Department, Joseph Grew, who had served as ambassador in Tokyo before the war, fashioned peace terms that would allow the Japanese emperor to retain his throne as a symbol of continuity. Grew found suppport from Henry Stimson and the War Department. Stimson's assistant secretary, John J. McCloy, remarked: "We should have our heads examined if we don't consider a political solution." The momentum of war, however, blocked this approach. President Truman and his new secretary of state, James F. Byrnes, feared American public opinion would not support any deviation from unconditional surrender. Therefore, for domestic political reasons, the Potsdam Proclamation of July 26 did not offer any concession to the emperor.

It is by no means certain that the Japanese would have surrendered if this concession had been offered. The emperor wanted peace, but the military planned to fight on. Civilian leaders had been putting out peace feelers, hoping that Russia would mediate while still neutral; but they held unrealistic hopes that peace terms might avoid complete defeat and enemy occupation. The Japanese-American war was ending as it began, in mutual misunderstanding, with each side talking past the other.

As it turned out, the Japanese emperor terminated hostilities by breaking all precedent and intervening directly at an imperial conference; but only after two atomic bombs had fallen on his country. The blast at Hiroshima on August 6, 1945, killed about 150,000 people, and the second bomb, at Nagasaki on August 9, nearly 100,000. (The decision to drop the A-bomb will be discussed further in the next chapter.) In between these two cataclysms, Russia declared war on August 8, invading Manchuria in force. These shocks moved the emperor to act. Hirohito signed the surrender document on August 14 and broadcast an appeal to his people the next day; for most Japanese it was the first time they had heard their emperor's voice. The war was over. It might have ended sooner except for the semantics of unconditional surrender.

The ghosts of World War I hovered over the battlefields of the second war. Franklin Roosevelt, remembering the sharp reaction against Woodrow Wilson's idealism, consciously undersold his own idealistic war aims. Rather than "a war to end wars" or to "make the world safe for democracy," FDR always referred to the struggle simply as "the survival war." Churchill had vivid nightmares of the slaughter in the trenches, so he delayed the launching of the second front until overwhelming force was available. Both Roosevelt and Churchill remembered the shattering collapse of Russia in 1917, so they funneled as many resources as they could to their Russian allies to keep them fighting this time. All three Allies fought on doggedly to avoid the misunderstandings of Woodrow Wilson's negotiated armistice in November 1918.

The coalition with greater resources and tighter cohesion won the war, but it did not attain its larger, more lofty goals. As Keith Sainsbury has pointed out, "Churchill hoped to restore the old world while Roosevelt aimed to build a new one." Stalin's aims fell in between, to save Russia, build a security perimeter around it, and ultimately to launch a world revolution. None of the Big Three achieved their long-range goals; but the improbable alliance of communist, conservative-imperialist, and liberal-democratic nations held together long enough to impose unconditional surrender on its enemies.

CHAPTER TWENTY-FOUR

The War of Extermination

People do things in wartime that they wouldn't even think of in times of peace. This depressing truism explains a great deal of otherwise inexplicable behavior. The government of Franklin D. Roosevelt ran huge budget deficits during World War II, borrowing and spending far more than it had in all the anti-depression programs of the 1930s. FDR laughingly explained that "Dr. New Deal" was yielding temporarily to "Dr. Win the War." In a less whimsical mood, Roosevelt signed Executive Order 9066 on February 19, 1942, uprooting 110,000 people of Japanese ancestry from their homes on the West Coast and interning them in concentration camps for the duration of the war. The majority of these Japanese internees were American citizens. Few protested the budget deficits or the internments. There was a war on!

In all the warring countries, governments exhorted their people to sacrifice and die for the nation. Japanese soldiers rarely surrendered, believing it dishonorable; instead, they mounted suicide charges when a battle turned against them. Hitler and Stalin also insisted, often against the best advice of their generals, that German and Soviet soldiers not retreat or surrender. Stalin disowned his own son Yakov as a traitor after learning he had turned up in a German prisoner-of-war camp. When Singapore was threatened by Japanese troops in January 1942, Winston Churchill cabled the commander of the beleaguered British garrison, "I want to make it absolutely clear that I expect every inch of ground to be defended, every scrap of material or defences to be blown to pieces to prevent capture by the enemy, and no question of surrender to be entertained until after protracted fighting among the ruins of Singapore City." General Douglas MacArthur, from his refuge in Australia, similarly ordered the American troops remaining behind in the Philippines to fight to the end. Both the British and American commanders in the field ignored these orders and capitulated, but their careers and reputations suffered. Soldiers are expected to defy common sense in wartime.

Hitler, as usual, carried disregard for his own people's well-being to an extreme with his euthanasia campaign. The führer had long been fascinated by the pseudo-science of eugenics, which aimed to improve the quality of the race by selective breeding. One of the earliest Nazi laws, in 1933, decreed the sterilization of mental defectives and others with "hereditary diseases." In doing this, the Nazis followed an American example, the compulsory sterilization law passed in 1907 by the state of Indiana to wipe out the Ben Ishmael tribe, a wandering group of mixed race. The outbreak of war, however, gave Hitler a chance to push his eugenics campaign beyond sterilization toward extermination. The Nazis converted six mental hospitals into killing centers, where they executed about 70,000 "inferior" Germans, first by lethal injection then later in gas chambers disguised as shower rooms. Underlining the point that this was a wartime measure, Hitler (either consciously or unconsciously) backdated the euthanasia order from October 1939, when he actually signed it, to September 1, 1939, the day his troops invaded Poland.

Despite the wartime hysteria, however, German church leaders, both Catholic and Protestant, did protest the euthanasia campaign, and Hitler suspended it after about a year. He learned a lesson from this that he later applied to other mass killings. Though people will commit unusual acts in wartime, it is easier to perform them out of sight, far from home.

Staff Sergeant Harrison Summers of the U.S. 82nd Airborne was far from home the day of the D-day landing in Normandy. Ordered to lead fifteen paratroopers against a coastal artillery barracks consisting of thick-walled stone farmhouses strung along seven hundred yards of road, he found his men reluctant to follow him. He therefore charged each farmhouse single-handedly, John Wayne style, kicking in the door and spraying the occupants with his Thompson submachine gun. After five hours of exertion, he had killed over fifty Germans and captured many more as prisoners. He then slumped on the ground, lit a cigarette, and exclaimed, "It was all kind of crazy." The crazy valor-terror of many such soldiers added up to a death toll for World War II similar to the slaughter of the First World War. The number of fatalities is estimated at 60 million.[1]

---

1. The First World War total of 60 million dead cited in chapter 9 is not directly comparable to the totals for World War II. It includes 15 million victims of the great influenza epidemic, which was only partially caused by the devastation of war; however, the World War II figures also include many millions who died from starvation and disease. The First World War figures also contain estimates of "population deficits" from the numbers of children who were never born due to the wartime separation and/or death of parents. I have not seen comparable figures for World War II. They would, undoubtedly, be large and would swell the total population deficit for the second catastrophe far above the first.

The Soviet Union suffered the heaviest losses. For many years, a figure of 20 million was quoted for the Soviet dead, though some questioned whether this might be inflated by Communist propaganda. In fact, when Soviet archives were recently opened, it was found that the figure was *too low*. The actual number may be as high as 25 million, about 11 or 12 percent of the total population of the Soviet Union. Much of the fighting on the eastern front took place in the Soviet republics of Ukraine and Byelorussia (today's Belarus), so the overall Soviet figure includes about 7 million Ukrainians and 2.25 million Byelorussians, 16 percent and 22 percent of those nations' prewar populations, respectively. Poland and Yugoslavia suffered comparable losses, about 6 million dead Poles (half Jewish, half Gentile), roughly 17 percent of their total population; and 1.7 million Yugoslavs (10 percent). Nearly 7 million Germans died (10 percent), half soldiers, half civilians. Casualties in the rest of Europe proved far lighter. The British lost 326,000 men in battle and suffered 62,000 civilian deaths. The United States military counted 295,000 deaths. The sum total for Europe and the United States was 40 million deaths.

In Asia, at least 10 million Chinese died during the war years, possibly many more. About 1.3 million of these were soldiers, the rest civilians swept away by disease and famine or else massacred by the Japanese. Perhaps 100,000 Malayans, 120,000 Filipinos, 1 million Vietnamese, and a staggering 4 million Indonesians similarly succumbed to a variety of disasters. The Japanese counted a total of 1,740,955 military fatalities, but perhaps another half million perished from other causes during the war. The Asian death count, therefore, approached 18 or 20 million.

In both world wars only a minority of fatalities occurred in battle. Both conflicts saw millions perish from disease or exposure, but warriors directly killed many more of the innocent or disarmed in the second war. Atrocities marked this struggle uniquely as a war of extermination.

Hitler set the tone on the eastern front with his *Untermensch* ("subhuman") campaign, an attempt to decimate and enslave the Slavic peoples of Eastern Europe. After the conquest of Poland in September 1939, the Nazis annexed outright the westernmost regions of Poznan and Pomerania, with a total population of 10.7 million. They intended to ruthlessly Germanize this territory by wiping out the Polish leadership class, deporting about half the Polish masses and enslaving the rest, then settling German agricultural colonists on the land. The remainder of Nazi-occupied Poland, including its largest cities of Warsaw and Cracow, were set up as the "General-Government," a dumping-ground for Jews, Poles, and Gypsies deported from the "Germanized" regions. The Nazis actually deported 3,000 Gypsies, 300,000 Jews, and 1.2 million Poles and killed about half the Polish intelligentsia, including 2,600 Catholic priests. One of these priests, the Franciscan Maximilian Kolbe, offered his own life at Auschwitz in place of a Polish officer with a family. Forty years later, a Polish pope, John Paul II, canonized Kolbe as a saint, in the presence of the soldier whose life he had saved.

The Nazis starved and neglected the Poles crowded into the General-Government, and they deported many of them once again, this time to labor in the fields and factories of Germany. Throughout the war, the German economy relied heavily on prisoners-of-war and civilians from the occupied territories to replace the millions of Germans drafted into the armed services. On May 31, 1940, after less than a year of war, 1.1 million foreign laborers were at work; 700,000 to 800,000 of these were Poles. Heinrich Himmler's SS required Polish "sub-humans" working in the Reich to wear a purple letter *P* on a yellow triangle and to avoid all contact with the "racially superior" Germans. Any Pole caught having sexual relations with a German was hanged.

During the whole course of the war, about 600,000 Poles were killed in battle or in the underground resistance and another 2.4 million Polish Christians were executed or died of neglect. About 1.5 million labored in Germany.

The Nazis applied the same kind of racial thinking to their invasion of the Soviet Union. One of the German generals, Walther von Reichenau, summed up the ground rules for the eastern campaign this way: "The soldier in the East is not only a fighter by the rules of war, but also the carrier of an inexorable racial concept *(volkische Idee)*." The overall plan for acquiring *Lebensraum* in the East required that many Slavs be exterminated, most of the remainder enslaved, and the rest driven east of the Urals into Asiatic Siberia where they could roam, starve, or die. Hitler modeled this policy on the European treatment of American Indians and the British Empire's rule over Asiatic Indians. He joked that he would supply the Slavs with "scarves, glass beads and everything that colonial peoples like." Centuries of European imperialism pointed toward Hitler's *Untermensch* campaign.

The SS organized *Einsatzgruppen* ("action teams") to follow closely behind the frontline troops and shoot captured Soviet commissars, Ukrainian or Russian intelligentsia, suspected partisans or saboteurs, and any Jews they could get their hands on. A ravine outside Kiev, named Babi Yar, became one of the most infamous killing grounds, where victims were lined up, machine-gunned, then tumbled into the abyss. The entire Jewish community of Kiev and many Slavs, including a Ukrainian soccer team that had the impertinence to defeat the German army team, perished at Babi Yar.

Yet before the SS could get very far in their murderous work, the invading Germans were overwhelmed by the vast numbers of Soviet prisoners who fell into their hands. Hitler had made few preparations to care for prisoners, not wishing to reduce living standards back home by devoting resources to captured "subhumans." As a result, at least 3.3 million of the 5.7 million Soviet POWs (58 percent) died during the war. The Germans shot many thousands outright, but most died of starvation or frostbite in makeshift prison camps. Hermann Göring wrote the Italian foreign minister during the winter of 1941-42 that the Russian POWs, "after eating everything possible including the soles of their boots, have begun to eat each other, and what is more serious, have also eaten a German sentry."

Many Soviet soldiers and civilians who survived that first horrible winter of occupation were deported for labor in the Third Reich. As *Ostarbeiters,* or Eastern workers, they too had to wear an identifying badge and were segregated, mistreated, overworked, and underpaid. They viewed Germany as another Siberia. At the peak of the compulsory labor program in December 1944, over 8 million foreigners labored for the Nazis, constituting 20 percent of the entire German workforce. These foreign workers fell into three rough categories: about a quarter of them came semi-voluntarily from Western Europe and were relatively well treated; half were dragooned from Poland and the Soviet Union, living and working in appalling conditions; most of the rest were truly slave laborers, inmates of concentration camps who were worked to death. Fritz Sauckel, Hitler's plenipotentiary for labor, decreed a general policy: "All the men must be fed, sheltered and treated in such a way as to exploit them to the highest possible extent at the lowest conceivable degree of expenditure."

Altogether, the *Untermensch* campaign, or the "other Holocaust," as it is sometimes called to distinguish it from the genocide of the Jews (discussed later in this chapter), claimed approximately 9 to 10 million victims. This includes 3 million Ukrainian and 2.4 million Polish Christian civilians, 1.4 million Byelorussians, and 3.3 million Soviet (which would include many nationalities) prisoners of war.

In East Asia the Japanese did not plan to exterminate or enslave "lesser races," as the Nazis did. Yet racial arrogance and pride in their military accomplishments prompted them to treat prisoners of war and civilians of occupied countries with great brutality. Japanese contempt for their enemies was not affected so much by racial theory as by moral and behavioral considerations. They disdained the Chinese as degenerate Asians who had too easily succumbed to European dominance, and they felt disgust for British and American soldiers who surrendered rather than fight to the end, as they themselves would have. The Japanese congratulated themselves for behaving better and more honorably than their foes. In actual fact, they often behaved atrociously. Japanese officers routinely slapped and beat their own enlisted men; these men in turn took out their frustrations on prisoners and civilians.

At Nanking in 1937 and at Manila in 1945, Japanese troops raged out of control, massacring civilians by the thousands. In early 1942, after the fall of Singapore, they executed over five thousand Chinese residents, for "collaborating" with their English rulers. Shortly thereafter, when the American commander in the Philippines surrendered the American and Filipino troops under his command, the infamous "Bataan Death March" ensued.

The Japanese commander in the Philippines, General Homma Masaharu, did not order the massacre or mistreatment of prisoners. He had devised plans for transporting prisoners from Bataan to a military base a hundred miles away, in the interior of Luzon. General Homma expected about 25,000 enemy prisoners, who could be moved in stages by truck, rail, or reasonable marches. When the Americans surrendered, however, about 70,000 prisoners, most of them half-dead from starvation and malaria, swamped these plans. Most were forced to march the full hundred miles from the tip of Bataan to their internment camp, under a blazing sun, with Japanese soldiers slapping and kicking them or prodding them with bayonets. Only about 54,000 of the original 70,000 reached the prison camp. Many, especially the Filipinos, escaped, but at least 7,000 Filipinos and 2,000 Americans died.

Those prisoners who survived the death march either rotted in jungle camps or were transported to Japan in the stifling holds of ships. Many of the latter died when American submarines sank their unmarked transports. Prisoners captured in Southeast Asia, however, were put to work building the Siam-Burma Railway, the so-called railway of death immortalized in the novel and movie *Bridge on the River Kwai.*

The 250-mile railway from Bangkok to Rangoon would shorten the sea voyage for supplying Japanese troops in Burma. In 1942 the military ordered completion of the line in a mere eighteen months, the sort of order Stalin gave routinely during his drive for industrialization in the 1930s. A quarter million or more Asians, from Malaya, Burma, and the Dutch East Indies, were dragooned into labor battalions, along with about sixty thousand prisoners of war, mostly British, Dutch, and Australian. The railway was completed on October 16, 1943, but at least one in five of the laborers died from disease, malnutrition, or overwork. The survivors looked like scarecrows, with their ribs protruding from famished bellies.

The most clearly evil of the Japanese atrocities were commited at the biological warfare research facility, called Unit 731, near Harbin in Manchuria. Japanese doctors experimented on Chinese prisoners, injecting them with deadly diseases, such as plague and typhoid, or else exposing them to severe weather and intentional injuries. The Japanese military also experimented with poison gas and employed it in limited quantities on battlefields in China. It was the only theater of war where poison gas, so common in World War I, was used. The Americans, British, and Germans reluctantly refrained from gas warfare so as not to give the other side any excuse for retaliation.

Comparative statistics for prisoner of war deaths summarize the brutality that reigned in both European and Asian theaters of war. About 60 percent of Soviet soldiers taken prisoner by the Germans did not survive; and the Soviet army reciprocated with nearly equal savagery. Approximately 45 percent of Germans captured in Russia died. The average death toll for prisoners taken by the Japanese was about 27 percent. Americans took few prisoners in the Pacific, since the Japanese refused to surrender and the Americans routinely strafed survivors of sunken ships or grounded airplanes. By way of comparison, only 4 percent of prisoners died on Europe's western front. Germans, British, and Americans, feeling racial kinship, treated each other's prisoners humanely. On the eastern front, however, and in Asia, World War II was a "war without mercy."

Yet no other atrocity of World War II rivaled the mass murder of the European Jews and Gypsies. The attempted extermination of these two ethnic groups prompted the international jurist, Raphael Lemkin, himself a Polish Jew, to coin a new word, *genocide*.[2] Jews and Gypsies were the only groups that the Nazis targeted for total genocide. They killed a greater number of Slavs, but not so high a proportion of the whole group. They did not attempt to annihilate all Slavs, but rather to subordinate and enslave them.

The Nazis proved more persistent and more successful in killing Jews than Gypsies. Jews had always held a special place in Hitler's demonology; he deemed Gypsies a nuisance, but Jews a mortal danger. Many more Gypsies escaped the Nazis' clutches, due to their nomadic way of life and long experience at evading arrest. As a result, at least 250,000 of Europe's 1.25 million Gypsies (20 percent) perished, whereas 6 million (67 percent) of the 8.8 million Jews of Europe were exterminated. The unique dimensions of the Jewish death toll have given it a distinctive name, the Holocaust. Philosopher and Holocaust survivor Elie Wiesel has aptly summed up the uniqueness of Jewish suffering: "While not all victims were Jews, all Jews were victims destined for annihilation."

Hitler's war against the Jews unfolded in three stages: (1) from 1933 to 1939, the German state legally circumscribed and harassed Jews, encouraging them to emigrate, preferably without their property and possessions; (2) from 1939 to 1941, the Nazis mounted more aggressive actions, ghettoizing Jews in the Polish General-Government and planning audacious killing strategies, while still exploring the possibility of mass expulsion or emigration; and (3) from 1941 until the end of the war, the Nazis pursued the Final Solution, systematic, "industrial-style" murder of all the Jews in Europe. Throughout this genocidal process, Hitler followed a strategy similar to the planning of his expansionist wars — dogged adherence to the final goal, in this case the elimination of all Jews, but infinite flexibility as to timing and means.

2. In his 1944 book, *Axis Rule in Occupied Europe*, Lemkin combined the Greek word *genos* ("people or tribe") with the common Latin ending *cide* ("killing") to create a word similar to *homicide*. Through the efforts of Lemkin and others, the United Nations passed a resolution on December 9, 1948, condemning genocide, which it defined as "acts committed with intent to destroy, in whole or in part, a national, ethnical, racial or religious group."

During the first year of Nazi ascendancy, 1933, the German state purged Jews from positions in the civil service, the universities, the press, and the professions. Then in 1935, with the passage of the so-called Nuremberg Laws, Jews were deprived of their citizenship and forbidden to intermarry with "pure" Germans. The Reich Citizenship Law of 1935 defined as Jewish anyone with three or more Jewish grandparents. Thus a job applicant had to produce seven baptismal certificates, his or her own and those of two parents and four grandparents.

This first stage of official harassment culminated in *Kristallnacht*, "The Night of Broken Glass," on November 9, 1938. Using the assassination of a German diplomat by a Jewish student in Paris as an excuse, Hitler's storm troopers raged throughout Germany smashing windows and setting fires in Jewish homes and shops. Nearly 100 Jews were killed and over 7,000 businesses were destroyed. The Nazis blamed the victims, levying an indemnity of one billion Reichsmarks on the Jewish community to pay for the damage. By this time, nearly 300,000 of Germany's 500,000 Jews had emigrated. More would have escaped except that Great Britain, the United States, and most other nations of the world imposed strict quotas and would not admit all who wished to flee.

On January 30, 1939, Hitler foretold what would happen to the Jews in the next two stages. In a speech to the Reichstag, he thundered: "Today I will be a prophet again: If international finance Jewry within Europe and abroad should succeed once more in plunging the peoples into a world war, then the consequence will be not the Bolshevization of the world and therewith a victory for Jewry, but on the contrary, the destruction of the Jewish race in Europe." Hitler later confirmed that such a Final Solution was only possible in wartime by misdating this speech to September 1, 1939, the day his troops invaded Poland. As with the euthanasia campaign, he consciously or unconsciously associated genocide with wartime.

German Jews had comprised only about one percent of the Reich's population, but the invasion of Poland delivered two million more into the Nazis' hands. The German government was initially unsure what to do with them. At first they confined the Jews in the gigantic, hunger-ravaged ghetto of the General-Government and toyed with the idea of mass deportations to the island of Madagascar in the Indian Ocean. Then, as plans for the invasion of Russia proceeded, with the prospect of many more millions of Jews coming under German rule, Hitler and the leaders of the SS moved towards the Final Solution, total, systematic extermination.

The *Einsatzgruppen* (special striking forces), which followed the German army into the Soviet Union, killed between one and two million Jews with machine-guns and mobile gas vans. Yet this method proved too slow and inefficient, so Heinrich Himmler and his lieutenants, Adolf Eichmann and Reinhard Heydrich, organized gigantic death camps to systematize the slaughter. The Nazis had built concentration camps, such as Dachau near Munich, as early as 1933, but their purpose had been detention, torture, and "political reeducation," not mass murder. In 1941 and 1942 they constructed six specialized extermination camps — Belzec, Chelmno, Majdanek, Sobibor, Treblinka, and Birkenau (the death camp at the previously organized Auschwitz concentration camp) — all located on Polish soil. They had learned the lesson of the euthanasia campaign that atrocious deeds were best perpetrated out of sight of the German public.

The Nazis decided, in the words of Reinhard Heydrich, that Europe was "to be combed through from west to east," until all the Jews of the occupied territories had been eliminated. They employed the euphemism "resettlement for work in the East" to herd Jewish families onto trains for the death camps. When the trains disgorged their human cargo, those few judged capable of heavy labor, about 10 percent, were separated out and worked until they expired. The remainder, the vast majority, were marched into gas chambers, and sprayed with zyklon-B, a cyanide gas first used in the euthanasia campaign. The bodies were then burned in gigantic crematoria.

Ninety percent of the Jews from Poland, the Baltic states, Germany, Austria, and the Czech lands died in the Holocaust. Smaller percentages from other occupied countries were eliminated. The government and people of Denmark, however, saved all 8,000 of their Jewish citizens, hiding them in their homes or smuggling them out to neutral Sweden. Six million Jews in all, two-thirds of Europe's prewar population, perished.

For much of World War II the British, American, and Russian Allies felt helpless to retaliate against the Germans, who were perpetrating such horrendous atrocities. Until the Russians turned the tide of battle at Stalingrad in January 1943 and the Anglo-Americans landed at Normandy in June 1944, the only way they could strike at Germany was through the air, fighting the fire of atrocities with fire from the heavens.

The British Royal Air Force had initially taken great care not to harm civilians in the vicinity of military targets. In the months after the invasion of Poland, therefore, the RAF contented itself with dropping propaganda leaflets and occasionally attacking naval installations or ships at sea. After Hitler's blitzkrieg through Holland and France, however, newly installed Prime Minister Winston Churchill ordered the first strategic bombing raid of the war, an attack on Hamburg and the industrial cities of the Ruhr on May 15, 1940. Shortly thereafter, Hermann Göring's Luftwaffe mounted the Blitz against military targets and major cities of Great Britain, in preparation for an invasion.

The British government then authorized retaliatory raids against German cities. The Luftwaffe's defenses proved so formidable, however, that the British limited their bombing attacks to nighttime, and they found it impossible to hit precise targets in the dark. A 1941 study found that only 20 percent of bombs fell within five miles of the target; this later improved to 60 percent within three miles. Therefore, a government directive of February 14, 1942, prescribed area bombing of German cities, "focused on the morale of the enemy civil population and in particular of the industrial workers." A week later, on February 23, a new commander, Arthur "Bomber" Harris, took over bomber command and pursued this policy with obsessive persistence. Churchill's science advisor, Frederick Lindemann (Lord Cherwell) explained the policy as one of "dehousing" the German worker. Another scientist, however, P. M. S. Blackett, ascribed it to a "Jupiter complex," righteous Britons avenging themselves with thunderbolts from on high.

The U.S. Army Air Force made its first appearance over European skies in August 1942, but did not attack Germany in force until the middle of the following year. The Americans, commanded by Generals Carl Spaatz and Ira Eaker, attempted precision bombing by day in contrast to the RAF's nighttime area bombing. They did this not so much for moral reasons, but because they believed it more effective "to cause a high degree of destruction in a few really essential industries than to cause a small degree of destruction in many industries." This proved militarily correct, but could not be pursued systematically until late in 1943 when a long-range fighter plane, the P-51 Mustang, made it possible to protect bombers right into the heart of Germany. In the final year of the war, both British and American planes targeted synthetic oil plants and vital transportation links in Germany. This finally brought on economic collapse; and as Albert Speer, German munitions minister, later testified, it might have ended the war sooner had it been pursued more consistently. "Bomber" Harris, however, still directed over 70 percent of British air sorties at cities.

The RAF carried strategic bombing to a new extreme one hot summer night over Hamburg in 1943. Harris's battle orders for Operation Gomorrah read simply "To destroy Hamburg." The first night, July 24, 1943, RAF bombers dropped a roughly equal amount of high explosive and incendiary bombs, setting fire to large residential quarters of the city. The next two days, American planes tried to hit the vital submarine yards on the waterfront, but smoke from the fires obscured their vision and little damage was done. Then on the night of July 27-28 the British returned, dropping incendiaries on a different residential district. This time, with city firefighters overwhelmed and atmospheric conditions just right, multiple fires merged into one vast blaze, sucking in oxygen to stoke hurricane winds of flame. The firestorm burned out eight square miles of Hamburg, equivalent in area to half of Manhattan island, killing about 45,000 German civilians, many of whom simply melted into pools of grease or were charred to ashes.

The setting of fires had been intentional, but no one had ever seen a firestorm before the Hamburg catastrophe. Thereafter, however, Allied bombers intentionally caused firestorms in one more German city, Dresden, on February 13-14, 1945 (vividly portrayed in Kurt Vonnegut's novel *Slaughterhouse Five*), and repeatedly in Japan in the final months of the war.

431

The Americans had bombed Tokyo from an aircraft carrier in 1942; but this hit-and-run raid commanded by General James Doolittle was basically a publicity stunt to lift American morale and annoy the Japanese, then at the height of their military success. Air attacks on the Japanese homeland could not be sustained until a new long-range plane, the B-29 Superfortress, was completed, and the islands of Saipan and Tinian in the Marianas were captured in 1944. Even then the strategy of precision bombing proved ineffective, since Japanese industries were small in scale and widely dispersed. So when General Curtis LeMay took over the B-29 force in the Marianas in early 1945, he turned to incendiaries, which thereafter made up about two-thirds of the U.S. bomb load. On May 9-10, over three hundred B-29s ignited the flimsy wood houses of Tokyo in a gigantic firestorm that ravaged sixteen square miles, twice the burned out area of Hamburg, incinerating 80,000 to 100,000 people and leaving a million homeless. General LeMay, the model for Stanley Kubrick's film villain Dr. Strangelove, declared that the Japanese had been "scorched and boiled and baked to death." Incendiary raids on other cities followed in the remaining months of the war.

All in all, Allied bombing killed at least 600,000 civilians in Germany and 200,000 in Japan. The great majority of these were society's most defenseless — women, children, and the elderly — for nearly all the males between ages eighteen and forty were absent on military duty. The bombing campaigns took a devastating toll on the aircrews as well. The British RAF alone lost 56,000 killed, half as many wounded, and 11,000 taken prisoner. Their overall casualty rate of 76 percent proved far higher than the slaughter in the trenches of World War I, and the number of British airmen who died nearly equaled the number of British civilians killed in the Blitz. Revenge had stretched the dimensions of the air war out of all proportion. Even Winston Churchill, one of the initiators of area bombing, wrote the Chiefs of Staff after the destruction of Dresden: "It seems to me that the moment has come when the question of bombing of German cities simply for the sake of increasing the terror, though under other pretexts, should be reviewed."

Yet before the war ended two more cities were utterly destroyed, by just a single bomb each. British and American scientists had been racing the Germans to create an explosion through the fission of uranium or plutonium atoms. When the Americans tested the first A-bomb in the deserts of New Mexico on July 16, 1945, it exceeded the expectations of the scientists. Robert Oppenheimer, the physicist in charge of atomic research at Los Alamos, quoted a chilling phrase from the Hindu scripture, the Bhagavad Gita, as he witnessed the first nuclear fireball: "Now I am become Death, the destroyer of worlds." By this time, Hitler was dead and Germany had surrendered. Therefore, as has been remarked many times, "the Japanese took Hitler's medicine."

On August 6, 1945, a uranium-based bomb, nicknamed Little Boy, leveled the city of Hiroshima, killing 100,000 instantly and 50,000 more from burns and radiation. On August 9, 1945, the plutonium bomb, Fat Man, dropped on Nagasaki, killing 75,000 before the end of the year and another 25,000 from lingering effects. In sum, the only two atom bombs ever dropped in wartime killed about 250,000 Japanese. Many who believe the bombing of Hiroshima was necessary to end the war, still consider Nagasaki an atrocity. The Americans left too little time for Japanese leaders to assess the damage at Hiroshima and decide whether or not to surrender. The momentum of wartime created an unnecessary rush.

President Harry S. Truman had inherited the atomic bomb program, code-named the Manhattan Project, from Franklin Roosevelt. This is important in analyzing his decision to drop the A-bombs. As an accidental president, chosen vice president for political reasons only a few months before, Truman naturally felt insecure and thus was predisposed to continue important programs initiated by his predecessor. A desire for political continuity, joined with the momentum of wartime, made Truman's decision almost automatic.

There were alternatives available, other methods for inducing Japan to admit defeat and end the war. Truman might have modified the unconditional surrender formula and explicitly guaranteed that Japan could retain its emperor in the postwar period. Then he could have waited for the Russians to declare war on Japan, as they had promised at Teheran and Yalta. There was no rush. The Allied invasion of the Japanese home islands was not scheduled to begin until November 1, 1945. The Russians had pledged to enter the war in August. The carrot and stick of a guarantee for the emperor coupled with the shock of a Russian war declaration might have produced a Japanese surrender.

Truman might also have issued the Japanese a warning about the atomic bomb and then arranged a demonstration shot, perhaps on an island in the Pacific or even over Tokyo Bay. Alternatively, he could have kept the A-bomb under wraps and continued to bomb and blockade Japan with conventional means. Or, in fact, the Allies could have declared a victory and gone home, merely retaining economic sanctions against Japan.

This is hindsight, yet all except the last alternative were actually discussed within the U.S. government during the spring and summer of 1945. Many government officials urged a guarantee for the emperor. Important military leaders, such as Generals Dwight Eisenhower and George Marshall, expressed reservations about using the bomb on cities. Admiral Leahy, the president's personal military advisor, later wrote: "My own feeling was that in being the first to use it, we had adopted an ethical standard common to the barbarians of the Dark Ages. I was not taught to make war in that fashion, and wars cannot be won by destroying women and children." There was little chance, however, that Truman would take such advice. Psychologists have demonstrated that individuals under stress only respond to certain other individuals, those they term "significant others." It didn't really matter how many people were advising Truman. Only two were significant others: James F. Byrnes, his closest friend in the government, whom he named as his secretary of state in July 1945, and Franklin D. Roosevelt, the dead president from whom he had inherited the bomb.

Byrnes believed that the atomic bomb would not only end the war before an American invasion, but possibly before the Russians entered the fray. Though the Americans had repeatedly begged Stalin to declare war against Japan, by 1945 they had backed off, fearing Russian advances in Asia. Byrnes hoped that use of the bomb would make the Russians more cooperative in the postwar world. He counseled Truman that the atomic bomb, originally invented to defeat Germany, should be dropped on Japan to impress Russia.

Though fear of the Russians was certainly an important motive for dropping the bomb, it was not the only or the primary one. Truman heeded his predecessor Roosevelt as much as his contemporary Byrnes. FDR had initiated the Manhattan Project as a war measure, and Truman wanted to use every weapon in the American arsenal, especially one that had cost over two billion dollars. As historian Daniel Boorstin has pointed out, the real decision regarding the A-bomb was "not whether, but when."

The belligerent nations had already crossed every moral threshold in the Second World War. Historian Barton J. Bernstein has summarized what he calls the "redefinition of morality" in World War II this way: "While the worst atrocities were perpetrated by the Axis, all the major nation-states sliced away at the moral code — often to the applause of their leaders and citizens alike." Since we are all likely to make moral judgments, at least implicitly, it might be useful to make mine explicit, by ranking World War II atrocities:

1. The Holocaust of the Jews and genocide of the Gypsies.
2. The *Untermensch* campaign, German murder and abuse of Slavic POWs and civilians, and similar Soviet abuses.
3. The East Asian "war without mercy," Japanese murder and abuse of POWs and civilians, and American reprisals.
4. Atomic bombing of Hiroshima and Nagasaki.
5. Area bombing and firestorms in Germany and Japan.

Two of the four terrible "isms" culminated in this list of atrocities.[3] Like a sorcerer's apprentice, Hitler transmuted German nationalism into a virulent racism and combined this with the imperialism that had dominated his, and this

---

3. Anarchists had committed many individual acts of terrorism but by definition could not organize the mass atrocities of a world war. Socialism, however, had led Stalin toward the only atrocities of the century that rival those of World War II, the party purges and the terror famine in Ukraine described in chapter 18.

century's, youth. The result was a war of extermination against nations and peoples. Ironically, the emphasis on national self-determination at the end of World War I contributed to the slaughter of World War II. By defining the ideal state as the ethnically pure nation-state, the peacemakers of Versailles had made ethnic minorities vulnerable.

The Japanese, too, were propelled by the imperialism that ruled Asia when they first sloughed off their isolation and by the racial nationalism of their own proud traditions. Both Japan and Germany missed opportunities to turn the nationalism of the occupied countries to their own advantage. Humane treatment of Ukrainians by Germany or Burmese by Japan could have won these subject nations to their cause. Instead, nationalism and imperialism exploded upon contact, just as the two hemispheres of plutonium brought together by the atomic scientists at Los Alamos.

Racial contempt for the Japanese made America's war in Asia far more brutal than the European struggle. As the famous war correspondent Ernie Pyle wrote when he was transferred from Germany to the Pacific in 1945, "Out here I soon gathered that the Japanese were looked upon as something subhuman and repulsive; the way some people feel about cockroaches or mice." Yet nationalism pushed to the point of racism does not explain all the war's atrocities. Both British and Americans dropped bombs on German civilians, who were their closest racial cousins.

At the highest level of generalization, the simplest explanation for the occurrence of atrocities is probably the best — people do things in wartime that they would not even think of in times of peace. As the title character of *Breaker Morant* observed (see chapter 1), "the tragedy of war is that these horrors are committed by normal men in abnormal situations."

On the level of individual behavior, the psychological mechanisms that permit normal people to commit atrocities include dehumanization of the enemy, a tradition of unquestioning obedience, a belief that the end justifies the means, and a detachment from reality. German soldiers and camp guards could murder Jews, Gypsies, and Slavs because Nazi racial doctrine had stripped these groups of their humanity. The Japanese, too, in their racial arrogance believed that other Asians, or surrendered soldiers, were less than human. In this, they followed the dynamics of imperialism quite closely. As we discussed in chapter 13, European imperialists had long justified their conquests, whether in Ireland, Africa, or Asia, as a process of uplifting or civilizing savages. Such contempt for the conquered led easily to massacres and genocide, such as the extermination of the Herero in South West Africa. Strategic bombing and the use of atom bombs was eased by a different process of dehumanization. Technology removed the personal element from such killing. Pilots and bombardiers could not see their victims from an altitude of thirty thousand feet.

Ordinarily, individuals will kill even a dehumanized enemy only if they are ordered to. All armies instill a code of absolute obedience. In some cultures, such as Germany and Japan, this code affects civilians as well. The German language, with its usual capacity to combine several words into one, has created an apt term for such blind obedience, *kadavergehorsam* (obedience of a corpse). Those who gave the orders believed they were furthering a great cause, and the end therefore justified the means.

Finally, the individual who commits atrocities usually must detach himself or herself from reality in order to remain sane. Nazi leaders employed verbal euphemisms, such as the Final Solution or "resettlement to the East," to describe the mass murder of the Jews. Similarly, British air commanders dubbed the purpose of their bombing missions the "dehousing" of civilians. Psychiatrist Robert Jay Lifton has noted another process of detachment, which he calls "doubling," in the Nazi doctors who experimented on concentration camp inmates. Doubling is an adaptive mechanism which creates a second self for an individual under stress. This second self can commit either good or evil, or perform deeds that are morally ambiguous. No doubt, Sergeant Harrison Summers created a heroic double for his "crazy" deeds on D-day. Similarly, both Holocaust survivors and concentration camp guards could say, "I was a different person in Auschwitz."

The ranking of atrocities I have presented is a purely personal endeavor on my part, using moral, not legal criteria. Yet international jurists have attempted to write rules and laws of warfare by which national leaders and ordinary soldiers can be judged. The European powers held a peace conference at The Hague, capital of the Netherlands, in 1899; and eight years later, in 1907, all but four of the independent countries of the world convened for the Second Hague Conference. Participating nations adopted extensive rules for the treatment of prisoners of war and the limiting of unnecessary damage to civilians. A parallel series of meetings, conducted at Geneva, Switzerland, resulted in a 1929 convention for the treatment of war prisoners.

There is something bizarre about "rules" of war, as if warfare were a football match. One of the British delegates to the Hague Conference, Admiral Sir John Fisher, found the whole idea of "humanizing" warfare laughable: "You might just as well talk of humanizing Hell." Yet "rules of war" possessed irresistible appeal for political leaders, none of whom wished to oppose them publicly.

Germany widely ignored the Hague rules during World War I, particularly in its violation of neutral countries and in its use of poison gas (which the other side quickly matched). The Treaty of Versailles, therefore, branded the kaiser a war criminal, but he escaped to neutral Holland, which refused to extradite him. The atrocities of World War II, however, seemed so excessive that the victorious Allies decided to cast a wider net this time.

From November 20, 1945, to October 1, 1946, the United States, Great Britain, the Soviet Union, and France conducted the International Military Tribunal in Nuremberg, Germany. Hitler and his closest collaborators, Joseph Goebbels and Heinrich Himmler, had committed suicide; but twenty-two other Germans were indicted for "crimes against peace," "war crimes," and "crimes against humanity." Twelve were condemned to death by hanging (including Martin Bormann, who was condemned in absentia and was actually dead already, and Hermann Göring, who cheated the hangman by committing suicide in prison). Three Germans were acquitted at Nuremberg, and the rest were given prison sentences ranging from ten years to life.

In Tokyo, from May 3, 1946, until November 12, 1948, eleven Allied nations tried twenty-eight Japanese leaders. Two died while the trial proceeded and one was declared mentally incompetent. Seven were hanged, including General Tojo Hideki, and none were acquitted. Besides these widely publicized international trials, thousands of other Japanese and Germans were tried in military courts by individual nations.

The procedures followed at Nuremberg were scrupulously fair. This was not a "show trial" like those staged by Stalin in the 1930s. No defendants were tortured or mistreated. They chose their own lawyers, and indeed about half the defense attorneys turned out to be former Nazis. The four-judge panel, particularly the tribunal president, Sir Geoffrey Lawrence from Great Britain, bent over backwards to ensure a fair trial. Three of the defendants were actually acquitted, almost a miracle given the circumstances.

Some of the procedures followed at the Tokyo trial were more questionable. For example, a simple majority of the eleven judges formed a quorum, and a majority of those present could decide any question, even life or death. Theoretically, therefore, as few as three justices (three out of a quorum of six, with the president breaking the tie) could sentence a man to death. In actual fact, one of the death sentences was imposed by a 6-5 vote. This contrasts with the usual requirement of unanimity in jury trials and the Nuremberg procedure which prescribed a 3 out of 4 majority.

All in all, however, the conclusion of legal historian Bradley Smith seems fair:

> Though some of the specific convictions and sentences might be argued, it is clear that the Tribunal generally acted like a court rather than a vigilante proceeding. Surely class bias, ideological blindness, and personal antipathy played a part in determining the fate of some defendants ... but it would be difficult to maintain that these failings were present in a noticeably greater degree at Nuremberg than in any court that regularly grinds out judgments on the ordinary people of the world.

This statement also applies, to a lesser extent, to the Tokyo trial.

Though generally equitable in their procedures, the World War II war crimes trials proved more deficient in their overall strategy and their long-range impact. The most glaring defect in the trials was their hypocrisy and one-sidedness. Rather than impartial, neutral, international bodies, the war crimes tribunals were gatherings of victors to try the defeated. As historian A. J. P. Taylor has cynically, but accurately, pointed out: "War criminals are leaders on the other side who have not so much caused the war as lost it. That is why war criminals get punished . . . because they were fools enough to lose it." A dissenting justice on the Tokyo tribunal, India's Radhabinod Pal, made the same point: "Indeed, when the conduct of the nations is taken into account the law will perhaps be found to be that only a lost war is a crime."

The victors also committed atrocities during the war, as this chapter has illustrated. The Russian prosecutors even had the audacity to charge the German defendants with the Katyn massacre of Polish army officers, which Stalin's soldiers themselves had committed. The Allies conducted the German trial amid the ruins of Nuremberg, a city in which their bombers had destroyed 91 percent of the buildings. The two German admirals on trial, Dönitz and Raeder, obtained a sworn affidavit from American Admiral Chester Nimitz that the U.S. Navy practiced unrestricted submarine warfare against the Japanese as fully as the Germans did in the Atlantic. Hypocrisy throughout the war crimes trials, therefore, tarnished the tribunals and lessened their moral impact.

The Nuremberg and Tokyo trials both prosecuted defendants for "conspiracy to wage aggressive war." Conspiracy prosecutions are unknown outside Anglo-American law and are notoriously controversial in the United States, where they are usually used against Mafia leaders or political protesters, when no hard evidence can be found. At Nuremberg, in addition, not just individuals but whole organizations (the SS, the Gestapo, and the inner core of the Nazi Party) were declared criminal. This was unprecedented in either domestic or international law. Branding an individual guilty merely for membership in an organization or in a loosely defined conspiracy comes dangerously close to the practice of the Nazis and the Stalinists.

Both the Nuremberg and Tokyo trials set disturbing precedents of "victor's justice." Along with unconditional surrender, war crimes trials are likely to make wars longer and more savage, for no defeated military leader will have any incentive to negotiate peace if he might suffer personal indictment as a war criminal.

Defenders of the Nuremberg and Tokyo trials argue that they documented the atrocities of World War II so vividly that no one can ever forget or forgive them. Yet this was unnecessary. Atrocities indelibly define wars, with or without war crimes trials. The American Civil War, for instance, is always remembered as the "war to free the slaves," even though slavery was not that war's immediate cause and no slaveowners were tried for their actions. In fact, only one war criminal was executed after the Civil War, Major Henry Wirz, the commander of the Andersonville prison camp. Few recall him, but everyone remembers the Emancipation Proclamation.

So too with World War II. Public opinion, even in Germany, remembers the war in Europe as Hitler's war against the Jews. The Japanese, and many other people worldwide, recall little of the East Asian war except the atomic bombings of Hiroshima and Nagasaki. A second dissenting justice at the Tokyo trial, Bernard Roling of the Netherlands, wrote a dozen years later: "From the Second World War above all two things are remembered: the German gas chambers and the American atomic bombings." Atrocities define wars. This one was a war of extermination.

CHAPTER TWENTY-FIVE

The Search for Alternatives

The devastation of World War II prompted a desperate search for alternatives. The unspeakable atrocities of the war challenged the most deeply held human assumptions about right and wrong, honor and duty, peace and war. To cut short the slaughter or prevent it from ever happening again, men and women began thinking the unthinkable, exploring risky options that in less extreme times might have seemed unrealistic or impossible.

The German officer corps had all sworn a personal oath of "unconditional obedience to the führer of the German Reich and people, Adolf Hitler, the supreme commander of the *Wehrmacht*"; yet a few officers attempted to assassinate the führer, overthrow his government, and bring the war to an end. Throughout the world, men of fighting age mobilized to resist Hitler and the Japanese imperialists, believing that if any war could be proclaimed just, this one certainly could. Yet a small number of individuals, particularly in Britain and the United States, decided that the answer to violence did not lie in more violence and therefore refused to serve in the military. Neither the assassins nor the pacifist war resisters stopped the fighting; so as the war drew to a close, the great majority of peacemakers throughout the world turned to the tarnished, but still hopeful, ideal of a world organization to prevent future wars.

Killing Hitler seemed the simplest alternative. Rarely in history had one man so dominated the unfolding of events as Hitler did in the years before and during World War II. If the führer could be removed, like a cancer, perhaps health could be restored to the German body politic, atrocities prevented, and the war brought to a speedy close. German historian Peter Hoffmann, who has studied the resistance to Hitler more exhaustively than any other scholar, has discovered no fewer than forty-six serious attempts on Hitler's life from the time he first entered public life in 1921.

One of these attempts, shortly after the German conquest of Poland in 1939, came within a few minutes of success. Every year Hitler and his *Alter Kampfer,* "old fighters" who had followed him unquestioningly since the earliest days of the National Socialist party, commemorated the anniversary of their unsuccessful 1923 putsch. On November 8, 1939, they gathered as usual in the Munich beer hall where the forlorn revolt had originated. At 9:20 P.M. a powerful bomb exploded in the hall, bringing the roof down upon the revelers, killing eight and injuring over sixty. Hitler, however, had left just a few minutes earlier.

The assassin of Munich, George Elser, had systematically planned his attempt for over three months, often concealing himself overnight in the beer hall to make a thorough inspection of the premises. He took a termporary job in a stone quarry, filched some explosives from his employer, then planted a bomb in the pillar where Hitler stood while addressing his comrades. The führer usually ranted from 8:30 P.M. until 10:00 at the earliest; yet the starting time was advanced to 8:00 and Hitler cut his speech short about 9:07. By the time of the explosion, his train was speeding toward Berlin.

The assassination of Hitler posed more problems than Elser had foreseen. Even if an assassin should succeed, this would not necessarily end the war and the atrocities. Though Hitler exercised unprecedented one-man authority, one of his leading followers, such as Hermann Göring or Heinrich Himmler, might well have seized power upon his death, proclaiming the führer a martyr for Germany. Therefore, many opponents of the Nazis preferred that Hitler be arrested and declared insane, or possibly tried for war crimes, to prevent his martyrdom and deification. Others who believed his death imperative realized it would not prove sufficient. Along with assassination, a full-scale coup d'etat was required.

A surprisingly large number of high officers in the German military were sympathetic to the idea of a coup against Hitler. Yet most satisfied their consciences by obeying their superiors, carrying out their duties with professional efficiency, and leading honorable private lives. Few if any would denounce fellow officers who plotted against Hitler, but only a handful would assist them. What distinguished the anti-Hitler conspirators from those who timidly held back was a "wholeness" or integrity of character, a close correspondence between their private and public morality. As we noted in the last chapter, concentration camp guards and others who carried out Hitler's evil commands often experienced a form of psychological "doubling." They became two persons: an honorable, decent private individual and a second, demoniac public official they barely recognized and tried not to think about. Those who resisted Hitler, however, remained whole.

Anti-Hitler conspirators, such as the Stauffenberg brothers, the Protestant pastor Dietrich Bonhoeffer, or the Jesuit priest Father Alfred Delp, drew on their Christian values and their classical education for role models of heroism and virtue. They possessed an aristocratic sense of noblesse oblige and personal honor, and were supported by close and satisfying family ties. Most came from families with a long tradition of public service and wished to pass on this legacy unsullied to the next generation. One conspirator quoted Shakespeare's *Henry V,* calling his fellows "we band of brothers." In fact, this was literally true, for many of those who plotted against Hitler were brothers, cousins, or other kin to each other.

From 1942 onwards the assassination and coup attempt centered around the Replacement Army headquarters in Berlin and its secret plans for Operation Valkyrie. The Replacement Army was the army reserve of Germany, responsible for supplying men and materiel to make up the losses at the front. After the attack on Russia, army staff formulated Operation Valkyrie as an emergency plan to mobilize the reserves in case of riot or rebellion by concentration camp inmates or foreign laborers. Hitler himself approved the plan, dated May 26, 1942. Resistance plotters within the military gradually infiltrated into positions at Replacement Army headquarters on the Bendlerstrasse in Berlin and began adapting the Valkyrie plans to a coup attempt. After a successful assassination of Hitler, Operation Valkyrie would be proclaimed from Berlin, the SS and other Nazi faithful would be neutralized by Replacement Army troops, and a provisional government would be proclaimed. The retired General Ludwig Beck agreed to act as head of state in the new government, and other civilian and military officials also consented to serve.

Before Valkyrie could be activated Hitler had to be killed; but the amazing luck which saved his life in November 1939 remained with the führer. On March 13, 1943, Hitler paid a rare visit to the Russian front, where Lieutenant-Colonel Henning von Tresckow planted a double dose of captured British explosive, shaped like two square bottles of Cointreau liqueur, in the führer's plane. The extreme cold of the return flight, however, prevented the bomb from exploding. Tresckow's aide managed to recover the explosives undetected, replacing them with two real bottles of Cointreau.

Shortly thereafter, another officer volunteered to blow himself up while accompanying Hitler through an exhibition of captured war booty on "Heroes Memorial Day." The führer seemed to possess a sixth sense for danger. Noting the officer's nervousness he literally ran through the exhibit without pausing at all. The would-be assassin managed to defuse the bomb in a washroom. Nearly a year later, another volunteer planned to shoot Hitler with a pistol at a military briefing, but failed to gain admittance.

Finally on July 20, 1944, Colonel Claus Schenk von Stauffenberg carried out a full-scale plan of assassination. Born on November 15, 1907, Count Stauffenberg belonged to an old noble family from Swabia in southwestern Germany. He and his brothers, Berthold and Alexander, had been raised as Catholics and given a rigorous humanist education at a 250-year-old *gymnasium* (high school) in

442

Stuttgart. Though originally attracted by the aura of national regeneration surrounding the Nazi takeover of power in Germany, the Stauffenbergs drew upon their family, religious, and educational values to make a complete break. When Claus met Hitler for the first time, on the eastern front in summer 1942, he found that he could resist the powerful gaze of the führer, which nearly always caused subordinates to lose their nerve in his presence.

Claus Stauffenberg was seriously wounded on the North African front in April 1943, losing his left eye, right hand, and two fingers of his left hand. He recovered his health by the end of August 1943 and took up a staff post with the Replacement Army. On July 1, 1944, the thirty-six-year-old colonel became chief of staff (second in command) to General Fritz Fromm, gaining direct access to Hitler. He determined to kill the führer himself. Stauffenberg's presence, however, would also be required at the Bendlerstrasse headquarters to direct the coup, since General Fromm could not be relied upon to support the conspiracy and the others lacked authority or nerve. The subsequent attack on Hitler, therefore, suffered from a fatal flaw. It required Stauffenberg to be in two places at once.

Early in the morning of July 20, 1944, Claus left the apartment of his brother Berthold, where he was staying in Berlin, and flew to Rastenburg in East Prussia for a military conference. His aide carried a briefcase with two bombs in it. Before entering the wooden briefing hut at 12:30 P.M., Stauffenberg ducked into a washroom to fuse the bombs but was interrupted by a sergeant after arming only one of them. He slipped the bomb into his briefcase, sat down next to Hitler, and put the briefcase underneath the heavy oak map table. A moment later, he muttered an excuse about an urgent phone call and left the room. About 12:40 the bomb exploded. Stauffenberg and his aide saw the flame and smoke, and swiftly escaped the compound for a flight back to Berlin.

In fact, four officers were killed by the bomb blast, and twenty others wounded. Hitler himself had his eardrums blown out and his clothing singed, but he survived. The heavy oak table leg had deflected part of the blast from the single bomb. Had both been armed as planned, no one would have lived through the explosion.

As Stauffenberg made the three-hour flight to Berlin, confused reports of the assassination attempt filtered back to the Bendlerstrasse causing the other conspirators to hesitate. They did not finally activate the Valkyrie plan until just before Stauffenberg arrived around five o'clock. By then it was too late, for counter-orders were already flowing from Hitler's Wolf's Lair. The coup unrolled fitfully, until it finally collapsed about eleven o'clock. General Fromm, who had been arrested in his office, was released by loyal soldiers. He then ordered Stauffenberg and three other conspirators summarily shot just after midnight. General Beck at the Bendlerstrasse, and Colonel von Tresckow, far away on the eastern front, both committed suicide. They proved to be the lucky ones. At least seven thousand people were arrested in connection with the plot. About two hundred ringleaders were tortured, tried, and executed. Hitler decreed that they be hanged with piano wire in such a way that their necks would not be broken and they would be slowly and painfully strangled to death.

The plot to assassinate Hitler had failed because too much depended upon one man. There were not enough conspirators with the values, the courage, and the organizational ability of Stauffenberg to successfully overthrow the Nazi regime.

One soldier who joined the assassination conspiracy thought, in retrospect, that another approach, nonviolent resistance, might have proven better. Captain Axel von dem Bussche witnessed the massacre of five thousand Jews at an airfield near the Ukrainian city of Dubno in 1942. At the time, he felt powerless to do anything, except vow to get even with Hitler; but he later believed he should have ostentatiously joined a row of Jewish victims, daring his military colleagues to shoot him as well.

The possibility of nonviolent resistance to Hitler is not so unthinkable as it might initially appear. If Captain Bussche had courageously followed his instincts at the Dubno airfield, he might have shamed his fellow soldiers and saved the remaining Jews of the city. Alternatively, he may have been shot along with the Jews, or arrested and sent to an insane asylum or concentration camp. Yet if Bussche were part of an organized movement of nonviolent resisters, he could have brought the whole killing machine to a halt. As Peter Brock, the foremost historian of pacifist movements, has concluded: "Even totalitarian regimes depend on the cooperation of their citizens and are sometimes amenable to the influence of world opinion; civil disobedience, *if* it could be organized on a wide enough scale, might topple them or at least bring sweeping concessions."

How widespread would a nonviolent resistance movement need to be? In 1930, Albert Einstein argued that if only 2 percent of the male population refused to fight, war would be impossible, for the jails could not hold so many conscientious objectors. It is unlikely that 2 percent would have been enough to overthrow Hitler, for the Nazis showed they could build, and fill, prisons and camps for vast numbers of their enemies. Einstein himself later recanted his own 2 percent solution and became a reluctant advocate of military force against the Nazis. The strategic placement of resisters might prove more crucial than sheer numbers. Before the Nazi takeover of Czechoslovakia in 1938, General Ludwig Beck, then the Army Chief of Staff, implored his fellow generals to take a "collective step" against the proposed aggression by resigning from their posts. None heeded his plea and Beck wound up resigning alone, quietly. If, however, the top-ranking officers had acted together, they might have stopped Hitler's war machine before it got started. The military possessed such great prestige in Germany that they could have removed Hitler's legitimacy.

These last few paragraphs have been necessarily hypothetical, for only a tiny handful of Germans refused military service during wartime. One of the few who did was an Austrian peasant, Franz Jagerstatter, from the mountain village of St. Radegund. Though he had a wife and three daughters, and his Catholic pastor urged him to comply with the draft, his inner convictions prompted him to refuse service. Consequently, he was tried by the military and beheaded on August 9, 1943.

Jagerstatter's resistance was a case of "solitary witness," in the words of his biographer Gordon Zahn. The Austrian peasant harbored no illusions that his action would change anything. In a remarkable letter from prison, he wrote: "Today one can hear it said repeatedly that there is nothing any more that an individual can do. . . . True, there is not much that can be done any more to change the course of world events . . . but as long as we live in this world, I believe it is never too late to save ourselves and perhaps some other soul for Christ." The long-range significance of such solitary witness should not be dismissed or underestimated. Decades after the war, Jagerstatter was awarded a posthumous honor by the Austrian government, and he has become something of a national hero. Similar heroes from the past served as role models for pacifists and for the Stauffenberg circle during World War II. Yet, in the immediate run of events, conscientious objection within the German Reich remained too exceptional to make any difference.

Yet other forms of noncooperation and nonviolent resistance did prove effective from time to time in the countries occupied by the Nazis. Norwegians mounted a violent underground resistance to the collaborationist government of Vidkun Quisling, but they also engaged in parallel acts of noncooperation. Throughout the occupation, for instance, Norwegians carried on a sports strike, boycotting all sports organizations and contests sponsored by either the Quisling regime or the German military. Such noncooperation forcefully stated the intransigence of Norway and necessitated a much larger occupying force than would otherwise be required. In Denmark and Finland, the citizens successfully saved the Jewish populations of their countries through nonviolent resistance, smuggling them out to neutral Sweden or hiding them in their own homes at great risk. Theologian Walter Wink has stated: "The tragedy is not that nonviolence did not work against the Nazis, but that it was so seldom utilized. . . . The churches as a whole were too docile or anti-Semitic, and too ignorant of the nonviolent message of the gospel, to act effectively to resist the Nazis or act in solidarity with the Jews."

The primary reason why nonviolent resistance within Germany and the occupied countries proved generally unsuccessful was its solitary, individualist, exceptional character. Mohandas Gandhi proved in India that collective injustice can be overcome only by collective resistance. As Walter Wink concludes:

It is wrong to compare nonviolence in its present, embryonic form with a system of violence that is in advanced stages of development, and deeply entrenched in the socioeconomic systems of the world. The comparison must rather be between our present system of violence and nonviolence as it might realistically be developed.

Few today would doubt that a nonviolent resistance from within Hitler's Germany would be just and desirable, though many, perhaps most, might judge it unrealistic or even foolhardy. But what of pacifism, conscientious objection, or nonviolent resistance to the Allied governments fighting against Hitler? For over fifty years the seemingly unanswerable question asked of pacifists has been, "Wouldn't you have fought against Hitler?"

In fact, far more English and Americans registered as conscientious objectors in World War II than in the previous war, about 60,000 in Great Britain and between 70,000 and 100,000 in the United States. The question "What about Hitler?" landed with less force at the time than it would today, for the facts about the Holocaust and other atrocities were not well known and not always believed during the war. The Japanese attack on Pearl Harbor posed a much stiffer challenge to American pacifists than the Holocaust did. Nevertheless, the number of conscientious objectors remained minuscule compared with the millions who mobilized for war. Most acted out of personal religious or political conviction, and like Franz Jagerstatter in Austria they felt powerless to alter the course of events. Historian Peter Brock, a very sympathetic chronicler of the pacifist movement, nevertheless concluded that "pacifism in World War II appeared a small and seemingly ineffective sect."

Only a large-scale, well-organized resistance movement, prepared by mass education and led by well-trained cadres of nonviolent resisters, could have exercised any impact on the outcome of World War II. Nonviolent resistance is difficult and dangerous; those who pursue it risk death, just as soldiers do. Effective pacifists are not passive, timid souls, but courageous peacemakers. Like soldiers, they believe in a cause worth dying for, but they do not believe any cause is worth killing for. Pacifists, however, need not be saints, or even religious believers. They simply need to cultivate the basic human stubbornness that can be observed in any child; a stubbornness to say "No." If people can be trained to be soldiers, they can be trained as pacifists.

One pacifist has recently suggested that the pope should convene an ecumenical council of all Christians, Catholic and non-Catholic alike, to proclaim the gospel of nonviolence. At such a council, religious leaders would reject the just war theory, asserting instead that modern means of warmaking are disproportionate to any imaginable good end. Such a gathering, perhaps with the participation of Indian leaders experienced in mass nonviolent protest and Jewish survivors of the Holocaust, might begin fashioning a credible alternative to warfare. Only when pacifists have their own peacekeeping "armies" can they challenge the weapons of national armies.

Nonviolent resistance to the Nazis still seems unthinkable to most citizens of the late twentieth century. If citizens of the nations threatened by Germany had adopted the noncooperation strategy suggested by Bertrand Russell during the first war, certainly Hitler would have greeted them with disdain, killing them outright or banishing them to slave labor camps. Thousands, perhaps millions, might have died. Yet warlike resistance with the world's most sophisticated weapons took six years to vanquish Hitler and in the process about 60 million people died worldwide. Any alternative that would result in fewer than 60 million deaths is not, therefore, unthinkable.

Cynthia Eller, an American sociologist who belongs to one of the historic peace churches, recently interviewed surviving conscientious objectors from World War II. When confronted with the indisputable facts about the Holocaust, some of them concluded that they were mistaken and should have taken up arms against Hitler. Many others, however, believed that knowledge of the Holocaust actually strengthened their adherence to pacifist principles. Even Hitler did not dare to attempt the Final Solution until he had unleashed a world war and been met with military resistance. "Wartime necessity" made it easier for people to collaborate in mass extermination. War is a warrant for genocide.

One American Jewish pacifist, Max Kleinbaum, told Cynthia Eller he was constantly asked "How can a Jew be a conscientious objector?" He answered that Jews above all people should refuse participation in war for three reasons: "(1) because war produces the conditions that result in the massacre of Jews; (2) because Jews always do better in peacetime; and (3) because Hitler is produced by the conditions that result from war."

Kleinbaum, Jagerstatter, and the other concientious objectors formed a tiny minority during World War II whose solitary witness remains inspiring and challenging. Yet their alternative failed, just as Stauffenberg's assassination plot did; and for much the same reason. The July 20 conspirators in Germany and pacifists of all nations remained too few, too isolated, and too individualist to overcome mass, collective evil. Like the anarchists at the beginning of the century, theirs was a lone cry against an overwhelming trend of the twentieth century, organized bigness.

The military and political leaders of the Allied powers realized the need for a collective response to aggression. Only the combined efforts of Great Britain, the United States, and the Soviet Union had defeated Germany and Japan. The victorous Allies, therefore, tried to forge a system of collective security to protect the hard-won peace and ensure against future aggression.

The previous collective security organization, the League of Nations, had proven inadequate. The League had considered over fifty international disputes in its two-decade-long history, and actually stopped four small wars (two minor Balkan imbroglios in the early 1920s, a dispute between Turkey and Iraq from 1924 to 1926, and a border battle between Colombia and Peru in 1932). It had arranged international reconstruction loans for Austria, Hungary, and Greece, and resettled hundreds of thousands of POWs and displaced persons after World War I. Specialized agencies associated with the League, such as the International Labor Organization, performed useful research, educational, and humanitarian tasks.

Yet the League was never taken seriously by the major powers of the world; in the words of historian Fred S. Northedge, it "tended to be left with the small change of diplomacy. . . ." Members of the League failed to stop the seizure of Manchuria by Japan in 1931 or Ethiopia by Italy in 1935-36. While Prime Minister Chamberlain met Hitler and Mussolini at the Munich Conference of 1938, the assembly of the League remained in session at Geneva, debating routine business, unconsulted on the fate of one of its members, Czechoslovakia. The League Council invoked sanctions only once, against Italy in 1935, but applied them halfheartedly and failed to stop Mussolini's conquest of Ethiopia. Though the French had suggested the formation of an international army to counter breaches of peace, this proposal was never adopted and the League never called on its member states for armed assistance. An oft-quoted phrase sums up the League's collective security machinery: it was not tried and found wanting, rather it was found difficult and not really tried at all.

The League of Nations had acquired such a stench of failure that when Roosevelt met Churchill for the first time, at the Atlantic Conference of August 1940, he refused to even use the term "international organization" in the final declaration. Churchill finally persuaded him to employ the more general phraseology, "a wider and permanent system of general security." The American president did not believe a League-like assembly of all nations would prove useful after the war. He envisioned instead a great power consortium, much like the old Concert of Europe, enforcing the peace. Roosevelt himself coined the term "United Nations," using it for the first time in the formal declaration of resistance to Nazi and Japanese aggression, signed by twenty-six nations on January 1, 1942. Yet this phrase originally applied to the wartime coalition, not a postwar organization.

The United States, as the strongest military power in World War II, and the only one undamaged by the war, necessarily took the lead in planning for peace. As Clark Eichelberger, a leading advocate of world organization, remarked: "One might say that the British [and the Russians] were too close to the war to engage in postwar planning, whereas the Americans were too far removed from it to have a sense of reality about it." FDR, however, possessed sufficient sense of reality to avoid the mistakes of Woodrow Wilson in planning for any new world organization. He used the failures of Wilson and the League as a kind of touchstone in all his subsequent thinking about the future United Nations organization.

The prime weaknesses of the League had been the absence of the strongest powers, such as the United States and the Soviet Union, and the failure of the remaining powers to exercise force or a credible threat of force at times of crisis. So Roosevelt determined that any "wider and permanent system of general security" must entail close cooperation of the four large nations who bore the brunt of resistance to Germany and Japan. These four — the United States, the United Kingdom, the Union of Soviet Socialist Republics, and the Republic of China — were listed first in the 1942 United Nations Declaration. Roosevelt often called them the "Four Policemen," and he originally believed that they alone should keep the peace after the defeat of the Axis, with the other nations of the world disarmed. Gradually, at the prompting of Cordell Hull, the secretary of state, FDR realized that world opinion would never assent to such a naked exercise of power. Thus the American State Department and the British Foreign Office formulated plans for an organization much like the League of Nations in form and structure.

The first definite decision about postwar organization was taken at the Foreign Ministers' Conference held in Moscow in October and November 1943. The final declaration of the conference stated that Great Britain, Russia, and the United States "recognize the necessity of establishing at the earliest practicable date a general international organization, based on the principle of the sovereign equality of all peace-loving states, and open to membership by all such states, large and small, for the maintenance of international peace and security." Roosevelt, Churchill, and Stalin personally ratified this commitment a few weeks later, when they met at the Teheran Conference.

To President Roosevelt the idea of forming an international organization "at the earliest practicable date" meant "before the war was over." Remembering how the League of Nations Covenant had gotten entangled in the arguments of the Paris Peace Conference, he determined to establish the UN while the wartime coalition remained intact, *before* the victors fell to wrangling about peace treaties. The State Department, therefore, prepared a preliminary draft proposal and invited representatives from Britain, the Soviet Union, and China to meet in Washington during the summer of 1944. Since Russia had not yet entered the Pacific War and Stalin did not respect or trust the Chinese leader Chiang Kai-shek, Soviet delegates refused to sit down with the Chinese. Therefore, this planning conference broke down into two sessions, the first consisting of England, the United States, and Russia, the second with England, the United States, and China.

The first, and more important, phase of the conference opened on August 21, 1944, at an old mansion named Dumbarton Oaks, in the Georgetown section of Washington, D.C. The delegates were not heads of state or government, or even foreign ministers, but high-ranking diplomats and bureaucrats; for this was a preliminary working conference, not one for ceremonies or final decisions. Over the next six weeks, Sir Alexander Cadogan of Great Britain, Edward R. Stettinius Jr. of the United States, and Andrei Gromyko of the Soviet Union, along with their staffs, hammered out the framework of a world organization. The brief follow-up session with the Chinese in early October merely ratified the decisions of the Big Three.

The Dumbarton Oaks Conference proved unable to settle two thorny questions. The first concerned voting procedure in the crucial body that the planners called the Security Council. The big powers were determined to dominate and control this council, for it would exercise the authority to resist aggression and ensure collective security. They agreed that the four permanent members of the Security Council, the Four Policemen (later joined by France as the fifth permanent member), would require unanimity for any decision to employ force. Each of the nations would enjoy veto power over Security Council actions. Yet what would happen if one of the "Policemen" initiated aggression? Who watches the watchman? Would the Big Four be allowed to vote on decisions concerning their own actions, or veto any discussion of their own misconduct? The relatively low-level delegates at Dumbarton Oaks could not settle this matter and reserved it for later decision by their superiors.

The other contentious matter was raised, out of the blue, by Soviet delegate Andrei Gromyko when he demanded that the USSR be granted sixteen votes in the General Assembly of the UN, one for each of the constituent republics of the Soviet Union. This was such a bombshell that the head of the American delegation, Edward Stettinius, begged the other delegates not to mention it to the press. He himself always referred to the question, even in his own diary, as the "X-matter."

The Soviet request for sixteen representatives in the new world body was not quite so outrageous as it initially seemed. We now know that Stalin was partly motivated by questions of internal politics. Ukraine, Byelorussia, and several of the other non-Russian republics had borne the brunt of the war in Eastern Europe and desired more freedom and recognition in the postwar years. Admission to the United Nations in their own names would be a relatively cheap reward for Stalin to grant. Furthermore, the arithmetic of international relations bothered the Russians. Great Britain would likely be supported by the votes of her dominions who would be admitted to the UN, and the United States could generally count on the votes of the Latin American nations. Thus, Stalin foresaw a situation where his Communist country would be outnumbered and isolated in the General Assembly. The extra Soviet votes would go some way towards righting the balance. In any case, the X-matter was not settled at Dumbarton Oaks and was also put over for further consideration by the Big Three.

Roosevelt, Churchill, and Stalin settled these outstanding questions about the United Nations relatively easily at the Yalta Conference in February 1945. The Russians themselves proposed a compromise on the number of Soviet republics to be represented in the organization, asking now that only three or two be admitted as members, not all sixteen. The Americans and British breathed a sigh of relief, and agreed to support the admission of Ukraine and Byelorussia, along with Russia, to the General Assembly. The Russians also accepted an American compromise on the veto power. The permanent members of the Security Council would be able to veto any decisions or actions of the Council, even if they themselves were a party to the dispute, but they could not veto procedural motions or prevent the council from discussing a dispute that concerned them.

Amid this planning and decision making, President Roosevelt was carefully preparing the way for American acceptance of the United Nations Organization. All the Allies feared that the United States would revert to isolationism after the war, as it had in 1919. So, with the ghost of Woodrow Wilson constantly before him, Roosevelt secured congressional approval in advance this time. In the summer of 1943, the House of Representatives passed a resolution introduced by Representative J. William Fulbright of Arkansas, "favoring the creation of appropriate international machinery with power adequate to maintain a just and lasting peace." On November 5, 1943, the Senate passed a similar resolution sponsored by Senator Tom Connally of Texas, the chairman of the Senate Foreign Affairs Committee. The Dumbarton Oaks Conference coincided with the presidential election campaign of 1944, but President Roosevelt convinced his challenger, Republican Thomas Dewey, not to make the postwar organization an issue.

American public opinion, therefore, was prepared for the founding of the United Nations, which took place at a conference in San Francisco, meeting from April 25 to June 26, 1945. President Roosevelt selected a politically well-balanced slate of delegates to this conference, including men from all sections of the country and one woman, Virginia Gildersleeve, dean of Barnard College. Unlike Woodrow Wilson, who had not included senators or prominent Republicans in his delegation at Paris, Roosevelt appointed both the House and Senate Foreign Affairs Committee chairmen and their ranking minority party members. FDR died in early April; but his successor, Harry Truman, confirmed on his first day in office that the San Francisco Conference would go ahead as planned. Continuity with his famous predecessor had influenced Truman's decision to drop the atomic bomb; it also predisposed him to favor the world organization.

The United Nations Charter, signed by fifty nations at San Francisco on June 26, 1945, and put into effect on October 24 of the same year, created a body that looked much like the discredited League of Nations. The structure of the UN contains the familiar four divisions — Security Council, General Assembly, Secretariat, and International Court of Justice. All member states send delegates to the General Assembly where they "may discuss any questions or any matters within the scope of the present Charter [and] . . . may make recommendations to the Members of the United Nations or to the Security Council." The Council originally consisted of five permanent members and six other nations, appointed by the Assembly to serve two-year terms, for a total membership of eleven; but it was expanded to fifteen members in 1965. The Security Council bears "primary responsibility for the maintenance of international peace and security" and may call on member nations to apply economic sanctions, blockades, or military force against aggressors. The Secretariat functions as the bureaucracy or civil service of the organization, under the direction of a secretary-general. The charter was unclear whether this officer would be primarily a secretary or a general. In practice he has always been selected from one of the small, neutral nations of the world and adopted a prudent, middle course, more than a faceless bureaucrat but less than a president of the world. The International Court of Justice remains at The Hague, where it had resided under the League of Nations, and it continues to adjudicate low-level disputes between nations.

The United Nations also took over the former "mandated territories" from the League of Nations as well as colonies stripped from Japan in the Pacific, administering them as "trust territories" in which "the interests of the inhabitants of these territories are paramount." Finally, the specialized economic and humanitarian agencies of the League, such as the International Labor Organization, were incorporated into the UN; and many more agencies, such as the Food and Agriculture Organization (FAO), the World Health Organization (WHO), and the United Nations Children's Fund (UNICEF), were established. These specialized agencies report to an Economic and Social Council of fifty-four members, selected by the General Assembly for three-year terms.

Three major differences distinguished the United Nations from the League of Nations: the location of its headquarters, the extent of its membership, and the voting procedures in the Assembly and the Council.

Although the League had completed a handsome new headquarters building in Geneva, Switzerland, the Palais des Nations, in 1937, the odor of failure hung so heavy over it that the Allied nations chose not to establish the new organization there but chose New York instead. A location in the United States provided insurance against another American isolationist withdrawal from the world. Furthermore, America's wealth, its freedom from wartime destruction, and the newly dominant position of the United States in the affairs of the world virtually dictated an American location. The Rockefeller family donated 8.5 million dollars to purchase a tract of land at Turtle Bay along the East River on New York's Manhattan Island. This site was cleared of tenements and old factories, and a modern headquarters building opened on the site in October 1952.

The League of Nations had been crippled by the defection of many important countries. After World War II, however, the victorious Allies stuck together, with fifty states signing the charter in 1945. Defeated countries were gradually admitted to the organization as were the numerous new nations that threw off colonial rule in the following two decades. By the 1960s the UN embraced 120 members; this number has grown to 185 at present. No member state has ever withdrawn or been expelled.

Instead of the unanimous approval that was necessary in League of Nations votes, the General Assembly of the United Nations decides "important questions," such as the admission of new member states and the election of nonpermanent members to the Security Council, by a two-thirds vote. All other resolutions and recommendations are determined by a simple majority of nations present and voting. The Security Council requires the affirmative vote of nine out of the fifteen members (originally seven out of eleven), but this must include all five permanent members. In the League of Nations all members could exercise a veto, but in the UN only the five major powers enjoy this privilege.

Despite its greater universality, more flexible voting procedures, and location within the world's most powerful nation, the UN possesses little more authority than its predecessor did. During the Second World War, the world organization's planners considered a number of measures to strengthen the enforcement power of the UN, such as control of strategic strong points throughout the world and the formation of an independent UN army or air force. President Roosevelt pointed out that if a world body had possessed its own force in 1935, when Mussolini invaded Ethiopia, it could have immediately closed the Suez Canal and choked off the Italian invasion. Yet the great powers, including the United States, ultimately rejected these measures as threats to their own control of the organization. All attempts to establish a true world government, with power and authority over the nations of the world, foundered on the rock of national sovereignty. Nationalism again proved the most powerful and persistent force in the twentieth-century world.

Without governmental authority of its own, the UN depends entirely on the cooperation of the permanent members of the Security Council — the Big Five or the Five Policemen — for its effectiveness as a collective security organization. Unfortunately, the Five Policemen did not cooperate for very long after the war's end. As we shall see in great detail in the second volume of this work, the Soviet Union and the United States became bitter enemies, and a Cold War between them dominated the second half of the century. The peace was kept, when it was kept at all, by a balance of armed terror between the two superpowers. The United Nations was only able to mount military force against aggression on two occasions. In 1950, since the Soviet Union was unwisely boycotting the Security Council, they could not veto the authorization of UN action against North Korea's invasion of the South. Then late in the century, in 1991, after Communist control of the Soviet Union had collapsed, the UN Security Council unanimously authorized military force to stop Iraq's annexation of Kuwait. On other occasions of international violence in the second half of the century, the United Nations proved as irrelevant as the League.

Yet the UN was not a total failure. It is fortunate that Anglo-American internationalists and the representatives of small states forced the great powers to compromise on their postwar plans for a world organization. Had Roosevelt's original idea of the Four Policemen, without any attendant General Assembly or specialized agencies, gone into effect in 1945, the resulting minimalist organization would have passed away within a short number of years. Once the policemen began fighting each other, nothing else would have been left.

By building a more complex organization, with a General Assembly to provide recognition and a debating forum for all the nations of the world, a secretary-general to rally worldwide public opinion, and a dense conglomeration of educational and humanitarian organizations, the United Nations has been able to accomplish a great deal. It has been ridiculed as a mere "talking shop," and for the most part that's what it is. Talk is cheap, but it is symbolically important for small nations, and it is always better than war. The "talking shop" on New York's East River has acquired some moral authority. As Conor Cruise O'Brien, a former UN delegate from Ireland, once wrote: "It [the UN] is basically a spiritual-political institution in the line of descent from the ancient shrine at Delhi and the medieval papacy." The worldwide journeys of modern popes such as Paul VI and John Paul II are striking examples of such spiritual-political authority in action. When the secretary-general of the United Nations attracts as much media publicity as the pope does, the UN will clearly have arrived as a moral force in the world.

Sometimes, the United Nations has gone beyond talk and symbolic politics. The humanitarian work of the UN is widespread and often effective. As just one example, the World Health Organization mounted a global campaign to eradicate smallpox in 1967. Forty-three countries had reported over 130,000 cases of the dread disease that year, but two decades later the WHO declared that the disease no longer existed anywhere on earth. In addition, the blue-helmeted UN peacekeeping forces have often prevented further bloodshed after regional wars. Though the UN has rarely been able to stop aggression by warlike states (collective security, or peace*making*), it has registered many notable successes preserving peace once the warring nations strike an armistice (peace*keeping*).

In 1933 President Franklin D. Roosevelt, in an address to the Woodrow Wilson Foundation, found a number of positive things to say about the League of Nations. His statement could equally well apply to the United Nations today:

> The League has provided a common meeting place; it has provided machinery which serves for international discussion; and in very many practical instances it has helped labor and health and commerce and education, and, last but not

least, the actual settlement of many disputes great and small among nations great and small.

Faint praise, perhaps, but better than no praise at all.

The victorious United Nations also tried to lay economic foundations for a more peaceful world. The economic collapse of the 1930s had dried up international investment and world trade, as the major industrialized nations closed in upon themselves, erecting high tariff barriers and forbidding the conversion of their currencies into gold or the currencies of other nations. Germany, Japan, Great Britain, and the United States all moved towards closed economic blocs, providing an illusion of protection but preventing the revival of world trade and economic prosperity. So during the war, economists in Britain and the United States planned a new international economic order, characterized by stable monetary exchange rates, orderly investment, and free international trade.

Both John Maynard Keynes and his American counterparts determined that monetary stability must come first, for no government, bank, or business would invest in a country where they could not freely convert their profits into their own currency at a predictable rate. Keynes envisioned a true world bank, which he called an International Clearing Union, that would issue its own currency and lend it to nations needing economic stimulus. The American Secretary of the Treasury, Henry Morgenthau, and his chief advisor for international economics, Harry Dexter White, rejected Keynes's scheme as too ambitious, but proposed two more limited international institutions, a stabilization fund that would prescribe stable exchange rates and an international investment bank that would make loans to war-devastated countries and underdeveloped nations.

From July 1 to 22, 1944, a month before the Dumbarton Oaks conference, economic and financial experts from forty-four nations met at the cool, mountain resort town of Bretton Woods in New Hampshire. John Kenneth Galbraith has remarked that "the Bretton Woods Conference was not a conference among nations. It was a conference of nations with Keynes. . . ." The eminent British economist was feted and celebrated; but in fact the Americans, particularly Harry Dexter White, set the agenda and dominated the discussions. The United States held nearly two-thirds of the world's gold at Fort Knox and produced as much in goods and services as the rest of the world combined. The British consoled themselves with a little ditty: "In Washington Lord Halifax, Once whispered to Lord Keynes: It's true *they* have the money bags, But we have all the brains." Nevertheless, whatever Uncle Money Bags wanted he got, at Bretton Woods as at Dumbarton Oaks.

The conference produced a plan for the International Monetary Fund, which would set and police exchange rates between national currencies and make short-term loans to support these rates, and the Bank for Reconstruction and

Development (usually called the World Bank), which would extend long-term loans for economic development projects. The headquarters of both institutions was established at Washington, D.C., and the voting process in both was established on a weighted basis, with the countries contributing the greatest amount of capital enjoying preponderant influence. Both institutions still exist, though they have changed greatly over the decades, and both have been thoroughly dominated by American economic interests. Like the United Nations itself, the Bretton Woods institutions have enjoyed some successes and they constitute an important symbolic achievement, but they have not replaced national self-interest and the dominance of the strongest with a true international order.

Ultimately the hardheaded, "realistic" alternatives to war pursued by the Big Power Policemen and by Uncle Moneybags failed almost as thoroughly as the quixotic plans of Hitler's assassins and the ineffectual dreams of the pacifists. The assassins and the pacifists were too isolated and individualistic, and the plans for a United Nations and a new economic order fell afoul of what might be called national individualism or national egoism. The task of building a collective alternative to war remained largely undone at midcentury, despite the idealism and the mortal fear engendered by two unprecedented world wars.

Afterword — Volume 1

The First World War was the watershed event of the twentieth century, for it led inexorably to worldwide economic depression and a second world war filled with atrocities. At root, it was caused by two of the terrible "isms," national sovereignty exercised imperialistically. Before 1914, Great Britain enjoyed hegemony, which means simply that it had to be consulted or considered in every international event. The Germans of Kaiser Wilhelm's day recognized this fact, resented it, and challenged it. Thus World War I ensued, and, after a generation, the second war.

The two world wars destroyed both Germany's potential for hegemony and England's actual hegemony. Neither side won and Europe's dominance in the world was mortally wounded. The two peripheral powers, Russia and the United States, filled the vacuum in the second half of the century, but the other countries of the world also rebelled against great power dominance. The Cold War between the two superpowers and the anti-imperialist rebellion of Asia and Africa are the two major themes of the second volume of this history of the world in the twentieth century.

The task of the twenty-first century is to replace a system of national sovereignty exercised imperialistically with a system of national sovereignty tempered by justice. The victorious powers after World War I tried to build such a system with the League of Nations but failed. They attempted this task again after the second war, with imperfect but somewhat greater success.

Isolated resistance to evil, whether violent or nonviolent, by either individuals or nations, satisfies the human urge to rebel and not give in. As Albert Camus, the mid-century novelist and philosopher, once wrote, *Je me revolte, donc je suis* — I rebel, therefore I am. The individual rebel suffers defeat, but asserts his own identity. To effect lasting change, however, the rebel must unite with others: *Je me revolte, donc nous sommes* — I rebel, therefore we are. The task remains.

457

Suggestions for Further Reading

L ife is too short to read bad books. Yet, some of the most important books of the twentieth century are nearly unreadable. I have read them so that you don't have to.

The following suggestions do not constitute a full scholarly bibliography. They are intended as a guide for the general reader and as a map of my own research. They include only English-language readings that I have personally consulted. They include classic texts, books that are unusually interesting, or those that I found especially useful. I have marked those I consider "must reading" (a highly subjective category) with an asterisk (*) and those which are unusually accessible and readable (an equally subjective judgment) with a plus sign (+). Some happy hybrids bear both marks!

Chapter 1. Europeans under Siege

Leo Marquard, *The People and Policies of South Africa,* 4th ed. (London: Oxford University Press, 1969), and T. R. H. Davenport, *South Africa: A Modern History* (London: Macmillan, 1977), provide excellent background on the broad sweep of South African history.

Military history bears an undeserved stigma among academic historians and enjoys an undeserved popularity among the general public. Thomas Pakenham's *+ The Boer War* (New York: Random House, 1979) is an example of military history at its best. Pakenham gives enough of the political background and larger significance to place the war in context but concentrates on describing the battles, largely in the words of the participants themselves. He engages in very little second-guessing or hindsight. Christopher Martin's +*The Boer War* (London: Abelard-Schuman, 1969) is much briefer and sketchier, but the book is useful for a quick overview.

Christopher Martin also wrote +*The Boxer Rebellion* (London: Abelard-Schuman, 1968). Richard O'Connor's +*The Spirit Soldiers: A Historical Narrative of the Boxer Rebellion* (New York: G. P. Putnam's Sons, 1973) provides a fuller account. Joseph Esherick's *The Origins of the Boxer Uprising* (Berkeley and Los Angeles: University of California Press, 1987) probes fully into the background of the Boxers.

The idea of a "revitalization movement" has been formulated by Anthony F. C. Wallace in "Revitalization Movements: Some Theoretical Considerations for their Comparative Study," *American Anthropologist* 58 (1956): 264-81, and applied to an American Indian nation in *The Death and Rebirth of the Seneca* (New York: Random House, 1969). Alice Beck Kehoe's *The Ghost Dance: Ethnohistory and Revitalization* (New York: Holt, Rinehart and Winston, 1989) is a brief but wide-ranging case study of the Ghost Dance as a revitalization movement. I am indebted to Stanley Coben's "A Study in Nativism: The American Red Scare of 1919-1920," *Political Science Quarterly* 79 (1964): 52-75, for suggesting a broader application of the revitalization concept.

Chapter 2. The Terrible "Isms"

In this chapter, and in the second section of the book, I have relied heavily on two marvelous, though very different books. Barbara Tuchman's *+The Proud Tower: A Portrait of the World before the War, 1890-1914* (New York: Macmillan, 1966) is a model of popular history on a grand scale. Laurence Lafore's *+The Long Fuse: An Interpretation of the Origins of World War I* (New York: J. B. Lippincott Company, 1971) represents academic history at its best — concise, interpretive, and balanced.

Wolfgang J. Mommsen's *Theories of Imperialism*, trans. P. S. Falla (Chicago: University of Chicago Press, 1980), provides an admirably brief and clear exposition of the various theories. Thomas Pakenham's +*The Scramble for Africa: White Man's Conquest of the Dark Continent from 1876 to 1912* (New York: Random House, 1991) narrates a tangled story of greed and rapacity. Pakenham illustrates how unplanned and chaotic imperialism often was, the product of a "scramble" rather than an ideologically or economically determined master plan. Ronald Robinson and John Gallagher, with Alice Denny, cover much the same territory as Pakenham in *Africa and the Victorians: The Climax of Imperialism* (New York: St. Martin's Press, 1961) but with a more explicit point of view. As the authors state in their introduction, "Africa is the hook on which we hang hypotheses about nationalism and world politics."

The two classic studies of nationalism are Hans Kohn's *Idea of Nationalism:*

A Study in Its Origins and Background (New York: Macmillan, 1944) and Carlton J. H. Hayes's *Nationalism: A Religion* (New York: Macmillan, 1960). Ernst Renan's lecture "Qu'est-ce qu'une nation?" was delivered at the Sorbonne on March 11, 1882, and is published in his *Oeuvres Completes,* ed. Henriette Psichari (Paris: Calmann-Levy, 1947-61). An abridged version of this lecture, translated into English, can be found in Hans Kohn's *+Nationalism: Its Meaning and History* (Princeton, N.J.: Van Nostrand, 1955), which provides a brief synopsis of Kohn's basic ideas accompanied by selected documents.

Arthur Mann taught me the importance of ethnicity and nationalism in history, first in course work at the University of Chicago, then as my mentor and friend, and finally in his book *+The One and the Many: Reflections on the American Identity* (Chicago: University of Chicago Press, 1979). I have developed some of my own ideas on ethnic nationalism in the "ethnicity" article in the *Encyclopedia of American Social History,* ed. Mary Kupiec Cayton et al. (New York: Charles Scribner's Sons, 1993). Illustrating my point that nationalism is often taken for granted, this encyclopedia does not contain a separate article on nationalism.

Most recent work on nationalism puts the idea in a worldwide context, devoting considerable attention to nationalism in Asia and Africa. Anthony D. Smith has been the most prolific, publishing *Theories of Nationalism* (New York: Homes & Meier, 1971), *Nationalism in the Twentieth Century* (New York: New York University Press, 1979), and *The Ethnic Origins of Nations* (Oxford: Blackwell, 1986). None of these books is easy reading, but the last is the most interesting and complete. Benedict Anderson's *Imagined Communities: Reflections on the Origin and Spread of Nationalism* (London: Verso, 1983) is highly original and very provocative. Liah Greenfeld's *Nationalism: Five Roads to Modernity* (Cambridge: Harvard University Press, 1992) contains some stimulating ideas but is overly long and jargon-laden.

The literary critic Edmund Wilson wrote a very readable history of socialist thought during the hundred years preceding the Russian Revolution: *To the Finland Station: A Study in the Writing and Acting of History* (New York: Harcourt, Brace, 1940). J. Hampden Jackson briefly surveys the development of both socialism and anarchism in *Marx, Proudhon and European Socialism* (London: English Universities Press, 1957), and in *The Second International, 1889-1914* (London: Weidenfeld & Nicolson, 1955) James Joll examines the organization within which the socialists and anarchists contended.

George Woodcock's *Anarchism: A History of Libertarian Ideas and Movements* (New York: New American Library, 1962) and James Joll's *The Anarchists* (London: Methuen, 1964) provide the best overviews of the anarchist movement; but see also David Miller's *Anarchism* (London: J. M. Dent & Sons, 1984), which focuses more on the ideas and ideology. *The Principle of Federation* by P.-J. Proudhon (Toronto: University of Toronto Press, 1979) is Richard Vernon's translation of the first two parts of Proudhon's major work on federalism. Most anarchists were fiercely antireligious, but Jacques Ellul shows that anarchism is not that far from gospel Christianity in *Anarchy and Christianity*, trans. Geoffrey W. Bromiley (Grand Rapids: William B. Eerdmans, 1991).

Chapter 3. East and West, North and South

Three unusual, brilliant, and sometimes disturbing books can provide a starting point for a consideration of colonialism and ethnocentrism: O. Mannoni's *Prospero and Caliban: The Psychology of Colonization*, trans. Pamela Powesland (New York: Praeger, 1956) combines literature and psychology to explore the relationship between rulers and ruled in the French colony of Madagascar; Edward Said's *Orientalism* (New York: Random House, 1978) dissects the persistent stereotypes with which Europeans approach "the Orient," and especially the Arab world; and Francis Jennings's *The Invasion of America: Indians, Colonialism, and the Cant of Conquest* (New York: W. W. Norton, 1976) throws new light on the English conquest of North America.

V. G. Kiernan's *European Empires from Conquest to Collapse, 1815-1960* (Leicester: Leicester University Press, 1982) provides a readable, brief survey of European colonialism with special emphasis on its military aspects, but his work occasionally shows signs of what Edward Said calls "Orientalism" — that is, a tendency to lapse into such stereotypical phrases as "the unchanging Orient" and "fanatical Muslims." An early novel by George Orwell, *Burmese Days* (New York: Harcourt, Brace and Company, 1934), offers a nice antidote to such unconscious imperialism by providing a savagely bitter look at the racism of the English in Asia. Burma (now Myanmar) was a frontier province of British India when Orwell served there as a young man.

Basil Davidson's *+*Africa in History: Themes and Outlines*, rev. ed. (New York: Macmillan, 1991), and Roland Oliver and J. D. Fage's *+*Short History of Africa*, 6th ed. (London: Penguin, 1995) are both widely used introductions to the history of Africa. Davidson is a bit more journalistic, Oliver and Fage more academic, but both are readable and thorough. For a more detailed look at the various regions of Africa in this century, see A. E. Afigbo, E. A. Ayandele, R. J. Gavin, and J. D. Omer-Cooper's *The Making of Modern Africa*, vol. 2, *The Twentieth Century*, rev. ed. (London: Longman, 1986). Walter Rodney's *How Europe Underdeveloped Africa* (London: Bogle-L'Ouverture Publications, 1972; Washington: Howard University Press, 1974) is an impassioned historical indictment of European colonialism. Rodney's overt Marxism may repel some readers, and his uncritical praise for the Soviet and Chinese Communist economic systems today seems laughable, but his book is wide-ranging and readable and asks many important questions.

461

Judith M. Brown's *Modern India: The Origins of an Asian Democracy*, 2d ed. (Oxford: Oxford University Press, 1994) is a valuable survey, but the author mars its readability by trying too hard to show the complexity of the subject. In *+The Sahibs and the Lotus: The British in India* (London: Constable, 1988), Michael Edwardes brilliantly evokes the everyday life of the British ruling class in India. Alain Peyrefitte's *+The Immobile Empire,* trans. Jon Rothschild (New York: Alfred A. Knopf, 1992), chronicles the Macartney mission to China in great detail, but the book, which is the product of a thirty-year obsession, holds much wider significance than its limited subject would suggest and raises numerous important questions about the relations between cultures.

Finally, I would like to acknowledge the helpful criticisms and suggestions of Theodore H. von Laue, with whom I corresponded in the pages of the American Historical Association's *Newsletter* in April and September 1993, and Michael Fuller, a theology student whom I taught at St. Mary of the Lake University in 1995-96. Both helped me clarify my thoughts about ethnocentrism.

Chapter 4. East Asian Responses to Europe

The starting point for any English speaker interested in China should be the works of John King Fairbank. Over a long lifetime he produced more than a score of books on China that were both scholarly and readable. His final book, *+China: A New History* (Cambridge: Belknap Press, 1992), is a superb introduction. Jonathan D. Spence's *+The Search for Modern China* (New York: W. W. Norton, 1990) is an equally fine survey of the more recent period. Jerome Ch'en's *China and the West: Society and Culture, 1815-1937* (Bloomington: Indiana University Press, 1979) is a wide-ranging study, full of insights, but poorly organized and sometimes maddening to read.

Daniel Boorstin's two epic volumes +*The Discoverers: A History of Man's Search to Know His World and Himself* (New York: Random House, 1983) and +*The Creators: A History of Heroes of the Imagination* (New York: Random House, 1992) contain several chapters comparing China to Europe. Especially striking is his analysis of the Cheng Ho voyages in *The Discoverers.*

For a collection of insights by a variety of authors, see *China in Revolution: The First Phase, 1900-1913,* ed. Mary Clabaugh Wright (New Haven: Yale University Press, 1968); Wright's lengthy introduction provides a good summary. Several of the contributors have expanded their work into book-length studies, most notably Michael Gasster in *China's Struggle to Modernize* (New York: Alfred A. Knopf, 1972). Harold Z. Schiffrin's +*Sun Yat-sen: Reluctant Revolutionary* (Boston: Little, Brown and Company, 1980) is a very readable brief biography.

Edwin O. Reischauer, who served with the American occupation of Japan after World War II and then spent his lifetime trying to understand the country, holds a place in the study of Japan similar to John King Fairbank's in China studies. Reischauer's *+*Japan: Story of a Nation* (New York: Alfred A. Knopf, 1974) is an updated version of his 1946 history of Japan. Ruth Benedict's *The Chrysanthemum and the Sword* (Boston: Houghton Mifflin, 1946) is a quirky study by an anthropologist trying to understand Japan's wartime behavior in the light of its history and culture.

W. G. Beasley's * *The Meiji Restoration* (Stanford: Stanford University Press, 1972) is the standard historical study. The same author's *Modern History of Japan* (London: Weidenfeld & Nicolson, 1963) provides a good survey. Richard Storry's * *Japan and the Decline of the West in Asia, 1894-1943* (New York: St. Martin's Press, 1979), ably examines the diplomacy surrounding Japan's emergence on the world stage; and Akira Iriye's *Across the Pacific: An Inner History of American East-Asian Relations* (New York: Harcourt, Brace and World, 1967) provides an interesting look at the interactions among the United States, China, and Japan. *The Modernization of Japan and Russia: A Comparative Study* (New York: Free Press, 1975), by Cyril E. Black et al., is a model of systematic comparative scholarship, with many useful suggestions for comparing China and Japan as well.

Bill Moyers's 1993 PBS series *Healing and the Mind* contains a fascinating episode dealing with Chinese traditional medicine. Bernardo Bertolucci's epic film *The Last Emperor* dramatizes the melancholy story of the last Manchu ruler, the boy emperor Pu-Yi.

Chapter 5. War and Revolution: The Preview

J. N. Westwood's * *Russia against Japan, 1904-05: A New Look at the Russo-Japanese War* (Albany: State University of New York Press, 1986) is an admirably brief and insightful study that draws on previously unused Russian sources. Christopher Martin's + *The Russo-Japanese War* (London: Abelard-Schuman, 1967) contains a marvelous prologue discussing the reasons why we should care about this almost forgotten war. John Albert White's *The Diplomacy of the Russo-Japanese War* (Princeton: Princeton University Press, 1964) is the standard study, but it should be supplemented by Richard Storry's *Japan and the Decline of the West in Asia* (cited in chapter 4).

For sketches of the history of tsarist Russia's last years, see Richard Charques, *The Twilight of Imperial Russia* (London: Phoenix House, 1958); Richard Pipes, *Russia under the Old Regime* (New York: Charles Scribner's Sons, 1974); and Miriam Kochan, + *The Last Days of Imperial Russia* (New York: Macmillan, 1976). Robert K. Massie's *+*Nicholas and Alexandra* (New York: Atheneum, 1967) is a poignant popular biography of the last tsar and his wife, with an emphasis on their son's hemophilia. Marc Ferro's *Nicholas II: Last of the Tsars,* trans. Brian Pearce (New York: Oxford University Press, 1993), is full of insights and contains a long investigative detective story about the murder of the tsar and his family, but the book can be confusing for a reader unfamiliar with the events it discusses. Better to read Charques and Massie first, then return to Ferro.

Sidney Harcave's *First Blood: The Russian Revolution of 1905* (New York: Macmillan, 1964) and Abraham Ascher's **The Revolution of 1905: Russia in Disarray* (Stanford: Stanford University Press, 1988) focus on the first Russian revolution; Lionel Kochan's *Russia in Revolution, 1890-1918* (London: Weidenfeld & Nicolson, 1966) places it in the broad sweep of Russian revolutionary events. Harrison Salisbury, *+Black Night, White Snow* (Garden City, N.Y.: Doubleday, 1978), is a vivid, anecdotal, but overly long and ultimately disappointing study of revolutionary Russia by a distinguished journalist.

Howard K. Beale's *Theodore Roosevelt and the Rise of America to World Power* (Baltimore: The Johns Hopkins University Press, 1956) is the standard study of the American president's diplomacy. Raymond Esthus has written two studies of Roosevelt's Far Eastern peacemaking: *Theodore Roosevelt and Japan* (Seattle: University of Washington Press, 1967) and *Double Eagle and Rising Sun: The Russians and Japanese at Portsmouth in 1905* (Durham, N.C.: Duke University Press, 1988).

Chapter 6. A Murder in Bosnia

Hugh and Christopher Seton-Watson combine a biography of their famous father, historian Robert Seton-Watson, with an analysis of the nationality problem in Austria-Hungary and the Balkans in **The Making of a New Europe: R. W. Seton-Watson and the Last Years of Austria-Hungary* (Seattle: University of Washington Press, 1981). Readers who find themselves intrigued can then consult the bibliography of the elder Seton-Watson's works and choose those which they wish to track down. Rebecca West's *Black Lamb, Grey Falcon* (New York: Viking Press, 1941) is a highly personal travelogue by an English writer who is violently anti-Austrian but a sympathetic observer of the Balkan lands and peoples. Charles and Barbara Jelavich provide a good historical overview of the small nations on the Balkan peninsula in *The Establishment of the Balkan National States, 1804-1920* (Seattle: University of Washington Press, 1977). Although Bosnia's role in the diplomacy of the Great Powers was long ago analyzed in such works as Bernadotte Schmitt's *The Annexation of Bosnia* (Cambridge: Cambridge University Press, 1937), little had been written about Bosnia itself until recently. Therefore, I relied primarily on Peter Sugar's *Industrialization of Bosnia-Hercegovina, 1878-1918* (Seattle: University of Washington Press, 1963) and the background chapter in Jozo Tomasevich's *Peasants, Politics, and Economic Change in Yugoslavia* (Stanford: Stanford University Press, 1955). Ivo Sivric's *Peasant Culture of Bosnia and Herzegovina* (Chicago: Franciscan Herald Press, 1982) exhibits a profoundly pro-Catholic Croatian bias, but it includes an appendix detailing the archeological use of medieval tombstones that is extremely informative about the beliefs of the Bosnian Bogomils, as is the introduction to John V. A. Fine Jr.'s *The Bosnian Church: A New Interpretation* (Boulder: East European Monographs, 1975).

In the midst of the Bosnian war of the early 1990s, new attention was paid to the history of that troubled region. Robert D. Kaplan's +*Balkan Ghosts* (New York: St. Martin's Press, 1993) is a best-selling account of how old quarrels still trouble the Balkans. Though he includes very little information about Bosnia, his pessimistic point of view tends to justify a policy of benign neglect by other countries. Robert J. Donia and John V. A. Fine Jr. offer a contrary point of view in *+Bosnia and Hercegovina: A Tradition Betrayed* (New York: Columbia University Press, 1994), arguing that until recently the various ethnic groups of Bosnia lived peaceably together and that forceful intervention is needed to restore this "betrayed tradition." Though Donia and Fine's book is very polemical, it also provides a readable brief history of Bosnia.

Ivo Andric, who won a Nobel Prize for literature in 1961, wrote a trilogy of historical novels about Bosnia. The second of these novels, *Travnicka Hronika*, published in Belgrade in 1945, was published in English as *Bosnian Chronicle* (New York: Alfred A. Knopf, 1963) and then reprinted under a new title, *The Days of the Consuls* (New York: Forest Books/Dufour Editions, 1993). It is set in the time of Napoleon but brilliantly evokes the clash of cultures that has persisted in Bosnia to this day.

Serbia, as a national state, has been the subject of more comprehensive historical works. Michael Boro Petrovich's *History of Modern Serbia, 1804-1918* (New York: Harcourt, Brace, Jovanovich, 1976) is a clear, balanced, and very detailed survey. More narrowly focused studies of Serbia include Wayne S. Vucinich's *Serbia between East and West: The Events of 1903-1908* (New York: AMS Press, 1954); Alex N. Dragnich's *Serbia, Nikola Pašić, and Yugoslavia* (New Brunswick, N.J.: Rutgers University Press, 1974); and *Kosovo: Legacy of a Medieval Battle*, ed. Wayne S. Vucinich and Thomas A. Emmert (Minneapolis: University of Minnesota, 1991). I have relied particularly on the essay by Dimitrije Djordjević in the latter volume.

A. J. P. Taylor's *+The Habsburg Monarchy, 1809-1918* (London: Hamish Hamilton, 1948) still provides the best introduction to the complicated state of Austria-Hungary. Taylor's book is quirky and opinionated but always interesting and insightful. Z. A. B. Zeman's *The Breakup of the Habsburg Empire, 1914-1918: A Study in National and Social Revolution* (London: Oxford University Press, 1961) is more balanced and traditional. Joachim Remak's "The Healthy Invalid: How Doomed the Habsburg Empire?" *Journal of Modern History* 41 (June 1969): 127-43 elegantly argues that Austria-Hungary would have remained viable had the war not cut short its lifespan. In *Austria-Hungary and the Origins of the First World War* (New York: St. Martin's Press, 1991), Samuel R. Williamson Jr. surveys the diplomatic events that led the empire to war. Alan Sked's *The Decline and Fall of the Habsburg Empire 1815-1918* (London: Longman, 1989), and *The Last Years of Austria-Hungary: Essays in Political and Military History 1908-1918*, ed. Mark Cornwall (Exeter: University of Exeter Press, 1990) both contain historiographical essays discussing the state of scholarship on the Dual Monarchy. Despite their brevity, they will probably be of most interest to readers wishing to eavesdrop on historians talking to each other.

The cityscape, politics, and culture of the two Habsburg capitals are brilliantly profiled by Carl E. Schorske in *Fin-de-Siècle Vienna: Politics and Culture* (New York: Alfred A. Knopf, 1980) and by John Lukacs in *Budapest 1900: A Historical Portrait of a City and Its Culture* (New York: Weidenfeld & Nicolson, 1988). The venturesome reader may want to sample the multivolume novel by Robert Musil *The Man without Qualities,* trans. Eithne Wilkins and Ernst Kaiser (New York: Coward-McCann, 1953).

Joachim Remak's +*Sarajevo: The Story of a Political Murder* (New York: Criterion Books, 1959) is an admirably readable narrative of the Archduke Franz Ferdinand's assassination that emphasizes the assassins' connections with the Black Hand. Vladimir Dedijer's *The Road to Sarajevo* (New York: Simon & Schuster, 1966) provides the most exhaustively researched study of that event. In contrast to Remak, Dedijer stresses the importance of the Bosnian context for an understanding of the murder.

Chapter 7. The Fatal Alliances

For brief, readable overviews of the origins of the First World War, see Laurence Lafore, *+ The Long Fuse: An Interpretation of the Origins of World War I* (cited in chapter 2); Joachim Remak, +*The Origins of World War I, 1871-1914* (New York: Holt, Rinehart and Winston, 1967); and James Joll, +*The Origins of the First World War,* 2d ed. (London: Longman, 1992).

St. Martin's Press has published a remarkable group of five books on the origins of the war, each dealing with one of the great powers, as part of Geoffrey Warner's "The Making of the 20th Century" series. The volumes are brief but so densely packed with facts and interpretation that they make for slow reading; nevertheless, they afford a rare opportunity to consider a single event, *Rashomon*-like, from several different perspectives. The individual books are V. R.

Berghahn's *Germany and the Approach of War in 1914 (1973); Zara S. Steiner's Britain and the Origins of the First World War (1977); D. C. B. Lieven's Russia and the Origins of the First World War (1983); John F. V. Keiger's France and the Origins of the First World War (1983); and Samuel R. Williamson Jr.'s Austria-Hungary and the Origins of the First World War (1991).

Fritz Fischer's Griff nach der Weltmacht has been published in English under the title *Germany's Aims in the First World War (New York: W. W. Norton, 1967). One of his disciples, Imanuel Geiss, has published a useful collection of documents, with a fine commentary; it has been published in English as +July 1914: The Outbreak of the First World War, Selected Documents (New York: W. W. Norton, 1967).

The Schlieffen plan and the war plans of the other powers are analyzed in The War Plans of the Great Powers, 1880-1914, ed. Paul M. Kennedy (London: George Allen & Unwin, 1979); Gerhard Ritter's *The Schlieffen Plan: Critique of a Myth (London: Oswald Wolff, 1958); and Barbara W. Tuchman's *+The Guns of August (New York: Macmillan, 1962).

Other books laying the background for war in the countries of Europe include Andrew Rossos's Russia and the Balkans: Inter-Balkan Rivalries and Russian Foreign Policy, 1908-1914 (Toronto: University of Toronto Press, 1981); Michael Balfour's +The Kaiser and His Times (London: Penguin, 1975); Eugen Weber's The Nationalist Revival in France, 1905-1914 (Berkeley and Los Angeles: University of California Press, 1968); Zara S. Steiner's The Foreign Office and Foreign Policy, 1898-1914 (Cambridge: Cambridge University Press, 1969); and Barbara W. Tuchman's *+The Proud Tower: A Portrait of the World before the War, 1890-1914 (cited in chapter 2).

Chapter 8. The War of Exhaustion

Winston Churchill published his history of the Great War, +The World Crisis, 1911-1918, in five volumes (New York: Charles Scribner's Sons, 1923-29) and then in a revised, combined edition (London: Landsborough, 1930). A combination memoir and narrative history, much of Churchill's work is preoccupied with justifying his role in the Gallipoli campaign, but when he writes of battles and events in which he did not participate, his writing is brilliant, concise, and insightful. The work proves especially useful since it was written before Churchill attained his exalted position in World War II and is thus free of anachronisms. It does, however, shed much light on Churchill's thoughts and actions in that later war.

Robin Prior's Churchill's 'World Crisis' as History (London: Croom Helm, 1983) is largely for nit-pickers, second-guessers, and military specialists. He ruthlessly criticizes Churchill's self-serving arguments about the Gallipoli campaign, but he indirectly supports the view that other sections of the book remain valuable by disclosing that Churchill had considerable documentation provided to him secretly by John Edmonds, the official British historian of the war. Prior also concludes that the book's literary values and the passionate commitment of the author "will ensure that *The World Crisis* continues to be read when many less committed though more accurate works have been long forgotten."

Bernadotte E. Schmitt and Harold C. Vedeler's *The World in the Crucible, 1914-1919* (New York: Harper & Row, 1984) is a good general history in the excellent "The Rise of Modern Europe" series edited by William L. Langer. Marc Ferro's *+La Grande Guerre* (Paris: Gallimard, 1969), translated as *The Great War, 1914-1918* (London: Routledge & Kegan Paul, 1973), is a brief, readable, wide-ranging book, easily the single best book on the war. In * *The Great War and Modern Memory* (New York: Oxford University Press, 1975), Paul Fussell imaginatively explores the language, literature, and grim realities of the war.

For analysis of the battles of the two major theaters of the war, see John Terraine, *The Western Front, 1914-1918* (Philadephia: J. B. Lippincott Company, 1965), and Norman Stone, *The Eastern Front, 1914-1917* (London: Hodder and Stoughton, 1975). Lyn Macdonald's *They Called It Passchendaele: The Story of the Third Battle of Ypres and of the Men Who Fought It* (London: Michael Joseph, 1978) recalls that horrendous battle through the reminiscences of survivors. Alan Moorehead's *Gallipoli* (New York: Harper and Bros., 1956) provides a full, well-rounded account of the battle.

John Swettenham's *To Seize the Victory: The Canadian Corps in World War I* (Toronto: The Ryerson Press, 1965) is a thorough, useful, but traditional and dry military history. Desmond Morton and J. L. Granatstein paint a much broader canvas in *+Marching to Armageddon: Canadians and the Great War, 1914-1919* (Toronto: Lester & Orpen Dennys, 1989), summarizing the battles and skillfully employing the diaries and memoirs of actual participants to discuss the impact of the war on Canadians. The book also uses numerous photographs intelligently and imaginatively. Australian historians have written two similar books. In *The Broken Years: Australian Soldiers in the Great War* (Canberra: Australian University Press, 1974), Bill Gammage follows the Anzac Corps throughout the war in their own words; and John Robertson's *+Anzac and Empire: The Tragedy and Glory of Gallipoli* (London: Leo Cooper, 1990) is a passionately written and lavishly illustrated volume that focuses on the defining Australian campaign of the war.

In *+Over There: The Story of America's First Great Overseas Crusade*, rev. ed. (Philadelphia: Temple University Press, 1990), Frank Freidel does for America's participation in the war what Morton and Granatstein do for Canada's and Gammage and Robertson do for Australia's. Arthur S. Link has devoted his life to writing about Woodrow Wilson and editing his papers. His early book *Woodrow*

Wilson and the Progressive Era, 1910-1917 (New York: Harper & Row, 1954), clearly narrates the events leading to America's entry into the war; and his volume of essays *Wilson the Diplomatist* (Baltimore: The Johns Hopkins University Press, 1957), reprinted in slightly revised form as *Woodrow Wilson: Revolution, War, and Peace* (Arlington Heights, Ill.: AHM Publishing, 1979), examines the twists and turns of American policy carefully but briefly. Barbara W. Tuchman's +*The Zimmermann Telegram* (New York: Viking Press, 1958) is a narrative, in the fashion of a thriller, of Germany's ill-fated attempt to ally with Mexico against the United States. David M. Kennedy's *Over Here: The First World War and American Society* (New York: Oxford University Press, 1980) examines the home front in the United States.

Chapter 9. Peace and Consequences

The clearest assessment of the consequences of the First World War can be found in Derek H. Aldcroft's *+"The Aftermath of War," chapter 2 in *From Versailles to Wall Street, 1919-1929* (Berkeley and Los Angeles: University of California Press, 1977). Marc Ferro's study *The Great War* (cited in chapter 8) also contains insightful analysis of the war's results. Arthur Marwick's *War and Social Change in the Twentieth Century: A Comparative Study of Britain, France, Germany, Russia and the United States* (London: Macmillan, 1974) is a pioneering study; chapter 9 of Marwick's earlier book *The Deluge: British Society and the First World War* (London: Bodley Head, 1965) is also useful. Harold Foster explains his disaster index in "Assessing Disaster Magnitude: A Social Science Approach," *Professional Geographer* 28 (August 1976): 241-47.

In *Pacifism and the Just War: A Study in Applied Philosophy* (London: Basil Blackwell, 1986) Jenny Teichman provides a brief, clear exposition of the two classic stances on war and peace. Arguing from a commonsense, nonreligious standpoint, Michael Walzer offers a fuller, more nuanced treatment of just-war theory in *Just and Unjust Wars: A Moral Argument with Historical Illustrations* (New York: Basic Books, 1977). Peter Brock narrates the history of anti-war movements in this century in *Twentieth-Century Pacifism* (New York: Van Nostrand Reinhold, 1970). Bertrand Russell sketches out an early, provocative case for nonviolent resistance to war in *"War and Non-Resistance," *Atlantic Monthly, August 1915, pp. 266-74.

In some ways, older books about the Paris Peace Conference remain the best. Winston Churchill's +*The Aftermath*, vol. 5 of *The World Crisis* (New York: Charles Scribner's Sons, 1929), is clear and concise without excessive self-justification, since Churchill was not heavily involved in the peacemaking process. Two other Englismen who were directly involved at Paris wrote passionate, critical accounts. The eminent economist John Maynard Keynes's *Economic Consequences of the Peace* (New York: Harcourt, Brace, and Howe, 1920) is uniformly negative, but Keynes writes elegant prose, unlike subsequent economists. Harold Nicolson's *Peacemaking 1919*, rev. ed. (London: Constable, 1943) is still probably the best brief analysis. Since Nicolson includes both his contemporary journal notes, his retrospective thoughts a decade later, and then a new introduction written during World War II, the book provides an almost archeological account of one diplomat's thinking about the peace conference. Harold W. V. Temperley's five-volume *History of the Paris Peace Conference* (London: Trowde, Hodder & Stoughton, 1920-24) is useful as an encyclopedic reference source, with complete texts of all the treaties.

Three works published in the second half of the century provide more detail than anyone could ever want about the peace process: Arthur Walworth's *Wilson and His Peacemakers: American Diplomacy at the Paris Peace Conference, 1919* (New York: W. W. Norton & Company, 1986), is voluminous and traditional, an updated version of Temperley; and two volumes by Arno J. Mayer, *Political Origins of the New Diplomacy, 1917-1918* (New Haven: Yale University Press, 1959), and *Politics and Diplomacy of Peacemaking: Containment and Counterrevolution at Versailles, 1918-1919* (New York: Alfred A. Knopf, 1967), have proven enormously influential among historians. Mayer stresses the interplay between domestic and international politics and highlights the context of revolutionary chaos in which the Paris Peace Conference took place.

Besides the numerous studies of Woodrow Wilson by Arthur S. Link cited in chapter 8, readers will find two other books very interesting: John Morton Blum's *+Woodrow Wilson and the Politics of Morality* (Boston: Little, Brown, 1956) and N. Gordon Levin Jr.'s *Woodrow Wilson and World Politics: America's Response to War and Revolution* (New York: Oxford University Press, 1968). The Fourteen Points address is a classic American text reprinted in +*An American Primer,* ed. Daniel J. Boorstin (Chicago: University of Chicago Press, 1966). For attempts to psychoanalyze Woodrow Wilson, see Sigmund Freud and William C. Bullitt, *Thomas Woodrow Wilson: A Psychological Study* (Boston: Houghton Mifflin, 1966) and Alexander L. and Juliette L. George, *Woodrow Wilson and Colonel House: A Personality Study* (New York: J. Day Co., 1956). The book by Freud (yes, it's *that* Freud) and Bullitt is a hatchet job by two men who, for different reasons, were disillusioned with Wilson's performance at Versailles. The Georges' study is more moderate but their knowledge of history is limited. Neither book should be taken seriously, but they make entertaining reading.

James Avery Joyce's +*Broken Star: The Story of the League of Nations (1919-1939)* (Swansea, U.K.: Christopher Davies, 1978) is a brief, passionate overview by a former member of the League civil service in Geneva. F. S. Northedge's *The League of Nations: Its Life and Times, 1920-1946* (Leicester: Leicester University

Press, 1986), provides a fuller, more critical history. In *Swords Into Plowshares: The Problems and Progress of International Organization*, 2d ed. (New York: Random House, 1959), Inis L. Claude Jr. provides useful background on the precedents for international organization and compares the League of Nations with the later United Nations Organization.

The rebirth of Poland is analyzed by Piotr S. Wandycz in * *The United States and Poland* (Cambridge: Harvard University Press, 1980) and by Louis L. Gerson in *Woodrow Wilson and the Rebirth of Poland, 1914-1920* (New Haven: Yale University Press, 1953). I examine the American political ramifications of the wartime events in Poland in *Polish-American Politics in Chicago, 1888-1936* (Chicago: University of Chicago Press, 1975). *The Immigrants' Influence on Wilson's Peace Policies*, ed. Joseph P. O'Grady (Lexington: University of Kentucky Press, 1967), includes chapters on each of the major ethnic groups, written by different authors. Finally, the East European quest for nationhood can be followed in Hugh and Christopher Seton-Watson's *The Making of a New Europe* (cited in chapter 6), but it is sometimes hard to untangle the narrative threads, since the authors interweave them with a biography of their famous father.

Chapter 10. Revolutions in Red, White, and Black

The tragic life of Tsar Nicholas II and his family has been well examined by Robert K. Massie in *+*Nicholas and Alexandra* and by Marc Ferro in *Nicholas II: Last of the Tsars* (both cited in chapter 5). Ferro also very insightfully examines the outburst of popular opinion that followed the February Revolution in *La Revolution de 1917* (Paris: Aubier Editions Montaigne, 1967), translated by J. F. Richards as *The Russian Revolution of February 1917* (Englewood Cliffs, N.J.: Prentice-Hall, 1972).

In * *Why Lenin? Why Stalin?: A Reappraisal of the Russian Revolution, 1900-1930* (Philadelphia: J. B. Lippincott, 1964), Theodore H. Von Laue provides a brief but wide-ranging overview of the entire course of revolution in Russia, with a special emphasis on its significance for the Third World. Robert V. Daniels provides a crisp account of the events of the October Revolution in *+*Red October: The Bolshevik Revolution of 1917* (New York: Charles Scribner's Sons, 1967). Daniels has also provided a good, brief collection of documents in *The Russian Revolution* (Englewood Cliffs, N.J.: Prentice-Hall, 1972). Edward Hallett Carr has condensed his massive multivolume *History of Soviet Russia* into one slim volume for the general reader, *The Russian Revolution: From Lenin to Stalin, 1917-1929* (London: Macmillan, 1979). Adam Ulam's * *The Bolsheviks* (New York: Macmillan, 1965) serves admirably as both a biography of Lenin and an intellectual background on the Communist Party. John Reed's *Ten Days That Shook the World* (New York:

Random House, 1960) is an overrated journalistic "classic" that does, however, convey the sense of excitement and confusion surrounding the revolution.

In *Russia and the West under Lenin and Stalin* (Boston: Little, Brown, 1961), George F. Kennan examines the Western intervention during the Russian revolution and civil war. Richard Pipes's *The Formation of the Soviet Union: Communism and Nationalism, 1917-1923* (Cambridge: Harvard University Press, 1954) serves as an excellent guide to the tangle of nationality conflicts during the civil war. In *Soviet Disunion: A History of the Nationalities Problem in the USSR* (New York: The Free Press, 1990), Bohdan Nahaylo and Victor Swoboda survey Soviet nationalities policy from Lenin to Gorbachev. And in *Lenin on the Question of Nationality* (New York: Bookman Associates, 1958), Alfred D. Low provides a brief analysis of Lenin's tortured hair-splitting on the nationality question. W. Bruce Lincoln's *+Red Victory: A History of the Russian Civil War* (New York: Simon and Schuster, 1989) and Evan Mawdsley's *The Russian Civil War* (Boston: Allen & Unwin, 1987) are both useful narratives of the course of that struggle.

Paul Avrich's *The Russian Anarchists* (Princeton: Princeton University Press, 1967) provides background on this minority strain of revolutionary thought and action; Avrich has also published an excellent collection of documents, *The Anarchists in the Russian Revolution* (Ithaca, N.Y.: Cornell University Press, 1973). Both Avrich and George Woodcock (the latter in *Anarchism,* cited in chapter 2) briefly mention Makhno in the Ukraine. Two full-length studies in English, Michael Palij's *The Anarchism of Nestor Makhno, 1918-1921: An Aspect of the Ukrainian Revolution* (Seattle: University of Washington Press, 1976) and Michael Malet's *Nestor Makhno in the Russian Civil War* (London: Macmillan, 1982), unfortunately manage to make the inherently thrilling story of Makhno's exploits boring.

Mikhail Sholokhov's fictional depiction of the Russian Revolution and the civil war in Cossack country, *Tikhii Don* ("The Silent Don"), was published in four volumes between 1928 and 1941. It is available in English in two volumes translated by Stephen Garry: *And Quiet Flows the Don* (New York: Alfred A. Knopf, 1946) and *The Don Flows Home to the Sea* (New York: Alfred A. Knopf, 1946).

Chapter 11. Gray Wolf on the Prowl

Bernard Lewis's *The Emergence of Modern Turkey* (London: Oxford University Press, 1961) is a classic study that is especially good on the Ottoman background. Geoffrey Lewis's +*Turkey,* 3d ed. (London: Ernest Benn Limited, 1965), is rather fussily British and extremely pro-Turkish, as this statement from the preface indicates: "I have learned never to despair of the Turks; they have an almost British talent for muddling through." Still, the book provides a useful, brief overview of the country's twentieth-century history. Feroz Ahmad's *The Making of Modern Turkey* (London: Routledge, 1993) is an equally brief, more up-to-date, but less interesting survey. Ahmad has also written a detailed study entitled *The Young Turks: The Committee of Union and Progress in Turkish Politics, 1908-1914* (Oxford: Clarendon Press, 1969). Jacob M. Landau's *Pan-Turkism in Turkey: A Study of Irredentism* (London: C. Hurst & Co. Ltd., 1981) sometimes degenerates into a list of nationalist writers, but it contains some very interesting material on the wilder pan-Turk aspirations of the Young Turks.

*+*Ataturk: The Rebirth of a Nation* (London: Weidenfeld and Nicolson, 1964), by Lord Kinross (John Patrick Douglas Balfour), is a very readable biography of the first Turkish president. Vamik D. Volkan and Norman Itzkowitz's *The Immortal Ataturk: A Psychobiography* (Chicago: University of Chicago Press, 1984) is much better than the average psychohistorical study. One of the authors is a psychoanalyst of Turkish origin and the other is a historian of the Ottoman Empire. Their biography is comprehensive and readable, and it's easy to ignore the psychobabble.

Christopher J. Walker's *Armenia: Survival of a Nation,* rev. ed. (New York: St. Martin's Press, 1990), is the best introduction to this ancient people. Two books by Richard G. Hovannisian, *Armenia on the Road to Independence, 1918* (Berkeley and Los Angeles: University of California Press, 1967), and *The Republic of Armenia: The First Year, 1919-1920* (Berkeley and Los Angeles: University of California Press, 1971), provide a detailed history of Armenia's short-lived independence.

Hovannisian has also edited a collection of essays entitled *The Armenian Genocide: History, Politics, Ethics* (New York: St. Martin's Press, 1992), but the best study of the atrocities is Robert Melson's *Revolution and Genocide: On the Origins of the Armenian Genocide and the Holocaust* (Chicago: University of Chicago Press, 1992), a brilliant comparative study. Many Jewish Holocaust survivors object to comparative studies, arguing that their experience is unique. Melson rejects this point of view, because, he says, "to hold that the Holocaust cannot be compared implies that it cannot be thought about," but he finesses the problem by placing historical pogroms, massacres, and genocides on a continuum and situating the Jewish Holocaust at the extreme end on the grounds that the Nazis intended to wipe all Jews from the face of the earth.

In *A Mandate for Armenia* (Kent, Ohio: Kent State University Press, 1967), James B. Gidney clearly narrates the melancholy story of how the great powers and the United States failed to protect Armenia's independence after World War I. In *Modern Greece* (New York: Praeger, 1968), John Campbell and Philip Sherrard provide a good account of the Greco-Turkish war and the ensuing population exchange.

473

Chapter 12. A Tangle of Promises

Two books by the English journalist Peter Mansfield, +*A History of the Middle East* (New York: Viking, 1991) and +*The Arabs,* 3d ed. (London: Penguin Books, 1990), are the best introductions for the general reader. Albert Hourani's best-selling *History of the Arab Peoples* (Cambridge: Belknap Press, 1991) is actually rather long and tedious.

George Antonius's **The Arab Awakening: The Story of the Arab National Movement* (New York: G. P. Putnam's Sons, 1939) is a classic text. Recent scholars agree that Antonius misinterpreted the origins of Arab nationalism, ascribing too much influence to Arab Christians in Beirut, but otherwise this book remains extremely readable and useful. Albert Hourani has assessed its strengths and weaknesses in the first of the commemorative Antonius Lectures at St. Antony's College, Oxford, "*The Arab Awakening* Forty Years After," which has been published in *Studies in Arab History: The Antonius Lectures, 1978-87,* ed. Derek Hopwood (London: Macmillan, 1990). Scholarly assessments of Arab nationalism can be sampled in C. Ernest Dawn's **From Ottomanism to Arabism: Essays on the Origins of Arab Nationalism* (Urbana: University of Illinois Press, 1973), and in **The Origins of Arab Nationalism,* ed. Rashhid Khalidi, Lisa Anderson, Muhammad Muslih, and Reeva S. Simon (New York: Columbia University Press, 1991). For those wishing to pursue the scholarly literature further, *The American Historical Review* published a special issue at the time of the Persian Gulf War (December 1991) containing nine articles analyzing key issues and identifying the best sources for the study of various Mideast countries. I found Rashid Khalidi's essay "Arab Nationalism: Historical Problems in the Literature" particularly useful for this chapter. Randall Baker's *King Husain and the Kingdom of Hejaz* (Cambridge: Oleander Press, 1979) is a brief, readable account of the Hashemite reign, and the first essay in Dawn's collection cited above, "The Amir of Mecca al-Husayn ibn-Ali and the Origin of the Arab Revolt," is clear and balanced.

Though the life of Colonel T. E. Lawrence was inherently dramatic, the controversy over his role in the Arab revolt has been tedious and unenlightening. Lawrence told his own story, with frequent exaggerations and embellishments, in his posthumously published autobiography, *Seven Pillars of Wisdom* (New York: Doubleday, 1935). Suleiman Mousa overreacts to the exaggerations of the Lawrence legend in *T. E. Lawrence: An Arab View,* trans. Albert Butros (London: Oxford University Press, 1966), but his book is basically fair and provides a good corrective. Jeremy Wilson's *Lawrence of Arabia: The Authorised Biography of T. E. Lawrence* (London: William Heinemann, 1989) is a massive, stolid volume. I readily admit that I have not read it through, but I did find it useful as a reference work.

Most of the general public will still rely mainly on David Lean's 1962 film *Lawrence of Arabia,* which is readily available on video. The film contains brilliant acting by Peter O'Toole as Lawrence and a literate screenplay by Robert Bolt that functions on three different levels: historical epic, personality study, and existential philosophy. Unfortunately, the historical level is the least satisfactory. The screenplay compresses events and invents characters for dramatic effect, which is normal and acceptable; but it also grossly exaggerates Lawrence's role and presents a very ethnocentric, "cowboys and Indians" view of the Arabs. The movie remains a classic, but it is best viewed and enjoyed as a fictional portrayal of a complicated individual, loosely set against the backdrop of the Arab revolt.

Walter Laqueur's *History of Zionism* (New York: Holt, Rinehart & Winston, 1972) is long but readable and balanced. Barbara W. Tuchman's first book, +Bible and Sword: England and Palestine from the Bronze Age to Balfour (1956; rpt., New York: Ballantine Books, 1984), is an odd but highly readable study of the origins of the Balfour Declaration, which traces the relationship betweeen England and Palestine back to prehistoric times. Ronald Sanders's The High Walls of Jerusalem: A History of the Balfour Declaration and the Birth of the British Mandate for Palestine (New York: Holt, Rinehart & Winston, 1983) is a more traditional and comprehensive study of the same subject, but the author tends to get bogged down in the minutiae of cable traffic. The best short interpretive study of the Balfour Declaration is Mayir Verete's essay *"The Balfour Declaration and Its Makers," which originally appeared in Middle Eastern Studies (January 1970) and has since been reprinted in From Palmerston to Balfour: Collected Essays of Mayir Verete, ed. Norman Rose (London: Frank Cass, 1992).

Neville J. Mandel's The Arabs and Zionism before World War I (Berkeley and Los Angeles: University of California Press, 1976) and Yehoshua Porath's The Emergence of the Palestinian-Arab National Movement, 1918-1929 (London: Frank Cass, 1974) survey the situation of the Zionist settlers in Palestine. Both books originated as doctoral dissertations and make for rather heavy reading, but they are worth digging into.

Sir Mark Sykes is a fascinating figure who deserves to be better known. Apparently a scholarly biography of him exists (Roger Adelson's Mark Sykes: Portrait of an Amateur [Leiden, 1975]), but I was unable to track it down. I had to rely on snatches of insight in Salutation to Five, by Shane Leslie; Two Studies in Virtue (New York: Alfred A. Knopf, 1953), by Christopher Sykes (Sir Mark's son); and frequent references to Sykes in all the standard histories. Ronald Sanders is particularly enlightening in The High Walls of Jerusalem (New York: Holt, Rinehart, & Winston, 1983).

Finally, there are two readable accounts of the rise of Saudi Arabia: David Holden and Richard Johns's +The House of Saud: The Rise and Rule of the Most Powerful Dynasty in the Arab World (New York: Holt, Rinehart & Winston, 1981) and Robert Lacey's +The Kingdom: Arabia and the House of Saud (New York: Harcourt Brace Jovanovich, 1981).

Chapter 13. The Beginning of the End

Three books by Irish-American historian Lawrence J. McCaffrey make a good starting point: *+*The Irish Question, 1800-1922* (Lexington: University of Kentucky Press, 1968), *The Irish Diaspora in America* (Bloomington: Indiana University Press, 1976), and *Ireland: From Colony to Nation State* (Englewood Cliffs, N.J.: Prentice-Hall, 1979). Mark Tierney's *Modern Ireland since 1850*, rev. ed. (Dublin: Gill & Macmillan, 1978), is another good survey. Joseph J. Lee's *Ireland, 1912-1985* (Cambridge: Cambridge University Press, 1989), is a very perceptive interpretive study, but it assumes a general knowledge of Irish history and so should be saved for last.

Alan J. Ward's *The Easter Rising: Revolution and Irish Nationalism* (Arlington Heights, Ill.: AHM Publishing, 1980) sketches the events of the rising, but his book is really another survey of the Irish question, with a special emphasis on the varieties of Irish nationalism. Charles Duff also goes far back in history for background in *Six Days to Shake an Empire* (London: J. M. Dent & Sons, 1966) but provides a fuller analysis of the Easter Rising than Ward does. Biographies by Ruth Dudley Edwards, *Patrick Pearse: The Triumph of Failure* (London: Victor Gollancz, 1977) and *James Connolly* (Dublin: Gill & Macmillan, 1981), profile two leaders of the rising.

A. T. Q. Stewart's *The Narrow Ground: Aspects of Ulster, 1609-1969* (London: Faber & Faber, 1977), consists of brilliant short essays reflecting on the Ulster Protestant experience. Donald Harman Akenson places that experience in a fascinating comparative perspective in *God's Peoples: Covenant and Land in South Africa, Israel, and Ulster* (Ithaca, N.Y.: Cornell University Press, 1992).

In *The Birth of the Irish Free State, 1921-1923* (Tuscaloosa: University of Alabama Press, 1980), Joseph M. Curran provides a rather dull but comprehensive account of the war for independence and the Anglo-Irish treaty negotiations. Charles Townshend's *The British Campaign in Ireland, 1919-1921: The Development of Political and Military Policies* (London: Oxford University Press, 1975) is a remarkably clear and balanced analysis of Britain's unsuccessful "Black and Tan" policy. The big authorized biography *Eamon de Valera* is by Thomas P. O'Neill and the Earl of Longford (Frank Pakenham) (London: Hutchinson & Co., 1970), but I have relied on the brief, highly interpretive study by Owen Dudley Edwards, *Eamon de Valera* (Washington: Catholic University of American Press, 1987). I have not read T. Desmond Williams's *The Irish Struggle, 1916-1926* (London, 1966), but I like his line, cited by Alan J. Ward, about Britain finding the answer after Ireland lost interest in the question.

Geoffrey Wheatcroft (an Englishman!) wrote a very perceptive and provocative essay on twentieth-century Ireland — "The Disenchantment of Ireland," *The Atlantic Monthly* (July 1993): 65-84. *The Atlantic* also published autobiographical sketches entitled "Twentieth Century Witness" by Ireland's most famous contemporary journalist, Conor Cruise O'Brien, beginning in January 1994 and continuing in July 1994. Finally, Neil Jordan's 1996 film *Michael Collins* is a magnificent, historically accurate dramatization of the Irish war for independence.

Chapter 14. Revolutions, Constitutions, and Institutions

Novelist Carlos Fuentes helped produce a television documentary for the Christopher Columbus Quincentenary in 1992; the accompanying book, +*The Buried Mirror: Reflections on Spain and the New World* (New York: Houghton Mifflin, 1992), provides a stimulating introduction not only to Mexico but to the whole of Latin America. Peter Calvert's *+*Mexico* (New York: Praeger, 1973) is a fine overview of Mexican history since independence.

Adolfo Gilly's *The Mexican Revolution,* trans. Patrick Camiller (London: Verso, 1983), is the single best book written on the subject. The author was a Marxist revolutionary from Argentina imprisoned in Mexico in the 1960s but later released and given a professorship at the Autonomous National University of Mexico. The book presents a relentlessly Marxist interpretation of "the interrupted revolution," as he calls it, but even the long quotations from Marx are interesting and the analysis is penetrating. Hector Aguilar Camin and Lorenzo Meyer's *In the Shadow of the Mexican Revolution: Contemporary Mexican History, 1910-1989,* trans. Luis Alberto Fierro (Austin: University of Texas Press, 1993), surveys the twentieth century and relies heavily on Gilly.

Essays on the Mexican Revolution: Revisionist Views of the Leaders, ed. George Wolfskill and Douglas W. Richmond (Austin: University of Texas Press, 1979), presents separate essays on Francisco Madero, Pancho Villa, Venustiano Carranza, Alvaro Obregon, and Lazaro Cardenas, by various authors. Since the materials were orginally delivered as public lectures, they are more accessible than the average academic essays. John Womack Jr.'s *+*Zapata and the Mexican Revolution* (New York: Alfred A. Knopf, 1969) is indispensable and fascinating. Manuel A. Machado Jr.'s *Centaur of the North: Francisco Villa, the Mexican Revolution, and Northern Mexico* (Austin: Eakin Press, 1988) is less satisfying but still interesting and useful. In "Pancho Villa and the Attack on Columbus, New Mexico," *American Historical Review* 83 (February 1978): 101-30, Friedrich Katz provides a convincing analysis of the background on Villa's raid. In *The Secret War in Mexico: Europe, the United States, and the Mexican Revolution* (Chicago: University of Chicago Press, 1981) Katz dissects the diplomatic ramifications of the revolution, including the Zimmermann Telegram. See also Barbara Tuchman, *The Zimmermann Telegram* (cited in chapter 8).

Ricardo Flores Magon's *Land and Liberty: Anarchist Influences in the Mexican Revolution,* ed. David Poole (Sanday, Orkney Islands: Cienfuegos Press, 1977), collects some of the anarchist's writings and presents a brief biography of him. Lowell L. Blaisdell's *The Desert Revolution: Baja California, 1911* (Madison: University of Wisconsin Press, 1962) chronicles the short-lived revolution that Flores Magon spearheaded.

William Cameron Townsend's *Lazaro Cardenas: Mexican Democrat* (Ann Arbor: George Wahr, 1952) is outrageously favorable to Cardenas but entertaining and informative. Dana Markiewicz's *The Mexican Revolution and the Limits of Agrarian Reform, 1915-1946* (Boulder: Lynne Rienner, 1993), presents a mechanical and academic Marxist interpretation of Mexican land reform, but it does contain much valuable information.

Robert E. Quirk (in *The Mexican Revolution and the Catholic Church, 1910-1929* [Bloomington: Indiana University Press, 1973]) and David C. Bailey (in *Viva Cristo Rey: The Cristero Rebellion and the Church-State Conflict in Mexico* [Austin: University of Texas Press, 1974]) cover much the same ground, thoroughly and evenhandedly. Jim Tuck's +*The Holy War in Los Altos: A Regional Analysis of Mexico's Cristero Rebellion* (Tucson: University of Arizona Press, 1982) is anecdotal and disjointed but fascinating.

Finally, Carlos Fuentes paints a marvelous tapestry of Mexican revolutionary history in *The Death of Artemio Cruz,* trans. Alfred MacAdam (New York: Farrar, Straus & Giroux, 1991), but in modernist fashion he fragments the narrative and presents it in nonlinear fashion. Graham Greene's classic novel of sin and redemption *The Power and the Glory* (New York: Viking Press, 1940) is set in the bleak, priestless landscape of revolutionary Tabasco.

Chapter 15. The Intoxicated Engineers

The best place to start is with John Kenneth Galbraith's brief, witty, and immensely readable study *+The Great Crash* (Boston: Houghton Mifflin, 1955). Robert W. Sobel's *The Great Bull Market: Wall Street in the 1920s* (New York: W. W. Norton, 1968) is also clear and concise.

For a broader assessment of the causes and consequences of the depression worldwide, three books are essential: Derek H. Aldcroft's *From Versailles to Wall Street, 1919-1929* (cited in chapter 9); Charles P. Kindleberger's *The World in Depression, 1929-1939* (Berkeley and Los Angeles: University of California Press, 1973); and John A. Garraty's *The Great Depression: An Inquiry into the Causes, Course, and Consequences of the Worldwide Depression of the Nineteen-Thirties, as Seen by Contemporaries and in the Light of History* (New York: Harcourt Brace Jovanovich, 1986). Despite its forbidding subtitle, Garraty's book is far more readable than Aldcroft's or Kindleberger's, and it contains a striking chapter comparing Hitler's and Roosevelt's responses to the depression. Peter Fearon's *The Origins and Nature of the Great Slump, 1929-1932* (London: Macmillan, 1979), a short pamphlet in the British series "Studies in Economic and Social History," provides a useful summation.

Frederick Lewis Allen's +*Only Yesterday: An Informal History of the 1920s* (New York: Harper & Bros., 1931) is a classic journalistic account of the Roaring Twenties in America. William E. Leuchtenberg surveys the same territory from a historian's perspective in *+The Perils of Prosperity, 1914-1932* (Chicago: University of Chicago Press, 1958). The three volumes of Arthur Schlesinger, Jr.'s *The Age of Roosevelt — The Crisis of the Old Order, 1919-1933* (Boston: Houghton Mifflin, 1957); *The Coming of the New Deal* (1958), and *The Politics of Upheaval, 1935-1936* (1960) — provide a detailed but fascinating political history of Franklin D. Roosevelt. William E. Leuchtenberg's *+Franklin D. Roosevelt and the New Deal* (New York: Harper & Row, 1963) is an excellent one-volume study. Paul K. Conkin's *The New Deal* (New York: Thomas Y. Crowell, 1967) furnishes both a very brief overview of the New Deal and a critical assessment of it, stressing its lack of coherence or direction.

In +*Britain since 1918*, 2d ed. (New York: St. Martin's Press, 1980), Bentley B. Gilbert provides a brief, readable survey of England's history between the wars. In *Depression and Recovery? British Economic Growth, 1918-1939* (London: Macmillan, 1972), another "Studies in Economic History" pamphlet, B. W. E. Alford analyzes England's economic performance during the period.

I hesitate to recommend a reading of John Maynard Keynes's *The General Theory of Employment, Interest and Money* (New York: Harcourt, Brace, 1935), for it is highly abstract and technical, often very tedious, and, in the words of John Kenneth Galbraith, "deeply ambiguous." On the other hand, it displays occasional flashes of Keynes's irreverent wit and requires very little mathematics. I read it for the first time at age fifty and do not regret it.

I would suggest that before reading Keynes himself, the reader first consult the chapter entitled "The Mandarin Revolution" in John Kenneth Galbraith's *The Age of Uncertainty* (Boston: Houghton Mifflin, 1977). This is the companion volume to a BBC television series of the same name that Galbraith narrated, and it presents the clearest explanation of Keynes's significance I have ever encountered. Finally, Robert Skidelsky, author of a standard study of the British response to the depression, *Politicians and the Slump* (London: Macmillan, 1967), has completed two volumes of a projected three-volume biography of John Maynard Keynes — *Hopes Betrayed, 1883-1920* (London: Macmillan, 1983), and *The Economist as Saviour, 1920-1937* (1992). I have relied heavily on the second volume, which is lengthy and often technical. Keynes's life is inherently fascinating, and Skidelsky successfully integrates his thoughts and writings with his personal life.

479

Chapter 16. Italy's "New Deal"

Denis Mack Smith's *Italy: A Modern History,* rev. ed. (Ann Arbor: University of Michigan Press, 1969), and Christopher Seton-Watson's *Italy from Liberalism to Fascism, 1870-1925* (London: Methuen, 1967), both provide a lengthy, detailed background survey of modern Italian history, but Seton-Watson's book is far superior in its organization and interpretation.

Alexander De Grand's *Italian Fascism: Its Origins and Development* (Lincoln: University of Nebraska Press, 1982) is the best brief overview of the fascist regime in Italy. In *Italian Fascism and Developmental Dictatorship* (Princeton: Princeton University Press, 1979), A. James Gregor explores the intellectual origins of fascism and also draws a provocative comparison between Italian Fascism and Russian Communism. David D. Roberts's *The Syndicalist Tradition and Italian Fascism* (Chapel Hill, N.C.: University of North Carolina Press, 1979) and Alexander De Grand's *The Italian Nationalist Association and the Rise of Fascism in Italy* (Lincoln: University of Nebraska Press, 1978) also examine the intellectual forerunners of the Fascists, but in a less interesting fashion than Gregor's work.

Unfortunately, the massive six-volume biography of Mussolini by Renzo De Felice has not been translated into English, but some idea of De Felice's interpretations can be gleaned from the brief volume *Fascism: An Informal Introduction to Its Theory and Practice — An Interview with Michael A. Ledeen* (New Brunswick, N.J.: Transaction Books, 1976).

Two large biographies in English are Ivone Kirkpatrick's *Mussolini: A Study in Power* (New York: Hawthorn Books, 1964) and Denis Mack Smith's *Mussolini* (New York: Alfred A. Knopf, 1982). These should be supplemented with A. James Gregor's *Young Mussolini and the Intellectual Origins of Fascism* (Berkeley and Los Angeles: University of California Press, 1979), which applies the author's previous work on the syndicalist roots of fascism directly to Mussolini. Both books by Gregor cited in this bibliography are unusual in that they take Mussolini's *ideas* seriously. These ideas can be sampled directly in the famous essay "The Doctrine of Fascism," cowritten by Musssolini and the philosopher Giovanni Gentile for the 1932 *Enciclopedia Italiana.* It has beeen translated by Michael Oakeshott and appears in *The Social and Political Doctrines of Contemporary Europe* (Cambridge: Cambridge University Press, 1939); it can also be found in *Communism, Fascism, and Democracy: The Theoretical Foundations,* ed. Carl Cohen (New York: Random House, 1962).

Many books attempt to define a generic concept of fascism and apply it to Mussolini's Fascists, the German Nazis, and other movements in Europe and elsewhere. One of the most noteworthy of these is Ernst Nolte's *Three Faces of Fascism: Action Francaise, Italian Fascism, National Socialism,* trans. Leila

Vennewitz (New York: Holt, Rinehart & Winston, 1966). I reread this volume recently after thirty years, and I readily confess that I still don't understand it. More accessible are F. L. Carsten's *The Rise of Fascism,* 2d ed. (Berkeley and Los Angeles: University of California Press, 1980), and *Fascism: A Reader's Guide — Analyses, Interpretations, Bibliography,* ed. Walter Laqueur (Berkeley and Los Angeles: University of California Press, 1976).

John P. Diggins's *Mussolini and Fascism: The View from America* (Princeton: Princeton University Press, 1972) is a lengthy but lively survey of American opinion about the Duce. Victoria De Grazia's *The Culture of Consent: Mass Organization of Leisure in Fascist Italy* (Cambridge: Cambridge University Press, 1981) reads rather ponderously but provides a fascinating glimpse at Mussolini's mass-mobilizing techniques. Finally, in *The Vatican and Italian Fascism, 1929-32* (Cambridge: Cambridge University Press, 1985), John F. Pollard explores an important topic that I have hardly mentioned in this chapter.

In sum, the English-language literature on Italian Fascism is quite disappointing, dominated by stereotyped images from the Second World War and a firm belief that Mussolini was an anti-intellectual opportunist. An adequate grasp of the subject, however, can be gleaned from just three books: Seton-Watson's *Italy from Liberalism to Fascism,* De Grand's *Italian Fascism,* and Gregor's *Italian Fascism and Developmental Dictatorship.*

Chapter 17. A Delayed-Action Fuse

Few authors have written short books about Adolf Hitler, including Hitler himself, whose autobiography ran over nine hundred pages. Yet some of these lengthy volumes are classics that amply repay the time required to read them. The two best-known biographies of Hitler — Alan Bullock's *+Hitler: A Study in Tyranny,* rev. ed. (New York: Harper & Row, 1962), and Joachim C. Fest's *Hitler,* trans. Richard and Clara Winston (New York: Harcourt Brace Jovanovich, 1974) — both fall in that category. Bullock's book focuses more on politics and Fest's contains more psychological and philosophical reflection, but both are excellent. William L. Shirer's + *The Rise and Fall of the Third Reich: A History of Nazi Germany* (New York: Simon & Schuster, 1960) was a runaway best-seller by a journalist who witnessed much of the story firsthand in Germany. Though historians have disagreed with some of Shirer's interpretations, his book still remains the most readable overview of the subject. Hitler's own massive autobiography and political testament, *Mein Kampf,* is also worth reading. Though he rants at great and obnoxious length about the "Jewish question," much of the book is lucid and interesting. It is essential reading in order to understand how little Hitler's views changed over time. I

481

used the unabridged volume edited and translated by John Chamberlain and a team of other American historians (New York: Reynal & Hitchcock, 1940), but many other editions are also available.

There *are* a few brief treatments of Hitler's rise, including A. J. Nicholls's *Weimar and the Rise of Hitler,* 2d ed. (New York: St. Martin's Press, 1979); Martin Broszat's *Hitler and the Collapse of Weimar Germany,* trans. V. R. Berghahn (Leamington Spa, U.K.: Berg Publishers, 1987); and Joseph W. Bendersky's *History of Nazi Germany* (Chicago: Nelson-Hall, 1985).

The following are useful for context: José Ortega y Gasset's *The Revolt of the Masses* (London: George Allen & Unwin, 1932); Hannah Arendt's *The Origins of Totalitarianism* (New York: Harcourt, Brace & World, 1951); Gordon A. Craig's *The Germans* (New York: G. P. Putnam's Sons, 1982); V. R. Berghahn's *Modern Germany: Society, Economy and Politics in the Twentieth Century,* 2d ed. (Cambridge: Cambridge University Press, 1987); and Hans W. Gatzke's "Hitler and Psychohistory," *American Historical Review* 78 (April 1973): 394-401. Two volumes cited in chapter 16, F. L. Carsten's *The Rise of Fascism* and Walter Laqueur's *Fascism: A Reader's Guide,* provide much comparative material on Nazism and Italian Fascism.

German hyperinflation is explained briefly by Derek H. Aldcroft in *From Versailles to Wall Street* (cited in chapter 9). Steven B. Webb provides a fuller analysis in *Hyperinflation and Stabilization in Weimar Germany* (New York: Oxford University Press, 1989), which is somewhat technical but basically readable. William Guttmann and Patricia Meehan focus on the human interest dimension of this economic tragedy in + *The Great Inflation: Germany 1919-1923* (London: Saxon House, 1975). John Dornberg provides a lively narrative of the Beer Hall Putsch in + *The Putsch That Failed: Munich 1923* (London: Weidenfeld & Nicolson, 1982).

Finally, two volumes edited by Peter D. Stachura — *The Shaping of the Nazi State* (London: Croom Helm, 1978) and *The Nazi Machtergreifung* (London: George Allen & Unwin, 1983) — provide interpretive articles by different historians on a variety of subjects. I found especially useful the articles by Michael Geyer on the German army and Ian Kershaw on Nazi ideology and propaganda, both in the latter volume.

Chapter 18. Socialism in One Country

Much of what we know about communism under Stalin has come from the writings of novelists and Soviet dissidents. Arthur Koestler's *+Darkness at Noon* (New York: Macmillan, 1941) presents a chilling fictionalized version of the party purges in the 1930s. Anatoli Rybakov's *Children of the Arbat,* trans. Harold

Shukman (Boston: Little, Brown, 1988), and *Fear,* trans. Antonina W. Bouis (Boston: Little, Brown, 1992), cover some of the same ground at greater length from the perspective of a young, idealist insider growing up in the Stalin years. Alexander Solzhenitsyn's *+*One Day in the Life of Ivan Denisovich,* trans. Max Hayward and Leopold Labedz (New York: Praeger, 1963), is a true classic that not only captures the feel of the Soviet Gulag but also gives testimony to the survival of the human spirit.

I readily admit that I did not have the nerve to read Solzhenitsyn's three-volume study of the Soviet prison camps, *The Gulag Archipelago,* or any of his other, more lengthy novels. Thousands of pages on such a depressing subject vanquished my good intentions, but I recommend these works to readers who are braver than I. For somewhat the same reasons, I also neglected dissident intellectual Roy Medvedev's massive study of Stalinism, *Let History Judge: The Origins and Consequences of Stalinism,* trans. Colleen Taylor, ed. David Joravsky and Georges Haupt (New York: Knopf, 1971). However, I did consult his later, briefer work, *Stalin and Stalinism,* trans. Ellen de Kadt (New York: Oxford University Press, 1979).

Two firsthand studies of Stalin that I recommend highly are Svetlana Alliluyeva's *+*Twenty Letters to a Friend,* trans. Priscilla Johnson McMillan (New York: Harper & Row, 1967), and Milovan Djilas's +*Conversations with Stalin,* trans. Michael B. Petrovich (New York: Harcourt, Brace & World, 1961). Svetlana Alliluyeva was Stalin's daughter; she adopted her mother's maiden name after her father's death. (For some reason, the library I used spelled her name "Allilueva" in the database, and I almost missed it. If you don't find the reference under the spelling above, which is used on the title page, try the alternate.) Her memoir is an absolutely riveting tale, akin to the story of a Mafia wife or daughter. Though it will not make anyone feel more kindly toward Stalin, it does portray him as a human being. Djilas's work contains fewer insights, for he met Stalin only three times, but it is interesting nonetheless. A more important study by Djilas, *The New Class: An Analysis of the Communist System* (New York: Praeger, 1957), is a classic critique of communism, written by a dissident Yugoslav Communist who spent much time in prison for his beliefs.

Edward Hallett Carr's one-volume synopsis of his work, *The Russian Revolution: From Lenin to Stalin* (cited in chapter 10) gives a brief, clear outline of the events surrounding Stalin's rise in the 1920s. Adam B. Ulam's *Stalin: The Man and His Era* (New York: The Viking Press, 1973) is an excellent one-volume biography. Ulam tends to go off on tangents, and his book probably contains more political and ideological detail than many readers will want, but the biography is worth a close reading because the author's comments are so insightful. In *Stalin: The Glasnost Revelations* (New York: Charles Scribner's Sons, 1990), Walter Laqueur provides a useful update from the perspective of the more open atmosphere in Russia in the late 1980s. Dmitri Volkogonov's *Stalin: Triumph and Tragedy,* trans. Harold Shukman (Rocklin, Calif.: Prima Publishing, 1992), is a recent biography by a Russian general who, as director of the Institute of Military History, had early access to Russian archives. Volkogonov's father was executed in the purges of the 1930s, so he is certainly not objective, but his account is passionate and fascinating. It does not, however, offer anything to drastically revise our understanding of Stalin's life and times.

Daniel Rancour-Laferriere's *The Mind of Stalin: A Psychoanalytic Study* (Ann Arbor: Ardis Publishers, 1988) is a brief, readable, but not particularly convincing psychological profile. Robert C. Tucker, who is completing a three-volume biography of Stalin, has reflected on his own psychological approach to the subject in "A Stalin Biographer's Memoir," in *Introspection in Biography: The Biographer's Quest for Self-Awareness,* ed. Samuel H. Baron and Carl Pletsch (Hillsdale, N.J.: Analytic Press, 1985). Readers who appreciate psychohistory should consult the first volume of Tucker's biography, *Stalin as Revolutionary* (New York: Norton, 1973).

Robert Conquest's * *The Harvest of Sorrow: Soviet Collectivization and the Terror-Famine* (New York: Oxford University Press, 1986) is a lengthy, definitive account. Robert Melson's *Revolution and Genocide: On the Origins of the Armenian Genocide and the Holocaust* (cited in chapter 11) contains only a few pages describing the Ukrainian terror famine, but the definitions and analysis in the early part of his book fit that event very well. The definitive study of the Stalin party purges is Robert Conquest's * *The Great Terror* (New York: Oxford University Press, 1971); an updated version of the volume was published in 1990 under the title *The Great Terror: A Reassessment.* However, research in newly opened Soviet archives has led to a further revision of some of the statistics in Conquest's book. See J. Arch Getty, Gabor T. Rittersporn, and Viktor N. Zemskov's "Victims of the Soviet Penal System in the Pre-War Years: A First Approach on the Basis of Archival Evidence," *American Historical Review* 98 (October 1993): 1017-49.

In + *The Ghost of the Executed Engineer: Technology and the Fall of the Soviet Union* (Cambridge: Harvard University Press, 1993), Loren R. Graham tells the fascinating story of Peter Palchinsky, one of the bourgeois specialists that Stalin executed, and reflects on the meaning of his life for the outcome of Soviet industrialization. John Scott's *+ *Behind the Urals: An American Worker in Russia's City of Steel,* rev. ed. (Bloomington: Indiana University Press, 1989) presents the unusual reflections of an American radical resident in Russia. Though Scott was an enthusiast of the Russian Revolution, his account is not uncritical.

Finally, I highly recommend Alan Bullock's *+ *Hitler and Stalin: Parallel Lives,* 2d ed. (New York: Alfred A. Knopf, 1993), a truly brilliant comparative study by the author of the best biography of Hitler (cited in chapter 17).

Chapter 19. The Spanish Tragedy

Two classic texts provide a fine starting point: Gerald Brenan's *+ *The Spanish Labyrinth: An Account of the Social and Political Background of the Civil War* (Cambridge: Cambridge University Press, 1943) and Hugh Thomas's *+*The Spanish Civil War* (London: Eyre & Spottiswoode, 1961). Both books have been reprinted frequently.

Paul Preston's *The Coming of the Spanish Civil War: Reform, Reaction and Revolution in the Second Republic, 1931-1936* (London: Macmillan, 1978), and Richard A. H. Robinson's *The Origins of Franco's Spain: The Right, the Republic and Revolution, 1931-1936* (Newton Abbot, U.K.: David & Charles Publishers, 1970), cover the same ground — the short, unhappy history of the Spanish Republic — but from opposite points of view (Preston sympathizes with the left, Robinson the right). It is best to read these books together and accept Preston's interpretation of the left and Robinson's interpretation of the right. Such a reading brings home the extreme polarization of Spanish politics.

Frank Sedwick's *The Tragedy of Manuel Azaña and the Fate of the Spanish Republic* (Columbus: Ohio State University Press, 1963) is barely adequate as a biography but does contain significant excerpts from Azana's speeches; the introduction by Salvador de Madariaga is very interesting. J. P. Fusi [Aizpurua]'s *Franco: A Biography*, trans. Felipe Fernandez-Armesto (New York: Harper & Row, 1987), is a rare brief biography that says much more than the usual thousand-page variety.

None of the following books makes for exciting reading, but they are all thorough and useful studies: Robert H. Whealey, *Hitler and Spain: The Nazi Role in the Spanish Civil War, 1936-1939* (Lexington: University Press of Kentucky, 1989); John F. Coverdale, *Italian Intervention in the Spanish Civil War* (Princeton: Princeton University Press, 1975); E. H. Carr, *The Comintern and the Spanish Civil War* (New York: Pantheon Books, 1984); and R. Dan Richardson, *Comintern Army: The International Brigades and the Spanish Civil War* (Lexington: University Press of Kentucky, 1982). Richardson's work is probably the most interesting. He explodes, somewhat too ferociously, the myth that the International Brigades consisted mainly of idealistic volunteers fighting for democracy against fascism.

George Orwell, author of *Animal Farm* and *1984*, fought in Spain and was swiftly disillusioned. His classic account, *+*Homage to Catalonia* (London: Folio Society, 1938), is still vivid and valuable. Chapter 5 contains the clearest explanation of the various left-wing political parties in Spain that I have ever read. Robert Hughes's +*Barcelona* (New York: Alfred A. Knopf, 1992) has little to do with the subject matter of this chapter, since he ends his book just before the start of the civil war and deals primarily with art and architecture, but his book is worth mentioning because it provides wonderful background on that fascinating city and is virtually the only such book in English.

Joan Connelly Ullman's *The Tragic Week: A Study of Anticlericalism in Spain, 1875-1912* (Cambridge: Harvard University Press, 1968), is a thorough study of that event. In * *The Spanish Civil War as a Religious Tragedy* (Notre Dame, Ind.: University of Notre Dame Press, 1987), José M. Sanchez discusses the anticlerical outrages during the civil war with perspective and balance.

Murray Bookchin's * *The Spanish Anarchists: The Heroic Years, 1868-1936* (New York: Free Life Editions, 1977), and Robert W. Kern's * *Red Years/Black Years: A Political History of Spanish Anarchism, 1911-1937* (Philadelphia: Institute for the Study of Human Issues, 1978), are both slightly disappointing but indispensable surveys.

The two most famous novels about the Spanish civil war are Ernest Hemingway's *For Whom the Bell Tolls* (New York: Charles Scribner's Sons, 1940) and André Malraux's *Man's Fate,* trans. Stuart Gilbert and Alastair Macdonald (New York: Random House, 1938). However, the best fictional account of the Spanish tragedy is contained in two long novels by Jose Maria Gironella: *+ *The Cypresses Believe in God,* trans. Harriet de Onis (New York: Alfred A. Knopf, 1955), and *+*One Million Dead,* trans. Joan MacLean (Garden City, N.Y.: Doubleday, 1963). Gironella portrays the absurdly tragic dimensions of the civil war by following a number of characters on both sides. My reading of these two novels thirty years ago helped confirm my own decision to become a pacifist.

Chapter 20. Incidents and Accidents in East Asia

The works cited in chapter 4 by John King Fairbank, Jonathan D. Spence, Michael Gasster, Richard Storry, Harold Z. Schiffrin, and Edwin O. Reischauer all contain significant sections relating to this chapter. I relied particularly on Jonathan D. Spence's excellent overview of Chinese history in *+ *The Search for Modern China* and Richard Storry's narration of Japanese foreign policy in *+*Japan and the Decline of the West in Asia, 1894-1943.*

Lucien Bianco's *+*Origins of the Chinese Revolution, 1915-1949,* trans. Muriel Bell (Stanford: Stanford University Press, 1971), is a brilliant interpretive history of Chinese Communism. The author is sympathetic to Mao's Communists but not uncritical. For an analysis of Chiang Kai-shek's regime, see *The Cambridge History of China,* vol. 13, *Republican China 1912-1949,* ed. John K. Fairbank and Albert Feuerwerker (Cambridge: Cambridge University Press, 1986); material from this volume has also been published separately as Lloyd E. Eastman, Jerome Ch'en, Suzanne Pepper, and Lyman P. Van Slyke's *The Nationalist Era in China, 1927-1937* (Cambridge: Cambridge University Press, 1991). Lloyd E. Eastman's long essay in this volume, *"Nationalist China during the Nanking Decade, 1927-1937," and his full-length treatment of the same subject,

The Abortive Revolution: China under Nationalist Rule, 1927-1937 (Cambridge: Harvard University Press, 1974), are basic treatments of the subject. William Morwood's +*Duel for the Middle Kingdom: The Struggle between Chiang Kai-shek and Mao Tse-tung for Control of China* (New York: Everest House, 1980) is a readable narrative, virtually a dual biography of Chiang and Mao.

William G. Beasley's *Japanese Imperialism, 1894-1945* (Oxford: Clarendon Press, 1987), is the best single study of the subject. One of his students, R. L. Sims, has written an overview of Japanese politics, *A Political History of Modern Japan, 1868-1952* (New Delhi: Vikas Publishing House, 1991). Sims's book can be mind-numbing in its detail, but it contains much useful information that is hard to find elsewhere. Akira Iriye's *After Imperialism: The Search for a New Order in the Far East, 1921-1931* (Cambridge: Harvard University Press, 1965), is the standard study of Japanese foreign policy in the 1920s, setting it in a very wide context. Richard Storry's *The Double Patriots: A Study of Japanese Nationalism* (London: Chatto and Windus, 1957) focuses on the rise of militant nationalism in the 1930s. In *Ishiwara Kanji and Japan's Confrontation with the West* (Princeton: Princeton University Press, 1975), Mark R. Peattie explores the life and times of this fascinating theorist and usefully sorts out the confusing welter of factions in the Japanese military. *The Japanese Colonial Empire, 1895-1945*, ed. Ramon H. Myers and Mark R. Peattie (Princeton: Princeton University Press, 1984), contains a number of articles by different authors analyzing the administration of Japan's "formal" colonies, primarily Korea and Taiwan.

Shortly after World War II a group of Japanese scholars in the Japan Association on International Relations launched a comprehensive research project on the origins of the war in the Pacific. The group published seven volumes in 1962 and 1963 under the title *Taiheiyo senso e no michi: kaisen gaiko shi* (The Road to the Pacific War: A Diplomatic History of the Origins of the War). James William Morley engaged English-speaking scholars to translate and publish five volumes of selections from this monumental work. Of these I consulted *Japan Erupts: The London Naval Conference and the Manchurian Incident, 1928-1932*, ed. James W. Morley (New York: Columbia University Press, 1984), and Morley's *The China Quagmire: Japan's Expansion on the Asian Continent, 1933-1941* (New York: Columbia University Press, 1983). Both volumes are overly detailed and light on interpretation, but they are about as close to primary sources as a non-Japanese speaker can get, and thus worth a look.

Finally, Alvin D. Coox and Hilary Conroy have edited a series of essays, *China and Japan: Search for Balance Since World War I* (Santa Barbara: ABC-Clio Inc., 1978), and Marius B. Jansen has written a fine, interpretive overview of the two countries' interactions, *Japan and China: From War to Peace, 1894-1972* (Chicago: Rand McNally College Publishing, 1975).

Chapter 21. The Onset of Hitler's War

P. M. H. Bell's *+*The Origins of the Second World War in Europe* (London: Longman, 1986) is the most thorough, comprehensive, and balanced, though not the most interesting, overview; it is clearly the place to start. On the other hand, Laurence Lafore's *+*The End of Glory: An Interpretation of the Origins of World War II* (Philadelphia: J. B. Lippincott Company, 1970) should be saved for the end, or near the end, when the reader already has the basic facts clearly in mind. Lafore's elegantly written, opinionated interpretation brilliantly paints the big picture, devoting nearly as much space to World War I and its consequences as to the immediate causes of World War II. He emphasizes the diminishing power of Europe on the world scene and the crucial absence of Russia and America in the years leading up to World War II. In *The Origins of the Second World War* (London: Hamish Hamilton, 1961), A. J. P. Taylor argues, among other things, that Hitler was a pure opportunist. Few historians today agree, but Taylor's brilliant, quirky, highly readable book is still stimulating. *"The Origins of the Second World War" Reconsidered: The A. J. P. Taylor Debate after Twenty-five Years,* ed. Gordon Martel (Boston: Allen & Unwin, 1986), ably analyzes the legacy of the English historian. My references to historian Norman Rich are drawn from his chapter, "Hitler's Foreign Policy," in this volume.

Adolf Hitler's *Mein Kampf* (cited in chapter 17) and Alan Bullock's *+*Hitler and Stalin: Parallel Lives* (cited in chapter 18) remain the best sources for Hitler's motives and actions. Bullock also considers Stalin's reactions and the events leading up to the Nazi-Soviet Nonaggression Pact and, later, the invasion of Russia. Klaus Hildebrand's **The Foreign Policy of the Third Reich,* trans. Anthony Fothergill (Berkeley and Los Angeles: University of California Press, 1973), is a short, densely reasoned, and essential analysis of the subject. William Carr's *Arms, Autarky and Aggression: A Study in German Foreign Policy, 1933-1939* (New York: W. W. Norton, 1972), focuses on the economic dimensions of Hitler's policy, which I neglect in my chapter. Fritz Fischer's *Germany's Aims in the First World War* (cited in chapter 7) provides a benchmark against which to assess the similar, but more expansive, aims of Hitler.

Ivone Kirkpatrick's *Mussolini: A Study in Power* (cited in chapter 16), and Anthony Adamthwaite's *France and the Coming of the Second World War, 1936-1939* (London: Frank Cass, 1977), provide detailed accounts of Italian and French policy, respectively.

R. A. C. Parker's **Chamberlain and Appeasement: British Policy and the Coming of the Second World War* (New York: St. Martin's Press, 1993) is a comprehensive and fair study of the much-maligned Neville Chamberlain, neither dismissing him as a fool nor defending his policy, but simply explaining the policy's origins and analyzing the reasons for its failure.

Martin Gilbert completed the eight volumes of the official biography of Winston Churchill that was begun by Churchill's son, Randolph, in the 1960s. Gilbert has also provided a hefty, thousand-page, one-volume version entitled *Churchill: A Life* (New York: Henry Holt, 1991), which is altogether long enough for my taste. It's actually more fun to read Churchill himself than Gilbert's books about him. Winston S. Churchill's *+ The Second World War*, vol. 1, *The Gathering Storm* (Boston: Houghton Mifflin, 1948) is a 667-page "I told you so" tale, arguing forcefully that Britain should have rearmed sooner and opposed Hitler's expansion earlier and more forcefully. The second volume, *+Their Finest Hour* (Boston: Houghton Mifflin, 1949), is more exciting, narrating the fall of France, the London blitz, and other tremendous events after Churchill became prime minister in 1940.

Matthew Cooper and James Lucas, *Panzer: The Armoured Force of the Third Reich* (New York: St. Martin's Press, 1976), is a brief, informative, profusely illustrated study of the theory and practice of blitzkrieg. In *+Blitzkrieg: From the Rise of Hitler to the Fall of Dunkirk* (New York: Alfred A. Knopf, 1980), Len Deighton provides a brilliant narrative history of the Battle of France that compares favorably with Barbara Tuchman's narrative of the 1914 invasion of France in *The Guns of August* (cited in chapter 7). Deighton's *+The Battle of Britain* (London: George Rainbird, 1980) is a fascinating illustrated study of the blitz.

Finally, *Paths to War: New Essays on the Origins of the Second World War*, ed. Robert Boyce and Esmonde M. Robertson (New York: St. Martin's Press, 1989), presents essays by various historians summarizing and analyzing the state of the question.

Chapter 22. The Coming of the Greater East Asia War

John Toland's *+ The Rising Sun: The Decline and Fall of the Japanese Empire, 1936-1945* (New York: Random House, 1970), is a long, wide-ranging, narrative history of the entire Greater East Asia War, written from a point of view sympathetic to Japan's culture. The first two sections of the book cover the subject matter of this chapter. Akira Iriye's *The Origins of the Second World War in Asia and the Pacific* (London: Longman, 1987) is the most reliable overview of the subject, though it does not make easy or enjoyable reading. Jonathan G. Utley's *Going to War with Japan, 1937-1941* (Knoxville: University of Tennessee Press, 1985), contains the best analysis of the American policy that led to war. Based on thorough archival research, the book makes some surprising revelations, such as the role of Assistant Secretary of State Dean Acheson in halting exports of gasoline to Japan.

Oka Yoshitake's *Konoe Fumimaro: A Political Biography*, trans. Shumpei Okamoto and Patricia Murray (Lanham, Md.: Madison Books, 1992), is useful but not particularly interesting. Robert J. C. Butow's *Tojo and the Coming of the War* (Princeton: Princeton University Press, 1961) deals more with the times than the life of the Japanese war leader. Though very long, rambling, and somewhat outdated, the book does a good job of demythologizing Tojo. Mark Peattie's *Ishiwara Kanji and Japan's Confrontation with the West* (cited in chapter 20) is the best biographical study of a Japanese leader in this period.

The Fateful Choice: Japan's Advance into Southeast Asia, 1939-1941, ed. James William Morley (New York: Columbia University Press, 1980), is another installment in the translation of *Taiheiyo senso e no michi* (cited in chapter 20). *Japan's Decision for War: Records of the 1941 Policy Conferences,* ed. and trans. Nobutaka Ike (Stanford: Stanford University Press, 1967), provides invaluable documents detailing Japan's decision for war. *Japan's Greater East Asia Co-Prosperity Sphere in World War II: Selected Readings and Documents,* ed. Joyce Lebra (Kuala Lumpur: Oxford University Press, 1975), furnishes fascinating and important evidence of Japan's goals in Asia, assessing both successes and failures in a balanced, lively fashion. Saburåo Ienaga's *The Pacific War: World War II and the Japanese, 1931-1945,* trans. Taiheiyåo Sensåo (New York: Pantheon Books, 1978), is a hard book to evaluate. Passionately written, it denounces Japan's prewar thought control and barbarous wartime behavior from a Marxist point of view. More anti-Japanese than most American wartime propaganda, it is probably not completely reliable, but it does provide fascinating material hard to find elsewhere. *Dilemmas of Growth in Prewar Japan,* ed. James William Morley (Princeton: Princeton University Press, 1971), is the record of an academic seminar discussing a wide range of topics dealing with Japan between the world wars. I relied particularly on the essays by Akira Iriye, Kentaro Hayashi, and Edwin O. Reischauer.

Gordon Prange's two massive volumes on Pearl Harbor represent the fruit of a thirty-seven-year obsession. Prange, a navy officer and professional historian who served in Japan during the war, read everything and interviewed everyone he could find, but his work remained unpublished when he died in May 1980. Two former students, Donald M. Goldstein and Katherine V. Dillon, brought the work to the public. *At Dawn We Slept: The Untold Story of Pearl Harbor* (New York: McGraw-Hill, 1981) is a narrative account of the Japanese attack, and *Pearl Harbor: The Verdict of History* (New York: McGraw-Hill, 1986) analyzes the controversy over American unpreparedness at Pearl Harbor. Both books made the best-seller list, though it's difficult to understand why; they're long and not particularly well written. Yet the research is voluminous, the judgments balanced, and the work definitive. They should, but probably won't, be the last word on the subject. John J. Stephan's *+Hawaii under the Rising Sun: Japan's Plans for Conquest after Pearl Harbor* (Honolulu: University of Hawaii Press, 1984) is a small gem, one of those rare books that delivers what it promises and more.

Chapter 23. Coalition Warfare, Unconditional Surrender

Gerhard L. Weinberg's massive one-volume history *A World at Arms: A Global History of World War II* (Cambridge: Cambridge University Press, 1994) reminds me of the old story about the dog walking on his hind legs, attributed to Doctor Samuel Johnson: "It's not that he does it so well, but it's amazing that he does it at all." Weinberg attempts a comprehensive account of military, political, diplomatic, economic, and technological history, stressing the simultaneity of events occurring around the world. I pushed myself through his 900 pages of text, both to see if I could do it and because of the information he provides. British military historian John Keegan has written a slightly briefer and more readable one-volume account, *The Second World War* (New York: Viking, 1990), which emphasizes the purely military aspects of the war.

Winston Churchill was the only one of the Big Three who lived to write his memoirs. His six-volume *The Second World War* is longer but more interesting to read than either Weinberg or Keegan. The first two volumes, *The Gathering Storm* and *Their Finest Hour,* were cited in chapter 21. *The Grand Alliance* (Boston: Houghton Mifflin, 1950), *The Hinge of Fate* (1950), *Closing the Ring* (1951), and *Triumph and Tragedy* (1953) cover the events of this chapter. Robert Sherwood, *Roosevelt and Hopkins: An Intimate History* (New York: Harper & Brothers, 1948), can serve as a memoir of FDR's close advisor Harry Hopkins, who died shortly after the war, and to some extent of the president himself. Herbert Feis's *Churchill, Roosevelt, Stalin: The War They Waged and the Peace They Sought* (Princeton: Princeton University Press, 1957) surveys the numerous wartime conferences of the Big Three in encyclopedic fashion. Keith Sainsbury's **Churchill and Roosevelt at War: The War They Fought and the Peace They Hoped to Make* (New York: New York University Press, 1994) is a rarity among Second World War volumes — a short book! It provides a mature, insightful analysis of this political partnership.

Alan Bullock's **+Hitler and Stalin: Parallel Lives* (cited in chapter 18) provides a full account of the Russo-German battles. I believe that Bullock's book is the single best work of history I have ever read. John Keegan's **+Six Armies in Normandy: From D-Day to the Liberation of Paris, June 6th–August 25th, 1944* (New York: Viking, 1982) is an innovative study of this famous invasion, told from the points of view of six different national traditions. John Toland's **+The Rising Sun* (cited in chapter 22) is a highly readable account of the East Asian war, narrated with unusual sensitivity to the Japanese point of view. Akira Iriye's *Power and Culture: The Japanese-American War, 1941-1945* (Cambridge: Harvard University Press, 1981), provides an interesting interpretive framework in which to place the Asian war. John A. Lorelli's ** To Foreign Shores: U.S. Amphibious Operations in World War II* (Annapolis: Naval Institute Press, 1995) offers a fascinating overview of all the amphibious battles, both in Europe and the Pacific. The writing does not sparkle, but the book is solid and insightful.

With the exception of Keegan's book on Normandy, I have not consulted studies of individual battles. The writing of such books, however, is a major industry of its own, and the reader who is interested will have no difficulty finding them. Any public library or bookstore will have many such battle histories. Indeed, that is all one can find in the history section of many bookstores.

Chapter 24. The War of Extermination

Alan Bullock's *Hitler and Stalin: Parallel Lives* (cited in chapter 18), Gerhard Weinberg's *A World at Arms* (cited in chapter 23), and John Toland's *The Rising Sun* (cited in chapter 22) narrate many of the atrocities discussed in this chapter. Bullock, in particular, provides admirably clear and balanced analyses of the Holocaust, the abuse of POWs on the Eastern Front, and the euthanasia campaign. The American precedent for Hitler's sterilization and euthanasia programs is discussed in a stunning article by Hugo P. Leaming, "The Ben Ishmael Tribe: A Fugitive 'Nation' of the Old Northwest," in *The Ethnic Frontier*, ed. Melvin G. Holli and Peter d'A. Jones (Grand Rapids: William B. Eerdmans, 1977).

Bohdan Wytwycky's * *The Other Holocaust: Many Circles of Hell* (Washington: Novak Report, 1980) is a brilliant brief analysis of the *Untermensch* campaign, with reasonable estimates of the numbers of victims. *A Mosaic of Victims: Non-Jews Persecuted and Murdered by the Nazis*, ed. Michael Berenbaum (New York: New York University Press, 1990), presents the results of an international scholarly conference held in 1987. Edward L. Homze's * *Foreign Labor in Nazi Germany* (Princeton: Princeton University Press, 1967) is a model monograph; on the other hand, Omer Bartov's *The Eastern Front, 1941-45: German Troops and the Barbarisation of Warfare* (New York: St. Martin's Press, 1986) is a clumsy, insufficiently revised doctoral dissertation that does not deliver as much information or analysis as its subtitle promises.

Richard Garrett's +*P.O.W.* (Newton Abbot, U.K.: David & Charles, 1981) is a well-written, brief overview of the POW experience throughout history, with primary emphasis on the twentieth century. In +*Prisoners of the Japanese: POWS of World War II in the Pacific* (New York: Morrow, 1994), Gavan Daws passionately indicts the behavior of the Japanese military. In * + *War without Mercy: Race and Power in the Pacific War* (New York: Pantheon Books, 1986), John W. Dower also presents the record of Japanese atrocities, but he matches it with American atrocities and places them both in a provocative context — the mutual racism felt by Americans and Japanese for each other. In *The Pacific War* (cited in chapter 22),

Saburåo Ienaga presents a stinging indictment of his own nation's behavior before and during World War II.

Leo Kuper's *Genocide: Its Political Use in the Twentieth Century* (New Haven: Yale University Press, 1981) is a brief, readable introduction; and Lucy Dawidowicz's *The War against the Jews, 1933-1945* (New York: Holt, Rinehart & Winston, 1975), provides a narrative overview of the Jewish Holocaust and a thorough analysis of the numbers of victims, country by country. Two comparative works are useful for assessing both the uniqueness of the Holocaust and its points of similarity with other atrocities: Robert Melson's *Revolution and Genocide* (cited in chapter 11) compares the Jewish Holocaust with the Armenian genocide; Eric Markusen and David Kopf's *The Holocaust and Strategic Bombing: Genocide and Total War in the Twentieth Century* (Boulder: Westview Press, 1995) surveys all the atrocities of the twentieth century before comparing the two highlighted in the title. Melson's is the better book, clear and forceful, certainly one of the best books ever written about genocide.

For surveys of the development of area bombing, see Charles Messenger, *"Bomber" Harris and the Strategic Bombing Offensive, 1939-1945* (New York: St. Martin's Press, 1984); Alan J. Levine, *The Strategic Bombing of Germany, 1940-1945* (Westport, Conn.: Praeger, 1992); and Conrad C. Crane, *Bombs, Cities, and Civilians: American Airpower Strategy in World War II* (Lawrence: University Press of Kansas, 1993). In *Ethics and Airpower in World War II: The British Bombing of German Cities* (New York: St. Martin's Press, 1993), Stephen A. Garrett provides a clearly reasoned and historically well-informed ethical analysis.

Richard Rhodes's *+ The Making of the Atomic Bomb* (New York: Simon & Schuster, 1986) is a massively thorough account of the atomic bomb's development. The book starts slowly, with a heavy emphasis on science and scientists, but from about page 378 on, the author presents an absolutely riveting account, which includes the firebombings in Europe and Japan as well as the atomic bombings themselves. The conventional justification for the A-bomb's use — that it was necessary to save the lives of American soldiers — is presented very forcefully by Henry L. Stimson in "The Decision to Use the Atomic Bomb," *Harper's*, February 1947, pp. 97-107, and by Harry S. Truman in the first volume of his memoirs, *1945: Year of Decisions* (Garden City, N.Y.: Doubleday, 1955). Gar Alperovitz has made the strongest revisionist case against the conventional interpretation, in *Atomic Diplomacy: Hiroshima and Potsdam: The Use of the Atomic Bomb and the American Confrontation with Soviet Power*, rev. ed. (New York: Simon & Schuster, 1985), and in *The Decision to Use the Atomic Bomb and the Architecture of an American Myth* (New York: Alfred A. Knopf, 1995). He argues that the dropping of the A-bomb was intended more to impress the Soviet Union than to end the war against Japan. Though I believe his latest book is essential reading, I find his arguments somewhat obsessive and exaggerated. Barton J. Bernstein presents a more balanced and persuasive revisionist analysis, but unfortunately most of his work has been published solely in scholarly journals rather than in easily accessible books. His essay *+"The Atomic Bombings Reconsidered," *Foreign Affairs* 74 (Jan.-Feb. 1995): 135-52, is the best brief treatment of the subject.

Calvin DeArmond Davis's *The United States and the Second Hague Peace Conference: American Diplomacy and International Organization, 1899-1914* (Durham, N.C.: Duke University Press, 1975), and James F. Willis's *Prologue to Nuremberg: The Politics and Diplomacy of Punishing War Criminals of the First World War* (Westport, Conn.: Greenwood Press, 1982) provide background on the development and application of the laws of war before World War II. In *+Nuremberg: Infamy on Trial* (New York: Viking, 1994), Joseph E. Persico presents a readable narrative of the European war crimes trial; Bradley F. Smith digs a little deeper in *Reaching Judgment at Nuremberg* (New York: Basic Books, 1977), focusing particularly on the decision-making process of the tribunal's judges. In "Misjudgment at Nuremberg," *New York Review of Books,* October 7, 1993, pp. 46-52, Istvan Deak offers a critical review of Telford Taylor's *Anatomy of the Nuremberg Trials: A Personal Memoir* (New York: Alfred A. Knopf, 1992) and of the war crimes trials themselves. Richard H. Minear's *+Victor's Justice: The Tokyo War Crimes Trial* (Princeton: Princeton University Press, 1971) is a scathing critique of the procedures employed at the Tokyo trial. In *The Japanese on Trial: Allied War Crimes Operations in the East, 1945-1951* (Austin: University of Texas Press, 1979), Philip R. Piccigallo surveys the Tokyo trial and the many other trials of individual Japanese in a dry, factual style.

Chapter 25. The Search for Alternatives

Peter Hoffmann's *The History of the German Resistance, 1933-1945,* trans. Richard Barry (Cambridge: MIT Press, 1977), and Eberhard Zeller's *The Flame of Freedom: The German Struggle against Hitler,* trans. R. P. Heller and D. R. Masters (London: Oswald Wolf, 1967), are both thorough, nearly encyclopedic accounts of the various plots to assassinate and overthrow Hitler. Robert Weldon Whelan's *Assassinating Hitler: Ethics and Resistance in Nazi Germany* (Selinsgrove, Pa.: Susquehanna University Press, 1993) and Michael Baigent and Richard Leigh's *Secret Germany: Claus von Stauffenberg and the Mystical Crusade against Hitler* (London: Jonathan Cape, 1994) are briefer, more interesting, and more interpretive.

Lisa Sowle Cahill's *Love Your Enemies: Discipleship, Pacifism, and Just War Theory* (Minneapolis: Fortress Press, 1994) and Walter Wink's *Engaging the Powers: Discernment and Resistance in a World of Domination* (Minneapolis: Fortress Press, 1992) both present a Christian theological argument in favor of pacifism. Wink's book is far more interesting and original, one of three volumes in which he discusses the biblical notion of "powers and principalities" as the functional equivalent of "the system," the political and economic forces that dominate the world. I am indebted to my colleague at Mundelein Seminary, the Reverend Leo Lefebure, and to one of our mutual students, Michael Fuller, for bringing Wink's work to my attention.

Gene Sharp's *Exploring Nonviolent Alternatives* (Boston: Extending Horizons, 1970) and *Civilian-Based Defense: A Post-Military Weapons System* (Princeton: Princeton University Press, 1990) present fascinating practical arguments for nonviolent means of countering aggression.

Peter Brock's *Twentieth-Century Pacifism* (cited in chapter 9) outlines the basic facts about conscientious objectors and war resisters in this century. Gordon Zahn's In Solitary Witness: The Life and Death of Franz Jagerstatter, rev. ed. (Springfield, Ill.: Templegate Publishers, 1986), profiles one of the few conscientious objectors in the Third Reich. In Conscientious Objectors and the Second World War: Moral and Religious Arguments in Support of Pacifism (New York: Praeger, 1991), Cynthia Eller analyzes interviews with American conscientious objectors from World War II.

James Avery Joyce's Broken Star, F. S. Northedge's The League of Nations, and Inis L. Claude Jr.'s Swords Into Plowshares (all cited in chapter 9) provide useful background on the failings of the League of Nations. The Big Three decisions that led to the founding of the United Nations organization can be followed in Robert Sherwood's Roosevelt and Hopkins and Herbert Feis's Churchill, Roosevelt, Stalin (both cited in chapter 23).

Clark Eichelberger's +Organizing for Peace: A Personal History of the Founding of the United Nations (New York: Harper & Row, 1977) provides a useful overview from an insider's perspective. Geoff Simons's The United Nations: A Chronology of Conflict (New York: St. Martin's Press, 1994) is an opinionated, anti-American tract. Robert C. Hilderbrand's *Dumbarton Oaks: The Origins of the United Nations and the Search for Postwar Security (Chapel Hill, N.C.: University of North Carolina Press, 1990) is the most thorough, detailed study of the postwar planning process. Stanley Meisler's *+United Nations: The First Fifty Years (New York: Atlantic Monthly Press, 1995) contains only a brief chapter on the UN's origins, but the rest of the book is a marvelously readable, sensible, balanced, and even exciting history of the organization's first fifty years.

The Historical Dictionary of the International Monetary Fund, ed. Norman K. Humphreys (Metuchen, N.J.: Scarecrow Press, 1993), provides a useful introduction to and chronology of the Bretton Woods institutions. Alfred E. Eckes Jr.'s *A Search for Solvency: Bretton Woods and the International Monetary System, 1941-1971 (Austin: University of Texas Press, 1975), and Armand Van Dormael's Bretton Woods: Birth of a Monetary System (New York: Holmes & Meier, 1978) both analyze the conference itself — Eckes from the American point of view and

Van Dormael from the British. Eckes's book is clearer and provides a fuller context for understanding Bretton Woods.

Index

Abdulhamid II, 179-81, 184, 200
Abdullah, 201, 203, 204, 214
Accidentalism, 331-32
Acheson, Dean, 395
Administrative Decentralization Party, 200
Africa, 34-37, 40, 125, 181, 276, 288, 368-69
The African Queen, 125
Afrikaners, 3-5
Ai-ling, 351
al-Ahd, 199
Albania, 101, 377
Alexandra, 70, 159-61, 169
Alexei, 70, 159-61, 169
Alfonso XIII, 328-29
Algeria, 198, 406
Ali, 201, 203, 204
Allenby, Gen. Edmund, 203, 204, 213
Alliluyeva, Nadezhda, 313
Alliluyeva, Svetlana, 313
Alsace (generic term), 20, 60, 87, 90, 153, 233
Alsace (province), 109, 116, 118, 149
Amerindians, 30, 216, 425
Anarchism: analyzed, xv, 20-27; in Mexico, 235, 236, 241-43; in Russian revolutions, 76-77, 160, 163, 167-68; in Spain, 329, 337, 340-44; in Ukraine, 172-74
Anarcho-syndicalism, 279 n. 2

Anders, Władyslaw, 378
Angell, Norman, 118, 121
Anschluss, 374
Anticlericalism, 240, 244-45, 247, 329-30, 342-44
Anti-Semitism, 295, 301, 307, 367
Appeasement, 371-73, 375-76
Arab Bureau, 203
Arab Legion, 204
Arabs: name explained, 196-97; in Ottoman Empire, 196, 199-200; in Palestine, 212; revolt, 201-4, 213-15, 251
Argentina, 403
Argonne Forest, 135
Armenia, 180, 186-88, 192, 205, 212
Arshinov, Peter, 173
Ascaso, Francisco, 341
Asquith, Herbert, 114, 211, 223
Ataturk, Mustafa Kemal: biographical sketch, 190; compared to other leaders, 232, 251, 352; founder of modern Turkey, 190-94; in World War I, 128, 184-86
Atomic bomb, 405, 420, 432-34
Attlee, Clement, 419
Auda Abu Tayeh, 203
Australia, 126-31, 140, 184, 386, 403, 405
Austria, 374
Austria-Hungary: analyzed, 90-93, 222;

Archduke assassinated, 95-99; Bosnia annexed by, 81, 83, 87-88, 93-95, 115; Serbia attacked by, 101-3, 111-13; terminated, 140
Axis alliance, 369, 377, 384-85, 386, 404
Azaña Diaz, Manuel, 329-30, 333

Babi Yar, 425
Baden-Powell, Robert, 6
Bakunin, Michael, 22, 23, 340
Baldwin, Stanley, 270, 382
Balfour, Arthur, 109, 207, 211, 221
Balfour Declaration, 207, 211, 212, 214
Balkan Wars, 88, 103, 182
Baring, Evelyn, 198
Basques, 327, 336 n. 3
Bataan Death March, 327
Battle of Britain, 382
Battle of the Bulge, 414
Beck, Gen. Ludwig, 442, 443, 444
Beer Hall Putsch, 299-300, 441
Belgium, 109-10, 112, 114, 131-32, 139, 378, 379-80
Bell, Gertrude, 203
Benedict XV, 277, 373
Beneš, Edvard, 375-76
Ben Ishmael tribe, 423
Berchtold, Leopold, 100-101, 103
Beria, Laurenti, 322
Bernstein, Edward, 24, 107
Bethmann Hollweg, Theodore von, 110, 111, 113, 134, 367
Biliński, Leon von, 100
Bismarck, Otto von, 91, 104, 274, 367
Black and Tans, 230, 284
Blackett, P. M. S., 431
Black Hand, 88, 96-97, 101
Blitzkrieg, 119-21, 368, 378-80
Blood River, battle of, 5
Bloody Sunday, 71-72, 160, 162
Boer War, 3-8, 66
Bogomils, 82
Bolshevik Revolution. See Russia: October Revolution
Bonhoeffer, Dietrich, 441
Bonillas, Ignacio, 246
Bonnet, Georges, 375

Bormann, Martin, 437
Bosnia-Hercegovina, 81-83, 93-95
Botha, Louis, 8
Boxer Rebellion, 8-12, 15, 51-52, 63
Braun, Eva, 415
Brazil, 403
Brazza, Pierre de, 16
Breaker Morant, 7, 435
Bresci, Gaetano, 276
Bretton Woods Conference, 455-56
Bridge on the River Kwai, 427
Brüning, Heinrich, 303
Brusilov, Gen. Alexei, 123
Bukharin, Nicholas, 310, 313, 321
Bulgaria, 87, 88, 103, 123, 382, 404
Bülow, Bernhard von, 105
Burian, Istvan, 102
Burma, 386, 390, 416, 427
Bushveldt Carbineers, 6
Bussche, Capt. Axel von dem, 444
Butt, Isaac, 220

Čabrinović, Nedjelko, 96-99
Cadogan, Alexander, 450
Calles, Gen. Plutarco Elias, 247, 249
Calvo Sotelo, Jose, 334
Cambon, Jules, 109, 116
Cambon, Paul, 106
Camus, Albert, 457
Canabal, Tomas Garrido, 247
Canada, 131-34, 140, 403, 405-6
Capital (Marx), 21
Caporetto, battle of, 278
Cardenas, Lazaro, 249-51
Carranza, Venustiano, 239-41, 243-44, 245-46
Carson, Edward, 223, 224
Casablanca Conference, 404, 406
Casement, Roger, 226, 229
Catalans, 327, 336 n. 3, 341
Catechism of the Catholic Church (John Paul II), 43
Catholic Church: in Germany, 293, 296, 307, 423, 441-42, 445; in Ireland, 217-19, 226, 229; in Italy, 275, 285; in Mexico, 234-35, 244-45, 246, 247-49; in Spain, 327-28, 329-30, 331-32, 342-44

Cavour, Camillo de, 274

CEDA *(Confederacion Espanola de Derechas Autonomas)*, 331-33

Chamberlain, Austen, 372

Chamberlain, Joseph, 371

Chamberlain, Neville, 371-73, 375-76, 377, 380, 448

Chang Hsueh-liang, 359, 361

Chang Tso-lin, 355, 359

CHEKA, 167, 171, 324 n. 2

Cheng Ho, 49

Ch'en Tu-hsiu, 349

Chiang Kai-shek, 349, 350-52, 354, 358-59, 361-62, 449

Ch'ien Lung, 38

China: Boxer Rebellion, 8-12, 51-52; Ch'ing dynasty, 8, 45-47, 50-51, 52-53, 57, 179; Communist movement, 348-49, 358-59; contact with Europeans, 37-38, 40, 45-53; Nationalist government, 349-52; Sino-Japanese War (1895), 51, 63; Sino-Japanese War (1930s), 355-62, 424; and United Nations, 449-50, 453

Chinese Eastern Railway, 66

Ch'ing-ling, 351

Chotek, Sophie, 95, 98, 100

Chou En-lai, 349, 361

Churchill, Randolph, 381

Churchill, Winston Spencer: biographical sketch, 381; in the interwar years, 257, 261, 381-82; in World War I, 122, 123-25, 128-30, 184; in World War II, 382, 401, 404-5, 411, 412, 414, 417, 419, 422, 430, 448, 450-51

Chu-Teh, 358

Ciano, Galeazzo, 369

Ciganović, Milan, 101, 102

Clarke, Tom, 222, 225, 226, 227, 228

Clemenceau, Georges, 147-49

Collective farms, 314-17

Collins, Michael, 231-32

Colonialism, 31-32. *See also* Imperialism

Columbus, Christopher, 29

Communism. *See* Socialism; Soviet Union

Communist Manifesto (Marx), 21

Concentration camps, 7, 248, 315, 320, 325, 429-30

Concert of Europe, 80, 104, 106, 111, 150

Confucianism, 47

Congress of Berlin, 83, 104

Connally, Tom, 451

Connolly, James, 225, 226, 227, 228-29

Conrad, Gen. Franz von Hotzendorf, 96, 100-103

Coolidge, Calvin, 255-56

Coral Sea, battle of, 416

Corradini, Enrico, 280

Cosgrave, William T., 232

Cossacks, 169, 172, 179

Cox, James M., 267

Craig, James, 223, 224

Cristero Rebellion, 247-48

Croatia, 83, 90

Crossing the Threshold of Hope (John Paul II), 42

Crowe, Eyre, 115, 116

Čubrilović, Vaso, 97-99

Cultural relativism, 38-44

Curragh Mutiny, 224

Currie, Gen. Arthur, 132-33, 136

Czech Legion, 169-70

Czechoslovakia, 140, 152, 374-76, 448

Dairen, 63

Daladier, Édouard, 375

Damascus, 203-4, 213

D'Annunzio, Gabriele, 278, 283, 284

D'Azeglio, Massimo, 275

The Death of Artemio Cruz (Fuentes), 249

Decolonization, 373, 406

Delcassé, Théophile, 106

Delp, Alfred, 441

Denikin, Gen. Anton, 170, 173

Denmark, 382, 445

Depression of the 1930s. *See* Great Depression

Depretis, Agostino, 276

De Valera, Eamon, 229-32

Dewey, Thomas, 451

Diaz, Porfirio, 234-35, 238, 241

Dieppe, 405-6, 412-14

Dimitrijević, Col. Dragutin, 86, 96-97, 101

Djilas, Milovan, 319, 323, 324, 405

Dneprostroi, 318-19

Dollfuss, Englebert, 333, 368
Donitz, Adm. Karl, 415, 438
Doolittle, Gen. James, 432
Dresden, 431
Drexler, Anton, 296, 306
Dr. Strangelove, 432
Dual Monarchy. *See* Austria-Hungary
Dumbarton Oaks Conference, 449-50
Dunkirk, 380
Durruti, Buenaventura, 341-42
Dutch East Indies, 386, 388, 389, 415
Dzerzhinsky, Felix, 171

Eaker, Gen. Ira, 431
Ebert, Friedrich, 293, 294, 300, 301
Economic Consequences of Mister Churchill
   (Keynes), 261
Economic Consequences of the Peace
   (Keynes), 260, 264
Egypt, 198, 211
Eichmann, Adolf, 429
Einstein, Albert, 444
Eisenhower, Gen. Dwight D., 411-12, 413,
   433
Eisenstein, Sergei, 72
Eisner, Kurt, 293
Elser, George, 441
Engels, Friedrich, 21
England. *See* Great Britain
Enver, 182, 183, 184, 187, 188, 189
España Invertebrada (Ortega y Gasset),
   328
Estonia, 140, 152
Ethiopia, 368-69, 448, 453
Ethnic cleansing, 187, 192, 194
Ethnocentrism, xvi, 37-44, 389-93, 401
Euthanasia, 423
Extraterritoriality, 48, 179

Facta, Luigi, 284, 285, 287
Falange, 332, 334, 337
Fanelli, Giuseppe, 340
Farinaci, Roberto, 283
Farouk, 198
Fascism: analyzed, 272, 274, 279-81, 289-
   90; compared to Nazism, 306-8; com-
   pared to New Deal, 286-88; in East

Asia, 351-52, 357- 58; Mussolini's lead-
   ership of, 283-86; in Spain, 332, 334,
   337
Fatalism, 136-37
al-Fatat, 200, 213
Fawcett, Millicent, 7
Federalism, xvii, 92-93, 153-55, 174-75,
   199-200
Feder, Gottfried, 306
Feisal, 201, 202, 203, 212-14
Female circumcision, 42
Feminism, 8-10, 42, 141, 162, 342
Feng Kuei-fen, 48
Fenians, 220, 222, 225
Ferrer y Guardia, Francisco, 340
Finland, 140, 152, 166, 382, 404, 445
Fisher, Adm. John, 436
Fitzgerald, F. Scott, 255
Fiume, 278, 283, 284
Flanders Fields (McCrae), 134
Foch, Marshal Ferdinand, 110
Food and Agriculture Organization, 452
Ford, Henry, 258
Fourteen Points, 146, 147, 407
France: and Africa, 16, 36; and Middle
   East, 202, 205, 213-14; in World War I,
   105-7, 111, 113-14, 118-19, 121, 124,
   147-49; in World War II, 377-80, 403-4,
   414
Franco Bahamonde, Gen. Francisco, 333,
   334, 336-37, 339, 373
Franz Ferdinand, 81, 95-98, 100, 103
Franz Joseph, 90, 92, 97, 100, 103
Freud, Sigmund, 92
Fromm, Gen. Fritz, 443
Fuchida Mutsuo, 399
Fuentes, Carlos, 249
Fukuda Hokosuke, 355
Fulbright, J. William, 451

Gaelic Athletic Association, 221
Gaelic League, 221, 222
Gallieni, Gen. Joseph, 121
Gallipoli campaign, 128-31, 184-86, 411
Gallipoli (film), 126
Gandhi, Mohandas, 144, 222, 230, 445
Gapon, Georgi, 71, 72

Garcia Oliver, Juan, 342
Garden of the Monks (Azana), 330
Garibaldi, Giuseppe, 274
Gaulle, Charles de, 414
Geisl, Vladimir, 102
Gekokujo, 389, 394, 395, 398
Genda Minoru, 399
General Idea of the Revolution in the
  Nineteenth Century (Proudhon), 22
General Theory of Employment, Interest
  and Money (Keynes), 265-66, 271
Genocide: Armenians, 86-88, 194-95; defined, 428; Gypsies, 428, 434; Hereros,
  16; Holocaust, 428-30, 434; terror-
  famine in Soviet Union, 316-17
Germany: and Africa, 16; economic prob-
  lems of, 149, 260, 266, 296-98, 302-3;
  and Spanish Civil War, 336, 337-38,
  339, 373; Third Reich, 367-71, 373-77;
  wartime atrocities, 423, 424-26, 428-30,
  434-36; Weimar Republic, 293-94, 299-
  305; in World War I, 103-4, 109-10,
  112-13, 118-26, 134-35, 147-50, 168,
  184; in World War II, 377-83, 404, 407-
  11, 412-15
Gestapo, 307, 438
Gildersleeve, Virginia, 451
Gil Robles y Quinones, José Maria, 331-
  33, 334
Giolitti, Giovanni, 276-77, 279, 284, 287
Gladstone, William, 220
Glass, Anna, 294
Goebbels, Joseph, 437
Gonzalez, Abraham, 236
Gonzalez Flores, Anacleto, 247-48
Gonzalez, Pablo, 242-43
Göring, Hermann, 307, 426, 437, 441
Grabez, Trifko, 96-99
Grand Illusion (Angell), 118
Great Britain: and Africa, 36; and China,
  37-38; economic leadership of, 259-60,
  261, 262, 270; and India, 29, 32-34; and
  Ireland, 216-33; and Japan, 64-65, 74;
  and Middle East, 201-15; and Nazi Ger-
  many, 366, 369, 371-73, 377-78; and
  United Nations, 403, 449-55; wartime
  atrocities, 430-31, 434; in World War I,

111, 114, 119, 125, 147, 149-50, 169-70;
  in World War II, 381-82, 399, 404-7,
  411, 412-14, 419, 424
Great Depression, 258-63, 266, 270-71,
  302-3, 318, 355, 365
Great Dictator, 287
Great Trek, 5
Greece, 189-90, 191-92, 382
Grew, Joseph, 392, 420
Grey, Edward, 111, 114, 116
Griffith, Arthur, 222, 229, 232
Gromyko, Andrei, 450
Guadalcanal, battle of, 416-17
Guajardo, Col. Jesus, 243
Guderian, Gen. Heinz, 378-80
Guernica, 338
Gypsies, 428, 434

Habsburg Monarchy. *See* Austria-Hungary
Hacha, Emil, 376
Hague Peace Conferences, 150, 436
Haig, Marshal Douglas, 132-33
Halsey, Adm. William, 417
Hamburg, 431
Hamilton, Gen. Ian, 128
Hankey, Maj. Maurice, 149
Harrer, Karl, 296
Harris, Gen. Arthur, 431
Harris, Townsend, 55
Hashim, House of, 200, 214
Hawaii, 386, 397, 398-401
Hejaz, 201, 214
Henlein, Konrad, 375
Hereros, 16, 186, 367
Herzl, Theodor, 208-9
Heydrich, Reinhard, 429, 430
Himmler, Heinrich, 307, 378, 425, 429,
  437, 441
Hindenburg, Gen. Paul von, 119, 123, 291,
  301, 303-5
Hirohito, 352-53, 397, 420
Hiroshima, 420, 432-33, 434
Hitler, Adolf: biographical sketch, 294-96;
  compared to Mussolini, 297, 299, 305,
  306-8; death of, 414-15; expansionist
  policy of, 365-68, 369-71, 373-77; leads
  Nazi movement, 296-305; resistance to,

440-46; and Spanish Civil War, 336, 337, 339; wartime atrocities, 423, 424-26, 428-30, 434-36; in World War II, 378-83, 401, 407-11

Hitler, Alois, 294

Hobhouse, Emily, 7

Holocaust, 428-30, 434

Homma Masaharu, 427

Hoover, Herbert, 257, 262, 267, 287

Hopkins, Harry, 268, 269, 404

Hornbeck, Stanley, 394

House, Col. Edward, 152

Hoyos, Alexander, 101

Huerta, Gen. Victoriano, 238-39

Hull, Cordell, 391-92, 394-96, 397, 398, 440

Hungary: in the Dual Monarchy, 90, 93, 101-2, 140; in World War II, 376, 382, 404

Hussein ibn Ali, 200-204, 207, 214-15

Hyde, Douglas, 221, 222, 223

Hyper-inflation, 297-99

Ibarruri, Dolores, 338

Ibn Saud, 214-15

Ilić, Danilo, 97-99

Imperialism: analyzed, xv, 13-16, 30-31; in Africa, 34-37, 181, 276, 288, 368-69; in the Balkans, 87, 93-95; in Ireland, 216-33; in India, 32-34; in Japan, 347, 353-58, 361-64; in Middle East, 197-99, 205-7, 213-15; in Nazi Germany, 365-66; in World War I, 115, 126, 140, 457; in World War II, 425, 434-35

Imperialism: The Highest Stage of Capitalism (Lenin), 16

India, 29, 32-34, 41, 381, 403, 405

Indochina, 386, 389, 395, 424

Indonesia. *See* Dutch East Indies

Influenza, 138

Inonu, Ismet, 191, 194

Intellectual proletariat, xvi, 284

International Brigades, 338

International Court of Justice, 452

International Labor Organization, 448, 452

International Telegraphic Union, 150

Iraq, 199, 205, 215, 454

Ireland (generic term), 20, 60, 90, 153, 233

Ireland (nation): compared to other countries, 251, 275; Easter Rising, 225-29; historical background, 216-19; home rule in, 219, 220, 222-23, 229; independence of, 229-33; nationalism in, 219-22

Irish Republican Army, 230-32

Irish Republican Brotherhood. *See* Fenians

Ishiwara Kanji, 355, 363, 390, 393

Islam, 178, 196-97, 201, 214

Israel. *See* Palestine; Zionism

Italy: Fascism in, 142, 279-89; historical background, 274-77; imperial conquests of, 181, 276, 288, 368-69, 377; and Spanish Civil War, 337-38, 339-40; in World War I, 103, 104, 148, 277-78, 280-81; in World War II, 380-81, 404

Itagaki Seishiro, 355

Ito Hirobumi, 58, 59

Iwo Jima, battle of, 418-19

Jagerstatter, Franz, 445

James I, 217

Japan: and China, 347-48, 354-62; creates co-prosperity sphere, 362-64, 385-89, 415-16; and Great Britain, 64-65, 74, 181, 347; historical background, 53-57; and Korea, 61-63, 347, 353; Meiji Restoration, 57-60, 181; and Russia, 65-69, 73-74, 130-31, 385, 397-98; and United States, 389-98; wartime atrocities, 426-28, 434-36; in World War I, 125-26, 140, 169, 347; in World War II, 398-401, 415-20, 424

Jaurès, Jean, 114

Jellicoe, Adm. John, 122

Jemal, 182, 189, 201, 209

Jerome, Jennie, 381

The Jewish State (Herzl), 208, 209

Jews: in Hitler's ideology, 295, 301, 307, 366-67; Holocaust, 428-30, 434; in Ottoman Empire, 178, 219; in Palestine, 207, 209

Joffe, Adolf, 349

Joffre, Gen. Joseph, 118
John Paul II, 42-43, 425, 454
Joyce, James, 92
Juarez, Benito, 234, 281
Julian calendar, 71 n. 1, 160 n. 1
Just war theory, 142-43

Kahn, Richard, 265
Kahr, Gustav von, 299
Kallay, Benjamin von, 94
Kamenev, Lev, 310, 314, 320-21
Kamikaze, 418
Kaneko Kentaro, 68
Karadjordjević, Peter, 86, 97
Katyn Massacre, 405, 438
Kazakhstan, 316-17
Kent, Edmund, 225
Kerensky, Alexander, 162, 165-67, 169
Keynes, John Maynard: biographical
    sketch, 263-64; economic theories of,
    169, 260, 264-66; influence of, 269-71,
    331, 455
Kiaochow Peninsula, 125, 347
Kimberley, 5-6
Kimmel, Adm. Husband, 400
King, Adm. Ernest, 418
King, Martin Luther, Jr., 144
Kipling, Rudyard, 16
Kirov, Sergei, 320-21
Kitchener, Gen. H. H., 6-7, 127
Kleinbaum, Max, 447
Kluck, Gen. Alexander von, 121
Kolbe, Maximilian, 424-25
Kolchak, Adm. Alexander, 169, 170
Komoto Daisaku, 355
Konoe Fumimaro, 385-86, 388, 396
Korea, 63, 347, 353, 453
Kornilov, Gen. Lar, 166, 168
Kosovo, battle of, 84, 95
Kristallnacht, 429
Krobatin, Gen. Alexander, 100
Krupskaya, Nadezhda, 164
Kuang-su, 8
Kulaks, 309, 315
Kung, H. H., 351
Kuomintang, 349, 351
Kurds, 187, 189, 194

Kuropatkin, Gen. A. N., 66
Kwantung Army, 353, 354, 355-57, 364

Ladysmith, 6
Largo Caballero, Francisco, 329, 333,
    342
Larkin, James, 225
Latvia, 140, 152
Lawrence, Geoffrey, 437
Lawrence of Arabia, 204
Lawrence, T. E., 203-4, 205
League of Nations, 150-52, 357, 369, 447-
    48, 452-53
Leahy, Adm. William, 433
Lebanon, 202, 205, 214
Lebensraum, 302, 307-8, 366, 425
Le May, Gen. Curtis, 432
Lemberg, battle of, 123
Lend-Lease Act, 401
Lenin, V. I. (born Vladimir Ilyich Ulanov);
    biographical sketch, 164; death of, 175,
    310; New Economic Policy of, 174, 309-
    10; in October Revolution, 164-68;
    mentioned, 16, 72, 145, 244
Leo XIII, 331
Lerroux Garcia, Alejandro, 332-33
Leyte Gulf, battle of, 418
Liaotung Peninsula, 63, 65, 69
Liaoyang, battle of, 66
Libya, 182, 369
Liddell-Hart, Gen. Basil, 378
Liège, 110, 112, 119, 123
Liman von Sanders, Gen. Otto, 182, 183,
    184
Lindemann, Frederick, 431
Lithuania, 140, 152
Lloyd George, David, 133, 147-49, 209,
    211, 230-31, 265
Lodge, Henry Cabot, 151
Long March, 359
Lopokova, Lydia, 264
Lossow, Gen. Otto von, 299
Ludendorff, Gen. Erich, 119, 123, 124,
    291, 299-301
Lueger, Karl, 295
Luftwaffe, 369, 377, 378, 382, 407, 430
Luxemburg, 109-10

MacArthur, Gen. Douglas, 415, 417, 418, 422

Macartney, George, 37-38

McCloy, John J., 420

McCrae, Col. John, 134

MacDermott, Sean, 225, 227, 228

MacDonagh, Thomas, 225

MacDonald, Ramsay, 270

McMahon, Gen. Henry, 201-2, 207

MacNeill, Eoin, 221, 224, 226

Madero, Francisco Indalecio, 235-38, 241, 251

Mafeking, 5-6

Maginot Line, 379

Magnitogorsk, 318-20, 322

Magon, Enriqué Flores, 242

Magon, Ricardo Flores, 235, 236, 242

Makhno, Nestor Ivanovych, 173-74, 242, 341

Malatesta, Enrico, 279

Malaya, 386, 389, 397, 415, 424

Mallin, Michael, 227

Manchuria, 353-54, 355-57, 364, 448

Manstein, Gen. Erich von, 379, 411

Man Without Qualities (Musil), 92

Mao Tse-tung, 349, 358-59

Marco Polo Bridge Incident, 361

Markiewicz, Constance, 227

Marne, battle of, 121

Marshall, Gen. George, 400, 401, 412, 433

Marx, Karl, 21-24, 207, 263

Masaryk, Thomas, 153

Masin, Draga, 85-86, 95

Matsuoka Yosuke, 386-88, 391

Matteoti, Giacomo, 286

Matzleberger, Franziska, 294

Max of Baden, 147, 291

Maxwell, Gen. John G., 228

al-Mazri, Aziz Ali, 199

Mehmedbasić, Muhamed, 97-99

Mehmed V, 181

Mehmed VI, 189, 192

Meiji, 57, 352

Mei-ling, 351

Mein Kampf (Hitler), 295, 300, 301-2, 366

Mensheviks, 164, 311

Mexico: constitutions of, 234, 239, 244-45; historical background, 234-35; revolution in, 235-51; in the world wars, 134-35, 243-44, 403

Mid-European Union, 153-55

Midway, battle of, 416

Miller, Herbert A., 153

Missionaries, 10, 15, 33

Mola Vidal, Gen. Emilio, 334, 336

Molotov, V. M., 321, 377, 412

Moltke, Gen. Helmuth von, 109-10, 111, 112, 118-19

Monash, Gen. John, 136

Montaño, Ottilio, 241

Montenegro, 88, 101

Montgomery, Gen. Bernard, 412, 417

Montseny, Federica, 342

Morgenthau, Henry, 455

Morocco, 106, 116, 333, 336, 406

Mosley, Oswald, 265

Mugica, Gen. Francisco, 244

Muhammad, 196, 200

Muhammad Ali, 197-98

Mukden, battle of, 66-67

Mukden Incident, 355-57

Muller, Hermann, 302

Munich Conference, 375-76, 448

Musil, Robert, 92

Mussolini, Benito: biographical sketch, 281-83; compared to Hitler, 297, 299, 305, 306-8, 368; compared to Roosevelt, 286-88; expansionist policy of, 368-69, 376, 377; leads Fascist movement, 283-86; and Spanish Civil War, 332, 337, 339; in World War II, 380-81, 404, 420

Mussolini, Rachelle, 282

Nagasaki, 420, 433, 434

Nagumo Chuichi, 398-99

Nansen, Fridtjof, 170

Nationalism: analyzed, xv, 17-20; in the Balkans, 87, 90, 91, 96, 180; cause of atrocities, 434-35; in China, 53, 347-48; in Ireland, 219-22, 226; in Italy, 275, 277, 280-81; in Japan, 60, 69, 76, 357-58; in the Middle East, 196, 199-200, 203, 213-15; religion and, 220, 226, 229, 244-45, 247-49, 278; in Russia, 171, 172,

174, 312; in Spain, 328; in Turkey, 176, 180-83; in World War I, 116, 121, 130, 134, 136, 152

Nazism: compared to Fascism, 306-8; Hitler's leadership of, 299-305; origins of, 142, 296-97. *See also* Hitler, Adolf

Netherlands, 109, 148, 378, 380

New Aristocracy (Panunzio), 279 n. 2

New Deal, 268-69, 286-88

New Zealand, 127, 140, 386, 403, 405

Nicholas II: biographical sketch, 70; death of, 169; and revolution of 1905, 71-73; and revolutions of 1917, 159-62; in World War I, 111, 112, 113, 116; mentioned 63, 64

Night of the Long Knives, 305, 322

Nikolayev, Leonid, 320

Nimitz, Adm. Chester, 417, 418, 438

Nomura Kichisaburo, 396, 397

Nonviolence, 222, 297, 444-46. *See also* Pacifism

Nordau, Max, 208

Normandy invasion, 412-14, 423

North African campaign, 406, 412

Norway, 379, 382, 445

Noske, Gustav, 293

Nuremberg laws, 429

Nuremberg trials, 436-39

Obregon, Gen. Alvaro, 239-40, 246-47, 249

Obrenović, Alexander, 85-86, 95

Obrenović, Milan, 84-85, 86

O'Connell, Daniel, 219

O'Farrell, Elizabeth, 228

Oil: in Mexico, 245, 246, 250; in the Middle East, 213-14, 215 n. 1; in the Pacific, 363, 388, 395-96

Okinawa, battle of, 418-19

O'Neill, Hugh, 216

Opium, 47-48, 52

Oppenheimer, Robert, 432

Ordzhonikidze, Sergo, 321

Origin of Species (Darwin), 31

Orlando, Vittorio, 147, 278

Orozco, Pascual, 236

Ortega y Gasset, José, 328

O'Shea, Kitty, 221

Ottoman Empire: Arab revolt, 196, 201-4; in the Balkans, 82-83, 84-85, 88; historical background, 176-79, 197, 219; in World War I, 126, 128-31, 183-86. *See also* Turkey

Oyama Iwao, 66, 67

Pacifism, 142-44, 373, 446-47. *See also* Nonviolence

Paderewski, Ignace Jan, 152-53

Paine, Thomas, 60

Pal, Radhabinod, 438

Palacky, Frantisek, 91

Paléologue, Maurice, 111

Palestine, 202, 205, 207, 209-12, 214

Panunzio, Sergio, 279 n. 2, 280

Papen, Franz von, 303-5

Paris Peace Conference, 147-49, 192, 212

Parliament of the World's Religions, 43

Parnell, Charles Stewart, 220-21, 223

Pašić, Nikola, 87, 97, 102

Passchendaele, battle of, 132-34

Paul VI, 454

Pearl Harbor, 65, 74, 394-95, 398-400

Pearse, Patrick, 225-27, 228, 229

Peron, Juan, 403

Perry, Com. Matthew C., 54-55, 63, 392, 393

Pershing, Gen. John J., 135, 136, 240

Philippines, 397, 415, 416, 418, 424, 427

Philippine Sea, battle of, 417

Picasso, Pablo, 338

Picot, Francois Georges, 205, 213

Piedmont, 274

Piłsudski, Gen. Josef, 153, 170

Pinyin system, 8n.2

Pius X, 276

Pius XI, 331

Plunkett, Joseph Mary, 225, 227, 228

Poincare, Raymond, 104, 111, 113, 114, 116

Poland: in World War I, 140, 149, 152-53, 170; in World War II, 376, 377-78, 405, 424-25

Polzl, Klara, 294

Popović, Cvijetko, 97-99

Popovici, Aurel, 93
Port Arthur, 65, 66-67, 69, 74
Potsdam Conference, 419, 420
The Presidential Succession in 1910 (Madero), 236
PRI *(Partido Revolucionario Institucional)*, 250-51
Prieto y Tuero, Indalecio, 329, 333
Primo de Rivera y Orbaneja, Gen. Miguel, 328, 337, 341
Primo de Rivera y Sáenz de Heredia, José Antonio, 332
Princip, Gavrilo, 81, 96-99, 101, 173
Propaganda by the deed, 24-26, 96, 114, 340
Protestants: in Germany, 423, 441; in Ireland, 217-19, 222, 223-24; in Spain, 343
Proudhon, Pierre-Joseph, 22-24
Pu-Yi, 53, 357
Pyatakov, Gregory, 310, 321

al-Qahtaniya, 191
Quadrigesimo Anno (Pius XI), 331
Quisling, Vidkun, 445

Racism, 28-29, 31, 33, 76, 301, 307, 401, 426, 434-35
Raeder, Adm. Erich, 438
Rape of Nanking, 362, 294
Rasputin, Gregory, 159-61
Rathenau, Walter, 298
Rauf, 184
Rauschning, Hermann, 366
Redmond, John, 222, 224, 229
Reed, John, 166
Renan, Ernst, 17
Reparations, 149, 260, 293, 297
The Resurrection of Hungary (Griffith), 222
Revitalization movements, 11-12
Rhineland, 371, 372
Rhodes, Cecil, 5, 6
Ribbentrop, Joachim von, 377, 388, 408
Ricci, Matteo, 45
Risorgimento, 274, 275
Rivera, Diego, 246
Roberts, Marshal Frederick, 6-7, 224

Rocco, Alfredo, 287
Röhm, Ernst, 305
Romania, 103, 109, 123, 382, 404
Rommel, Gen. Erwin, 379, 404, 405, 412, 413, 417
Roosevelt, Eleanor, 266, 271
Roosevelt, Franklin Delano: biographical sketch, 266-68; compared to Mussolini, 286-88; death of, 419, 451; New Deal of, 141, 268-71; in World War II, 394, 396, 399-401, 404-5, 412, 414, 422, 434, 448-49, 450-51
Roosevelt, James, 266
Roosevelt, Sara Delano, 266
Roosevelt, Theodore, 68-69, 76, 236, 267
Rosenthal, Joe, 419
Rothschild, Lionel, 207
Ruhr, 297-98
Russell, Bertrand, 143-44, 447
Russia: empire of, 61, 69-70; February Revolution, 159-63; October Revolution, 163-68; revolution of 1905, 71-73, 74; in World War I, 105-6, 107, 111-12, 113, 119. *See also* Soviet Union
Russo-Japanese War, 65-69, 73-74, 130-31, 397-98
Ruth, Babe, 256

SA *(Sturmabteilung)*, 303, 305
Saionji Kimmochi, 357
Saipan, battle of, 417
Salandra, Antonio, 277, 285
Samuel, Herbert, 209, 212
San Francisco Conference, 451
Sanjak of Novipazar, 87
Sanjurjo Sacanel, Gen. José, 329, 334, 336
San Remo Agreement, 214
Sarajevo, 95-98
Saud, House of, 197, 214-15
Sazanov, Sergei, 111, 113
Schicklgruber, Maria Anna, 294
Schleicher, Gen. Kurt von, 303, 305
Schlieffen, Gen. Alfred von, 109
Schlieffen Plan, 109-10, 112, 118-21, 239, 378
Scott, John, 319-20, 322, 324
Seeckt, Gen. Hans von, 300

Seisser, Col. Hans von, 299
Selassie, Haile, 369
Sepoy Mutiny, 33-34
Serbia: historical background, 84-87;
  struggles with Austria-Hungary, 87-88,
  96-97, 101-3, 109, 111-12; in World
  War I, 123
Servan-Schreiber, Jean Jacques, xviii
Seton-Watson, Robert, 90, 91, 93
Seymour, Adm. Edward, 10
Seyss-Inquart, Arthur, 374
Shakespear, William, 203
Shidehara Kijuro, 354
Short, Gen. Walter, 399-400
Sinn Fein, 222, 229, 230
Skoropadski, Gen. Paul, 172
Slaughterhouse Five (Vonnegut), 431
Slavery, 31, 438-39
Slovakia, 376
Smith, F. E., 229
Smoot-Hawley Tariff, 263
Social Darwinism, 115-16, 295, 302
Social Democratic Workers' Party, 164-67
Socialism: analyzed, xv, 20-23; in China,
  348-49, 358-59; in Germany, 291-93,
  297, 306; in Ireland, 225; in Italy, 276,
  278-80, 284, 286, 306; in revolution of
  1905, 71-73, 74, 76-77; in revolutions of
  1917, 159-75; in Soviet Union, 309-10,
  313, 314-20; in Spain, 329, 330-31, 333,
  337, 341-42; in World War I, 114
Socialist Revolutionaries, 162, 164
Socio-nationalism, xvi, 297, 325
Somaliland, 369
Sonnino, Sydney, 277
Soong, Charles, 351
South Africa, 3-8, 140, 403
South America, 403
South Manchuria Railway, 65
South West Africa, 16
Soviet of Workers' Deputies (1905), 72,
  165
Soviet of Workers' and Soldiers' Deputies
  (1917), 162-63, 167
Soviet Union: civil war in, 168-71; eco-
  nomic development of, 174, 309-10,
  313, 314-20; party purges in, 320-24;

and Spanish Civil War, 338, 339; and
  United Nations, 449-55; wartime atroc-
  ities, 427-28, 434; in World War II,
  377, 404-6, 407-11, 414-15, 419, 424
Spatz, Gen. Carl, 431
SS *(Schutzstaffeln)*, 307, 378, 425, 438
Stalin, Joseph (born Joseph
  Vissarionovich Djugashvili): biographi-
  cal sketch, 311-13; comes to power,
  313-14; economic policies of, 314-20;
  party purges of, 320-24; and Spanish
  Civil War, 338, 339; in World War II,
  377-78, 404-5, 407-11, 412, 414, 419,
  422, 450-51
Stalingrad, battle of, 410-11, 417
Stark, Adm. Harold, 400
Stauffenberg, Berthold von, 443
Stauffenberg, Col. Claus Schenk von, 442-
  44
Steed, Henry Wickham, 90
Stephens, James, 220
Stettinius, Edward R., Jr., 450
Stimson, Henry, 420
Stock market crash, 255-57
Stoessel, Gen. A. M., 67
Strasser, Gregor, 304, 305, 306
Strategic bombing, 430-32, 434
Stürgkh, Karl, 100
Sudetenland, 375-76
Suez Canal, 198, 211, 369, 453
Sukhomlinov, Gen. Vladimir, 111
Summers, Harrison, 423, 436
Sun Yat-sen, 52-53, 69, 349-50
Suzuki Keiji, 390
Svanidze, Catherine Semyonovna, 311
Sweden, 379, 445
Switzerland, 152, 382, 452
Sykes, Mark, 205-7, 211, 213
Sykes-Picot Agreement, 205, 207, 213
Syndicalism, 26, 279-80, 340-41
Syria, 204, 205, 213-14

Taisho, 352
Talat, 182, 189
Tanaka Giichi, 354, 363
Tankosić, Maj. Voja, 96, 101, 102
Tanks, 124, 378-80, 411

Tannenberg, battle of, 119
Taranto, 399
Teheran Conference, 405, 412, 419, 449
Ten Days That Shook the World (Reed), 166
Thailand, 386, 427
Thousand and One Nights, 197
Tientsin, 10, 11
Tirpitz, Adm. Alfred von, 105
Tisza, Istvan, 100, 102
Togo Heihachiro, 66, 68
Tojo Hideki, 396-98, 437
Tokugawa shoguns, 54-57
Tokyo trials, 437-39
Tonghak Rebellion, 63
Totalitarianism, 289-90, 306-7
Transjordan, 214
Trans-Siberian Railway, 61, 68, 169
Treaty of Kanagawa, 55
Treaty of Lausanne, 192
Treaty of Locarno, 254, 371
Treaty of London, 277, 278
Treaty of Nanking, 48
Treaty of Neuilly, 152 n. 2
Treaty of Portsmouth, 69, 76
Treaty of Saint Germain, 152 n. 2
Treaty of Sevres, 189, 192
Treaty of Shimoda, 55
Treaty of Shimonoseki, 51
Treaty of Trianon, 152 n. 2
Treaty of Versailles. *See* Versailles Treaty
Treaty of Washington, 354
Tresckow, Col. Henning von, 442, 443
Trident Conference, 412
Trieste, 278
Triple Alliance, 103-4, 277
Triple Entente, 105-7, 114, 277
Triple Intervention, 51, 60, 63, 125
Trotha, Gen. Lothar von, 16
Trotsky, Leon (born Lev Davidovich Bronstein): in revolution of 1905, 72; in revolutions of 1917, 165, 166, 168, 170; as rival to Stalin, 310, 313-14, 324
Truman, Harry S., 419-20, 433-34, 451
Ts'u-hsi, 8-11, 50, 53
Tsushima, battle of, 67-68, 69, 73, 398
Tuan Ch'i-jui, 348

Tukachevsky, Marshal Michael, 322
Tunisia, 198
Turkey: Armenian genocide, 186-88; Ataturk's nationalist revival, 190-94; Young Turk revolution, 180-82, 199. *See also* Ottoman Empire

U-boats, 122, 134-35
Ukraine, 172-75, 315, 316-17, 424, 450-51
Ulster, 217, 223-24, 232
Ulysses (Joyce), 92
Unamuno y Jugo, Miguel de, 344
Unconditional surrender, 406-7, 418, 420
Union of Democratic Control, 145
United Nations, 403, 448-55
United Nations Children's Fund, 455
United States: coming of age in world politics, 75-76; economic leadership of, 253, 258-59, 260, 261-62, 270-71; and Japan, 389-98; and Mexico, 234, 240, 243, 250; and United Nations, 403, 448-56; wartime atrocities, 422, 431-34, 435; in World War I, 134-35, 140, 147-52, 169; in World War II, 398-401, 404-7, 411-20, 424
United States of Greater Austria (Popovici), 93
Universal Declaration of Human Rights (UN), 43
Universal Postal Union, 150
Untermensch campaign, 424-26, 434
Upper Silesia, 149, 153

Venizelos, Eleutherios, 189, 191
Verdun, battle of, 124, 125
Versailles Treaty, 149-52, 293, 365, 369-71, 407
Victor Emmanuel II, 274, 275
Victor Emmanuel III, 285, 369, 420
Victoria, 8, 34, 104, 160
Vietnam. *See* Indochina
Villa, Francisco "Pancho" (born Doroteo Arango), 238, 239-40, 247
Vittorio Veneto, battle of, 278
Viva Zapata, 251
Viviani, René, 111
Vonnegut, Kurt, 431

Vyrubova, Anna, 160

Wagner, Robert F., 269
Wedemeyer, Gen. Albert, 411
Weizmann, Chaim, 211, 212
Weltpolitik, 105, 115, 301
What Is to be Done? (Lenin), 25
White, Harry Dexter, 455
White Man's Burden, 16, 94, 353
White Sea canal, 319
Wiesner, Friedrich von, 101
Wilhelm II: biographical sketch, 104; and
    the coming of World War I, 101, 105,
    106, 111, 112, 113, 116; and war strat-
    egy, 118, 122, 134, 148; and "yellow
    peril," 63; mentioned, 68, 95, 100,
    367
William of Orange, 217
Wilson, Gen. Henry, 107, 110, 224, 233
Wilson, Henry Lane, 238
Wilson, Woodrow: biographical sketch,
    145; and Mexico, 236, 239, 240; peace
    program of, 145-55, 192, 278; war lead-
    ership of, 134-35
Witte, Sergei, 70-71, 72-73
World Bank, 455-56
World Health Organization, 452, 454
World War I: casualties, 138-40; causes,
    95-117; Eastern front, 119, 122-23, 165,
    168; Gallipoli campaign, 128-31; naval
    warfare, 121-22, 126, 134-35; peace ne-
    gotiations, 147-50, 168; Western front,
    118-21, 123-25, 131-33; and World War
    II, 345, 365, 402, 457
World War II: atrocities, 424-36; casual-
    ties, 423-24, 426, 427-28, 430; causes in
East Asia, 352-58, 361-64, 389-98;
    causes in Europe, 365, 367-77; coalition
    warfare, 404-7, 411-12, 419, 420-21;
    German invasion of France, 378-80;
    German invasion of Poland, 377-78;
    German invasion of Russia, 407-11;
    Japanese attack on Pearl Harbor, 398-
    401; Pacific war, 415-20; second front
    in Europe, 411-14; war crimes trials,
    436-39; war resistance, 440-47
Wrangel, Gen. Peter, 170

Yalta Conference, 405, 414, 419, 450-51
Yamagata Aritomo, 58, 59
Yamamoto Isoroku, 398-99, 401, 415-16
Yellow Sea, battle of, 66
Yezhov, Nicholas, 321-22
Yoshinobu, 57
Young Bosnia, 88, 96
Young Ireland, 219
Young Turks, 180-82, 186-89, 199, 358
Ypres, First battle of, 131-31
Ypres, Third battle of. *See* Passchendaele
Yuan Shi-kai, 53, 347
Yudenich, Gen. Nicholas, 170
Yugoslavia, 87, 140, 152, 278, 382, 424

Zapata, Emiliano, 239-40, 241-43, 246,
    251
Zerajić, Bogdan, 95
Zhukov, Gen. Georgi, 408
Zimmermann Telegram, 134-35, 243
Zinoviev, Gregory, 310, 314, 320-21
Zionism, 208-12, 251
Zorian, Rostom, 188
Zulus, 5